Computerized Accounting with

QuickBooks®
2013

Kathleen Villani, CPA
Queensborough Community College

James B. Rosa, CPA
Queensborough Community College

Paradigm
PUBLISHING

St. Paul

Managing Editor	Christine Hurney
Developmental Editor	Spencer Cotkin
Production Editor	Lori Michelle Ryan
Cover Designer	Valerie King
Senior Production Specialist	Jack Ross

Care has been taken to verify the accuracy of information presented in this book. However, the authors, editors, and publisher cannot accept responsibility for Web, e-mail, newsgroup, or chat room subject matter or content, or for consequences from application of the information in this book, and make no warranty, expressed or implied, with respect to its content.

Trademarks: Some of the product names and company names included in this book have been used for identification purposes only and may be trademarks or registered trade names of their respective manufacturers and sellers. The authors, editors, and publisher disclaim any affiliation, association, or connection with, or sponsorship or endorsement by, such owners.

QuickBooks© is a registered trademark of Intuit, Inc. Windows, Microsoft Word, and Microsoft Excel are registered trademarks of Microsoft Corporation in the United States and other countries.

We have made every effort to trace the ownership of all copyrighted material and to secure permission from copyright holders. In the event of any question arising as to the use of any material, we will be pleased to make the necessary corrections in future printings. Thanks are due to the aforementioned authors, publishers, and agents for permission to use the materials indicated.

ISBN 978-0-76385-314-3 (text and CDs)
ISBN 978-0-76385-312-9 (text)

© 2014 by Paradigm Publishing, Inc.
875 Montreal Way
St. Paul, MN 55102
Email: educate@emcp.com
Website: www.emcp.com

Printed in the United States of America

22 21 20 19 18 17 16 15 14 13   2 3 4 5 6 7 8 9 10

Brief Contents

Contents

Appendices

Preface

Computerized Accounting with QuickBooks® 2013 teaches both the accountant and non-accountant student how to use QuickBooks 2013, one of the most popular general ledger software packages for small- and medium-sized businesses. With this program, businesses can maintain a general ledger; track vendor, customer, and inventory activities; process payroll for company employees; prepare bank reconciliations; track time for employees and jobs; and complete other key accounting procedures.

In addition to learning how to use QuickBooks, students gain an understanding of the accounting concepts as they are processed in the software.

Textbook Features

Computerized Accounting with QuickBooks 2013 is designed around features that support student mastery of skills and concepts while providing flexibility in approach for instructors.

- Chapter Objectives are listed for each chapter.
- Each chapter compares a manual accounting system with the elements of QuickBooks for the topics covered in the chapter.
- Accounting definitions are provided in the margins.
- Each chapter reviews accounting concepts and then presents a tutorial of the procedural steps needed to process accounting data in QuickBooks.
- Software steps are fully explained and illustrated with many screen captures.
- For each transaction completed in QuickBooks, the accounting concepts are illustrated in traditional debit and credit format using T-accounts.
- Each task presented in QuickBooks is followed by a Practice Exercise to provide immediate reinforcement.
- A company called Kristin Raina Interior Designs is used to illustrate the topics of each chapter; this company also is the basis for the intra-chapter Practice Exercises.
- The topics presented in every chapter build on the topics covered in the previous chapters.

- At the end of each chapter is a Procedure Review, which summarizes the QuickBooks steps illustrated in the chapter.
- End-of-chapter exercises called Key Concepts and Procedure Check offer review and assessment questions for students to answer.
- In each chapter there are two case problems, which include companies called Lynn's Music Studio and Olivia's Web Solutions, to be completed in QuickBooks to review the topics of that chapter.

Chapters at a Glance

This text is organized to follow the four levels of operation in QuickBooks: New Company Setup, Lists/Centers, Activities, and Reports.

Students learn the New Company Setup more effectively if they understand the basic operations of the QuickBooks software. Therefore, Chapters 1–5 present how to use QuickBooks following a normal business flow. After the basic software operations are mastered in Chapters 1–5, the New Company Setup level of operation is explained in Chapters 6 and 7. Chapters 8 and 9 discuss the setup and processing of payroll transactions. Throughout these chapters, students view and print many reports and financial statements. Upon completion of Chapters 1–9, readers will have a thorough understanding of the four levels of operation in QuickBooks. Chapters 10–12 discuss banking, jobs accounting, time tracking, and customization features.

Chapter 1 – QuickBooks 2013

Chapter 1 introduces the student to some basic steps for installing the software and the company files that accompany the text; navigating in the QuickBooks software; and opening, backing up, and restoring company files.

Chapter 2 – Vendors

Chapter 2 describes the steps involved when bills are received and subsequently paid; or when bills are paid immediately.

Chapter 3 – Customers

Chapter 3 illustrates the process followed when a company earns revenue; creates an invoice for services rendered for a customer and either immediately (cash) or subsequently collects payment; and makes bank deposits.

Chapter 4 – Period-End Procedures

Chapter 4 presents the use of the general journal to record adjusting journal entries and to complete the accounting cycle.

Chapter 5 – Inventory

Chapter 5 shows how to work with the purchase and sale of inventory items, sales tax, and sales discounts.

Chapter 6 – New Company Setup— Detailed Start

Chapter 6 describes the New Company Setup process using the Detailed Start method and the QuickBooks Setup window to enter data.

Chapter 7 – New Company Setup— Express Start

Chapter 7 illustrates the New Company Setup process with the alternative method—Express Start.

Chapter 8 – Payroll Setup

Chapter 8 presents the setup of the company file for payroll.

Chapter 9 – Payroll Processing

Chapter 9 describes the processing of payroll.

Chapter 10 – Banking

Chapter 10 explains QuickBooks banking features, including bank transfers, bank reconciliations, and the use of credit cards.

Chapter 11 – Jobs and Time Tracking

Chapter 11 presents the software capabilities of job accounting and time-tracking.

Chapter 12 – Customizing Your Company File

Chapter 12 describes more advanced features available in QuickBooks, such as customizing the desktop, lists and centers, activities, and reports, and preparing for fiscal year end and the new fiscal year.

Appendices

Ten appendices are included in this text. Appendices A, B, C, and F are summaries of information discussed in the book; these appendices can be used by students as a quick reference guide. Appendix G illustrates an alternative payroll setup method. Appendices D, E, H, I, and J present additional topics that supplement material covered in the book.

Appendix A – Open or Restore a Company File

Appendix A summarizes and compares how to open a company file and how to restore (open) a backup company file.

Appendix B – Manual Accounting versus QuickBooks

Appendix B summarizes and compares a manual accounting system to QuickBooks.

Appendix C – Journal Report Types

Appendix C is a summary of the journal report types used in QuickBooks.

Appendix D – Purchase Orders

Appendix D illustrates the use of purchase orders when ordering inventory part items.

Appendix E – Customer Credits and Bad Debt Write-offs

Appendix E describes the recording of customer credits and writing off a customer's bad debt.

Appendix F – New Company Setup Methods

Appendix F summarizes and compares the New Company Setup process using the Detailed Start method, including the QuickBooks Setup window to enter data, to the New Company Setup process using the Express Start method, excluding the QuickBooks Setup window to enter data.

Appendix G – QuickBooks Payroll Setup Window

Appendix G describes payroll setup using the QuickBooks Payroll Setup window, rather than the custom payroll setup, which was described in Chapter 8.

Appendix H – Sick and Vacation Paid Time

Appendix H illustrates how to track sick and vacation paid time in payroll.

Appendix I – Setting Up QuickBooks for Multiple Users

Appendix I describes how to set up the company file for multi-users.

Appendix J – Setting Up Passwords and Users

Appendix J demonstrates how to set up passwords and users for a company file.

Prerequisites for Using the Text

Computerized Accounting with QuickBooks 2013 provides students with detailed instruction and thorough practice for learning how to use this popular software. It is assumed that students know some basic accounting. For effective use of this book, QuickBooks 2013 must be installed on a computer. Students also should be familiar with using a personal computer and understand basic Windows terminology. Where knowledge of specific Windows procedures would enhance the operation of QuickBooks, those procedures are explained.

Student Resources

Two CDs are provided with the text:
(1) QuickBooks 2013 Student Trial Edition, restricted to be used within 140 days of installation; (2) Student Resources CD. See Chapter 1 for instructions on installing the QuickBooks 2013 Student Trial Edition software and the company files from the Student Resources CD.

The other major student supplement is the Internet Resource Center for the book at www.paradigmcollege.net/quickbooks2013.

QuickBooks 2013 Software CD

QuickBooks 2013 must be installed on a computer to effectively use this book. To support an installation of QuickBooks 2013, a computer must have the following:

- Windows XP (SP3), Vista (SP1 incl 64-bit), Windows 7 (incl 64-bit), or Windows 8 (incl 64-bit)
- Processor with at least 2.0 GHz speed (2.4 GHz recommended)
- 1 GB of RAM for a single user
- 2 GB of RAM recommended for multiple users
- minimum 2.5 GB of disk space (additional space required for data files)

- 1024 × 786 screen resolution, 16-bit or higher color
- 4x CD-ROM drive
- minimum of Microsoft Word 2003 or Microsoft Excel 2003 to use the features in QuickBooks that integrate with Word and Excel

Be sure to register the software as directed in the installation process. If you do not register the software, it will stop working. After installing the software on your computer, store the CD in a safe place.

Student Resources CD

This CD contains the sample company files that are used to illustrate the concepts presented in the text and to complete the two cases at the end of each chapter. Each company file contains the opening balances needed to perform the steps in the chapter and the chapter-end cases. The companies discussed in this text are:

- Kristin Raina Interior Designs is the sample company illustrated in each chapter.
- Lynn's Music Studio is the company to be used for Case 1 at the end of each chapter.
- Olivia's Web Solutions is the company to be used for Case 2 at the end of each chapter.

There are company files for each chapter except Chapters 6 and 7. In these two chapters, students learn how to create a new company file.

It is advisable to copy company files onto the hard drive of your computer. See Chapter 1 of the text for instructions on installing the company files from the Student Resources CD onto your computer. By default, QuickBooks stores company files in the path:

In Windows 8:
C:\Users\Public\Public Documents\ Intuit\QuickBooks\Sample Company Files\ QuickBooks 2013

In Windows 7:
C:\Users\Public\Public Documents\Intuit\ QuickBooks\Company Files

In Vista:
C:\Public\Public Documents\Intuit\ QuickBooks\Company Files

In Windows XP:
C:\Documents and Settings\All Users\(Shared) Documents\Intuit\QuickBooks\Company Files

After installing the company files onto your computer, store the CD in a safe place.

Internet Resource Center

The Internet Resource Center for this text is available at www.paradigmcollege.net/quickbooks2013 free of charge. Information resources include tips for studying, for taking tests, and for succeeding in academic courses. The site also provides technical support information and web links.

eBook

For students who prefer studying with an eBook, *Computerized Accounting with QuickBooks 2013* is available in an electronic form. The Web-based, password-protected eBook features dynamic navigation tools, including bookmarking, a linked table of contents, and the ability to jump to a specific page.

Instructor Resources

An Instructor Resources CD, the Computerized Accounting Internet Resource Center, and online course management tools are available for instructors. Although the Education Version of QuickBooks 2013 is packaged with the text, instructors should be aware that QuickBooks can be purchased in retail stores or directly from Intuit (1-888-2-Intuit or 1-888-246-8848). An Education site license, purchased directly from Intuit (1-866-570-3843), is available for schools that wish to load the software on several computers in a computer laboratory. Education site licenses are available for groups of 10, 25, or 50 workstations. When ordering the Education site license, Intuit provides the QuickBooks Premier Accountant Edition version of the software.

Instructor Resources CD

The following teaching resources are included on the Instructor Resources CD:

- Model Answers (PDF): Reports for Case 1 and Case 2.
- Model Answers (QBW): Solutions in QuickBooks files for Kristin Raina Interior Designs, Case 1, and Case 2.
- Teaching Materials
  - About This Text
  - Overview
  - Chapter Objectives
  - Sample Course Syllabi
  - Teaching Hints
  - Lecture Notes by Chapter
  - Reference Tables
  - End-of-Chapter Case Studies Check Figures
  - Review and Assessment by Chapter (solutions to the Key Concepts and Procedure Checks)
  - Objective Midterm and Final Exams
  - Comprehensive Problem

Internet Resource Center

All of the materials included on the Instructor Resources CD is available on the book-specific Internet Resource Center but is password-protected. Contact your sales representative to arrange for secure access. Both students and instructors can access the student resources on the Internet Resource Center free of charge, no password required, at www.paradigmcollege.net/quickbooks2013.

Blackboard Course Files

Blackboard course files are available for use on various platforms. Using these files, instructors can provide a syllabus, assignments, quizzes, study aids, and other course materials online; hold e-discussions and group conferences; send and receive email and assignments from students; and manage grades electronically.

DEDICATION

With love and thanks to my husband…
   Harry Whitbeck

and our daughters…
   Kristin, Jennifer, and Lynnann Whitbeck

With love and thanks to my wife…
   Renee Rosa

and our daughters…
   Raina and Olivia Rosa

In loving memory of Ray Waszak

CHAPTER 1

QuickBooks 2013

Overview, Open a Company File, Create Backup Copy, and Restore a Backup Copy

Chapter Objectives

- Describe the differences and similarities between manual and computerized accounting

- Identify the four levels of operation within QuickBooks

- Open QuickBooks

- Open a company file

- Make a backup copy of a company file

- Restore a backup copy of a company file

- Change the company name in a company file

Introduction

Accounting for the financial activity of any company involves repetitive recording of day-to-day business activities. Recording common business activities such as paying bills, purchasing merchandise, selling merchandise, and processing payroll involves repeating the same steps again and again. Many of these activities can occur several times in the course of one day, requiring much repetitive recording.

With the introduction of mainframe computers, certain processes such as payroll became simple to perform on computers. Companies appeared that used mainframe computers to process payrolls for local businesses. Eventually, other accounting activities were processed by mainframe computers, such as maintaining the general ledger and journals. As personal computers became more common, several computerized accounting software packages became available that enabled the processing of all routine business activities—from paying bills to buying and selling merchandise to paying payroll—all without the user needing a mainframe computer.

With a computerized accounting software package, as business activities are recorded, all necessary reports—from the journals to the general ledger to the payroll reports and the **financial statements**—are instantly prepared. This makes them available on a more timely basis. Also, with accounting software, if an error is noticed it can be easily corrected and a revised report immediately printed.

Originally, only people trained in accounting commonly used accounting software. But as more people began to use personal computers, business owners and non-accounting people started to record business activities on their own using accounting software.

QuickBooks® 2013 is an example of an accounting software package used to record all types of business and accounting activities and prepare a variety of reports, including financial statements. However, unlike many accounting software products, it is designed with the non-accountant in mind. Many of the data entry windows are described in everyday, non-accounting terms. Behind the scenes, QuickBooks uses traditional accounting procedures to record, summarize, and report financial information. Therefore, a basic understanding of accounting terms and procedures allows you to operate the software more efficiently. Throughout the text, accounting terms and concepts are displayed in the margins to describe the accounting going on behind the scenes in QuickBooks.

Accounting with QuickBooks versus Manual and Other Computerized Accounting Systems

In accounting, every **transaction** that involves money must be recorded. In a manual accounting system, all transactions are recorded chronologically in a **general journal**. At the end of the month, these transactions are posted (rewritten) in a book called the general ledger. The **general ledger** summarizes the information by descriptive names, called accounts. Examples of accounts are Cash, Accounts Receivable, and Inventory (assets); Accounts Payable and Notes Payable (liabilities); Capital and Drawings, and Stock and Retained Earnings (equity); Fees Earned and Sales (revenue); and Rent, Insurance, Salaries, and Depreciation (expenses). After routine transactions and any necessary adjustments are recorded in the journal and posted to the

trial balance A report containing all the general ledger account names, their debit and credit balances, and the total debits and credits.

general ledger, a **trial balance** is prepared to confirm that the general ledger is in balance, and then the financial statements are prepared.

To facilitate the recording of so many transactions in a manual accounting system, several journals are used. Similar transactions are recorded in each journal. Typically, a purchases journal is used to record purchases of merchandise on account; a sales journal is used to record sales of merchandise on account; a cash receipts journal is used to record collections of sales on account, cash sales, or any other cash receipt activity; and a cash payments journal is used to record payment of purchases on account, cash purchases, or any other cash payment activity. These journals are often referred to as **special journals** Journals such as the purchases journal, sales journal, cash receipts journal, and cash payments journal. These journals can be used instead of the general journal to chronologically record similar transactions. At the end of the month, transactions in the special journals are posted (rewritten) to the general ledger.

special journals. Any transaction that is not appropriately recorded in a special journal is recorded in the general journal. Month-end adjusting journal entries and fiscal year-end closing entries are recorded in the general journal.

Many computerized accounting software packages follow the procedures used in a manual accounting system. Transactions are recorded in special journals and the general journal as appropriate, and transactions from the journals are then posted to the general ledger. Users of other accounting software packages need to analyze the transaction, determine the correct journal in which to record the transaction, enter the data, view the journal entry for correctness, and then post the journal entry to the general ledger.

QuickBooks, on the other hand, is designed for the non-accountant as well as the accountant. QuickBooks does not do its recording in special journals; instead, it identifies transactions by business function: vendors, customers, employees, and banking. The language used in recording transactions is common business language: enter bills, pay bills, create invoices, receive payments, and so on. The user enters the transaction based on the nature of the activity. Then, behind the scenes, the software updates the appropriate accounting reports—the journal, general ledger, and trial balance—and financial statements, based on the activity entered into the system.

Four Levels of Operation

Although much of the accounting is conducted behind the scenes in QuickBooks, an understanding of the accounting concepts used by the software will help you determine how to record financial information correctly. The operations conducted by QuickBooks can be classified into four levels: New Company Setup, Lists/Centers, Activities, and Reports. (See figure 1–A.)

FIGURE 1–A
Four Levels of Operation in QuickBooks

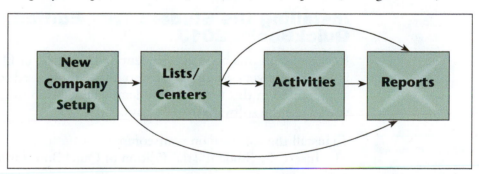

NEW COMPANY SETUP: The first level of operation is creating and setting up a new company file with the background information for the new company. This involves recording the company name, address, identification numbers, fiscal periods, type of business, accounts, and balances.

The second level of operation is recording background information in Lists and Centers. These Lists and Centers include Chart of Accounts, Item, Fixed Asset Item, Price Level, Billing Rate Level, Sales Tax Code, Payroll Item, Customer, Vendor, Employee, and so on. Information is initially recorded in Lists and Centers as part of New Company Setup, but it can be revised by adding, deleting, or editing information.

The Lists/Centers in QuickBooks function similarly to a database. Certain information is stored on these Lists/Centers, and as business activities involving any item on the Lists/Centers are processed, the information can simply be recalled and plugged into the windows rather than requiring you to re-key the data.

In QuickBooks 2013, the difference between Lists and Centers lies in how the List information is accessed. For the Customer, Vendor, and Employee Lists, the information is accessed through their respective Centers. For the Chart of Accounts, Item, Fixed Asset Item, Price Level, Billing Rate Level, Sales Tax Code, and Payroll Item Lists, the Lists are accessed using Lists from the main menu bar.

ACTIVITIES:
The third level of operation is recording daily business activity in QuickBooks. This is where most of the routine accounting work is processed. Activities are identified using common language such as enter bills, write checks, create invoices, receive payments, and so on. In addition, the information in Lists/Centers is frequently used to eliminate repetitive keying of data while recording daily activities.

REPORTS:
At certain times, it is necessary to display and print a variety of reports and financial statements based on information entered into QuickBooks. The fourth level of operation is using QuickBooks to display and print an assortment of Reports—for example, management reports related to each activity, such as vendor, customer, inventory, and payroll reports; accounting reports, such as the journal, general ledger, and trial balance; and financial statements, including the income statement and balance sheet.

Information that appears on the Reports is gathered during other operations within QuickBooks. As data is entered in the New Company Setup, Lists/Centers, and Activities levels of operation, the information is simultaneously recorded in the Reports level. QuickBooks provides for simple as well as more elaborate reporting. All the Reports can be customized according to the user's needs.

Installing the Student Trial Edition of QuickBooks 2013

Enclosed with this book is a Student Trial Edition of QuickBooks 2013. This is a complete version of the software that will be used to learn the software as presented in this text. The Student Trial Edition of QuickBooks allows you to use the software for 140 days.

HINT

The installation can take several minutes.

To install the software on your computer—

1. Insert the Student Trial Edition of QuickBooks into the disc drive.

   If your computer allows Autoplay, click *Run setup.exe* and go to step 5, or if the installation begins automatically, go to step 5.

   If the installation does not begin automatically, continue with step 2.

2. Right-click the Start button, and click Open Windows Explorer or Explore.

3. In the next window, on the left slide, click the disk drive that contains the CD. The files on the CD should appear on the right side of the window.
4. On the right side of the window, double-click *Setup.exe*.
5. Follow the instructions on the screen.
6. You will be prompted to enter a license number and a product number. These numbers are on the yellow sticker on the sleeve that contained the Student Trial Edition of QuickBooks.
7. After entering these numbers, continue to follow the instructions on the screen to complete the installation.

Note: If you were directed to an Intuit QuickBooks Installer message, click Finish. If the Intuit QuickBooks Installer Help window appears, close the window. If you receive a message How QuickBooks uses your Internet connection window, click OK. If the QuickBooks Setup window appears, close the window.

8. If you are prompted to register QuickBooks, you should do this immediately. **If you do not register the Student Trial Edition of QuickBooks within 30 days, you will no longer be able to use the software.**

Installing the Company Files Needed for This Text

QuickBooks must be installed on your computer for you to use this book. In addition to the Student Trial Edition of QuickBooks, also enclosed with the text is a Student Resources CD that contains the company files you will use to learn the topics presented in each chapter and do the two case problems at the end of the chapters. There are company files for all chapters except chapters 6 and 7, where you will learn how to create a new company file.

Throughout the text, you will be called on to open and use the company files provided on the Student Resources CD. The company files first need to be installed onto your hard drive or network. By default, QuickBooks stores company files at a location accessed by a path determined by your computer's operating system. Specifically:

If your computer is using *Windows 7*, the path would be as follows:
    C:\Users\Public\Public Documents\Intuit\QuickBooks\Company Files

If your computer is using *Windows Vista*, the path would be as follows:
    C:\Public\Public Documents\Intuit\QuickBooks\Company Files

If your computer is using *Windows XP*, the path would be as follows:
    C:\Documents and Settings\All Users\(Shared) Documents\Intuit\QuickBooks\Company Files

This textbook assumes that you store company files in the subfolder Company Files. However, you or your instructor can also install the company files in some other directory on your hard drive or on a network. If you use a subfolder other than Company Files, you must adjust the instructions below accordingly.

To install the company files from the Student Resources CD onto the hard drive—
1. Insert the Student Resources CD into the disc drive.

If your computer allows Autoplay, click *Run QBFilesSetup.exe* and go to step 5, or if the installation begins automatically, go to step 5.

If the installation does not begin automatically, continue with step 2.

2. Right-click the Start button, and click Open Windows Explorer or Explore.
3. In the next window, on the left slide, click the disk drive that contains the CD. The files on the CD should appear on the right side of the window.
4. On the right side of the window, double-click *QBFilesSetup.exe*.
5. At the Choose Destination Location dialog box, the Destination Directory text box will show the default path of QuickBooks company files based on the version of Windows installed on your computer as indicated above. If that is where you want the files installed, click Next. If you want to put them in another location, click Browse, find the alternative location, click OK, and then click Next.
6. For the next two steps in the installation wizard, click Next.
7. Finally, click Close.

Note: The Student Resources CD also includes a folder labeled Company Files that also contains all the Company Files. You could select all the company files in this folder and use the copy and paste commands to copy the company files to the destination of your choice.

Opening QuickBooks

To open QuickBooks—
1. Click Start on the Windows desktop taskbar.
2. At the Start menu, click *All Programs*.
3. At the All Programs menu, click *QuickBooks*.
4. At the QuickBooks menu, click *QuickBooks Premier-Accountant Edition 2013*. (See figure 1–B.)

Note: You may also use the QuickBooks Premier-Accountant Edition 2013 desktop icon.

FIGURE 1–B
Desktop Icon and
QuickBooks Menus

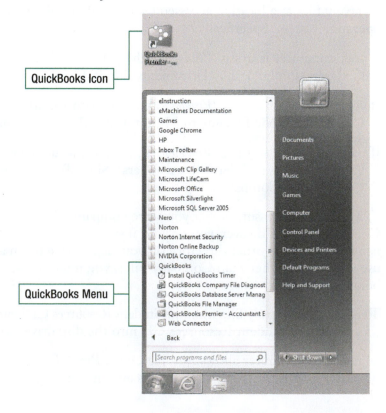

Note: If you receive a message How QuickBooks uses your Internet connection window, click OK. If the QuickBooks Setup window appears, close the window.

When QuickBooks is opened, the QuickBooks main window appears. In addition, a window titled *No Company Open* will appear. (See figure 1–C.)

Note: If a company file was previously used on this computer, the company file may automatically be opened. In this case, click File, then click Close Company, and you should see a window as in figure 1–C.

FIGURE 1–C
QuickBooks Main
Window—No
Company Open
Window

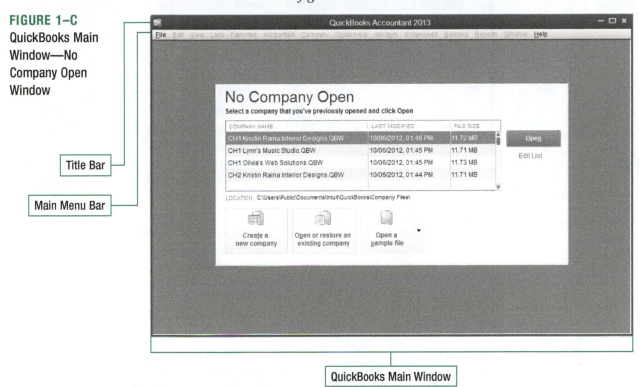

Title Bar

Main Menu Bar

QuickBooks Main Window

In the No Company Open window, the first time QuickBooks is opened, no company files will be listed. Thereafter, company files previously opened will be listed; you can use this window to select a company name and then click the Open button. Notice under the box listing the company files that the Location path is indicated. This path will be useful later as you begin to open several different company files. You also have three additional choices: Create a new company, Open or restore an existing company, or Open a sample file.

In chapters 1–5 and 8–12, you will open an existing company file from those provided on the Student Resources CD. In chapters 6 and 7, you will learn how to create a new company file.

HINT

If the *menu title* is in dark print, the menu is active and can be chosen. When a menu title is dimmed ("grayed out"), or in a lighter color, it is inactive and cannot be chosen.

Using Drop-Down Menus and Dialog Boxes

Whether a company file is open or not, notice the QuickBooks main window shown in figure 1–C. Along the top is the QuickBooks title bar, which will include a company name when a company file is open. Below the title bar is the main menu bar, which includes the menu choices of File, Edit, View, Lists, Favorites, Accountant, Company, Customers, Vendors, Employees, Banking, Reports, Window, and Help. When no company is open, only the menus File and Help are active and can be chosen. You can choose a menu by clicking the menu name with the mouse or by pressing the Alt key and the underlined letter from the menu name on the keyboard. Whenever you choose a menu, a drop-down menu appears that lists additional choices or commands. Choices on the menus will vary depending on the data entered into the company file, and depending on which of the open windows is active.

On the main menu bar, click File. The File drop-down menu appears, displaying commands or choices. (See figure 1–D.)

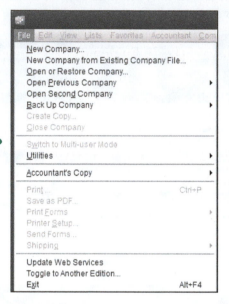

FIGURE 1–D
File Menu in
QuickBooks

HINT

If the *command* is in dark print, the command is active and can be chosen. If the command is dimmed ("grayed out"), it is inactive and cannot be chosen.

When you choose a command followed by an ellipsis (…), a window, called a dialog box, will appear. Additional information must be entered in the dialog box for the command to be processed. Included in dialog boxes are command buttons (such as Open, Cancel, Help). The active command button will have a slightly darker line around it. You can activate a command button by clicking the button. If the button is active, you can also activate the command by pressing the Enter key.

When you choose a command followed by an arrow, an additional drop-down menu, called a submenu, appears. Submenus list additional commands or choices.

QuickBooks

Intuit, the maker of QuickBooks, offers several versions of the QuickBooks software: Pro, Premier, and Enterprise Solutions. In addition, the QuickBooks Premier version is available in several editions: Accountant Edition, General Business Edition, Contractor Edition, and so on. The fundamentals of each version and edition of the QuickBooks software are the same. QuickBooks Pro is the basic version of the software with Premier and Enterprise Solutions offering additional features. Usually QuickBooks Pro would be used by small business owners. Larger businesses, businesses that have large inventories, or specific industries may use QuickBooks Enterprise Solutions or QuickBooks Premier. The QuickBooks Premier Accountant Edition is often used by the accountant who may have clients that use various versions or editions of QuickBooks. The QuickBooks Premier Accountant Edition software allows the accountant to toggle (switch) to different versions and editions of QuickBooks so the accountant can view the accounting records of their clients using their clients' version or edition of QuickBooks.

QuickBooks also offers an online version of the software on a monthly charge basis. There are three versions available: QuickBooks Online Simple Start, QuickBooks Online Essentials, and QuickBooks Online Plus. Although the functionality of the online version is similar to the traditional QuickBooks, the graphic interface of the menus, data entry windows, and reports differs significantly.

This book is prepared using the QuickBooks Premier Accountant Edition, and the Student's Trial version of the software is also QuickBooks Premier Accountant Edition. When schools purchase the Education packs of the software to install in computer laboratories, Intuit provides the schools with the QuickBooks Premier Accountant Edition version of the software.

To toggle to other versions or editions of QuickBooks, in the QuickBooks Premier Accountant Edition—

1. At the main menu bar, click File.
2. On the File menu, click Toggle to Another Edition. The Select QuickBooks Industry-Specific Edition dialog box appears. (See figure 1-E.)

FIGURE 1–E
Select QuickBooks
Industry-Specific Edition
Dialog Box

3. At the Select QuickBooks Industry-Specific Edition dialog box, you would click the desired version or edition of QuickBooks.
4. Click Next. The next window confirms the version or edition of QuickBooks that you have selected.

   If you click Toggle, QuickBooks Premier Accountant Edition closes and then reopens in the version or edition of QuickBooks that you have selected. Since the text is prepared using QuickBooks Accountant Edition, do not change to another version of the software.

5. Click Cancel.

QuickBooks Editions

There are several ways to determine which edition of QuickBooks you are using. The QuickBooks edition is listed in the title bar. In figure 1-C note the title bar displays QuickBooks Accountant 2013. If you toggle to a different edition of QuickBooks, the title bar will change to reflect which edition you are using.

You can also determine the edition that is currently open in the Select QuickBooks Industry-Specific Edition window. See figure 1-E, which notes the edition that is currently open.

The Help menu also displays the edition of QuickBooks you are using.

To determine the edition of QuickBooks using the Help menu—
1. Click Help on the main menu bar.
2. At the drop-down menu, notice the last command.

   The last command on the drop-down Help menu displays the edition of QuickBooks that is open.

3. Click Help to remove the Help drop-down menu.

Opening a Company File

The sample company file that came with this textbook, Kristin Raina Interior Designs, will be used to illustrate the topics in each chapter.

To open Kristin Raina Interior Designs—
1. At the No Company Open window, click the Open or restore an existing company button, or at the main menu bar, click File and then click Open or Restore Company. The Open or Restore Company window appears.

2. In the Open or Restore Company window, choose *Open a company file*. (See figure 1–F.)

FIGURE 1–F
Open or Restore
Company Window—
Open a Company File
Selected

Open a
Company File

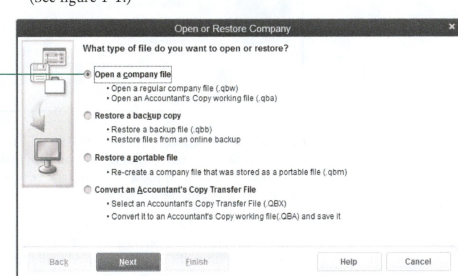

3. Click Next.

   The Open a Company dialog box appears. Most likely, the subfolder *Company Files* will appear in the *Look in* text box. QuickBooks automatically assigns the extension .QBW to each company file.

4. In the Open a Company dialog box in the *Look in* text box, choose *Company Files* or whatever subfolder contains the company files.

5. Select the company *CH1 Kristin Raina Interior Designs.QBW*.

   When you select a company name, the name also appears in the *File name* text box. (See figure 1–G.)

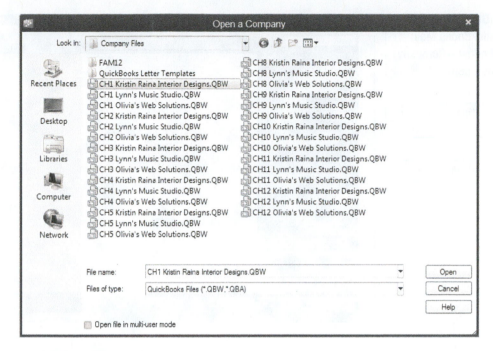

6. Click Open.

At various times when opening a company file or when operating QuickBooks, various pop-up messages will appear. In general, just close the messages. On some occasions you may be provided a choice to not show the message again. Also, in some situations, the QuickBooks default can be changed so the messages will no longer appear. Throughout this book suggestions will be made to close the message, choose not to show the message again, or change the default.

For now, when opening a company file, if a window appears titled Accountant Center, remove the check mark in the box to the left of Show Accountant Center when opening a company file, and then click the X to close the window.

Once a company file is open, the main window of QuickBooks changes. (See figure 1–H.)

FIGURE 1–H

QuickBooks Main
Window—Company
File Open

Title Bar with
Company Name

Left Icon Bar

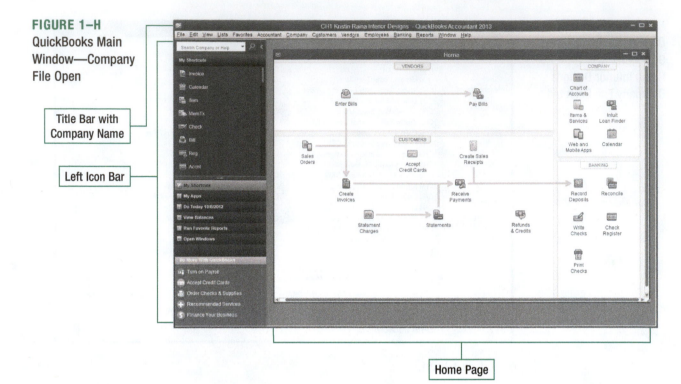

Home Page

HINT

Chapter 12 illustrates customizing and using the home page and icon bars.

The company name, CH1 Kristin Raina Interior Designs, is now displayed in the title bar. Along the left side of the window is the left icon bar. The remainder of the screen displays the home page. The left icon bar and the home page are additional methods that can be used to access information in QuickBooks as an alternative to using the main menu bar. In this text, only the main menu bar is used. The left icon bar and the home page will be closed to allow more screen space for the windows.

To close the left icon bar—
1. At the main menu bar, click View.
2. At the View menu, click Hide Icon Bar.

To close the home page—
1. Click the X.

You can change the default if you do not want the home page window to open each time QuickBooks is opened:

To change the default to close the home page window—
1. At the main menu bar, click Edit.
2. At the Edit menu, click Preferences.
3. Along the left, click the Desktop View icon.
4. Choose the My Preferences tab.
5. Remove the check mark to the left of Show home page when opening a company file.
6. Click OK.

Multi-User and Single-User Mode

multi-user mode
A setting in QuickBooks that allows up to five users to access a company file at the same time, each on their own computers.

single-user mode
A setting in QuickBooks that allows only one user at a time to access a company file.

QuickBooks is designed so that several people can use one company file at the same time. Assume a business has three bookkeepers, each with their own computer on their desk. When using QuickBooks, each bookkeeper can access the company records at the same time on their own computers. This is referred to as running the software in **multi-user mode**. Multi-user mode allows each bookkeeper to do his or her work individually; but at the same time, all information entered individually updates the company file as a whole. QuickBooks Premier allows for up to five users at one time. When QuickBooks is used on a single computer, it is referred to as **single-user mode**.

In the computer laboratory environment, you will use QuickBooks in single-user mode. Each person is using the company files individually; your work is not and should not be connected to anyone else's work. When QuickBooks is in single-user mode, the menu choice in the File menu is Switch to Multi-user Mode; when in multi-user mode, the menu choice is Switch to Single-user Mode. Because you should be working in single-user mode, the menu choice should be Switch to Multi-user Mode.

HINT

See Appendix I for information about setting up multi-users in QuickBooks.

Backing Up a Company File

In business, it is advisable to make backup copies of records on a regular basis and store the backup copies in a safe place, separate from the business location. In the event of damage to a company's computer and/or files, the backup copies can be used to restore the lost or damaged data.

Why Backing Up a File Is Important

In this text, you will use the Back Up command for two purposes. First, Backup will be used to make a copy of the original company file. The original company file will then be preserved intact for others to use; the backup copy will be restored for you to use in the practice exercises.

Second, as in business, you will use the Backup command to make backup copies of the exercise company files on removable storage devices or on a network directory. In the event your copy is deleted from the hard drive that you are working on, you will have a backup copy. This copy will also be helpful in case you use a different computer each time in the computer lab.

Naming Backup Files

Two types of names are used in QuickBooks to identify a company file—the file name and the company name. When your backup copy is made and restored, it is recommended that you include your name, or your initials, as part of the company *file* name, to distinguish your individual copy of the file from those of other students. In the restored copy (your exercise copy), the *company name* will also be changed to include your name, or your initials, to further identify the exercise copy of the company file as your copy.

In each chapter, the original company file name is preceded with the prefix CH1, CH2, and so on, to represent the chapter number. The backup copies are assigned the prefix EX1, EX2, and so on. EX stands for exercise and is the prefix used to identify the company file as a backup copy exercise file.

QuickBooks automatically assigns the extension .QBB to a backup copy and condenses the file. Condensed backup copies cannot be used for work; they are strictly for use as stored copies.

Backup copies can be made to the *Company Files* subfolder, to a subfolder of your choice, or to a removable storage device. It is recommended that you create your own subfolder on the hard drive, using Windows Explorer, and use your subfolder to store your backup copy of the company file. The following instructions assume you have created your own subfolder.

To make a backup copy of the CH1 Kristin Raina Interior Designs company file—

1. At the main menu bar, click File and then click *Back Up Company*.
2. At the Back Up Company submenu, click *Create Local Backup*. The Create Backup window—Do you want to save your backup copy online or locally? page appears.

   At certain times in QuickBooks, the title in a window will remain the same, but as you click the Next button, there will be a series of pages, within that window title, that will ask for or inform you of additional information.

3. In the Create Backup window, at the Do you want to save your backup copy online or locally? page, *Local backup* should be selected. (See figure 1–I.)

FIGURE 1–I

Create Backup Window—Do You Want to Save Your Backup Copy Online or Locally? Page

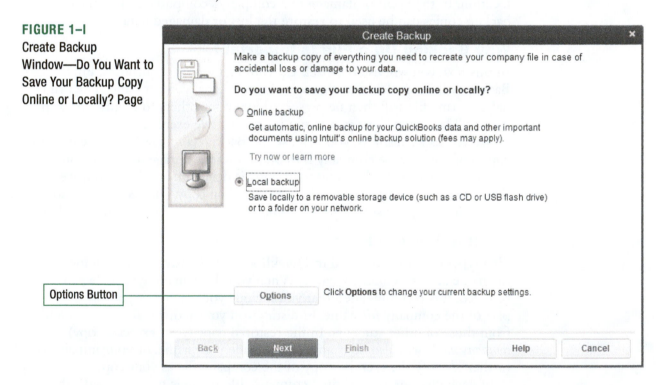

Options Button

4. Click Next. The Backup Options window appears. (See figure 1–J.)

Add the date
and time
option

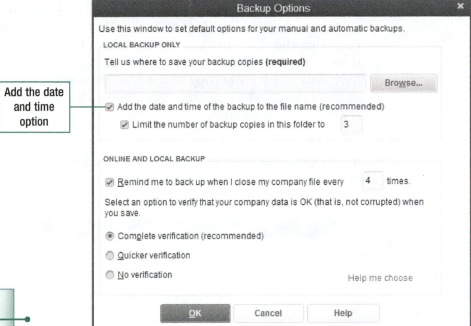

Note: The first time you make a backup copy of a company file, the Backup Options window appears. For subsequent backup copies of the same file, this window will not appear; you would not need to do steps 5–9 of this procedure.

HINT

Use the Options button to open the Backup Options window when it does not open automatically. The Backup Options window is used for settings regarding Backup.

5. At the Backup Options window, click the Browse button. The Browse for Folder window appears. (See figure 1–K.)

6. At the Browse for Folder window, choose your subfolder, a network directory designated by your instructor, or a removable storage device.
7. Click OK. You are returned to the Backup Options window, and the Tell us where to save your backup copies (required) field is completed.

By default, the date and time are listed in the file name of the Backup copy of a company file. When you make many backup copies of a company file, you will have several backup files, each with its individual date and time in the backup file name. You can remove this option by removing the check mark in the box to the left of Add the date and time of the backup to the file name. (See figure 1–J.) You would then have only one backup copy of the file, which would be replaced each time you updated the backup copy. Other Option settings can also be changed in this window.

8. Click OK.
9. At the QuickBooks message, click Use this Location. The Create Backup window—When do you want to save your backup copy? page appears. (See figure 1–L.)

FIGURE 1–L
Create Backup
Window—When Do
You Want to Save Your
Backup Copy? Page

10. At the When do you want to save your backup copy? page, choose *Save it now*, then click Next. The Save Backup Copy dialog box appears.
11. In the *Save in* text box, choose your subfolder, a network directory designated by your instructor, or a removable storage device, if it is not correct.
12. In the *File name* text box, key **EX1 [*Your Name*] Kristin Raina Interior Designs**. (See figure 1–M.)

FIGURE 1–M
Save Backup Copy
Dialog Box

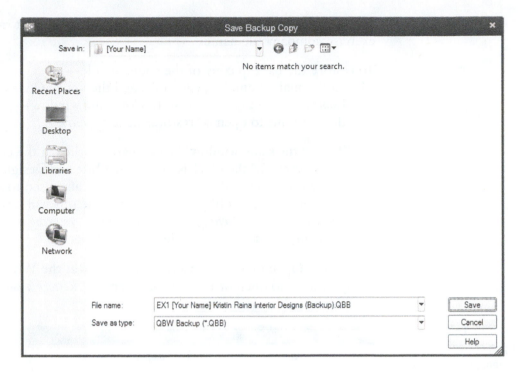

13. Click Save.

    If you use a file name that already exists, you will receive a Confirm Save As message asking if you want to replace the existing file. If you want to replace or update the existing file, click Yes. If you do not want to replace the existing file, click No and then use a different file name in the Save Backup Copy dialog box.

    If the QuickBooks message appears, click *Use this Location.*

14. At the QuickBooks Information message, click OK.

   You have now made a backup copy of the company file, but the *original file is still open.* To work on the backup copy of the company file that you just created, you must *restore* the backup copy.

Restoring a Company File

You use the Restore command to *open a backup copy* of a company file. Recall that backup copies are automatically assigned the extension .QBB and that they are condensed copies of a company file. QuickBooks gives the restore copy a .QBW extension, which denotes the working copies of the company file. If you are using removable storage devices to store your backup copies of company files, it is recommended that you use the hard drive for the exercises and use the removable storage devices only for backup. Using removable storage devices for the exercises may be slow, and all your work for one company file may not fit onto one removable storage device.

   Restoring a backup file is a two-step process. In the first step you determine which backup copy you wish to *open* (Open Backup Copy); in the second step you indicate where you wish to restore the backup copy *to* (Save Company File as). In business, the backup company file would be restored to the original company file name. In this book, however, the intent is to retain the original company file intact for others to use, so the backup company will *not* be restored to the original company file name but rather to your exercise company file name.

To restore the backup copy of the company file—

1. At the main menu bar, click File, and then click *Open or Restore Company*. The Open or Restore Company window—What type of file do you want to open or restore? page appears.

   This is the same window that appeared earlier in the chapter when you first *opened* the CH1 Kristin Raina Interior Designs company file as seen in figure 1–F. This window is now also used to *restore* a backup copy of a company file. Whenever you use this window, be clear as to whether you are *opening* a company file or *restoring a backup copy* of a company file so you make the correct choice.

2. In the Open or Restore Company window at the What type of file do you want to open or restore? page, choose *Restore a backup copy*. (See figure 1–N.)

FIGURE 1–N

Open or Restore Company Window— Restore a Backup Copy Selected

Restore a Backup Copy

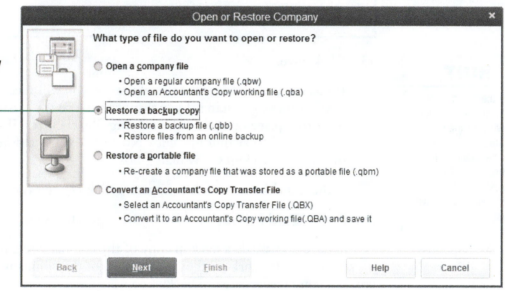

3. Click Next. The Is the backup copy stored locally or online? page appears.
4. At the Is the backup copy stored locally or online? page, choose *Local backup*, and then click Next. The Open Backup Copy dialog box appears.
5. In the *Look in* text box, choose the location where you saved your back-up copy.
6. Select the company file EX1 [*Your Name*] Kristin Raina Interior Designs (Backup).QBB. (See figure 1–O.)

FIGURE 1–O

Open Backup Copy
Dialog Box—EX1
[Your Name] Kristin
Raina Interior Designs
Selected

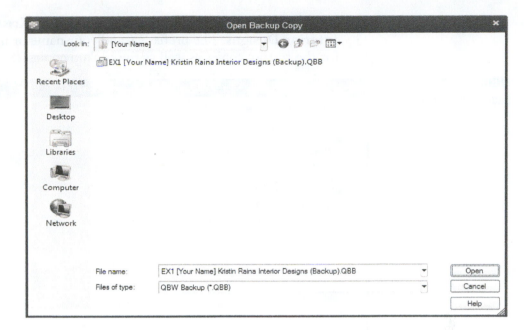

Compare figure 1–F with figure 1–N, and compare figure 1–G with figure 1–O. When you *open* a company file, on the Open or Restore Company window, you choose the option *Open a company file* (see figure 1–F). This window is followed by the *Open a Company* dialog box. All the files in this dialog box have the extension .QBW (see figure 1–G).

Conversely, when you want to open a backup copy of a company file, you must *restore* the file. On the Open or Restore Company window, you choose the option *Restore a backup copy* (see figure 1–N). This window is followed by the *Open Backup Copy* dialog box. All the files in this dialog box have the extension .QBB (see figure 1–O).

You must use the *restore* command to open a *backup* copy of a file. If you do not see your backup copy file listed, you may be in the wrong window. Go back to the Open or Restore Company window, and be sure you selected the Restore a backup copy choice.

HINT

See Appendix A for a comparison of the windows used to Open a Company File and Restore (Open) a Backup Copy of a Company File.

7. If the Open Backup Copy window is correct, click Open. The Where do you want to restore the file? page appears.
8. At the Where do you want to restore the file? page, click Next. The Save Company File as dialog box appears.
9. In the *Save in* text box, choose the subfolder where you will be opening and working on your copies of the company files.

10. In the *File name* text box, key **EX1 [*Your Name*] Kristin Raina Interior Designs**. The prefix EX and your name or initials will be used for the restore copies as well as the backup copies. (See figure 1–P.)

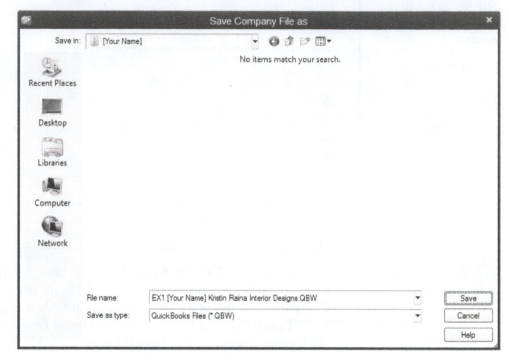

When a backup copy of a company file is restored, it becomes a working copy of the company file and QuickBooks assigns it a .QBW extension.

11. If the information is correct, click Save.

    If you use a file name that already exists, a Confirm Save As message appears indicating that this company file exists and asking if you want to replace it. If this is what you want to do, click Yes. You must then key **yes** in the box in the Delete Entire File message and click OK. If the name shown in the Confirm Save As message is not the correct file name, click No, and enter the correct file name in the Save Company File as dialog box.

12. A message stating *Your data has been restored successfully* should appear. Click OK at the message.

13. If the Accountant Center appears, remove the check mark in the box to the left of Show Accountant Center when opening a company file, and then click the X to close the window. If the home page window appears, click the X to close it. If the left icon bar appears, click View on the main menu bar, then click Hide Icon bar to remove it.

After your backup copy is successfully restored, your exercise copy of the company file appears in the QuickBooks window, but the title bar indicates the original company file name. Before you begin working, you should change the company name in the Company Information window to match your exercise company file name. This will then further identify this company file as your individual company file.

To change the company name—

1. Click Company on the main menu bar, then click *Company Information*.
2. At the Company Information window, in the *Company Name* text box, change the company name to **EX1 [*Your Name*] Kristin Raina Interior Designs**. (See figure 1–Q.)

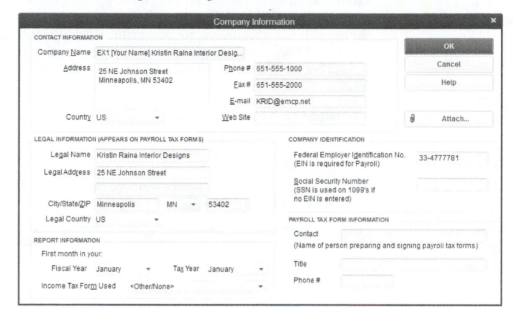

3. If the information is correct, click OK.

The company name is changed in the title bar. This company name will now appear in the heading of the reports. The name in the title bar comes from the Company Information window. The name of the company file in the Open a Company dialog box is based on the file name typed in the Backup and Restore dialog boxes. Be careful to type the *same* name in both places. This will help you to more easily keep track of your files.

In business, backup is used to maintain a copy of your company financial records. You would make backup copies of your company file on a regular basis. You would only need to restore the backup copy in the event your computer was damaged or you upgraded your computer system. An accountant may use backup and restore procedures when reviewing their clients' accounting records.

Because you may be working in a computer laboratory environment, where many students might be working on the same company files, the backup and restore procedures are used to make your own personal copy of the company file so that you may practice the work in each chapter in your own copy of each company file. You also use the backup procedures to make a copy to your personal removable device to retain a copy of the company file in the event your personal copy in a computer laboratory environment is deleted.

If you are unsure as to which location the company file you are working on is, click File, then click Open Previous Company. The file listed on the top of the list is the current file that is open.

QuickBooks Updates

QuickBooks will occasionally provide product updates to the current version of software that you are using. Product updates, sometimes referred to as maintenance releases by QuickBooks, are delivered via the Internet. Your computer can be set up so that the product updates are automatically downloaded (which is the default), or you can disable the automatic updates. If the updates are not automatic, when updates are available, upon opening QuickBooks, a message will appear inquiring if you wish to update QuickBooks. You can also check for QuickBooks updates using the Help menu.

To update QuickBooks using the Help menu—
1. At the main menu bar, click Help.
2. On the Help menu, click Update QuickBooks. The Update QuickBooks window appears.
3. At the Update QuickBooks window, click the Update Now button or click the Update Now tab. (See figure 1-R.)

FIGURE 1–R

Update QuickBooks Window

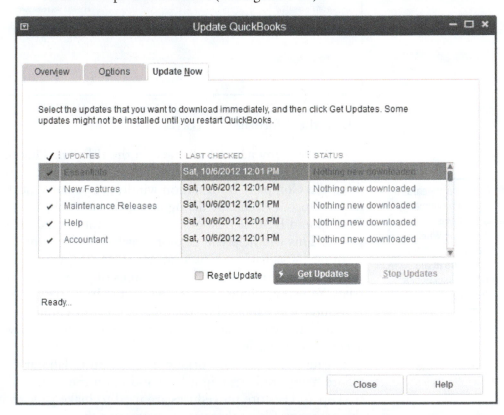

4. At the Update Now tab, click the Get Updates button. If any updates are available they will be downloaded. Follow the instructions to download the updates.

The product updates are noted by release numbers, such as R2, R3, and so on. To determine the most recent update downloaded onto your computer, press the F2 key on the keyboard, or press Ctrl + 1, which will display the Product Information window. In the Product Information window, on the first line next to Product, the edition of

QuickBooks is displayed along with the latest release number. (See figure 1–S.)

FIGURE 1–S
Product Information Window

Product Edition and Release Number

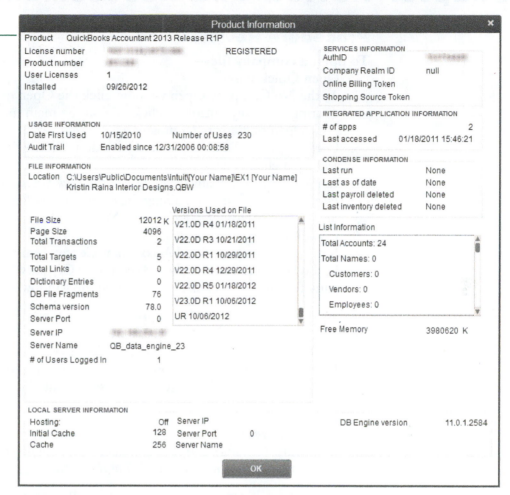

5. Close the Product Information window and close the Update QuickBooks window.

Exiting QuickBooks

Most work is automatically saved in QuickBooks when the correct command button is chosen. At the end of a session, it is recommended that you use the Backup command to save your work onto a removable storage device or a network directory designated by your instructor. For the security of your work, you should also close your company file before exiting QuickBooks. However, it is not necessary to make a backup copy of the exercise file for this session.

To close your company file, click File and then *Close Company*. To exit QuickBooks, click X (Close button) on the QuickBooks title bar, or click File and then *Exit*.

Chapter Review and Assessment

Procedure Review

To open a company file—

1. Open QuickBooks.
2. At the No Company Open window, click the Open or restore an existing company button or click File on the main menu bar, and then click Open or Restore Company.
3. In the Open or Restore Company window, choose *Open a company file* and then click Next.
4. In the Open a Company dialog box in the *Look in* text box, choose *Company Files*, or the subfolder containing the company files for this course.
5. Select the company *CH# Company Name.QBW*.
6. Click Open.
7. If a window appears titled Accountant Center, remove the check mark in the box to the left of Show Accountant Center when opening a company file, and then click the X to close the window.

To make a backup copy of a company file—

1. Click File, then click *Back Up Company*.
2. At the Back Up Company submenu, click *Create Local Backup*.
3. In the Create Backup window, at the Do you want to save your backup copy online or locally? page, *Local backup* should be selected, then click Next.

Note: The first time you make a backup copy of a company file, the Backup Options window appears. For subsequent backup copies of the same file, this window will not appear; you would not need to do steps 4–7 of this procedure.

4. At the Backup Options window, click the Browse button.
5. At the Browse for Folder window, choose your subfolder, a network directory designated by your instructor, or a removable storage device, and then click OK.
6. At the Backup Options window, you can remove the check mark to the left of Add the date and time of the backup to the file name, if you do not want multiple backup copies of the company file, and then click OK.
7. At the QuickBooks message, click *Use this Location*.
8. At the Create Backup window, at the When do you want to save your backup copy? page, choose *Save it now*, then click Next.
9. At the Save Backup Copy dialog box, in the *Save in* text box, choose your subfolder, a network directory designated by your instructor, or a removable storage device if it is not correct.
10. In the *File name* text box, key **EX# [*Your Name*] Company Name**.
11. Click Save. If the QuickBooks message appears, click *Use this Location*.
12. At the QuickBooks Information message, click OK.

To restore the backup copy of the company file—

1. Click File and then click *Open or Restore Company*.
2. In the Open or Restore Company window, at the What type of file do you want to open or restore? page, choose *Restore a backup copy* and then click Next.
3. At the Is the backup copy stored locally or online? page, choose *Local backup* and then click Next.
4. At the Open Backup Copy dialog box, in the *Look in* text box, choose the location where you saved your backup copy.
5. Select the company file *EX# [Your Name] Company Name.QBB.*
6. Click Open.
7. At the Where do you want to restore the file? page, click Next.
8. At the Save Company File as dialog box, in the *Save in* text box, choose the subfolder where you will be opening and working on your copies of the company files.
9. In the *File name* text box, key **EX# [*Your Name*] Company Name.**
10. Click Save.
11. At the *Your data has been restored successfully* message, click OK.
12. If the Accountant Center appears, remove the check mark in the box to the left of Show Accountant Center when opening a company file, and then click the X to close the window. If the home page window appears, click the X to close it. If the left icon bar appears, click View on the main menu bar, then click Hide Icon Bar to remove it.

To change the company name—

1. Click Company and then click *Company Information*.
2. In the Company Information dialog box at the *Company Name* text box, key **EX# [*Your Name*] Company Name.**
3. Click OK.

Key Concepts

Select the letter of the item that best matches each definition.

a. Company Name	f. Reports
b. Ellipsis	g. New Company Setup
c. Activities	h. Main Menu Bar
d. QuickBooks	i. Back Up Company
e. File Name	j. Lists/Centers

_____ 1. A software package used to record business and accounting activities, designed with the non-accountant in mind.

_____ 2. The level of operation that creates a new company file.

_____ 3. The level of operation that records background information.

_____ 4. The level of operation where most routine work is processed.

_____ 5. The level of operation where information can be displayed and printed.

_____ 6. Follows a command on a menu and means additional information must be entered in a second window called a dialog box.

_____ 7. The name that appears in the title bar of QuickBooks. The source is the Company Information window.

_____ 8. The part of the QuickBooks window where the File, Edit, View, Lists, Favorites, Accountant, Company, Customers, Vendors, Employees, Banking, Reports, Window, and Help menus are displayed.

_____ 9. The name indicated in the Backup and Restore windows.

_____ 10. The command used to make a copy of the original company file.

Procedure Check

1. What is QuickBooks?
2. What does single-user mode and multi-user mode mean in QuickBooks?
3. List the steps for opening a company file called Mary's Marathon Track Club, which is stored in the Company Files subfolder on the hard drive.
4. Assume you are instructed to work on a company file named CH1 Hercules Body Building Equipment. List the steps to make a backup copy called EX1 [*Your Name*] Hercules Body Building Equipment and then restore the backup copy. Assume the company file is stored in the Company Files subfolder and backed up and restored in the [*Your Name*] subfolder. If you backed up the file to a removable storage device, how would the steps be different? The same?
5. Assume you are working on a company file previously backed up and restored as EX1 [*Your Name*] Lynette's Boutique but are unable to finish the work today. When you return the next day to complete the work, explain how you would open the company file assuming no additional backup copy was made.

6. Discuss the advantages of using a computerized accounting software package instead of using non-computerized accounting methods. Discuss the specific advantages of using QuickBooks.

Case Problems

Case Problem 1

On April 1, 2014, Lynn Garcia started her business, called Lynn's Music Studio, as a music instructor.

1. Open the company file CH1 Lynn's Music Studio.QBW.
2. Make a backup copy of the company file using the file name LMS1 [*Your Name*] Lynn's Music Studio.
3. Restore the backup copy of the company file. In both the Open Backup Copy and the Save Company File as windows, use the file name LMS1 [*Your Name*] Lynn's Music Studio.
4. Change the company name to **LMS1 [*Your Name*] Lynn's Music Studio**.
5. Close the company.

Case Problem 2

On June 1, 2014, Olivia Chen started her business as an Internet consultant and web page designer, Olivia's Web Solutions.

1. Open the company file CH1 Olivia's Web Solutions.QBW.
2. Make a backup copy of the company file using the file name OWS1 [*Your Name*] Olivia's Web Solutions.
3. Restore the backup copy of the company file. In both the Open Backup Copy and the Save Company File as windows, use the file name OWS1 [*Your Name*] Olivia's Web Solutions.
4. Change the company name to **OWS1 [*Your Name*] Olivia's Web Solutions**.
5. Close the company.

CHAPTER 2

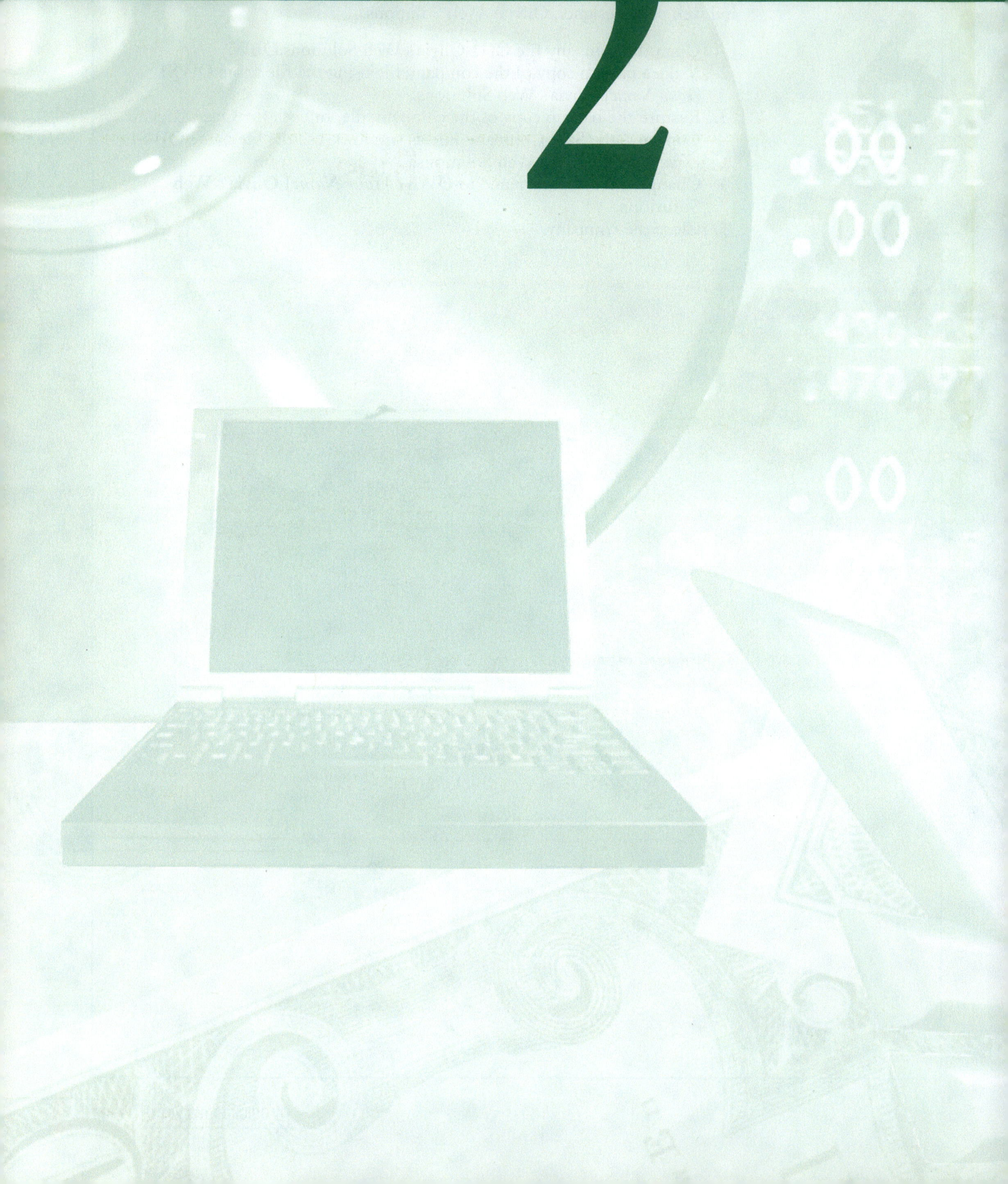

Vendors

Enter Bills, Pay Bills, and Cash Payments

Chapter Objectives

- Identify the system default accounts for vendors

- Update the Vendor Center

- Record purchases on account in the Enter Bills window

- Process credit memos in the Enter Bills window

- Record payments of accounts payable in the Pay Bills window

- Record cash purchases in the Write Checks window

- Display and print vendor-related reports

Introduction

QuickBooks allows you to track all vendor transactions. A **vendor** is someone from whom a company buys goods or services, either on account or for cash. You should establish a file for each vendor before entering transactions for that vendor. The collection of all vendor files comprises the vendor list, which is contained in the *Vendor Center* (Lists/Centers).

Once a vendor file is established, transactions (Activities) such as receiving a bill from a vendor, paying that bill, or paying for a cash purchase can be entered in the *Enter Bills, Pay Bills,* and *Write Checks* windows. As transactions are recorded in the activities windows, QuickBooks simultaneously updates the vendor's file in the Vendor Center, and any related reports (Reports), with information about the transaction for a particular vendor.

In this chapter, you will record and pay bills received by our sample company, Kristin Raina Interior Designs, for non-inventory purchases of goods and services, such as operating expenses and assets acquisitions. In addition, you will record cash purchases when bills have not been previously received or entered.

QuickBooks versus Manual Accounting: Vendor Transactions

In a manual accounting system, all purchases of goods on account are recorded in a multi-column **purchases journal**. At the conclusion of the month, the totals are posted to the asset, expense, and liability (Accounts Payable) accounts affected by the transactions. As each purchase transaction is recorded, the appropriate vendor's account in the accounts payable subsidiary ledger is updated for the new liability on a daily basis. Payments for open accounts payable balances and payments for cash purchases of goods/services are recorded in a multi-column **cash payments journal**. As in the purchases journal, monthly totals are posted to the general ledger accounts, while payment information is recorded daily in the vendor's subsidiary ledger record.

In QuickBooks, the Vendor Center serves as the accounts payable subsidiary ledger for the company. The Vendor Center contains a file for all companies and individuals from whom the company buys goods and services. Relevant information, such as name, address, contact, credit limit, and so on, should be entered at the time the vendor's file is created in the Vendor Center.

When the company receives a bill for goods or services, the bill is recorded in the Enter Bills window. The Enter Bills window is equivalent to the multi-column purchases journal. QuickBooks automatically updates the **Chart of Accounts List** and general ledger; at the same time, it updates the vendor's file in the Vendor Center for the new liability. When the bill is to be paid, you enter the transaction in the Pay Bills window. The Pay Bills window is equivalent to the part of the cash payments journal that records payment of open accounts payable. This transaction also updates the Chart of Accounts List and general ledger and at the same time updates the vendor's file in the Vendor Center for the payment of the liability.

For a cash payment for a bill not previously entered, you use the Write Checks window. This is equivalent to the part of the cash payments journal that records payment for cash purchases of goods/services. Again, the Chart of Accounts List, general ledger, and the vendor's file in the Vendor Center are simultaneously updated.

---

vendor Someone from whom a company buys goods or services, either on account or for cash.

purchases journal A journal used to record all purchases of goods on account; can be in a single-column or multi-column format.

cash payments journal A journal used to record all cash payment activities, including payment of accounts payable.

HINT

See Appendix B for a comparison of Manual Accounting versus QuickBooks.

Chart of Accounts List A list of all accounts a business uses.

System Default Accounts

To process transactions expeditiously and organize data for reporting, QuickBooks establishes specific general ledger accounts as default accounts in each activity window. When you enter transactions, QuickBooks automatically increases or decreases certain account balances depending on the nature of the transaction. For example, when you enter a vendor invoice in the Enter Bills window, QuickBooks automatically increases (credits) the Accounts Payable account because the Enter Bills window is used to record purchases on account. When you write a check in the Pay Bills window, QuickBooks automatically decreases (debits) the Accounts Payable account. Therefore, you do not have to enter the account number or name for these default accounts, because they have been pre-established by QuickBooks.

Throughout the text, we will identify the default accounts for each type of transaction, such as vendor, customer, inventory, and payroll.

Chapter Problem

In this chapter, you will enter and track vendor transactions for Kristin Raina Interior Designs, a sole proprietorship providing interior decorating and design services to both residential and commercial clients. The owner of the business, Kristin Raina, began operations on January 1, 2014, by investing $50,000 in the business. During January, Kristin Raina devoted most of her time to organizing the business, securing office space, and buying assets. Beginning February 1, 2014, she wishes to begin tracking vendor transactions. Information for several vendors has been entered in the Vendor Center. This information, along with February 1, 2014, beginning balances, is contained in the company file CH2 Kristin Raina Interior Designs.

Begin by opening the company file—
1. Open QuickBooks.
2. At the No Company Open window, click *Open or restore an existing company*; or click File and then click *Open or Restore Company*.
3. At the Open or Restore Company window, choose *Open a company file* and then click Next.
4. At the Open a Company dialog box, in the *Look in* text box, choose the Company Files subfolder, or the subfolder containing the company files.
5. Select the company file CH2 Kristin Raina Interior Designs.QBW, then click Open.
6. If a window appears titled Accountant Center, remove the check mark in the box to the left of Show Accountant Center when opening a company file, and then click the X to close the window.

Next, make a backup copy of the company file—
1. At the main menu bar, click File and then click *Back up Company*.
2. At the Back Up Company submenu, click *Create Backup Copy*.
3. In the Create Backup window, at the Do you want to save your backup copy online or locally? page, *Local backup* should be selected, then click Next.
4. At the Backup Options window, click the Browse button.
5. At the Browse for Folder window, choose your subfolder, a network directory designated by your instructor, or a removable storage device, and then click OK.

<aside>
HINT

In Windows XP, you must press the Alt key to see the underlined letter in the menu name.
</aside>

<aside>
HINT

The first time you make a backup copy of a company file, the Backup Options window appears. For subsequent backup copies of the same file, this window will not appear; you would not need to do steps 4-7 of this procedure.
</aside>

HINT

QuickBooks auto-
matically assigns an
extension of .QBB to a
backup copy.

6. At the Backup Options window, you can remove the check mark to the left of the Add the date and time of the backup to the file name if you do not want multiple backup copies, then click OK.
7. At the QuickBooks message, click Use this Location.
8. In the Create Backup window at the When do you want to save your backup copy? page, choose *Save it now* and then click Next.
9. In the Save Backup Copy dialog box, in the *Save in* text box, choose your subfolder, network directory designated by your instructor, or removable storage device, if it is not correct.
10. In the *File name* text box, key **EX2 [*Your Name*] Kristin Raina Interior Designs**.
11. Click Save. If the QuickBooks message appears, click *Use this Location*.
12. At the QuickBooks Information message, click OK.

Now restore the backup copy of the company file—
1. Click File and then click *Open or Restore Company*.
2. In the Open or Restore Company window, at the What type of file do you want to open or restore? page, choose the *Restore a backup copy* and then click Next.
3. At the Is the backup copy stored locally or online? page, choose *Local backup* and then click Next.
4. At the Open Backup Copy dialog box, in the *Look in* text box, choose the location where you saved your file.
5. Select the company file EX2 [*Your Name*] Kristin Raina Interior Designs.QBB, then click Open.
6. At the Where do you want to restore the file? page, click Next.
7. At the Save Company File as dialog box, in the *Save in* text box, choose the subfolder where you will be opening and working on your copies of the company file.
8. In the *File name* text box, key **EX2 [*Your Name*] Kristin Raina Interior Designs**, then click Save.
9. At the *Your data has been restored successfully* message, click OK.
10. If the Accountant Center appears, remove the check mark in the box to the left of Show Accountant Center when opening a company file, and then click the X to close the window. If the home page window appears, click the X to close it. If the left icon bar appears, click View on the main menu bar, then click Hide Icon bar to remove it.

The backup copy has been restored, but the company name still reads CH2 Kristin Raina Interior Designs.

HINT

QuickBooks automati-
cally assigns the exten-
sion .QBW to a restored
copy.

Change the company name—
1. At the main menu bar, click Company and then click *Company Information*.
2. Change the company name to **EX2 [*Your Name*] Kristin Raina Interior Designs**.
3. Click OK.

LISTS/CENTERS:

The Vendor Center

The Vendor Center contains a file for each vendor with which the company does business. For example, the utility company that supplies electricity, the company that provides advertising, and the company from which equipment for the business is purchased are all vendors. The Vendor Center contains important information on each vendor, such as company name, address, contact person, type of vendor, terms, credit limit, tax ID, and current balance owed. All vendors the company does business with should be included in the Vendor Center.

You should enter the information for each vendor in the Vendor Center before recording transactions. However, if you inadvertently omit a vendor, you can add that vendor during the Activities level of operation with a minimum of disruption.

You will need to periodically revise the Vendor Center to add new vendors, delete vendors no longer used in the business, or make modifications as background information on vendors changes. These adjustments to the vendor files in the Vendor Center are referred to as *updating* the Vendor Center, and they are part of the second level of operation in QuickBooks.

Kristin Raina has entered information for existing and anticipated vendors in the Vendor Center of her company file.

To review the Vendor Center—
1. Click Vendors and then click *Vendor Center*. If a window appears titled New Feature - Attach Documents to QuickBooks, click OK or X to close. The Vendor Center appears with the vendor file for Galeway Computers displayed. (See figure 2–A.)

FIGURE 2–A
Vendor Center—Galeway Computers Vendor File Displayed

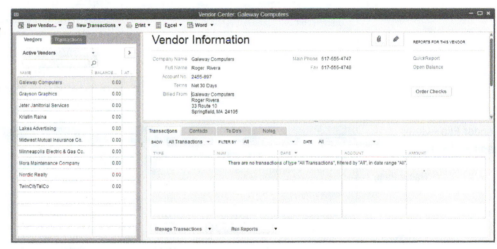

The Vendor Center contains the following parts:

Vendors tab	Lists all vendors with current balance owed. You can display all vendors, active vendors, or vendors with balances.
Transactions tab	Lists all transactions for a selected vendor. The Transactions tab in the Vendor Information section contains the same information.
New Vendor button	Used to add a new vendor.
New Transactions button	Used to enter a bill or pay a bill.
Vendor Information	Displays background and transaction information for the vendor selected in the Vendor tab.
Attach Icon	Used to attach documents via QuickBooks Document Management feature.

Edit Icon	Used to edit background information for the vendor selected in the Vendor Tab.
Reports for this Vendor	Lists the reports available in the Vendor Center.
Contacts tab	When you enter a name in the FULL NAME field it will be added to the Contacts tab. You can also right-click the tab to add, edit, or delete a contact.
To Do's tab	Used to view the To Do List for this vendor.
Notes tab	Used to include narrative information specific to a vendor.

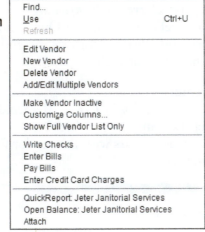

FIGURE 2–B
Vendor Center Drop-Down
Menu

In addition, after selecting a vendor, you can right-click the mouse on the Vendor tab to display a shortcut menu to accomplish most vendor-related activities. (See figure 2–B.)

To view a specific vendor file—
1. Move the mouse pointer to *Jeter Janitorial Service*, then double-click to open the file. If a window appears titled New Feature Add/Edit Multiple List Entries, place a check mark in the box to the left of the *Do not display this message in the future* field and click OK to close. This will open the file in Edit Vendor mode. (See figure 2–C.)

FIGURE 2–C
Vendor File—Jeter
Janitorial Services

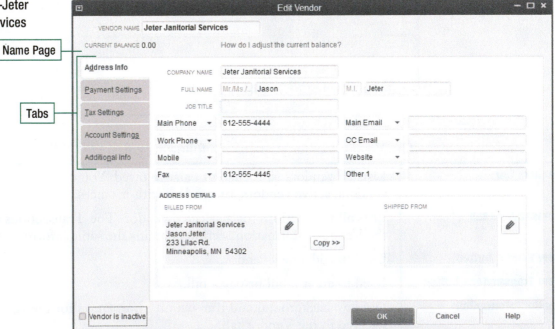

The vendor's file contains six parts:

Name page	This portion displays the vendor's name, current balance, and three command buttons: OK, Cancel, and Help.
Address Info tab	This tab allows you to enter the vendor's company name, address, contact person, telephone and fax numbers, and email address. The Edit icon can be used to edit address information.
Payment Settings tab	This tab allows you to enter information, such as the vendor's account number, credit limit, payment terms, and name to be printed on checks.
Tax Settings tab	This tab allows you to enter the vendor's tax identification number (TIN) and indicate if the vendor is to receive a 1099.
Account Settings tab	This tab allows you to identify up to three default general ledger posting accounts for each vendor. Once a vendor is selected in an activity window, the first account listed will be identified as the general ledger posting account for that transaction. The use of this tab is optional.
Additional Info tab	This tab allows you to enter the vendor type and gives you the ability to create customized fields.

2. Close the Edit Vendor window.
3. Close the Vendor Center.

Adding a Vendor

Kristin Raina has just hired a new accountant who will provide accounting services each month for the business. She wishes to add this vendor to the Vendor Center by creating a vendor file.

To add a new vendor—

1. At the main menu bar, click Vendors and then click *Vendor Center*. The Vendor Center opens with a list of vendors on the Vendor tab and information displayed for the first vendor on the list.
2. At the Vendor Center window, click the New Vendor button, and select New Vendor. The New Vendor window appears. (See figure 2–D.)

FIGURE 2–D
New Vendor Window

HINT

QuickBooks defaults to the current date. Be sure to change the date to match the problem.

3. Enter the data below on the name page and the Address Info tab. (The Edit button can be used to enter the address but is not necessary.)

HINT

Use Tab to move to each field and Shift + Tab to move back a field. In the *BILLED FROM* field, at the end of each line in the address, use the Enter key or the Down Arrow key to move to the next line.

Name page

VENDOR NAME:	**[Your Name] Accounting Service**
OPENING BALANCE:	**0 AS OF February 1, 2014**

Address Info

COMPANY NAME:	**[Your Name] Accounting Service**
FULL NAME:	
First:	**[Your First Name]**
Last:	**[Your Last Name]**
Main Phone:	**651-555-2222**
Fax:	**651-555-2223**
Main Email:	**[Your Initials]@emcp.net**
BILLED FROM:	**One Main Plaza**
	St. Paul, MN 53602

Your New Vendor window should look similar to figure 2–E.

FIGURE 2–E
New Vendor Window— Name Page and Address Info Tab Completed

HINT

You can click the Edit icon to access the address information window.

4. Click the Payment Settings tab and complete the information below.

Payment Settings

ACCOUNT NO.   **99-2014-XX**
PAYMENT TERMS: **Net 30 Days**
PRINT NAME ON CHECK AS: **[Your Name] Accounting Service**

(See figure 2–F.)

FIGURE 2–F
New Vendor Window—
Payments Settings Tab
Completed

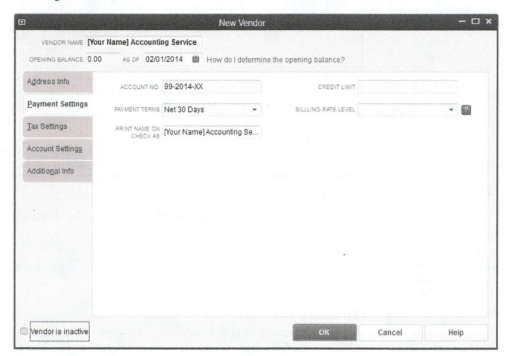

5. Click the Account Settings tab, and complete the information below.

Account Settings

Select accounts to pre-fill transactions:
6020 Accounting Expense

(See figure 2–G.)

FIGURE 2–G

New Vendor Window—
Account Settings Tab
Completed

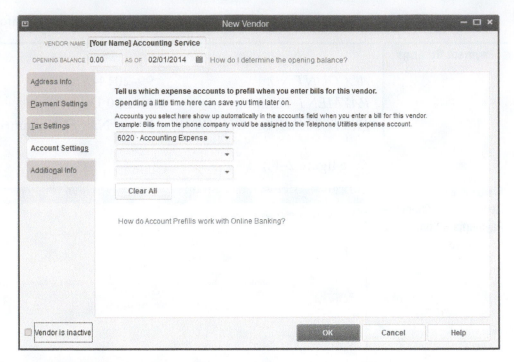

HINT

Remember you must click OK to save the information. If you exit the window by clicking the Close button (X), the information will be lost.

6. If the information is correct, click OK.
7. Click X (Close button) to close the Vendor Center.

Deleting a Vendor

Kristin Raina wishes to delete Lakes Advertising from the Vendor Center because the company has ceased to operate.

To delete a vendor—

1. At the main menu bar, click Vendors and then click *Vendor Center*.
2. At the Vendor Center window, select (highlight) *Lakes Advertising*, but do not open the file. (See figure 2–H.)

FIGURE 2–H

Vendor Center—Lakes Advertising Selected

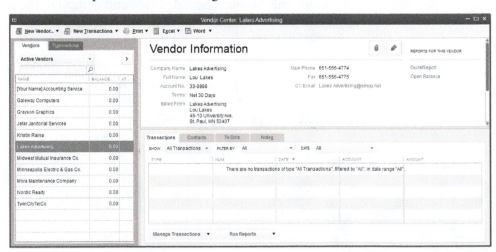

3. From the main menu bar, click Edit and then click *Delete Vendor*.
4. The Delete Vendor warning appears. Click OK. The vendor file will be deleted.
5. Close the Vendor Center window.

QuickBooks cannot delete a vendor who has a balance or a vendor who has been part of a transaction for the fiscal period. If a vendor will no longer be used but there has been activity to the file for the period, you can place a check mark in the *Vendor is inactive* box. The vendor's name is no longer displayed in the reports, but the vendor information is retained in QuickBooks and can be accessed as needed.

Editing a Vendor

Kristin Raina needs to edit the file for Minneapolis Electric & Gas Co. because the billing address has changed.

To edit a vendor file—
1. At the menu bar, click Vendors and then click *Vendor Center*. Double-click *Minneapolis Electric & Gas Co.* This will open the vendor file in the edit mode. (See figure 2–I.)

HINT

An alternate method to access the Edit Vendor window is to select the vendor in the Vendor Center and then click the Edit icon.

FIGURE 2–I
Edit Vendor Window

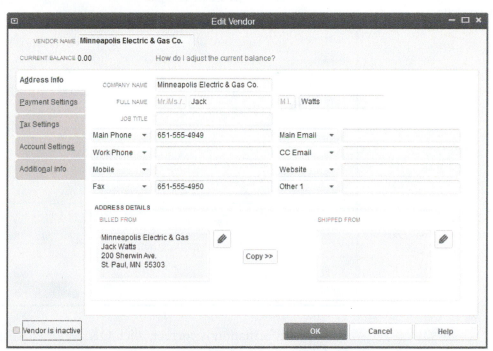

2. Since this is an edit of an address, click the Edit icon ✐. The Edit Address Information window will appear. (See figure 2–J.)

FIGURE 2–J
Edit Address Information
Window

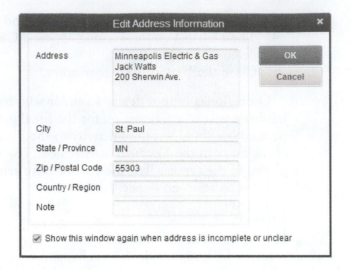

3. At the *Address* field, delete the current street address; in its place, key **150 Douglas Ave**. Click OK. (See figure 2–K.)

FIGURE 2–K
Edit Vendor Window—
Completed

4. If the information is correct, click OK.
5. Close the Vendor Center window.

Practice Exercise

Add the following vendor:

Name page

VENDOR NAME:	**Williams Office Supply Company**
OPENING BALANCE:	**0 AS OF February 1, 2014**

Address Info

COMPANY NAME:	**Williams Office Supply Company**
FULL NAME:	
First:	**Bernard**
Last:	**Williams**
Main Phone:	**612-555-2240**
Fax:	**612-555-2241**
Main Email:	**Wilsup@emcp.net**
BILLED FROM:	**One Main Plaza**
	St. Paul, MN 53602

Payment Settings

ACCOUNT NO.:	**55-8988**
PAYMENT TERMS:	**Net 30 Days**
PRINT NAME ON CHECK AS:	**Williams Office Supply Company**

Delete the following vendor:
   Mora Maintenance Company

Edit the following vendor:
   New phone/fax for Grayson Graphics:

Main Phone:	**612-555-0002**
Fax:	**612-555-0003**

QuickCheck: The updated Vendor Center appears in figure 2–L.

FIGURE 2–L
Updated Vendor Center

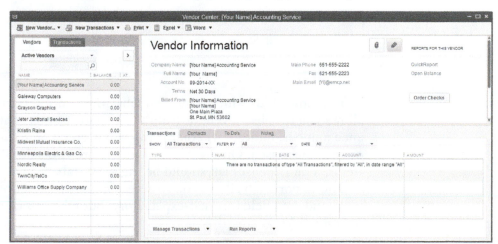

The Enter Bills Window

In QuickBooks, the Enter Bills window is used to record a **purchase on account**. This window allows you to identify the vendor sending the bill, the invoice date, due date, terms of payment, and nature of purchase (expense, asset, or item). QuickBooks uses the default Accounts Payable account from the Chart of Accounts to post all open bill liabilities. Certain recurring bills can be set up to be recorded automatically as they become due. In addition, you can use this window to record credit memos.

QuickBooks records a transaction that is a purchase on account as follows:

		Asset/Expense/Drawings	XXX	
		Accounts Payable		XXX

At the same time, QuickBooks updates the vendor's file in the Vendor Center to reflect the new liability.

Recall from chapter 1 that the third level of operation in QuickBooks is Activities. In this case, the Activity is the recording of purchases on account in the Enter Bills window. Accounts Payable is the default general ledger posting account. All transactions entered in this window will result in a credit to the Accounts Payable account. The *ACCOUNT* field in this window is used to indicate the asset, expense, or drawings account to be debited.

The QuickBooks Enter Bills window appears in figure 2–M.

FIGURE 2–M

Enter Bills Window—
Expenses Tab

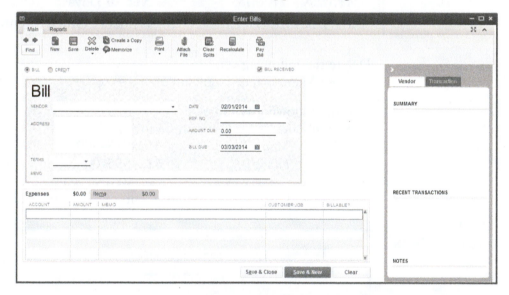

The Enter Bills window has two tabs: Main and Reports. The Main tab allows you to select a vendor from the Vendor Center, enter a bill reference number, indicate whether it is a bill or credit, and indicate the expense or item purchased. On the Main tab, there are two sub-tabs: Expenses and Items. The Expenses tab should be the active tab.

The Reports tab allows you to access various transactions reports. Most icons and data fields are self-explanatory, but take special note of the following on the Main tab:

purchase on account
When a company receives a bill for goods or services from a vendor but plans to pay it at a later date.

Find Previous/Next arrows	Used to move from the current transaction to the previous ◀ or next ▶ transaction. The current transaction will be saved before moving to the previous or next window. Also used to find previously recorded bills by vendor, date range, reference number, and amount.
New button	Used to open a blank transactions window and save current transactions.
Delete button	Used to delete or void the transaction.
Clear Splits button	Used to erase entries in the Expenses or Items tabs.
Recalculate button	Used to add up multiple entries on the Expenses and Items tabs to fill the *AMOUNT DUE* field.
Pay Bill button	Used to open the Pay Bills window.
BILL RECEIVED	Indicates that the bill has been received for this expense or item. If unchecked, the expense or item was received, but the bill will follow at a later date.
Expenses/Items tabs	For non-item purchases, such as expenses, non-inventory assets, and so on, click Expenses. If this is a purchase of an item, such as inventory, click the Items tab. The Items tab will be covered in chapter 5.
Save & Close button	Used to save (post) the transaction and close the window.
Save & New button	Used to save (post) the transaction and clear the window for a new transaction.
Clear button	Used to clear the entire screen if errors are made.
Vendor Name/ Transaction tabs	Displays a summary of information about the vendor, recent trsnsactions, and notes.
Edit icon 🖉	Allows you to edit vendor information while remaining in the Enter Bills window.
SUMMARY	Lists phone number, email address, and open balance for selected vendor.
RECENT TRANSACTIONS	Displays recent transactions for selected vendor. Also allows you to access a Quick Report for this vendor.
NOTES	Clicking 🖉 allows you to post notes concerning selected vendor.

Entering a Bill

On February 2, 2014, Kristin Raina received a bill for utilities services from Minneapolis Electric & Gas Co. in the amount of $350, Ref. No. 125-55. The bill is due March 4, 2014, terms **Net 30 Days**.

To enter a bill—
1. At the main menu bar, click Vendors and then click *Enter Bills.*
2. Click the BILL option and the *BILL RECEIVED* box, if necessary.
3. To display the VENDOR drop-down list, click the down arrow in the *VENDOR* field and then click *Minneapolis Electric & Gas Co.*
4. At the *DATE* field, choose *02/02/2014.* (Click the calendar icon, click through the months to find February 2014, then click 2.)
5. At the *REF. NO.* field, key **125-55.**
6. At the *AMOUNT DUE* field, key **350.**
7. At the *BILL DUE* field, choose *03/04/2014.*
8. At the *TERMS* field, click *Net 30 Days*, if necessary.

Net 30 Days Full payment of an invoice within 30 days of the invoice date is requested.

9. At the Expenses tab in the *ACCOUNT* field, click the first line to display the drop-down list arrow. At the account drop-down list, click *6500 Utilities Expense*. (See figure 2–N.)

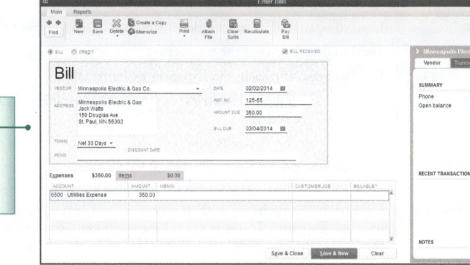

HINT

Click the arrow on the Vendor Name/ Transactions tabs to hide it. Click it again to display.

10. If the information is correct, click Save & Close.

Recall that Save & Close will save the information and close the window. The Next arrow will save the information and then clear the fields for the next transaction. The Previous arrow will display the window for the previous transaction. Since this is the first transaction, the Previous arrow cannot yet be used.

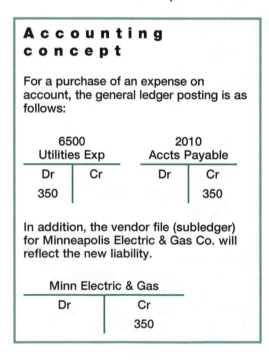

Accounting concept

For a purchase of an expense on account, the general ledger posting is as follows:

6500 Utilities Exp		2010 Accts Payable	
Dr	Cr	Dr	Cr
350			350

In addition, the vendor file (subledger) for Minneapolis Electric & Gas Co. will reflect the new liability.

Minn Electric & Gas	
Dr	Cr
	350

Updating the Vendor Center While in an Activities Window

On February 2, 2014, Kristin Raina received a bill for prepaid advertising services from Cuza and Carl Associates in the amount of $600, Invoice No. X-145. The bill is due March 4, 2014, terms Net 30 Days. Cuza and Carl Associates is a new vendor.

To update the Vendor Center from the Enter Bills window—

1. Click Vendors and then click *Enter Bills*.
2. At the VENDOR drop-down list, click < Add New >.

   The New Vendor window appears. This is the same window that appears after choosing the New Vendor button in the Vendor Center window.

3. Enter the information for the new vendor as listed on the next page.

VENDOR NAME:	**Cuza and Carl Associates**
OPENING BALANCE:	**0 AS OF February 2, 2014**
COMPANY NAME:	**Cuza and Carl Associates**

Address Info

FULL NAME:	**Carrie Cuza**
First Name:	**Carrie**
Last Name:	**Cuza**
Main Phone:	**651-555-8855**
Fax:	**651-555-8856**
Main Email:	**CC@emcp.net**
BILLED FROM:	**23 W. University Ave.**
	St. Paul, MN 53603

Payment Settings

ACCOUNT NO.:	**KR569**
TERMS:	**Net 30 Days**
PRINT NAME ON CHECK AS:	**Cuza and Carl Associates**

4. Click OK to save the information. You will exit the New Vendor window, and the new vendor is now listed in the *Vendor* field.
5. Complete the remaining fields of the Enter Bills window.
6. On the Expenses tab, click the account *1410 Prepaid Advertising*.

You use the Expenses tab to indicate which account should be debited. The account can be an asset, expense, or drawings account. Remember when using this window that by default, Accounts Payable is the account credited. (See figure 2–O.)

FIGURE 2–O
Enter Bills Window—
Completed

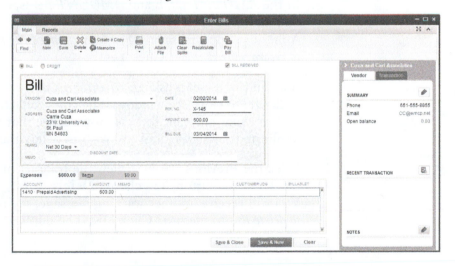

HINT

You can display transactions previously entered by clicking the Previous arrow ⬅ on the Find button; any errors can then be corrected. Clicking the Next arrow ➡ returns you to the current transaction or will bring you to a clear window.

7. If the information is correct, click Save & New.

Correcting Errors

There are several ways to correct an error in a recorded transaction. One way is to open the window that contains the transaction and use the ◀ on the Find button to view it. You can then make the necessary correction and save the transaction by choosing the Save icon. As an alternative to correcting an error in a transaction, you can delete the transaction by clicking the Delete button (in this example) or by selecting Edit on the main menu bar, clicking *Delete Bill*, and re-entering the transaction correctly.

Assume on February 2, 2014, that Kristin Raina inadvertently records a Prepaid Advertising amount for $300, realizes the correct amount is $600, and further realizes that the invoice had already been recorded. The bill is from Cuza and Carl Associates, Invoice No. X-145, due March 4, 2014, terms Net 30 Days.

To record an erroneous transaction, make corrections, and delete the transaction—

1. Click Vendors and then click *Enter Bills* (if necessary).
2. At the VENDOR drop-down list, click *Cuza and Carl Associates*.
3. Enter information in the *DATE, REF. NO., BILL DUE, TERMS*, and *ACCOUNT* fields.
4. In the *AMOUNT DUE* field, key **300**.
5. Click Save & New.
6. You will receive a warning that the Reference No. has already been used. This means that you are incorrectly recording an invoice for the second time. For now, ignore the warning, and click Keep Number. The transaction is recorded.
7. Click the Previous ◀ arrow.

   Upon reviewing the transaction, you realize the correct amount should have been $600.

8. In the *AMOUNT DUE* and *AMOUNT* fields, change the amount to **600** and then click Save & New.
9. A message appears, saying *You have changed the transaction. Do you want to record your changes?* Click Yes.

   If a window appears asking: *Want to reclassify several transactions at once?*, click OK to close the window. The corrected transaction is then saved with the new amount. But you now realize that this transaction is a duplicate transaction, and you wish to delete the transaction completely.

10. Click the Previous arrow to view the transaction.
11. Click Delete button, and choose **Delete**.
12. You will receive another warning message, saying *Are you sure you want to delete this transaction?* Click OK. The duplicate transaction is deleted.

Practice Exercise

Record the following transactions in the Enter Bills window:

Feb. 3	Received bill from Nordic Realty for February rent, Invoice No. F-14, $800. Due date February 13, 2014 (charge to Rent Expense Account No. 6400).
Feb. 6	Received bill from Williams Office Supply Company for purchase of office supplies, Invoice No. K-222, $475. Due date March 8, 2014 (charge to Office Supplies Account No. 1305).
Feb. 9	Received bill from Midwest Mutual Insurance Co. for 1-year insurance policy, Invoice No. 01-21, $2,400. Due date March 11, 2014 (charge to Prepaid Insurance Account No. 1420).
Feb. 13	Received bill from Galeway Computers for a new computer, Invoice No. 556588, $3,600. Due date March 15, 2014 (charge to Computers, Cost Account No. 1825).
Feb. 23	Received bill from [Your Name] Accounting Service for accounting service, Invoice No. Feb14, $300. Due date March 25, 2014. (Note that Account 6020—Accounting Expense automatically filled the general ledger posting account line on the Expenses tab because the Account Settings tab was completed for this vendor).

Processing a Credit Memo

credit memo
A reduction of Accounts Payable as a result of a return or an allowance by a vendor.

QuickBooks allows you to process a **credit memo** from a vendor using the Enter Bills window. The resulting credit will reduce the balance owed to that vendor.

On February 24, 2014, Kristin Raina returned $75 of damaged office supplies to Williams Office Supply Company for credit, using credit memo CM-245.

To record a vendor credit—

1. Click Vendors and then click *Enter Bills* if it is not already open.
2. At the VENDOR drop-down list, click *Williams Office Supply Company*. Note on the Vendor tab the balance due and bill for the purchase of supplies dated 2/6/2014.
3. Click the CREDIT option button. When this button is chosen, the default entry is a debit to Accounts Payable.
4. Enter the appropriate information in the *DATE*, *REF. NO.*, and *CREDIT AMOUNT* fields.
5. At the *MEMO* field, key **Return damaged office supplies**.
6. At the Expenses tab in the *ACCOUNT* field, click *1305 Office Supplies*. (See figure 2–P.) If the information is correct, click Save & Close.

For a return of office supplies for credit, the general ledger posting is as follows:

In addition, the vendor file for Williams Office Supply Company will reflect the reduced liability amount:

2010 Accts Payable		1305 Office Supplies	
Dr	Cr	Dr	Cr
75			75

Williams Office Supply Co.

Dr		Cr	
CM	75	Bill	475
		Bal	400

FIGURE 2–P
Credit Memo—
Completed

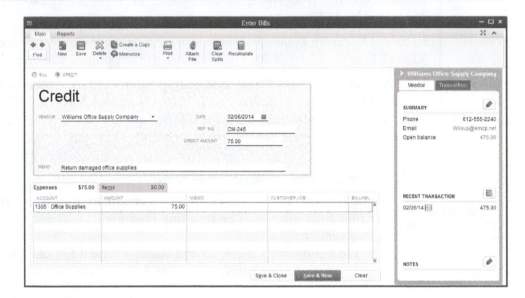

○ **The Pay Bills Window**

In QuickBooks, the Pay Bills window is used to record the **payment on account**. These are the bills previously recorded in the Enter Bills window. This window displays all open bills as of a selected date. Bills can be paid in full or a partial payment can be made. Payment can be in the form of check, credit card, or online payment. In addition, several bills can be paid at one time.

payment on account
Payment of an outstanding account payable.

The Pay Bills window is designed only for payments of existing bills. The default accounts are Accounts Payable and Cash. The transaction is recorded as follows:

	Accounts Payable		XXX	
	Cash			XXX

At the same time, the vendor's file in the Vendor Center is updated to reflect the payment. The QuickBooks Pay Bills window appears in figure 2–Q.

FIGURE 2–Q
Pay Bills Window

This window allows you to select a bill or bills to be paid, pay all or part of each bill, and designate checks to be printed by the computer. Note the following fields:

Show bills	Displays all bills or bills due by a certain date.
Filter By	Allows you to display bills for all vendors or a selected vendor from the drop-down list.
Sort By	Lists bills by due date, discount date, vendor, or amount due.
Go to Bill button	Allows you to view selected bill in the Enter Bills window.
Set Discount/Set Credits buttons	Used to activate any discount or credit for a bill selected for payment.
PAYMENT Account	Lists accounts from which this payment can be made.
PAYMENT Method	Lists methods of payment. If the *To be printed* option button is selected, a check number starting with 1 is assigned to each check in sequence. When the Assign check number option is chosen, a new dialog box appears where a check number can be assigned.
PAYMENT Date	Indicates the date of payment that will appear on the payment check and on all reports.

If you make an error in this window, and have chosen Pay Selected Bills, you cannot correct the error in this window. However, you can correct the error in the Write Checks window, as will be explained later.

Activities identified as purchases on account were recorded in the Enter Bills window. Subsequently, activities identified as payment of the outstanding accounts payable (previously recorded in the Enter Bills window) are then recorded in the Pay Bills window. Accounts Payable and Cash are the default general ledger posting accounts. All transactions entered in this window will result in a debit to the Accounts Payable account and a credit to the Cash account.

Paying a Bill in Full

On February 10, 2014, Kristin Raina wishes to pay the bill from Nordic Realty Corp. for the rent bill received on February 3, 2014 (Check No. 1). Do not print the check.

To pay a bill—

1. At the main menu bar, click Vendors and then click *Pay Bills*.
2. At the Show bills options, click *Show all bills*.
3. At the *Filter By* field, choose *Nordic Realty*.
4. At the *PAYMENT Method* field, choose *Check* and then *Assign check number*.
5. At the *PAYMENT Account* field, click *1010 Cash - Operating*.
6. At the *PAYMENT Date* field, choose *02/10/2014*.
7. Choose the bill from *Nordic Realty* by clicking in the box (❑) to place a check mark. (See figure 2–R.)

FIGURE 2–R
Pay Bills Window—
Vendor Bill Selected

8. Click Pay Selected Bills. The Assign Check Numbers window will appear.
9. Click the *Let me assign the check numbers below* option.
10. In the *CHECK NO.* field, key **1**. (See Figure 2–S.)

FIGURE 2–S
Assign Check Numbers
Window

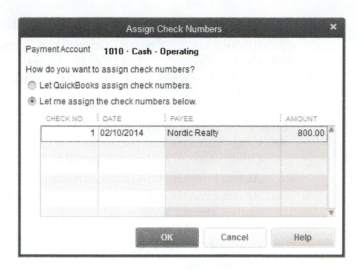

11. Click OK.
12. The Payment Summary window appears. (See figure 2–T.)

FIGURE 2–T
Payment Summary
Window

HINT

If the information is incorrect, it cannot be corrected here. It can be corrected later in the Write Checks window.

13. Click Done.

Even though a check is not printed, for accounts payable and general ledger purposes, the bill is now considered paid. The vendor balance owed has been reduced along with the cash balance. Each time you click Pay Selected Bills in this window, the Assign Check Numbers window appears. After assigning the first check number, you can either use the foregoing procedure and indicate a check number, or you can click the *Let QuickBooks assign check numbers* option. Subsequent check numbers will then be assigned in sequence. You will not see a check number in this window, but you will see the check number for these transactions in the Write Checks window and reports.

Accounting concept

For a payment of an existing Accounts Payable, the general ledger posting is as follows:

2010 Accts Payable		1010 Cash - Operating	
Dr	Cr	Dr	Cr
800			800

In addition, the vendor file (subledger) for Nordic Realty Corp. will reflect the payment:

Nordic Realty Corp.	
Dr	Cr
Pay 800	800 Bill
	0

Making a Partial Payment of a Bill

QuickBooks allows a partial payment to be made toward an outstanding bill. On February 23, 2014, Kristin Raina wishes to make a partial payment of $200 toward the Cuza and Carl Associates outstanding bill of $600 (Check No. 2).

To make a partial payment—
1. Click Vendors and then click *Pay Bills.*
2. Click *Show all bills* to display all bills.
3. At the *Filter By* field, choose *Cuza and Carl Associates.*
4. At the *PAYMENT Method* field, choose *Check;* the *Assign check no.* option should be selected.
5. At the *PAYMENT Date* field, set the payment date for *02/23/2014.*
6. In the *AMT. TO PAY* field, on the line for the Cuza and Carl Associates bill, key **200**.

   When you move to another field, the bill is automatically checked off for payment. (See figure 2–U.)

FIGURE 2–U
Pay Bills Window—
Partial Payment

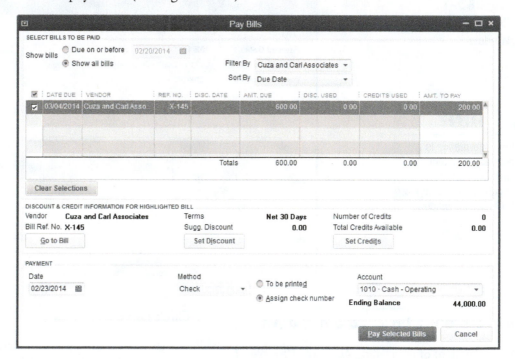

7. Click Pay Selected Bills.
8. At the Assign Check Numbers window, click the *Let QuickBooks assign check numbers* option.
9. Click OK.
10. At the Payment Summary window, you will notice the Check number is 2.
11. Click Done.

Practice Exercise

Record the following transactions in the Pay Bills window:

Use the Scroll Down
arrow if you do not see
the invoice in the Pay
Bills window.

| Feb. 27 | Paid [*Your Name*] Accounting Services bill in full (Check No. 3). |
| Feb. 27 | Made a partial payment of $1,000 toward Galeway Computers bill of $3,600 (Check No. 4). |

ACTIVITIES:

The Write Checks Window

cash purchase
Payment of any bill
or item other than
accounts payable.

In QuickBooks, the Write Checks window is used to record a **cash purchase** that has not been previously entered into the system. The Write Checks window is useful for companies that usually pay on account but occasionally receive bills and remit payments immediately, or for companies that do not purchase goods or services on account and therefore do not need to track vendor data. Accounts Payable is not used, which allows for the recording of a cash purchase in one step. The data fields in this window are similar to those in the Enter Bills window—payee (vendor name), date, expense, asset, or item purchased.

The Write Checks window is used for all cash purchases, whether the payment is by check, PayPal, electronic transfer, or debit card. The default account is Cash. The transaction is recorded as follows:

| | | Asset/Expense/Drawing | | XXX | | |
| | | Cash | | | XXX | |

A transaction entered in this window will not be tracked through the *Accounts Payable* or *Vendor* reports.

Activities identified as cash purchases are recorded in the Write Checks window. In this window, the Cash account is the default credit posting account because all transactions result in a cash payment. All transactions entered in this window will result in a credit to the Cash account. The account field in this window is used to indicate the asset, expense, or drawings account to be debited.

On February 28, 2014, Kristin Raina receives a bill for $125 for monthly janitorial services from Jeter Janitorial Services. She pays it with Check No. 5.

To write a check—
1. At the main menu bar, click Banking and then click *Write Checks*.
2. At the *BANK ACCOUNT* field, make sure *1010 Cash - Operating* is displayed; also make sure the *Print Later* box is not checked, and the check number is 5.
3. At the *DATE* field, choose *02/28/2014*.
4. At the PAY TO THE ORDER OF drop-down list, click *Jeter Janitorial Services*.
5. At the *$* field, key **125**.
6. At the Expenses tab in the *ACCOUNT* field, click *6300 Janitorial Expenses*. (See figure 2–V.)

FIGURE 2–V
Write Checks Window—
Completed

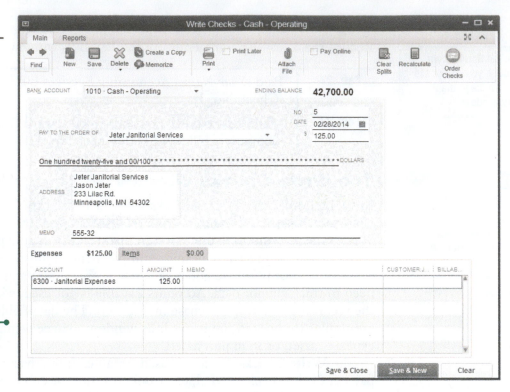

HINT

Errors can be corrected in the Write Checks window, or you can click the Delete button and choose Delete Check.

7. If the information is correct, click Save & New. Even though a check is not printed, the bill is now considered paid.

Accounting concept

For a cash payment of an expense, the general ledger posting will be as follows:

6300 Janitorial Expenses

Dr	Cr
125	

1010 Cash - Operating

Dr	Cr
	125

The vendor file is unaffected because payment was made immediately.

If you click the Previous arrow at this time, you will see the payments recorded in this window as well as the payments recorded in the Pay Bills window. Activities recorded in the Pay Bills window are actually checks written that subsequently appear in the Write Checks window, in addition to the checks written in the Write Checks window. The payments are recorded in check number sequence. Remember, since checks are not being printed, the program automatically assigns the next check number. Any errors recorded in the Pay Bills window cannot be corrected in the Pay Bills window, but they can be corrected in the Write Checks window.

To see an example of this, click the Previous arrow several times. Each time, notice that the payments include those entered in both the Write Checks and Pay Bills windows. As you scroll through the windows, notice the window is different for payments made in the Write Checks and Pay Bills windows. Notice also that the check numbers are in sequence.

Practice Exercise

Record the following transactions in the Write Checks window:

Feb. 28	Received bill from Grayson Graphics for design supplies, $200. Pay immediately with Check No. 6 (charge to Design Supplies Account No. 1300).
Feb. 28	Received bill from TwinCityTelCo for telephone service for February, $275. Pay immediately with Check No. 7 (charge to Telephone Expense Account No. 6450).
Feb. 28	The owner, Kristin Raina, withdrew $400 for personal use. Pay immediately with Check No. 8 (charge to Kristin Raina, Drawings Account No. 3020).

Debit Card Payments

As previously mentioned, the Write Checks window is used for all cash payments, including those made using a debit card. The steps for entering a purchase by debit card are the same as the steps for payment by check, except instead of entering a check number in the NO. field, another identifier (such as "DC-1, DC-2) would be used. All other steps remain the same.

REPORTS:

Vendor Reports and Accounting Reports

Reports, the fourth level of operation in QuickBooks, reflect the information and activities recorded in the various Lists/Centers and Activities windows. QuickBooks can display and print a variety of internal management reports as well as typical accounting and financial reports, many of which should be printed monthly.

Vendor Reports

The Accounts Payable and vendor-related reports help a company manage its liability payments, ensure timely and correct remittances, control cash flow, and retain an accurate record of all vendor-related transactions. Among these reports are the *Unpaid Bills Detail* report, the *Vendor Balance Detail* report, and the *Vendor Contact List* report.

Unpaid Bills Detail Report

The *Unpaid Bills Detail* report lists all unpaid bills for each vendor at a specific date. The report will list each open bill (with date and invoice number) for a vendor, along with any credit memos applied. The report may be customized to show all vendors or only those with outstanding bills.

To view and print the *Unpaid Bills Detail* report—
1. At the main menu bar, click Reports and then click *Vendors & Payables*.
2. At the Vendors & Payables submenu, click *Unpaid Bills Detail*.
3. At the Date calendar, choose *02/28/2014* and then click the Refresh button on the top of the report. The *Unpaid Bills Detail* report appears. (See figure 2–W.)

FIGURE 2–W
Unpaid Bills Detail Report

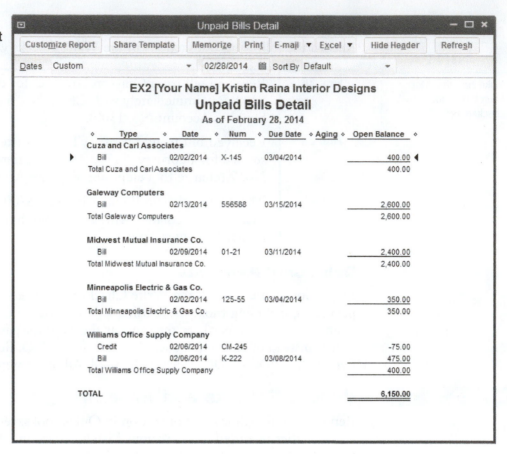

Along the top of the *Unpaid Bills Detail* report window are several buttons (Customize Report, Share Template, Memorize, Print, and so on). Notice the diamond shape before each of the column headings in the report text. If you wish to change the width of a column, you can click and drag the diamond in either direction.

4. To print the report, click the Print button on the top of the report.

   If you receive a message about Printing Features, place a check mark in the box to the left of the *Do not display this message in the future* field and then click OK. The Print Reports dialog box appears. (See figure 2–X.)

FIGURE 2–X
Print Reports Dialog Box

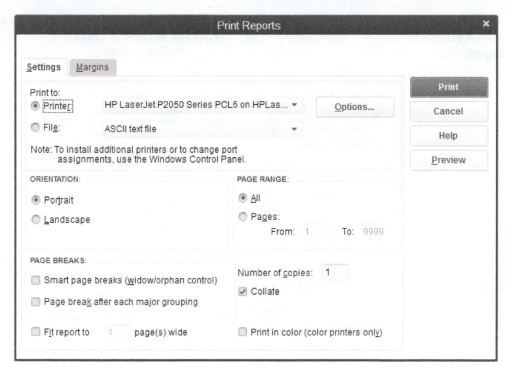

At the Print Reports dialog box, settings, fonts, and margins can be changed. The orientation of the report may also be changed. There is a Preview button if you wish to preview the report before printing. At this time, do not change any settings other than the orientation. For most reports, the portrait orientation is fine, but for some wider reports, the landscape orientation may be more useful.

5. At the Print Reports dialog box, choose Portrait in the *Orientation* section, then click Print.
6. Close the report.

If you receive a message about Memorize Report, place a check mark in the box to the left of the *Do not display this message in the future* option, then click No.

Vendor Balance Detail Report

The *Vendor Balance Detail* report displays all transactions for each vendor and shows the remaining balance owed. This report is similar to an accounts payable subsidiary ledger in a manual system. The report shows all vendor-related transactions—that is, all bills, payments, and credit memos for each vendor—in chronological order.

To view and print the *Vendor Balance Detail* report—
1. Click Reports and then click *Vendors & Payables*.
2. At the Vendors & Payables submenu, click *Vendor Balance Detail*.
3. Click the Print button on the top of the report.
4. At the Print Reports dialog box, choose Portrait orientation and then click Print. Your printout should look like figure 2–Y.
5. Close the report.

FIGURE 2–Y

Vendor Balance Detail
Report

EX2 [Your Name] Kristin Raina Interior Designs
Vendor Balance Detail
All Transactions

Type	Date	Num	Account	Amount	Balance
[Your Name] Accounting Service					
Bill	02/23/2014	Feb14	2010 · Accounts Payable	300.00	300.00
Bill Pmt -Check	02/27/2014	3	2010 · Accounts Payable	-300.00	0.00
Total [Your Name] Accounting Service				0.00	0.00
Cuza and Carl Associates					
Bill	02/02/2014	X-145	2010 · Accounts Payable	600.00	600.00
Bill Pmt -Check	02/23/2014	2	2010 · Accounts Payable	-200.00	400.00
Total Cuza and Carl Associates				400.00	400.00
Galeway Computers					
Bill	02/13/2014	556588	2010 · Accounts Payable	3,600.00	3,600.00
Bill Pmt -Check	02/27/2014	4	2010 · Accounts Payable	-1,000.00	2,600.00
Total Galeway Computers				2,600.00	2,600.00
Midwest Mutual Insurance Co.					
Bill	02/09/2014	01-21	2010 · Accounts Payable	2,400.00	2,400.00
Total Midwest Mutual Insurance Co.				2,400.00	2,400.00
Minneapolis Electric & Gas Co.					
Bill	02/02/2014	125-55	2010 · Accounts Payable	350.00	350.00
Total Minneapolis Electric & Gas Co.				350.00	350.00
Nordic Realty					
Bill	02/03/2014	F-14	2010 · Accounts Payable	800.00	800.00
Bill Pmt -Check	02/10/2014	1	2010 · Accounts Payable	-800.00	0.00
Total Nordic Realty				0.00	0.00
Williams Office Supply Company					
Bill	02/06/2014	K-222	2010 · Accounts Payable	475.00	475.00
Credit	02/06/2014	CM-245	2010 · Accounts Payable	-75.00	400.00
Total Williams Office Supply Company				400.00	400.00
TOTAL				**6,150.00**	**6,150.00**

Vendor Contact List Report

The *Vendor Contact List* report displays information, for all vendors, that has been entered in each vendor's file. This report displays the name of each vendor, account number, address, contact person, and telephone and fax numbers. It also shows the present balance owed.

HINT

The *Vendor Contact list* may also be accessed from the Vendors & Payables submenu.

To view the *Vendor Contact List* report—
1. At the main menu bar, click Reports and then click *List*.
2. At the List submenu, click *Vendor Contact List*. The *Vendor Contact List* appears. (See figure 2–Z.)
3. Close the report.

FIGURE 2–Z

Vendor Contact List

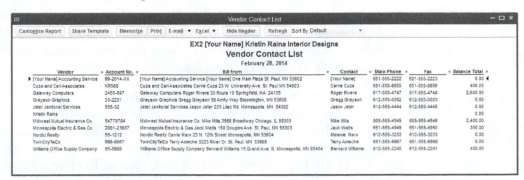

Drilling Down to a Transaction Window

While viewing reports, it is frequently helpful to see the originating transaction or document that gave rise to the report figures. Most of the reports provide a drill-down feature. When reviewing a report, QuickBooks, like many computerized accounting programs, allows you to "drill down" from a report to the original window where data has been entered. If the transaction is incorrect, you can edit or remove the transaction at that time. Any changes to the transactions are automatically reflected in subsequent reports.

When Kristin Raina reviewed the *Unpaid Bills Detail* report, she discovered that the bill from Minneapolis Electric & Gas Co. was entered incorrectly at $350, while the correct amount was $450.

To drill down from a report and correct an error—
1. Click Reports and then click *Vendors & Payables*.
2. At the Vendors & Payables submenu, click *Unpaid Bills Detail*.
3. Set the date for *02/28/2014*, and click the Refresh button on the top of the report.
4. Place the mouse pointer over the Minneapolis Electric & Gas Co. bill. Notice that the mouse pointer turns into a magnifying glass with a Z in the center. This is called the zoom glass.
5. With the zoom glass over the Minneapolis Electric & Gas Co. bill, double-click the mouse. The original bill entry will appear. (See figure 2–AA.)

FIGURE 2–AA

Minneapolis Electric & Gas Bill Transaction

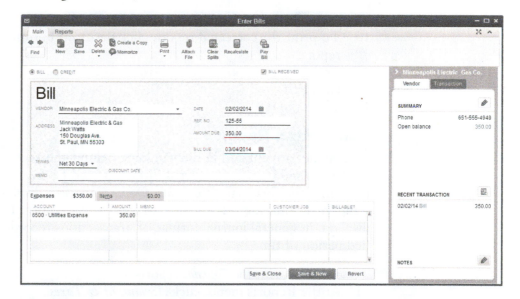

6. In the *AMOUNT DUE* field, change the amount to **450**.
7. After completing the change, click Save & Close.
8. At the Recording Transaction window, click Yes.
9. If the Report needs to be refreshed window appears, click Yes.

You will be returned to the report with the corrected figure in place. (See figure 2–BB.)

FIGURE 2–BB

Corrected Unpaid Bills Report

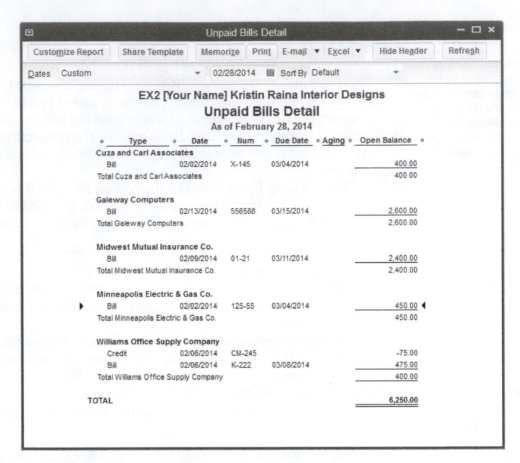

Customize Report | Share Template | Memorize | Print | E-mail ▼ | Excel ▼ | Hide Header | Refresh

Dates Custom ▾ 02/28/2014 📅 Sort By Default ▾

EX2 [Your Name] Kristin Raina Interior Designs
Unpaid Bills Detail
As of February 28, 2014

◇ Type ◇	Date ◇	Num ◇	Due Date ◇	Aging ◇	Open Balance ◇
Cuza and Carl Associates					
Bill	02/02/2014	X-145	03/04/2014		400.00
Total Cuza and Carl Associates					400.00
Galeway Computers					
Bill	02/13/2014	556588	03/15/2014		2,600.00
Total Galeway Computers					2,600.00
Midwest Mutual Insurance Co.					
Bill	02/09/2014	01-21	03/11/2014		2,400.00
Total Midwest Mutual Insurance Co.					2,400.00
Minneapolis Electric & Gas Co.					
Bill	02/02/2014	125-55	03/04/2014		450.00 ◄
Total Minneapolis Electric & Gas Co.					450.00
Williams Office Supply Company					
Credit	02/06/2014	CM-245			-75.00
Bill	02/06/2014	K-222	03/08/2014		475.00
Total Williams Office Supply Company					400.00
TOTAL					**6,250.00**

10. To print the corrected report, click the Print button on the top of the report.
11. At the Print Reports dialog box, choose Landscape orientation and then click Print.
12. Close the report.

Accounting Reports

As activities are entered in the windows, behind-the-scenes accounting activity is recorded in general journal format, posted to the general ledger, and flows into the financial statements. QuickBooks can display and print these standard accounting reports, such as the *Journal* report. The *Journal* report displays, in general journal format, all transactions recorded during a specified period of time.

To view and print the *Journal* report—
1. At the Reports menu, click *Accountant & Taxes*.
2. At the Accountant & Taxes submenu, click *Journal*.
3. At the *From* and *To* fields, choose *02/01/2014* and *02/28/2014* and then click the Refresh button on the top of the report. The *Journal* report is displayed.
4. To print the report, click the Print button on the top of the report.
5. At the Print Reports dialog box, choose Landscape orientation and then click Print. (See figure 2–CC.)
6. Close the report.

FIGURE 2–CC
Journal Report

EX2 [Your Name] Kristin Raina Interior Designs
Journal
February 2014

Trans #	Type	Date	Num	Name	Memo	Account	Debit
3	Bill	02/02/2014	125-55	Minneapolis Electric & Gas Co. Minneapolis Electric & Gas Co.		2010 · Accounts Payable 6500 · Utilities Expense	 450.00
							450.00
4	Bill	02/02/2014	X-145	Cuza and Carl Associates Cuza and Carl Associates		2010 · Accounts Payable 1410 · Prepaid Advertising	 600.00
							600.00
6	Bill	02/03/2014	F-14	Nordic Realty Nordic Realty		2010 · Accounts Payable 6400 · Rent Expense	 800.00
							800.00
7	Bill	02/06/2014	K222	Williams Office Supply Company Williams Office Supply Company		2010 · Accounts Payable 1305 · Office Supplies	 475.00
							475.00
8	Bill	02/09/2014	0121	Midwest Mutual Insurance Co. Midwest Mutual Insurance Co.		2010 · Accounts Payable 1420 · Prepaid Insurance	 2,400.00
							2,400.00
9	Bill	02/13/2014	556588	Galeway Computers Galeway Computers		2010 · Accounts Payable 1825 · Computers, Cost	 3,600.00
							3,600.00
10	Bill	02/23/2014	Feb14	[Your Name] Accounting Service [Your Name] Accounting Service		2010 · Accounts Payable 6020 · Accounting Expense	 300.00
							300.00
11	Credit	02/24/2014	CM245	Williams Office Supply Company Williams Office Supply Company	Return damaged office supplies Return damaged office supplies	2010 · Accounts Payable 1305 · Office Supplies	75.00
							75.00
12	Bill Pmt -Check	02/10/2014	1	Nordic Realty Nordic Realty	55-1212 55-1212	1010 · Cash □Operating 2010 · Accounts Payable	 800.00
							800.00
13	Bill Pmt -Check	02/23/2014	2	Cuza and Carl Associates Cuza and Carl Associates	KR569 KR569	1010 · Cash - Operating 2010 · Accounts Payable	 200.00
							200.00
14	Bill Pmt -Check	02/27/2014	3	[Your Name] Accounting Service [Your Name] Accounting Service	9992014XX 9992014XX	1010 · Cash - Operating 2010 · Accounts Payable	 300.00
							300.00
15	Bill Pmt -Check	02/27/2014	4	Galeway Computers Galeway Computers	2455897 2455897	1010 · Cash - Operating 2010 · Accounts Payable	 1,000.00
16	Check	02/28/2014	5	Jeter Janitorial Services Jeter Janitorial Services	555-32 555-32	1010 · Cash - Operating 6300 · Janitorial Expenses	 125.00
							125.00
17	Check	02/28/2014	6	Grayson Graphics Grayson Graphics	332221 332221	1010 · Cash - Operating 1300 · Design Supplies	 200.00
							200.00
18	Check	02/28/2014	7	TwinCityTelCo TwinCityTelCo	666-6667 666-6667	1010 · Cash - Operating 6450 · Telephone Expense	 275.00
							275.00
19	Check	02/28/2014	8	Kristin Raina Kristin Raina		1010 · Cash □Operating 3020 · Kristin Raina, Drawings	 400.00
							400.00
TOTAL							12,000.00

QuickBooks automatically assigns transaction numbers (Trans #). You cannot change them. Notice in figure 2–CC that there is no transaction number 5 because this transaction was deleted earlier in the chapter. The software deletes the transaction but will move to the next transaction number for the next transaction. When comparing your work to the solutions, do not be concerned if you have different transaction numbers as long as you have the correct journal entries.

The Type column in figure 2–CC indicates the window where the activity was recorded. In this column, the *Bill* entries represent transactions entered in the Enter Bills window. Notice that each of these *Bill* transactions has a credit to Accounts Payable because this is the default for that account. The *Credit* entry represents the credit memo entered in the Enter Bills window. Recall that when the credit memo option is chosen, the default account becomes a debit to Accounts Payable. The *Bill Pmt–Check* entries represent transactions entered in the Pay Bills window. All these transactions are a debit to Accounts Payable and a credit to Cash; these two accounts are the default for this window. The *Check* entries are from the Write Checks window, which all have a credit to Cash because that is the default account for this window.

Exiting QuickBooks

After completing this session, you should make a backup copy of your exercise company file to a removable storage device or network directory using the backup procedures explained in chapter 1. When you back up to a removable storage device, be sure to change the *Save in* text box to the location where you keep your backup files, and carefully type in the correct file name.

After making a backup copy of the company file, close the company, exit QuickBooks, and then return to the Windows desktop by clicking File and then *Exit*.

Chapter Review and Assessment

Procedure Review

To add a vendor—
1. At the main menu bar, click Vendors and then click *Vendor Center*.
2. At the Vendor Center window, click the New Vendor menu button, and select New Vendor.
3. Enter the background data for the vendor.
4. Click OK.
5. Close the Vendor Center window.

To delete a vendor—
1. Click Vendors and then click *Vendor Center*.
2. At the Vendor Center window, select the vendor you wish to delete.
3. From the main menu bar, click Edit and then click *Delete Vendor*.
4. Click OK at the warning.
5. Close the Vendor Center window.
   You cannot delete a vendor who has a balance or who was used in a transaction during the period.

To edit a vendor—
1. Click Vendors and then click *Vendor Center*.
2. At the Vendor Center window, select the vendor you wish to edit, then double-click the vendor name.
3. Change the appropriate information.
4. Click OK.
5. Close the Vendor Center window.

To enter a bill—
1. At the main menu bar, click Vendors and then click *Enter Bills*.
2. Click the BILL option.
3. At the VENDOR drop-down list, click the vendor name.
4. Enter the bill date in the *DATE* field.
5. Enter the invoice number in the *REF.NO.* field.
6. Enter the amount in the *AMOUNT DUE* field.
7. Enter the due date in the *BILL DUE* field.
8. Select the terms in the *TERMS* field.
9. Select the account to be debited in the Expenses tab.
10. Click Save & Close.

To update the Vendor Center while in an Activity window—
1. Click Vendors and then click *Enter Bills*.
2. At the VENDOR drop-down list, click < Add New >.
3. Follow the procedures to add a vendor.
4. Click OK.

To process a credit memo—
1. Click Vendors and then click *Enter Bills*.
2. Click the CREDIT option button.
3. Follow the procedures for entering a bill.

To pay a bill—
1. Click Vendors and then click *Pay Bills*.
2. Click Show all bills.
3. At the *Filter By* field, choose the appropriate vendor whose bill you wish to pay.
4. At the *PAYMENT Method* field, choose Check and the *Assign check no.* option.
5. At the *PAYMENT Account* field, choose the appropriate cash account.
6. Enter the payment date in the *PAYMENT Date* field.
7. Choose the bill to be paid by clicking in the ❏ field to the left of the bill. Accept the full amount or enter a partial amount.
8. Click Pay Selected Bills. The Assign Check Numbers window will appear.
9. Click the *Let me assign the check numbers below* option.
10. Enter the check number.
11. Click OK.
12. At the Payment Summary window, click Done.

To record a cash purchase—
1. At the main menu bar, click Banking and then click *Write Checks*.
2. At the *BANK ACCOUNT* field, choose the appropriate account.
3. Enter the payment date in the *DATE* field.
4. Choose the payee from the PAY TO THE ORDER OF drop-down list.
5. At the *$* field, enter the amount of the payment.
6. At the Expenses tab, choose the account to be debited.
7. Click Save & Close.

To view and print vendor reports from the Reports menu—
1. At the main menu bar, click Reports and then click *Vendors & Payables*.
2. At the Vendors & Payables or List submenu, choose a report.
3. Indicate the appropriate dates for the report, then click the Refresh button on the top of the report.
4. Click the Print button on the top of the report.
5. At the Print Reports dialog box, review the settings and click Print.
6. Close the report.

Key Concepts

Select the letter of the item that best matches each definition.

a. *Journal* report   f. Credit Memo
b. Write Checks window   g. Pay Bills window
c. System Default account   h. Vendor
d. Vendor Center   i. Enter Bills window
e. *Unpaid Bills* report   j. *Vendor Contact List* report

_____ 1. Someone from whom the business buys goods or services.
_____ 2. Contains a file for all vendors with whom the company does business.
_____ 3. A report that lists all unpaid vendor bills at a specific date.
_____ 4. Processed through the Enter Bills window to reflect a reduction of the vendor's liability due to a credit for return or allowance.

_____ 5. Activity window used to record vendor bills to be paid at a later date.

_____ 6. Activities displayed in general journal format for a specified period of time.

_____ 7. Report that lists all vendors from whom the company buys goods and services.

_____ 8. A pre-identified general ledger account that will increase or decrease automatically depending on the type of transaction entered.

_____ 9. Activity window used to record cash purchase of goods or services from a vendor.

_____ 10. Activity window used to pay bills previously entered in the Enter Bills window.

Procedure Check

1. Your company has changed its telephone carrier. Describe the steps to add the new vendor to the system.
2. Upper management requests a list of all businesses from which the company buys goods or services. How would you use QuickBooks to quickly produce this information?
3. You receive a batch of bills that must be paid immediately. You do not need to maintain an Accounts Payable record of these payments. How would you use QuickBooks to expeditiously enter these payments into the system and write the appropriate payment checks?
4. A vendor calls your company to complain that a bill forwarded 45 days ago remains unpaid. How would you use QuickBooks to verify this complaint?
5. You wish to view all the bills received from a vendor and all payments to that vendor. How would you use QuickBooks to obtain the required information?

6. Compare and contrast a manual accounting system with a computerized accounting system for processing vendor transactions. How does the accounts payable subsidiary ledger compare with the Vendor Center?

Case Problems

Case Problem 1

On April 1, 2014, Lynn Garcia started her business, called Lynn's Music Studio, as a music instructor. She began by depositing $10,000 cash in a bank account in the business name. She also contributed a piano and some guitars. The musical instruments have an outstanding note balance of $2,000, which will now be assumed by the business. The cash, musical instruments, note payable, and capital have all been recorded in the opening balances of the books. Lynn anticipates spending the beginning of the month setting up her studio and expects to provide piano and guitar lessons later in the month. Record the transactions listed below for the month of April.

1. Open the company file CH2 Lynn's Music Studio.QBW.
2. Make a backup copy of the company file LMS2 [*Your Name*] Lynn's Music Studio.

3. Restore the backup copy of the company file. In both the Open Backup Copy and Save Company File as windows, use the file name LMS2 [*Your Name*] Lynn's Music Studio.

4. Change the company name to **LMS2 [*Your Name*] Lynn's Music Studio**.

5. Add the following vendors to the Vendor Center:

VENDOR NAME:	**Pioneer Phone**
OPENING BALANCE:	**0 AS OF April 1, 2014**
COMPANY NAME:	**Pioneer Phone**
First Name:	**Customer**
Last Name:	**Service**
Main Phone:	**570-555-6000**
Fax:	**570-555-6500**
Main Email:	**pioph@emcp.net**
BILLED FROM:	**1000 Route 6**
	Carbondale, PA 18407
PAYMENT TERMS:	**Net 15 Days**

VENDOR NAME:	**Steamtown Electric**
OPENING BALANCE:	**0 AS OF April 1, 2014**
COMPANY NAME:	**Steamtown Electric**
First Name:	**Customer**
Last Name:	**Service**
Main Phone:	**570-555-2500**
Fax:	**570-555-3000**
Main Email:	**steam@emcp.net**
BILLED FROM:	**150 Vine Lane**
	Scranton, PA 18501
PAYMENT TERMS:	**Net 15 Days**

Delete the following vendor:
 Universal Electric

Edit the following vendor:
 Mutual Insurance Company telephone number: **570-555-5600**

6. Using the appropriate window, record the following transactions for April 2014:

Apr. 2 Received bill for rent for the month of April from Viewhill Realty Management, $600, paid immediately, Check No. 1. Do not print check.

Apr. 2 Received a bill for a 1-year insurance policy on account from Mutual Insurance Company, Invoice No. 4010102, $1,200, Net 30 Days.

Apr. 5 Purchased furniture on account from Mills Family Furniture, Invoice No. 1257, $2,500, Net 30 Days.

Apr. 6 Purchased a computer system on account from Computer Town, Invoice No. X234, $3,000, Net 30 Days.

Apr. 9 Purchased music supplies on account from Strings, Sheets, & Such, Invoice No. 1290, $500, Net 15 Days.

Apr. 9	Received bill for tuning of piano and guitars from Tune Tones, $100, paid immediately, Check No. 2. Tune Tones is a new vendor:

VENDOR NAME:	**Tune Tones**
OPENING BALANCE:	**0 AS OF April 1, 2014**
COMPANY NAME:	**Tune Tones**
First Name:	**Tony**
Last Name:	**Tune**
Main Phone:	**570-555-1111**
Fax:	**570-555-2222**
Main Email:	**TUNE@emcp.net**
BILLED FROM:	**500 Monroe Ave.**
	Dunmare, PA 18512
PAYMENT TERMS:	**Net 30 Days**

Apr. 9	Purchased office supplies on account from Paper, Clips, and More, Invoice No. 01-1599, $400, Net 30 Days.
Apr. 12	Received the telephone bill from Pioneer Phone, Invoice No. pp401, $50, Net 15 Days.
Apr. 13	Received utilities bill from Steamtown Electric, Invoice No. SE401, $70, Net 15 Days.
Apr. 20	Paid in full Strings, Sheets, & Such, Invoice No. 1290 (Check No. 3). Do not print check.
Apr. 23	Received a credit memo from Paper, Clips, and More, Invoice No. CM250, $50, for office supplies returned.
Apr. 26	Paid in full Pioneer Phone, Invoice No. pp401 (Check No. 4).
Apr. 27	Paid in full Steamtown Electric, Invoice No. SE401 (Check No. 5).
Apr. 30	Made a partial payment of $1,000 to Mills Family Furniture (Check No. 6).
Apr. 30	Made a partial payment of $1,000 to Computer Town (Check No. 7).
Apr. 30	The owner, Lynn Garcia, withdrew $1,000, for personal use (Check No. 8).

7. Display and print the following reports for April 1, 2014, to April 30, 2014:
   a. *Unpaid Bills Detail*
   b. *Vendor Balance Detail*
   c. *Vendor Contact List*
   d. *Journal*

Case Problem 2

On June 1, 2014, Olivia Chen started her business as an Internet consultant and web page designer, Olivia's Web Solutions. She began by depositing $25,000 cash in a bank account in the business name. She also contributed a computer system. The computer has an outstanding note balance of $2,500 that will be assumed by the business. The cash, computer, note payable, and capital have all been recorded in the opening balances of the books. Olivia anticipates spending the beginning of the month setting up her office and expects to provide Web design and Internet consulting services later in the month. You will record the transactions listed below for the month of June.

1. Open the company file CH2 Olivia's Web Solutions.QBW.
2. Make a backup copy of the company file OWS2 [*Your Name*] Olivia's Web Solutions.
3. Restore the backup copy of the company file. In both the Open Backup Copy and Save Company File as windows, use the file name OWS2 [*Your Name*] Olivia's Web Solutions.
4. Change the company name to **OWS2 [*Your Name*] Olivia's Web Solutions**.
5. Add the following vendors to the Vendor Center:

VENDOR NAME:	**Comet Computer Supplies**
OPENING BALANCE:	**0 AS OF June 1, 2014**
COMPANY NAME:	**Comet Computer Supplies**
First Name:	**Customer**
Last Name:	**Service**
Main Phone:	**631-555-4444**
Fax:	**631-555-4455**
Main Email:	**CometCs@emcp.net**
BILLED FROM:	**657 Motor Parkway**
	Center Island, NY 11488
PAYMENT TERMS:	**Net 15 Days**

VENDOR NAME:	**Chrbet Advertising**
OPENING BALANCE:	**0 AS OF June 1, 2014**
COMPANY NAME:	**Chrbet Advertising**
First Name:	**Chris**
Last Name:	**Chrbet**
Main Phone:	**212-555-8777**
Fax:	**212-555-8778**
Main Email:	**Cadv@emcp.net**
BILLED FROM:	**201 East 10th Street**
	New York, NY 10012
PAYMENT TERMS:	**Net 30 Days**

Delete the following vendor:
   Johnson Ad Agency

Edit the address for Martin Computer Repairs:
   366 North Franklin Street
   Garden City, NY 11568

6. Using the appropriate window, record the following transactions for June 2014:

   Jun. 1   Received bill for rent for the month of June from ARC Management, $800, paid immediately. Check No. 1. Do not print check.

   Jun. 4   Received a 1-year insurance policy on account from Eastern Mutual Insurance, Invoice No. 87775, $1,800, Net 30 Days.

Jun. 4	Purchased software on account from Netsoft Development Co., Invoice No. 38745, $3,600, Net 30 Days.
Jun. 7	Purchased office furniture on account from Lewis Furniture Co., Invoice No. O9887, $3,200, Net 30 Days.
Jun. 8	Purchased 6 months of advertising services on account from Chrbet Advertising, Invoice No. O-989, $1,200, Net 30 Days.
Jun. 11	Purchased computer supplies on account from Comet Computer Supplies, Invoice No. 56355, $600, Net 15 Days.
Jun. 14	Received bill for online Internet services, from Systems Service, $150, paid immediately (Check No. 2). Systems Service is a new vendor:

VENDOR NAME:	**Systems Service**
OPENING BALANCE:	**0 AS OF June 1, 2014**
COMPANY NAME:	**Systems Service**
First Name:	**Jeremy**
Last Name:	**Jones**
Main Phone:	**516-555-2525**
Fax:	**516-555-2526**
Main Email:	**Sysser@emcp.net**
ADDRESS DETAILS:	**36 Sunrise Lane**
	Hempstead, NY 11004
PAYMENT TERMS:	**Net 30 Days**

Jun. 15	Purchased office supplies on account from Office Plus, Invoice No. 3665, $450, Net 30 Days.
Jun. 18	Received the telephone bill from Eastel, Invoice No. 6-2568, $350, Net 30 Days.
Jun. 21	Received utilities bill from LI Power Company, Invoice No. OWS-23556, $125, Net 15 Days.
Jun. 21	Returned office supplies to Office Plus for a $75 credit, CM789.
Jun. 21	Paid in full Eastern Mutual Insurance, Invoice No. 87775 (Check No. 3). Do not print check.
Jun. 25	Paid in full Comet Computer Supplies, Invoice No. 56355 (Check No. 4).
Jun. 28	Paid in full LI Power Company, Invoice No. OWS-23556 (Check No. 5).
Jun. 30	Made a partial payment of $2,000 to Netsoft Development Co. (Check No. 6).
Jun. 30	Made a partial payment of $1,500 to Lewis Furniture Co. (Check No. 7).
Jun. 30	The owner, Olivia Chen, withdrew $500, for personal use (Check No. 8).

7. Display and print the following reports for June 1, 2014, to June 30, 2014:
   a. *Unpaid Bills Detail*
   b. *Vendor Balance Detail*
   c. *Vendor Contact List*
   d. *Journal*

CHAPTER 3

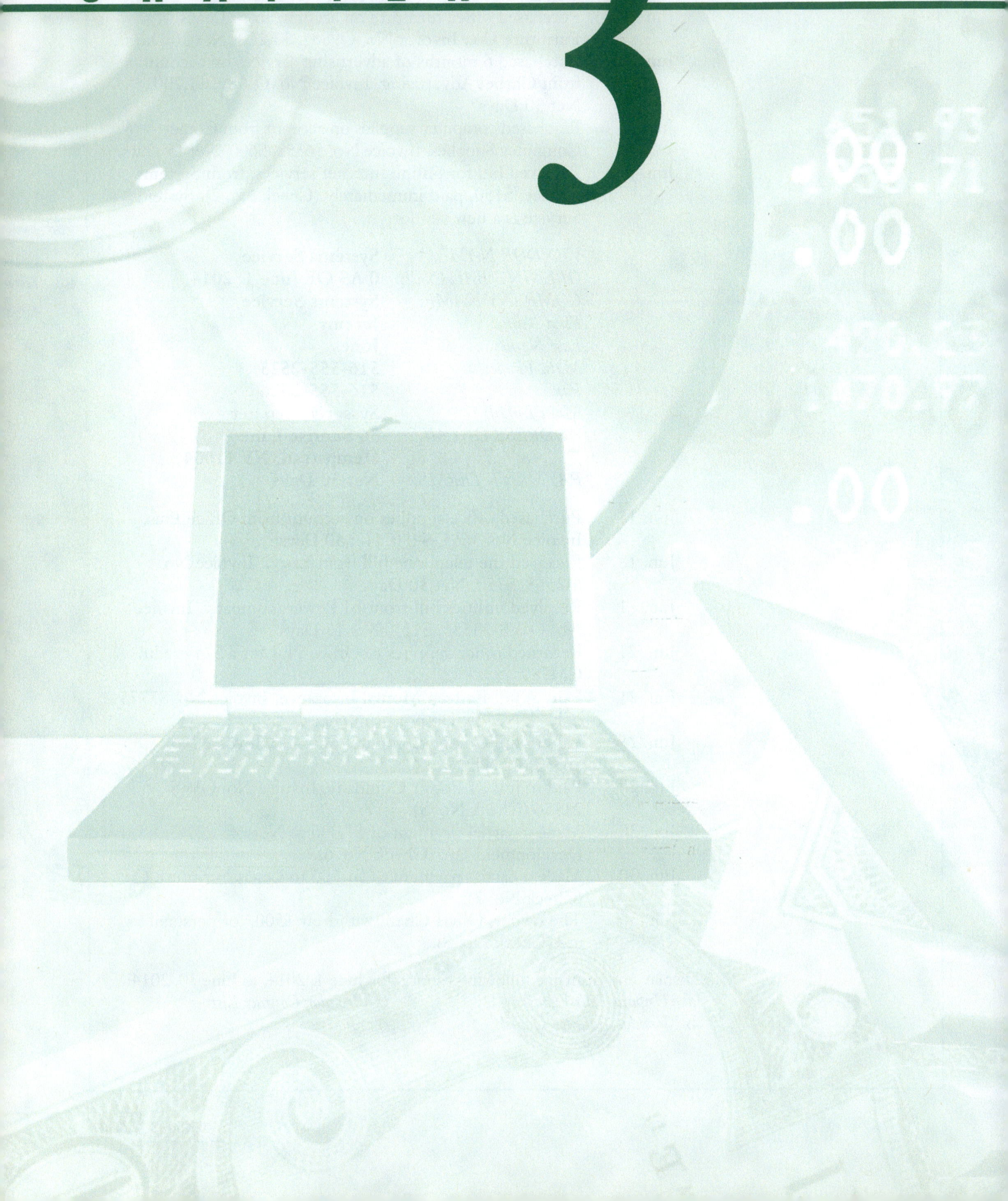

Customers

Create Invoices, Receive Payments, Enter Sales Receipts, and Make Deposits

Chapter Objectives

- Identify the system default accounts for customers

- Update the Customer Center

- Record sales on account in the Create Invoices window

- Record collections of accounts receivable in the Receive Payments window

- Record cash sales in the Enter Sales Receipts window

- Record deposits in the Make Deposits window

- Display and print customer-related reports

Introduction

customer A person or business that the company sells goods or services to, either on account or for cash.

QuickBooks allows you to track all customer transactions. A **customer** is a person or business that the company sells goods or services to, either on account or for cash. A file for each customer should be established before entering transactions for a particular customer. The collection of all customer files comprises the customer list, which is contained in the *Customer Center* (Lists/Centers).

Once a customer file is established, transactions (Activities) such as creating an invoice for a customer, receiving payment from that customer, or making a cash sale can be entered in the *Create Invoices, Receive Payments, Enter Sales Receipts,* and *Make Deposits* windows. As transactions are recorded in these activities windows, QuickBooks simultaneously updates the customer's file in the Customer Center to include information about the transactions for that customer. At the same time, QuickBooks updates any related reports (Reports).

In this chapter, our sample company, Kristin Raina Interior Designs, will create invoices for design and decorating services, receive payments for invoices, make cash sales, and deposit funds.

QuickBooks versus Manual Accounting: Customer Transactions

sales journal A journal used to record all sales of goods or services on account; can be in single-column or multi-column format.

In a manual accounting system, all sales of goods or services on account are recorded in a multi-column **sales journal**. At the conclusion of the month, the totals are posted to the accounts receivable and revenue accounts affected by the transactions. As each sales transaction is recorded, the appropriate customer's account in the accounts receivable subsidiary ledger is updated for the new receivable on a daily basis. Collections of open accounts receivable balances and cash sales of goods/services are recorded in a multi-column **cash receipts journal**. As was done with the sales journal, monthly totals are posted to the general ledger accounts while payment information is recorded daily in the customer's subsidiary ledger record.

cash receipts journal A journal used to record all cash receipt activities including collection of accounts receivable.

In QuickBooks, the Customer Center serves as the accounts receivable subsidiary ledger for the company. The Customer Center contains a file for all companies and individuals to whom the company sells goods and services. Relevant information, such as name, address, contact, credit limit, and so on, is entered when the customer's file is created in the Customer Center.

When the company creates an invoice for goods or services, the invoice is created in the Create Invoices window. The Create Invoices window is equivalent to the multi-column sales journal. This transaction will update the Chart of Accounts List and general ledger while simultaneously updating the customer's file in the Customer Center for the new receivable. When the customer pays the invoice, the company enters this transaction in the Receive Payments window. The Receive Payments window is equivalent to the part of the cash receipts journal that records collection of open accounts receivable. QuickBooks automatically updates the Chart of Accounts List and general ledger while at the same time updating the customer's file in the Customer Center for the payment of the receivable.

To record a check received for an invoice not previously entered, the Enter Sales Receipts window is used. This window is equivalent to the remainder of the cash receipts journal, which records all cash receipts other than collection of accounts receivable. Again, the Chart of Accounts List and general ledger and the customer's file in the Customer Center are simultaneously updated.

System Default Accounts

As we saw in chapter 2, to process transactions expeditiously and organize data for reporting, QuickBooks establishes specific general ledger accounts as default accounts in each window. When you enter transactions, QuickBooks automatically increases or decreases certain account balances, depending on the nature of the transaction.

For example, for vendors, when you enter a transaction in the Enter Bills window, QuickBooks automatically increases (credits) the Accounts Payable account; when you pay the bills in the Pay Bills window, QuickBooks automatically decreases (debits) the Accounts Payable account. Similarly, for customers, when you enter a transaction in the Create Invoices window, QuickBooks automatically increases (debits) the Accounts Receivable account because the Create Invoices window is used to record sales on account. When you record a collection of accounts receivable in the Receive Payments window, QuickBooks automatically decreases (credits) the Accounts Receivable account. Therefore, you do not have to enter the account number or name for these default accounts because they have been pre-established by QuickBooks.

Chapter Problem

In this chapter, you will enter and track customer transactions for Kristin Raina Interior Designs. Kristin Raina provides interior design and decorating services both on account and for cash. Customers and clients remit payment for invoices; these funds are periodically deposited in the company checking account. Information for several customers has been entered in the Customer Center. This information, along with February 1, 2014, beginning balances and vendor activity from chapter 2, is contained in the company file CH3 Kristin Raina Interior Designs.

Begin by opening the company file—
1. Open QuickBooks.
2. At the No Company Open window, click the *Open or restore an existing company* button; or click File and then click *Open or Restore Company*.
3. At the Open or Restore Company window, choose *Open a Company file* and then click Next.
4. At the Open a Company dialog box in the *Look in* text box, choose the Company Files subfolder, or the subfolder containing the company files.
5. Select the company file CH3 Kristin Raina Interior Designs.QBW, then click Open.
6. If a window appears titled Accountant Center, remove the check mark in the box to the left of Show Accountant Center when opening a company file, and then click the X to close the window.

Next, make a backup copy of the company file—

1. Click File and then click *Back Up Company*.
2. At the Back up Company submenu, click *Create Backup Copy*.
3. In the Create Backup window at the Do you want to save your backup copy online or locally? page, *Local backup* should be selected, then click Next.
4. At the Backup Options window, click the Browse button.
5. At the Browse for Folder window, choose your subfolder, a network directory designated by your instructor, or a removable storage device, and then click OK.
6. At the Backup Options window, you can remove the check mark to the left of Add the date and time of the backup to the file name if you do not want multiple backups, then click OK.
7. At the QuickBooks message, click Use this Location.
8. In the Create Backup window at the When do you want to save your backup copy? page, choose *Save it now* and then click Next.
9. In the Save Backup Copy dialog box, in the *Save in* text box, choose your subfolder, network directory designated by your instructor, or removable storage device if it is not correct.
10. In the *File name* text box, key **EX3 [*Your Name*] Kristin Raina Interior Designs**.
11. Click Save. If the QuickBooks message appears, click *Use this Location*.
12. At the QuickBooks Information message, click OK.

Now restore the backup copy of the company file—

1. Click File and then click *Open or Restore Company*.
2. In the Open or Restore Company window, at the What type of file do you want to open or restore? page, choose *Restore a backup copy* and then click Next.
3. At the Is the backup copy stored locally or online? page, choose *Local backup* and then click Next.
4. At the Open Backup Copy dialog box, in the *Look in* text box, choose the location where you saved your file.
5. Select the company file EX3 [*Your Name*] Kristin Raina Interior Designs.QBB, then click Open.
6. At the Where do you want to restore the file? page, click Next.
7. At the Save Company File as dialog box, in the *Save in* text box, choose the subfolder where you will be opening and working on your copies of the company file.
8. In the *File name* text box, key **EX3 [*Your Name*] Kristin Raina Interior Designs** and then click Save.
9. At the *Your data has been restored successfully* message, click OK.
10. If the Accountant Center appears, remove the check mark in the box to the left of Show Accountant Center when opening a company file, and then click the X to close the window. If the home page window appears, click the X to close it. If the left icon bar appears, click View on the main menu bar, click Hide Icon Bar to remove it.

The backup copy has been restored, but the company name still reads CH3 Kristin Raina Interior Designs.

> **HINT**
>
> The first time you make a backup copy of a company file, the Backup Options window appears. For subsequent backup copies of the same file, this window will not appear; you would not need to do steps 4-7 of this procedure.

Change the company name—
1. Click Company and then click *Company Information*.
2. Change the company name to **EX3 [*Your Name*] Kristin Raina Interior Designs**.
3. Click OK.

The Customer Center

The Customer Center contains a file for each customer to whom the company sells goods or services. Each file contains important information, such as company name, address, contact person, type of customer, terms, credit limit, preferred payment method, and current balance owed. You should include all customers the company does business with in the Customer Center.

Recall from chapter 1 that the second level of operation in QuickBooks is recording background information on Lists/Centers. The Customer Center is revised periodically when new customers are added, customers not used in the business are deleted, and modifications are made to customer information. These adjustments to the customer files are referred to as updating the Customer Center.

As previously stated, the Customer Center contains a file for each customer with whom the company does business. You should try to enter the information for each customer in the Customer Center before recording transactions. However, if you inadvertently omit a customer, you can add that customer during the Activities level of operation with a minimum of disruption.

Kristin Raina has entered information for existing and anticipated customers in the Customer Center.

To view the Customer Center—
1. Click Customers and then click *Customer Center*. If a window appears titled New Feature - Attach Documents to QuickBooks, click OK or X to close.

The Customer Center appears with the customer file for Alomar Company displayed. (See figure 3–A).

FIGURE 3–A
Customer Center—
Alomar Company File
Displayed

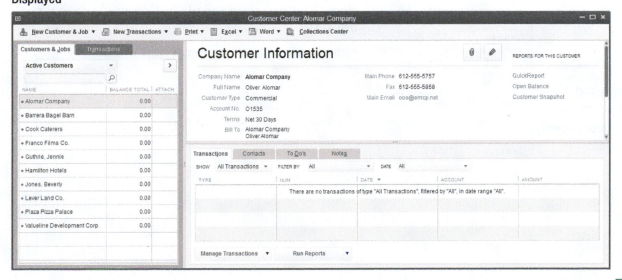

The Customer Center contains the following parts:

Customers & Jobs tab	Lists all customers and jobs with current balance due. You can display all customers, active customers, or only customers with balances.
Transactions tab	Lists all transactions for a selected customer. The Transactions tab in the Customer Information section contains the same information.
New Customer & Job button	Used to add a new customer or job.
New Transactions button	Used to create an invoice and to enter sales receipts, payments, and credit memos.
Customer Information	Displays background and transaction information for the customer selected in the Customer & Jobs tab.
Attach icon	Used to attach documents via QuickBooks Document Management feature.
Contacts tab	When entering a name in the FULL NAME field, it will be added to the Contacts tab. You can also right click the tab to add, edit, or delete a contact.
Edit icon	Used to edit background information for the customer selected in the Customer & Jobs tab.
To Do's tab	Used to view the To Do List for this customer.
Notes tab	Used to include narrative information specific to a customer.
Reports for this Customer	Lists the reports available in the Customer Center.

FIGURE 3–B
Customer Center Drop-Down Menu

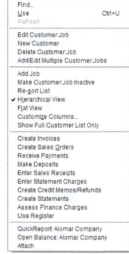

FIGURE 3–C
Customer File— Alomar Company Selected

In addition to the foregoing, once a customer is selected, you can right-click the mouse on the Customers & Jobs tab to display a shortcut menu. Use this menu to accomplish most customer-related activities. (See figure 3–B.)

To view a specific customer file—
1. Move the mouse pointer to Alomar Company, then double-click to open the file. If a window appears titled New Feature Add/Edit Multiple List Entries, place a check mark in the box to the left of the *Do not display this message in the future* field and click OK to close. This will open the file in Edit mode. (See figure 3–C.)

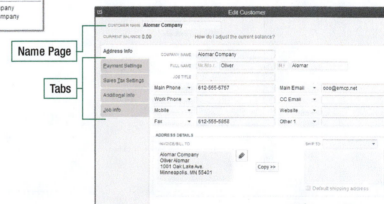

The customer file contains six parts:

Name page	This portion displays the customer's name, current balance, and three command buttons: OK, Cancel, and Help.
Address Info tab	This tab allows you to enter the customer's company name, billing and shipping address, contact person, telephone and fax numbers, and email address. The Edit icon can be used to edit address information.
Payment Settings tab	This tab allows you to enter information such as the customer's account number, credit limit, payment terms and preferred send method.
Sales Tax Settings tab	This tab allows you to enter the customer's sales tax code and resale number.
Additional Info tab	This tab allows you to enter the customer type and gives you the ability to create customized fields.
Job Info tab	This tab allows you to enter information, such as job status and start and end dates for a job for this customer.

    2. Close the Edit Customer window.

    3. Close the Customer Center.

Adding a Customer

Kristin Raina has just been hired by a new client, Maria Omari, to provide interior decorating services for Omari's new residence.

To add a new customer—

    1. Click Customers and then click *Customer Center*.

        The Customer Center opens, displaying a list of customers on the Customers & Jobs tab and information for the first customer on the list.

    2. At the Customer Center window, click the New Customer & Job button, and select New Customer. The New Customer window appears. (See figure 3–D.)

FIGURE 3–D
New Customer Window

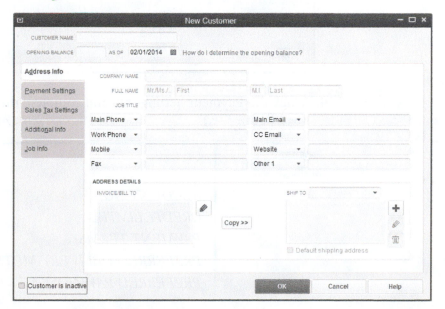

To move from field to field, press Tab or Shift + Tab. In the *INVOICE/ BILL TO* box, use the Down Arrow key to enter each line of the address.

3. Enter the data below on the Name Page and Address Info tab. (See figure 3–E.)

Name page

Address Info

CUSTOMER NAME:	**Omari, Maria**
OPENING BALANCE:	**0 AS OF February 1, 2014**
FULL NAME:	
First:	**Maria**
Last:	**Omari**
Main Phone:	**612-555-9999**
Fax:	**612-555-9998**
Main Email:	**MO@emcp.net**
INVOICE/BILL TO:	**210 NE Lowry Ave.**
	Minneapolis, MN 54204

FIGURE 3–E
New Customer Window—Name Page and Address Info Tab Completed

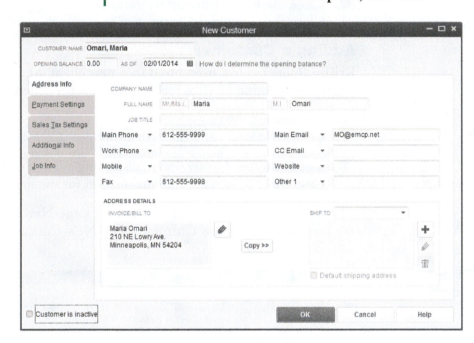

4. Click the Payment Settings tab and complete the information below. (See figure 3–F.)

Payment Settings

ACCOUNT NO:	**01545**
CREDIT LIMIT:	**10,000**
PAYMENT TERMS:	**Net 30 Days**
PREFERRED DELIVERY METHOD:	**None**
PREFERRED PAYMENT METHOD:	**Check**

FIGURE 3–F
New Customer
Window—Payment
Settings Tab Completed

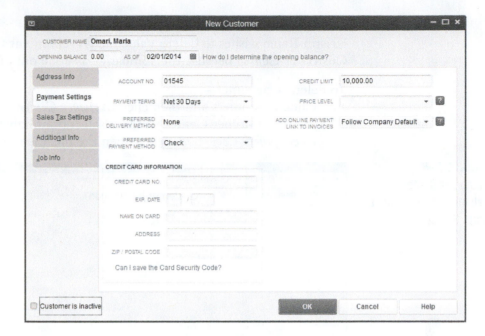

5. Click the Additional Info tab and complete the information below. (See figure 3–G.)

Additional Info

CUSTOMER TYPE: **Residential**

FIGURE 3–G
New Customer
Window—Additional Info
Tab Completed

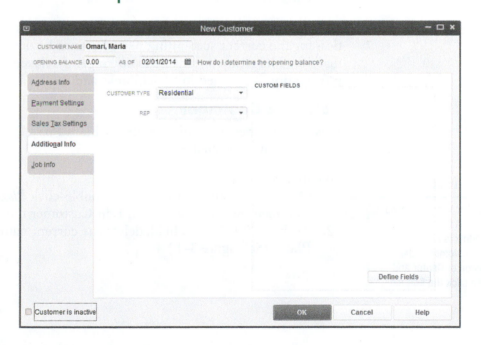

6. If the information is correct, click OK.
7. Close the Customer Center.

Deleting a Customer

Kristin Raina wishes to delete Valueline Development Corp. from the Customer Center because the company has gone out of business.

To delete a customer—
1. Click Customers and then click *Customer Center*.
2. At the Customer Center window, select (highlight) *Valueline Development Corp.* but do not open the file. (See figure 3–H.)

FIGURE 3–H
Customer Center—
Valueline Development
Corp. Selected

3. At the main menu bar, click Edit and then click *Delete Customer:Job*.
4. Click OK at the *Delete Customer:Job* warning. The customer file is now deleted.
5. Close the Customer Center window.

A customer with a balance or a customer who has been part of a transaction for the current accounting period cannot be deleted but can be marked inactive. The customer's name is no longer displayed in the reports, but the information is retained in QuickBooks and can be accessed if needed.

Editing a Customer

Kristin Raina needs to edit the file for Plaza Pizza Palace because the contact person has changed.

To edit a customer file—
1. Open the Customer Center and double-click *Plaza Pizza Palace*. This will open the customer file in Edit Customer mode.
2. At the *FULL NAME* field, delete the current name and then key **Mikey Plaza**. (See figure 3–I.)

> **HINT**
>
> Another way to access the Edit Customer window is to select the customer in the Customer Center and then click the Edit icon.

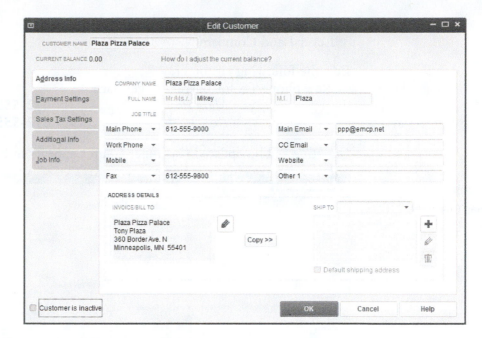

FIGURE 3–I
Edit Customer Window—
Plaza Pizza Palace

Practice Exercise

Add the following customer:

Name page		
	CUSTOMER NAME:	**Berger Bakery Company**
	OPENING BALANCE:	**0 AS OF February 1, 2014**
Address Info		
	COMPANY NAME:	**Berger Bakery Company**
	First Name:	**Barry**
	Last Name:	**Berger**
	Main Phone:	**612-555-2240**
	Fax:	**612-555-2241**
	Main Email:	**BBC@emcp.net**
	INVOICE/BILL TO:	**18 N Grand Ave.**
		Minneapolis, MN 55403
Payment Settings		
	ACCOUNT NO:	**R1825**
	CREDIT LIMIT:	**10,000**
	PAYMENT TERMS:	**Net 30 Days**
	PREFERRED DELIVERY METHOD:	**None**
	PREFERRED PAYMENT METHOD:	**Check**
Additional Info		
	CUSTOMER TYPE:	**Commercial**

Delete the following customer:
Lever Land Company

Edit the following customer:
New phone/fax for Barrera Bagel Barn:

Main Phone:	**612-555-1233**
Fax:	**612-555-1234**

QuickCheck: The updated Customer Center appears in figure 3–J.

FIGURE 3–J
Updated Customer
Center

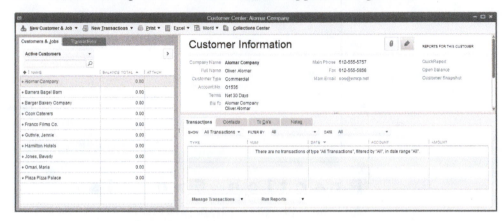

ACTIVITIES:

○ The Create Invoices Window

Recall from chapter 1 that the third level of operation in QuickBooks is Activities. In QuickBooks, Activities identified as **sales on account** are recorded in the Create Invoices window. Accounts Receivable is the default general ledger posting account. All transactions entered in this window will result in a debit to the Accounts Receivable account. The account to be credited, usually a revenue account, is determined based on the item chosen.

sale on account
A sale on account occurs when a company sells goods or services to a customer but does not receive payment until a future date.

QuickBooks records a sales-on-account transaction as follows:

Accounts Receivable	XXX	
Revenue		XXX

At the same time, QuickBooks updates the customer's file in the Customer Center to reflect the new receivable. The QuickBooks Create Invoices window appears in figure 3-K.

FIGURE 3–K
Create Invoices Window

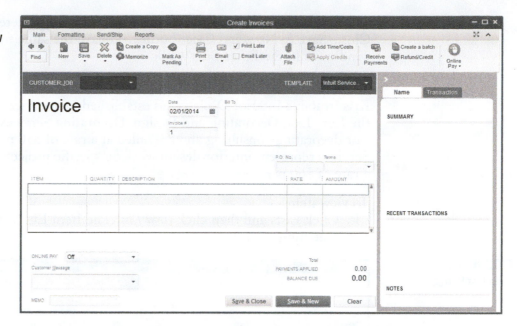

The Create Invoices window has four tabs: Main, Formatting, Send/Ship and Reports. The Main tab allows you to select a customer from the Customer Center, enter an invoice number and terms of payment, and identify items sold or services provided. The Formatting tab allows you to customize the design and presentation of invoices. Customizing invoices will be covered in chapter 12. The Send/Ship tab allows you to select a carrier for a shipment. The Reports tab accesses various transaction reports. Most icons and data fields are self-explanatory, but take special note of the following on the Main tab:

TEMPLATE	QuickBooks allows for eight types of invoice formats. Choose the one that best describes the items sold. For this chapter, Intuit Service Invoice will be used. In addition, you can customize or download additional formats.
ITEM	When you click in the item field, a drop-down arrow appears, which allows you to access the Item List. Choose the item of service or inventory sold from the drop-down list. Once an item is selected, the description and rate are filled in automatically based on data entered in the Item List window.
	Allows you to print this invoice immediately rather than using the Print Forms submenu of the File menu.
Customer Name/ Transactions tabs	Displays a summary of information about the customer, recent transactions, and notes.
Edit Icon	Allows you to edit customer information while remaining in the Create Invoices window.
SUMMARY	Lists phone number, email address, credit limited, and open balance for selected customer.
RECENT TRANSACTIONS	Displays recent transactions for selected customer.
NOTES	By clicking Edit, allows you to post notes concerning selected customer.

The Find, Previous, and Next arrows, New, Save, Delete, and the Save & Close, Save & New, and Clear buttons all have the same functions in this window as in the Enter Bills window.

Items

Kristin Raina Interior Designs has established two service revenue items in the Item List, Decorating and Design. Decorating Services represent interior decorating consulting and are billed at a rate of $50 per hour. Design Services represent interior design work on specific projects and are billed at a rate of $60 per hour.

To view items—

1. Click Lists and then click *Item List*. The Item List window appears. (See figure 3–L.)

FIGURE 3–L

Item List Window

2. To view the data for the Decorating Services item, double-click the item. The Edit Item window will appear. (See figure 3–M.)

FIGURE 3–M

Edit Item Window—
Decorating Services

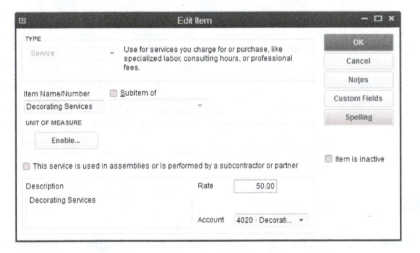

Decorating Services is indicated as a service item (rather than inventory or payroll). The window also contains a description, rate per unit (hour), and default general ledger posting account. QuickBooks uses this data when you create an invoice for a customer for this service.

3. Close the Edit Item and Item List windows.

Creating an Invoice

On February 1, 2014, Kristin Raina provided 12 hours of decorating services on account to Beverly Jones.

To create an invoice—

1. Click Customers and then click *Create Invoices*.
2. At the CUSTOMER:JOB drop-down list, click *Jones, Beverly*.
3. At the TEMPLATE drop-down list, accept the default choice, *Intuit Service Invoice*.
4. At the *Date* field, choose *02/01/2014*.
5. In the *Invoice #* field, key **1001**.
6. At the *Terms* drop-down list, accept the default choice, *Net 30 Days*.
7. In the *ITEM* field, click the first line to display the drop-down Item List, then click *Decorating Services*. The data from the Decorating Services file in the Item List will complete the *DESCRIPTION* and *RATE* fields. (See figure 3–N.)

FIGURE 3–N

Create Invoices Window—Partially Completed

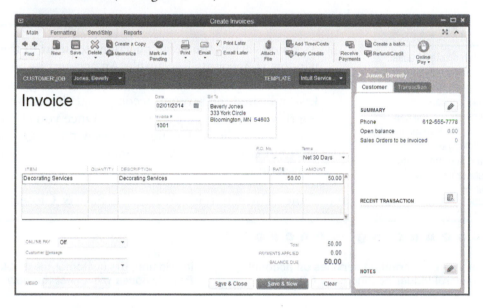

8. At the *QUANTITY* field, key **12**.

   When you move to the next field, the *AMOUNT* box will be completed based on the hourly rate times the hours invoiced.

9. The *Print Later* and *Email Later* boxes should not have a check mark in them. The *ONLINE PAY* box should say Off. (See figure 3–O.)

FIGURE 3–O
Create Invoices
Window—Completed

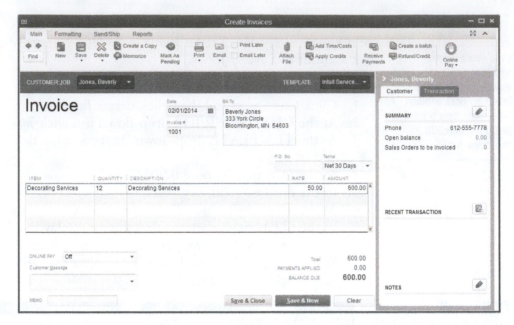

HINT

You can display transactions previously entered by clicking the Previous arrow. You can correct errors, or you can remove the transaction by clicking the Delete button and then either delete or void the invoice.

As stated earlier, the default account to debit in the Create Invoices window is Accounts Receivable. An account to be credited is not indicated in this window. The item for Decorating Services in the Item List indicated the revenue account that should be credited when entering this item in an activity window. Once you choose the Decorating Services item in the Create Invoices window, QuickBooks knows from the Item List to credit the revenue account Decorating Services for this transaction.

10. If the information is correct, click Save & Close.

A c c o u n t i n g   c o n c e p t

For a sale of decorating services on account, the general ledger posting is as follows:

In addition, the customer file (subledger) for Beverly Jones will reflect the new receivable:

1200 Accts Rec		4020 Decor Serv		Jones, Beverly	
Dr	Cr	Dr	Cr	Dr	Cr
600			600	600	

Practice Exercise

HINT

If there is more than one item, move to the next line in the *ITEM* field.

HINT

The Formatting tab offers the choices of Insert Line and Delete Line.

Record the following transactions in the Create Invoices window:

Feb. 6	Provided 16 hours of design services to Jennie Guthrie on account. Invoice No. 1002. *QuickCheck:* 960
Feb. 13	Provided 8 hours of decorating services and 16 hours of design services to Cook Caterers. Invoice No. 1003. *QuickCheck:* 1360
Feb. 17	Provided 24 hours of design services to Franco Films Co. Invoice No. 1004. *QuickCheck:* 1440
Feb. 23	Provided 24 hours of decorating services to Berger Bakery Company. Invoice No. 1005. *QuickCheck:* 1200
Feb. 27	Provided 6 hours of decorating services and 15 hours of design services to Cook Caterers. Invoice No. 1006. *QuickCheck:* 1200

ACTIVITIES:

The Receive Payments Window

collection of accounts receivable
Collection of accounts receivable occurs when a customer pays part or all of their outstanding balance due the company; this Activity is sometimes referred to as payment of accounts receivable.

In QuickBooks, the Receive Payments window is used to record the **collection of accounts receivable** from customers previously invoiced in the Create Invoices window. This window displays all open invoices for a specific customer. Payment can be in the form of cash, check, or credit card. In addition, customer credit memos can be recorded.

The Receive Payments window is designed only for collection of existing invoices. The default accounts are Accounts Receivable and Cash or Undeposited Funds (discussed later in this chapter). The transaction is recorded as follows:

Cash (or Undeposited Funds)	XXX	
Accounts Receivable		XXX

At the same time, the customer's file in the Customer Center is updated to reflect the payment. The QuickBooks Receive Payments window appears in figure 3–P.

FIGURE 3–P
Receive Payments Window

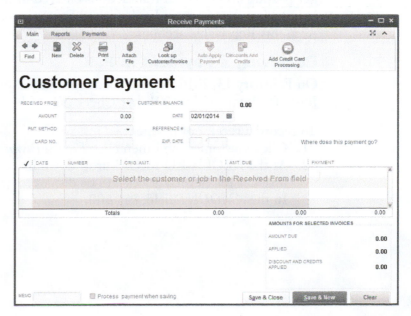

Once a customer is identified, a list of open invoices will be displayed. Note the following fields in the Receive Payments window:

CUSTOMER BALANCE	Indicates the balance owed by this customer for all open invoices.
AMOUNT	Used to enter the current payment. When an amount is entered, it is applied to the oldest invoice, with a check mark appearing on the left side of the invoice line. If you wish to have the payment applied to an alternate invoice, you will need to select that invoice by manually placing a check mark next to it.
PMT. METHOD	Indicates whether customer is paying invoice by cash, check, e-check, or credit card.
Look up Customer/ Invoice button	Used to search for all open invoices. Search can be by invoice number, customer name, amount, date, and so on.
Auto Apply/Un-Apply Payment button	Auto Apply Payment is the default button. If no invoice has been selected, Auto Apply will automatically apply payment to the oldest invoice. When a payment is applied, the button switches to Un-Apply Payment, which allows you to select the invoice to be paid.
Discounts and Credits button	Used to apply discounts for early payments and unused credits.

Activities identified as sale on account were recorded in the Create Invoices window. Subsequently, Activities identified as collection of an outstanding account receivable (previously recorded in the Create Invoices window) are now recorded in the Receive Payments window. Cash or Undeposited Funds and Accounts Receivable are the default general ledger posting accounts. All transactions entered in this window will result in a debit to the Cash or Undeposited Funds account and a credit to the Accounts Receivable account.

Receiving a Payment in Full

On February 13, 2014, Kristin Raina receives a $600 payment from Beverly Jones for Invoice No. 1001, her Check No. 6544.

To record a receipt of payment—
1. Click Customers and then click *Receive Payments.*
2. At the RECEIVED FROM drop-down list, click *Jones, Beverly.* All open invoices for Beverly Jones will be displayed. (See figure 3–Q.)
3. In the *AMOUNT* field, key **600.**

FIGURE 3–Q

Receive Payments
Window—Beverly Jones

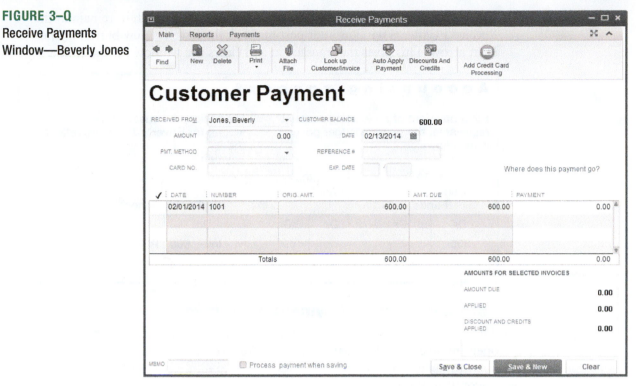

Once the amount is entered and you move to the next field, a check mark will appear next to open Invoice No. 1001, indicating the $600 payment will be applied to that invoice automatically (since this is the only open invoice).

4. At the *DATE* field, choose *02/13/2014.*
5. At the PMT. METHOD drop-down list, click *Check.*
6. At the *CHECK #* field, key **6544**. (See figure 3–R.)

FIGURE 3–R

Receive Payments
Window—Completed

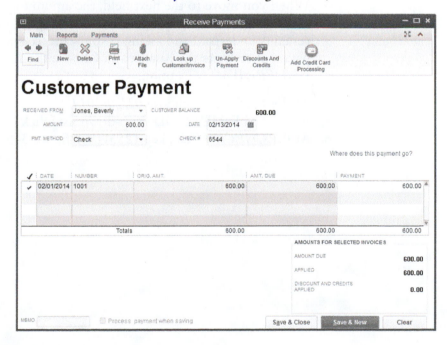

7. Click Save & Close.

Save & Close returns you to the main window. If you wish to remain in the Receive Payments window after posting, click the Save & New button or the Next arrow. This posts the transaction and clears the window for the next entry.

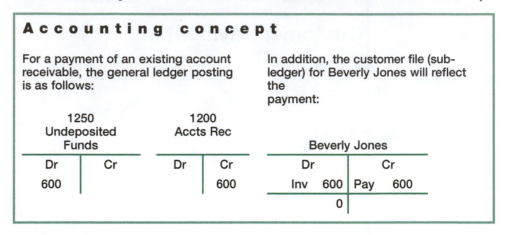

Accounting concept

For a payment of an existing account receivable, the general ledger posting is as follows:

In addition, the customer file (sub-ledger) for Beverly Jones will reflect the payment:

1250 Undeposited Funds		1200 Accts Rec		Beverly Jones	
Dr	Cr	Dr	Cr	Dr	Cr
600			600	Inv 600	Pay 600
					0

Entering a Partial Payment of an Invoice

The Receive Payments window allows you to record partial payments of open invoices. On February 20, 2014, Franco Films remits $500 toward their open Invoice No. 1004 in the amount of $1,440, their Check No. 1255. No discount is allowed.

To record a partial payment of an invoice—
1. Click Customers and then click *Receive Payments*.
2. At the RECEIVED FROM drop-down list, click *Franco Films Co.* The open invoice will be displayed along with the unpaid amount of $1,440 in the *CUSTOMER BALANCE* field.
3. In the *AMOUNT* field, key **500**.

   When you move to the next field, the amount appears in the *PAYMENT* field. A pop-up window will appear, indicating that $940 remains underpaid and asking if you want to leave it as an underpayment or write the balance off. Choose the *LEAVE THIS AS AN UNDERPAYMENT* option.

4. At the *DATE* field, choose *02/20/2014*.
5. At the PMT. METHOD drop-down list, click *Check*.
6. At the *CHECK #* field, key **1255**. (See figure 3–S.)

FIGURE 3–S
Receive Payments
Window—Partial
Payment

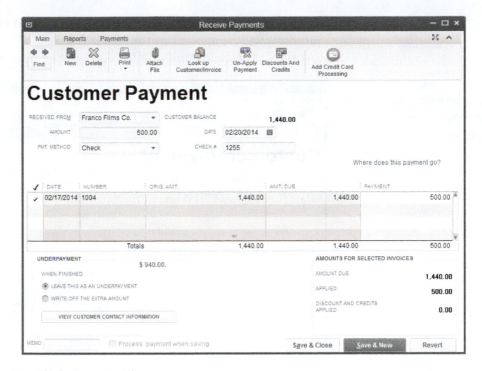

7. Click Save & Close.

Receiving Payment for More Than One Invoice

QuickBooks allows you to record a payment of several invoices at the same time. On February 27, 2014, Cook Caterers remits $2,560 in full payment of Invoices No. 1003 and 1006, their Check No. 655.

To record payment of more than one invoice—
1. Click Customers and then click *Receive Payments*.
2. At the RECEIVED FROM drop-down list, click *Cook Caterers*. All open invoices are displayed. (See figure 3–T.)

FIGURE 3–T
Receive Payments
Window—Invoices
Displayed

3. At the *AMOUNT* field, key **2560**. When you move to the next field, the amount will be applied to the two invoices.
4. At the *DATE* field, choose *02/27/2014*. (See figure 3–U.)

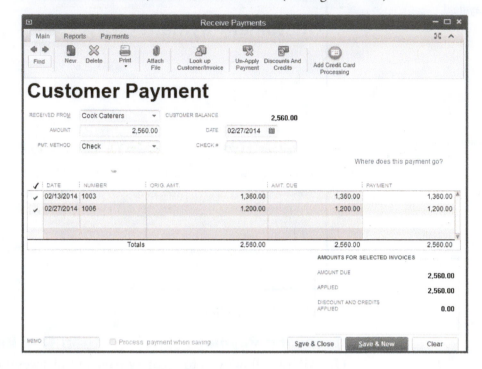

5. Complete the *PMT. METHOD* and *CHECK #* fields. (See figure 3–V.)

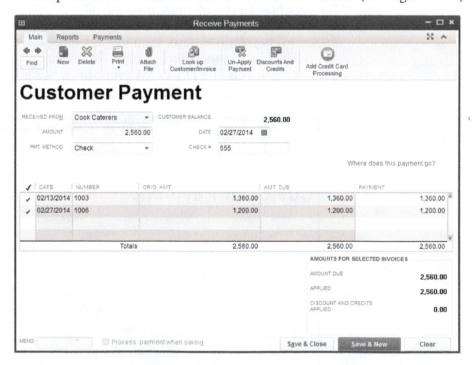

6. If the information is correct, click Save & Close.

Practice Exercise

Record the following transactions in the Receive Payments window:

Feb. 28	Received $960 from Jennie Guthrie in full payment of Invoice No. 1002, her Check No. 674.
Feb. 28	Received $600 from Berger Bakery Company in partial payment of Invoice No. 1005. Leave as underpayment, their Check No. 12458.

ACTIVITIES:

The Enter Sales Receipts Window

cash sale A sale for which payment is received immediately.

In QuickBooks, you use the Enter Sales Receipts window to record sales where payment is received immediately. Since you do not use Accounts Receivable, this window allows you to record a **cash sale** in one step. The data fields in this window are similar to those of the Create Invoices window: customer, date, item sold, service provided, and so on.

The Enter Sales Receipts window is used for all cash sales of goods and services. As with the Receive Payments window, the default account is Cash or Undeposited Funds. The transaction is recorded as follows:

	Cash (or Undeposited Funds)	XXX	
	Revenue		XXX

A transaction entered in this window will not be tracked through the Accounts Receivable or Customer reports.

Activities identified as cash sales are recorded in the Enter Sales Receipts window. In this window, the Cash or Undeposited Funds account is the default debit posting account because all transactions result in a cash receipt. All transactions entered in this window will result in a debit to the Cash or Undeposited Funds account. The account to be credited is based on the item selected. As in the Create Invoices window, when an item is selected, QuickBooks uses the information from the Item List window to determine which account should be credited.

On February 24, 2014, Kristin Raina provided 8 hours of design services to Hamilton Hotels on Invoice No. 1007. Hamilton Hotels issued Check No. 25546 in full payment.

HINT

After entering the quantity, you must move to another field for the amount to be computed.

To record a cash sale—
1. Click Customers and then click *Enter Sales Receipts*.
2. At the CUSTOMER:JOB drop-down list, click *Hamilton Hotels*.
3. Enter the appropriate date, then key **1007** in the *Sale No.* field.
4. At the Payment Method drop-down list, click *Check*.
5. Key **25546** in the *Check No.* field. The *Print Later* and the *Email Later* boxes should not be checked.
6. Complete the balance of the window in the same manner as you would complete an invoice. (See figure 3–W.)

FIGURE 3–W

Enter Sales Receipts
Window—Completed

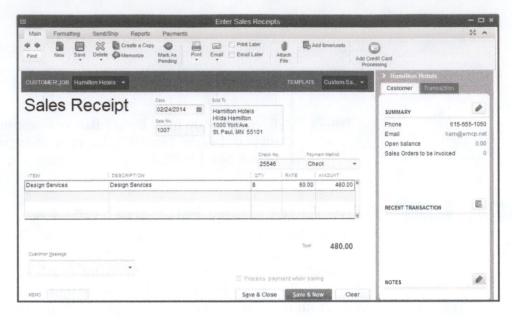

7. If the information is correct, click Save & Close.

The customer file is unaffected because the payment was received at point of sale.

A c c o u n t i n g   c o n c e p t

For a cash sale, the general ledger posting is as follows:

1250 Undeposited Funds		4010 Design Serv	
Dr	Cr	Dr	Cr
480			480

The Make Deposits Window

Most accounting textbooks assume that when cash is received, it is immediately posted to a Cash account. However, many businesses post to the Cash account only when funds are actually deposited in the checking account. This may occur several days after the funds are received. For these businesses, the receipt of funds is posted to a current asset account, titled Undeposited Funds, until a deposit is made. At that point, a second transaction is recorded to show the undeposited funds transferred to the Cash - Operating account. Debits to the Cash - Operating account should coincide with deposits recorded on the bank statement. This allows the company to more easily track deposits during the month-end bank reconciliation process.

When the Undeposited Funds account is utilized, cash receipts are recorded as follows:

	Undeposited Funds		XXX	
	Accounts Receivable/Revenue			XXX

This entry results from activities entered in the Receive Payments and Enter Sales Receipts windows.

When funds previously received and recorded in the Receive Payments or Sales Receipts windows are subsequently deposited in the bank, the Make Deposits window is used. The default accounts are Cash and Undeposited Funds. The transaction is recorded as follows:

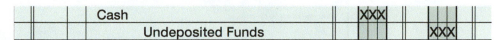

	Cash	XXX	
	Undeposited Funds		XXX

Activities identified as a deposit of funds are recorded in the Make Deposits window. In this window, Cash and Undeposited Funds are the default general ledger posting accounts. All transactions entered in this window will result in a debit to the Cash account and a credit to the Undeposited Funds account.

In this chapter, Kristin Raina will deposit all receipts at one time at month-end. In a real-world setting, deposits are made more frequently depending on collection volume. This window allows you either to deposit each receipt individually or deposit several receipts, or to deposit all receipts at one time. On February 28, 2014, Kristin Raina deposits all collections for the month.

To deposit all receipts collected and previously recorded as Undeposited Funds—

1. Click Banking and then click *Make Deposits*. The Payments to Deposit window is displayed, showing all undeposited receipts.

2. At the Sort payments by drop-down list, click Date. (See figure 3–X.)

FIGURE 3–X
Payments to Deposit Window

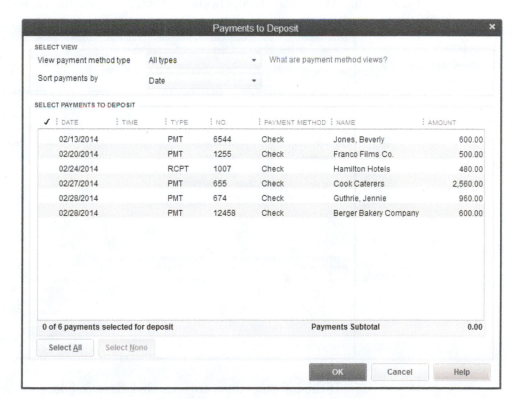

3. Since all receipts will be deposited, click Select All. All receipts will be checked for deposit. (See figure 3–Y.)

FIGURE 3–Y
Payments to Deposit Window—All Receipts Selected

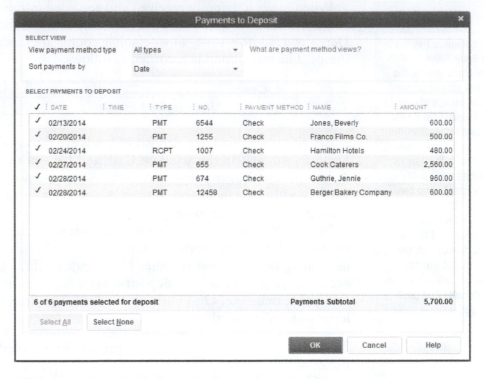

4. If the information is correct, click OK. You will be forwarded to the Make Deposits window.
5. In the Deposit To drop-down list, click *1010 Cash - Operating*.
6. At the *Date* field, choose *02/28/2014*. (See figure 3–Z.)

FIGURE 3–Z
Make Deposits Window—Completed

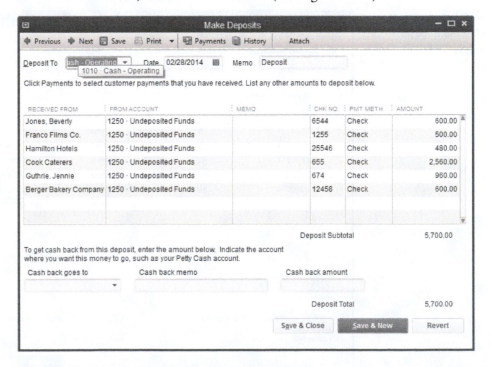

7. If the information is correct, click Save & Close.

Accounting concept

The deposit of receipts as a separate transaction is recorded as follows:

1010 Cash - Operating		1250 Undeposited Funds	
Dr	Cr	Dr	Cr
5,700		5,700	5,700
			0

REPORTS:

Customer Reports and Accounting Reports

Recall from chapter 1 that Reports, the fourth level of operation, display the information and activities recorded in the various Lists/Centers and Activities windows. QuickBooks can display and print a variety of internal management reports as well as typical accounting and financial reports, many of which should be printed monthly.

Customer Reports

The Accounts Receivable and customer-related reports help the company to manage its collections, control cash flow, and retain an accurate record of all customer-related transactions. Among these reports are the *Open Invoices* report, the *Customer Balance Detail* report, and the *Customer Contact List* report.

Open Invoices Report

The *Open Invoices* report lists all unpaid invoices for each customer at a specific date. The report lists each open invoice, with date and invoice number, for a customer; it also lists the terms and due date. The report may be customized to show all customers or only those with outstanding bills.

To view and print the *Open Invoices* report—
1. Click Reports and then click *Customers & Receivables.*
2. At the Customers & Receivables submenu, click *Open Invoices.*
3. At the *Date* field, choose *02/28/2014.*
4. Click the Refresh button on the top of the report. The report will be displayed. (See figure 3–AA.)

FIGURE 3–AA
Open Invoices Report

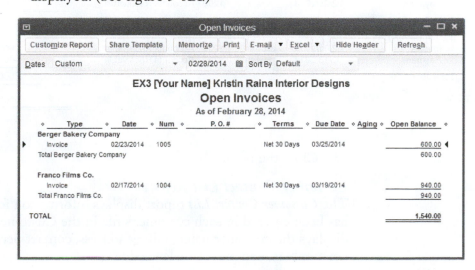

5. To print the report, click the Print button on the top of the report.
6. At the Print Reports dialog box, choose Portrait orientation and then click Print.
7. Close the report.

Customer Balance Detail Report

The *Customer Balance Detail* report displays all transactions for each customer with the remaining balance owed. This report is similar to an accounts receivable subsidiary ledger in a manual accounting system.

To view and print the *Customer Balance Detail* report—

1. Click Reports and then click *Customers & Receivables*.
2. At the Customers & Receivables submenu, click *Customer Balance Detail*.

   The report will show all invoices, payments, and credit memos for each customer in chronological order.

3. To print the report, click the Print button on the top of the report.
4. At the Print Reports dialog box, choose Landscape orientation and then click Print. Your printout should look like figure 3–BB.

<table>
<tr><td colspan="7">**HINT**
To change the width of a column, use your mouse to click and drag the diamonds between each column heading.</td></tr>
</table>

HINT

To change the width of a column, use your mouse to click and drag the diamonds between each column heading.

FIGURE 3–BB
Customer Balance Detail Report

EX3 [Your Name] Kristin Raina Interior Designs
Customer Balance Detail
All Transactions

Type	Date	Num	Account	Amount	Balance
Berger Bakery Company					
Invoice	02/23/2014	1005	1200 · Accounts Receivable	1,200.00	1,200.00
Payment	02/28/2014	12458	1200 · Accounts Receivable	-600.00	600.00
Total Berger Bakery Company				600.00	600.00
Cook Caterers					
Invoice	02/13/2014	1003	1200 · Accounts Receivable	1,360.00	1,360.00
Invoice	02/27/2014	1006	1200 · Accounts Receivable	1,200.00	2,560.00
Payment	02/27/2014	655	1200 · Accounts Receivable	-2,560.00	0.00
Total Cook Caterers				0.00	0.00
Franco Films Co.					
Invoice	02/17/2014	1004	1200 · Accounts Receivable	1,440.00	1,440.00
Payment	02/20/2014	1255	1200 · Accounts Receivable	-500.00	940.00
Total Franco Films Co.				940.00	940.00
Guthrie, Jennie					
Invoice	02/06/2014	1002	1200 · Accounts Receivable	960.00	960.00
Payment	02/28/2014	674	1200 · Accounts Receivable	-960.00	0.00
Total Guthrie, Jennie				0.00	0.00
Jones, Beverly					
Invoice	02/01/2014	1001	1200 · Accounts Receivable	600.00	600.00
Payment	02/13/2014	6544	1200 · Accounts Receivable	-600.00	0.00
Total Jones, Beverly				0.00	0.00
TOTAL				**1,540.00**	**1,540.00**

5. Close the report.

Customer Contact List Report

The *Customer Contact List* report displays information for all customers that has been entered in each customer's file in the Customer Center. This report displays the customer name, billing address, contact person, telephone and fax numbers, and present balance due.

To view the *Customer Contact List* report—
1. Click Reports and then click *List*.
2. At the List submenu, click *Customer Contact List*. The Customer Contact List appears. (See figure 3–CC.)
3. Close the report.

FIGURE 3–CC
Customer Contact List Report

	Customer Contact List						— ☐ ✕

| Customi<u>z</u>e Report | Share Template | Memori<u>z</u>e | Print | E-mai<u>l</u> ▾ | E<u>x</u>cel ▾ | Hide He<u>a</u>der | Re<u>f</u>resh | Sort By Default ▾ |

EX3 [Your Name] Kristin Raina Interior Designs
Customer Contact List
February 28, 2014

◇	Customer	◇	Bill to	◇	Contact	◇	Main Phone	◇	Fax	◇	Balance Total	◇
▸	Alomar Company		Alomar Company Oliver Alomar 1001 Oak Lake Ave. Minneapolis, MN 55401		Oliver Alomar		612-555-5757		612-555-5858		0.00 ◂	
	Barrera Bagel Barn		Barrera Bagel Barn Belinda Barrera 148 46th Ave. N Plymouth, MN 53406		Belinda Barrera		612-555-1233		612-555-1234		0.00	
	Berger Bakery Company		Berger Bakery Company Barry Berger 18 N Grand Ave. Minneapolis, MN 55403		Barry Berger		612-555-2240		612-555-2241		600.00	
	Cook Caterers		Cook Caterers Stephen Cook 275 Oak Lake Ave. Minneapolis, MN 55401		Stephen Cook		612-555-7896		612-555-7599		0.00	
	Franco Films Co.		Franco Films Co. Fred Franco 100 Pleasant Ave. S Minneapolis, MN 55409		Fred Franco		612-555-4566		612-555-4567		940.00	
	Guthrie, Jennie		Jennie Guthrie 165 Terrace Ct. St. Paul, MN 55101		Jennie Guthrie		615-555-1515				0.00	
	Hamilton Hotels		Hamilton Hotels Hilda Hamilton 1000 York Ave. St. Paul, MN 55101		Hilda Hamilton		615-555-1050		615-555-1060		0.00	
	Jones, Beverly		Beverly Jones 333 York Circle Bloomington, MN 54603		Beverly Jones		612-555-7778				0.00	
	Omari, Maria		Maria Omari 210 NE Lowry Ave. Minneapolis, MN 54204		Maria Omari		612-555-9999		612-555-9998		0.00	
	Plaza Pizza Palace		Plaza Pizza Palace Tony Plaza 360 Border Ave. N Minneapolis, MN 55401		Mikey Plaza		612-555-9000		612-555-9800		0.00	

Accounting Reports

As activities are entered in the windows, behind-the-scenes accounting activity is recorded in general journal format, posted to the general ledger, and flowed into the financial statements. You can display and print standard accounting reports showing this activity, such as the *Journal* report. The *Journal* report displays, in general journal format, all transactions recorded during a specified period of time.

To view and print the *Journal* report—
1. Click Reports and then click *Accountant & Taxes*.
2. At the Accountant & Taxes submenu, click *Journal*.
3. At the *From* and *To* fields, choose *02/01/2014* to *02/28/2014*.
4. Click the Refresh button on the top of the report. The *Journal* report is displayed.
5. To print the report, click the Print button on the top of the report.
6. At the Print Reports dialog box, choose the Landscape orientation and then click Print. The last portion of your printout should look like figure 3–DD.
7. Close the report.

FIGURE 3–DD
Journal Report—Partial

EX3 [Your Name] Kristin Raina Interior Designs
Journal
February 2014

Trans #	Type	Date	Num	Name	Memo	Account	Debit	Credit
20	Invoice	02/01/2014	1001	Jones, Beverly		1200 · Accounts Receivable	600.00	
				Jones, Beverly		4020 · Decorating Services		600.00
							600.00	600.00
21	Invoice	02/06/2014	1002	Guthrie, Jennie		1200 · Accounts Receivable	960.00	
				Guthrie, Jennie		4010 · Design Services		960.00
							960.00	960.00
22	Invoice	02/13/2014	1003	Cook Caterers		1200 · Accounts Receivable	1,360.00	
				Cook Caterers		4020 · Decorating Services		400.00
				Cook Caterers		4010 · Design Services		960.00
							1,360.00	1,360.00
23	Invoice	02/17/2014	1004	Franco Films Co.		1200 · Accounts Receivable	1,440.00	
				Franco Films Co.		4010 · Design Services		1,440.00
							1,440.00	1,440.00
24	Invoice	02/23/2014	1005	Berger Bakery Company		1200 · Accounts Receivable	1,200.00	
				Berger Bakery Company		4020 · Decorating Services		1,200.00
							1,200.00	1,200.00
25	Invoice	02/27/2014	1006	Cook Caterers		1200 · Accounts Receivable	1,200.00	
				Cook Caterers		4020 · Decorating Services		300.00
				Cook Caterers		4010 · Design Services		900.00
							1,200.00	1,200.00
26	Payment	02/13/2014	6544	Jones, Beverly		1250 · Undeposited Funds	600.00	
				Jones, Beverly		1200 · Accounts Receivable		600.00
							600.00	600.00
27	Payment	02/20/2014	1255	Franco Films Co.		1250 · Undeposited Funds	500.00	
				Franco Films Co.		1200 · Accounts Receivable		500.00
							500.00	500.00
28	Payment	02/27/2014	655	Cook Caterers		1250 · Undeposited Funds	2,560.00	
				Cook Caterers		1200 · Accounts Receivable		2,560.00
							2,560.00	2,560.00
29	Payment	02/28/2014	674	Guthrie, Jennie		1250 · Undeposited Funds	960.00	
				Guthrie, Jennie		1200 · Accounts Receivable		960.00
							960.00	960.00
30	Payment	02/28/2014	12458	Berger Bakery Company		1250 · Undeposited Funds	600.00	
				Berger Bakery Company		1200 · Accounts Receivable		600.00
							600.00	600.00
31	Sales Receipt	02/24/2014	1007	Hamilton Hotels		1250 · Undeposited Funds	480.00	
				Hamilton Hotels		4010 · Design Services		480.00
							480.00	480.00
32	Deposit	02/28/2014			Deposit	1010 · Cash - Operating	5,700.00	
				Jones, Beverly	Deposit	1250 · Undeposited Funds		600.00
				Franco Films Co.	Deposit	1250 · Undeposited Funds		500.00
				Hamilton Hotels	Deposit	1250 · Undeposited Funds		480.00
				Cook Caterers	Deposit	1250 · Undeposited Funds		2,560.00
				Guthrie, Jennie	Deposit	1250 · Undeposited Funds		960.00
				Berger Bakery Company	Deposit	1250 · Undeposited Funds		600.00
							5,700.00	5,700.00
TOTAL							**30,160.00**	**30,160.00**

HINT

If the name field displays Multiple, you can click the Expand button at top of the report to display more detail.

Notice on your printout that all activity for February is displayed in the order that it was entered. The earlier transactions are the vendor activities recorded in chapter 2. The later transactions are the customer activities recorded in this chapter. Scroll down to the transactions for this chapter, and look in the Type column. This indicates the window where the activity was recorded. The *Invoice* type is from the Create Invoices window. Each of these transactions has a debit to Accounts Receivable, because this is the default for that window. The *Payment* type is from the Receive Payments window. All these transactions are a debit to Undeposited Funds and a credit to Accounts Receivable, which are the default accounts for this window. The *Sales Receipt* type is from the Enter Sales Receipts window, which all have a debit to Undeposited Funds because that is the default account for this window. The *Deposit* type is from the Make Deposits window. This transaction by default is a debit to Cash and a credit to Undeposited Funds.

Exiting QuickBooks

Upon completing this session, make a backup copy of your practice exercise company file to a removable storage device using the Backup command. Be sure to change the *Save in* text box to the removable storage device, and carefully key the correct file name. Close the company before exiting.

Chapter Review and Assessment

Procedure Review

To add a customer—
1. Click Customers and then click *Customer Center*.
2. At the Customer Center window, click the New Customer & Job button and then select New Customer.
3. Enter the background data for the customer.
4. Click OK.
5. Close the Customer Center window.

To delete a customer—
1. Click Customers and then click *Customer Center*.
2. At the Customer Center window, select the customer you wish to delete.
3. At the main menu bar, click Edit and then click *Delete Customer:Job*.
4. Click OK at the warning.
5. Close the Customer Center window.

   You cannot delete a customer who has a balance or who was used in a transaction during the current accounting period.

To edit a customer—
1. Click Customers and then click *Customer Center*.
2. At the Customer Center window, double-click to select the customer you wish to edit.
3. Change the appropriate information.
4. Click OK.
5. Close the Customer Center window.

To create an invoice—
1. Click Customers and then click *Create Invoices*.
2. At the CUSTOMER:JOB drop-down list, click the customer name.
3. At the TEMPLATE drop-down list, accept *Intuit Service Invoice*.
4. Enter the invoice date in the *Date* field.
5. Enter the invoice number in the *Invoice #* field.
6. Select the terms in the Terms drop-down list.
7. Click the first line in the *ITEM* field, and the drop-down arrow will appear for the Item List. Then select the appropriate item(s) at the Item drop-down list.
8. Enter the quantity.
9. Make sure the *Print Later* and *Email Later* boxes are not checked. The *ONLINE PAY* box should say Off.
10. Click Save & Close.

To receive a payment—
1. Click Customers and then click *Receive Payments*.
2. At the RECEIVED FROM drop-down list, click the customer name.
3. Enter the amount in the *AMOUNT* field.
4. Enter the payment date in the *DATE* field.

5. At the PMT.METHOD drop-down list, click *Check*.
6. Enter the check number in the *CHECK #* field.
7. Click Save & Close.

To enter a cash sale—
1. Click Customers and then click *Enter Sales Receipts*.
2. At the CUSTOMER:JOB drop-down list, click the customer name.
3. Complete the balance of the window in the same manner as an invoice.
4. Click Save and Close.

To make a deposit—
1. Click Banking and then click *Make Deposits*.
2. At the Payments to Deposit window, click Select All to deposit all receipts.
3. Click OK.
4. At the Make Deposits window in the *Deposit To* field, accept or choose *1010 Cash - Operating* account.
5. Enter the deposit date in the *Date* field.
6. Click Save & Close.

To view and print customer reports from the Reports menu—
1. Click Reports and then click *Customers & Receivables*.
2. At the Customers & Receivables submenu, choose a report.
3. Choose the appropriate dates for the report, then click the Refresh button on the top of the report.
4. Click the Print button on the top of the report.
5. At the Print Reports dialog box, review the settings, and click Print.
6. Close the report.

Key Concepts

Select the letter of the item that best matches each definition.

a. Customer Center
b. Receive Payments window
c. Cash Sales
d. Create Invoices window
e. *Open Invoices* report
f. Customer
g. Undeposited Funds
h. Enter Sales Receipts window
i. Deposit Funds window
j. *Customer Balance Detail* report

_____ 1. Contains a file for all customers with whom the company does business.
_____ 2. A report that displays all transactions for a customer.
_____ 3. Window used to deposit funds collected.
_____ 4. A person or business the company provides services for or sells a product to.
_____ 5. Window used to record the payment of invoices.
_____ 6. Sales where payment is received immediately.
_____ 7. Window used to record sales on account.
_____ 8. Collections not yet deposited in the bank.
_____ 9. A report that lists all unpaid invoices for each customer.
_____ 10. Window used to record sales for cash.

Procedure Check

1. Your company has obtained a new major client. Describe the steps to add the new client to the system.
2. Your company has the type of business that makes cash sales to many customers and rarely tracks accounts receivable. How would you use QuickBooks to record your sales?
3. Your business wishes to track all the deposits made to the bank to facilitate the month-end bank reconciliation process. How would you record collection of funds to accomplish this?
4. You wish to determine the oldest unpaid invoices. How would you use QuickBooks to obtain that information?
5. Upper management requests a report for each customer with contact information. How would you use QuickBooks to develop this information?

6. Compare and contrast a manual accounting system with a computerized accounting system for processing customer transactions. Include an explanation of how the accounts receivable subsidiary ledger compares with the Customer Center.

Case Problems

Case Problem 1

On April 1, 2014, Lynn Garcia started her business of Lynn's Music Studio. Lynn began by depositing $10,000 cash in a bank account in the business name. She also contributed a piano and some guitars. The musical instruments have an outstanding note balance of $2,000 that has been assumed by the business. The cash, musical instruments, note payable, and capital have all been recorded in the opening balances of the books. For the first part of the month, Lynn set up her studio. She has now begun providing piano and guitar lessons. Piano lessons are billed at $35 per hour, and guitar lessons are billed at $30 per hour. You will record the transactions listed below for the month of April. The company file for this chapter includes the beginning information for Lynn's Music Studio along with the transactions recorded in chapter 2.

1. Open the company file CH3 Lynn's Music Studio.QBW.
2. Make a backup copy of the company file, and name it LMS3 [*Your Name*] Lynn's Music Studio.
3. Restore the backup copy of the company file. In both the Open Backup Copy and Save Company File as windows, use the file name LMS3 [*Your Name*] Lynn's Music Studio.
4. Change the company name to **LMS3 [*Your Name*] Lynn's Music Studio**.
5. Add the following customer to the Customer Center:

> *CUSTOMER NAME:* **Musical Youth Group**
> *OPENING BALANCE:* **0 AS OF April 1, 2014**
> *COMPANY NAME:* **Musical Youth Group**
> *First Name:* **Dana**
> *Last Name:* **Thompson**

Main Phone:	570-555-6642
Fax:	570-555-6700
Main Email:	**myg@emcp.net**
INVOICE/BILL TO:	**550 Marion Lane**
	Scranton, PA 18504
CREDIT LIMIT:	**20,000**
PAYMENT TERMS:	**Net 30 Days**
TYPE:	**Group**

Delete the following customer:
  Rivera Family

6. Using the appropriate window, record the following transactions for April 2014:

Apr. 9   Provided 15 hours guitar lessons and 10 hours piano lessons on account to Jefferson High School, Invoice No. 2001, Net 10 Days.

Apr. 12   Provided 3 hours piano lessons to the Schroeder Family, Invoice No. 2002. Received payment immediately, Check No. 478.

Apr. 13   Provided 12 hours piano lessons to Highland School, Invoice No. 2003, Net 30 Days.

Apr. 16   Provided 8 hours guitar lessons and 5 hours piano lessons to Twin Lakes Elementary School, Invoice No. 2004, Net 30 Days.

Apr. 16   Provided 6 hours guitar lessons to the Patterson Family, Invoice No. 2005. Received payment immediately, Check No. 208.

Apr. 20   Provided 5 hours guitar lessons and 7 hours piano lessons to Mulligan Residence, Invoice No. 2006, Net 30 Days.

Apr. 20   Received payment in full from Jefferson High School for Invoice No. 2001, Check No. 28759.

Apr. 23   Provided 5 hours of piano lessons to Douglaston Senior Center, Invoice No. 2007, Net 30 Days. Douglaston Senior Center is a new client:

CUSTOMER NAME:	**Douglaston Senior Center**
OPENING BALANCE:	**0 AS OF April 1, 2014**
COMPANY NAME:	**Douglaston Senior Center**
First Name:	**Herbie**
Last Name:	**Richardson**
Main Phone	**570-555-7748**
Fax:	**570-555-8800**
Main Email:	**DSC@emcp.net**
INVOICE/BILL TO:	**574 S Beech Street**
	Scranton, PA 18506

CREDIT LIMIT:	**25,000**
PAYMENT TERMS:	**Net 30 Days**
TYPE:	**Group**

Apr. 23   Provided 10 hours guitar lessons and 10 hours piano lessons to the Musical Youth Group, Invoice No. 2008. Received payment immediately, Check No. 578.

Apr. 26   Provided 15 hours guitar lessons and 10 hours piano lessons on account to Jefferson High School, Invoice No. 2009, Net 10 Days.

Apr. 26   Received payment in full from Highland School for Invoice No. 2003, Check No. 75281.

Apr. 27   Provided 2 hours guitar lessons for the Patel Family, Invoice No. 2010. Received payment immediately, Check No. 629.

Apr. 30   Provided 8 hours guitar lessons and 5 hours piano lessons to Twin Lakes Elementary School, Invoice No. 2011, Net 30 Days.

Apr. 30   Received partial payment of $145 from Mulligan Residence for Invoice No. 2006, Check No. 715.

Apr. 30   Deposited all receipts for the month.

7. Display and print the following reports for April 1, 2014, to April 30, 2014:
   a. *Open Invoices*
   b. *Customer Balance Detail*
   c. *Customer Contact List*
   d. *Journal*

Case Problem 2

On June 1, 2014, Olivia Chen began her business, Olivia's Web Solutions. Olivia began by depositing $25,000 cash in a bank account in the business name. She also contributed a computer. The computer has an outstanding note balance of $2,500 that has now been assumed by the business. The cash, computer, note payable, and capital have all been recorded in the opening balances of the books. For the first part of the month, Olivia set up her office. She has now begun providing web design and Internet consulting services to individuals and small businesses. The Web Page Design Services are billed at $125 per hour, and the Internet Consulting Services at $100 per hour. You will record the transactions listed below for the month of June. The company file includes the beginning information for Olivia's Web Solutions along with the transactions recorded in chapter 2.

1. Open the company file CH3 Olivia's Web Solutions.QBW.
2. Make a backup copy of the company file, and name it OWS3 [*Your Name*] Olivia's Web Solutions.
3. Restore the backup copy of the company file. In both the Open Backup Copy and Save Company File as windows, use the file name OWS3 [*Your Name*] Olivia's Web Solutions.
4. Change the company name to **OWS3 [*Your Name*] Olivia's Web Solutions**.

5. Add the following customer to the Customer Center:

CUSTOMER NAME:	**Thrifty Stores**
OPENING BALANCE	**0 AS OF June 1, 2014**
COMPANY NAME:	**Thrifty Stores**
First Name:	**William**
Last Name:	**Way**
Main Phone:	**718-555-2445**
Fax	**718-555-2446**
Main Email:	**Thrifty@emcp.net**
INVOICE/BILL TO:	**23 Boston Ave.**
	Bronx, NY 11693
CREDIT LIMIT:	**25,000**
PAYMENT TERMS:	**Net 30 Days**
TYPE:	**Commercial**

Delete the following customer:
   Printers Group

6. Using the appropriate window, record the following transactions for June 2014:

Jun. 11	Provided 8 hours of Internet Consulting Services and 10 hours of Web Page Design Services on account to Long Island Water Works, Invoice No. 1001, Net 30 Days.
Jun. 14	Provided 8 hours of Web Page Design Services on account to Sehorn & Smith, Invoice No. 1002, Net 30 Days.
Jun. 15	Provided 8 hours of Web Page Design Services on account to the Schneider Family, Invoice No. 1003.
Jun. 17	Provided 4 hours of Internet Consulting Services and 8 hours of Web Page Design Services on account to Miguel's Restaurant, Invoice No. 1004, Net 30 Days.
Jun. 18	Provided 4 hours of Internet Consulting Services to the Singh Family, Invoice No. 1005. Received payment immediately, Check No. 687.
Jun. 21	Provided 8 hours of Web Page Design Services on account to Breathe Easy, Invoice No. 1006, Net 30 Days.
Jun. 25	Received payment in full from Long Island Water Works for Invoice No. 1001, Check No. 124554.
Jun. 25	Provided 12 hours of Web Page Design Services on account to Thrifty Stores, Invoice No. 1007, Net 30 Days.
Jun. 28	Provided 8 hours of Internet Consulting Services on account to Artie's Auto Repair, Invoice 1008, Net 30 Days. Artie's Auto Repair is a new client:

CUSTOMER NAME:	**Artie's Auto Repair**
OPENING BALANCE:	**0 AS OF June 1, 2014**
COMPANY NAME:	**Artie's Auto Repair**
First Name:	**Leon**

Last Name:	Artie
Main Phone:	516-555-1221
Fax	516-555-1231
Main Email:	ArtieAuto@emcp.net
INVOICE/BILL TO:	32 West 11th Street
	New Hyde Park, NY 11523
CREDIT LIMIT::	25,000
PAYMENT TERMS:	Net 30 Days
TYPE:	Commercial

Jun. 28	Received payment in full from Sehorn & Smith for Invoice No. 1002, Check No. 3656.
Jun. 29	Provided 12 hours of Internet Consulting Services on account to South Shore School District, Invoice No. 1009, Net 30 Days.
Jun. 29	Received payment in full from Miguel's Restaurant for Invoice No. 1004, Check No. 3269.
Jun. 30	Provided 8 hours of Internet Consulting Services on account to Sehorn & Smith, Invoice No. 1010, Net 30 Days.
Jun. 30	Received partial payment of $250 from Breathe Easy for Invoice No. 1006, Check No. 1455.
Jun. 30	Deposited all receipts for the month.

7. Display and print the following reports for June 1, 2014, to June 30, 2014:
   a. *Open Invoices*
   b. *Customer Balance Detail*
   c. *Customer Contact List*
   d. *Journal*

CHAPTER 4

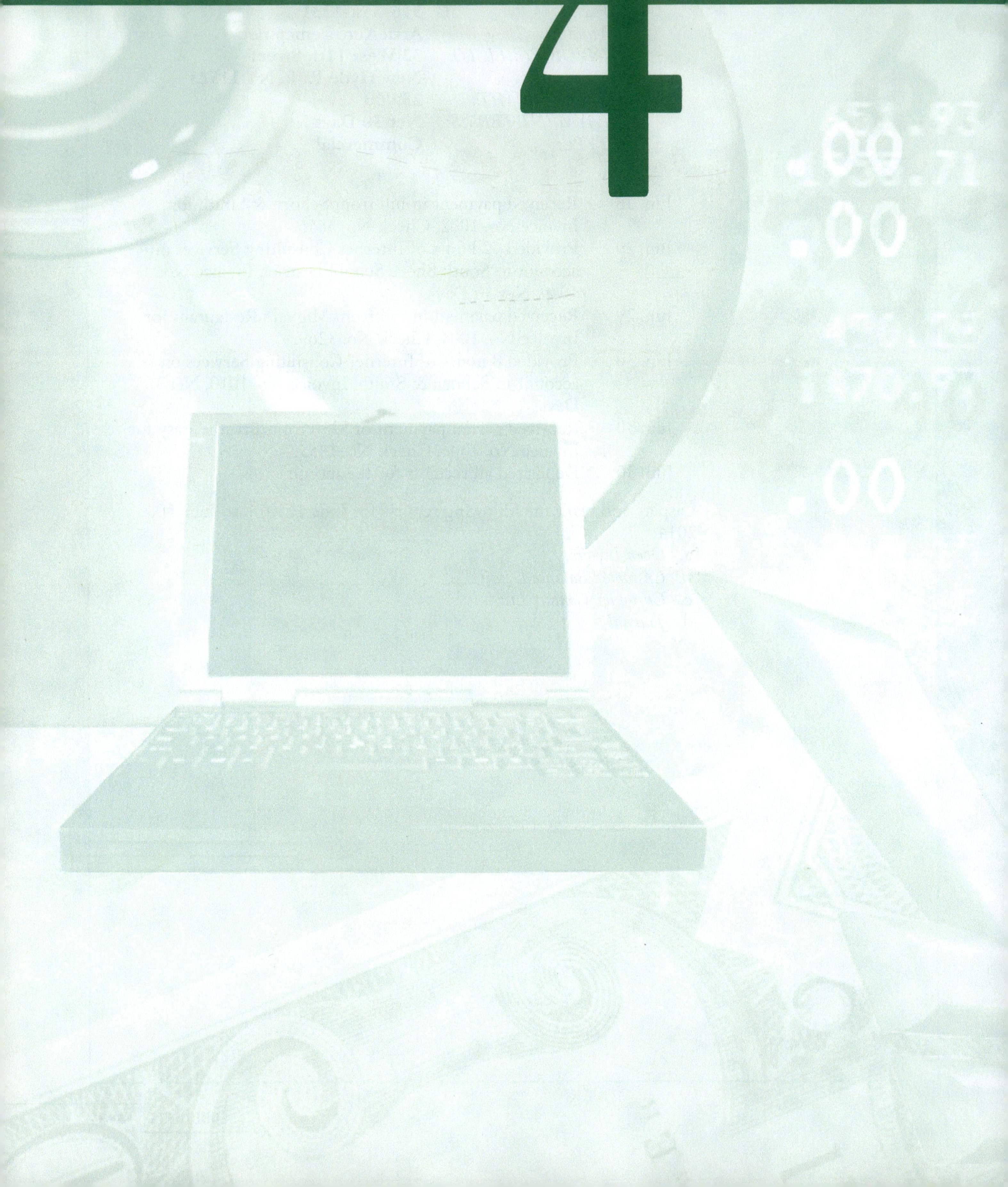

Period-End Procedures

Make General Journal Entries

Chapter Objectives

- Update the Chart of Accounts List

- Record adjustments in the Make General Journal Entries window

- View the effect of period-end adjustments on the trial balance

- Display and print period-end accounting reports

- Change the reports display using the Customize Report button

- Display and print accounting reports and financial statements

Introduction

general journal In a manual accounting system, the document in which transactions are initially recorded chronologically.

generally accepted accounting principles (GAAP) Principles used to prepare the financial statements of a company. They consist of both formal accounting regulations and procedures mandated by regulatory agencies, and of traditionally used accounting procedures.

adjusting journal entries Adjustments made to accounts at certain periods of time, such as the end of the month or the end of the fiscal year, to bring the balances up to date

debit Dollar amount recorded in the *left* column of an account. Depending on the account, it either increases or decreases the balance in the account.

credit Dollar amount recorded in the *right* column of an account. Depending on the account, it either increases or decreases the balance in the account.

special journals The purchases journal, sales journal, cash receipts journal, and cash payments journal.

QuickBooks allows you to record journal entries in general journal format. As seen in chapters 2 and 3, QuickBooks records daily activities in windows such as Enter Bills, Pay Bills, Write Checks, Create Invoices, Receive Payments, and so on. However, behind the scenes, QuickBooks also records the activities in **general journal** format using debits and credits. The accounts used to record the activities come from the *Chart of Accounts* (Lists/Centers).

At times, some account balances (Activities) will need to be adjusted based on information that does not appear in the daily activities so that the financial statements can be properly prepared in accordance with **generally accepted accounting principles (GAAP)**. These adjustments to the accounts are called **adjusting journal entries** and are recorded in the *Make General Journal Entries* window. As you record the daily activities and adjusting journal entries, QuickBooks simultaneously updates the accounting records and financial statements (Reports).

In this chapter, our sample company, Kristin Raina Interior Designs, will make the necessary adjusting journal entries for February—the end of the first month of operations.

QuickBooks versus Manual Accounting: General Journal Entries

In a manual accounting system, the general journal is the document in which transactions are initially recorded chronologically. For each transaction, the dollar value of at least one account must be recorded as a **debit** amount, and the dollar value of at least one account must be recorded as a **credit** amount. The total dollar value of debits must equal the total dollar value of credits. Companies have the option of recording all transactions exclusively in the general journal or, alternatively, for frequent similar transactions, in **special journals**. In either case, at month-end, the transactions from all journals are posted to the general ledger.

Periodically, certain adjustments that are not daily business activities must be made to the accounts to update the balances. These adjustments, called adjusting journal entries, are always recorded in the general journal. They are then posted to the general ledger to update the balances in the accounts. The adjusted balances are used to prepare the financial statements. These adjusting journal entries must always be made on the date the financial statements are prepared, but they can be recorded more often. Most large companies typically prepare the adjusting journal entries monthly.

QuickBooks does not follow the format of the special journals for daily transactions. Instead, all activities are recorded in the different windows depending on the nature of the activity. Behind the scenes, QuickBooks records the activity in general journal format, as seen in the *Journal* report. However, for adjusting journal entries, QuickBooks uses the Make General Journal Entries window in a manner similar to that of a manual accounting system. As you save information entered in each of the windows, including the Make General Journal Entries window, the general ledger balances, the Chart of Accounts List balances, the trial balance, and the financial statements are simultaneously updated. Due to the ease of updating balances in a computerized accounting system, even small companies can now record adjusting journal entries monthly.

Chapter Problem

In this chapter, you will record the adjusting journal entries for the end of the first month of business, February 28, 2014, for Kristin Raina Interior Designs. The February 1, 2014, beginning balances, along with all vendor and customer activities for the month of February as illustrated in chapters 2 and 3, are contained in the company file CH4 Kristin Raina Interior Designs.

Before you begin, open the company file CH4 Kristin Raina Interior Designs. QBW. Make a backup copy of the file, name it **EX4 [*Your Name*] Kristin Raina Interior Designs**, and then restore the file. Finally, change the company name in the file to **EX4 [*Your Name*] Kristin Raina Interior Designs**.

LISTS/CENTERS:

The Chart of Accounts List

Recall from chapter 1 that the second level of operation in QuickBooks is recording background information in Lists/Centers. Lists and Centers need to be revised periodically when new accounts need to be added, accounts not used in the business need to be deleted, or modifications need to be made to an account. When you make these revisions to the accounts, you are updating the Chart of Accounts List.

Chart of Accounts List The list of accounts a company uses as it conducts its business.

The **Chart of Accounts List** is the list of accounts a company uses as it conducts its business. In a manual accounting system, all the individual accounts are placed together in a book called the **general ledger**. Each account in the general ledger shows all the increases and decreases in the account, reflected as debits and credits, and the balance in each account. In computerized accounting systems, a general ledger is also maintained showing the increases, decreases, and the balance for each account. In addition, the Chart of Accounts List displays the balance next to each account name. Because of this, the Chart of Accounts List has become synonymous with the general ledger in computerized systems, although it indicates only the balance and not all the detail activity.

general ledger The document where transactions are summarized by account.

In QuickBooks, the Chart of Accounts List consists of the account number, name, type, and balance. The account numbers are optional but are used in this text. The name you assign an account is the name that appears in the windows and reports. The balance is determined by the original amount entered (if any) when the account is first created and then subsequently updated by Activities entered in the windows.

The account types are used by the software to determine where to place the account name and balance on the financial statements and to establish the system default accounts.

The account types consist of—

Assets:
Bank
Accounts Receivable
Other Current Asset
Fixed Asset
Other Asset

Liabilities:
Accounts Payable
Credit Card
Other Current Liability
Long Term Liability

Equity:
Equity

Income and Expenses:
Income
Cost of Goods Sold
Expense
Other Income
Other Expense

As was seen in chapters 2 and 3, QuickBooks identifies certain accounts as system default accounts and uses them to identify the transactions recorded in the windows. For example, the Accounts Payable account type is used to identify the Accounts Payable liability account when transactions are recorded in the Enter Bills window. The Accounts Receivable account type is used to identify the Accounts Receivable asset account when transactions are recorded in the Create Invoices window. When QuickBooks looks for an account, it looks for the account type, not the account name.

Kristin Raina previously entered information to establish the Chart of Accounts List that was then used for the February activities recorded in chapters 2 and 3.

To review the Chart of Accounts List—
1. Click Reports and then click *List*.
2. At the List submenu, click *Account Listing*. The Account Listing is displayed. (See figure 4–A.)

FIGURE 4–A
Account Listing

Account Listing window

EX4 [Your Name] Kristin Raina Interior Designs
Account Listing
February 28, 2014

Account	Type	Balance Total	Description	Accnt. #	Tax Line
1010 · Cash - Operating	Bank	47,400.00		1010	<Unassigned>
1200 · Accounts Receivable	Accounts Receivable	1,540.00		1200	<Unassigned>
1250 · Undeposited Funds	Other Current Asset	0.00		1250	<Unassigned>
1300 · Design Supplies	Other Current Asset	200.00		1300	<Unassigned>
1305 · Office Supplies	Other Current Asset	400.00		1305	<Unassigned>
1410 · Prepaid Advertising	Other Current Asset	600.00		1410	<Unassigned>
1420 · Prepaid Insurance	Other Current Asset	2,400.00		1420	<Unassigned>
1700 · Furniture and Fixtures	Fixed Asset	12,000.00		1700	<Unassigned>
1700 · Furniture and Fixtures:1725 · Furniture, Cost	Fixed Asset	12,000.00		1725	<Unassigned>
1700 · Furniture and Fixtures:1750 · Accum. Dep., Furniture and Fix	Fixed Asset	0.00		1750	<Unassigned>
1800 · Computers	Fixed Asset	3,600.00		1800	<Unassigned>
1800 · Computers:1825 · Computers, Cost	Fixed Asset	3,600.00		1825	<Unassigned>
1800 · Computers:1850 · Accum. Dep., Computers	Fixed Asset	0.00		1850	<Unassigned>
2010 · Accounts Payable	Accounts Payable	6,250.00		2010	<Unassigned>
2020 · Notes Payable	Other Current Liability	7,000.00		2020	<Unassigned>
2030 · Interest Payable	Other Current Liability	0.00		2030	<Unassigned>
3010 · Kristin Raina, Capital	Equity	50,000.00		3010	<Unassigned>
3020 · Kristin Raina, Drawings	Equity	-400.00		3020	<Unassigned>
3030 · Accumulated Earnings	Equity			3030	<Unassigned>
4010 · Design Services	Income			4010	<Unassigned>
4020 · Decorating Services	Income			4020	<Unassigned>
6020 · Accounting Expense	Expense			6020	<Unassigned>
6030 · Administrative Expense	Expense			6030	<Unassigned>
6175 · Deprec. Exp., Furniture	Expense			6175	<Unassigned>
6200 · Insurance Expense	Expense			6200	<Unassigned>
6300 · Janitorial Expenses	Expense			6300	<Unassigned>
6350 · Promotion Expense	Expense			6350	<Unassigned>
6400 · Rent Expense	Expense			6400	<Unassigned>
6450 · Telephone Expense	Expense			6450	<Unassigned>
6500 · Utilities Expense	Expense			6500	<Unassigned>

HINT

Recall that in a Report, you can click and drag on the diamond shape before the column heading to change the width of the column.

In QuickBooks, the account balances that flow into the financial statements are based on the account type. If you want to subtotal two or more accounts on the financial statements, you can identify an account as a *subaccount*. Subaccounts show a subtotal amount on the financial statements in addition to the regular account balances. When an account is identified as a subaccount, the account it is a subaccount of is called the *parent* account.

In Kristin Raina's Chart of Accounts List, the asset cost and accumulated depreciation accounts were marked as subaccounts of the related asset account. This was done to see the accumulated depreciation account as a deduction from the cost of an asset on the financial statements and to display the net amount.

In the Account Listing Report window, when parent and subaccounts are used, subaccount names by default display the parent account name left aligned and the subaccount name to the right of the parent account name all on one line. Review the Account Listing in figure 4–A. Look at the *1700 Furniture and Fixtures* account. The accounts below it are *1700 Furniture and Fixtures: 1725 - Furniture, Cost* and *1700 Furniture and Fixtures: 1750 - Accum. Dep., Furniture and Fix*. This means accounts 1725 and 1750 are subaccounts of 1700. Account 1700 is a parent account because it has a subaccount. Notice the same setup with accounts 1800, 1825, and 1850 on the Account Listing.

To view a specific account—
1. With the Account Listing open, place the zoom glass over the *Cash - Operating* account.
2. Choose *Cash - Operating* by double-clicking the mouse. The Edit Account window for Cash - Operating is displayed. (See figure 4–B.)

FIGURE 4–B
Edit Account Window

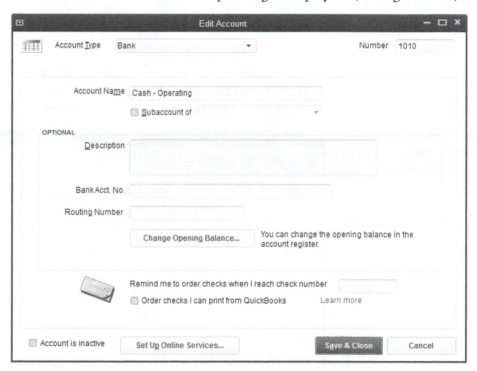

The Edit Account window contains the following account information:

Account Type	Use the drop-down list to display and choose the account type. QuickBooks uses the account type for system default accounts in windows and for placement on financial statements.
Number	An account number is optional. Account numbers will be used in this text and have been established in the company files.
Account Name	Fill in an account name of your choice. The software uses the account type, not the account name, for necessary identification (default accounts and placement on financial statements). The name keyed in this field appears in the windows and on reports.
Subaccount of	Accounts can be identified as subaccounts of another account. To activate this field, click the mouse to place a check mark in the box. Once this box is activated, use the drop-down list to determine in which account this will become a subaccount.
Description	This field is optional. A description entered here will appear on certain reports.
Bank Acct. No. and Routing Number	These fields are optional. They are listed as references for the user.

3. Close the Edit Account window.
4. At the *Account Listing* report, double-click *1800 Computers: 1850 - Accum. Dep., Computers*. At the Edit Account window, notice how this account is marked as a subaccount of 1800 - Computers. (See figure 4–C.)

FIGURE 4–C
Edit Account Window—
Subaccount Checked

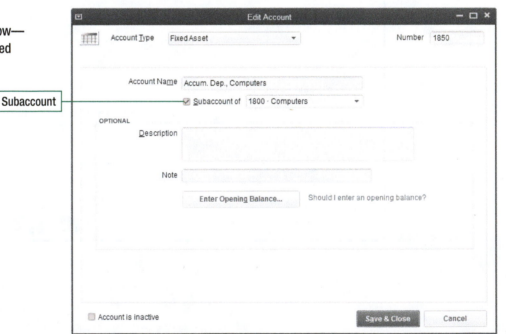

5. Close the Edit Account window.
6. Close the *Account Listing* report window.

Adding an Account

In preparation for recording month-end adjusting journal entries, Kristin Raina has determined that she needs to add an Advertising Expense account to the Chart of Accounts List.

To add a new account—
1. Click Lists and then click *Chart of Accounts*.

· The Chart of Accounts List window appears. (See figure 4–D.)

NAME	⚡	TYPE	BALANCE TOTAL	ATTACH
◇ 1010 · Cash - Operating		Bank	47,400.00	
◇ 1200 · Accounts Receivable		Accounts Receivable	1,540.00	
◇ 1250 · Undeposited Funds		Other Current Asset	0.00	
◇ 1300 · Design Supplies		Other Current Asset	200.00	
◇ 1305 · Office Supplies		Other Current Asset	400.00	
◇ 1410 · Prepaid Advertising		Other Current Asset	600.00	
◇ 1420 · Prepaid Insurance		Other Current Asset	2,400.00	
◇ 1700 · Furniture and Fixtures		Fixed Asset	12,000.00	
◇ 1725 · Furniture, Cost		Fixed Asset	12,000.00	
◇ 1750 · Accum. Dep., Furniture and Fix		Fixed Asset	0.00	
◇ 1800 · Computers		Fixed Asset	3,600.00	
◇ 1825 · Computers, Cost		Fixed Asset	3,600.00	
◇ 1850 · Accum. Dep., Computers		Fixed Asset	0.00	
◇ 2010 · Accounts Payable		Accounts Payable	6,250.00	
◇ 2020 · Notes Payable		Other Current Liability	7,000.00	
◇ 2030 · Interest Payable		Other Current Liability	0.00	
◇ 3010 · Kristin Raina, Capital		Equity	50,000.00	
◇ 3020 · Kristin Raina, Drawings		Equity	-400.00	
◇ 3030 · Accumulated Earnings		Equity		
◇ 4010 · Design Services		Income		
◇ 4020 · Decorating Services		Income		
◇ 6020 · Accounting Expense		Expense		
◇ 6030 · Administrative Expense		Expense		
◇ 6175 · Deprec. Exp., Furniture		Expense		
◇ 6200 · Insurance Expense		Expense		
◇ 6300 · Janitorial Expenses		Expense		
◇ 6350 · Promotion Expense		Expense		
◇ 6400 · Rent Expense		Expense		
◇ 6450 · Telephone Expense		Expense		
◇ 6500 · Utilities Expense		Expense		

Account ▼ Activities ▼ Reports ▼ Attach ☐ Include inactive

List Window Drop-Down Menu Buttons

Notice that most of the account names are left aligned. In the Chart of Accounts List window, when parent and subaccounts are used, by default the parent account name is left aligned and the subaccounts names are indented under the parent account name. For example, account 1700 is the parent account, and the subaccounts of 1725 and 1750 are indented under account 1700.

The presentation of parent accounts and subaccounts in the Chart of Accounts List window is different than the presentation of parent and subaccounts on the Account Listing Report. Recall in the Account Listing report in figure 4-A, for each subaccount listed, both the parent account and subaccount are listed on one line, with the parent account name left aligned and the subaccount name listed to the right of the parent account name.

The Chart of Accounts List is displayed in a List window. List windows have drop-down menu buttons at the bottom of the window. The first menu button in all List windows represents the name of the List, in this case Account. In almost all List windows there is also a Reports button. The remaining buttons vary according to the List window displayed. In the Chart of Accounts List window, the first button is Account, the second menu button is Activities, the third menu button is Reports, and the fourth menu button is Attach. The Activities and Reports buttons are shortcuts you can use instead of using the main menu bar drop-down menus to access commands. The Attach button can be used to attach documents using the QuickBooks Document Management feature. The Attach button may or may not be an active button.

2. At the Chart of Accounts List window, click the Account menu button. A drop-down menu appears. (See figure 4–E.)

FIGURE 4–E

Account Drop-Down Menu

3. At the Account menu, click New. The Add New Account: Choose Account Type window appears. (See figure 4–F.)

FIGURE 4–F

Add New Account: Choose Account Type Window

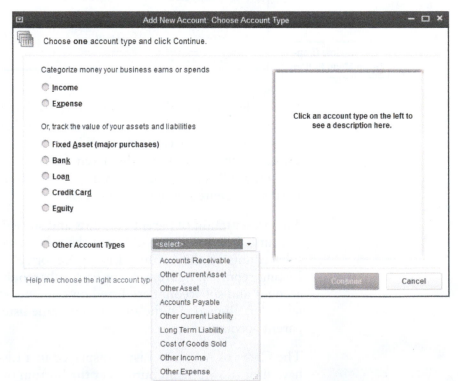

4. Click Expense and then click Continue. The Add New Account window appears, with the Account Type drop-down list completed with Expense. (See figure 4–G.)

If you chose an incorrect account type, you can simply change it here. Click the Account Type arrow, and a drop-down list displays all of the account types. (See figure 4–H.)

5. Enter the data below for the account number and name.

Number:	**6050**
Name:	**Advertising Expense**

(See figure 4–I.)

FIGURE 4–I

Add New Account
Window—Completed

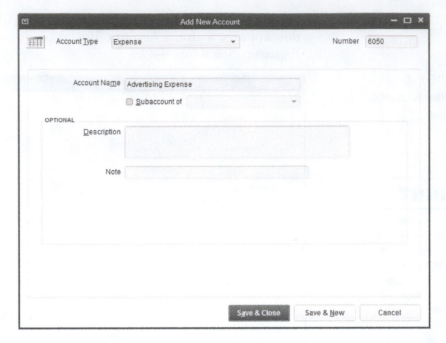

6. If the information is correct, click Save & Close. Notice the account was added to the Chart of Accounts List.
7. Close the Chart of Accounts List window.

Deleting an Account

Kristin Raina has decided the Promotion Expense account is not necessary and should be deleted.

To delete an account—
1. Click Lists and then click *Chart of Accounts*.
2. At the Chart of Accounts List window, select (highlight) *6350 Promotion Expense*. (See figure 4–J.)

FIGURE 4–J

Chart of Accounts List—
Promotion Expense
Selected

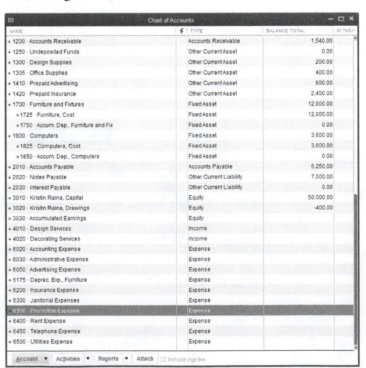

3. Click the Account menu button.
4. At the Account menu, click Delete Account.
5. The Delete Account warning appears. Click OK. The account will be deleted.
6. Close the Chart of Accounts List window.

An account with a balance or that has been used in a transaction cannot be deleted. It can instead be marked inactive and will no longer appear in reports.

Editing an Account

Kristin Raina decides to change the account name Furniture and Fixtures to simply Furniture.

To edit an account—

1. Open the Chart of Accounts List and select the *1700 Furniture and Fixtures* account.
2. At the Chart of Accounts List window, click the Account menu button.
3. At the Account menu, click Edit Account. The Edit Account window appears.
4. At the *Name* field, delete the part of the name *and Fixtures*. (See figure 4–K.)

FIGURE 4–K

Edit Account Window—Completed

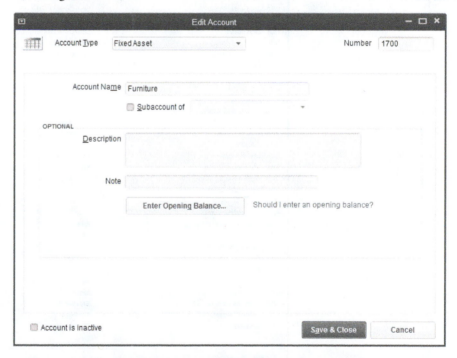

5. If the information is correct, click Save & Close.
6. Close the Chart of Accounts List window.

Practice Exercise

Add the following accounts:

Type:	**Expense**
Number:	**6325**
Name:	**Office Supplies Expense**
Type:	**Other Expense**
Number:	**7000**
Name:	**Interest Expense**

Delete the following account:
6030 Administrative Expense

Edit the following account:
Change the name of account 1750 to *Accum. Dep., Furniture*

QuickCheck: The updated Chart of Accounts List window appears in figure 4–L.

FIGURE 4–L
Updated Chart of Accounts List Window

The Trial Balance

REPORTS:

trial balance A report containing all the general ledger account names, their respective debit or credit balances, and the total debits and total credits.

In a manual accounting system, as journal entries are recorded and posted to the general ledger, errors can occur when posting to the general ledger or when doing arithmetic computations. The **trial balance** is used to verify that the total debits equal the total credits, which means the general ledger is in balance. In a computerized system, on the other hand, there is less chance of the accounts being out of balance because the postings to the general ledger and arithmetic computations occur automatically.

But a trial balance is still useful. It allows you to view the accounts and their debit or credit balances without having to look at all the detail in the general ledger. It is often useful to review the trial balance before adjusting journal entries.

To view and print the trial balance—
1. Click Reports and then click *Accountant & Taxes.*
2. At the Accountant & Taxes submenu, click *Trial Balance.*
3. At the *From* and *To* fields, choose *01/01/2014* and *02/28/2014*, then click the Refresh button on the top of the report. The trial balance is displayed. (See figure 4–M.)

FIGURE 4–M
Trial Balance Report

HINT

Print the Trial Balance at this time. Once you record adjusting journal entries, you will no longer be able to view and print a preadjusted Trial Balance.

	Debit	Credit
1010 · Cash - Operating	47,400.00	
1200 · Accounts Receivable	1,540.00	
1250 · Undeposited Funds	0.00	
1300 · Design Supplies	200.00	
1305 · Office Supplies	400.00	
1410 · Prepaid Advertising	600.00	
1420 · Prepaid Insurance	2,400.00	
1700 · Furniture:1725 · Furniture, Cost	12,000.00	
1800 · Computers:1825 · Computers, Cost	3,600.00	
2010 · Accounts Payable		6,250.00
2020 · Notes Payable		7,000.00
3010 · Kristin Raina, Capital		50,000.00
3020 · Kristin Raina, Drawings	400.00	
4010 · Design Services		4,740.00
4020 · Decorating Services		2,500.00
6020 · Accounting Expense	300.00	
6300 · Janitorial Expenses	125.00	
6400 · Rent Expense	800.00	
6450 · Telephone Expense	275.00	
6500 · Utilities Expense	450.00	
TOTAL	70,490.00	70,490.00

EX4 [Your Name] Kristin Raina Interior Designs
Trial Balance
As of February 28, 2014
Accrual Basis

4. To print the report, click the Print button on the top of the report.
5. At the Print Reports dialog box, check the settings and then click Print.
6. Close the report.

The Make General Journal Entries Window

To adjust account balances based on accounting rules, you usually need to enter adjusting journal entries before preparing financial statements. In QuickBooks, adjusting journal entries are recorded in the Make General Journal Entries window. This window is set up similar to that for a manual accounting system. It lists the account and amount of the debit entry, the account and amount of the credit entry, and an explanation.

The QuickBooks Make General Journal Entries window appears in figure 4–N.

FIGURE 4–N
Make General Journal Entries Window

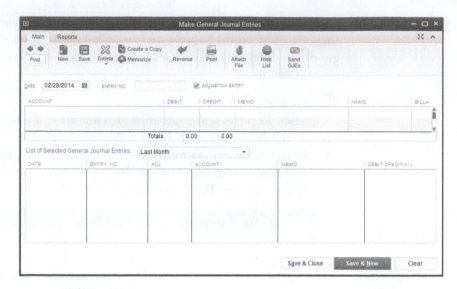

The Make General Journal Entries window contains the following fields:

ADJUSTING ENTRY	A check mark in this box identifies the journal entry as an adjusting journal entry. Adjusting journal entries appear on the Adjusted Trial Balance (worksheet) report and the Adjusting Journal Entries report. In the Journal report, any adjusting entries will be noted with a check mark.
ACCOUNT	Indicates the general ledger account to be adjusted.
DEBIT	Indicates the amount to debit to the account.
CREDIT	Indicates the amount to credit to the account.
MEMO	This field is optional. Any memo entry recorded here will appear in reports.
List of Selected General Journal Entries:	Displays a list of journal entries recorded in the Make General Journal Entries window. If the journal entry was checked off as an adjusting entry it will have a check mark in this list.
Hide List Icon	Click this button to hide the List of Selected General Journal Entries. When you hide the List of Selected General Journal Entries, the button changes to Show List.

As you recall from chapter 1, the third level of operation in QuickBooks is Activities. Activities identified as adjustments to account balances are entered in the Make General Journal Entries window. There are no default accounts in this window, because each adjusting journal entry will be different. The account to debit and the account to credit must be indicated. Adjusting journal entries are usually dated the last day of the month.

The first adjusting journal entry Kristin Raina makes on February 28, 2014, is to record (debit) Advertising Expense and reduce (credit) the Prepaid Advertising account for 1 month of service. The prepaid advertising was originally purchased on February 1 for $600 and represents a 6-month prepayment. One month of Advertising Expense is $100 ($600/6 months).

To record an adjusting journal entry—

1. Click Company and then click *Make General Journal Entries*. The Make General Journal Entries window appears.

   A message *Assigning Numbers to Journal Entries* may appear. As you know, QuickBooks automatically assigns a transaction number (Trans. #) to each transaction recorded in each of the windows. You cannot change the transaction number. If a transaction is deleted, that transaction number is also deleted; the next transaction would then be assigned the next transaction number in sequence. QuickBooks allows the user to assign journal entry numbers to each transaction. In this book, journal entry numbers are used for the adjusting journal entries. Once you start a sequence of numbers in the Make General Journal Entries window, QuickBooks will automatically assign the next adjusting journal entry number in sequence; however, you can edit or delete the automatically assigned journal entry number. If you receive the message box, place a check mark in the box to the left of *Do not display this message in the future*, and click OK.

2. Choose *02/28/2014* in the *DATE* field.
3. In the *ENTRY NO.* field, key **AJE1**.
4. Place a check mark in the box to the left of ADJUSTING ENTRY by clicking on the box, if necessary.

5. In the first line of the *ACCOUNT* field, click the drop-down arrow and then click *6050 Advertising Expense*.
6. In the *DEBIT* field, key **100**.
7. Move to the second line in the *ACCOUNT* field, click the drop-down arrow, and click *1410 Prepaid Advertising*.
8. In the *CREDIT* field, *100* should appear; if it does not, key **100**.
9. In the *MEMO* field, key **To record one month advertising expense**. The *MEMO* field is optional; you do not have to enter an explanation. (See figure 4–O.)

FIGURE 4–O
Make General Journal Entries Window—Completed

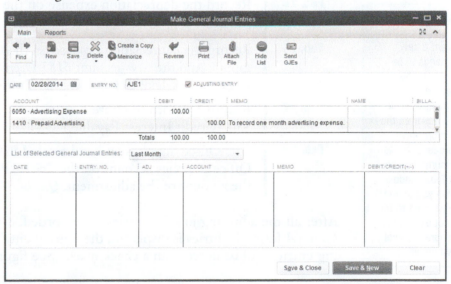

10. If the entry is correct, click Save & Close.

As in the other windows, the Find arrows can be used to view previous and subsequent journal entries. Choosing one of the arrows saves the entry. The Save & New button can be used when entering more than one journal entry.

Accounting concept

For this adjusting journal entry, the general ledger posting is as follows:

6050 Advertising Exp		1410 Prepaid Advertising	
Dr	Cr	Dr	Cr
100		Bill 600	100 Adj
		Bal 500	

In all journal entries the total dollar value of debits must equal the total dollar value of credits. In the Make General Journal Entries window, if you attempt to save an entry that is not in balance, a warning window appears that gives you the opportunity to correct the journal entry. If the journal entry is not corrected, you will not be able to save it.

Practice Exercise

Record the following adjusting journal entries in the Make General Journal Entries window:

Feb. 28	Record 1 month of insurance expense. The insurance was purchased for $2,400 in February and recorded as Prepaid Insurance. It is a 1-year policy effective February 1. *QuickCheck:* 200
Feb. 28	Record the depreciation expense on the Furniture of $100 per month.
Feb. 28	Record the depreciation expense on the Computer of $60 per month. Add the new account *6185 Deprec. Exp., Computers* while in the Make General Journal Entries window.
Feb. 28	Record 1 month of interest expense on the note payable of $50. (Credit Interest Payable.)
Feb. 28	The Office Supplies on hand totaled $200. Refer to the Office Supplies account on the Trial Balance to determine the amount of the adjustment. *QuickCheck:* 200

After all the adjusting journal entries are recorded, if the List of Selected General Journal Entries is displayed, the journal entries identified as adjusting entries will be noted with a check mark. (See figure 4-P.)

HINT

If the Tracking Fixed Assets on Journal Entries message appears, place a check mark in the box to the left of *Do not display this message in the future,* and click OK.

HINT

In the event a new account needs to be added while in the Make General Journal Entries window, click *< Add New >* from the account drop-down list. This opens the Add New Account: Choose Account Type window and allows you to add the new account to the list without exiting the Make General Journal Entries window.

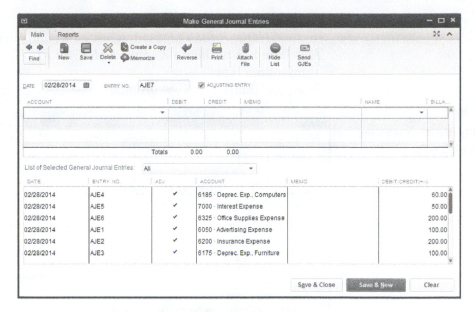

Period-End Accounting Reports and Financial Statements

REPORTS:

Reports, the fourth level of operation in QuickBooks, reflect the Activities and adjustments recorded in the windows as well as the information compiled in the Lists/Centers. When you complete the adjusting journal entries, you should display and print the period-end accounting reports and the financial statements.

Accounting Reports

The period-end accounting reports consist of the *Journal*, the *General Ledger*, and the *Adjusted Trial Balance* reports. These reports should be printed at the end of each month.

Journal Report

In the previous chapters, the *Journal* report was printed for the entire month. However, it is not necessary to reprint all the journal entries when you wish to view only the adjusting journal entries. All reports can be customized to modify the appearance of the report or the fields of information to be displayed. In this case, we will customize the report using the Filter feature, which will display only the adjusting journal entries in the *Journal* report.

To view and print only the adjusting journal entries in the *Journal* report—
1. Click Reports and then click *Accountant & Taxes*.
2. At the Accountant & Taxes submenu, click *Journal*.
   Note: *Do not choose the Adjusting Journal Entries report at this time.*
3. At the *From* and *To* fields, choose *02/01/2014* and *02/28/2014* and then click the Refresh button on the top of the report. The Journal report is displayed.

   All transactions for February, from all windows, are displayed. Scroll to the bottom of the entries. Notice the account type General Journal. These are the adjusting journal entries entered in the Make General Journal Entries window.

4. Click the Customize Report button on the top of the report. The Modify Report: Journal dialog box appears.

5. Click the Filters tab.
6. In the *CHOOSE FILTER* field, scroll down and click *Transaction Type*. The box to the right of the *CHOOSE FILTER* field changes to Transaction Type.
7. From the Transaction Type drop-down list, click *Journal*. (See figure 4–Q.)

FIGURE 4–Q
Modify Report: Journal—
Filters Tab—Completed

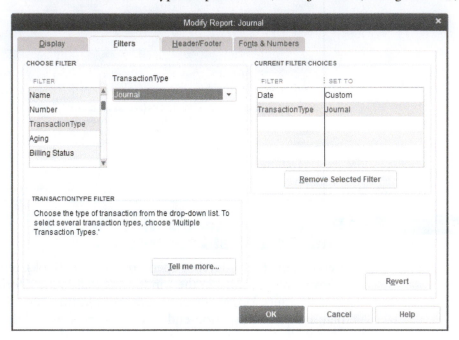

8. Click OK. Only the journal entries recorded in the Make General Journal Entries window are displayed. (See figure 4–R.)

FIGURE 4–R
Journal Report—
Adjusting Journal Entries

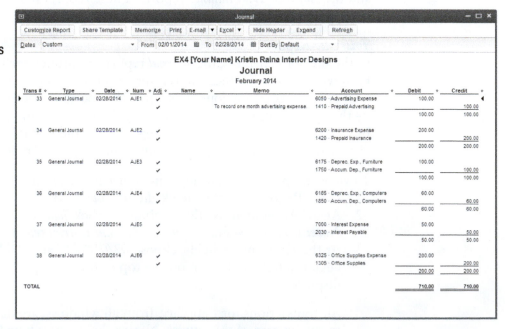

9. To print the report, click the Print button on the top of the report.
10. At the Print Reports dialog box, check the settings and then click Print.
11. Close the report.

Because it is usually the accountant that views the adjusting journal entries, instead of displaying the Journal report and filtering the adjusting journal entries, QuickBooks Premier Accountant Edition provides an Adjusting Journal Entries report.

To view and print the Adjusting Journal Entries report in QuickBooks Premier Accountant Edition—

1. Click Reports and then click *Accountant & Taxes*.
2. At the Accountant & Taxes submenu, click *Adjusting Journal Entries*.
3. At the *From* and *To* fields, choose *02/01/2014* and *02/28/2014* and then click the Refresh button on the top of the report. The Adjusting Journal Entries report is displayed.

This report displays the adjusting journal entries recorded in the Make General Journal Entries window that were checked off as an Adjusting Entry. The adjusting journal entries are the same entries displayed in the Journal report in figure 4-R. Notice, however, in this report that the title of the report is Adjusting Journal Entries and the columns labeled Trans#, Type, and Adj are not displayed.

4. To print the report, click the Print button on the top of the report.
5. At the Print Reports dialog box, check the settings and then click Print.
6. Close the report.

General Ledger Report

All transactions recorded in any of the windows are posted to the general ledger. The *General Ledger* report displays all activity in each account and lists the balance after each activity.

To view and print the *General Ledger* report—

1. Click Reports and then click *Accountant & Taxes*.
2. At the Accountant & Taxes submenu, click *General Ledger*.
3. At the *From* and *To* fields, choose *01/01/2014* and *02/28/2014* and then click the Refresh button on the top of the report. The general ledger is displayed. (See figure 4–S.)

FIGURE 4–S
General Ledger Report—
Partial

4. To print the report, click the Print button on the top of the report.
5. At the Print Reports dialog box, check the settings and then click Print.
6. Close the report.

Adjusted Trial Balance Report

The trial balance of February 28, 2014 (figure 4–M), was reviewed before preparing the adjusting journal entries. Typically, the trial balance is printed again after the adjusting journal entries have been recorded. The second trial balance is referred to as the *Adjusted Trial Balance* report. To distinguish between the two printed trial balances, you will modify the report by changing the name in the heading of the second trial balance to *Adjusted Trial Balance*.

HINT

Once you record the adjusting journal entries, you can no longer create a pre-adjusted trial balance.

To view and print the *Adjusted Trial Balance* report—
1. Click Reports and then click *Accountant & Taxes.*
2. At the Accountant & Taxes submenu, click *Trial Balance.*
   Note: *Do not choose the Adjusted Trial Balance report at this time.*
3. At the *From* and *To* fields, choose *01/01/2014* and *02/28/2014*, and click the Refresh button on the top of the report. The trial balance is displayed. Notice that the heading includes the default heading Trial Balance. You will use the Customize Report button to change the heading to Adjusted Trial Balance.
4. Click the Customize Report button on the top of the report. The Modify Report:Trial Balance dialog box appears.
5. Click the Header/Footer tab.
6. In the *Report Title* field, key the word **Adjusted** before *Trial Balance*. (See figure 4–T.)

FIGURE 4–T

Modify Report: Trial Balance—Header/Footer Tab Completed

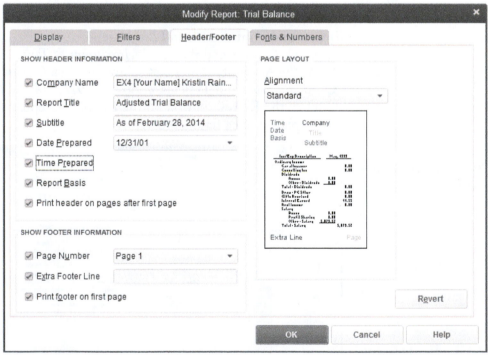

7. If the information is correct, click OK. The trial balance heading is now displayed as *Adjusted Trial Balance*. (See figure 4–U.)

FIGURE 4–U

Trial Balance Report—
Renamed Adjusted
Trial Balance

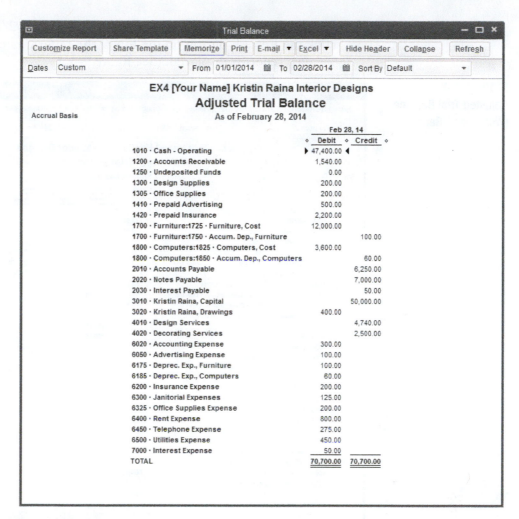

8. To print the report, click the Print button on the top of the report.
9. At the Print Reports dialog box, check the settings and then click Print.
10. Close the report.

Compare the effect of the adjusting journal entries on the account balances by comparing the Trial Balance (figure 4–M) to the Adjusted Trial Balance (figure 4–U). *Note: The earlier amount showed $70,490, while the Adjusted Trial Balance now shows $70,700.*

Once again, because the text is using the Accountant edition of the QuickBooks software, instead of displaying the Trial Balance report and modifying the report to display the name Adjusted Trial Balance, QuickBooks Premier Accountant Edition provides for an Adjusted Trial Balance (worksheet) report. Not only does this report have the name Adjusted Trial Balance, it also displays the original trial balance, the adjusting journal entries, and the adjusted trial balance. It is similar to a worksheet an accountant might prepare.

To view, make a correction, and print the Adjusted Trial Balance (worksheet) report in QuickBooks Premier Accountant Edition—
1. Click Reports and then click *Accountant & Taxes*.
2. At the Accountant & Taxes submenu, click *Adjusted Trial Balance*.

3. At the *From* and *To* fields, choose *01/01/2014* and *02/28/2014* and then click the Refresh button on the top of the report. The Adjusted Trial Balance report is displayed. (See figure 4–V.)

FIGURE 4–V
Adjusted Trial Balance
(Worksheet) Report

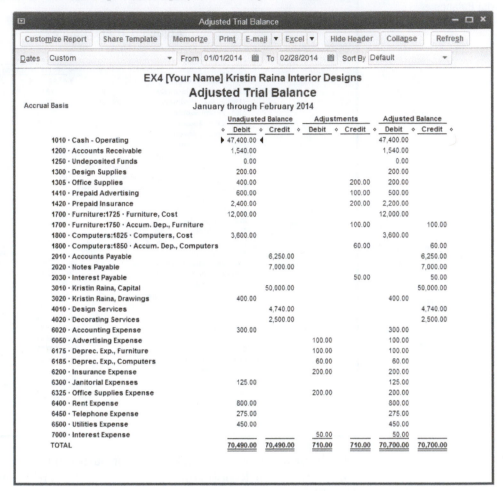

Look at the first two columns labeled Unadjusted Balance. This is the original trial balance of February 28, 2014. Compare this to figure 4–M. Next, look at the third and fourth columns, which are labeled Adjustments. These are the adjusting journal entries displayed in the Journal report in figure 4–R. Finally, look at the fifth and sixth column of this report. This is the adjusted trial balance that was displayed in figure 4–U.

Recall that on most reports in QuickBooks, you can drill down to the original window where an activity was recorded and make any necessary changes. This can also be done in this report. Assume you realize the Office Supplies on hand was $250, not $200 as noted in the Practice Exercise on page 4–16. The last adjusting journal entry originally recorded as $200 needs to be changed to $150 ($400 Office Supplies - $250 supplies on hand = $150 Supplies Expense).

4. In the Adjustments - Debit column, on the line that displays 6325 Office Supplies Expense, double-click the 200. You are drilled down to the Transactions by Account Report.

5. In the Transactions by Account report, on the line that displays AJE6, double-click the 200. You are drilled down to the Make General Journal Entries window where the adjusting journal entry for Supplies Expense was originally recorded.

6. Change the amount to 150 in both the debit column and the credit column. (See figure 4–W.)

FIGURE 4–W
Make General Journal Entries Window— Correction Completed

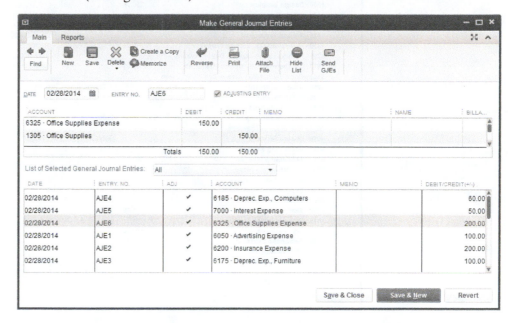

The List of Selected General Journal Entries still displays 200 for AJE6. This List will be updated after the change to the adjusting journal entry is saved.

7. If the information is correct, click Save & Close. At the Recording Transaction message, click Yes.

8. You are returned to the Transactions by Account report with the adjusting journal entry updated for the correction. Close the Transactions by Account report.

9. You are returned to the Adjusted Trial Balance (worksheet) report. Click the Refresh button. The report is updated. (See figure 4–X.)

HINT

Be sure to click the Refresh button in the Adjusted Trial Balance (worksheet) report to update the balances to reflect any changes or corrections.

FIGURE 4–X

Adjusted Trial Balance (Worksheet) Report—Correction Completed

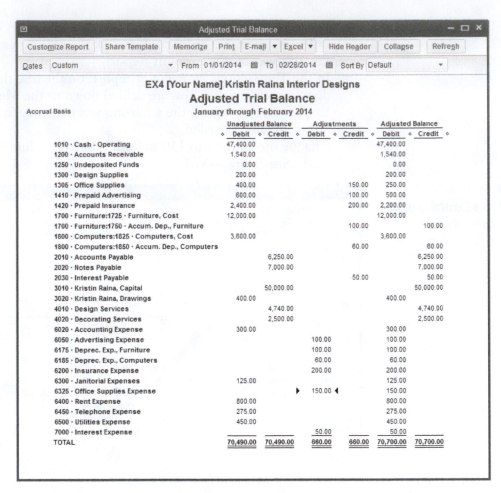

	Unadjusted Balance		Adjustments		Adjusted Balance	
	Debit	Credit	Debit	Credit	Debit	Credit
1010 · Cash - Operating	47,400.00				47,400.00	
1200 · Accounts Receivable	1,540.00				1,540.00	
1250 · Undeposited Funds	0.00				0.00	
1300 · Design Supplies	200.00				200.00	
1305 · Office Supplies	400.00			150.00	250.00	
1410 · Prepaid Advertising	600.00			100.00	500.00	
1420 · Prepaid Insurance	2,400.00			200.00	2,200.00	
1700 · Furniture:1725 · Furniture, Cost	12,000.00				12,000.00	
1700 · Furniture:1750 · Accum. Dep., Furniture				100.00		100.00
1800 · Computers:1825 · Computers, Cost	3,600.00				3,600.00	
1800 · Computers:1850 · Accum. Dep., Computers				60.00		60.00
2010 · Accounts Payable		6,250.00				6,250.00
2020 · Notes Payable		7,000.00				7,000.00
2030 · Interest Payable				50.00		50.00
3010 · Kristin Raina, Capital		50,000.00				50,000.00
3020 · Kristin Raina, Drawings	400.00				400.00	
4010 · Design Services		4,740.00				4,740.00
4020 · Decorating Services		2,500.00				2,500.00
6020 · Accounting Expense	300.00				300.00	
6050 · Advertising Expense			100.00		100.00	
6175 · Deprec. Exp., Furniture			100.00		100.00	
6185 · Deprec. Exp., Computers			60.00		60.00	
6200 · Insurance Expense			200.00		200.00	
6300 · Janitorial Expenses	125.00				125.00	
6325 · Office Supplies Expense			150.00		150.00	
6400 · Rent Expense	800.00				800.00	
6450 · Telephone Expense	275.00				275.00	
6500 · Utilities Expense	450.00				450.00	
7000 · Interest Expense			50.00		50.00	
TOTAL	70,490.00	70,490.00	660.00	660.00	70,700.00	70,700.00

10. To print the report, click the Print button on the top of the report.
11. At the Print Reports dialog box, check the settings and then click Print.
12. Close the report.

Financial Statements

The financial statements include the income statement and the balance sheet. Companies must prepare financial statements at least once a year, but they can be prepared more frequently, such as quarterly or even monthly.

Profit & Loss Standard Report (Income Statement)

The income statement is known as the *Profit & Loss* report in QuickBooks. The *Profit & Loss* report displays revenue and expenses for a specified period of time. The *Profit & Loss* report can be displayed in a standard or comparative format. In addition, a detailed *Profit & Loss* report can also be produced that lists all transactions affecting a particular item on the report.

To view and print a year-to-date *Profit & Loss Standard* report—
1. Click Reports and then click *Company & Financial*.
2. At the Company & Financial submenu, click *Profit & Loss Standard*.
3. At the *From* and *To* fields, choose *01/01/2014* and *02/28/2014* and then click the Refresh button on the top of the report. The report for the period will be displayed. (See figure 4–Y.)

FIGURE 4–Y
Profit & Loss Standard Report

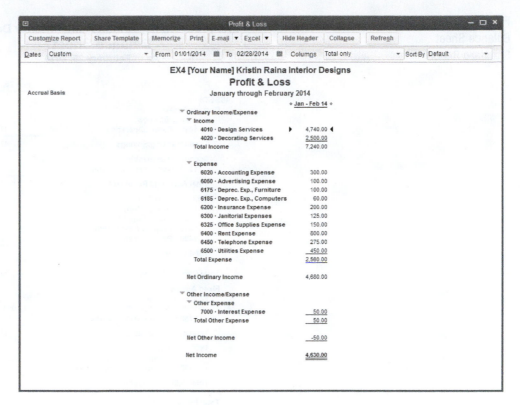

EX4 [Your Name] Kristin Raina Interior Designs
Profit & Loss
January through February 2014

Accrual Basis

	Jan - Feb 14
Ordinary Income/Expense	
Income	
4010 · Design Services	4,740.00
4020 · Decorating Services	2,500.00
Total Income	7,240.00
Expense	
6020 · Accounting Expense	300.00
6050 · Advertising Expense	100.00
6175 · Deprec. Exp., Furniture	100.00
6185 · Deprec. Exp., Computers	60.00
6200 · Insurance Expense	200.00
6300 · Janitorial Expenses	125.00
6325 · Office Supplies Expense	150.00
6400 · Rent Expense	800.00
6450 · Telephone Expense	275.00
6500 · Utilities Expense	450.00
Total Expense	2,560.00
Net Ordinary Income	4,680.00
Other Income/Expense	
Other Expense	
7000 · Interest Expense	50.00
Total Other Expense	50.00
Net Other Income	-50.00
Net Income	4,630.00

4. To print the report, click the Print button on the top of the report.
5. At the Print Reports dialog box, check the settings and then click Print.
6. Close the report.

Balance Sheet Standard Report

In QuickBooks, the *Balance Sheet* report, which shows the assets, liabilities, and equity balances as of a certain date, may be displayed in a standard, summary, or comparative format. In addition, a detailed report, showing all transactions affecting balance sheet accounts, can be produced.

To display and print a *Balance Sheet Standard* report—
1. Click Reports and then click *Company & Financial*.
2. At the Company & Financial submenu, click *Balance Sheet Standard*.
3. In the *As of* field, choose *02/28/2014* and then click the Refresh button on the top of the report. The balance sheet in standard format is displayed.
4. To print the report, click the Print button on the top of the report.
5. At the Print Reports dialog box, check the settings and then click Print. (See figure 4–Z.)

FIGURE 4–Z
Balance Sheet
Standard Report

EX4 [Your Name] Kristin Raina Interior Designs
Balance Sheet
As of February 28, 2014

Accrual Basis

	Feb 28, 14
ASSETS	
Current Assets	
Checking/Savings	
1010 · Cash □Operating	47,400.00
Total Checking/Savings	47,400.00
Accounts Receivable	
1200 · Accounts Receivable	1,540.00
Total Accounts Receivable	1,540.00
Other Current Assets	
1300 · Design Supplies	200.00
1305 · Office Supplies	250.00
1410 · Prepaid Advertising	500.00
1420 · Prepaid Insurance	2,200.00
Total Other Current Assets	3,150.00
Total Current Assets	52,090.00
Fixed Assets	
1700 · Furniture	
1725 · Furniture, Cost	12,000.00
1750 · Accum. Dep., Furniture	-100.00
Total 1700 · Furniture	11,900.00
1800 · Computers	
1825 · Computers, Cost	3,600.00
1850 · Accum. Dep., Computers	-60.00
Total 1800 · Computers	3,540.00
Total Fixed Assets	15,440.00
TOTAL ASSETS	**67,530.00**
LIABILITIES & EQUITY	
Liabilities	
Current Liabilities	
Accounts Payable	
2010 · Accounts Payable	6,250.00
Total Accounts Payable	6,250.00
Other Current Liabilities	
2020 · Notes Payable	7,000.00
2030 · Interest Payable	50.00
Total Other Current Liabilities	7,050.00
Total Current Liabilities	13,300.00
Total Liabilities	13,300.00
Equity	
3010 · Kristin Raina, Capital	50,000.00
3020 · Kristin Raina, Drawings	-400.00
Net Income	4,630.00
Total Equity	54,230.00
TOTAL LIABILITIES & EQUITY	**67,530.00**

Look at the Fixed Assets section of the Balance Sheet Report. Recall that in the Chart of Accounts List, parent and subaccounts were used for the fixed assets. When parent and subaccounts flow into the financial statements, the parent account name becomes a 'heading' and a 'total' for the related subaccounts. Under the parent account name heading, the subaccounts names are indented on the financial statements. The account balances for the subaccounts are displayed and subtotaled, and then shown as the total for the parent account. For example, the parent account 1700 Furniture is a heading; the subaccounts 1725 Furniture, Cost and 1750 Accum. Dep., Furniture are indented and displayed under the parent account; and then the parent account 1700 Furniture is again displayed this time as the total for the subaccounts. On the printout of the report, the balances of the subaccounts (12,000 and -100) are displayed to the left of the dollar-value column and the subtotal of these subaccounts (11,900) is displayed in the dollar-value column and labeled as the total for the parent account.

6. Close the report.

Registers

Because QuickBooks is designed for the non-accountant, it includes an alternative method for reviewing daily activity by using *registers*. Registers are available for any balance sheet account—that is, any asset, liability, or equity account. They are not available for income and expense accounts.

The register format is similar to that of a personal checkbook, but the information displayed in the registers is similar to the information displayed in the general ledger.

To view a register—
1. Click Lists and then click *Chart of Accounts.*
2. In the Chart of Accounts List window, double-click the *1010 Cash - Operating* account. The 1010 Cash - Operating register appears. (See figure 4–AA.)

FIGURE 4–AA
Cash - Operating Register

HINT

An alternate method of displaying the register is to select *1010 Cash - Operating* in the Chart of Accounts List window, click the Activities menu button, and click Use Register.

Transactions that were entered in any of the other windows that affected the 1010 Cash - Operating account are also displayed here. Scroll through the transactions and compare them with the 1010 Cash - Operating account in the general ledger (figure 4–S). You can use the register to correct any activity already recorded by drilling down to the source of the activity.

To drill down using the register—

1. At the 1010 Cash - Operating register, choose the *February 23, Cuza and Carl Associates* transaction by double-clicking. The Bill Payments (Check) window appears. (See figure 4–BB.)

FIGURE 4–BB
Bill Payments (Check)
Window

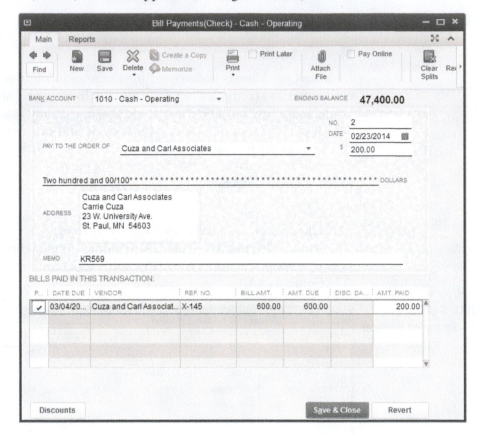

HINT

An alternative method of drilling down from the register to the activity window is to select the transaction in the register and click Edit Transaction in the register.

This transaction was originally recorded in the Pay Bills window. Recall that after a transaction is saved in the Pay Bills window, it cannot subsequently be edited in that window. However, the Write Checks window will show all payments, both those entered through the Pay Bills window and those entered in the Write Checks window. So even though this transaction was initially recorded in the Pay Bills window, you can drill down to the Bill Payments (Check) window and correct any errors if necessary.

2. Close all the windows.

Registers are available only for balance sheet accounts. For income statement accounts—that is, income and expenses—a register is not available; but an *Account QuickReport* is available that displays all the activity to the account, again similar to the general ledger information.

To view an income *Account QuickReport*—

1. Click Lists and then click *Chart of Accounts*.
2. At the Chart of Accounts window, double-click *4020 Decorating Services*.
3. At the *From* and *To* fields, choose *02/01/2014* and *02/28/2014* and then click the Refresh button on the top of the report. The *Account QuickReport* is displayed, listing all of the activity to this account during the time period chosen. (See figure 4–CC.)

FIGURE 4–CC
Account QuickReport

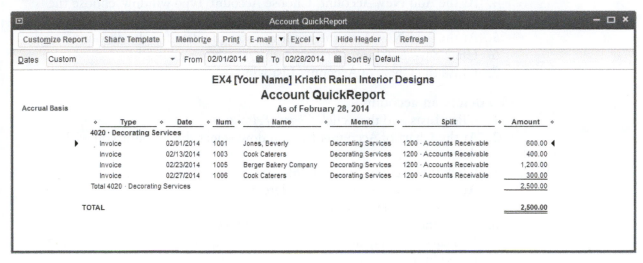

From this report, as with others, you can drill down to the window where the original activity was recorded.

4. Close the report.
5. Close the Chart of Accounts window.

Chapter Review and Assessment

Procedure Review

To add an account—

1. Click Lists and then click *Chart of Accounts*.
2. At the Chart of Accounts List window, click the Account menu button.
3. At the Account menu, click New.
4. At the Add New Account: Choose Account Type window, choose the account type and then click Continue.
5. At the Add New Account window, enter the data for the account.
6. Click Save & Close.
7. Close the Chart of Accounts List window.

To delete an account—

1. Click Lists and then click *Chart of Accounts*.
2. At the Chart of Accounts List window, select the account you wish to delete.
3. Click the Account menu button.
4. At the Account menu, click Delete Account.
5. Click OK at the warning.
6. Close the Chart of Accounts List window.
    You cannot delete an account that has a balance or has been used in a transaction.

To edit an account—

1. Click Lists and then click *Chart of Accounts*.
2. At the Chart of Accounts List window, select the account you wish to edit.
3. Click the Account menu button.
4. At the Account menu, click Edit Account.
5. Change the appropriate information.
6. Click Save & Close.
7. Close the Chart of Accounts List window.

To record an adjusting journal entry—

1. Click Company and then click *Make General Journal Entries*.
2. Enter the date in the *DATE* field.
3. In the *ENTRY NO.* field, key in the original journal entry number, if necessary; thereafter, QuickBooks will assign the entry numbers in sequence.
4. Place a check mark in the box to the left of ADJUSTING ENTRY.
5. In the first line of the *ACCOUNT* field, click once to access the drop-down list of accounts, then choose the account to debit.
6. Enter the amount to debit in the *DEBIT* field.
7. Move to the second line in the *ACCOUNT* field, and from the drop-down list of accounts, choose the account to credit.
8. Enter the amount to credit in the *CREDIT* field, if necessary.
9. In the *MEMO* field, key in a brief explanation (optional).
10. Click Save & Close.

To view and print accounting reports from the Reports menu—
1. Click Reports and then click *Accountant & Taxes*.
2. At the Accountant & Taxes submenu, choose a report.
3. Indicate the appropriate dates for the report and then click the Refresh button on the top of the report.
4. Click the Print button on the top of the report.
5. At the Print Reports dialog box, review the settings and then click Print.
6. Close the report.

To view and print financial statements from the Reports menu—
1. Click Reports and then click *Company & Financial*.
2. At the Company & Financial submenu, choose a financial statement.
3. Indicate the appropriate dates for the statement and then click the Refresh button on the top of the report.
4. Click the Print button on the top of the report.
5. At the Print Reports dialog box, review the settings and then click Print.
6. Close the statement.

To filter the information displayed in a report or financial statement—
1. Open a report or financial statement, enter the correct dates, and click the Refresh button. Then click the Customize Report button on the top of the report.
2. At the Modify Report dialog box, click the Filters tab.
3. In the CHOOSE FILTER field, select the category of information you wish to filter, for example, transaction type.
4. The field to the right changes to the filter chosen. Choose the specific information you wish to filter, for example, in transaction type you might choose the Journal.
5. Click OK. The report now displays the information chosen on the Filters tab.

To change the heading in a report or financial statement—
1. Open a report or financial statement, enter the correct dates, and click the Refresh button. Then click the Customize Report button on the top of the report.
2. At the Modify Report dialog box, click the Header/Footer tab.
3. In the Report Title field change the name of the report to the desired title.
4. Click OK. The report now displays the new title of the report.

To view and print a register or *Account QuickReport* from the Lists menu—
1. Click Lists and then click *Chart of Accounts*.
2. Double-click the account for which you want the register or *Account QuickReport*. (Registers are used for assets, liabilities, and equity accounts; Account QuickReports are used for revenues and expenses accounts.)
3. For the *Account QuickReport*, indicate the dates and then click the Refresh button.
4. Click the Print button on the top of the report.
5. At the Print Reports dialog box, review the settings and then click Print.
6. Close the register.

Key Concepts

Select the letter of the item that best matches each definition.

a. Make General Journal Entries window   f. Registers
b. Filters   g. Header/Footer
c. *Profit & Loss* report   h. *Trial Balance* report
d. *General Ledger* report   i. Adjusting Journal Entries
e. Chart of Accounts   j. *Balance Sheet* report

_____ 1. Recorded periodically so financial statements can be prepared according to accounting rules.

_____ 2. The report that shows assets, liabilities, and equity balances at a specified date.

_____ 3. The list of accounts a company uses in business.

_____ 4. The tab in the Customize Report - Modify Report dialog box that is used to identify categories of information to be displayed in a report.

_____ 5. The report that lists the activity increases, decreases, and balances for each account.

_____ 6. Similar to a manual accounting system, this allows for the recording of a debit entry, a credit entry, and an explanation.

_____ 7. The report that displays the revenue and expenses for a specified period of time.

_____ 8. The tab in the Customize Report - Modify Report dialog box that is used to change the heading on a report.

_____ 9. The format is similar to that of a checkbook and can be used to view the activities for any balance sheet account.

_____ 10. A report that displays all accounts and their debit or credit balance.

Procedure Check

1. The manager has requested a list of all accounts the company uses. Which is the best report to print to provide this information, and how would you obtain it?

2. The manager wants to know the balance in each of the company's accounts. Which is the best report to print to provide this information, and how would you obtain it?

3. You have been asked to review the adjusting journal entries and have located an error. How would you correct the error in the adjusting journal entry?

4. Which report provides the information on the revenue and expenses of a company, and how would you obtain the report? If you wanted to change the title of this report to Income Statement, how would you do it?

5. Which report provides the information on the assets, liabilities, and equity of the company, and how would you obtain the report?

6. Explain the purpose of adjusting journal entries. Compare and contrast recording adjusting journal entries in a manual accounting system and QuickBooks, and explain why there are not any default accounts in the Make General Journal Entries window.

Case Problems

Case Problem 1

On April 1, 2014, Lynn Garcia began her business, called Lynn's Music Studio. All the daily activities for the month of April—including entering and paying bills, writing checks, recording of sales (both cash and on account), collection of receivables, and depositing receipts—have been recorded. It is the end of the first month of business; the adjusting journal entries need to be recorded, and financial statements need to be printed. You will record the adjusting journal entries for April 30 using the information provided below. The company file includes the beginning information for Lynn's Music Studio along with the transactions recorded in chapters 2 and 3.

1. Open the company file CH4 Lynn's Music Studio.QBW.
2. Make a backup copy of the company file LMS4 [*Your Name*] Lynn's Music Studio.
3. Restore the backup copy of the company file. In both the Open Backup Copy and Save Company File as windows, use the file name LMS4 [*Your Name*] Lynn's Music Studio.
4. Change the company name to **LMS4 [*Your Name*] Lynn's Music Studio**.
5. Add the following accounts to the Chart of Accounts List:

Type:	**Expense**
Number:	**6300**
Name:	**Music Supplies Expense**

Type:	**Expense**
Number:	**6325**
Name:	**Office Supplies Expense**

   Delete the following account:
   Advertising Expense

6. Display and print the *Trial Balance* report before preparing the adjusting journal entries (April 1, 2014–April 30, 2014).
7. Use the information below to prepare adjusting journal entries. Record each adjusting journal entry separately, and use April 30, 2014, for the date.
   a. The prepaid insurance represents a 1-year policy. Record insurance expense for 1 month. Refer to the trial balance to determine the amount in the Prepaid Insurance account. For Entry No., use AJE1.
   b. Monthly depreciation on the assets: $60 for the Music Instruments, $40 for the Furniture, and $35 for the Computers. Record each depreciation expense as a separate adjusting journal entry.
   c. The music supplies on hand total $430. Compare with the amount in the Music Supplies account to determine how much of the music supplies has been used, then record the music supplies expense.
   d. The office supplies on hand total $300. Compare with the amount in the Office Supplies account to determine how much of the office supplies has been used, then record the office supplies expense.

e. The interest on the note payable for 1 month is $51. Record the interest expense. Add to the Chart of Accounts List, the Interest Payable account, Other Current Liability, number 2030.

8. Display and print the following reports for April 30, 2014:
   a. *Adjusted Trial Balance* (worksheet): Change Interest Expense to $15 (April 1, 2014–April 30, 2014)
   b. *Journal:* Only the adjusting journal entries (April 30, 2014–April 30, 2014)
   c. *Trial Balance:* Change name in header of the report to Adjusted Trial Balance (April 1, 2014–April 30, 2014)
   d. *Profit & Loss Standard* (April 1, 2014–April 30, 2014)
   e. *Balance Sheet Standard* (April 30, 2014)

Case Problem 2

On June 1, 2014, Olivia Chen began her business, which she named Olivia's Web Solutions. All daily activities for the month of June, including entering and paying bills, writing checks, recording of sales (both cash and on account), collection of receivables, and depositing receipts have been recorded. It is the end of the first month of business; the adjusting journal entries need to be recorded, and financial statements need to be printed. You will record the adjusting journal entries for June 30 using the information provided below. The company file includes the beginning information for Olivia's Web Solutions along with the transactions recorded in chapters 2 and 3.

1. Open the company file CH4 Olivia's Web Solutions.QBW.
2. Make a backup copy of the company file OWS4 [*Your Name*] Olivia's Web Solutions.
3. Restore the backup copy of the company file. In both the Open Backup Copy and Save Company File as windows, use the file name OWS4 [*Your Name*] Olivia's Web Solutions.
4. Change the company name to **OWS4 [*Your Name*] Olivia's Web Solutions**.

5. Add the following accounts to the Chart of Accounts List:

Type:	**Expense**
Number:	**6300**
Name:	**Computer Supplies Expense**

Type:	**Expense**
Number:	**6325**
Name:	**Office Supplies Expense**

Delete the following account:
   Repair Expense

6. Display and print the *Trial Balance* report before preparing the adjusting journal entries (June 1, 2014–June 30, 2014).

7. Use the information below to prepare adjusting journal entries. Record each adjusting journal entry separately, and use June 30, 2014, for the date.
   a. The prepaid insurance represents a 1-year policy. Record insurance expense for 1 month. Refer to the trial balance to determine the amount in the Prepaid Insurance account. For Entry No., use AJE1.
   b. The prepaid advertising represents a 6-month contract. Record the advertising expense for 1 month.
   c. Monthly depreciation on the assets: $75 for the Computer, $50 for the Furniture, and $100 for the Software. Record each depreciation expense as a separate adjusting journal entry.
   d. The computer supplies on hand total $350. Compare with the amount in the Computer Supplies account to determine how much of the computer supplies has been used, then record the computer supplies expense.
   e. The office supplies on hand total $325. Compare with the amount in the Office Supplies account to determine how much of the office supplies has been used, then record the office supplies expense.
   f. The interest on the note payable for 1 month is $52. Record the interest expense. Add to the Chart of Accounts List, the Interest Payable account, Other Current Liability, number 2030.

8. Display and print the following reports for June 30, 2014:
   a. *Adjusted Trial Balance* (worksheet): Change Interest Expense to $25 (June 1, 2014–June 30, 2014)
   b. *Journal:* Only the adjusting journal entries: (June 30, 2014–June 30, 2014)
   c. *Trial Balance:* Change name in header of the report to Adjusted Trial Balance (June 1, 2014–June 30, 2014)
   d. *Profit & Loss Standard* (June 1, 2014–June 30, 2014)
   e. *Balance Sheet Standard* (June 30, 2014)

CHAPTER 5

Inventory

Receive Items, Sell Items, Process Sales Discounts, Adjust Quantity/Value on Hand, and Pay Sales Tax

Chapter Objectives

- Identify the two inventory systems

- Update the Item List

- Record purchases of inventory items in the Enter Bills and Write Checks windows

- Identify transactions requiring sales tax

- Process sales discounts

- Record adjustments to inventory items in the Adjust Quantity/Value on Hand window

- Record payment of sales tax in the Pay Sales Tax window

- Display and print inventory-related reports

- Display and print accounting reports and financial statements

Introduction

inventory Merchandise that is sold to customers for a profit.

QuickBooks allows you to track inventory transactions. **Inventory** is ready-made merchandise that is sold to customers for a profit. Before you can enter inventory transactions, you must establish a file for each inventory item. Inventory item files are included in the *Item List* (Lists/Centers).

Once you establish an inventory item file, transactions for the item (Activities) can be entered in the Enter Bills, Write Checks, Create Invoices, Enter Sales Receipts, and *Adjust Quantity/Value on Hand* activity windows in much the same manner as was done in prior chapters. Every time the company receives merchandise for resale, sells merchandise, or adjusts the inventory because of loss or damage, QuickBooks will record that information in the Item List. This allows you to accurately determine inventory quantity, value, and profit on sales. In addition, QuickBooks will automatically change balance sheet and income statement accounts based on the inventory information on the Item List (Reports).

In this chapter, our sample company, Kristin Raina Interior Designs, begins to purchase and sell decorative accessories to clients in addition to providing design and decorating services. This means that Kristin Raina must now be concerned with keeping an inventory.

QuickBooks versus Manual Accounting: Inventory Transactions

As discussed in previous chapters, in a manual accounting system, purchases on account are recorded in a purchases journal while sales on account are recorded in a sales journal. This is true whether the purchase or sale is for services or for merchandise. Cash transactions are recorded in the cash receipts or cash payments journals, again for both inventory and non-inventory items.

In QuickBooks, the Item List serves as an inventory subsidiary ledger for the company. The list includes all items the company sells, both inventory and service items. Relevant information for each inventory item, such as name/number, type, description, cost, sales price, and related general ledger accounts, is entered at the time the item file is created and is updated as necessary.

When the company purchases an inventory item from a vendor on account, the transaction is recorded in the Enter Bills activity window in much the same manner as non-inventory purchases were recorded. When the inventory items are sold on account, the invoice will be recorded in the Create Invoices activity window in a manner similar to that done for other revenues. When you enter these transactions, QuickBooks updates the Chart of Accounts List (general ledger) and at the same time updates each vendor and customer file. In addition, it updates the Item List to reflect the purchase and sale of the inventory items. Cash purchases of inventory items are recorded in the Write Checks activity window, while cash sales of inventory are recorded in the Enter Sales Receipts activity window. Changes in inventory not due to a sale or purchase are recorded in the Adjust Quantity/Value on Hand window. In all instances where inventory items are purchased, sold, or adjusted, the Item List is updated to reflect the new inventory quantity and value.

Accounting for Inventory Transactions

periodic inventory system Values the inventory periodically based on a physical count of the merchandise; usually done once a year.

There are two types of inventory systems: periodic and perpetual. Under the **periodic inventory system**, separate records are *not* maintained for inventory items, and no attempt is made to adjust the inventory account for purchases and sales. Instead, inventory is counted periodically to determine inventory quantity, value, cost of goods sold, and gross profit. In the past, the periodic system was often used by businesses that sold high-volume, low-cost goods, for which keeping individual inventory records was not practical.

perpetual inventory system Values the inventory after every purchase and sale of inventory items.

Under the **perpetual inventory system**, accounting records are maintained that continuously show the current inventory quantity and value. When inventory is purchased, the inventory (asset) account is increased. When inventory is sold, the inventory account is reduced. In addition, the cost of goods sold is simultaneously computed to arrive at gross profit. Before the availability of low-cost computer hardware and software, only businesses with low-volume, high-cost goods used the perpetual system. Now, with computers pervasive in business, most companies are able to use a perpetual inventory system.

QuickBooks, like almost all general ledger accounting software programs, uses the perpetual system because it not only allows the user to know the current inventory quantity and value at any given moment but also calculates the cost of goods sold and gross profit after each sale without the need for a periodic physical inventory count.

Chapter Problem

In this chapter, you will track inventory transactions for Kristin Raina Interior Designs, which has decided to begin selling decorative inventory items in addition to providing decorating and design services. Information for inventory items has been entered in the Item List. This information along with the March 1, 2014, beginning balances is contained in the company file CH5 Kristin Raina Interior Designs.

Before you begin, open the company file CH5 Kristin Raina Interior Designs.QBW. Make a backup copy of the file, name it **EX5 [*Your Name*] Kristin Raina Interior Designs**, and then restore the file. Finally, change the company name in the file to **EX5 [*Your Name*] Kristin Raina Interior Designs**.

LISTS/CENTERS:

The Item List

Recall from chapter 1 that the second level of operation in QuickBooks is to record background information in Lists/Centers. The Item List contains a file for each type of service or inventory item sold by the company. If the item sold is an inventory product, QuickBooks calls this an *inventory part* as opposed to a service item. You should enter the information for each inventory item in the Item List before recording transactions. This will make the Activities function run more smoothly. However, if you inadvertently omit an item, you can add that item during the Activities level of operation with a minimum of disruption.

The Item List contains important information on each product, such as type of item; number; descriptions; cost; general ledger posting accounts for inventory asset, cost of goods sold, and sales; preferred vendor; and sales tax status. All products or services sold by the company should be included in the Item List. Periodically, these files will need to be updated as products are added, or discontinued, or background information changes.

Kristin Raina has entered information for various inventory items in the Item List.

To review the Item List—
1. Click Lists and then click *Item List*.
2. The *Item List* appears. (See figure 5–A.)

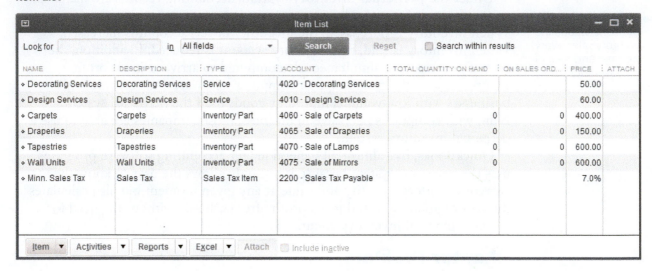

To view a specific inventory item file—
1. Place the mouse over the item name *Carpets* and double-click. The inventory item file will appear in Edit Item mode. (See figure 5–B.)

Note the following fields in this window:

TYPE	If this is an inventory item, select *Inventory Part*. Other selections include *Service* for service revenue items, *Non-inventory Part* for products sold that are not maintained in inventory, *Inventory Assembly*, *Other Charge*, and so on.
Item Name/Number	Used to assign an identifying name or number to each item.
Subitem of	Used if item is a component of another item, such as in a construction or manufacturing company.
Description on Purchase Transactions/ Description on Sales Transactions	Used to enter a description of the item for purchase or sales activity windows.
Cost	Used to enter the typical unit cost for the item. This amount will appear in the purchase activity windows (Enter Bills and Write Checks) as the default cost amount. Can override as needed.
COGS Account	Lists the default general ledger posting account for cost of goods sold when the item is sold. Can override this account as needed.
Sales Price	This is the default unit-selling price that will appear in sales activity windows (Create Invoices and Enter Sales Receipts). Can override this entry as needed.
Tax Code	Used to indicate if the item is taxable or non-taxable for sales tax purposes.
Income Account	This is the default general ledger posting account for revenue when the item is sold. Can override this account as needed.
Asset Account	This is the default general ledger posting account for the inventory balance sheet account when items are purchased. Can override this entry as needed.

2. Close the Edit Item window.
3. Close the Item List window.

The Item List is revised periodically when new inventory items are added, unused items are deleted, or modifications are made to inventory items. These adjustments to the inventory item files are referred to as updating the Item List.

Adding an Item

The company has decided to sell a line of modern lamps to its clients and needs to add this inventory item to the Item List.

To add an item—
1. Click Lists and then click *Item List*.
2. At the Item List window, click the Item menu button. The Item menu appears. (See figure 5–C.)

FIGURE 5–C
Item Menu

3. At the Item menu, click *New*. The New Item window appears. (See figure 5–D.)

FIGURE 5–D
New Item Window

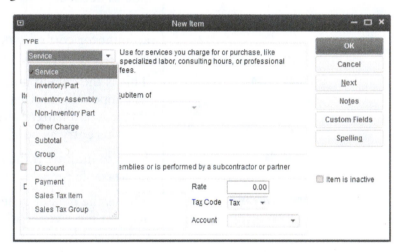

4. At the TYPE drop-down list, click *Inventory Part*.
5. Complete the balance of the window with the following information:

Item Name/Number:	**Lamps**
Description on Purchase/Sales Transactions:	**Lamps**
Cost:	**100**
COGS Account:	**5070 Cost of Lamps Sold**
Preferred Vendor:	**Lumiare Lighting Company**
Sales Price:	**200**
Tax Code:	**Tax – Taxable Sales**
Income Account:	**4070 Sale of Lamps**
Asset Account:	**1270 Inventory of Lamps**

Reorder Point:	**5**	
Date:	**March 1, 2014**	

Your screen should look like figure 5–E.

FIGURE 5–E
New Item Window—
Completed

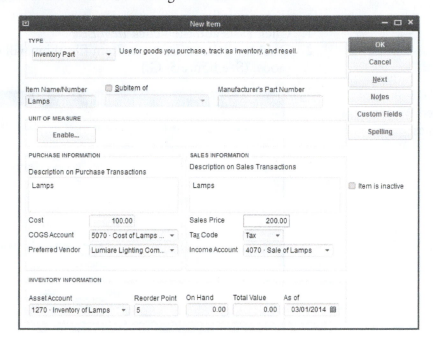

6. If the information is correct, click OK.
7. Close the Item List window.

Deleting an Item

Kristin Raina wishes to delete Tapestries from the Item List because the company has decided not to sell this product.

To delete an item—
1. Click Lists and then click *Item List*.
2. At the Item List, select *Tapestries* but do not open the file. (See figure 5–F.)

FIGURE 5–F
Item List—Tapestries
Selected

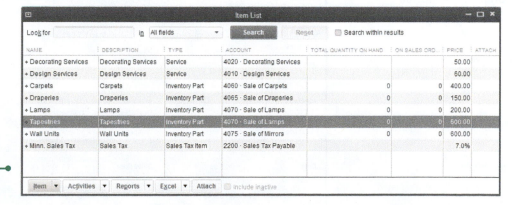

If you delete the wrong item, click Edit and then Undo Delete Item immediately after deleting the item. If you do not do this immediately, you will not be able to undo the deletion and you will have to enter the record again.

3. Click the Item menu button. At the Item menu, click *Delete Item*.
4. A warning screen will appear. Click OK. The Item file will be deleted.
5. Close the Item List window.

You cannot delete an item with a balance or an item that has been part of a transaction for the period.

Editing an Item

Kristin Raina needs to edit the file for Draperies because the unit cost has increased to $125 and the sales price to $250.

To edit an item file—
1. Click Lists and then click *Item List*.
2. Double-click the *Draperies* Item file. This will open the file in Edit mode. (See figure 5–G.)

FIGURE 5–G
Edit Item Window—
Draperies

3. At the *Cost* and *Sales Price* fields, delete the current information and then enter the new amounts shown in figure 5–H.

FIGURE 5–H
Edit Item Window—
Draperies—Updated

4. If the information is correct, click OK and then close the Item List window.

Practice Exercise

Add the following item:

Type:	**Inventory Part**
Item Name/Number:	**Mirrors**
Description on Purchase/Sales Transactions:	**Decorative Mirrors**
Cost:	**150**
COGS Account:	**5075 Cost of Mirrors Sold**
Preferred Vendor:	**Ace Glass Works**
Sales Price:	**300**
Tax Code:	**Tax – Taxable Sales**
Income Account:	**4075 Sale of Mirrors**
Asset Account:	**1275 Inventory of Mirrors**
Reorder Point:	**5**
Date:	**March 1, 2014**

Delete the following item:

  Wall Units

QuickCheck: The updated Item List appears in figure 5–I.

FIGURE 5–I
Updated Item List

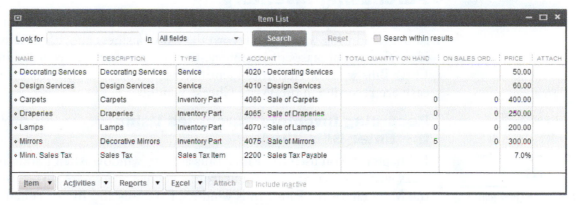

Inventory Center

Many of the procedures reviewed in this chapter, such as adding or editing an inventory item or recording a sale of inventory, can be accomplished through the Inventory Center. The Inventory Center can be found by clicking the Vendors menu, then clicking Inventory Activities (See Figure 5-J).

The Inventory Center window is similar to the Vendor Center and Customer Center windows. The Inventory Center window contains a file for each inventory item. Each file contains important information, such as inventory item name, description, cost, sales price, quantity on hand, and so on. The Inventory Center duplicates the information contained in the Item List. However, the Inventory Center maintains only files for Inventory Part items as seen on the Item List. The Inventory Center does not display non-inventory part items from the Item List.

FIGURE 5-J
Inventory Center

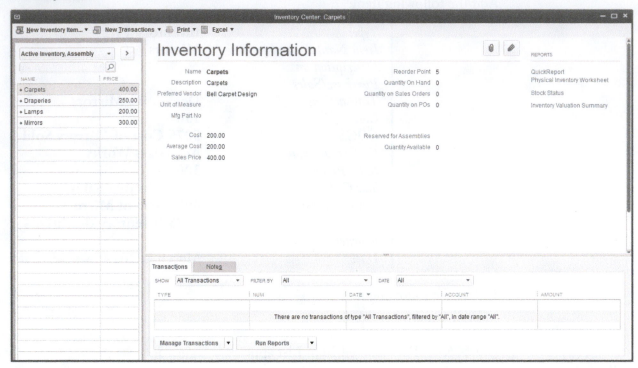

Purchasing Inventory

ACTIVITIES:

Recall from chapter 1 that the third level of operation in QuickBooks is Activities, during which you record the daily business activities. Activities identified as purchases of inventory items on account are recorded in the Enter Bills window. Activities identified as purchases of inventory items for cash are recorded in the Write Checks window.

Recording Inventory Purchases Using the Enter Bills Window

HINT

If you click Enter Bills instead of Receive Items and Enter Bill, simply click the Items tab in the Enter Bills window.

In chapter 2, you used the Enter Bills activity window when goods and services were purchased on account from a vendor. There are two sub-tabs on the Main tab of the Enter Bills window: Expenses and Items. When you choose Enter Bills from the Vendors pull-down menu, the Enter Bills window opens with the Expenses tab as the active tab. When a company wishes to use the inventory feature, the Vendors pull-down menu offers an additional choice of Receive Items and Enter Bill. When you click Receive Items and Enter Bill, the Enter Bills window is opened, but the Items tab is the active tab. In the Enter Bills window, the Items tab is similar to the Expenses tab but provides for additional fields that relate to inventory. In addition, you will find buttons that can be used when purchase orders are used in the purchase of inventory.

In some instances, items will be received before the vendor forwards a bill. If this occurs, a different procedure is employed to record the transactions. However, for this chapter, it is assumed that a bill from the vendor accompanies the receipt of the inventory item and that you will record the transaction in the Enter Bills window—Items tab by clicking Vendors and then Receive Items and Enter Bill. (See figure 5–K.)

FIGURE 5–K

Enter Bills Window—
Items Tab

The Enter Bills window—Items tab contains the following new fields:

ITEM	Click the inventory item purchased from the drop-down list. Once an item is chosen, the *DESCRIPTION* and unit *COST* fields will automatically be filled based on information in the Item file.
QTY	Enter the quantity purchased. QuickBooks multiplies the quantity purchased by the unit cost to arrive at the AMOUNT and AMOUNT DUE figures.

Notice that a field for the general ledger accounts is not displayed. Recall that when you entered items in the Item List, the general ledger accounts for the purchase (inventory asset account) and sale (income account and COGS account) of inventory items that were indicated. QuickBooks uses the information in the Item List and the information entered in the Enter Bills window to adjust the correct accounts automatically.

The Enter Bills window—Items tab is designed for purchases of inventory items on account. The default accounts are the Inventory asset account and the Accounts Payable account. QuickBooks uses the information on the Item List to correctly record the amount and account for the inventory asset. The transaction is recorded as follows:

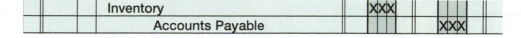

	Inventory		XXX			
	Accounts Payable				XXX	

Recording a Purchase and Receipt of an Inventory Item on Account

On March 1, 2014, Kristin Raina purchases and receives 10 mirrors from Ace Glass Works at a cost of $150 each, their Invoice No. K-588. The bill is due March 31, 2014, terms Net 30 Days.

To record a purchase and receipt of inventory items on account—

1. Click Vendors and then click *Receive Items and Enter Bill.*
2. At the VENDOR drop-down list, click *Ace Glass Works.*
3. Complete the *DATE, REF. NO., BILL DUE,* and *TERMS* fields in the same way as you would for non-inventory purchases. Make sure the Items tab is the active tab. (See figure 5–L.)

FIGURE 5–L
Enter Bills Window—
Partially Completed

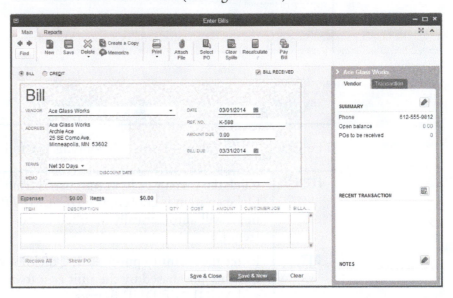

4. At the ITEM drop-down list, click *Mirrors.* The *DESCRIPTION* and *COST* fields will fill automatically.
5. At the *QTY* field, key **10** and then move to the next field. The *AMOUNT* and *AMOUNT DUE* fields will be completed automatically. (See figure 5–M.)

FIGURE 5–M
Enter Bills Window—
Completed

HINT

Remember: You can enter the quantity while the inventory icon is displayed.

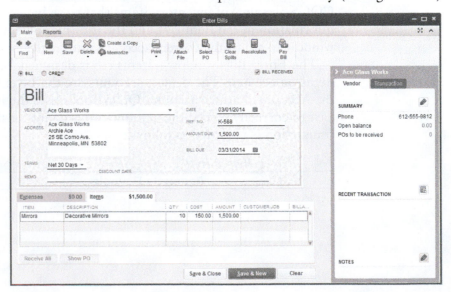

6. If all data is correct, click Save & Close.

Accounting concept

For a purchase of inventory on account, the general ledger posting is as follows:

1275 Mirror Inventory		2010 Accts Payable	
Dr	Cr	Dr	Cr
1,500			1,500

In addition, the vendor file (subledger) for Ace Glass Works will reflect the new liability.

Ace Glass Works	
Dr	Cr
	1,500

In addition to the general ledger and vend... this transaction will update the item file for N... reflect a quantity of 10 on hand with an inven... of $1,500.

Recording Inventory Purchases Usin... the Write Checks Window

Like the Enter Bills window, the Write Checks window has an Expenses tab and an Items tab. For purchase of inventory items for cash, you switch to the Items tab after opening the Write Checks window. The fields to enter information for inventory items in the Write Checks window Items tab are similar to those in the Enter Bills window—Items tab.

The Write Checks window—Items tab is designed for purchases of inventory items for cash. The default accounts are the Inventory asset account and the Cash account. QuickBooks uses the information on the Item List to correctly record the amount and account for the inventory asset. The transaction is recorded as follows:

		Inventory		XXX		
		Cash			XXX	

Recording a Purchase and Receipt of an Inventory Item for Cash

On March 2, 2014, Kristin Raina purchases and receives 16 lamps from Lumiare Lighting Company at a cost of $100 each, their Invoice No. 6844, paid with Check No. 9.

To record a purchase and receipt of inventory items for cash—
1. Click Banking and then click *Write Checks*.
2. At the Write Checks window, make sure BANK ACCOUNT *1010 Cash - Operating* is displayed, the NO. is *9*, and the *Pay Online* box and *Print Later* box are not checked.
3. At the *DATE* field, choose *03/02/2014*.
4. At the PAY TO THE ORDER OF drop-down list, click *Lumiare Lighting Company*.
5. Click the Items tab.
6. At the ITEM drop-down list, click *Lamps*.
7. At the *QTY* field, key **16** and then move to the next field. QuickBooks will complete the *AMOUNT* fields. (See figure 5–N.)

FIGURE 5–N
Write Checks Window—
Completed

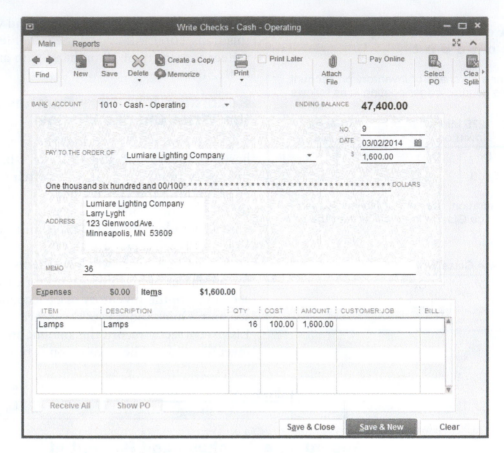

8. Click Save & Close.

Accounting concept

For a cash payment for the purchase of inventory, the general ledger posting will be as follows:

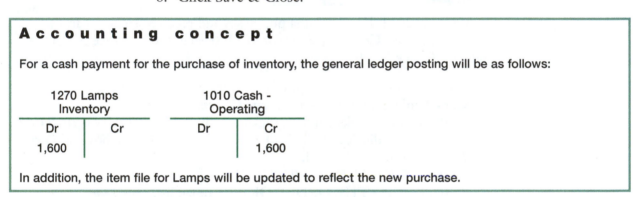

1270 Lamps Inventory		1010 Cash - Operating	
Dr	Cr	Dr	Cr
1,600			1,600

In addition, the item file for Lamps will be updated to reflect the new purchase.

Practice Exercise

HINT

Many companies use purchase order forms to order inventory items from their suppliers. After completing Chapter 5, refer to Appendix D to see how QuickBooks uses Purchase Orders as part of the inventory purchase cycle.

Record the following transactions in the Enter Bills or Write Checks window:

Mar. 6	Purchased and received 10 carpets from Bell Carpet Design at a cost of $200 each, their Invoice No. 12-5585. The bill is due April 5, 2014. *QuickCheck:* $2,000
Mar. 13	Purchased and received 12 sets of draperies from Weaver Fabrics at a cost of $125 each. Pay immediately with Check No. 10. *QuickCheck:* $1,500

Sales Tax

sales tax An amount charged on the sale of merchandise, usually a percentage of the sales price. It is collected by the company as part of the sale and later remitted to the appropriate government agency.

When it sells a product to a customer, a company is usually required to collect **sales tax** on the sale. The sales tax amount charged is added to the invoice price of the product. For example, a customer purchases an item with a retail price of $1,000 and the applicable sales tax rate is 6%. The retailer will add $60 to the invoice and collect $1,060 from the customer. At a later date, the retailer will remit the tax collected from customers to the appropriate state sales tax collection agency. Rules for applying and collecting sales tax are complex and beyond the scope of this text. However, QuickBooks, like most general ledger software programs, is equipped to track sales-taxable transactions and to facilitate the collection and payment of taxes due.

In this chapter, Kristin Raina Interior Designs will be selling decorative accessories to its customers. All sales of these products are subject to a sales tax charge of 7%, which is added to the invoice total. The tax will be payable to the Minnesota Department of Revenue at the end of each month. Sales tax will not be collected on services (decorating and design) in this text, because services generally are not subject to sales tax. Note, however, that in some communities, services also are subject to sales tax.

As you know from chapter 3, a sale on account is recorded in the Create Invoices window, and a sale for cash is recorded in the Enter Sales Receipts window. The default account in the Create Invoices window is a debit to Accounts Receivable, and the default account in the Enter Sales Receipts window is a debit to Cash or Undeposited Funds. When sales tax is charged on the sale of an item, a default Sales Tax Payable account is credited in both the Create Invoices and Enter Sales Receipts windows. The sale of taxable products either for cash or on account results in the following general ledger posting:

Accounts Receivable/Cash (or Undeposited Funds)	XXX			
Sales			XXX	
Sales Tax Payable			XXX	

Sale of Inventory

Activities identified as sales of inventory items on account are recorded in the Create Invoices window. Activities identified as sales of inventory items for cash are recorded in the Enter Sales Receipts window. Activities recorded in these windows are similar to those in chapter 3, but additional fields in the window are used that relate to inventory.

Inventory Sales on Account in the Create Invoices Window

When you record the sale of inventory items in the Create Invoices window, you use a template to access the additional fields needed for inventory items. In chapter 3, for the sale of services, you used the Intuit Service Invoice Template. For the sale of inventory items on account, you will use the Intuit Product Invoice Template.

The Create Invoices window—Intuit Product Invoice is designed for the sale of inventory items on account. The default accounts are Accounts Receivable, Cost of Goods Sold, Inventory, Sales Tax Payable, and Sales. QuickBooks uses the inventory Item List to determine the correct amount and account for the Cost of Goods Sold, Inventory, and Sales accounts. If an item is marked as taxable, QuickBooks uses the Item List to determine the correct amount of sales tax to be recorded in the Sales Tax Payable account.

The transaction is recorded as follows:

	Accounts Receivable	XXX	
	Cost of Goods Sold	XXX	
	Inventory		XXX
	Sales Tax Payable		XXX
	Sales		XXX

Recording a Sale of an Inventory Item on Account

On March 15, 2014, Kristin Raina sells the following items to Jennie Guthrie on account, Invoice No. 1008. Terms 2/10, Net 30 Days:

2 lamps	$ 400.00
3 carpets	1,200.00
1 mirror	300.00
total sale of merchandise	$ 1,900.00
sales tax (0.07 × $1,900)	133.00
decorating services (8 hours)	400.00
total sale on account	$ 2,433.00

To record a sale of inventory on account—
1. Click Customers and then click *Create Invoices*.
2. At the CUSTOMER:JOB drop-down list, click *Guthrie, Jennie*.
3. At the TEMPLATE drop-down list, click *Intuit Product Invoice*. Additional fields for inventory item information appear.
4. Enter the information listed above for the *Date* and *Invoice #* fields.
5. At the Terms drop-down list, click *2/10, Net 30 Days*.
6. At the *QUANTITY* field, key **2**.
7. Click the *ITEM CODE* field. At the ITEM CODE drop-down list, click *Lamps*. QuickBooks will automatically fill the *DESCRIPTION, PRICE EACH, AMOUNT* and *TAX* fields. (See figure 5–O.)

FIGURE 5–O
Create Invoices Window—Partially Completed

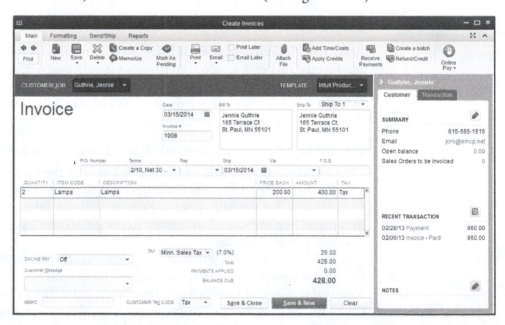

Note that the word *Tax* should appear in the TAX field for taxable items, and *Non* should appear for the non-taxable service item. If the correct coding for tax does not appear, use the drop-down list in the field to indicate the correct tax code.

8. Move to the second line of the *QUANTITY* field, and key **3**.
9. At the ITEM CODE drop-down list, click *Carpets*. QuickBooks will fill the *DESCRIPTION, PRICE EACH, AMOUNT,* and *TAX* fields.
10. Move to the third line of the *QUANTITY* field, and key **1**.
11. At the ITEM CODE drop-down list, click *Mirrors*. QuickBooks will fill the remaining fields.
12. Move to the fourth line of the *QUANTITY* field, and key **8**.
13. At the ITEM CODE drop-down list, click *Decorating Services*. QuickBooks will fill the remaining fields. Note that the TAX field indicates Non because Decorating Services are not subject to sales tax.
14. Click the arrow at the TAX drop-down list, and click *Minn. Sales Tax*, if necessary. The *Print Later* and *Email Later* boxes should not be checked. The ONLINE PAY box should say Off. The Tax from the CUSTOMER TAX CODE drop-down list should be selected. (See figure 5–P.)

FIGURE 5–P
Create Invoices Window—Completed

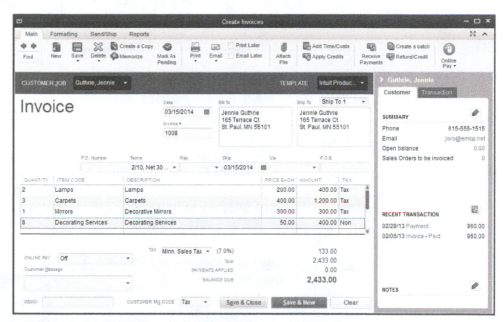

15. If the information is correct, click Save & Close.

Accounting concept

For a sale of inventory products on account, the general ledger posting is as follows:

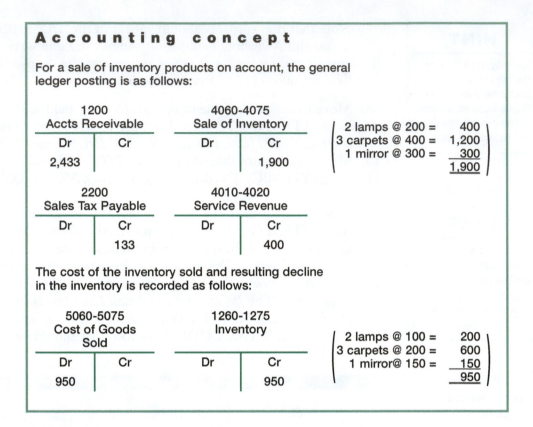

1200 Accts Receivable			4060-4075 Sale of Inventory			
Dr	Cr		Dr	Cr	2 lamps @ 200 =	400
2,433				1,900	3 carpets @ 400 =	1,200
					1 mirror @ 300 =	300
						1,900

2200 Sales Tax Payable			4010-4020 Service Revenue		
Dr	Cr		Dr	Cr
	133			400

The cost of the inventory sold and resulting decline in the inventory is recorded as follows:

5060-5075 Cost of Goods Sold			1260-1275 Inventory			
Dr	Cr		Dr	Cr	2 lamps @ 100 =	200
950				950	3 carpets @ 200 =	600
					1 mirror @ 150 =	150
						950

Inventory Sales for Cash in the Enter Sales Receipts Window

The Enter Sales Receipts window is designed for cash received for both the sale of services and the sale of inventory items for cash. Once an inventory item is chosen, QuickBooks uses the information from the Item List to correctly record the Cost of Goods Sold, Inventory, and Sales accounts. If an item is marked as taxable, QuickBooks uses the Item List to determine the correct amount of sales tax to be recorded in the Sales Tax Payable account. The transaction is recorded as follows:

	Cash (or Undeposited Funds)	XXX	
	Cost of Goods Sold	XXX	
	Inventory		XXX
	Sales Tax Payable		XXX
	Sales		XXX

Recording a Sale of an Inventory Item for Cash

On March 22, 2014, Kristin Raina sells the following items to Beverly Jones, Invoice No. 1009, receiving payment immediately, her Check No. 5477.

1 carpet	$ 400.00
2 draperies	500.00
total sale of merchandise	$ 900.00
sales tax (0.07 × $900)	63.00
decorating services (4 hrs)	200.00
Total sale for cash	$ 1,163.00

To record a sale of inventory for Cash—

1. Click Customers and then click *Enter Sales Receipts*.
2. At the CUSTOMER:JOB drop-down list, click *Jones, Beverly*.
3. Choose the appropriate date, and key **1009** in the *Sale No.* field.
4. At the Payment Method drop-down list, click *Check*, and key **5477** in the *NO.* field. The *Print Later* and *Email Later* boxes should not be checked. The TAX from the CUSTOMER TAX CODE drop-down list should be selected.
5. Complete the balance of the window for each item in the same manner as you would in the Create Invoices window. (See figure 5–Q.)

FIGURE 5–Q

Enter Sales Receipts
Window—Completed

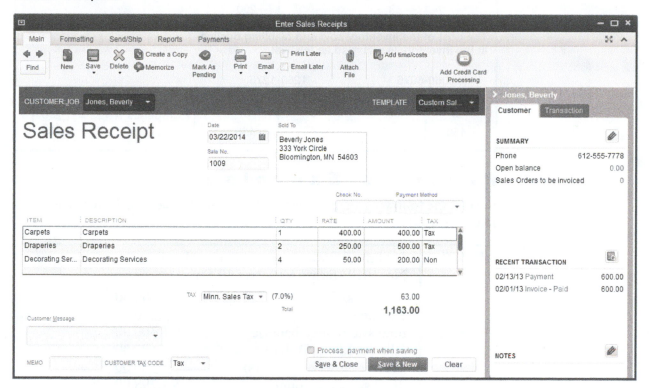

6. If all information is correct, click Save & Close.

For a sale of inventory products for cash, the general ledger posting is as follows:

1250 Undeposited Funds		4060-4075 Sale of Inventory	
Dr	Cr	Dr	Cr
1,163			900

$$\left.\begin{array}{lr} \text{1 carpet @ 400 =} & 400 \\ \text{2 draperies @ 250 =} & \underline{500} \\ & \underline{900} \end{array}\right)$$

2200 Sales Tax Payable		4010-4020 Service Revenue	
Dr	Cr	Dr	Cr
	63		200

The cost of the inventory sold and resulting decline in the inventory is recorded as follows:

5060-5075 Cost of Goods Sold		1260-1275 Inventory	
Dr	Cr	Dr	Cr
450			450

$$\left.\begin{array}{lr} \text{1 carpet @ 200 =} & 200 \\ \text{2 draperies @ 125 =} & \underline{250} \\ & \underline{450} \end{array}\right)$$

Practice Exercise

Record the following transactions in the Create Invoices or Enter Sales Receipts window:

Mar. 27	Sold the following on account to Hamilton Hotels, Invoice No. 1010, Terms 2/10, Net 30 Days:

2 mirrors	$ 600.00
2 carpets	800.00
total sale of merchandise	$ 1,400.00
sales tax (.07 × $1,400)	98.00
decorating services (6 hrs)	300.00
Total sale on account	$ 1,798.00

Mar. 29	Sold the following for cash to Franco Films Co., Invoice No. 1011, their Check No. 1361:

4 lamps	$ 800.00
2 draperies	500.00
total sale of merchandise	$ 1,300.00
sales tax (.07 × $1,300)	91.00
design services (4 hrs)	240.00
Total sale for cash	$ 1,631.00

Sales Discounts

sales discount
A reduction in the selling price if the invoice payment is made shortly after the invoice date.

Sales discounts are offered to customers to encourage early payment of outstanding invoices. Generally, companies provide for a 1% or 2% reduction of the invoice amount if the payment is made within 10 days of the invoice date.

On March 23, 2014, Kristin Raina receives full payment from Jennie Guthrie of Invoice No. 1008, her Check No. 2453, less the appropriate discount.

To record a receipt of payment within the discount period—
1. Click Customers and then click *Receive Payments*.
2. At the RECEIVED FROM drop-down list, click *Guthrie, Jennie*. The open invoice in the full amount for Jennie Guthrie appears.
3. At the *DATE* field, choose *03/23/2014*. Enter the payment method and check number. (See figure 5–R.)

FIGURE 5–R

Receive Payments Window—Jennie Guthrie—Partially Completed

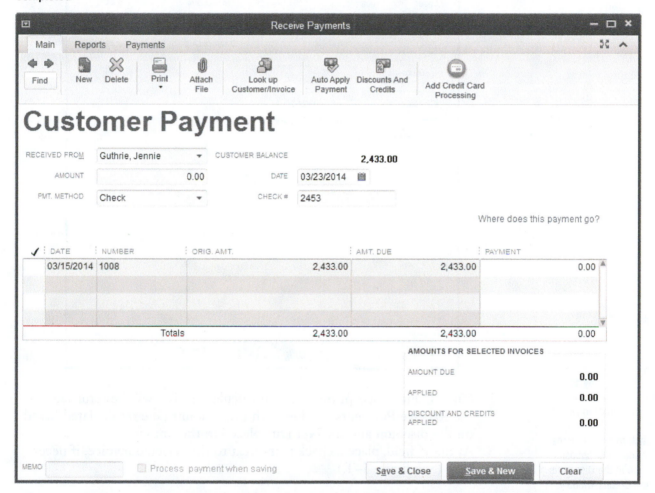

4. Select the invoice by clicking in the ✓ column next to the open invoice.

   The Automatically Calculate Payments window warning appears inquiring if in the Company Preferences for Payments, the Automatically calculate payments option should be selected. Place a check mark in the box to the left of *Do not display this message in the future*, and click Yes. If you chose No, go to Edit, click *Preferences*, and choose Payments. On the Company Preferences tab, place a check mark next to Automatically calculate payments.

5. Click the Discount and Credits button. This will display the Discount and Credits window.

   This window will display information concerning the selected invoice, including the date the discount is available. The window will compute the default discount amount based on information contained in the customer file.

6. At the Discount Account drop-down list, click *4100 Sales Discounts*. (See figure 5–S.)

FIGURE 5–S
Discount and Credits
Window

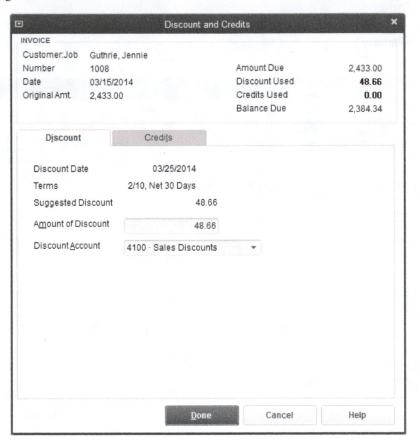

HINT

If you forget to record the discount and go back to edit the transaction, after choosing Done in the Discounts and Credits window, you must correct the amount in the amount field—it is not corrected automatically.

7. Click Done to accept the discount calculation. You will be returned to the Receive Payments window with the Amount Due recalculated based on the discount and the Net Due placed in the Amount field.
8. At the ✓ field, place a check mark next to the selected invoice, if necessary. (See figure 5–T.)

FIGURE 5–T
Receive Payments
Window—Completed

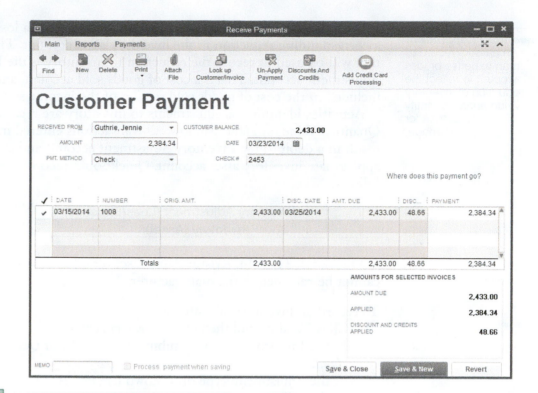

Accounting concept

For a collection of an accounts receivable with a sales discount, the general ledger posting is as follows:

1010 Cash - Operating		1200 Accts Receivable		4100 Sales Discounts	
Dr	Cr	Dr	Cr	Dr	Cr
2,384.34		Bill 2,433	Coll 2,433	48.66	
		Bal 0			

In addition, the Customer File (subledger) for Jennie Guthrie will reflect the new collection.

HINT

See Appendix E for the steps to record a customer credit for returned inventory and to write-off uncollectable receivables.

HINT

If you make an error on the payment, you can correct changes and resave, or click Edit and then Delete Payment and start over.

9. If the information is correct, click Save & Close.

Practice Exercise

Record the following transaction in the Receive Payments window:

Mar. 30	Received full payment from Hamilton Hotels for Invoice No. 1010, their Check No. 6555, less applicable discount. *QuickCheck:* $1,762.04

ACTIVITIES:

The Adjust Quantity/Value on Hand Window

In QuickBooks, you use the Adjust Quantity/Value on Hand activity window to record changes in the inventory from events other than a purchase or sale. If inventory items are lost, stolen, damaged, or spoiled, the resulting change in the inventory quantity and/or value will be recorded in this window as an **inventory adjustment**. The reduction is considered a loss/expense with a corresponding reduction in the inventory asset account. The account that will be used to record the reduction to inventory is the Inventory Adjustment account. This is a cost of goods sold account, and it will be included in the cost of goods sold section of the income statement.

Activities identified as adjustments to inventory are recorded in the Adjust Quantity/Value on Hand window. All transactions entered in this window result in a debit to the Inventory Adjustment account and a credit to the appropriate inventory asset account. QuickBooks records the transaction as follows:

			Inventory Adjustment (Loss/Expense)	XXX		
			Inventory (Asset)		XXX	

On March 31, 2014, Kristin Raina discovers that a mirror is damaged and cannot be returned to the manufacturer.

To record an inventory adjustment—
1. Click Vendors and then click *Inventory Activities*.
2. At the Inventory Activities submenu, click *Adjust Quantity/Value on Hand*.
3. At the Adjustment Type drop-down list, choose *Quantity and Total Value*.
4. At the Adjustment Date drop-down list, choose *03/31/2014*.
5. At the *Reference No.* field, key **Inv. Adj. 1**.
6. At the Adjustment Account drop-down list, click *5900 Inventory Adjustment*. If the Income or Expense expected window appears, place a check mark in the box to the left of *Do not display this message in the future* and then click OK.
7. At the ITEM drop-down list, click *Mirrors*. The description and current quantity are displayed. (See figure 5–U.)

FIGURE 5–U
Adjust Quantity/Value on Hand Window

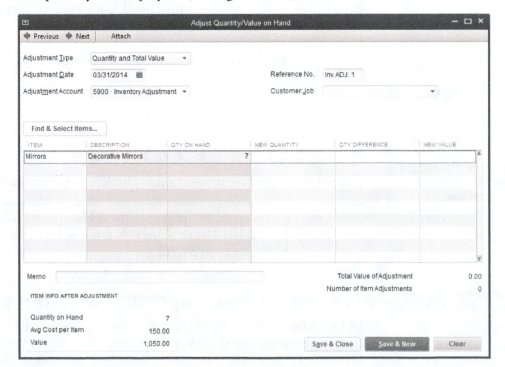

8. At the *NEW QUANTITY* field, key **6**.

When you move to the next field, QuickBooks fills the *QTY DIFFERENCE* and *NEW VALUE* fields and enters the Total Value of Adjustment amount. (See figure 5–V.)

FIGURE 5–V
Adjust Quantity/Value on Hand Window— Completed for Quantity

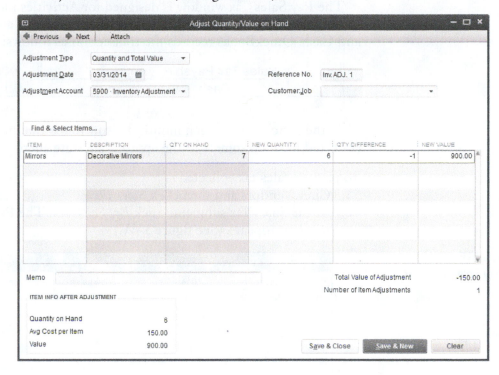

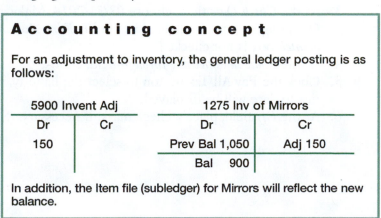

HINT

If you make an error in this window, click Edit and then Delete Inventory Adjustment and redo the transaction.

9. If the information is correct, click Save & Close.

If the inventory adjustment was a result of a change in value only, without a change in quantity, the *Total Values* selection should be chosen from the adjustment type drop-down list. This allows you to adjust the value without changing the quantity.

Accounting concept

For an adjustment to inventory, the general ledger posting is as follows:

5900 Invent Adj		1275 Inv of Mirrors	
Dr	Cr	Dr	Cr
150		Prev Bal 1,050	Adj 150
		Bal 900	

In addition, the Item file (subledger) for Mirrors will reflect the new balance.

○ **The Pay Sales Tax Window**

In QuickBooks, the Pay Sales Tax window is used to record the remittance of sales tax charged to customers to the proper tax agency. QuickBooks uses the default accounts Sales Tax Payable and Cash.

The Pay Sales Tax window is designed for Activities identified as payment of sales tax charged to customers. The default accounts are Sales Tax Payable and Cash. QuickBooks records the transaction as follows:

| | | Sales Tax Payable | XXX | |
| | | Cash | | XXX |

At the conclusion of each month, Kristin Raina remits the sales tax collected from customers to the appropriate state agency.

To pay the sales tax collected—
1. Click Vendors and then click *Sales Tax*.
2. At the Sales Tax submenu, click *Pay Sales Tax*. The Pay Sales Tax window appears. (See figure 5–W.)

FIGURE 5–W
Pay Sales Tax Window

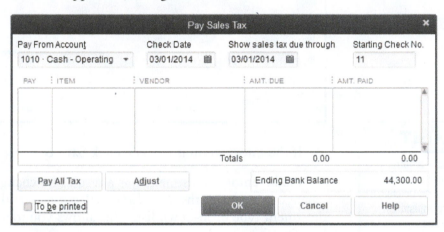

3. At the *Check Date* field, choose *03/31/2014*. Make sure the *1010 Cash - Operating* account is selected in the *Pay From Account* field and the *To be printed* box is not checked.
4. At the *Show sales tax due through* field, choose *03/31/2014*.
5. Click the Pay All Tax button to select the liability. The sales tax liabilities to date will be displayed.
6. At the *Pay* field, place a check mark, if necessary. (See figure 5–X.)

FIGURE 5–X

Pay Sales Tax Window—
Liabilities Displayed

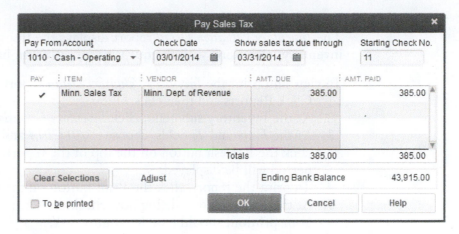

7. If the information is correct, click OK. The liability is now paid.

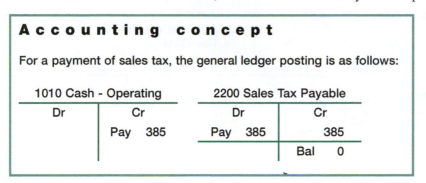

Accounting concept

For a payment of sales tax, the general ledger posting is as follows:

1010 Cash - Operating		2200 Sales Tax Payable	
Dr	Cr	Dr	Cr
	Pay 385	Pay 385	385
			Bal 0

ACTIVITIES:

Make Deposits

Recall from chapter 3 that Kristin Raina Interior Designs deposits all funds collected from customers at the end of the month. Before reviewing the reports for the month, the deposits should be recorded.

Practice Exercise

Record the following transaction in the Make Deposits window:

Mar. 31	Deposit all undeposited funds to the Cash - Operating account. *QuickCheck:* $6,940.38

REPORTS:

Inventory Reports, Accounting Reports, and Financial Statements

Recall from chapter 1 that Reports, the fourth level of operation, reflect the activities recorded in the various Lists/Centers and Activities windows. Inventory activities entered in the various windows flow into the reports, many of which should be displayed and printed at the end of the month.

Inventory Reports from the Reports Menu

Inventory reports, such as the *Inventory Valuation Detail* report, *Inventory Stock Status by Item* report, and the *Purchases by Item Detail* report, help the company track and manage its inventory.

Inventory Valuation Detail Report

The *Inventory Valuation Detail* report displays the transactions affecting each inventory item along with the quantity and value on hand for each.

To view and print the *Inventory Valuation Detail* report—
1. Click Reports and then click *Inventory*.
2. At the Inventory submenu, click *Inventory Valuation Detail*.
3. At the *From* and *To* fields, choose *03/01/2014* and *03/31/2014*, then click the Refresh button on the top of the report. The report for the period will be displayed.
4. To print the report, click the Print button on the top of the report.
5. At the Print Reports dialog box, check the settings and then click Print. Your printout should look like figure 5–Y.

FIGURE 5–Y

Inventory Valuation Detail Report

EX5 [Your Name] Kristin Raina Interior Designs
Inventory Valuation Detail
March 2014

Type	Date	Name	Num	Qty	Cost	On Hand	Avg Cost	Asset Value
Inventory								
Carpets (Carpets)								
Bill	03/06/2014	Bell Carpet Design	12-5585	10	2,000.00	10	200.00	2,000.00
Invoice	03/15/2014	Guthrie, Jennie	1008	↿3		7	200.00	1,400.00
Sales Receipt	03/22/2014	Jones, Beverly	1009	-1		6	200.00	1,200.00
Invoice	03/27/2014	Hamilton Hotels	1010	↿2		4	200.00	800.00
Total Carpets (Carpets)						4.00		800.00
Draperies (Draperies)								
Check	03/13/2014	Weaver Fabrics	10	12	1,500.00	12	125.00	1,500.00
Sales Receipt	03/22/2014	Jones, Beverly	1009	-2		10	125.00	1,250.00
Sales Receipt	03/29/2014	Franco Films Co.	1011	-2		8	125.00	1,000.00
Total Draperies (Draperies)						8.00		1,000.00
Lamps (Lamps)								
Check	03/02/2014	Lumiare Lighting ...	9	16	1,600.00	16	100.00	1,600.00
Invoice	03/15/2014	Guthrie, Jennie	1008	↿2		14	100.00	1,400.00
Sales Receipt	03/29/2014	Franco Films Co.	1011	↿4		10	100.00	1,000.00
Total Lamps (Lamps)						10.00		1,000.00
Mirrors (Decorative Mirrors)								
Bill	03/01/2014	Ace Glass Works	K-588	10	1,500.00	10	150.00	1,500.00
Invoice	03/15/2014	Guthrie, Jennie	1008	↿1		9	150.00	1,350.00
Invoice	03/27/2014	Hamilton Hotels	1010	↿2		7	150.00	1,050.00
Inventory Adjust	03/31/2014		Inv. Adj. 1	-1		6	150.00	900.00
Total Mirrors (Decorative Mirrors)						6.00		900.00
Total Inventory						28.00		3,700.00
TOTAL						**28.00**		**3,700.00**

6. Close the report.

Inventory Stock Status by Item Report

The *Inventory Stock Status by Item* report displays the on-hand status of each inventory item. The report indicates whether an item should be ordered based upon on-hand quantity and the reorder amount.

To view and print the *Inventory Stock Status by Item* report—
1. Click Reports and then click *Inventory*.
2. At the Inventory submenu, click *Inventory Stock Status by Item*.
3. At the *From* and *To* fields, choose *03/01/2014* and *03/31/2014*, and click the Refresh button on the top of the report. The report for the period will be displayed. (See figure 5–Z.)

FIGURE 5–Z
Inventory Stock Status by
Item Report

4. To print the report, click Print, check the settings, and click Print.
5. Close the report.

Purchases by Item Detail Report

The *Purchases by Item Detail* report displays all purchase information for each inventory item. The report shows vendor name, cost per unit, quantity purchased, and total cost.

To view and print the *Purchases by Item Detail* report—

1. Click Reports and then click *Purchases.*
2. At the Purchases submenu, click *Purchases by Item Detail.*
3. At the *From* and *To* fields, choose *03/01/2014* and *03/31/2014,* and click the Refresh button on the top of the report. The report for the period will be displayed.
4. To print the report, click the Print button on the top of the report, check the settings, and click Print. Your printout should look like figure 5–AA.

FIGURE 5–AA
Purchases by Item Detail
Report

EX5 [Your Name] Kristin Raina Interior Designs
Purchases by Item Detail
March 2014

Accrual Basis

Type	Date	Num	Memo	Source Name	Qty	Cost Price	Amount	Balance
Inventory								
Carpets (Carpets)								
Bill	03/06/2014	12-5585	Carpets	Bell Carpet Design	10	200.00	2,000.00	2,000.00
Total Carpets (Carpets)					10		2,000.00	2,000.00
Draperies (Draperies)								
Check	03/13/2014	10	Draperies	Weaver Fabrics	12	125.00	1,500.00	1,500.00
Total Draperies (Draperies)					12		1,500.00	1,500.00
Lamps (Lamps)								
Check	03/02/2014	9	Lamps	Lumiare Lighting Company	16	100.00	1,600.00	1,600.00
Total Lamps (Lamps)					16		1,600.00	1,600.00
Mirrors (Decorative Mirrors)								
Bill	03/01/2014	K588	Decorative Mirrors	Ace Glass Works	10	150.00	1,500.00	1,500.00
Total Mirrors (Decorative Mirrors)					10		1,500.00	1,500.00
Total Inventory					48		6,600.00	6,600.00
TOTAL					48		6,600.00	6,600.00

This report, like several of those reviewed in prior chapters, allows you to drill down to view the source transaction. Kristin Raina wishes to see the detail of the purchase of carpets on March 6, 2014.

To drill down to the purchase transaction of carpets—

1. Place the mouse pointer over the carpet purchase transaction until the zoom glass appears.
2. Double-click the transaction. The Enter Bills window for this transaction is displayed.
3. Close the Enter Bills window and the report.

Inventory Reports from the Lists Menu

QuickBooks allows you to view and print several inventory reports from the Lists windows. Once a list is accessed, a report list is available that is accessed by clicking the Reports menu button in the List window.

The *Sales by Item Detail* report shows sales of all inventory items both on account and for cash.

To view and print an Item List report such as *Sales by Item Detail*—

1. Click Lists and then click *Item List*.
2. At the Item List window, click the Reports menu button.
3. At the Reports menu, click *Reports on All Items*.
4. At the Reports on all Items submenu, click *Sales Reports*.
5. At the Sales Reports submenu, click *By Item Detail*.
6. At the *From* and *To* fields, choose *03/01/2014* and *03/31/2014*, and click the Refresh button on the top of the report. The report for the period will be displayed.
7. To print the report, click the Print button on the top of the report, check the settings, and click Print. Your printout should look like figure 5–BB.

FIGURE 5–BB

Sales by Item Detail Report

EX5 [Your Name] Kristin Raina Interior Designs
Sales by Item Detail
March 2014

Accrual Basis

Type	Date	Num	Memo	Name	Qty	Sales Price	Amount	Balance
Inventory								
Carpets (Carpets)								
Invoice	03/15/2014	1008	Carpets	Guthrie, Jennie	3	400.00	1,200.00	1,200.00
Sales Receipt	03/22/2014	1009	Carpets	Jones, Beverly	1	400.00	400.00	1,600.00
Invoice	03/27/2014	1010	Carpets	Hamilton Hotels	2	400.00	800.00	2,400.00
Total Carpets (Carpets)					6		2,400.00	2,400.00
Draperies (Draperies)								
Sales Receipt	03/22/2014	1009	Draperies	Jones, Beverly	2	250.00	500.00	500.00
Sales Receipt	03/29/2014	1011	Draperies	Franco Films Co.	2	250.00	500.00	1,000.00
Total Draperies (Draperies)					4		1,000.00	1,000.00
Lamps (Lamps)								
Invoice	03/15/2014	1008	Lamps	Guthrie, Jennie	2	200.00	400.00	400.00
Sales Receipt	03/29/2014	1011	Lamps	Franco Films Co.	4	200.00	800.00	1,200.00
Total Lamps (Lamps)					6		1,200.00	1,200.00
Mirrors (Decorative Mirrors)								
Invoice	03/15/2014	1008	Decorative Mirrors	Guthrie, Jennie	1	300.00	300.00	300.00
Invoice	03/27/2014	1010	Decorative Mirrors	Hamilton Hotels	2	300.00	600.00	900.00
Total Mirrors (Decorative Mirrors)					3		900.00	900.00
Total Inventory					19		5,500.00	5,500.00
Service								
Decorating Services (Decorating Services)								
Invoice	03/15/2014	1008	Decorating Services	Guthrie, Jennie	8	50.00	400.00	400.00
Sales Receipt	03/22/2014	1009	Decorating Services	Jones, Beverly	4	50.00	200.00	600.00
Invoice	03/27/2014	1010	Decorating Services	Hamilton Hotels	6	50.00	300.00	900.00
Total Decorating Services (Decorating Services)					18		900.00	900.00
Design Services (Design Services)								
Sales Receipt	03/29/2014	1011	Design Services	Franco Films Co.	4	60.00	240.00	240.00
Total Design Services (Design Services)					4		240.00	240.00
Total Service					22		1,140.00	1,140.00
TOTAL					41		6,640.00	6,640.00

8. Close the report.

In addition to the *Sales* reports, *Purchase, Inventory, Item*, and *Price* reports can be viewed from the Reports menu of the Item List.

Practice Exercise

1. From the Inventory Reports menu, view and print the *Inventory Stock Status by Vendor* report.

2. From the Item List window, view and print the *Item Profitability* report (from the Reports on All Items—Project submenu).

Accounting Reports and Financial Statements

At the end of each month, the *Journal, Profit & Loss Standard (or Income Statement)*, and *Balance Sheet Standard* reports should be viewed and printed. Your printouts should look like figures 5–CC, 5–DD, and 5–EE, respectively.

FIGURE 5–CC
Journal Report—Partial
March 1, 2014–March 31, 2014

EX5 [Your Name] Kristin Raina Interior Designs
Journal
March 2014

Trans #	Type	Date	Num	Name	Memo	Account	Debit	Credit
39	Bill	03/01/2014	K-588	Ace Glass Works		2010 · Accounts Payable		1,500.00
				Ace Glass Works	Decorative Mirrors	1275 · Inventory of Mirrors	1,500.00	
							1,500.00	1,500.00
40	Check	03/02/2014	9	Lumiare Lighting Company	36	1010 · Cash - Operating		1,600.00
				Lumiare Lighting Company	Lamps	1270 · Inventory of Lamps	1,600.00	
							1,600.00	1,600.00
41	Bill	03/06/2014	12-5585	Bell Carpet Design		2010 · Accounts Payable		2,000.00
				Bell Carpet Design	Carpets	1260 · Inventory of Carpets	2,000.00	
							2,000.00	2,000.00
42	Check	03/13/2014	10	Weaver Fabrics	9878	1010 · Cash - Operating		1,500.00
				Weaver Fabrics	Draperies	1265 · Inventory of Draperies	1,500.00	
							1,500.00	1,500.00
43	Invoice	03/15/2014	1008	Guthrie, Jennie		1200 · Accounts Receivable	2,433.00	
				Guthrie, Jennie	Lamps	4070 · Sale of Lamps		400.00
				Guthrie, Jennie	Lamps	1270 · Inventory of Lamps		200.00
				Guthrie, Jennie	Lamps	5070 · Cost of Lamps Sold	200.00	
				Guthrie, Jennie	Carpets	4060 · Sale of Carpets		1,200.00
				Guthrie, Jennie	Carpets	1260 · Inventory of Carpets		600.00
				Guthrie, Jennie	Carpets	5060 · Cost of Carpets Sold	600.00	
				Guthrie, Jennie	Decorative Mirrors	4075 · Sale of Mirrors		300.00
				Guthrie, Jennie	Decorative Mirrors	1275 · Inventory of Mirrors		150.00
				Guthrie, Jennie	Decorative Mirrors	5075 · Cost of Mirrors Sold	150.00	
				Guthrie, Jennie	Decorating Services	4020 · Decorating Services		400.00
				Minn. Dept. of Revenue	Sales Tax	2200 · Sales Tax Payable		133.00
							3,383.00	3,383.00
44	Sales Receipt	03/22/2014	1009	Jones, Beverly		1250 · Undeposited Funds	1,163.00	
				Jones, Beverly	Carpets	4060 · Sale of Carpets		400.00
				Jones, Beverly	Carpets	1260 · Inventory of Carpets		200.00
				Jones, Beverly	Carpets	5060 · Cost of Carpets Sold	200.00	
				Jones, Beverly	Draperies	4065 · Sale of Draperies		500.00
				Jones, Beverly	Draperies	1265 · Inventory of Draperies		250.00
				Jones, Beverly	Draperies	5065 · Cost of Draperies Sold	250.00	
				Jones, Beverly	Decorating Services	4020 · Decorating Services		200.00
				Minn. Dept. of Revenue	Sales Tax	2200 · Sales Tax Payable		63.00
							1,613.00	1,613.00

Figure Continued

FIGURE 5–CC
Journal Report *Continued*

EX5 [Your Name] Kristin Raina Interior Designs
Journal
March 2014

Trans #	Type	Date	Num	Name	Memo	Account	Debit	Credit
45	Invoice	03/27/2014	1010	Hamilton Hotels		1200 · Accounts Receivable	1,798.00	
				Hamilton Hotels	Decorative Mirrors	4075 · Sale of Mirrors		600.00
				Hamilton Hotels	Decorative Mirrors	1275 · Inventory of Mirrors		300.00
				Hamilton Hotels	Decorative Mirrors	5075 · Cost of Mirrors Sold	300.00	
				Hamilton Hotels	Carpets	4060 · Sale of Carpets		800.00
				Hamilton Hotels	Carpets	1260 · Inventory of Carpets		400.00
				Hamilton Hotels	Carpets	5060 · Cost of Carpets Sold	400.00	
				Hamilton Hotels	Decorating Services	4020 · Decorating Services		300.00
				Minn. Dept. of Revenue	Sales Tax	2200 · Sales Tax Payable		98.00
							2,498.00	2,498.00
46	Sales Receipt	03/29/2014	1011	Franco Films Co.		1250 · Undeposited Funds	1,631.00	
				Franco Films Co.	Lamps	4070 · Sale of Lamps		800.00
				Franco Films Co.	Lamps	1270 · Inventory of Lamps		400.00
				Franco Films Co.	Lamps	5070 · Cost of Lamps Sold	400.00	
				Franco Films Co.	Draperies	4065 · Sale of Draperies		500.00
				Franco Films Co.	Draperies	1265 · Inventory of Draperies		250.00
				Franco Films Co.	Draperies	5065 · Cost of Draperies Sold	250.00	
				Franco Films Co.	Design Services	4010 · Design Services		240.00
				Minn. Dept. of Revenue	Sales Tax	2200 · Sales Tax Payable		91.00
							2,281.00	2,281.00
47	Payment	03/23/2014	2453	Guthrie, Jennie		1250 · Undeposited Funds	2,384.34	
				Guthrie, Jennie		1200 · Accounts Receivable		2,384.34
				Guthrie, Jennie		1200 · Accounts Receivable		48.66
				Guthrie, Jennie		4100 · Sales Discounts	48.66	
							2,433.00	2,433.00
48	Payment	03/30/2014	6555	Hamilton Hotels		1250 · Undeposited Funds	1,762.04	
				Hamilton Hotels		1200 · Accounts Receivable		1,762.04
				Hamilton Hotels		1200 · Accounts Receivable		35.96
				Hamilton Hotels		4100 · Sales Discounts	35.96	
							1,798.00	1,798.00
49	Inventory Adj...	03/31/2014	Inv. Adj. 1			5900 · Inventory Adjustment	150.00	
					Mirrors Inventory Adjustment	1275 · Inventory of Mirrors		150.00
							150.00	150.00
50	Sales Tax Pa...	03/31/2014	11	Minn. Dept. of Revenue		1010 · Cash - Operating		385.00
				Minn. Dept. of Revenue		2200 · Sales Tax Payable	385.00	
							385.00	385.00
51	Deposit	03/31/2014			Deposit	1010 · Cash - Operating	6,940.38	
				Jones, Beverly	Deposit	1250 · Undeposited Funds		1,163.00
				Guthrie, Jennie	Deposit	1250 · Undeposited Funds		2,384.34
				Franco Films Co.	Deposit	1250 · Undeposited Funds		1,631.00
				Hamilton Hotels	Deposit	1250 · Undeposited Funds		1,762.04
							6,940.38	6,940.38
TOTAL							**28,081.38**	**28,081.38**

Accrual Basis

EX5 [Your Name] Kristin Raina Interior Designs
Profit & Loss
January through March 2014

	Jan ☐Mar 14
Ordinary Income/Expense	
Income	
4010 · Design Services	4,980.00
4020 · Decorating Services	3,400.00
4060 · Sale of Carpets	2,400.00
4065 · Sale of Draperies	1,000.00
4070 · Sale of Lamps	1,200.00
4075 · Sale of Mirrors	900.00
4100 · Sales Discounts	-84.62
Total Income	13,795.38
Cost of Goods Sold	
5060 · Cost of Carpets Sold	1,200.00
5065 · Cost of Draperies Sold	500.00
5070 · Cost of Lamps Sold	600.00
5075 · Cost of Mirrors Sold	450.00
5900 · Inventory Adjustment	150.00
Total COGS	2,900.00
Gross Profit	10,895.38
Expense	
6020 · Accounting Expense	300.00
6050 · Advertising Expense	100.00
6175 · Deprec. Exp., Furniture	100.00
6185 · Deprec. Exp., Computers	60.00
6200 · Insurance Expense	200.00
6300 · Janitorial Expenses	125.00
6325 · Office Supplies Expense	150.00
6400 · Rent Expense	800.00
6450 · Telephone Expense	275.00
6500 · Utilities Expense	450.00
Total Expense	2,560.00
Net Ordinary Income	8,335.38
Other Income/Expense	
Other Expense	
7000 · Interest Expense	50.00
Total Other Expense	50.00
Net Other Income	-50.00
Net Income	**8,285.38**

EX5 [Your Name] Kristin Raina Interior Designs
Balance Sheet
As of March 31, 2014

	Mar 31, 14
ASSETS	
Current Assets	
Checking/Savings	
1010 · Cash □Operating	50,855.38
Total Checking/Savings	50,855.38
Accounts Receivable	
1200 · Accounts Receivable	1,540.00
Total Accounts Receivable	1,540.00
Other Current Assets	
1260 · Inventory of Carpets	800.00
1265 · Inventory of Draperies	1,000.00
1270 · Inventory of Lamps	1,000.00
1275 · Inventory of Mirrors	900.00
1300 · Design Supplies	200.00
1305 · Office Supplies	250.00
1410 · Prepaid Advertising	500.00
1420 · Prepaid Insurance	2,200.00
Total Other Current Assets	6,850.00
Total Current Assets	59,245.38
Fixed Assets	
1700 · Furniture	
1725 · Furniture, Cost	12,000.00
1750 · Accum. Dep., Furniture	-100.00
Total 1700 · Furniture	11,900.00
1800 · Computers	
1825 · Computers, Cost	3,600.00
1850 · Accum. Dep., Computers	-60.00
Total 1800 · Computers	3,540.00
Total Fixed Assets	15,440.00
TOTAL ASSETS	**74,685.38**
LIABILITIES & EQUITY	
Liabilities	
Current Liabilities	
Accounts Payable	
2010 · Accounts Payable	9,750.00
Total Accounts Payable	9,750.00
Other Current Liabilities	
2020 · Notes Payable	7,000.00
2030 · Interest Payable	50.00
Total Other Current Liabilities	7,050.00
Total Current Liabilities	16,800.00
Total Liabilities	16,800.00
Equity	
3010 · Kristin Raina, Capital	50,000.00
3020 · Kristin Raina, Drawings	-400.00
Net Income	8,285.38
Total Equity	57,885.38
TOTAL LIABILITIES & EQUITY	**74,685.38**

Chapter Review and Assessment

Procedure Review

To add an item—
1. Click Lists and then click *Item List*.
2. At the Item List window, click the Item menu button.
3. At the Item menu, click *New*.
4. Enter the background data for the item.
5. Click OK.
6. Close the Item List window.

To delete an item—
1. Click Lists and then click *Item List*.
2. At the Item List window, select the item you wish to delete.
3. Click the Item menu button.
4. At the Item menu, click *Delete Item*.
5. Click OK at the warning.
6. Close the Item List window.

   You cannot delete an item that has a balance or is used in a transaction.

To edit an item—
1. Click Lists and then click *Item List*.
2. At the Item List window, select the item you wish to edit.
3. Click the Item menu button.
4. At the Item menu, click *Edit Item*.
5. Change the appropriate information.
6. Click OK.
7. Close the Item List window.

To record a purchase and receipt of an inventory item on account—
1. Click Vendors and then click *Receive Items and Enter Bill*.
2. At the VENDOR drop-down list, click the vendor name.
3. Enter data into the *DATE, REF. NO., BILL DUE,* and *TERMS* fields in the usual manner.
4. Click the item from the ITEM drop-down list.
5. Enter the quantity; the *AMOUNT* and *AMOUNT DUE* fields will fill automatically.
6. Click Save & Close.

To record a purchase and receipt of an inventory item for cash—
1. Click Banking and then click *Write Checks*.
2. At the Write Checks window, click the appropriate bank account.
3. Enter the check date in the *DATE* field.
4. Click the payee from the PAY TO THE ORDER OF drop-down list.
5. Click the Items tab.
6. Click the item from the ITEM drop-down list.
7. Enter the quantity; the *AMOUNT* field will fill automatically.
8. Click Save & Close.

To record a sale of inventory on account—
1. Click Customers and then click *Create Invoices*.
2. At the CUSTOMER:JOB drop-down list, click the customer name.
3. At the TEMPLATE drop-down list, click *Intuit Product Invoice*.
4. Enter data into the *Date*, *Invoice #*, and *Terms* fields in the usual manner.
5. Enter the quantity.
6. Click the item from the ITEM drop-down list; the *DESCRIPTION*, *PRICE EACH*, and *AMOUNT* field will fill automatically.
7. At the TAX drop-down list, click the applicable sales tax. Make sure the Tax from the CUSTOMER TAX CODE drop-down list is selected.
8. Click Save & Close.

To enter a cash sale of inventory—
1. Click Customers and then click *Enter Sales Receipt*.
2. At the CUSTOMER:JOB drop-down list, click the customer name.
3. Enter the date, invoice number, payment method, and check number.
4. Complete the balance of the window in the same manner as a sale on account.
5. Click Save & Close.

To record a receipt of payment within the discount period—
1. Click Customers and then click *Receive Payments*.
2. At the RECEIVED FROM drop-down list, click the customer name.
3. Enter the payment date in the *DATE* field. Enter the payment method and check number.
4. Select the invoice by clicking in the ✓ column next to the open invoice.
5. Click YES at the warning, then click the Discounts and Credits button.
6. At the Discount Account drop-down list, click the Sales discount GL account.
7. Click Done to accept the discount calculation.
8. At the ✓ field, place a check mark next to the selected invoice, if necessary.
9. Click Save & Close.

To record an inventory adjustment—
1. Click Vendors and then click *Inventory Activities*.
2. At the Inventory Activities menu, click *Adjust Quantity/Value on Hand*.
3. At the Adjustment Type drop-down list, choose *Quantity and Total Value*.
4. Enter data into the *Date* and *Reference No.* fields.
5. At the Adjustment Account drop-down list, click *Inventory Adjustment*.
6. Select the item from the drop-down list.
7. Enter the new quantity in the *NEW QUANTITY* field.
8. Click Save & Close.

To pay sales tax—
1. Click Vendors and then click *Sales Tax*.
2. At the Sales Tax submenu, click *Pay Sales Tax*.
3. Enter the payment date.
4. Click the Cash account.
5. Enter the correct date in the *Show sales tax due through* field.
6. Click the Pay All Tax button.
7. Place a check mark in the *Pay* field.
8. Click OK.

To view and print inventory reports from the Reports menu—
1. Click Reports and then click *Inventory*.
2. At the Inventory submenu, choose a report.
3. Indicate the appropriate dates for the report.
4. Click the Print button on the top of the report.
5. At the Print Reports dialog box, review the settings, and click Print.
6. Close the report.

To view and print inventory reports from the Lists menu—
1. Click Lists and then click *Item List*.
2. Click the Reports menu button.
3. Click Reports on All Items.
4. From the submenu, click a category.
5. From the second submenu, click a report.
6. Indicate the appropriate dates for the report.
7. Click the Print button on the top of the report.
8. At the Print Reports dialog box, review the settings, and click Print.
9. Close the report.

Key Concepts

Select the letter of the item that best matches each definition.

a. Enter Bills window—Items tab
b. Adjust Quantity/Value on Hand activity window
c. Item List
d. Sales Discounts
e. *Purchases by Item Detail* report
f. Sales Tax
g. Pay Sales Tax window
h. *Inventory Valuation Detail* report
i. *Sales by Item Detail* report
j. *Inventory Stock Status by Item* report

_____ 1. Report that displays all transactions affecting each inventory item.

_____ 2. Reduction of invoice amount due when customer pays by a specific date.

_____ 3. Window used to record purchases and receipt of inventory items.

_____ 4. Window used to adjust quantity or value of inventory as a result of damage or loss.

_____ 5. Contains a file of all inventory items.

_____ 6. Window used to remit sales tax collected from customers to the appropriate state tax agency.

_____ 7. Report that displays each purchase transaction for inventory items.

_____ 8. Report that displays the on-hand status of every inventory item.

_____ 9. Report from the Item List that shows sales information for each inventory item.

_____ 10. Tax collected by a retailer from a customer on sales of goods.

Procedure Check

1. Your company will be selling a new product. Describe the steps that must be taken to add the new item to the system.
2. Explain the difference between using Enter Bills or Receive Items and Enter Bills from the Vendors pull-down menu.
3. Which QuickBooks report(s) would you use to view the sales and purchases of specific inventory items?
4. At year-end, you wish to confirm the quantity on hand for each inventory item. How would you use QuickBooks reports to determine the quantity and value of the ending inventory?
5. Your company wishes to view the profitability of each inventory item. How could you use QuickBooks to develop this information?
6. Discuss the advantages of using a computerized accounting system to maintain a perpetual inventory system.

Case Problems

Case Problem 1

On April 1, 2014, Lynn Garcia began her business, called Lynn's Music Studio. In the first month of business, Lynn set up the music studio, provided guitar and piano lessons, and recorded month-end activity. In May, the second month of business, Lynn decides to purchase and sell inventory items of guitars, keyboards, music stands, and sheet music. For customers that purchase merchandise inventory, the terms of payment are 2/10, Net 30 Days. For illustration purposes, assume a 7% sales tax is charged on the sale of all inventory items. The company file includes the information for Lynn's Music Studio as of May 1, 2014.

1. Open the company file CH5 Lynn's Music Studio.QBW.
2. Make a backup copy of the company file LMS5 [*Your Name*] Lynn's Music Studio.
3. Restore the backup copy of the company file. In both the Open Backup Copy and Save Company File as windows use the file name LMS5 [*Your Name*] Lynn's Music Studio.
4. Change the Company Name to **LMS5 [*Your Name*] Lynn's Music Studio**.
5. Add the following inventory items to the Item List:

Type:	**Inventory Part**
Item Name/Number:	**Keyboards**
Description on	
Purchase/Sales Transactions:	**Keyboards**
Cost:	**75**
COGS Account:	**5065 Cost of Keyboards Sold**
Preferred Vendor:	**Katie's Keyboards**
Sales Price:	**150**
Tax Code:	**Tax – Taxable Sales**
Income Account:	**4065 Sale of Keyboards**
Asset Account:	**1265 Inventory of Keyboards**
Reorder Point:	**10**

Type:	**Inventory Part**
Item Name/Number:	**Sheet Music**
Description on	
Purchase/Sales Transactions:	**Sheet Music**
Cost:	**3**
COGS Account:	**5075 Cost of Sheet Music Sold**
Preferred Vendor:	**Strings, Sheets & Such**
Sales Price:	**6**
Tax Code:	**Tax – Taxable Sales**
Income Account:	**4075 Sale of Sheet Music**
Asset Account:	**1275 Inventory of Sheet Music**
Reorder Point:	**50**

Delete the following inventory item:
   Harmonicas

6. Using the appropriate window, record the following transactions for May:

May 3	Purchased 30 guitars on account from Music Instruments, Inc., at $50 each, their Invoice No. GU75998.
May 3	Purchased 30 keyboards on account from Katie's Keyboards at $75 each, their Invoice No. 10089-30.
May 3	Purchased 30 music stands from Melody Music Equipment at $20 each, paid immediately, Check No. 9. Do not print check.
May 3	Purchased 300 sheets of music of various themes from Strings, Sheets & Such at $3 each, paid immediately, Check No. 10. Do not print check.
May 4	Sold 15 guitars for $100 each, 15 keyboards for $150 each, and 15 music stands for $40 each to Jefferson High School, Invoice No. 2012, terms 2/10, Net 30 Days. In addition, provided 15 hours of guitar lessons and 10 hours of piano lessons.
May 4	Sold 10 keyboards for $150 each to Highland School, Invoice No. 2013, terms 2/10, Net 30 Days. In addition, provided 12 hours of piano lessons.
May 7	Received full payment from Jefferson High School for Invoice 2009, Check No. 30531.
May 10	Record the weekly cash sales of sheet music, 75 sheets at $6 each, Sale No. 2014. Leave the *Customer:Job* field blank.
May 11	Sold 3 guitars for $100 each, 3 keyboards for $150 each, and 3 music stands for $40 each to Mulligan Residence, Invoice No. 2015, terms 2/10, Net 30 Days. In addition, provided 5 hours of guitar lessons and 7 hours of piano lessons.
May 11	Received full payment net of discount from Jefferson High School for Invoice No. 2012, Check No. 30711.

May 14	Received full payment net of discount from Highland School, Check No. 76115.
May 17	Purchased 20 keyboards on account from Katie's Keyboard Company at $75 each, their Invoice No. 10758-20.
May 17	Purchased 10 music stands from Melody Music Equipment at $20 each, paid immediately, Check No. 11. Do not print check.
May 17	Record the weekly cash sales of sheet music, 100 sheets at $6 each, Sale No. 2016.
May 21	Sold 5 guitars for $100 each, 5 keyboards for $150 each, and 5 music stands to Twin Lakes Elementary, Invoice No. 2017, terms 2/10, Net 30 Days. In addition, provided 8 hours of guitar lessons and 5 hours of piano lessons.
May 24	Received a payment of $830 from Twin Lakes Elementary for Invoices 2004 and 2011, Check No. 7266.
May 24	Record the weekly cash sales of sheet music, 115 sheets at $6 each, Sale No. 2018.
May 24	Purchased 300 sheets of music of various themes from Strings, Sheets, & Such at $3 each, paid immediately, Check No. 12. Do not print check.
May 25	Received full payment net of discount from Twin Lakes Elementary for Invoice No. 2017, Check No. 7384.
May 25	Paid in full Music Instruments, Inc. (Check No. 13). Do not print check.
May 25	Paid in full Katie's Keyboard Company, Invoice No. 10089-30 (Check No. 14). Do not print check.
May 31	Record the weekly cash sales of sheet music, 145 sheets at $6 each, Invoice No. 2019.
May 31	Upon reviewing the inventory, Lynn discovers that one guitar is damaged, through no fault of the manufacturer, and cannot be sold. Adjust the inventory on hand to remove the one guitar from the inventory. Inv. Adj. 1.
May 31	Remit all sales taxes collected to the PA Dept. of Revenue, Check No. 15.
May 31	Deposit all undeposited funds to the Cash - Operating account.

7. Display and print the following reports for May 1, 2014, to May 31, 2014:
a. *Inventory Valuation Detail*
b. *Inventory Stock Status by Item*
c. *Purchases by Item Detail*
d. *Sales by Item Detail*
e. *Journal*
f. *Profit & Loss Standard* (April 1, 2014–May 31, 2014)
g. *Balance Sheet Standard*

Case Problem 2

On June 1, 2014, Olivia Chen began her business, which she named Olivia's Web Solutions. In the first month of business, Olivia set up the office, provided web page design and Internet consulting services, and recorded month-end activity. In July, the second month of business, Olivia decides to purchase and sell inventory items of computer hardware and software. For customers that purchase merchandise inventory, the terms of payment are 2/10, Net 30 Days. For illustration purposes, assume an 8% sales tax is charged on the sale of all inventory items. The company file includes the information for Olivia's Web Solutions as of July 1, 2014.

1. Open the company file CH5 Olivia's Web Solutions.QBW.
2. Make a backup copy of the company file OWS5 [*Your Name*] Olivia's Web Solutions.
3. Restore the backup copy of the company file. In both the Open Backup Copy and Save Company File as windows use the file name OWS5 [*Your Name*] Olivia's Web Solutions.
4. Change the Company Name to **OWS5 [*Your Name*] Olivia's Web Solutions**.
5. Add the following inventory items to the Item List:

Type:	**Inventory Part**
Item Name/Number:	**Scanners**
Description on	
Purchase/Sales Transactions:	**Scanners**
Cost:	**300**
COGS Account:	**5065 Cost of Scanners Sold**
Preferred Vendor:	**Scanntronix**
Sales Price:	**600**
Tax Code:	**Tax – Taxable Sales**
Income Account:	**4065 Sale of Scanners**
Asset Account:	**1265 Inventory of Scanners**
Reorder Point:	**5**

Type:	**Inventory Part**
Item Name/Number:	**Desktop Publishing Software**
Description on	
Purchase/Sales Transactions:	**Desktop Publishing Software**
Cost:	**100**
COGS Account:	**5075 Cost of Desktop Pub. Soft. Sold**
Preferred Vendor:	**Textpro Software, Inc.**
Sales Price:	**200**
Tax Code:	**Tax – Taxable Sales**
Income Account:	**4075 Sale of Desktop Pub. Soft.**
Asset Account:	**1275 Inventory of Desktop Pub. Soft.**
Reorder Point:	**5**

Delete the following inventory item:
Printers

6. Using the appropriate window, record the following transactions for July:

Jul. 2   Purchased 10 computers on account from Computec Computers at $1,000 each, their Invoice No. 068788.

Jul. 2   Purchased 20 scanners on account from Scanntronix at $300 each, their Invoice No. 10089-30.

Jul. 2   Purchased 10 desktop publishing software packages from Textpro Software, Inc. at $100 each, paid immediately, Check No. 9. Do not print check.

Jul. 2   Purchased 20 HTML software packages from InterSoft Development Co. at $75 each, paid immediately, Check No. 10. Do not print check.

Jul. 5   Sold 3 computers for $2,000 each, 2 scanners for $600 each, and 1 desktop publishing software package for $200 on account to Long Island Water Works, Invoice No. 1011, terms 2/10, Net 30 Days. In addition, provided 10 hours of Internet consulting services.

Jul. 6   Sold 2 computers on account to Miguel's Restaurant, Invoice No. 1012, terms 2/10, Net 30 Days. In addition, provided 8 hours of Web page design services.

Jul. 9   Sold 1 scanner for $600 and 1 desktop publishing software package for $200 to the Singh family, Invoice No. 1013. Received payment immediately, their Check No. 901.

Jul. 12   Sold 1 computer for $2,000, 2 scanners for $600 each, and 1 HTML software package for $150 on account to Breathe Easy, Invoice No. 1014, Net 30 Days. In addition, provided 12 hours of Internet consulting services.

Jul. 13   Received full payment net of discount from Long Island Water Works for Invoice No. 1011, Check No. 125671.

Jul. 16   Purchased 5 computers on account from Computec Computers at $1,000 each, their Invoice No. 072445.

Jul. 16   Purchased 5 desktop publishing software packages from Textpro Software, Inc. at $100 each, paid immediately, Check No. 11. Do not print check.

Jul. 19   Sold 1 computer for $2,000 and 1 desktop publishing software package for $200 to the Schneider Family, Invoice No. 1015. Received payment immediately, their Check No. 899.

Jul. 20   Sold 3 computers for $2,000 each, 3 scanners for $600 each, and 2 desktop publishing software packages for $200 each to South Shore School District, Invoice No. 1016, terms 2/10, Net 30 Days. In addition, provided 16 hours of Web page design services.

Jul. 26   Received full payment, no discount, from Miguel's Restaurant, for Invoice No. 1012, Check No. 4110.

Jul. 27   Received full payment, no discount, from Breathe Easy for Invoices Nos. 1006 (remaining balance) and 1014, Check No. 1874.

Jul. 30	Purchased 5 computers on account from Computec Computers at $1,000 each, their Invoice No. 073111.
Jul. 30	Paid in full Computec Computers Invoice No. 068788 (Check No. 12). Do not print check.
Jul. 30	Paid in full Scanntronix, Invoice No. 10089-30 (Check No. 13). Do not print check.
Jul. 30	Upon reviewing the inventory, Olivia discovers one HTML software package was damaged, through no fault of the manufacturer, and cannot be sold. Adjust the inventory on hand to remove the one HTML software package from the inventory. Inv. Adj. 1
Jul. 31	Remit all sales taxes collected to New York State, Check No. 14.
Jul. 31	Deposit all undeposited funds to the Cash - Operating account.

7. Display and print the following reports for July 1, 2014, to July 31, 2014:

a. *Inventory Valuation Detail*
b. *Inventory Stock Status by Item*
c. *Purchases by Item Detail*
d. *Sales by Item Detail*
e. *Journal*
f. *Profit & Loss Standard* (June 1, 2014–July 31, 2014)
g. *Balance Sheet Standard*

New Company Setup— Detailed Start

EasyStep Interview and QuickBooks Setup

Chapter Objectives

- Create a new company file and establish preferences using the QuickBooks Detailed Start method and EasyStep Interview window

- Set up the Customer Center, Vendor Center, and Item List using the QuickBooks Setup window

- Review information recorded in the EasyStep Interview and QuickBooks Setup windows

- Customize the Chart of Accounts List, System Default Accounts, and Terms List

- Update the Chart of Accounts and Item Lists

- Update the Customer and Vendor Centers

- Adjust the new company file to follow the accrual basis of accounting

- Display and print accounting reports and financial statements

Introduction

In this chapter, you will learn how to create a new company file in QuickBooks. As you know, the four levels of operation for QuickBooks are New Company Setup, Lists/Centers, Activities, and Reports. In chapters 2 through 5, you learned and used the Lists/Centers, Activities, and Reports levels for both a service company and a merchandise company. In those chapters, you opened an existing company file, updated Lists/Centers, recorded Activities in the various windows, and viewed and printed Reports. You will now learn the first level of operation for QuickBooks—New Company Setup.

QuickBooks provides two methods of New Company Setup: Detailed Start and Express Start. Chapter 6 presents the Detailed Start method and chapter 7 presents the Express Start method.

QuickBooks provides two windows to help with New Company Setup. One window is the *EasyStep Interview* window. When you choose the Detailed Start method, you are moved to the EasyStep Interview window, which is designed to assist you in creating and setting up a new company file. The EasyStep Interview window involves entering some basic company information and answering some questions about your company. QuickBooks also provides a *QuickBooks Setup* window. The QuickBooks Setup window is first used to select the method of New Company Setup (Detailed Start or Express Start). But then, the QuickBooks Setup window further assists you in setting up your new company file. The QuickBooks Setup window allows you to enter information on customers, vendors, service items, and inventory part items. You do not have to use the QuickBooks Setup window to enter information after using EasyStep Interview but it will be used in this chapter. Using the EasyStep Interview and QuickBooks Setup windows is only part of the process of setting up a new company file. You then take the information set up in the EasyStep Interview and QuickBooks Setup windows and customize and update it according to your company's preferences. Finally, the new company file is prepared for the accrual basis of accounting.

In this chapter, you will create and set up a new company file for our sample company, Kristin Raina Interior Designs. It is assumed that Kristin Raina Interior Designs was recording accounting activities using a manual accounting system and has decided to convert the company's accounting records to QuickBooks.

QuickBooks versus Manual Accounting: New Company Setup

In a manual accounting system, a company's records are set up by creating the Chart of Accounts and the general ledger. The Chart of Accounts is the list of accounts (assets, liabilities, equity, revenues, and expenses) the company intends to use. The general ledger is the book of all accounts with the beginning balance for each account. If desired, subsidiary ledgers are also created and beginning balances recorded. The subsidiary ledgers typically include accounts receivable and accounts payable. If the perpetual inventory system is used, an inventory subsidiary ledger would also be created.

In QuickBooks, a company's records are set up by creating a new company file and establishing the Chart of Accounts List. As the opening balances are entered, QuickBooks simultaneously sets up the general ledger. The Customer Center and Vendor Center are set up; these centers are equivalent to the accounts receivable and accounts payable subsidiary ledgers. The Item List is set up, which is equivalent to an inventory subsidiary ledger. However, in QuickBooks, the Item List also includes service revenue items and sales tax items in addition to inventory items.

In this chapter, you will first use the EasyStep Interview window to create a new company file, establish some preferences, and begin the Item List, and Chart of Accounts List. After the company file is created, you leave the EasyStep Interview and then use the QuickBooks Setup window to enter information on customers, vendors, and inventory part items. This will set up the Customer Center, Vendor Center, and add to the Item List, which begins in EasyStep Interview. You will next customize and update the company file. Finally, there are three journal entries you need to make to complete the New Company Setup. One journal entry records the opening balance in the accounts that were not included in the EasyStep Interview or QuickBooks Setup windows; the other two journal entries reverse accounts QuickBooks sets up during New Company Setup that are not used in the accrual basis of accounting.

Chapter Problem

In this chapter, there is no prepared company file to open from the company files. Instead, you will create and set up the company file for Kristin Raina Interior Designs.

Assume that Kristin Raina began operating her interior design business in January 2014 and has maintained accounting records with a manual accounting system for January through March. Effective April 1, 2014, Kristin Raina has decided to convert the company's accounting records to QuickBooks using the Detailed Start method.

Before you create a new company file, you would gather all the information you need including: company information (name, address, tax identification numbers); general ledger account names and account numbers; customer information (name, address, telephone numbers, and so on) and outstanding balances; vendor information (name, address, telephone numbers, and so on) and outstanding balances; services items and billing amounts; inventory part items (name, cost, selling price, and quantity on hand); and sales tax information. You will enter this information into QuickBooks as you create and set up the new company file.

To begin New Company Setup—
1. Open QuickBooks.
2. At the No Company Open window, click *Create a new company;* or click File and then click *New Company.* The QuickBooks Setup window appears with the Let's get your business set up quickly! page displayed. This is the page where you select the method of New Company Setup. (See figure 6–A.)

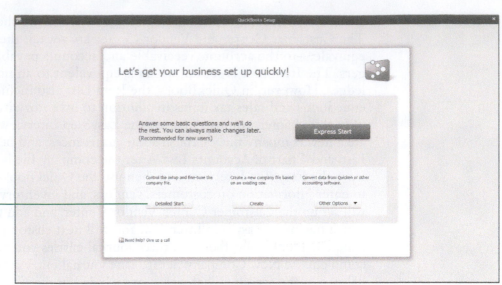

Detailed
Start Button

Detailed Start and EasyStep Interview Window

In New Company Setup, the first level of operation in QuickBooks, you will enter the information needed to create and set up a company file for Kristin Raina Interior Designs using the Detailed Start method, which uses the EasyStep Interview window.

The EasyStep Interview window is designed to guide you through the steps needed to create and set up a new company file. (EasyStep Interview is not the only way to create a company file in QuickBooks; an alternative method is covered in chapter 7.)

With EasyStep Interview, you proceed through a series of pages by clicking the Next button. On each of the pages, you enter some basic company information and answer some questions that QuickBooks uses to create the new company file. As you answer the questions, QuickBooks establishes some preferences for your company. Company preferences enable or disable features available in QuickBooks. When a feature is enabled, it allows for choices to be listed on the pull-down menus and on the home page. If a feature is disabled, you will not see that choice on the pull-down menu or home page.

The company information can later be edited by clicking Company and then Company Information. The preferences can be edited by clicking Edit and then Preferences.

At any time, you can click the Leave button to leave the EasyStep Interview window. However, although you may leave the EasyStep Interview window at any time, it is advisable not to leave before saving the company file. If you leave the window before saving the company file, all information will be lost.

If you leave EasyStep Interview after saving the company file, QuickBooks goes to the No Company Open window. The next time you open the company file, you return to the same page where you left off as long as the company file has been saved.

To create a new company file using the Detailed Start method and the EasyStep Interview window—

1. At the QuickBooks Setup window on the Let's get your business set up quickly! page, click the Detailed Start button. The EasyStep Interview window appears with the Enter your company information page displayed.

2. At the Enter your company information page, key the company name **CH6 [*Your Name*] Kristin Raina Interior Designs** in the *Company Name* field.

   When you tab to the *Legal name* field, the same name is automatically filled in. The legal name is the name that will be used on tax forms. If the company name and legal name are not the same, you can make any necessary changes. For our sample company, the company name and legal name are the same.

3. At the Enter your company information page, key in or click the following information:

Tax ID:	**33-4777781**
Street address:	**25 NE Johnson Street**
City:	**Minneapolis**
State:	**MN**
Zip:	**53402**
Country:	**U.S.**
Phone:	**651-555-1000**
Fax:	**651-555-2000**
E-mail address:	**KRID@emcp.net**

   (See figure 6–B.)

HINT

If you key the letter **M** in the *State* field, the first state that begins with *M (MA)* is displayed. To choose *MN,* keep pressing the M key. You will scroll through all states beginning with M. An alternative is to click the drop-down arrow to display the list of states.

FIGURE 6–B
EasyStep Interview Window—Enter Your Company Information Page

HINT

If you want to activate the Next button using the keyboard, press Alt + N.

4. If the information is correct, click Next.

5. At the Select your industry page, scroll down the Industry list and click *General Product-based Business*. (See figure 6–C.)

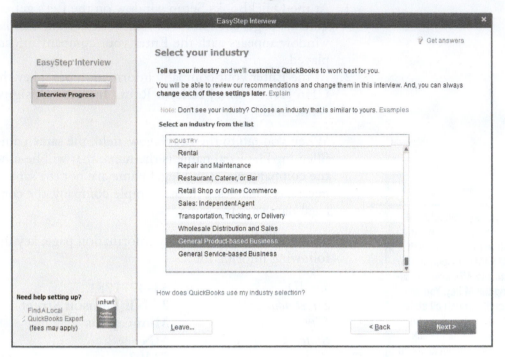

QuickBooks provides for several sample-type industries to assist you in creating your new company file. Based on the industry you select, QuickBooks will inquire if you wish to use particular features or may recommend that you use certain features. In addition, QuickBooks will create a Chart of Accounts including some accounts typical for the industry you chose. Later in the EasyStep Interview, you will have the opportunity to review and edit the suggested revenue and expense accounts to be included in the Chart of Accounts List.

6. If the information is correct, click Next.
7. At the How is your company organized? page, click *Sole Proprietorship* and then click Next.
8. At the Select the first month of your fiscal year page, at the *My fiscal year starts in* field, click *January* and then click Next.
9. At the Setup your administrator password page, click Next.

In business, it is advisable to password-protect access to financial records. QuickBooks has the ability to password-protect not only the entire company file but also specific sections of the company's file. This allows a company to limit employee access to their respective areas of responsibility. For instance, the accounts receivable bookkeeper may be permitted to access only the information pertaining to the customers' accounts; the payroll bookkeeper may be permitted to access only the payroll information, and so on.

In the classroom environment, we will not password-protect access to QuickBooks.

10. At the Create your company file page, click Next. The Filename for New Company dialog box appears.
11. Choose your subfolder in the *Save in* text box, and accept the file name CH6 [*Your Name*] Kristin Raina Interior Designs.QBW.
12. If the information is correct, click Save. The new company file has been created and saved.

At this point, the company file has been saved. It is now safe to use the Leave button at any time from this point on. If you do leave the EasyStep Interview at this point, QuickBooks will close the company file. The next time you open QuickBooks, and open the company file, you will return to the EasyStep Interview window to the last page you opened.

13. At the Customizing QuickBooks for your business page, read the page and then click Next.
14. At the What do you sell? page, click *Both services and products*, then click Next.
15. At the Do you charge sales tax? page, click *Yes* and then click Next.
16. At the Do you want to create estimates in QuickBooks? page, click *No* and then click Next.
17. At the Tracking customer orders in QuickBooks page, click *No* and then click Next.
18. At the Using statements in QuickBooks page, click *No* and then click Next.
19. At the Using invoices in QuickBooks page, click *Yes* and then click Next.
20. At the Using progress invoicing page, click *No* and then click Next.
21. At the Managing bills you owe page, click *Yes* and then click Next.
22. At the Tracking inventory in QuickBooks page, click *Yes* and then click Next.
23. At the Tracking time in QuickBooks page, click *No* and then click Next.
24. At the Do you have employees? page, click *No* and then click Next.
25. At the Using accounts in QuickBooks page, read the page and then click Next.
26. At the Select a date to start tracking your finances page, click *Use today's date or the first day of the quarter or month*, then click *04/01/2014*.

This identifies the date the company began to use QuickBooks. For our sample company Kristin Raina Interior Designs, the fiscal start date is January 1, 2014. The QuickBooks start date is April 1. You will enter the balances as of April 1, which represent January 1 to March 31 activities, in the new company file as part of the New Company Setup. (See figure 6–D.)

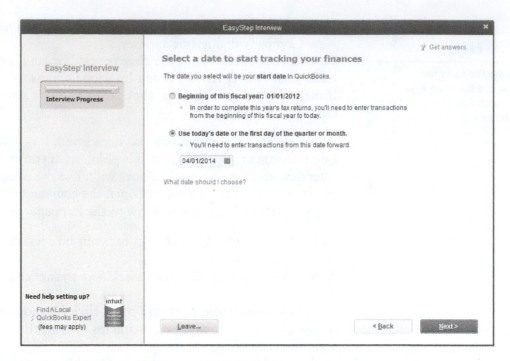

27. If the information is correct, click Next.

The Review income and expense accounts page appears. (See figure 6–E.)

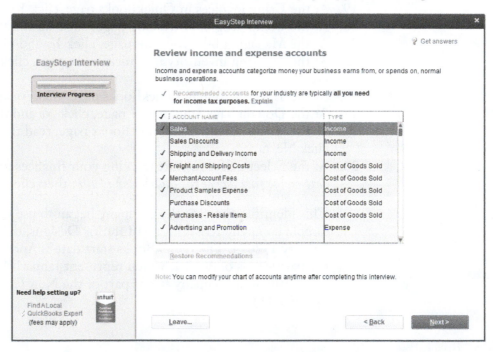

This page lists common Chart of Accounts income and expense accounts names. Those with the check mark to the left of the Account Name are the accounts that QuickBooks recommends for your company based on the industry type you selected earlier in the EasyStep Interview window. You can remove the check mark for any account your company does not use, and you can add a check mark for any account that your company does use. At any time, you can click the Restore Recommendations button to replace the original check marks placed by QuickBooks.

Any account checked will be created in the Chart of Accounts List by QuickBooks. After you finish the EasyStep Interview window, you can add, delete, and modify any account on the Chart of Accounts List using the procedures presented in chapter 4.

28. Remove the check mark from the following accounts, since Kristin Raina Interior Designs does not use these accounts:

   Shipping and Delivery Income
   Freight and Shipping Costs
   Merchant Account Fees
   Product Samples Expense
   Purchases - Resale Items
   Automobile Expense
   Bank Service Charges
   Computer and Internet Expenses
   Dues and Subscriptions
   Meals and Entertainment
   Postage and Delivery
   Professional Fees
   Repairs and Maintenance Expense
   Travel Expense

29. Place a check mark to the left of the following accounts, as these are accounts Kristin Raina Interior Designs uses:

   Sales Discounts
   Janitorial Expense

30. Click Next. The EasyStep Interview is complete. The Congratulations! window appears.

31. Click Go to Setup.
   After completing the EasyStep Interview window, you are returned to the QuickBooks Setup window with the You've got a company file! Now add your info. page displayed. (See figure 6–F.)

FIGURE 6–F
QuickBooks Setup Window—You've Got a Company File! Now Add Your Info. Page

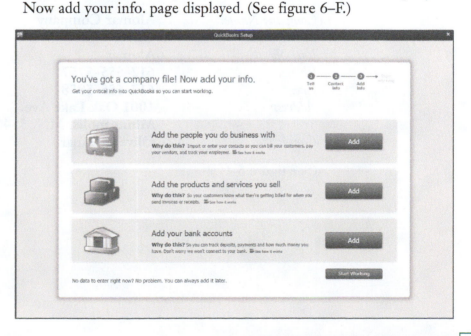

HINT

The Add button may change to Add More.

QuickBooks Setup Window

You can use the QuickBooks Setup window – You've got a company file! Now add your info. page to enter your customers (Customer Center), vendors (Vendor Center), service items and inventory items (Item List), and banking (Cash – Operating) information or you can go directly into QuickBooks.

For Kristin Raina Interior Designs, the QuickBooks Setup window will be used to continue setting up the new company file and to create the Customer Center, Vendor Center, and add to the Item List that begins in EasyStep Interview.

If you wish to leave the QuickBooks Setup window, click the X. You will enter QuickBooks in the new company file. To return to the QuickBooks Setup window, click Help on the main menu bar, then click Quick Start Center. At the Quick Start Center window, click Return to Add Info.

Setting Up the Customer Center

The Customer Center records the information for all customers with whom the company does business. Kristin Raina has 10 customers. Two of the customers have outstanding balances. When you record the outstanding balances, QuickBooks creates the accounts receivable for that customer.

To add customers to the Customer Center using the QuickBooks Setup window—

1. In the QuickBooks Setup window, at the You've got a company file! Now add your info. page, in the *Add the people you do business with* field, click the Add button.
2. At the next Add the people you do business with page, choose the *Paste from Excel or enter manually* button, then click Continue.
3. At the next Add the people you do business with page, in the Customer column, click *Select all* and all of the circles will be filled in.
4. At the *Name* field, key **Alomar Company**. Press the tab key to move to the next field.
5. Enter the information listed below in the appropriate columns:

Company Name:	**Alomar Company**
First Name:	**Oliver**
Last Name:	**Alomar**
Phone:	**612-555-5757**
Fax:	**612-555-5858**
Address:	**1001 Oak Lake Ave.**
	Minneapolis, MN 55401
Contact:	**Oliver Alomar**

(See figure 6–G.)

<figure>

FIGURE 6–G
Add the People You Do
Business With Page—
Customers—Partially
Complete

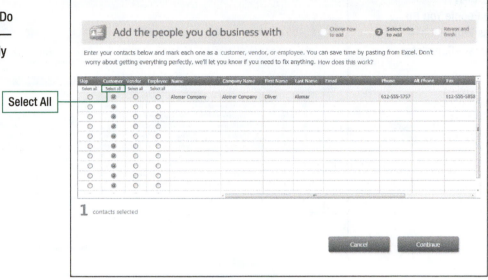

Select All

6. Using the information in table 6–1, key in the information for all customers.

TABLE 6–1
Customers

Customer/ Company Name	Name/Contact	Phone/Fax	Address
Barrera Bagel Barn	Belinda Barrera	612-555-1233 612-555-1234	148 46th Ave. N Plymouth, MN 53406
Berger Bakery Company	Barry Berger	612-555-2240 612-555-2241	18 N. Grand Ave. Minneapolis, MN 55403
Cook Caterers	Stephen Cook	612-555-7896 612-555-7599	275 Oak Lake Ave. Minneapolis, MN 55401
Franco Films Co.	Fred Franco	612-555-4566 612-555-4567	100 Pleasant Ave. S. Minneapolis, MN 55409
Guthrie, Jennie	Jennie Guthrie	651-555-1515	165 Terrace Ct. St. Paul, MN 55101
Hamilton Hotels	Hilda Hamilton	651-555-1050 651-555-1060	1000 York Ave. St. Paul, MN 55101
Jones, Beverly	Beverly Jones	612-555-7778	333 York Circle Bloomington, MN 54603
Omari, Maria	Maria Omari	612-555-9999 612-555-9998	210 NE Lowry Ave. Minneapolis, MN 54204
Plaza Pizza Palace	Mikey Plaza	612-555-9000 612-555-9800	360 Border Ave. N Minneapolis, MN 55401

HINT

If you have information in an Excel spread sheet, you can copy an entire column and paste into the Add the people you do business with page, but you must use CTRL + V to paste.

After entering the information in table 6–1, the screen should look like figure 6–H.

FIGURE 6–H

Add the People You Do
Business With Page—
Customers—Complete

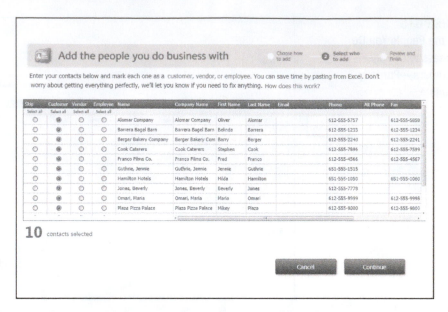

7. If the information is correct, click Continue. At the next Add the people you do business with page, it should indicate that 10 contacts are ready to be added. If it is incorrect, you will have an opportunity to make corrections later. (See figure 6–I)

FIGURE 6–I

Add the People You Do
Business With Page—
Enter Opening Balances
Link

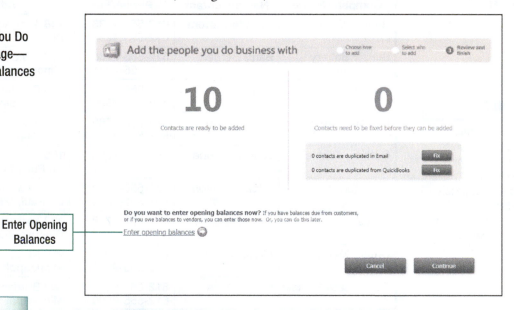

Enter Opening
Balances

HINT

Exercise care in clicking the Enter Opening Balances link. If you do not click the Enter Opening Balances link here, then you will subsequently have to re-enter the customers with balances.

---

8. Click *Enter opening balances*. At the Enter opening balances for customers and vendors page, enter the balances for the following customers and change the date to 04/01/2014:

Berger Bakery Company	$600
Franco Films Co.	940

(See figure 6–J)

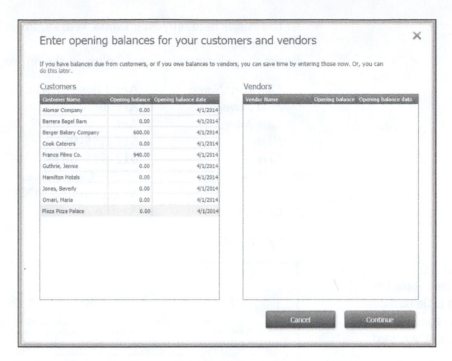

9. If the information is correct, click Continue. You are returned to the Add the people you do business with page, click Continue.
10. You are returned to the QuickBooks Setup window – You've got a company file! Now add your info. page.

A c c o u n t i n g   c o n c e p t

1200 Accounts Receivable		49900 Uncategorized Income	
Dr	Cr	Dr	Cr
600			600
940			940
Bal 1,540			Bal 1,540

Setting Up the Vendor Center

The Vendor Center records the information for all vendors with whom the company does business. Kristin Raina has 17 vendors. Seven of the vendors have outstanding balances. When you record the outstanding balances, QuickBooks creates the accounts payable for that vendor.

To add vendors to the Vendor Center using the QuickBooks Setup window—

1. In the QuickBooks Setup window at the You've got a company file! Now add your info. page, in the *Add the people you do business with* field, click the Add More button.
2. At the Add the people you do business with page, choose the *Paste from Excel or enter manually* button, then click Continue.
3. At the next Add the people you do business with page, in the Vendor column, click *Select all*.

4. At the *Name* field, key **Ace Glass Works**. Press the tab key to move to the next field.

5. Enter the information listed below in the appropriate columns:

Company Name:	**Ace Glass Works**
First Name:	**Archie**
Last Name:	**Ace**
Phone:	**612-555-9812**
Fax:	**612-555-6813**
Address:	**25 SE Como Ave.**
	Minneapolis, MN 53602
Contact:	**Archie Ace**

(See figure 6–K.)

Select All

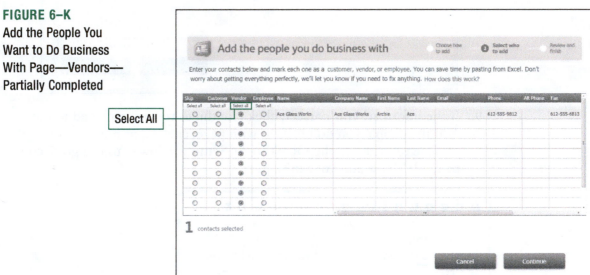

6. Using the information in table 6–2, key in the information for all vendors.

TABLE 6–2
Vendors

Vendor/Company Name	Name/Contact	Phone/Fax	Address
Bell Carpet Design	Bill Bell	651-555-8823 651-555-8824	55 North Main Ave. St. Paul, MN 54603
Cuza and Carl Associates	Carrie Cuza	651-555-8855 651-555-8856	23 W. University Ave. St. Paul, MN 54603
Darren Tapestry	Donna Darren	612-555-2221 612-555-2222	10 W. Larpenteur Ave. Minneapolis, MN 52604
Galeway Computers	Roger Rivera	617-555-4747 617-555-4748	33 Route 10 Springfield, MA 24105
Grayson Graphics	Gregg Grayson	612-555-0002 612-555-0003	56 Amity Way Bloomington, MN 53608
Jeter Janitorial Services	Jason Jeter	612-555-4444 612-555-4445	233 Lilac Rd. Minneapolis, MN 54302
Kristin Raina	Kristin Raina		
Lumiare Lighting Company	Larry Lyght	612-555-4790 612-555-4795	123 Glenwood Ave. Minneapolis, MN 53609
Midwest Mutual Insurance Co.	Mike Mills	805-555-4545 805-555-4546	3566 Broadway Chicago, IL 58303
Minn. Dept. of Revenue			
Minneapolis Electric & Gas Co.	Jack Watts	651-555-4949 651-555-4950	150 Douglas Ave. St. Paul, MN 55303
Nordic Realty	Melanie Marx	612-555-3232 612-555-3233	23 N. 12th St. Minneapolis, MN 53604
TwinCityTelCo	Terry Ameche	651-555-6667 651-555-6668	3223 River Dr. St. Paul, MN 53908
Weaver Fabrics	Jon Weaver	612-555-8777 612-555-8778	355 W. 70th St. Minneapolis, MN 53604
Williams Office Supply Company	Bernard Williams	612-555-2240 612-555-2241	15 Grand Ave. S Minneapolis, MN 55404
[Your Name] Accounting Service	Your Name	612-555-2222 612-555-2223	One Main Plaza St. Paul, MN 53602

After entering the information in table 6–2, your screen should look like figure 6–L.

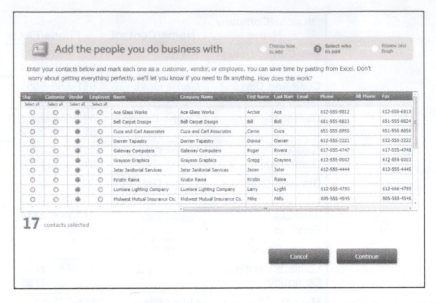

7. Scroll down the list of vendors and make sure the Vendor button was selected on each line. If the information is correct, click Continue. At the next Add the people you do business with, it should indicate that 17 contacts are ready to be added. If it is incorrect, you will have an opportunity to make corrections later.

8. Click *Enter opening balances*. At the Enter opening balances for customers and vendors page, enter the balances for the following vendors and change all of the dates to 04/01/2014:

Ace Glass Works	$1,500
Bell Carpet Design	2,000
Cuza and Carl Associates	400
Galeway Computers	2,600
Midwest Mutual Insurance Co.	2,400
Minneapolis Electric & Gas Co.	450
Williams Office Supply Company	400

(See figure 6–M.)

HINT

Exercise care in clicking the Enter Opening Balances link. If you do not click the Enter Opening Balances link here, you will subsequently have to re-enter the vendors with balances.

FIGURE 6–M

Enter Opening Balances for Your Customers and Vendors Page— Vendors—Completed

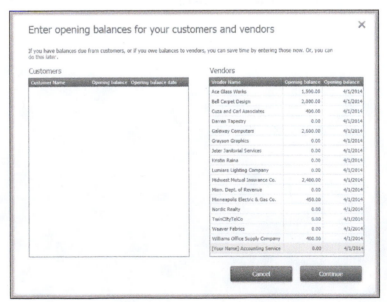

9. If the information is correct, click Continue. You are returned to the Add the people you do business with page, click Continue.
10. You are returned to the QuickBooks Setup window – You've got a company file! Now add your info. page.

Accounting concept

69800 Uncategorized Expenses		2010 Accounts Payable	
Dr	Cr	Dr	Cr
1,500			1,500
2,000			2,000
400			400
2,600			2,600
2,400			2,400
450			450
400			400
Bal 9,750			Bal 9,750

Adding to the Item List

The Item List stores information about the service items, the inventory part items, and the sales tax. As transactions are recorded in the Activities windows, QuickBooks uses information in the Item List to record the transaction in the correct accounts. Kristin Raina has two service items and four inventory part items. When you record the quantity on hand for inventory parts, QuickBooks creates the inventory asset for that inventory part.

To add service items to the Item List using the QuickBooks Setup window—
1. In the QuickBooks Setup window at the You've got a company file! Now add your info. page, in the *Add the products and services you sell* field, click the Add button.
2. At the Add the products and services you sell page, choose the *Service* button, then click Continue.
3. In the Name field, key **Design Services**.
4. In the Description field, key **Design Services**.
5. In the Price field, key **60**.
6. Enter the information below for the next service item:

Name:	**Decorating Services**
Description:	**Decorating Services**
Price:	**50**

   (See figure 6–N.)

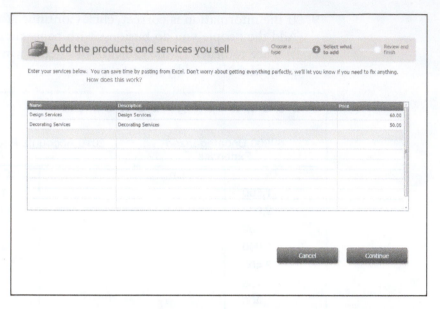

7. If the information is correct, click Continue. You are returned to the Add the products and services you sell page, which should indicate 2 Items are ready to be added. If it is incorrect you will have an opportunity to make corrections later.

8. Click Continue. You are returned to the QuickBooks Setup window – You've got a company file! Now add your info. page.

To add inventory part items to the Item List using the QuickBooks Setup window—

1. In the QuickBooks Setup window at the You've got a company file! Now add your info. page, in the *Add the products and services you sell* field, click the Add More button.

2. At the Add the products and services you sell page, choose the *Inventory part* button, then click Continue.

3. In the Name field, key **Carpets**.

4. In the Description field, key **Carpets**.

5. In the Price field, key **400**.

6. In the Cost field, key **200**.

7. In the On Hand field, key **4**. When you move to the next field, the amount in the Total Value field is computed automatically based on cost times quantity.

8. In the As of date field, choose **04/01/14**.

9. Using the information in table 6-3, key in the information for all inventory part items as of 04/01/14.

TABLE 6–3
Inventory Part Items

Name and Description	Price	Cost	On Hand	Total Value
Draperies	$250	$125	8	$1,000
Lamps	200	100	10	1,000
Mirrors	300	150	6	900

After entering the information in table 6–3, your screen should look like figure 6–O.

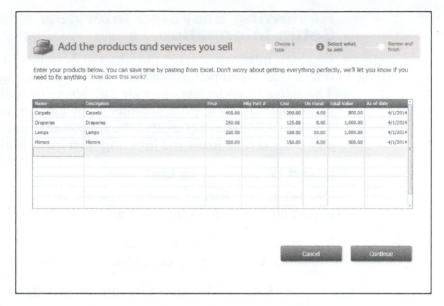

10. If the information is correct, click Continue. You are returned to the Add the products and services you sell page, which should indicate 4 Items are ready to be added. If it is incorrect you will have an opportunity to make corrections later.

11. Click Continue. You are returned to the QuickBooks Setup window – You've got a company file! Now add your info. page.

12. Exit the QuickBooks Setup window by clicking the X. You will enter QuickBooks in the new company file. The QuickBooks home page and the left icon bar appear. Close the home page by clicking on the X and remove the left icon bar by clicking on View and then click Hide Icon Bar.

HINT

Recall you can change the default so the home page does not appear when opening a company file. Click Edit on the main menu bar, then click Preferences. Along the left, click the Desktop View icon. Choose the My Preferences tab. Remove the check mark to the left of Show Home page when opening a company file and then click OK.

Accounting concept

Inventory Asset		Opening Balance Equity	
Dr	Cr	Dr	Cr
800			800
1,000			1,000
1,000			1,000
900			900

Reviewing EasyStep Interview and QuickBooks Setup Information

EasyStep Interview created the Chart of Accounts List and the Item List. It also established preferences that enabled certain features in QuickBooks. The activated preferences provide for choices to be listed on the drop-down menus and the home page, and they allow for accessing Activities windows. The QuickBooks Setup created the Customer Center, Vendor Center, and added the service items and inventory part items to the Item List.

Chart of Accounts List

Reviewing the Chart of Accounts List allows you to see the accounts set up as part of the EasyStep Interview and QuickBooks Setup.

To view the Chart of Accounts List—
1. Click Lists and then click *Chart of Accounts.*

The Chart of Accounts List appears. (See figure 6–P.)

FIGURE 6–P

Chart of Accounts List Window

System Default Accounts Created by QuickBooks as Part of EasyStep Interview and QuickBooks Setup

NAME	⚡ TYPE	BALANCE TOTAL	ATTACH
Accounts Receivable	Accounts Receivable	1,540.00	
Inventory Asset	Other Current Asset	3,700.00	
Accumulated Depreciation	Fixed Asset	0.00	
Furniture and Equipment	Fixed Asset	0.00	
Accounts Payable	Accounts Payable	9,750.00	
Sales Tax Payable	Other Current Liability	0.00	
Opening Balance Equity	Equity	3,700.00	
Owners Draw	Equity	0.00	
Owners Equity	Equity		
Sales	Income		
Sales Discounts	Income		
Sales Income	Income		
Uncategorized Income	Income		
Cost of Goods Sold	Cost of Goods Sold		
Advertising and Promotion	Expense		
Depreciation Expense	Expense		
Insurance Expense	Expense		
Interest Expense	Expense		
Janitorial Expense	Expense		
Office Supplies	Expense		
Rent Expense	Expense		
Telephone Expense	Expense		
Uncategorized Expenses	Expense		
Utilities	Expense		
Ask My Accountant	Other Expense		

Account ▾ | Activities ▾ | Reports ▾ | Attach | ☐ Include Inactive

You can correct any errors by adding, deleting, or editing the account as illustrated in chapter 4.

Upon reviewing the Chart of Accounts List, observe that Kristin Raina Interior Designs uses many more accounts that are not included in the Chart of Accounts List created by the EasyStep Interview and QuickBooks Setup or uses different account names. Notice also that an account number was not assigned to each account.

2. Close the Chart of Accounts List.

Item List

Reviewing the Item List allows you to see the items set up as part of the EasyStep Interview and QuickBooks Setup.

To view the Item List—

1. Click Lists and then click *Item List*. The Item List appears. (See figure 6–Q.)

FIGURE 6–Q

Item List Window

In the QuickBooks Setup window at the Add new products and services page, when you added service items and inventory part items, these items were added to the Item List.

2. Choose the *Decorating Services* service item by double-clicking. The Edit Item window appears. (See figure 6–R.)

FIGURE 6–R

Edit Item Window—
Service Item

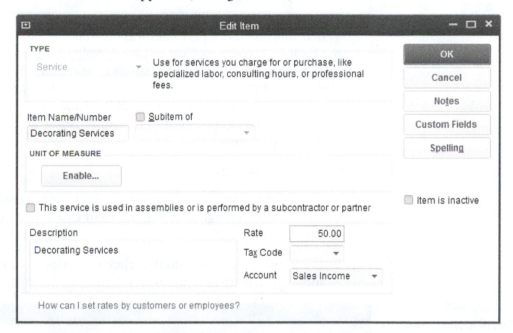

When this service item was created, QuickBooks Setup recorded Sales Income in the Account field. If you double-click Design Services, you will notice that QuickBooks Setup also uses Sales Income as the Account for the Design Services.

3. Close the Edit Item window.
4. In the Item List window, choose the *Carpets* inventory part item by double-clicking. The Edit Item window appears. (See figure 6–S.)

FIGURE 6–S
Edit Item Window—
Inventory Part Item

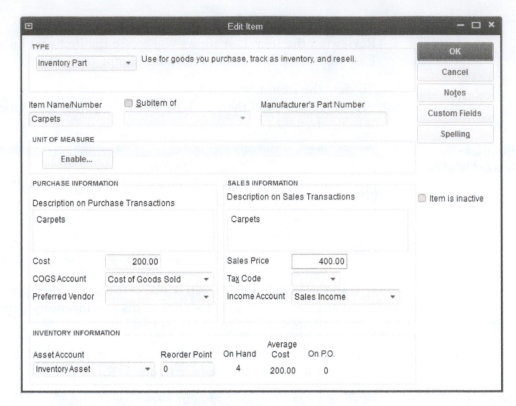

When this inventory part item was created, QuickBooks Setup recorded the COGS Account as Cost of Goods Sold, the Income Account as Sales Income, and the Asset Account as Inventory Asset. If you double-click each of the other inventory part items – Draperies, Lamps, and Mirrors – you will notice that QuickBooks Setup also used Cost of Goods Sold, Sales Income, and Inventory Asset as the accounts for each inventory part item.

5. Close the Edit Item window.

In the EasyStep Interview window, when you answered the question that yes you do charge sales tax, the Item List was created with this sales tax item.

6. In the Item List window, double-click the Sales Tax item. The Edit Item window appears. (See figure 6–T.)

FIGURE 6–T
Edit Item Window—Sales
Tax Item

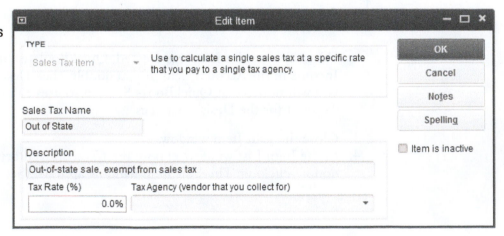

EasyStep Interview created this item in the Item List, but it does not include an appropriate name for the Kristin Raina Interior Designs tax item, a tax rate, or a tax agency. These will be added later.

7. Close the Edit Item and Item List windows.

Errors in the Item List Window

If there is an error in the type, name, cost, or price amounts in any of the service items, inventory part items, or sales tax, you can correct it in the Edit Item window. If there is an error in the quantity on hand, you can correct it when viewing journal entries. If there is no quantity on hand for an inventory part item, delete the inventory part item, and then go back to the QuickBooks Setup – Add the products and services you sell window.

To return to the QuickBooks Setup, click Help, and then click Quick Start Center. At the Quick Start Center window, click Return to Add Info. At the Add the products and services you sell field, click Add More, and then re-enter the inventory part item with the correct quantity on hand and the correct date as previously illustrated.

Customer Center

Reviewing the Customer Center allows you to see the customers set up as part of the QuickBooks Setup.

To review the Customer Center—
1. Click Customers, then click *Customer Center*. The Customer Center appears. (See figure 6–U.)

FIGURE 6–U
Customer Center Window

2. Choose *Berger Bakery Company* by double-clicking. The Edit Customer window appears. (See figure 6–V.)

FIGURE 6–V
Edit Customer Window

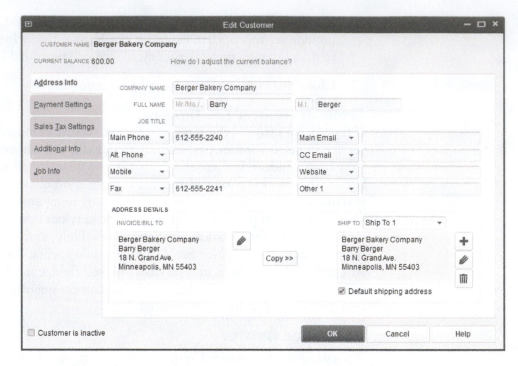

QuickBooks created this customer based on the information entered in QuickBooks Setup – Add the people you do business with pages. If you entered an opening balance, the balance is displayed in the CURRENT BALANCE field. If you did not enter an opening balance, the CURRENT BALANCE field indicates a zero. You can correct all information in the Edit Customer window, except the CURRENT BALANCE.

3. Close the Edit Customer window and the Customer Center window.

Errors in the Customer Center Window

If there is an error in the name, address, phone or fax numbers, or contact for any of the customers, you can correct it in the Edit Customer window. If there is an error in the CURRENT BALANCE, you can correct it when viewing journal entries. If there is no CURRENT BALANCE for a customer with an outstanding balance, delete the customer, and then go back to the QuickBooks Setup – Add people you do business with pages.

To return to the QuickBooks Setup, click Help, and then click Quick Start Center. At the Quick Start Center window, click Return to Add Info. At the Add the people you do business with field, click Add More, and then re-enter the customer. Continue to the enter opening balances page and enter the correct balance and the correct date as previously illustrated.

Vendor Center

Reviewing the Vendor Center allows you to see the items set up as part of the QuickBooks Setup.

To review the Vendor Center—
1. Click Vendors, then click *Vendor Center*. The Vendor Center appears. (See figure 6–W.)

FIGURE 6–W
Vendor Center Window

2. Choose *Ace Glass Works Company* by double-clicking. The Edit Vendor window appears. (See figure 6–X.)

FIGURE 6–X
Edit Vendor Window

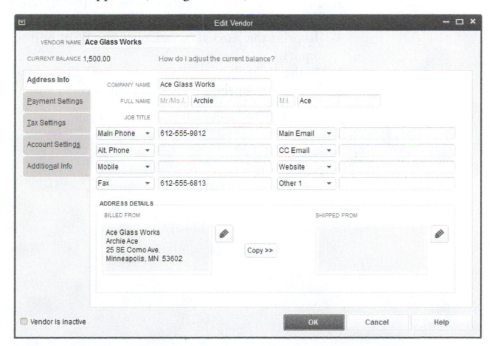

QuickBooks created this vendor based on the information entered in QuickBooks Setup – Add the people you do business with pages. If you entered an opening balance, the balance is displayed in the CURRENT BALANCE field. If you did not enter an opening balance, the CURRENT BALANCE field indicates a zero. You can correct all information in the Edit Vendor window, except the CURRENT BALANCE.

3. Close the Edit Vendor window and the Vendor Center window.

Errors in the Vendor Center Window

If there is an error in the company name, address, phone or fax numbers, or contact name for any of the vendors, you can correct it in the Edit Vendor window. If there is an error in the CURRENT BALANCE, you can correct it when viewing journal entries. If there is no CURRENT BALANCE for a vendor with an outstanding balance, delete the vendor, and then go back to the QuickBooks Setup – Add people you do business with pages.

To return to the QuickBooks Setup, click Help, and then click Quick Start Center. At the Quick Start Center window, click Return to Add Info. At the Add the people you do business with field, click Add More, and then re-enter the vendor. Continue to the enter opening balances page and enter the correct balance and the correct date as previously illustrated.

Journal Report

Reviewing the *Journal* report allows you to see the journal entries created as part of the QuickBooks Setup.

To view and print the *Journal* report—
1. Click Reports and then click *Accountant & Taxes*.
2. At the Accountant & Taxes submenu, click *Journal*. If the Collapsing and Expanding Transactions message appears, read the message, then place a check mark in the box to the left of Do not display this message in the future, and then click OK.
3. In the *From* and *To* fields, choose from *04/01/2014* to *04/01/2014* and then click the Refresh button on the top of the report.
4. To print the *Journal* report, click the Print button on the top of the report.
5. At the Print Reports dialog box, check the settings and then click Print. Your printout should look like figure 6–Y.

FIGURE 6–Y
Journal Report

CH6 [Your Name] Kristin Raina Interior Designs
Journal
April 1, 2014

Trans #	Type	Date	Num	Adj	Name	Memo	Account	Debit	Credit
1	Invoice	04/01/2014			Berger Bakery Company	Opening balance	Accounts Receivable	600.00	
					Berger Bakery Company	Opening balance	Uncategorized Income		600.00
								600.00	600.00
2	Invoice	04/01/2014			Franco Films Co.	Opening balance	Accounts Receivable	940.00	
					Franco Films Co.	Opening balance	Uncategorized Income		940.00
								940.00	940.00
3	Bill	04/01/2014			Ace Glass Works	Opening balance	Accounts Payable		1,500.00
					Ace Glass Works	Opening balance	Uncategorized Expenses	1,500.00	
								1,500.00	1,500.00
4	Bill	04/01/2014			Bell Carpet Design	Opening balance	Accounts Payable		2,000.00
					Bell Carpet Design	Opening balance	Uncategorized Expenses	2,000.00	
								2,000.00	2,000.00
5	Bill	04/01/2014			Cuza and Carl Associates	Opening balance	Accounts Payable		400.00
					Cuza and Carl Associates	Opening balance	Uncategorized Expenses	400.00	
								400.00	400.00
6	Bill	04/01/2014			Galeway Computers	Opening balance	Accounts Payable		2,600.00
					Galeway Computers	Opening balance	Uncategorized Expenses	2,600.00	
								2,600.00	2,600.00
7	Bill	04/01/2014			Midwest Mutual Insurance Co.	Opening balance	Accounts Payable		2,400.00
					Midwest Mutual Insurance Co.	Opening balance	Uncategorized Expenses	2,400.00	
								2,400.00	2,400.00
8	Bill	04/01/2014			Minneapolis Electric & Gas Co.	Opening balance	Accounts Payable		450.00
					Minneapolis Electric & Gas Co.	Opening balance	Uncategorized Expenses	450.00	
								450.00	450.00
9	Bill	04/01/2014			Williams Office Supply Company	Opening balance	Accounts Payable		400.00
					Williams Office Supply Company	Opening balance	Uncategorized Expenses	400.00	
								400.00	400.00
10	Inventory Adjust	04/01/2014				Carpets Opening balance	Opening Balance Equity		800.00
						Carpets Opening balance	Inventory Asset	800.00	
								800.00	800.00
11	Inventory Adjust	04/01/2014				Draperies Opening balance	Opening Balance Equity		1,000.00
						Draperies Opening balance	Inventory Asset	1,000.00	
								1,000.00	1,000.00
12	Inventory Adjust	04/01/2014				Lamps Opening balance	Opening Balance Equity		1,000.00
						Lamps Opening balance	Inventory Asset	1,000.00	
								1,000.00	1,000.00
13	Inventory Adjust	04/01/2014				Mirrors Opening balance	Opening Balance Equity		900.00
						Mirrors Opening balance	Inventory Asset	900.00	
								900.00	900.00
TOTAL								14,990.00	14,990.00

HINT

There should be 13 journal entries. If all the journal entries do not appear in the Journal Report, change the dates of the report from 01/01/2014 – 04/01/2014. The date on each journal entry should be 04/01/2014. If the date, or the amount, on a journal entry is incorrect, double-click the journal entry. At the window you drill-down to, change the date to 04/01/2014, correct the amount if necessary, and then click Save & Close. Click Yes at the warning.

HINT

If the Future Transactions message appears, click Yes. To change this preference, click Edit on the main menu bar, then click *Preferences*. Along the left, click the Accounting icon. Choose the Company Preferences tab. Remove the check marks in the DATE WARNINGS field, and then click OK.

HINT

If the Report needs to be refreshed message appears, place a check mark in the box to the left of Do not ask again (apply to all reports and graphs), and then click Yes.

As you added customers, vendors, and inventory part items on the appropriate page in QuickBooks Setup, behind the scenes QuickBooks recorded the information in general journal format and updated the appropriate balances.

In the Journal report, QuickBooks recorded 13 journal entries based on information recorded in the QuickBooks Setup. The journal entries can be categorized as follows:

a. The two journal entries labeled as Invoice were created when customers with balances were recorded in the Add people you do business with pages. QuickBooks debits the Accounts Receivable with the customers outstanding balances and credits an account called Uncategorized Income.

b. The seven journal entries labeled as Bill were created when vendors with outstanding balances were recorded in the Add people you do business with pages. QuickBooks credits the Accounts Payable with the vendors outstanding balances and debits an account called Uncategorized Expenses.

c. The four journal entries labeled as Inventory Adjust were created when the inventory part items with balances were recorded in the Add new products and services page. QuickBooks debits the Inventory Asset account with the total value for each inventory part item and credits the Opening Balance Equity account.

6. Close the *Journal* report. If you receive a message to Memorize Report, place a check mark to the left of *Do not display this message in the future* and then click No.

Errors in the Journal Report

HINT

QuickBooks created the Opening Balance Equity, Owners Draw, and Owners Equity accounts.

If you determine an error in the Journal report, you can drill down to the original source, as seen in prior chapters. The original source you drill down to is based on the transaction type. The transaction type is the same as seen in prior chapters.

For a transaction type of Invoice, if you double-click that transaction, you will be drilled down to the Create Invoices window. You can make corrections to a customer's opening balance or date in this window.

For a transaction type of Bill, if you double-click that transaction, you will be drilled down to the Enter Bills window. You can make corrections to a vendor's opening balance or date in this window.

For a transaction type of Inventory Adjust, if you double-click that transaction, you will be drilled down to the Adjust Quantity/Value on Hand window. You can make corrections to an inventory part quantity on hand or date in this window. The value of the inventory part item is automatically computed by QuickBooks as the quantity on hand multiplied by the cost for the inventory part. If you change the quantity on hand in the Adjust Quantity/ Value on Hand window but the value does not change to the correct amount, go to the Item List and edit the inventory part item and make sure the cost is the correct amount.

Trial Balance

Reviewing the Trial Balance will allow you to see the balances in the accounts you created as part of the QuickBooks Setup.

To view the Trial Balance—
1. Click Reports and then click *Accountant & Taxes*.
2. At the Accountant & Taxes submenu, click *Trial Balance*.
3. In the *From* and *To* fields, choose from *04/01/2014* to *04/01/2014* and then click the Refresh button on the top of the report. (See figure 6–Z.)

FIGURE 6–Z
Trial Balance
April 1, 2014
(after EasyStep Interview and QuickBooks Setup)

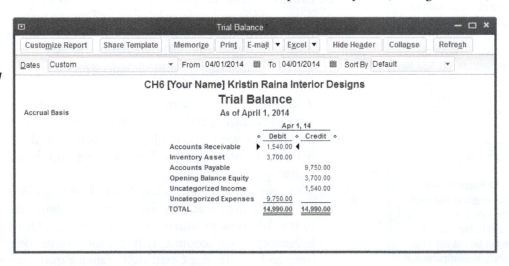

A review of the trial balance indicates the following:
a. The amount in the Accounts Receivable account equals the amount in the Uncategorized Income account.

b. The amount in the Inventory Asset account equals the amount in the Opening Balance Equity account.

c. The amount in the Accounts Payable account equals the amount in the Uncategorized Expenses account.

4. Close the report.

Figure 6–AA shows the Trial Balance from EX5 [*Your Name*] Kristin Raina Interior Designs. It reflects the activities of January 1 to March 31, 2014, which were recorded in chapters 2 through 5. Compare the trial balance of April 1, 2014 (figure 6–Z) with the trial balance of March 31, 2014 (figure 6–AA).

FIGURE 6–AA
Trial Balance
March 31, 2014
(from Chapter 5)

EX5 [Your Name] Kristin Raina Interior Designs
Trial Balance
As of March 31, 2014

	Mar 31, 14	
	Debit	Credit
1010 · Cash - Operating	50,855.38	
1200 · Accounts Receivable	1,540.00	
1250 · Undeposited Funds	0.00	
1260 · Inventory of Carpets	800.00	
1265 · Inventory of Draperies	1,000.00	
1270 · Inventory of Lamps	1,000.00	
1275 · Inventory of Mirrors	900.00	
1300 · Design Supplies	200.00	
1305 · Office Supplies	250.00	
1410 · Prepaid Advertising	500.00	
1420 · Prepaid Insurance	2,200.00	
1700 · Furniture:1725 · Furniture, Cost	12,000.00	
1700 · Furniture:1750 · Accum. Dep., Furniture		100.00
1800 · Computers:1825 · Computers, Cost	3,600.00	
1800 · Computers:1850 · Accum. Dep., Computers		60.00
2010 · Accounts Payable		9,750.00
2020 · Notes Payable		7,000.00
2030 · Interest Payable		50.00
2200 · Sales Tax Payable	0.00	
3010 · Kristin Raina, Capital		50,000.00
3020 · Kristin Raina, Drawings	400.00	
4010 · Design Services		4,980.00
4020 · Decorating Services		3,400.00
4060 · Sale of Carpets		2,400.00
4065 · Sale of Draperies		1,000.00
4070 · Sale of Lamps		1,200.00
4075 · Sale of Mirrors		900.00
4100 · Sales Discounts	84.62	
5060 · Cost of Carpets Sold	1,200.00	
5065 · Cost of Draperies Sold	500.00	
5070 · Cost of Lamps Sold	600.00	
5075 · Cost of Mirrors Sold	450.00	
5900 · Inventory Adjustment	150.00	
6020 · Accounting Expense	300.00	
6050 · Advertising Expense	100.00	
6175 · Deprec. Exp., Furniture	100.00	
6185 · Deprec. Exp., Computers	60.00	
6200 · Insurance Expense	200.00	
6300 · Janitorial Expenses	125.00	
6325 · Office Supplies Expense	150.00	
6400 · Rent Expense	800.00	
6450 · Telephone Expense	275.00	
6500 · Utilities Expense	450.00	
7000 · Interest Expense	50.00	
TOTAL	**80,840.00**	**80,840.00**

Although EasyStep Interview and QuickBooks Setup guide you in creating a new company file, it does not enter all the information for a company. Upon completion of the next parts of New Company Setup—customizing and updating the new company file, and preparing for the accrual basis of accounting—the trial balance of April 1 will be the same as the trial balance of March 31.

Profit & Loss Standard (Income Statement) Report

Reviewing the Profit & Loss Standard report will allow you to see the balances created as part of the QuickBooks Setup that flow into the Profit & Loss Standard report.

To view the *Profit & Loss Standard* report—
1. Click Reports and then click *Company & Financial.*
2. At the Company & Financial submenu, click *Profit & Loss Standard.*
3. In the *From* and *To* fields, choose *from 01/01/2014 to 04/01/2014* and then click the Refresh button on the top of the report. (See figure 6–BB.)

FIGURE 6–BB
Profit & Loss Standard Report

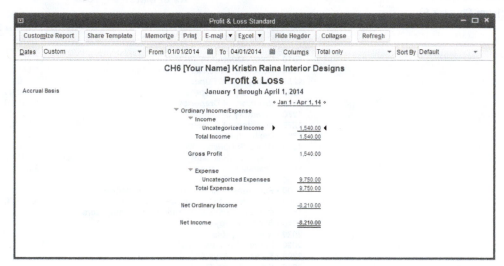

The *Profit & Loss Standard* report indicates only Uncategorized Income and Uncategorized Expenses. These amounts are offsetting amounts of the Accounts Receivable and Accounts Payable accounts. This is not a proper representation of the income and expenses of this company.

4. Close the report.

Balance Sheet Standard Report

Reviewing the Balance Sheet Standard Report will allow you to see the balances created as part of the QuickBooks Setup that flow into the Balance Sheet Standard Report.

To display the *Balance Sheet Standard* report—
1. Click Reports and then click *Company & Financial.*
2. At the Company & Financial submenu, click *Balance Sheet Standard.*
3. In the *As of* field, choose *04/01/2014* and then click the Refresh button at the top of the report. (See figure 6–CC.)

FIGURE 6-CC

Balance Sheet Standard Report

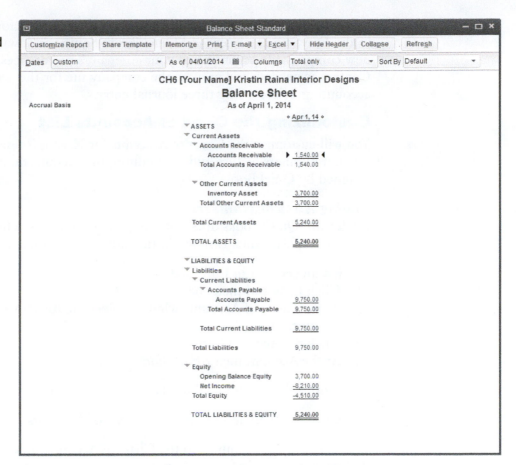

A review of the balance sheet indicates the following:

a. The only assets recorded so far are Accounts Receivable and Inventory Asset.

b. The only liabilities recorded so far are the Accounts Payable.

c. The balance in the Opening Balance Equity account is the amount in Inventory Asset.

d. The net income is incorrect as seen in the Income Statement (Profit and Loss Report) because of incomplete information.

4. Close the report.

NEW COMPANY SETUP:

Customizing the New Company File

When you use the EasyStep Interview and QuickBooks Setup windows only part of the New Company Setup is completed. The EasyStep Interview window is used to create the new company file, enable or disable some preferences, record a sales tax item, which begins the Item List, and begin the setup of the Chart of Accounts List. When you enter information in the QuickBooks Setup window, you create the Customer Center, the Vendor Center, and update the Item List to include service items and inventory part items. At the same time, the information entered in the QuickBooks Setup window records opening balances for Accounts Receivable, Accounts Payable, and Inventory Asset.

The next part of the process is to continue with the information set up in the EasyStep Interview and QuickBooks Setup windows to customize the new company file according to your company's preferences, update the Lists/Centers as needed, and prepare the company file for the accrual basis of accounting by recording three journal entries.

Customizing the Chart of Accounts List

You will customize the Chart of Accounts for Kristin Raina by enabling the account numbers feature and then editing the account numbers and names assigned by QuickBooks.

Adding Account Numbers

By default, QuickBooks does not use account numbers. This can be seen in the Chart of Accounts List and in the individual accounts.

To view an account in Edit mode—
1. Click Lists and then click *Chart of Accounts*.
2. At the Chart of Accounts window, select the Accounts Receivable account.
3. Click the Account button.
4. At the Account menu, click *Edit Account*.

   Notice there is no field to place an account number.

5. Close the Edit account and the Chart of Accounts List windows.

   To add account numbers to the Chart of Accounts List, you must activate the account numbers feature in the Preferences window.

To activate the account numbers feature—
1. Click Edit and then click *Preferences*. The Preferences window appears.

   Along the left side of the window are 23 icons that represent the different categories of features. For each category, there is a My Preferences tab and a Company Preferences tab. The Company Preferences tab is used for most customizations when setting up a new company file. The My Preferences tab records the preferences for each user. When using the EasyStep Interview window, most preferences are established based on the responses to the questions in the EasyStep Interview.

2. Along the left frame of the Preferences window, click the *Accounting* icon.
3. Click the Company Preferences tab.
4. At the *ACCOUNTS* field, place a check mark in the box to the left of *Use account numbers* to turn on the account numbers feature. (See figure 6–DD.)

FIGURE 6-DD

Preferences Window—
Accounting—Company
Preferences Tab

Use account
numbers

DATE
WARNINGS

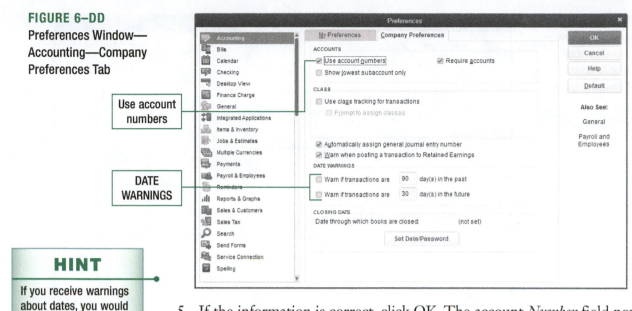

5. If the information is correct, click OK. The account *Number* field now appears in the New Account and Edit Account windows in the Chart of Accounts List.

Editing Account Numbers and Names

When you activate the account numbers feature, QuickBooks assigns account numbers to most accounts. You can change or delete these numbers.

To edit the account numbers and names—

1. Click Lists and then click *Chart of Accounts*.
2. At the Chart of Accounts window, select the Furniture and Equipment account.
3. Click the Account button.
4. At the Account menu, click *Edit Account*. Notice a number field has now been added.
5. In the *Number* field, key **1700** and in the Account Name field delete **and Equipment**. (See figure 6–EE.)

6. If the information is correct, click Save & Close.
7. Edit each of the accounts created by QuickBooks, changing the account numbers and names as listed below. If an edited name is not listed, keep the name assigned by QuickBooks.

	QuickBooks		Edited	
Number	Account Name	Number	Account Name	
17000	Accumulated Depreciation	1750	Accum. Dep., Furniture [Subaccount of 1700 Furniture]	
30800	Owners Draw	3020	Kristin Raina, Drawings	
	Sales Income	4060	Sale of Carpets	
48300	Sales Discounts	4100		
60000	Advertising and Promotion	6050	Advertising Expense	
62400	Depreciation Expense	6175	Deprec. Exp., Furniture	
63300	Insurance Expense	6200		
63400	Interest Expense	7000	[Type: Other Expense]	
63500	Janitorial Expense	6300		
64900	Office Supplies	6325	Office Supplies Expense	
67100	Rent Expense	6400		
68100	Telephone Expense	6450		
68600	Utilities	6500	Utilities Expense	
80000	Ask My Accountant	6020	Accounting Expense [Type: Expense]	

8. Close the Chart of Accounts List.

Deleting an Account

As part of the EasyStep Interview and QuickBooks Setup, QuickBooks created two sales accounts: Sales Income and 47900 Sales. The Sales Income account was not assigned an account number by QuickBooks but was the revenue account QuickBooks used in the Item List whenever an income account was needed. This account now has the number 4060 and the name has been changed to Sale of Carpets. Kristin Raina does not need the 47900 Sales account and will delete it.

To delete an account—
1. Click Lists and then click *Chart of Accounts*.
2. At the Chart of Accounts window, select the 47900 Sales account.
3. Click the Account button.
4. At the Account menu, click *Delete Account*.
5. At the Delete Account warning, click OK. The account is now deleted from the Chart of Accounts.

The customized Chart of Accounts List appears in figure 6–FF.

FIGURE 6–FF
Chart of Accounts List—
Customized with Account
Numbers and Names

6. Close the Chart of Accounts List.

Customizing System Default Accounts

As you saw in prior chapters, QuickBooks establishes default accounts and uses those accounts when recording transactions in the Activities windows. QuickBooks looks for these accounts in the Chart of Accounts List; if it cannot find an account, it creates one. Some system default accounts you have learned so far are Accounts Receivable, Undeposited Funds, Accounts Payable, Sales Tax Payable, Inventory Asset, and Cost of Goods Sold. Other system default accounts include the equity accounts (capital and accumulated earnings).

When you created the company file using EasyStep Interview and QuickBooks Setup, QuickBooks created some of the system default accounts (Accounts Receivable, Accounts Payable, Sales Tax Payable, and the equity accounts) as part of the Chart of Accounts, as seen in figure 6–P. You will customize the system default accounts that were created as part of the EasyStep Interview (Sales Tax Payable and the equity accounts) and QuickBooks Setup (Accounts Receivable and Accounts Payable), by editing the account names and numbers to follow the company's pattern for naming and numbering accounts on the Chart of Accounts List. Then you will learn how to force QuickBooks to create additional system default accounts that were not created as part of EasyStep Interview or QuickBooks Setup (undeposited funds, inventory asset, and cost of goods sold). After QuickBooks creates the additional system default accounts, you will then customize these account names and numbers.

Customizing System Default Accounts Created in a New Company File

When you created the company and indicated it was a sole proprietorship, QuickBooks automatically created three equity accounts: Opening Balance Equity, Owners Draw, and Owners Equity. When you activated the sales tax feature, QuickBooks created a Sales Tax Payable account. When you added customers in QuickBooks Setup, QuickBooks created the Accounts Receivable account. When you added vendors in QuickBooks Setup, QuickBooks created the Accounts Payable account. When you added inventory parts in QuickBooks Setup, QuickBooks created the Inventory Asset and Cost of Goods Sold accounts. The numbers and names for each of these accounts can be edited. The Opening Balance Equity account will be renamed as Kristin Raina, Capital, and the Owners Draw account was already renamed Kristin Raina, Drawings. QuickBooks uses the Opening Balance Equity account as an offsetting account when certain opening balances are entered in the accounts. The Owners Equity account is created for the purpose of capturing net income at the end of the fiscal year. In chapter 12, you will see how QuickBooks uses the Owner's Equity account in a company file. This account will be renamed as Accumulated Earnings. As we will soon see, QuickBooks recognizes the Accounts Receivable, Accounts Payable, Sales Tax Payable, Kristin Raina, Capital (Opening Balance Equity), and Accumulated Earnings (Owners Equity) accounts as system default accounts, but QuickBooks does not recognize the Inventory Asset and Cost of Goods Sold accounts as system default accounts. QuickBooks usually identifies a system default account by graying, or dimming, the account type. As you edit each of these accounts, notice that the account type is dimmed.

To edit system default account numbers and account names—
1. Click Lists and then click *Chart of Accounts*.
2. At the Chart of Accounts window, select *30000 Opening Balance Equity*.
3. Click the Account button.
4. At the Account menu, click *Edit Account*.
5. In the *Number* field, delete 30000 and key **3010**.
6. In the *Account Name* field, delete Opening Balance Equity, and key **Kristin Raina, Capital**. (See figure 6–GG.)

FIGURE 6–GG
Edit Account Window—
System Default Account

Account Type
Dimmed

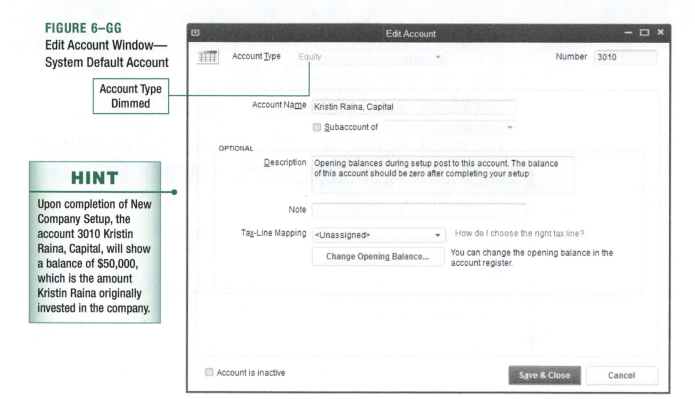

HINT

Upon completion of New Company Setup, the account 3010 Kristin Raina, Capital, will show a balance of $50,000, which is the amount Kristin Raina originally invested in the company.

7. If the information is correct, click Save & Close.
8. Edit the other system default accounts created by EasyStep Interview and QuickBooks Setup as follows:

QuickBooks		Edited	
Number	Account Name	Number	Account Name
11000	Accounts Receivable	1200	
20000	Accounts Payable	2010	
25500	Sales Tax Payable	2200	
32000	Owners Equity	3030	Accumulated Earnings

9. Close the Chart of Accounts List window.

Customizing System Default Accounts Created for Use in Activities Windows

Recall that in the Create Invoices window, the system default account is a debit to Accounts Receivable; in the Enter Bills window, the system default is a credit to Accounts Payable. When you chose an inventory item in any of the Activities windows, QuickBooks knew—from the Item List—which inventory asset account, cost of goods sold account, and sale of inventory account was the system default account to use for properly recording the transaction. You also know that you can create accounts in the Chart of Accounts List. However, sometimes QuickBooks does not find an account already created; you must let QuickBooks create the account for the software to identify it as a system default account.

To illustrate how QuickBooks creates its own system default accounts, you will first add an account to the Chart of Accounts List and then open some Activities windows and the Item List. You will see that QuickBooks cannot locate the account you created and some accounts created in QuickBooks

Setup, and creates its own accounts.

To add a new account—
1. Click Lists and then click *Chart of Accounts*.
2. At the Chart of Accounts window, click the Account button and then click *New*. The Add New Account: Choose Account Type window appears.
3. Click *Other Account Types*. The drop-down list appears. (See figure 6–HH.)

FIGURE 6–HH

Add New Account: Choose Account Type Window

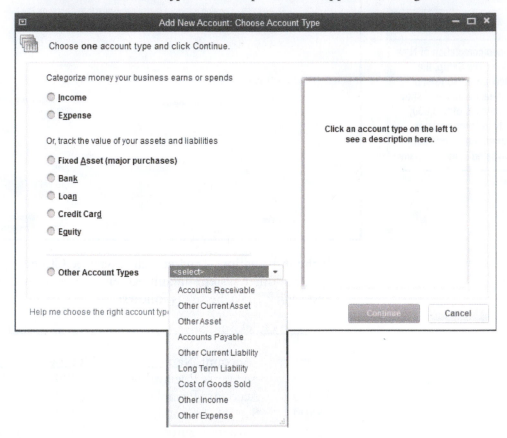

4. From the Other Account Types drop-down list, click *Other Current Asset*.
5. Click Continue. The Add New Account window appears.
6. In the *Number* field, key **1250**.
7. In the *Account Name* field, key **Undeposited Funds**. (See figure 6–II.)

FIGURE 6–II

Add New Account
Window—Completed

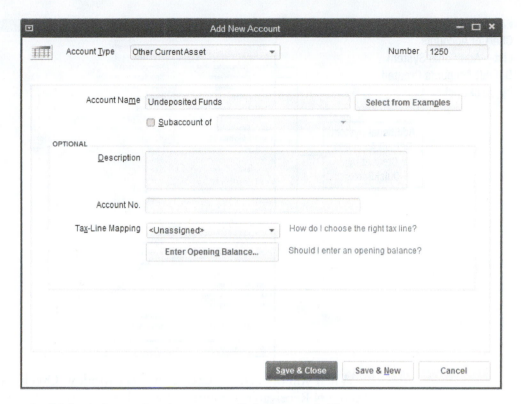

8. If the information is correct, click Save and Close.
9. Close the Chart of Accounts List window.

To allow QuickBooks to create system default accounts—

1. Click Customers and then click *Create Invoices*. Close the Create Invoices window.
2. Click Customers and then click *Enter Sales Receipts*. Close the Enter Sales Receipts window.
3. Click Vendors and then click *Enter Bills*. Close the window.
4. Click Lists and then click *Item List*.
5. At the Item List window, click the Item button.
6. At the Item menu, click *New*.
7. At the New Item window, in the *TYPE* field, click *Inventory Part*.
8. Close the New Item window. Close the Item List.

> **HINT**
>
> QuickBooks sometimes needs to create its own system default accounts. Opening and closing these windows forces QuickBooks to create system default accounts. After QuickBooks creates these accounts, you can then edit the account name and number.

As you opened each of these windows, QuickBooks looked for certain system default accounts; when they could not be identified, QuickBooks created new system default accounts. Review the Chart of Accounts List, and observe that QuickBooks created the following accounts as shown in figure 6–JJ:

12000	*Undeposited Funds
12100	*Inventory Asset
50000	*Cost of Goods Sold

Additional System
Default Accounts
Created by
QuickBooks

When you opened the Create Invoices window, QuickBooks looked for the Accounts Receivable account and was able to locate it because of the accounts receivable account type in that account. Similarly, when you opened the Enter Bills window, QuickBooks looked for the Accounts Payable account and was able to locate it because of the accounts payable account type.

But, when you opened the Enter Sales Receipts window, QuickBooks looked for an Undeposited Funds account; even though you created this account, QuickBooks could not locate it and created the new account 12000 *Undeposited Funds. Likewise, when you chose the new inventory part type in the Item List, QuickBooks looked for an inventory asset account and cost of goods sold account. Even though an Inventory Asset account and Cost of Goods Sold account were created when you entered inventory part items in the QuickBooks Setup window, QuickBooks did not identify these accounts as system default accounts and therefore did not locate them and created a new account 12100 *Inventory Asset account and a new account 50000 *Cost of Goods Sold. In some situations—such as these—you must allow QuickBooks to create its own accounts, then you can edit them to your liking. In all cases, accounts created by QuickBooks will have dimmed account types; you will not be able to change the account type, but you can change the account numbers and account names.

Before you can edit the accounts that QuickBooks created, delete the 1250 Undeposited Funds account you created. This account name and number can then be used when editing the accounts created by QuickBooks.

To delete an account—
1. Click Lists and then click *Chart of Accounts*.
2. At the Chart of Accounts window, select *1250 Undeposited Funds*.
3. Click the Account button and then click *Delete Account*.
4. At the warning, click OK.

At this time, you cannot delete the Inventory Asset account and Cost of Goods Sold account (the accounts without numbers) created in QuickBooks Setup because they are used in the Item List and in the Journal report. In the upcoming section on Updating the Item List with the updated Chart of Accounts, you will be able to then delete these two accounts.

Now edit the accounts created by QuickBooks, noting that for each of these accounts created by QuickBooks, the account type is dimmed:

	QuickBooks		Edited
Number	Account Name	Number	Account Name
12000	*Undeposited Funds	1250	Undeposited Funds
12100	*Inventory Asset	1260	Inventory of Carpets
50000	*Cost of Goods Sold	5060	Cost of Carpets Sold

After QuickBooks creates an inventory account and a cost of goods sold account, you can create as many additional inventory and cost of goods sold accounts as desired. This will be done in the upcoming section, Updating the Chart of Accounts List.

6. Close the Chart of Accounts List.

Customizing Payment Terms

In QuickBooks a list with payment terms is accessed in customer files, vendor files, and activities windows when needed. As seen in prior chapters, payment terms such as Net 30 Days, 2/10 Net 30 Days, and so on can be identified in both the customer and vendor files if they relate to a particular customer or vendor.

When you create a new company file, QuickBooks automatically creates a list of payment terms. As with all other Lists in QuickBooks, you can add, delete, or edit the Terms List to customize it for your company.

To add a payment term—
1. Click Lists and then click *Customer & Vendor Profile Lists*.
2. At the Customer & Vendor Profile Lists submenu, click *Terms List*.

The Terms List window appears with the terms of payment that were created by QuickBooks. (See figure 6–KK.)

FIGURE 6–KK
Terms List Created by QuickBooks

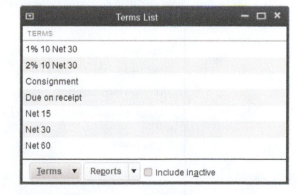

3. At the Terms List window, click the Terms button.
4. At the Terms menu, click *New*. The New Terms window appears.
5. In the *Terms* field, key **Net 10 Days**.
6. In the *Net due in days* field, key **10**. (See figure 6–LL.)

FIGURE 6–LL

New Terms Window—
Net 10 Days—Completed

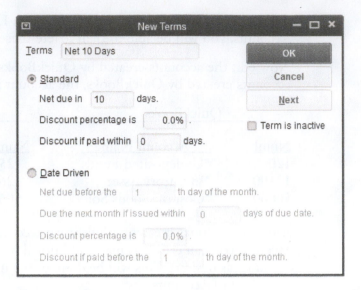

7. If the information is correct, click OK.

To delete a payment term—
1. At the Terms List, select *1% 10 Net 30,* but do not open it.
2. Click the Terms menu button. At the Terms menu, click *Delete Terms.*
3. A warning screen will appear. Click OK. The payment terms will be deleted.
4. Delete the following terms of payment:

Consignment
Due on Receipt
Net 60

To edit a payment term—
1. At the Terms List, double-click *2% 10 Net 30* terms to open the Edit Terms window.
2. At the *Terms* field, change the name to **2/10, Net 30 Days**. (See figure 6–MM.)

FIGURE 6–MM

Edit Terms Window—
2/10, Net 30 Days—
Completed

3. If the information is correct, click OK.
4. Edit the following terms of payment:

   Net 15 to **Net 15 Days**
   Net 30 to **Net 30 Days**

   The updated Terms List appears in figure 6–NN.

FIGURE 6–NN
Terms List—Customized

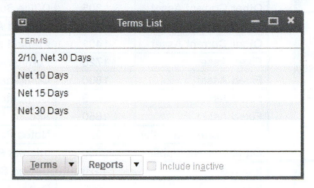

5. Close the Terms List window.

LISTS/CENTERS: ── ○ **Updating Lists/Centers**

In the EasyStep Interview and QuickBooks Setup windows, QuickBooks created the Chart of Accounts List, which has now been customized for Kristin Raina Interior Designs. But our sample company uses many more accounts that must be added to the Chart of Accounts List. Also, as part of EasyStep Interview and QuickBooks Setup, the Item List was created, but requires some modifications.

The QuickBooks Setup created the Customer Center and the Vendor Center, which may also require some modifications. So the next part of customizing the company file is to update the Chart of Accounts and Item Lists as well as the Customer and Vendor Centers.

Updating the Chart of Accounts List

As just noted, QuickBooks has already created some accounts in the new company file. However, many additional accounts must be added to the Chart of Accounts List for Kristin Raina Interior Designs. Most of these accounts have opening balances. These opening balances will be entered later by general journal entry.

Using the information in table 6–4, key in all remaining accounts. The updated Chart of Accounts List appears in figure 6–OO.

TABLE 6–4

Chart of Accounts List

Account Type	Number	Account Name
Bank	1010	Cash - Operating
Other Current Asset	1265	Inventory of Draperies
Other Current Asset	1270	Inventory of Lamps
Other Current Asset	1275	Inventory of Mirrors
Other Current Asset	1300	Design Supplies
Other Current Asset	1305	Office Supplies
Other Current Asset	1410	Prepaid Advertising
Other Current Asset	1420	Prepaid Insurance
Fixed Asset	1725	Furniture, Cost [Subaccount of 1700]
Fixed Asset	1800	Computers
Fixed Asset	1825	Computers, Cost [Subaccount of 1800]
Fixed Asset	1850	Accum. Dep., Computers [Subaccount of 1800]
Other Current Liability	2020	Notes Payable
Other Current Liability	2030	Interest Payable
Income	4010	Design Services
Income	4020	Decorating Services
Income	4065	Sale of Draperies
Income	4070	Sale of Lamps
Income	4075	Sale of Mirrors
Cost of Goods Sold	5065	Cost of Draperies Sold
Cost of Goods Sold	5070	Cost of Lamps Sold
Cost of Goods Sold	5075	Cost of Mirrors Sold
Cost of Goods Sold	5900	Inventory Adjustment
Expense	6185	Deprec. Exp., Computers

HINT

In the *Account Type* field, instead of looking for the type in the drop-down list, press the first letter of the type.

HINT

If a message appears stating the account number is being used, click Cancel. You recorded an account incorrectly; review the Chart of Accounts List to locate your error and edit the account to correct it.

FIGURE 6–00

Chart of Accounts List—Updated

HINT

If you incorrectly labeled an account as a parent or subaccount, you can edit the account or you can move the entry. To move the entry, click the diamond to the left of the account number. If you drag the diamond to the left, a subaccount will become a parent account. If you drag the diamond to the right, a parent account will become a subaccount. You can also click and drag up or down to reorganize the list.

Updating the Item List

In QuickBooks, the Item List stores information about the service items, the inventory part items, and the sales tax. As transactions are recorded in the Activities windows, QuickBooks uses information in the Item List to record the transaction in the correct accounts.

Open and review the Item List. In EasyStep Interview when responding yes to the question if sales tax is used, QuickBooks created a sales tax item. In QuickBooks Setup, service and inventory part items were added on the Add products and services you sell pages. As this information was entered in EasyStep Interview and QuickBooks Setup windows, QuickBooks recorded the information in the Item List. Earlier in the chapter, you reviewed the Item List (figure 6–Q) and saw that for service items and inventory part items (figure 6–R and figure 6–S), QuickBooks used the same Sales Income account as the income account for each item. In addition, for each inventory part item (figure 6–S) QuickBooks used the same Cost of Goods Sold account and Inventory Asset account. When customizing the system default accounts, some of the account names and numbers were changed. Sales Income was changed to 4060 Sale of Carpets, 12100 Inventory Asset was changed to 1260 Inventory of Carpets, and 50000 Cost of Goods Sold was changed to 5060 Cost of Carpets Sold. In addition, when updating the Chart of Accounts List, you added additional inventory accounts, income accounts, and cost of goods sold accounts. When you changed the account names and numbers of the system default accounts, these changes flowed into the Item List. You will now edit the service items and inventory part items to reflect the accounts used by Kristin Raina Interior Designs.

When you entered the service items and inventory part items in the QuickBooks Setup window, it did not allow for you to indicate if the item was taxable or non-taxable. For inventory part items, the QuickBooks Setup window did not include a column for the reorder point. When you edit the service and inventory part items for the correct accounts, you will also indicate if the item is taxable or non-taxable, and for inventory part items, you will also record the reorder point. In addition, the sales tax item (figure 6–T) does not have the necessary information for Kristin Raina Interior Designs sales tax and must be edited.

To edit a service item—
1. Click Lists and then click *Item List*.
2. At the Item List window, choose the Decorating Services item by double-clicking. The Edit Item window appears.
3. In the Tax Code field, click *Non Non-Taxable Sales*.
4. In the Account field, click 4020 Decorating Services. (See figure 6–PP).

FIGURE 6–PP

Edit Item Window—
Service—Completed

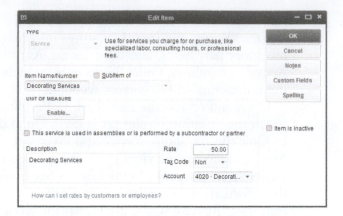

5. If the information is correct, click OK. At the warning, click Yes.
6. Choose the *Design Services* service item by double-clicking.
7. In the Tax Code field, click *Non Non-Taxable*, and in the account field, click *4010 Design Services*.
8. Click OK, and then at the warning click Yes.

To edit an inventory part item—
1. Choose the *Carpets* inventory part item by double-clicking. The Edit Item window appears.
2. In the COGS Account field, click *5060 Cost of Carpets Sold*.
3. In the Tax Code field, click *Tax Taxable Sales*.
4. In the Income Account field, *4060 Sale of Carpets* should appear.
5. In the Asset Account field, click *1260 Inventory of Carpets*.
6. In the Reorder Point filed, key **5**. (See figure 6–QQ.)

FIGURE 6–QQ

Edit Item Window—
Inventory Part—
Completed

7. If the information is correct, click OK. At the warning, click Yes.
8. Using the information in table 6–5, update the remainder of the inventory part items. All inventory part items are taxable, and the reorder point is 5.

TABLE 6–5

Update Inventory
Part Items

Inventory Part Item	COGS Account	Income Account	Asset Account
Draperies	5065	4065	1265
Lamps	5070	4070	1270
Mirrors	5075	4075	1275

After completing the updating of the accounts for the inventory part items, the Inventory Asset account and Cost of Goods Sold account (the accounts without numbers) can be deleted from the Chart of Accounts List.

To edit the sales tax item—
1. Double-click the Sales Tax item. The Edit Item window appears.
2. In the *Sales Tax Name* field, delete Out of State and key **Minn. Sales Tax**.
3. At the *Description* field, delete the description and key **Sales Tax**.
4. In the *Tax Rate (%)* field, key **7**.
5. At the Tax Agency drop-down list, click Minn. Dept. of Revenue. The Edit Item window is complete. (See figure 6–RR.)

FIGURE 6–RR
Edit Item Window—Sales Tax Item—Completed

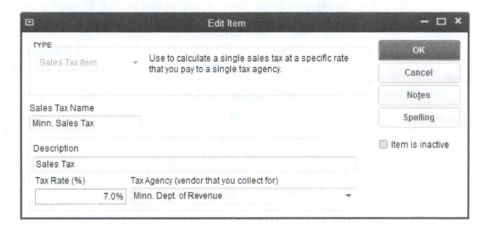

6. If the information is correct, click OK.

The updated Item List appears in figure 6–SS. Compare to figure 6–Q.

FIGURE 6–SS
Item List—Updated

7. Close the Item List window.

Accounting concept

1260 Inventory of Carpets		1265 Inventory of Draperies		1270 Inventory of Lamps		1275 Inventory of Mirrors		3010 Kristin Raina, Capital	
Dr	Cr	Dr	Cr	Dr	Cr	Dr	Cr	Dr	Cr
800		1,000		1,000		900			800
									1,000
									1,000
									900

Updating the Customer Center and Vendor Center

The Customer Center and Vendor Center were created when information was entered in the QuickBooks Setup window – Add the people you do business with pages. You reviewed them when the QuickBooks Setup was complete. (See figures 6–U and 6–W.) At this time if you want to include additional information in the Customer Center or Vendor Center that was not included in the QuickBooks Setup, such as terms of payment, email addresses, account numbers, and so on, you could edit each customer and vendor to add the additional information.

Adjusting for the Accrual Basis of Accounting

You have now created, customized, and updated the Lists and Centers in the new company file. The final part is to enter the remaining opening balances and prepare the company file for the **accrual basis of accounting**.

Accrual Basis of Accounting versus Cash Basis of Accounting

accrual basis of accounting An accounting method that requires the recording of revenue when it is earned and the recording of expenses when they are incurred regardless of cash receipts or cash payments.

You may have noticed in many of the reports that the label *accrual basis* was in the upper left-hand corner of the report. In QuickBooks, by default, the accounting reports and financial statements are prepared using the accrual basis of accounting, which records revenue when earned and expenses when incurred regardless of cash receipts and cash payments. The accrual basis of accounting follows GAAP – generally accepted accounting principles—and is the basis used in this text.

cash basis of accounting An accounting method that records revenue when cash is received for services provided or for a product sold, and records expenses only when payments have been made.

An alternative basis is called the **cash basis of accounting**, which records revenue only when the cash has been received for services provided or for a product sold, and records expenses only when cash payments have been made. QuickBooks allows you to switch individual reports from the accrual basis of accounting to the cash basis.

To view a report using the cash basis of accounting, open the report and click the Customize Report button. Then on the Display tab, choose REPORT BASIS – Cash, and click OK. The report is converted to reflect the cash basis of accounting. The accounts that are typically affected are Accounts Receivable, Accounts Payable, revenues, and expenses.

The default for all reports can be changed to the cash basis of accounting in the Preferences window. To change the default, click Edit, then click Preferences. Choose the Reports & Graphs icon and the Company Preferences tab. The SUMMARY REPORTS BASIS field is where the default can be changed to the cash basis.

Completing New Company Setup Using the Accrual Basis of Accounting

Recall that you entered the opening balances for the Accounts Receivable, Accounts Payable, and Inventory accounts when you entered the information in the QuickBooks Setup window. When you added new accounts to the Chart of Accounts list, you also could have entered the opening balances for assets (excluding Accounts Receivable), liabilities (excluding Accounts Payable), and equity accounts at that time. But you cannot enter opening balances for some system default accounts (such as Accounts Receivable, Accounts Payable, and Sales Tax Payable) and you cannot enter opening balances for revenue and expense accounts when creating new accounts in the Chart of Accounts List. Therefore, all opening balances (excluding inventory, accounts receivable, and accounts payable) will be entered in one journal entry.

As you saw in the *Journal* report (figure 6–Y), every time an Accounts Receivable account was recorded, a corresponding Uncategorized Income account was recorded; every time an Accounts Payable account was recorded, a corresponding Uncategorized Expenses account was recorded. The Uncategorized Income and Uncategorized Expenses accounts are not used in the accrual basis of accounting and therefore must be reversed to eliminate them. You do this by using **reversing entries**.

To complete New Company Setup using the accrual basis of accounting, you will prepare three journal entries: entering opening balances, reversing uncategorized income account, and reversing uncategorized expenses account.

reversing entries
Entries recorded in the general journal to offset a balance in an account.

Entering Opening Balances

You will enter all opening balances for Kristin Raina Interior Designs, excluding inventory, accounts receivable, and accounts payable, as one large compound journal entry.

To enter opening balances in the Make General Journal Entries window—
1. Click Company and then click *Make General Journal Entries*. At the Assigning Numbers to Journal Entries message, place a check mark in the box to the left of *Do not display this message in the future*, and click OK. The Make General Journal Entries window appears.
2. At the *DATE* field, choose *04/01/2014*.
3. At the *ENTRY NO.* field, accept the default ENTRY NO. 1.
4. Remove the check mark from ADJUSTING ENTRY and click the Hide List icon to allow more space to record this large journal entry.
5. Enter the following accounts and amounts as debits:

Number	Account Name	Balance
1010	Cash - Operating	50,855.38
1300	Design Supplies	200.00
1305	Office Supplies	250.00
1410	Prepaid Advertising	500.00
1420	Prepaid Insurance	2,200.00
1725	Furniture, Cost	12,000.00
1825	Computers, Cost	3,600.00
3020	Kristin Raina, Drawings	400.00
4100	Sales Discounts	84.62
5060	Cost of Carpets Sold	1,200.00
5065	Cost of Draperies Sold	500.00
5070	Cost of Lamps Sold	600.00
5075	Cost of Mirrors Sold	450.00
5900	Inventory Adjustment	150.00
6020	Accounting Expense	300.00
6050	Advertising Expense	100.00
6175	Deprec. Exp., Furniture	100.00
6185	Deprec. Exp., Computers	60.00

HINT

Maximize the Make General Journal Entries window and click the Hide List icon before recording this journal entry so that you can see more of the entries.

HINT

You can key in the account number for each account or use the drop-down list.

continued

6200	Insurance Expense	200.00
6300	Janitorial Expense	125.00
6325	Office Supplies Expense	150.00
6400	Rent Expense	800.00
6450	Telephone Expense	275.00
6500	Utilities Expense	450.00
7000	Interest Expense	50.00

QuickCheck: $75,600.00

6. Enter the following accounts and amounts as credits:

Number	Account Name	Balance
1750	Accum. Dep., Furniture	100.00
1850	Accum. Dep., Computers	60.00
2020	Notes Payable	7,000.00
2030	Interest Payable	50.00
4010	Design Services	4,980.00
4020	Decorating Services	3,400.00
4060	Sale of Carpets	2,400.00
4065	Sale of Draperies	1,000.00
4070	Sale of Lamps	1,200.00
4075	Sale of Mirrors	900.00

QuickCheck: $54,510.00

7. Record the credit balance of $54,510.00 as a credit to account 3010
Kristin Raina, Capital. (See figure 6–TT.)

FIGURE 6–TT
Make General Journal
Entries Window—
Opening Balances

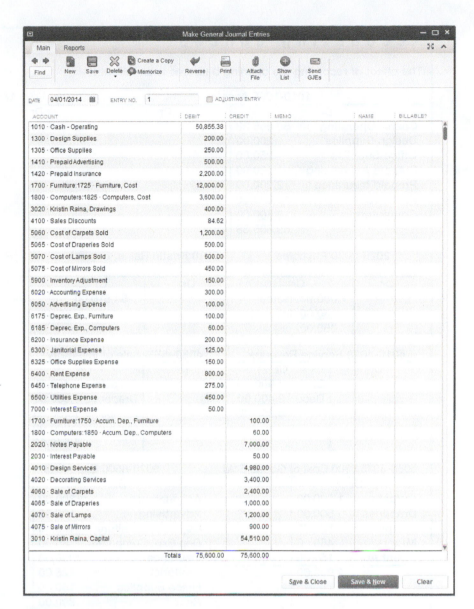

Figure: Make General Journal Entries window showing:

ACCOUNT	DEBIT	CREDIT
1010 · Cash - Operating	50,855.38	
1300 · Design Supplies	200.00	
1305 · Office Supplies	250.00	
1410 · Prepaid Advertising	500.00	
1420 · Prepaid Insurance	2,200.00	
1700 · Furniture:1725 · Furniture, Cost	12,000.00	
1800 · Computers:1825 · Computers, Cost	3,600.00	
3020 · Kristin Raina, Drawings	400.00	
4100 · Sales Discounts	84.62	
5060 · Cost of Carpets Sold	1,200.00	
5065 · Cost of Draperies Sold	500.00	
5070 · Cost of Lamps Sold	600.00	
5075 · Cost of Mirrors Sold	450.00	
5900 · Inventory Adjustment	150.00	
6020 · Accounting Expense	300.00	
6050 · Advertising Expense	100.00	
6175 · Deprec. Exp., Furniture	100.00	
6185 · Deprec. Exp., Computers	60.00	
6200 · Insurance Expense	200.00	
6300 · Janitorial Expense	125.00	
6325 · Office Supplies Expense	150.00	
6400 · Rent Expense	800.00	
6450 · Telephone Expense	275.00	
6500 · Utilities Expense	450.00	
7000 · Interest Expense	50.00	
1700 · Furniture:1750 · Accum. Dep., Furniture		100.00
1800 · Computers:1850 · Accum. Dep., Computers		60.00
2020 · Notes Payable		7,000.00
2030 · Interest Payable		50.00
4010 · Design Services		4,980.00
4020 · Decorating Services		3,400.00
4060 · Sale of Carpets		2,400.00
4065 · Sale of Draperies		1,000.00
4070 · Sale of Lamps		1,200.00
4075 · Sale of Mirrors		900.00
3010 · Kristin Raina, Capital		54,510.00
Totals	75,600.00	75,600.00

DATE 04/01/2014   ENTRY NO. 1   ADJUSTING ENTRY

HINT

If the Future Transactions
message appears, click
Yes. To change this
preference, click Edit
on the main menu bar,
then click *Preferences.*
Along the left, click
the Accounting icon.
Choose the Company
Preferences tab. Remove
the check marks in the
DATE WARNINGS field,
and then click OK.

8. If the information is correct, click Save & New. If a message appears about Tracking fixed assets, place a check mark in the box to the left of *Do not display this message in the future*, and click OK.

Reversing Uncategorized Income Account

Recall that in the *Journal* report of figure 6–Y, two journal entries are recorded that debit the Accounts Receivable and credit Uncategorized Income for two customers as follows:

Berger Bakery Company	$ 600
Franco Films Co.	940
	$1,540

The debit entries to the Accounts Receivable account are correct and will stay in that account. The credits to the Uncategorized Income account will be reversed by debiting Uncategorized Income for the total of $1,540 and crediting the account 3010 Kristin Raina, Capital (formerly the Opening Balance Equity account), for $1,540.

HINT

As part of customizing
the Chart of Accounts,
the account Opening
Balance Equity, created
by QuickBooks, was
changed to 3010 Kristin
Raina, Capital.

Accounting concept

The effect of recording the opening balances is as follows:

1010-1825 Assets

Dr		Cr
Cash - Operating	50,855.38	
Design Supplies	200.00	
Office Supplies	250.00	
Prepaid Advertising	500.00	
Prepaid Insurance	2,200.00	
Furniture	12,000.00	
Computers	3,600.00	
	69,605.38	

1750-1850 Accum Dep

Dr	Cr
	100.00
	60.00
	160.00

2020-2030 Payables

Dr	Cr	
	7,000.00	Notes
	50.00	Interest
	7,050.00	

3010 Kristin Raina, Capital

Dr	Cr
	54,510.00

3020 Kristin Raina, Drawings

Dr	Cr
400.00	

4010-4020 Service Revenue

Dr	Cr	
	Design	4,980.00
	Decor	3,400.00
		8,380.00

4060-4075 Sale of Inventory

Dr	Cr	
	Carpets	2,400.00
	Draperies	1,000.00
	Lamps	1,200.00
	Mirrors	900.00
		5,500.00

4100 Sales Discounts

Dr	Cr
84.62	

5060-5075,5900 Cost of Goods Sold

Dr		Cr
Carpets	1,200.00	
Draperies	500.00	
Lamps	600.00	
Mirrors	450.00	
Invent Adj	150.00	
	2,900.00	

6020-6500 Expenses

Dr		Cr
Accounting	300.00	
Advertising	100.00	
Dep Exp, Furniture	100.00	
Dep Exp, Computers	60.00	
Insurance	200.00	
Janitorial	125.00	
Office Supplies	150.00	
Rent	800.00	
Telephone	275.00	
Utilities	450.00	
Bal	2,560.00	

7000 Interest Exp

Dr	Cr
50.00	

To reverse the Uncategorized Income account—

1. At the Make General Journal Entries window, choose the date, *04/01/2014*, and at the *ENTRY NO.* field, accept ENTRY NO. 2.
2. Remove the check mark from ADJUSTING ENTRY, if necessary.
3. Debit account 49900 Uncategorized Income for 1,540, and credit account 3010 Kristin Raina, Capital, for 1,540. (See figure 6–UU.)

FIGURE 6–UU

Make General Journal
Entries Window—
Reverse Uncategorized
Income

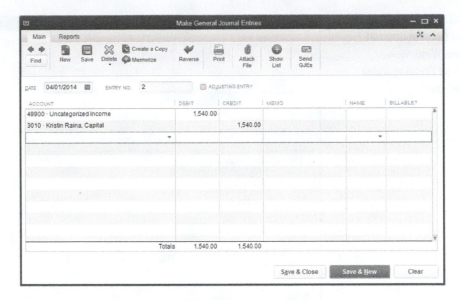

4. If the information is correct, click Save & New.

Accounting concept

49900 Uncategorized Income		3010 Kristin Raina, Capital	
Dr	Cr	Dr	Cr
Rev 1,540	1,540		1,540
0	Bal 0		

Reversing the Uncategorized Expenses Account

In the *Journal* report shown in figure 6–Y, there are seven journal entries
that credit Accounts Payable and debit Uncategorized Expenses for seven
vendor balances as follows:

Ace Glass Works	$1,500
Bell Carpet Design	2,000
Cuza and Carl Associates	400
Galeway Computers	2,600
Midwest Mutual Insurance Co.	2,400
Minneapolis Electric & Gas Co.	450
Williams Office Supply Company	400
	$9,750

The credit entries to the Accounts Payable account are correct and will
stay in that account. The debits to the Uncategorized Expenses, however,
have to be reversed by crediting Uncategorized Expenses for the total of
$9,750 and debiting the 3010 Kristin Raina, Capital, account for $9,750.

To reverse the Uncategorized Expenses account—
1. At the Make General Journal Entries window, choose the date
   04/01/2014, and at the *ENTRY NO.* field, accept ENTRY NO. 3.
2. Remove the check mark from ADJUSTING ENTRY, if necessary.
3. Debit account 3010 Kristin Raina, Capital, for 9,750, and credit account
   69800 Uncategorized Expenses for 9,750. (See figure 6–VV.)

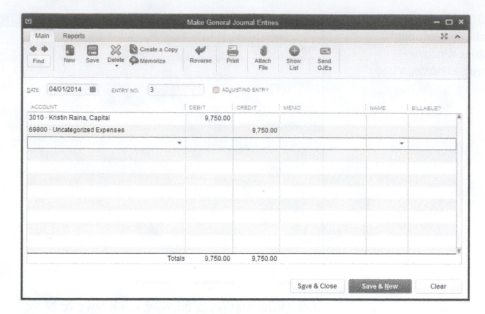

4. If the information is correct, click Save & Close.

A c c o u n t i n g   c o n c e p t

69800 Uncategorized Expenses		3010 Kristin Raina, Capital	
Dr	Cr	Dr	Cr
9,750	Rev 9,750	9,750	
0			

Accounting Reports and Financial Statements

Upon completing the New Company Setup, you should display and print the accounting reports and financial statements.

Accounting Reports

HINT

To display only the last three journal entries in the *Journal* report, click the Customize Report button. Then click the Filters tab. In the *CHOOSE FILTER* field, click *Transaction Type*. In the *Transaction Type* field, click *Journal*. Then click OK.

The accounting reports you need to print and review consist of the *Journal* and the *Trial Balance*.

Journal Report

You displayed and printed the *Journal* report after the EasyStep Interview and QuickBooks Setup windows were completed (figure 6–Y). After recording the opening balances and reversing the Uncategorized Income and Uncategorized Expenses accounts, three more journal entries have been added to the *Journal* report. You can view and print all of the journal entries for April 1, 2014. Figure 6–WW displays only the additional three journal entries.

FIGURE 6–WW
Additional Journal Entries

CH6 [Your Name] Kristin Raina Interior Designs
Journal
April 1, 2014

Trans #	Type	Date	Num	Adj	Name	Memo	Account	Debit	Credit
14	General Journal	04/01/2014	1				1010 · Cash - Operating	50,855.38	
							1300 · Design Supplies	200.00	
							1305 · Office Supplies	250.00	
							1410 · Prepaid Advertising	500.00	
							1420 · Prepaid Insurance	2,200.00	
							1725 · Furniture, Cost	12,000.00	
							1825 · Computers, Cost	3,600.00	
							3020 · Kristin Raina, Drawings	400.00	
							4100 · Sales Discounts	84.62	
							5060 · Cost of Carpets Sold	1,200.00	
							5065 · Cost of Draperies Sold	500.00	
							5070 · Cost of Lamps Sold	600.00	
							5075 · Cost of Mirrors Sold	450.00	
							5900 · Inventory Adjustment	150.00	
							6020 · Accounting Expense	300.00	
							6050 · Advertising Expense	100.00	
							6175 · Deprec. Exp., Furniture	100.00	
							6185 · Deprec. Exp., Computers	60.00	
							6200 · Insurance Expense	200.00	
							6300 · Janitorial Expense	125.00	
							6325 · Office Supplies Expense	150.00	
							6400 · Rent Expense	800.00	
							6450 · Telephone Expense	275.00	
							6500 · Utilities Expense	450.00	
							7000 · Interest Expense	50.00	
							1750 · Accum. Dep., Furniture		100.00
							1850 · Accum. Dep., Computers		60.00
							2020 · Notes Payable		7,000.00
							2030 · Interest Payable		50.00
							4010 · Design Services		4,980.00
							4020 · Decorating Services		3,400.00
							4060 · Sale of Carpets		2,400.00
							4065 · Sale of Draperies		1,000.00
							4070 · Sale of Lamps		1,200.00
							4075 · Sale of Mirrors		900.00
							3010 · Kristin Raina, Capital		54,510.00
								75,600.00	75,600.00
15	General Journal	04/01/2014	2				49900 · Uncategorized Income	1,540.00	
							3010 · Kristin Raina, Capital		1,540.00
								1,540.00	1,540.00
16	General Journal	04/01/2014	3				3010 · Kristin Raina, Capital	9,750.00	
							69800 · Uncategorized Expenses		9,750.00
								9,750.00	9,750.00
TOTAL								**86,890.00**	**86,890.00**

Page 1

> **HINT**
> If you display all the journal entries, the total debits and credits is $101,880.

Trial Balance Report

Next, view and print the *Trial Balance* report for April 1, 2014.
(See figure 6–XX.)

FIGURE 6–XX
Trial Balance Report

CH6 [Your Name] Kristin Raina Interior Designs
Trial Balance
As of April 1, 2014

Accrual Basis

	Apr 1, 14	
	Debit	Credit
1010 · Cash - Operating	50,855.38	
1200 · Accounts Receivable	1,540.00	
1260 · Inventory of Carpets	800.00	
1265 · Inventory of Draperies	1,000.00	
1270 · Inventory of Lamps	1,000.00	
1275 · Inventory of Mirrors	900.00	
1300 · Design Supplies	200.00	
1305 · Office Supplies	250.00	
1410 · Prepaid Advertising	500.00	
1420 · Prepaid Insurance	2,200.00	
1700 · Furniture:1725 · Furniture, Cost	12,000.00	
1700 · Furniture:1750 · Accum. Dep., Furniture		100.00
1800 · Computers:1825 · Computers, Cost	3,600.00	
1800 · Computers:1850 · Accum. Dep., Computers		60.00
2010 · Accounts Payable		9,750.00
2020 · Notes Payable		7,000.00
2030 · Interest Payable		50.00
3010 · Kristin Raina, Capital		50,000.00
3020 · Kristin Raina, Drawings	400.00	
4010 · Design Services		4,980.00
4020 · Decorating Services		3,400.00
4060 · Sale of Carpets		2,400.00
4065 · Sale of Draperies		1,000.00
4070 · Sale of Lamps		1,200.00
4075 · Sale of Mirrors		900.00
4100 · Sales Discounts	84.62	
49900 · Uncategorized Income	0.00	
5060 · Cost of Carpets Sold	1,200.00	
5065 · Cost of Draperies Sold	500.00	
5070 · Cost of Lamps Sold	600.00	
5075 · Cost of Mirrors Sold	450.00	
5900 · Inventory Adjustment	150.00	
6020 · Accounting Expense	300.00	
6050 · Advertising Expense	100.00	
6175 · Deprec. Exp., Furniture	100.00	
6185 · Deprec. Exp., Computers	60.00	
6200 · Insurance Expense	200.00	
6300 · Janitorial Expense	125.00	
6325 · Office Supplies Expense	150.00	
6400 · Rent Expense	800.00	
6450 · Telephone Expense	275.00	
6500 · Utilities Expense	450.00	
69800 · Uncategorized Expenses	0.00	
7000 · Interest Expense	50.00	
TOTAL	**80,840.00**	**80,840.00**

The accounts and balances on this trial balance should match the trial balance of March 31, 2014 (figure 6–AA), after transactions were recorded in chapters 2 through 5.

Recall that QuickBooks created the Uncategorized Income and Uncategorized Expenses accounts when you entered outstanding accounts receivable and accounts payable balances in the Customer Center and Vendor Center, respectively. The balances in these uncategorized accounts were subsequently reversed when the company file was prepared for the accrual basis of accounting. These accounts are no longer needed and can be marked inactive in the Chart of Accounts List.

Financial Statements

The financial statements consist of the *Profit & Loss Standard* report (see figure 6–YY) and the *Balance Sheet Standard* report (see figure 6–ZZ). Upon completion of the New Company Setup, these reports should be the same as the financial statements printed at the end of chapter 5.

FIGURE 6–YY
Profit & Loss Standard Report

CH6 [Your Name] Kristin Raina Interior Designs
Profit & Loss
January 1 through April 1, 2014

Accrual Basis

	Jan 1 – Apr 1, 14
Ordinary Income/Expense	
Income	
4010 · Design Services	4,980.00
4020 · Decorating Services	3,400.00
4060 · Sale of Carpets	2,400.00
4065 · Sale of Draperies	1,000.00
4070 · Sale of Lamps	1,200.00
4075 · Sale of Mirrors	900.00
4100 · Sales Discounts	-84.62
49900 · Uncategorized Income	0.00
Total Income	13,795.38
Cost of Goods Sold	
5060 · Cost of Carpets Sold	1,200.00
5065 · Cost of Draperies Sold	500.00
5070 · Cost of Lamps Sold	600.00
5075 · Cost of Mirrors Sold	450.00
5900 · Inventory Adjustment	150.00
Total COGS	2,900.00
Gross Profit	10,895.38
Expense	
6020 · Accounting Expense	300.00
6050 · Advertising Expense	100.00
6175 · Deprec. Exp., Furniture	100.00
6185 · Deprec. Exp., Computers	60.00
6200 · Insurance Expense	200.00
6300 · Janitorial Expense	125.00
6325 · Office Supplies Expense	150.00
6400 · Rent Expense	800.00
6450 · Telephone Expense	275.00
6500 · Utilities Expense	450.00
69800 · Uncategorized Expenses	0.00
Total Expense	2,560.00
Net Ordinary Income	8,335.38
Other Income/Expense	
Other Expense	
7000 · Interest Expense	50.00
Total Other Expense	50.00
Net Other Income	-50.00
Net Income	8,285.38

FIGURE 6–ZZ
Balance Sheet
Standard Report

CH6 [Your Name] Kristin Raina Interior Designs
Balance Sheet
As of April 1, 2014

Accrual Basis

	Apr 1, 14
ASSETS	
Current Assets	
Checking/Savings	
1010 · Cash - Operating	50,855.38
Total Checking/Savings	50,855.38
Accounts Receivable	
1200 · Accounts Receivable	1,540.00
Total Accounts Receivable	1,540.00
Other Current Assets	
1260 · Inventory of Carpets	800.00
1265 · Inventory of Draperies	1,000.00
1270 · Inventory of Lamps	1,000.00
1275 · Inventory of Mirrors	900.00
1300 · Design Supplies	200.00
1305 · Office Supplies	250.00
1410 · Prepaid Advertising	500.00
1420 · Prepaid Insurance	2,200.00
Total Other Current Assets	6,850.00
Total Current Assets	59,245.38
Fixed Assets	
1700 · Furniture	
1725 · Furniture, Cost	12,000.00
1750 · Accum. Dep., Furniture	-100.00
Total 1700 · Furniture	11,900.00
1800 · Computers	
1825 · Computers, Cost	3,600.00
1850 · Accum. Dep., Computers	-60.00
Total 1800 · Computers	3,540.00
Total Fixed Assets	15,440.00
TOTAL ASSETS	**74,685.38**
LIABILITIES & EQUITY	
Liabilities	
Current Liabilities	
Accounts Payable	
2010 · Accounts Payable	9,750.00
Total Accounts Payable	9,750.00
Other Current Liabilities	
2020 · Notes Payable	7,000.00
2030 · Interest Payable	50.00
Total Other Current Liabilities	7,050.00
Total Current Liabilities	16,800.00
Total Liabilities	16,800.00
Equity	
3010 · Kristin Raina, Capital	50,000.00
3020 · Kristin Raina, Drawings	-400.00
Net Income	8,285.38
Total Equity	57,885.38
TOTAL LIABILITIES & EQUITY	**74,685.38**

Backing Up the New Company File

You should make a backup copy of the new company file in the event there is damage to the file or the computer, or you are working on a different computer. Using the procedures learned in previous chapters, make a backup copy of the new company file to your subfolder and/or a removable storage device and name it **EX6 [*Your Name*] Kristin Raina Interior Designs**. Restore the backup copy, and change the company name to **EX6 [*Your Name*] Kristin Raina Interior Designs**.

Upon completion of the New Company Setup level of operation, customizing and updating the Lists/Centers, recording the appropriate journal entries, viewing and printing Reports, and making a backup copy of the new company file, your accounting records are now ready for recording daily activities. Activities would be recorded in the new company file using the procedures illustrated in prior chapters.

Chapter Review and Assessment

Procedure Review

To begin New Company Setup and create a new company file using the Detailed Start method and the EasyStep Interview window—
1. Open QuickBooks.
2. At the No Company Open window, click *Create a new company;* or click File and then click *New Company*. The QuickBooks Setup window appears with the Let's get your business setup quickly! page displayed. This is the page where you select the method of New Company Setup.
3. At the QuickBooks Setup window on the Let's get your business set up quickly! page, click the Detailed Start button. The EasyStep Interview window appears.
4. At the EasyStep Interview window, read and complete each of the pages. Click Next after each page is completed.
5. At the Congratulations! window, click Go to Setup. Continue New Company Setup using the QuickBooks Setup window or exit the QuickBooks Setup window and go directly into the new company file.

To leave the EasyStep Interview window—
Click the Leave button. Click OK at the EasyStep Interview message.

You should not leave the EasyStep Interview window until the new company file has been saved.

To re-enter the EasyStep Interview window—
Click File and then click *Open Company*. Open the new company file. Click OK at the QuickBooks Information message.

When you open the company file, you are returned to the page you were last using.

To enter the QuickBooks Setup window—
1. Click Help, then click Quick Start Center.
2. At the Quick Start Center window, click Return to Add Info.

To add customers to the Customer Center using the QuickBooks Setup window—
1. In the QuickBooks Setup window, at the You've got a company file! Now add your info. page, in the *Add the people you do business with* field, click the Add button.
2. At the next Add the people you do business with page, choose the *Paste from Excel or enter manually* button, then click Continue.
3. At the next Add the people you do business with page, in the Customer column, click *Select all*.
4. Enter the information for the customers in the appropriate columns.
5. After all customer information is entered, click Continue.
6. At the next Add the people you do business with page, click *Enter opening balances*.
7. At the Enter opening balances for customers and vendors page, enter the balances for the customers and enter the correct date.

8. Click Continue. You are returned to the Add the people you do business with page.

9. Click Continue. You are returned to the QuickBooks Setup window – You've got a company file! Now add your info. page.

10. Click Add More to enter additional customers, vendors, or items, or exit the QuickBooks Setup window by clicking the X.

To add vendors to the Vendor Center using the QuickBooks Setup window—

1. In the QuickBooks Setup window, at the You've got a company file! Now add your info. page, in the *Add the people you do business with* field, click the Add button.

2. At the next Add the people you do business with page, choose the *Paste from Excel or enter manually* button, then click Continue.

3. At the next Add the people you do business with page, in the Vendor column, click *Select all*.

4. Enter the information for the vendors in the appropriate columns.

5. After all vendor information is entered, click Continue.

6. At the next Add the people you do business with page, click *Enter opening balances.*

7. At the Enter opening balances for customers and vendors page, enter the balances for the vendors and enter the correct date.

8. Click Continue. You are returned to the Add the people you do business with page.

9. Click Continue. You are returned to the QuickBooks Setup window – You've got a company file! Now add your info. page.

10. Click Add More to enter additional vendors, customers, or items, or exit the QuickBooks Setup window by clicking the X.

To add service items to the Item List using the QuickBooks Setup window—

1. In the QuickBooks Setup window, at the You've got a company file! Now add your info. page, in the *Add the products and services you sell* field, click the Add button.

2. At the Add the products and services you sell page, choose the *Service* button, then click Continue.

3. Enter the information for the service items in the appropriate columns.

4. After all the service items information is entered, click Continue. You are returned to the Add the products and services you sell page.

5. Click Continue. You are returned to the QuickBooks Setup window – You've got a company file! Now add your info. page.

6. Click Add More to enter additional items, customers, or vendors, or exit the QuickBooks Setup window by clicking the X.

To add inventory part items to the Item List using QuickBooks Setup—

1. In the QuickBooks Setup window, at the You've got a company file! Now add your info. page, in the *Add the products and services you sell* field, click the Add or Add More button.

2. At the Add the products and services you sell page, choose the *Inventory part* button, then click Continue.

3. Enter the information for the inventory part items in the appropriate columns and choose the correct date.

4. After all the inventory part items information is entered, click Continue. You are returned to the Add the products and services you sell page.

5. Click Continue. You are returned to the QuickBooks Setup window – You've got a company file! Now add your info. page.

6. Click Add More to enter additional items, customers, or vendors, or exit the QuickBooks Setup window by clicking the X.

To correct an error in the *Journal* report—

1. In the Journal report, double-click the transaction with the error.
   The Invoice type will bring you to the Create Invoices window.
   The Bill type will bring you to the Enter Bills window.
   The Inventory Adjust type will bring you to the Adjust Quantity/Value on Hand window.

2. Make the correction in the appropriate window, and then click Save and Close.

3. At the warning, click Yes.

To activate the account numbers feature—

1. Click Edit and then click *Preferences*.
2. Along the left frame of the Preferences window, click the *Accounting* icon.
3. Click the Company Preferences tab.
4. At the *ACCOUNTS* field, place a check mark in the box to the left of *Use account numbers* to turn on the account numbers feature.
5. Click OK.

To customize the accounts on the Chart of Accounts List created in EasyStep Interview and QuickBooks Setup windows and change account numbers and names—

1. Click Lists and then click *Chart of Accounts*.
2. Select the account to edit.
3. Click the Account button.
4. At the Account menu, click *Edit Account*.
5. Make any necessary changes to the account and then click Save and Close.

To allow QuickBooks to create system default accounts—

1. Open and close Activities windows, such as the Create Invoices, Enter Sales Receipts, and Enter Bills windows. Also open the Item List and the New Item window, and select *Inventory Part*.

This process will create the system default accounts: Undeposited Funds, Inventory Asset, and Cost of Goods Sold. After QuickBooks creates these accounts, you can edit the account number and name. If you created an accounts receivable–type account and an accounts payable–type account, QuickBooks will accept the accounts. If you did not previously create them, when you open and close the Create Invoices and Enter Bills windows, QuickBooks will create the accounts receivable and accounts payable accounts, respectively.

2. Follow the steps to customize the Chart of Accounts List and to customize the number and names of the system default accounts created by QuickBooks.

To customize the payment terms created in the EasyStep window—
1. Click Lists and then click *Customer & Vendor Profile Lists*.
2. At the Customer & Vendor Profile Lists submenu, click *Terms List*.
3. At the Terms List window, select the terms created by QuickBooks that you wish to edit.
4. Click the Terms menu button; from the Terms menu, click *Edit Terms*.
5. Change the appropriate information and then click OK.
6. At the Terms List window, select the terms created by QuickBooks that you wish to delete.
7. Click the Terms menu button; from the Terms menu, click *Delete Terms*. Click OK at the warning.
8. At the Terms List window, click the Terms menu button.
9. At the Terms menu, click *New*.
10. At the New Terms window, key the appropriate information for any terms QuickBooks did not create that you wish to create.
11. Click Next or OK.

To update the Chart of Accounts List—
1. Click Lists and then click *Chart of Accounts*.
2. Click the Account button.
3. At the Account menu, click *New*.
4. At the Add New Account: Choose Account Type window, choose the type and click Continue.
5. At the Add New Account window, key in the information and then click Save and New or Save and Close.

To edit the Item List for service items created in the QuickBooks Setup window—
1. Click Lists and then click *Item List*.
2. At the Item List window, choose the service item by double-clicking. The Edit Item window appears.
3. In the Tax Code field, click Non Non-Taxable Sales.
4. In the Account field, click the correct account.
5. If the information is correct, click OK.

To edit an inventory part item created in the QuickBooks Setup window—
1. Click Lists and then click *Item List*.
2. At the Item List window, choose the inventory part item by double-clicking. The Edit Item window appears.
3. In the COGS Account field, click the correct account.
4. In the Tax Code field, click Tax Taxable Sales.
5. In the Income Account field, click the correct account.
6. In the Asset Account field, click the correct account.
7. In the Reorder Point field, key in the amount.
8. If the information is correct, click OK.

To edit the Item List for sales tax created in EasyStep Interview—
1. Click Lists and then click *Item List*.
2. At the Item List window, double-click the sales tax item to display the Edit window for that item.
3. Review the sales tax information, and make any necessary changes.
4. Click OK.

To enter opening balances in the Make General Journal Entries window—
1. Click Company and then click *Make General Journal Entries*.
2. Choose the date and make or accept the entry in the *ENTRY NO.* field.
3. Remove the check mark from ADJUSTING ENTRY.
4. Enter the accounts and amounts to be debited.
5. Enter the accounts and amounts to be credited.
6. Record the balancing amount as a credit (or debit) to the capital account.
7. Click Save & Close.

To reverse the Uncategorized Income account—
1. Click Company and then click *Make General Journal Entries*.
2. Choose the date, and check the entry in the *ENTRY NO.* field.
3. Remove the check mark from ADJUSTING ENTRY.
4. Debit the Uncategorized Income account for the full amount in that account, and credit the Capital account for the same amount.
5. Click Save & Close.

To reverse the Uncategorized Expenses account—
1. Click Company and then click *Make General Journal Entries*.
2. Choose the date, and check the entry in the *ENTRY NO.* field.
3. Remove the check mark from ADJUSTING ENTRY.
4. Debit the Capital account for the full amount in the Uncategorized Expenses account, and credit the Uncategorized Expenses account for the same amount.
5. Click Save & Close.

To view and print accounting reports from the Reports menu—
1. Click Reports and then click *Accountant & Taxes*.
2. At the Accountant & Taxes submenu, choose a report.
3. Indicate the start and end dates for the report.
4. Click the Print button on the top of the report.
5. At the Print Reports dialog box, review the settings and then click Print.
6. Close the report.

To view and print financial statements from the Reports menu—
1. Click Reports and then click *Company & Financial*.
2. At the Company & Financial submenu, choose a financial report.
3. Indicate the start and end dates for the report.
4. Click the Print button on the top of the report.
5. At the Print Reports dialog box, review the settings and then click Print.
6. Close the report.

Key Concepts

Select the letter of the item that best matches each definition.

a. System Default Accounts
b. EasyStep Interview
c. Account Numbers
d. Uncategorized Expenses
e. Customizing the Chart of Accounts List
f. Inventory Asset and Cost of Goods Sold

g. Lists - Customer & Vendor Profile Lists - Terms
h. Uncategorized Income
i. Edit - Preferences
j. Dimmed Account Type

_____ 1. The way QuickBooks recognizes system default accounts.
_____ 2. A feature in a company file to identify accounts; must be activated in the Preferences window.
_____ 3. Menu choice used to customize payment terms.
_____ 4. Window where a new company file is created.
_____ 5. Account created by QuickBooks as an offsetting amount for Accounts Receivable.
_____ 6. Accounts created by QuickBooks to be used in the Activities windows and journal entries.
_____ 7. Menu choice used to make account numbers active.
_____ 8. Adding and editing account numbers and names.
_____ 9. Accounts created by QuickBooks as an offsetting amount of Accounts Payable.
_____ 10. System default accounts QuickBooks looks for when an inventory part item is set up.

Procedure Check

1. What is New Company Setup? What is one method of New Company Setup?
2. You have switched your company accounting records to QuickBooks using the EasyStep Interview window and QuickBooks Setup window. What would you do to customize the Chart of Accounts List created by QuickBooks?
3. How and why would you adjust the Uncategorized Income and Uncategorized Expenses accounts?
4. You are reviewing the new company file you created in QuickBooks using EasyStep Interview and QuickBooks Setup, and you notice there are no balances in the revenue and expense accounts. Why is this, and how would you correct it?
5. How does QuickBooks identify system default accounts?
6. Your manager is just learning QuickBooks. He has asked you to explain what EasyStep Interview and QuickBooks Setup mean. Provide the manager with a written explanation of the EasyStep Interview and QuickBooks Setup windows. Be sure to explain what is included in the EasyStep Interview window and QuickBooks Setup window, and describe the additional procedures necessary to complete the New Company Setup after completing the EasyStep Interview and QuickBooks Setup windows.

Case Problems

Case Problem 1

On April 1, 2014, Lynn Garcia began her business, called Lynn's Music Studio. In the first month of business, Lynn set up the music studio, provided guitar and piano lessons, and recorded month-end activity. In May, the second month of business, Lynn started purchasing and selling inventory items of guitars, keyboards, music stands, and sheet music. In April and May, Lynn was recording the financial activities using a manual accounting system. On June 1, 2014, Lynn decides to switch her accounting method to QuickBooks. Lynn has organized the information about the company but has hired you to convert the accounting records to QuickBooks.

1. Use the following information to create the company file and record the information for the company using the Detailed Start method and the EasyStep Interview window. Where no specific information is given, accept the EasyStep Interview window default setting.

Company Name:	**CH6 [*Your Name*] Lynn's Music Studio**
Tax ID:	**45-6123789**
Address:	**228 Pearl Street**
	Scranton, PA 18501
Country:	**U.S.**
Phone:	**570-555-0400**
Fax:	**570-555-0500**
E-mail:	**LYNN@emcp.net**
Industry:	**General Product-based Business**
Company:	**Sole Proprietorship**
Fiscal Year Start:	**April**
Password:	**(none)**
Save As:	**CH6 [Your Name] Lynn's Music Studio**
Sell:	**Both services and products**
Sales Tax:	**Yes**
Estimates:	**No**
Tracking Customer Orders:	**No**
Statements:	**No**
Invoices:	**Yes**
Progress Invoicing:	**No**
Bills You Owe:	**Yes**
Tracking Inventory:	**Yes**
Tracking Time:	**No**
Employees:	**No**
Start Tracking:	**06/01/2014**

Remove the check mark from the following accounts:
     Shipping and Delivery Income
     Freight and Shipping Costs
     Merchant Account Fees
     Product Samples Expense
     Purchases - Resale Items
     Advertising and Promotion
     Automobile Expense
     Bank Service Charges
     Computer and Internet Expenses
     Dues and Subscriptions
     Meals and Entertainment
     Postage and Delivery
     Professional Fees
     Repairs and Maintenance
     Travel Expense
     Ask My Accountant

Place a check mark to the left of the following account:
     Sales Discounts

2. Use the information in table LMS—Customers to create and update the Customer Center using the QuickBooks Setup window. Be sure to use the date June 1, 2014.

TABLE LMS—Customers

Customer/Company Name	Name/Contact	Phone/Fax	Address	Balance
Douglaston Senior Center	Herbie Richardson	570-555-7748 570-555-8800	574 S Beech Street Scranton, PA 18506	175.00
Highland School	Asst. Principal Office	570-555-6963 570-555-6970	115 Forrest Street Waymart, PA 18472	
Jefferson High School	Music Department	570-555-9600 570-555-9700	500 Apple Street Dunmore, PA 18512	
Mulligan Residence	Adam Smith	570-555-3325 570-555-3500	299 Hickory Lane Scranton, PA 18504	1575.90
Musical Youth Group	Dana Thompson	570-555-6642 570-555-6700	550 Marion Lane Scranton, PA 18504	
Patel Family	Ari Patel	570-555-1132	574 Kenwood Drive Dickson City, PA 18519	
Patterson Family	Jonathan Patterson	570-555-6321	650 Memory Lane Dickson City, PA 18519	
Schroeder Family	Betty Schroeder	570-555-1897	98 Belmont Rd. Carbondale, PA 18407	
Twin Lakes Elementary	Miss Brooks	570-555-4474 570-555-4485	515 Hobson Street Honesdale, PA 18431	

3. Use the information in table LMS—Vendors to create and update the Vendor Center using the QuickBooks Setup window. Be sure to use the date June 1, 2014.

TABLE LMS—Vendors

Vendor/Company Name	Name/Contact	Phone/Fax	Address	Balance
Computer Town	Customer Service	570-555-1500 570-555-1550	1000 Carbondale Highway Scranton, PA 18502	2,000.00
Katie's Keyboards	Katie Shea	570-555-7777 570-555-8888	158 Clay Road Scranton, PA 18505	1,500.00
Lynn Garcia				
Melody Music Equipment	Melody Arhmand	570-555-1120 570-555-1125	780 Roselyn Ave. Scranton, PA 18505	
Mills Family Furniture	Edna Mills	570-555-7144 570-555-7200	150 Amelia Street Scranton, PA 18503	1,500.00
Music Instruments, Inc.	Matilda Molloy	570-555-9630 570-555-9635	25 Monroe Ave. Scranton, PA 18505	
Mutual Insurance Company	Bob Maxwell	570-555-5600 570-555-5900	1 Main Street Honesdale, PA 18431	1,200.00
PA Dept. of Revenue				
Paper, Clips, and More	Justin Daves	570-555-8558 570-555-5555	157 Waymart Lane Waymart, PA 18472	350.00
Pioneer Phone	Customer Service	570-555-6000 570-555-6500	1000 Route 6 Carbondale, PA 18407	
Steamtown Electric	Customer Service	570-555-2500 570-555-3000	150 Vine Lane Scranton, PA 18501	
Strings, Sheets & Such	Manuela Perez	570-555-3636 570-555-3700	250 Lincoln St. Scranton, PA 18505	
Tune Tones	Tony Tune	570-555-1111 570-555-2222	500 Monroe Ave. Dunmore, PA 18512	
Viewhill Realty	Matt Snyder	570-555-1000 570-555-1200	100 Commerce Blvd. Scranton, PA 18501	

4. Use the information in table LMS—Items to update the Item List using the QuickBooks Setup window. Be sure to use the date June 1, 2014.

TABLE LMS—Items

Item Name and Description	Price	Cost	On Hand	Total Value
Service Items				
Guitar Lessons	$30			
Piano Lessons	35			
Inventory Part Items				
Guitars	100	$50	6	$ 300
Keyboards	150	75	17	1,275
Music Stands	40	20	17	340
Sheet Music	6	3	165	495

5. Activate the account numbers feature. Use the following information to customize the Chart of Accounts List:

QuickBooks		Edited
Number	Account Name	Number or Account Name
15000	Furniture and Equipment	1700 Music Instruments
17000	Accumulated Depreciation	1750 Accum. Dep., Music Instruments [Subaccount of 1700 Music Instruments]
30800	Owners Draw	3020 Lynn Garcia, Drawings
	Sales Income	4060 Sale of Guitars
48300	Sales Discounts	4100
62400	Depreciation Expenses	6075 Deprec. Exp., Music Instruments
63300	Insurance Expense	6200
63400	Interest Expense	7000 [Type: Other Expense]
64900	Office Supplies	6325 Office Supplies Expense
67100	Rent Expense	6400
68100	Telephone Expense	6450
68600	Utilities	6500 Utilities Expense

6. Delete the following account: 47900 Sales

7. Open and close the following windows to allow QuickBooks to create default accounts:

Create Invoices
Enter Sales Receipts
Enter Bills
Item List: New Item: Inventory Part

8. Customize the system default accounts:

QuickBooks		Edited	
Number	Account Name	Number	Account Name
11000	Accounts Receivable	1200	
12000	Undeposited Funds	1250	Undeposited Funds
12100	*Inventory Asset	1260	Inventory of Guitars
20000	Accounts Payable	2010	
25500	Sales Tax Payable	2200	
30000	Opening Balance Equity	3010	Lynn Garcia, Capital
32000	Owners Equity	3030	Accumulated Earnings
50000	*Cost of Goods Sold	5060	Cost of Guitars Sold

9. Customize the payment Terms List to list only the following:

   2/10, Net 30 Days
   Net 10 Days
   Net 15 Days
   Net 30 Days

10. Use the information in table LMS—New Accounts to update the Chart of Accounts List.

TABLE LMS—New Accounts

Account Type	Number	Account Name
Bank	1010	Cash - Operating
Other Current Asset	1265	Inventory of Keyboards
Other Current Asset	1270	Inventory of Music Stands
Other Current Asset	1275	Inventory of Sheet Music
Other Current Asset	1300	Music Supplies
Other Current Asset	1305	Office Supplies
Other Current Asset	1410	Prepaid Advertising
Other Current Asset	1420	Prepaid Insurance
Fixed Asset	1725	Music Instruments, Cost [Subaccount of 1700]
Fixed Asset	1800	Furniture
Fixed Asset	1825	Furniture, Cost [Subaccount of 1800]
Fixed Asset	1850	Accum. Dep., Furniture [Subaccount of 1800]
Fixed Asset	1900	Computers
Fixed Asset	1925	Computers, Cost [Subaccount of 1900]
Fixed Asset	1950	Accum. Dep., Computers [Subaccount of 1900]
Other Current Liability	2020	Notes Payable
Other Current Liability	2030	Interest Payable
Income	4010	Piano Lessons
Income	4020	Guitar Lessons
Income	4065	Sale of Keyboards
Income	4070	Sale of Music Stands
Income	4075	Sale of Sheet Music
Cost of Goods Sold	5065	Cost of Keyboards Sold
Cost of Goods Sold	5070	Cost of Music Stands Sold
Cost of Goods Sold	5075	Cost of Sheet Music Sold
Cost of Goods Sold	5900	Inventory Adjustment
Expense	6085	Deprec. Exp., Furniture
Expense	6095	Deprec. Exp., Computers
Expense	6150	Instrument Tuning Expense
Expense	6300	Music Supplies Expense

11. Use the information in table LMS-Update Item List to update the Item List for items created as part of QuickBooks Setup.

LMS-Update Item List

Item Name and Description	COGS Account	Income Account	Asset Account	Reorder Point
Service Items (nontaxable):				
Guitar Lessons		4020		
Piano Lessons		4010		
Inventory Part Items (taxable):				
Guitars	5060	4060	1260	10
Keyboards	5065	4065	1265	10
Music Stands	5070	4070	1270	10
Sheet Music	5075	4075	1275	50

After updating the Item List, you can delete the Inventory Asset account and Cost of Goods Sold account (the accounts with no numbers).

12. Edit the Item List for the sales tax item created in the EasyStep Interview:

Sales Tax Name:	**PA Sales Tax**
Description:	**Sales Tax**
Tax Rate:	**7%**
Tax Agency:	**PA Dept. of Revenue**

13. Make three journal entries on June 1, 2014 (accept the default Entry Nos.):
    a. Enter the opening balances listed below. Enter the following accounts and amounts as debits:

Number	Account Name	Balance
1010	Cash - Operating	14,615.18
1300	Music Supplies	430.00
1305	Office Supplies	300.00
1420	Prepaid Insurance	1,100.00
1725	Music Instruments, Cost	4,000.00
1825	Furniture, Cost	2,500.00
1925	Computers, Cost	3,000.00
3020	Lynn Garcia, Drawings	1,000.00
4100	Sales Discounts	188.92
5060	Cost of Guitars Sold	1,150.00
5065	Cost of Keyboards Sold	2,475.00
5070	Cost of Music Stands Sold	460.00
5075	Cost of Sheet Music Sold	1,305.00
5900	Inventory Adjustment	50.00
6075	Deprec. Exp., Music Instruments	60.00
6085	Deprec. Exp., Furniture	40.00
6095	Deprec. Exp., Computers	35.00
6150	Instrument Tuning	100.00

continued

Number	Account Name	Balance
6200	Insurance Expense	100.00
6300	Music Supplies Expense	70.00
6325	Office Supplies Expense	50.00
6400	Rent Expense	600.00
6450	Telephone Expense	50.00
6500	Utilities Expense	70.00
7000	Interest Expense	15.00

Enter the following accounts and amounts as credits:

Number	Account Name	Balance
1750	Accum. Dep., Music Instruments	$ 60.00
1850	Accum. Dep., Furniture	40.00
1950	Accum. Dep., Computers	35.00
2020	Notes Payable	2,000.00
2030	Interest Payable	15.00
4010	Piano Lessons	3,535.00
4020	Guitar Lessons	2,910.00
4060	Sale of Guitars	2,300.00
4065	Sale of Keyboards	4,950.00
4070	Sale of Music Stands	920.00
4075	Sale of Sheet Music	2,610.00

    b. Make a journal entry to reverse the Uncategorized Income account.
    c. Make a journal entry to reverse the Uncategorized Expenses account.

14. Display and print the following reports for June 1, 2014:

    a. *Journal*
    b. *Trial Balance*
    c. *Profit & Loss Standard* (04/01/2014–06/01/2014)
    d. *Balance Sheet Standard*
    e. *Item Listing*
    f. *Customer Contact List*
    g. *Vendor Contact List*

15. Make a backup copy of the new company file. Use the name **LMS6 [*Your Name*] Lynn's Music Studio**. Restore the backup copy, and change the company name to **LMS6 [*Your Name*] Lynn's Music Studio**.

Case Problem 2

On June 1, 2014, Olivia Chen began her business, called Olivia's Web Solutions. In the first month of business, Olivia set up the office, provided web page design and Internet consulting services, and recorded month-end activity. In July, the second month of business, Olivia began to purchase and sell inventory items of computer hardware and software. In June and July, Olivia was recording the financial activities using a manual accounting system. On August 1, 2014, Olivia decides to switch her accounting method to

QuickBooks. Olivia has organized the information about the company but has hired you to convert the accounting records to QuickBooks.

1. Use the information below to create the company file and record the information for the company using the Detailed Start method and the EasyStep Interview window. Where no specific information is given, accept the EasyStep Interview window default setting.

Company Name:	**CH6 [*Your Name*] Olivia's Web Solutions**
Tax ID:	**55-5656566**
Address:	**547 Miller Place**
	Westport, NY 11858
Country:	**U.S.**
Phone:	**516-555-5000**
Fax:	**516-555-6000**
E-mail:	**LIV@emcp.net**
Industry:	**General Product-based Business**
Company:	**Sole Proprietorship**
Fiscal Year Start:	**June**
Password:	**(none)**
Save As:	**CH6 [Your Name] Olivia's Web Solutions**
Sell:	**Both services and products**
Sales Tax:	**Yes**
Estimates:	**No**
Tracking Customer Orders:	**No**
Statements:	**No**
Invoices:	**Yes**
Progress Invoicing:	**No**
Bills You Owe:	**Yes**
Tracking Inventory:	**Yes**
Tracking Time:	**No**
Employees:	**No**
Start Tracking:	**08/01/2014**

Remove the check mark from the following accounts:

      Shipping and Delivery Income
      Freight and Shipping Costs
      Merchant Account Fees
      Product Samples Expense
      Purchases - Resale Items
      Automobile Expense
      Bank Service Charges
      Computer and Internet Expenses
      Dues and Subscriptions
      Meals and Entertainment
      Postage and Delivery
      Professional Fees
      Repairs and Maintenance
      Travel Expense
      Ask My Accountant

Place a check mark to the left of the following account:
Sales Discounts

2. Use the information in table OWS—Customers to create and update the Customer Center using the QuickBooks Setup window. Be sure to use the date August 1, 2014.

TABLE OWS—Customers

Customer/ Company Name	Name/ Contact	Phone/Fax	Address	Balance
Artie's Auto Repair	Leon Artie	516-555-1221 516-555-1231	32 W. 11th Street New Hyde Park, NY 11523	800.00
Breathe Easy A/C Contractors	Allen Scott	516-555-6868 516-555-6869	556 Atlantic Ave. Freeport, NY 11634	
Long Island Water Works	Customer Service	516-555-4747 516-555-4748	87-54 Bayview Ave. Glen Cove, NY 11563	
Miguel's Restaurant	Miguel Perez	516-555-3236 516-555-3237	30 Willis Ave. Roslyn, NY 11541	
Schneider Family	Johnny Schneider	516-555-8989 516-555-8990	363 Farmers Rd. Syosset, NY 11547	1,000.00
Sehorn & Smith Attorneys	Jerry Sehorn	212-555-3339 212-555-3338	510 Fifth Ave. New York, NY 10022	800.00
Singh Family	David Singh	718-555-3233 718-555-3239	363 Marathon Parkway Little Neck, NY 11566	
South Shore School District	Joseph Porter	516-555-4545 516-555-4546	3666 Ocean Ave. South Beach, NY 11365	12,056.00
Thrifty Stores	William Way	718-555-2445 718-555-2446	23 Boston Ave. Bronx, NY 11693	1,500.00

3. Use the information in table OWS—Vendors to create and update the Vendor Center using the QuickBooks Setup window. Be sure to use the date August 1, 2014.

TABLE OWS—Vendors

Vendor/Company Name	Name/Contact	Phone/Fax	Address	Balance
ARC Management	Alvin R. Clinton	516-555-6363 516-555-6364	668 Lakeville Ave. Garden City, NY 11678	
Chrbet Advertising	Chris Chrbet	212-555-8777 212-555-8778	201 E. 10th Street New York, NY 10012	1,200.00
Comet Computer Supplies	Customer Service	631-555-4444 631-555-4455	657 Motor Parkway Center Island, NY 11488	
Computec Computers	Customer Service	702-555-6564 702-555-6563	3631 Gate Blvd. Greenboro, NC 27407	10,000.00
Eastel	Customer Service	212-555-6565 212-555-6566	655 Fifth Ave. New York, NY 10012	350.00
Eastern Mutual Insurance	Customer Service	212-555-6363 212-555-6364	55 Broadway Room 55 New York, NY 10001	
InterSoft Development Co.	Customer Service	631-555-3634 631-555-3635	556 Route 347 Hauppauge, NY 11654	
Lewis Furniture Co.	Manny Lewis	631-555-6161 631-555-6162	1225 Route 110 Farmingdale, NY 11898	1,700.00
LI Power Company	Customer Service	516-555-8888 516-555-8889	5444 Northern Ave. Plainview, NY 11544	
Martin Computer Repairs	Ken Martin	516-555-7777 516-555-7778	366 N. Franklin St. Garden City, NY 11568	
Netsoft Development Co.	Customer Service	974-555-7873 974-555-7874	684 Mountain View Rd Portland, OR 68774.	1,600.00
NYS Tax Dept.				
Office Plus	Customer Service	516-555-3214 516-555-3213	45 Jericho Tpke. Jericho, NY 11654	375.00
Olivia Chen				
Scanntronix	Customer Service	617-555-8778 617-555-8776	2554 Bedford Rd. Boston, MA 02164	
Systems Service	Jeremy Jones	516-555-2525 516-555-2526	36 Sunrise Lane Hempstead, NY 11004	
Textpro Software, Inc.	Customer Service	615-555-4545 615-555-4546	877 Route 5 Ft. Lauderdale, FL 70089	

4. Use the information in table OWS—Items to update the Item List using the QuickBooks Setup window. Be sure to use the date August 1, 2014.

TABLE OWS—Items

Item Name and Description	Price	Cost	On Hand	Total Value
Service Items:				
Internet Consulting Services	$100			
Web Page Design Services	125			
Inventory Part Items:				
Computers	2,000	$1,000	10	$10,000
Scanners	600	300	12	3,600
HTML Software	150	75	18	1,350
Desktop Pub. Software	200	100	10	1,000

5. Activate the account numbers feature. Use the following information to customize the Chart of Accounts List:

	QuickBooks	Edited
Number	Account Name	Number/Account Name
15000	Furniture and Equipment	1700 Computers
17000	Accumulated Depreciation	1750 Accum. Dep., Computers Subaccount of 1700]
30800	Owners Draw	3020 Olivia Chen, Drawings
	Sales Income	4060 Sale of Computers
48300	Sales Discounts	4100
60000	Advertising and Promotion	6050 Advertising Expense
62400	Depreciation Expense	6075 Deprec. Exp., Computers
63300	Insurance Expense	6100
63400	Interest Expense	7000 [Type: Other Expense]
64900	Office Supplies	6325 Office Supplies Expense
67100	Rent Expense	6400
68100	Telephone Expense	6450
68600	Utilities	6500 Utilities Expense

6. Delete the following account: 47900 Sales

7. Open and close the following windows to allow QuickBooks to create default accounts:

Create Invoices
Enter Sales Receipts
Enter Bills
Item List: New Item: Inventory Part

8. Customize the system default accounts:

	QuickBooks		Edited
Number	Account Name	Number	Account Name
11000	Accounts Receivable	1200	
12000	Undeposited Funds	1250	Undeposited Funds
12100	*Inventory Asset	1260	Inventory of Computers
20000	Accounts Payable	2010	
25500	Sales Tax Payable	2200	
30000	Opening Balance Equity	3010	Olivia Chen, Capital
32000	Owners Equity	3030	Accumulated Earnings
50000	*Cost of Goods Sold	5060	Cost of Computers Sold

9. Customize the payment Terms List to list only the following:

2/10, Net 30 Days
Net 10 Days
Net 15 Days
Net 30 Days

10. Use the information in table OWS—New Accounts to update the Chart of Accounts List.

TABLE OWS—New Accounts

Account Type	Number	Account Name
Bank	1010	Cash - Operating
Other Current Asset	1265	Inventory of Scanners
Other Current Asset	1270	Inventory of HTML Software
Other Current Asset	1275	Inventory of Desktop Pub. Soft.
Other Current Asset	1300	Computer Supplies
Other Current Asset	1305	Office Supplies
Other Current Asset	1410	Prepaid Advertising
Other Current Asset	1420	Prepaid Insurance
Fixed Asset	1725	Computers, Cost [Subaccount of 1700]
Fixed Asset	1800	Furniture
Fixed Asset	1825	Furniture, Cost [Subaccount of 1800]
Fixed Asset	1850	Accum. Dep., Furniture [Subaccount of 1800]
Fixed Asset	1900	Software
Fixed Asset	1925	Software, Cost [Subaccount of 1900]
Fixed Asset	1950	Accum. Dep., Software [Subaccount of 1900]
Other Current Liability	2020	Notes Payable
Other Current Liability	2030	Interest Payable
Income	4010	Web Page Design Fees
Income	4020	Internet Consulting Fees
Income	4065	Sale of Scanners
Income	4070	Sale of HTML Software
Income	4075	Sale of Desktop Pub. Software
Cost of Goods Sold	5065	Cost of Scanners Sold
Cost of Goods Sold	5070	Cost of HTML Software Sold
Cost of Goods Sold	5075	Cost of Desktop Pub. Soft. Sold
Cost of Goods Sold	5900	Inventory Adjustment
Expense	6085	Deprec. Exp., Furniture
Expense	6095	Deprec. Exp., Software
Expense	6300	Computer Supplies Expense
Expense	6350	Online Service Expense

11. Use the information in table OWS-Update Item List to update the Item List for items created as part of QuickBooks Setup.

TABLE OWS-Update Item List

Item Name and Description	COGS Account	Income Account	Asset Account	Reorder Point
Service Items (nontaxable):				
Internet Consulting Services		4020		
Web Page Design Services		4010		
Inventory Part Items (taxable):				
Computers	5060	4060	1260	3
Scanners	5065	4065	1265	5
HTML Software	5070	4070	1270	5
Desktop Pub. Software	5075	4075	1275	5

After updating the Item List, you can delete the Inventory Asset account and Cost of Goods Sold account (the accounts with no numbers).

12. Edit the Item List for the sales tax item created in the EasyStep Interview:

Sales Tax Name:	**NY Sales Tax**
Description:	**Sales Tax**
Tax Rate:	**8%**
Tax Agency:	**NYS Tax Dept.**

13. Make three journal entries on August 1, 2014 (accept the default Entry Nos.):
    a. Enter the opening balances listed below. Enter the following accounts and amounts as debits:

Number	Account Name	Balance
1010	Cash - Operating	24,489.16
1300	Computer Supplies	350.00
1305	Office Supplies	325.00
1410	Prepaid Advertising	1,000.00
1420	Prepaid Insurance	1,650.00
1725	Computers, Cost	5,000.00
1825	Furniture, Cost	3,200.00
1925	Software, Cost	3,600.00
3020	Olivia Chen, Drawings	500.00
4100	Sales Discounts	179.84
5060	Cost of Computers Sold	10,000.00
5065	Cost of Scanners Sold	2,400.00
5070	Cost of HTML Software Sold	75.00
5075	Cost of Desktop Pub. Soft. Sold	500.00
5900	Inventory Adjustment	75.00
6050	Advertising Expense	200.00
6075	Deprec. Exp., Computers	75.00
6085	Deprec. Exp., Furniture	50.00
6095	Deprec. Exp., Software	100.00

continued

Number	Account Name	Balance
6100	Insurance Expense	150.00
6300	Computer Supplies Expense	250.00
6325	Office Supplies Expense	50.00
6350	Online Service Expense	150.00
6400	Rent Expense	800.00
6450	Telephone Expense	350.00
6500	Utilities Expense	125.00
7000	Interest Expense	25.00

Enter the following accounts and amounts as credits:

Number	Account Name	Balance
1750	Accum. Dep., Computers	$ 75.00
1850	Accum. Dep., Furniture	50.00
1950	Accum. Dep., Software	100.00
2020	Notes Payable	2,500.00
2030	Interest Payable	25.00
4010	Web Page Design Fees	9,750.00
4020	Internet Consulting Fees	6,600.00
4060	Sale of Computers	20,000.00
4065	Sale of Scanners	4,800.00
4070	Sale of HTML Software	150.00
4075	Sale of Desktop Pub. Software	1,000.00

b. Make a journal entry to reverse the Uncategorized Income account.
c. Make a journal entry to reverse the Uncategorized Expenses account.

14. Display and print the following reports for August 1, 2014:

   a. *Journal*
   b. *Trial Balance*
   c. *Profit & Loss Standard* (06/01/2014–08/01/2014)
   d. *Balance Sheet Standard*
   e. *Item Listing*
   f. *Customer Contact List*
   g. *Vendor Contact List*

15. Make a backup copy of the new company file. Use the name **OWS6 [*Your Name*] Olivia's Web Solutions**. Restore the backup copy, and change the company name to **OWS6 [*Your Name*] Olivia's Web Solutions**.

CHAPTER 7

New Company Setup—Express Start

Set Up Company Preferences

Chapter Objectives

- Create a new company file using the QuickBooks Express Start method

- Establish preferences

- Update the Chart of Accounts List

- Customize the System Default Accounts and Terms List

- Update the Item List

- Update the Customer and Vendor Centers

- Adjust the new company file to follow the accrual basis of accounting

- Display and print accounting reports and financial statements

Introduction

In this chapter, you will learn an alternative method for creating a new company file in QuickBooks. As you know, the four levels of operation for QuickBooks are New Company Setup, Lists/Centers, Activities, and Reports. In chapters 2 through 5, the Lists, Activities, and Reports levels were presented for both a service company and a merchandise company. In those chapters, you opened an existing company file, updated the Lists/Centers, recorded Activities in the various windows, and viewed and printed Reports. You will now learn the first level of operation for QuickBooks – New Company Setup.

QuickBooks provides two methods of New Company Setup: Detailed Start and Express Start. In chapter 6, the New Company Setup level of operation was presented using the Detailed Start method, which moves you to the EasyStep Interview window. In addition you used the QuickBooks Setup window to continue with the New Company Setup.

In chapter 7, you will learn how to conduct New Company Setup using the Express Start method. With this method, you do not use the EasyStep Interview window; instead, you directly enable the features you desire. In addition, you will not use the QuickBooks Setup window to enter information. Instead you will use many of the procedures you learned earlier for updating the Lists/Centers to enter information in the new company file. Finally, the new company file is prepared for the accrual basis of accounting.

In this chapter, you will again create and set up a new company file for our sample company, Kristin Raina Interior Designs. It is assumed that Kristin Raina Interior Designs was recording accounting activities using a manual accounting system and has decided to convert the company's accounting records to QuickBooks.

QuickBooks versus Manual Accounting: New Company Setup

In a manual accounting system, a company's records are set up by creating the Chart of Accounts and creating a general ledger. The Chart of Accounts is the list of accounts (assets, liabilities, equity, revenues, and expenses) the company intends to use. The general ledger is the book of each account with the beginning balance for each account. If desired, subsidiary ledgers are also created and beginning balances recorded. The subsidiary ledgers typically include accounts receivable and accounts payable. If the perpetual inventory system is used, an inventory subsidiary ledger would also be created.

In QuickBooks, a company's records are set up by creating a new company file and establishing the Chart of Accounts List. As the opening balances are entered, QuickBooks simultaneously sets up the general ledger. The Customer Center and Vendor Center are set up; these centers are equivalent to the accounts receivable and accounts payable subsidiary ledgers. The Item List is set up, which is equivalent to an inventory subsidiary ledger. However, in QuickBooks, the Item List also includes service revenue items and sales tax items in addition to inventory items.

When you set up a new company file using the Express Start method, that is, without using the EasyStep Interview window, you must first identify certain company preferences. After that, you customize parts of the company file. If you choose not to use the QuickBooks Setup window to enter information, you then use the Lists/Centers windows to continue with the setup of the new company file. Entering information in the Lists/Centers is similar to creating a Chart of Accounts, general ledger, and subsidiary ledgers in a manual accounting system. Finally, there are three journal entries you need to make to complete the New Company Setup. One journal entry records the opening balances in the accounts that were not included when you set up the Lists/Centers; the other two journal entries reverse accounts set up by QuickBooks during New Company Setup that are not used in the accrual basis of accounting.

Chapter Problem

In this chapter, there is no prepared company file to open from the company files. Instead, you will create and set up the company file for Kristin Raina Interior Designs.

Assume that Kristin Raina began her interior design business in January 2014 and has maintained accounting records with a manual accounting system for January through March. Effective April 1, 2014, Kristin Raina has decided to convert the company's accounting records to QuickBooks using the Express Start method.

Before you create a new company file, you would gather all the information you need, including: company information (name, address, tax identification numbers); general ledger account names and account numbers; customer information (name, address, telephone numbers, and so on) and outstanding balances; vendor information (name, address, telephone numbers, and so on) and outstanding balances; services items and billing amounts; inventory part items (name, cost, selling price, and quantity on hand); and sales tax information. You will enter this information into QuickBooks as you create and set up the new company file.

To begin New Company Setup—
1. Open QuickBooks.
2. At the No Company Open window, click *Create a new company*; or click File and then click *New Company*. The QuickBooks Setup window appears with the Let's get your business set up quickly! page displayed. This is the page where you select the method of New Company Setup. (See figure 7–A.)

FIGURE 7–A
QuickBooks Setup Window—Let's Get Your Business Set Up Quickly! Page

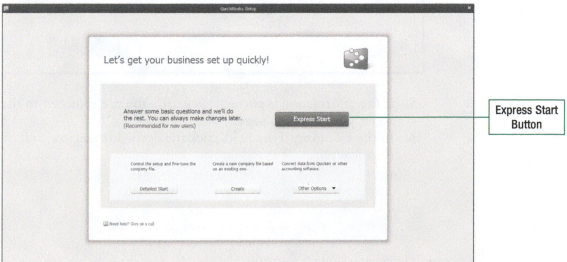

○ **Express Start**

In New Company Setup, the first level of operation in QuickBooks, you will enter the information needed to create and set up a company file for Kristin Raina Interior Designs using the Express Start method. With the Express Start method of New Company Setup, you will enter some information about the company and identify the type of industry for your business. You will then save the company file.

To create a new company file using the Express Start method—

1. At the QuickBooks Setup window on the Let's get your business set up quickly! page, click the Express Start button. The Tell us about your business page appears.
2. At the Tell us about your business page, in the *Company Name* field, key **CH7 [*Your Name*] Kristin Raina Interior Designs**.
3. Move to the *Industry* field and click *Help me choose*. The Select Your Industry page appears.
4. At the Select Your Industry page, in the *Industry* field, scroll to the bottom and select *Other/None*. (See figure 7-B.)

FIGURE 7–B
Select Your Industry Page

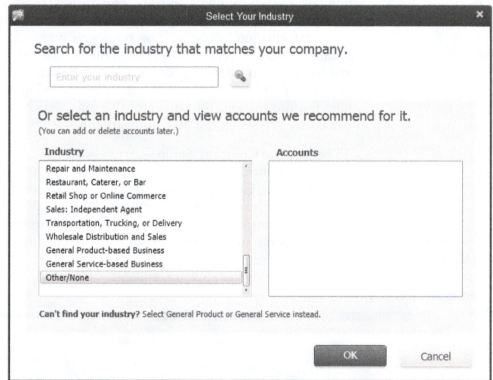

5. If the information is correct, click OK. You are returned to the Tell us about your business page.
6. In the Company Type field, click the drop-down arrow, and choose *Sole Proprietorship*.

7. At the Tax ID# field, key **33-4777781**. (See figure 7-C.)

FIGURE 7–C

Tell Us About Your
Business Page—
Complete

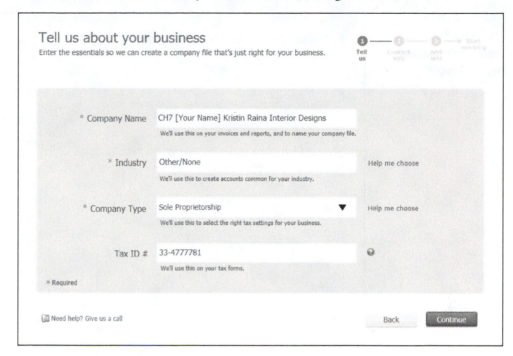

8. If the information is correct, click Continue. You are moved to the Enter your business contact information page.

The company name is automatically filled in the *Legal Name* field. The legal name is the name that will be used on tax forms. If the company name and legal name are not the same, any necessary changes can be made. For our sample company, the names are the same.

9. At the Enter your business contact information page, key the following information:

Legal Name:	**CH7 [*Your Name*] Kristin Raina Interior Designs**
Address:	**25 NE Johnson Street**
City:	**Minneapolis**
State:	**MN**
Zip:	**53402**
Country:	**U.S.**
Phone:	**651-555-1000**
Email:	**KRID@emcp.net**

When you are finished, your screen should look like figure 7–D.

FIGURE 7–D

Enter Your Business
Contact Information
Page—Completed

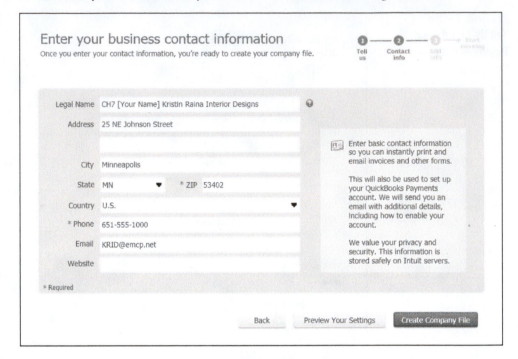

10. If the information is correct, click the Preview Your Settings button.
11. At the Preview Your Company Settings page, click the Company File Location tab.
12. On the Company File Location tab, click the Change Location button. You are moved to the Browse For Folder window.
13. At the Browse For Folder window, scroll through the list and choose the folder where you save your files, and then click OK. You are returned to the Company File Location tab with the path and folder displayed.
14. If the path and folder are correct, click OK. You are returned to the Enter your business contact information page.
15. Click the Create Company File button. The company file CH7 [*Your Name*] Kristin Raina Interior Designs is saved in the path and folder you indicated above.

    The QuickBooks Setup window appears with You've got a company file! Now add your info. page displayed. The QuickBooks Setup window can now be used to enter information for customers, vendors, service items, and inventory part items, as was illustrated in chapter 6. However, in this chapter, the QuickBooks Setup window will not be used. Instead you will enter information directly into Lists and Centers.

16. Click the X to close the QuickBooks Setup window. The home page and left icon bar appear. Click the X to close the home page. To remove the left icon bar, click View and then click Hide Icon Bar.

To continue the New Company Setup using the Express Start method, and not using the QuickBooks Setup window to enter information, you must take the following steps: establish Preferences; update the Chart of Accounts List, customize System Default Accounts and Terms List; update the Item List, Customer Center, and Vendor Center with beginning balances; enter opening balances in accounts by journal entry; and record two journal entries to offset two accounts created by QuickBooks that are not used in the accrual basis of accounting.

Establishing Preferences

When you use the EasyStep Interview window in the Detailed Start method of New Company Setup, QuickBooks asks questions and, based on your responses, establishes preferences for your company. When you use the Express Start method of New Company Setup, the EasyStep Interview window is not used. Therefore, you must establish the preferences for the new company file yourself. Company preferences enable or disable features available in QuickBooks. When a feature is enabled, it allows for choices to be listed on the pull-down menus and on the home page. If a feature is disabled, then you will not see some choices on the drop-down menu or home page.

You set these preferences in the Preferences window. You will use the Preferences window to activate the account *Number* field in the Chart of Accounts List window, activate the inventory feature, activate sales tax, and disable the payroll feature.

Account Numbers

By default, QuickBooks does not use account numbers. You must activate the account numbers feature to add them.

To activate the account numbers feature—
1. Click Edit and then click *Preferences*. The Preferences window appears.

   Along the left side of the window are 23 icons representing the different categories of features. For each category there is a My Preferences tab and a Company Preferences tab. The Company Preferences tab is used for most preferences when setting up a new company file. The My Preferences tab records the preferences for each user.

2. Along the left frame of the Preferences window, click the *Accounting* icon.
3. Click the Company Preferences tab.
4. At the *ACCOUNTS* field, place a check mark in the box to the left of *Use account numbers* to turn on the account numbers feature. (See figure 7–E.)

FIGURE 7–E

Preferences Window—
Accounting—Company
Preferences Tab

Use account
numbers

DATE WARNINGS

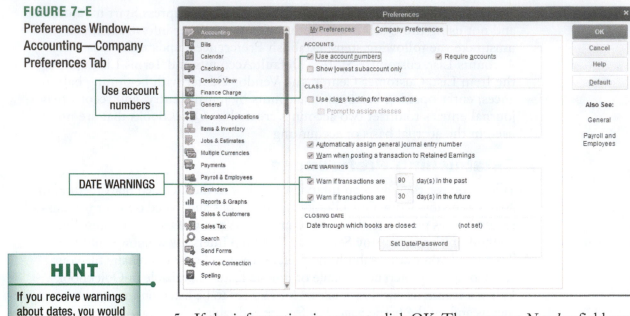

If you receive warnings
about dates, you would
uncheck the DATE
WARNINGS boxes.

5. If the information is correct, click OK. The account *Number* field now appears in the New Account and Edit Account windows in the Chart of Accounts List.

Inventory

QuickBooks provides you with the ability to maintain inventory records, but the inventory feature must be activated.

To activate the inventory feature—

1. Click Edit and then click *Preferences*. The Preferences window appears.
2. Along the left frame of the Preferences window, click the *Items & Inventory* icon.
3. Click the Company Preferences tab.
4. At the *PURCHASE ORDERS AND INVENTORY* section, place a check mark in the box to the left of *Inventory and purchase orders are active* to turn on the inventory feature. (See figure 7–F.)

FIGURE 7–F

Preferences Window—
Items & Inventory—
Company Preferences
Tab

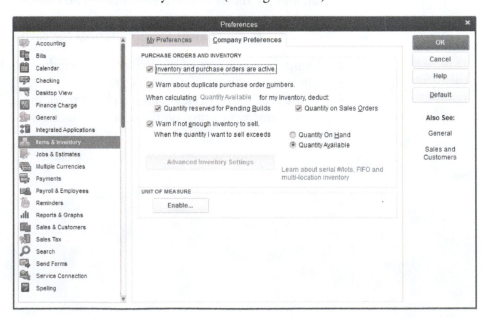

5. If the information is correct, click OK. The inventory feature is now activated, and fields of information relevant to inventory will now appear in the Activities windows.

Sales Tax

QuickBooks also provides you with the ability to charge and maintain sales tax information, but the sales tax feature must be activated.

To activate the sales tax feature—
1. Click Edit and then click *Preferences*.
2. Along the left frame of the Preferences window, click the *Sales Tax* icon.
3. Click the Company Preferences tab.
4. At the *Do you charge sales tax?* field, click *Yes*.

   The other fields of information that were dimmed now become activated.

   You must complete the *Your most common sales tax item* field.

5. Move to the *Your most common sales tax item* field, and click the drop-down arrow.

   Because this is a new company, there is no information regarding sales tax. You will add it in this window.

6. Click < Add New >.

   The New Item window appears. This allows you to add sales tax to the Item List.

7. Key the sales tax item information listed below:

TYPE:	**Sales Tax Item**
Sales Tax Name:	**Minn. Sales Tax**
Description:	**Sales Tax**
Tax Rate (%):	**7**

8. Move to the *Tax Agency (vendor that you collect for)* field, and click the drop-down arrow. Again, because this is a new company file, vendors have not yet been entered into the file.
9. At the Tax Agency drop-down list, click < Add New >. The New Vendor window appears.
10. In both the *VENDOR NAME* and *COMPANY NAME* fields, key **Minn. Dept. of Revenue**, and move to the next field. (See figure 7–G.)

> **HINT**
>
> You could also click *Add sales tax item.*

FIGURE 7–G
New Vendor Window

11. If the information is correct, click OK. The Minn. Dept. of Revenue has been added to the Vendor Center and the New Item window is complete. (See figure 7–H.)

FIGURE 7–H
New Item Window—
Completed

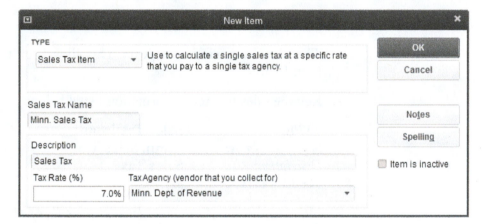

12. If the information is correct, click OK. The Sales Tax Item has been added to the Item List and the Preferences window for Sales Tax is complete. (See figure 7–I.)

FIGURE 7–I
Preferences Window—
Sales Tax—Completed

FIGURE 7–I
Preferences Window—
Sales Tax—Completed

FIGURE 7–J
Updating Sales Tax
Dialog Box

13. If the information is correct, click OK.

The Updating Sales Tax dialog box appears. In this dialog box, QuickBooks is inquiring if all existing customers and all non-inventory and inventory parts should be made taxable. (See figure 7–J.)

14. Click OK. The sales tax item is established.

Payroll

When you create a new company file using the Express Start method, QuickBooks assumes you will be using the Payroll feature and by default activates it. When QuickBooks activated the payroll feature, it automatically created a Payroll Liabilities account and Payroll Expenses account in the Chart of Accounts List. Our sample company, Kristin Raina Interior Designs, has not yet used the payroll feature and does not need it activated.

To disable the payroll feature—
1. Click Edit and then click *Preferences*.
2. Along the left frame of the Preferences window, click the *Payroll & Employees* icon.
3. Click the Company Preferences tab.
4. At the *QUICKBOOKS PAYROLL FEATURES* field, click *No payroll*. The other fields of information are now dimmed.
5. Click OK.

Even though you have disabled the payroll feature, the Payroll Liabilities account and the Payroll Expenses account will still appear on the Chart of Accounts List.

> **HINT**
>
> When you use the Detailed Start method of New Company Setup, you have the choice to enable or disable the payroll feature.

Updating the Chart of Accounts List

When you created the new company file and established some of the preferences, QuickBooks began to set up the Chart of Accounts List. Open the Chart of Accounts List window and review the list.

To open and review the Chart of Accounts List—
1. Click Lists and then click *Chart of Accounts*. (See figure 7–K.)

FIGURE 7–K

Chart of Accounts List Window

System Default Accounts Created by QuickBooks

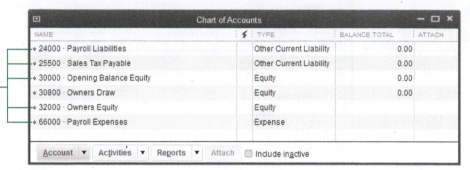

There are many additional accounts that must be added to the Chart of Accounts List for Kristin Raina Interior Designs. Most of these accounts have opening balances. These balances will be entered later by general journal entry.

You add accounts to the Chart of Accounts List by using the Chart of Accounts List window as illustrated in prior chapters.

To add a new account—
1. Open the Chart of Accounts List, if it is not already open.
2. At the Chart of Accounts window, click the Account button and then click New. The Add New Account: Choose Account Type window appears.
3. At the Choose Account Type window, click Bank and then click Continue. The Add New Account window appears.
4. At the Add New Account window, enter the following information:

> *Number:* **1010**
> *Account Name:* **Cash - Operating**

Your screen should look like figure 7–L.

> **HINT**
>
> You can enter the opening balances when you create a new account in the Chart of Accounts List for most assets, liabilities, and equity accounts, or you can enter account balances by journal entry.

FIGURE 7–L

Add New Account Window

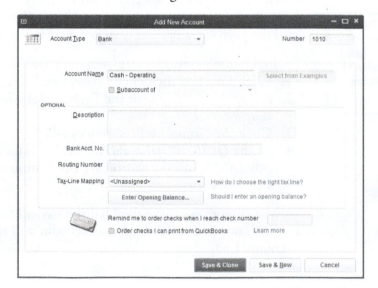

5. If the information is correct, click Save & New. The New Account window is displayed with the fields cleared for the next account.
6. Using the information in table 7–1, key in all the accounts.

TABLE 7–1
Chart of Accounts List

HINT

In the *Account Type* field, instead of looking for the type in the drop-down list, key the first letter of the type name.

HINT

The Inventory of Carpets and Cost of Carpets Sold accounts will be added in the next section of this chapter.

Account Type	Number	Account Name
Accounts Receivable	1200	Accounts Receivable
Other Current Asset	1250	Undeposited Funds
Other Current Asset	1265	Inventory of Draperies
Other Current Asset	1270	Inventory of Lamps
Other Current Asset	1275	Inventory of Mirrors
Other Current Asset	1300	Design Supplies
Other Current Asset	1305	Office Supplies
Other Current Asset	1410	Prepaid Advertising
Other Current Asset	1420	Prepaid Insurance
Fixed Asset	1700	Furniture
Fixed Asset	1725	Furniture, Cost [Subaccount of 1700]
Fixed Asset	1750	Accum. Dep., Furniture [Subaccount of 1700]
Fixed Asset	1800	Computers
Fixed Asset	1825	Computers, Cost [Subaccount of 1800]
Fixed Asset	1850	Accum. Dep., Computers [Subaccount of 1800]
Accounts Payable	2010	Accounts Payable
Other Current Liability	2020	Notes Payable
Other Current Liability	2030	Interest Payable
Income	4010	Design Services
Income	4020	Decorating Services
Income	4060	Sale of Carpets
Income	4065	Sale of Draperies
Income	4070	Sale of Lamps
Income	4075	Sale of Mirrors
Income	4100	Sales Discounts
Cost of Goods Sold	5065	Cost of Draperies Sold
Cost of Goods Sold	5070	Cost of Lamps Sold
Cost of Goods Sold	5075	Cost of Mirrors Sold
Cost of Goods Sold	5900	Inventory Adjustment
Expense	6020	Accounting Expense
Expense	6050	Advertising Expense
Expense	6175	Deprec. Exp., Furniture
Expense	6185	Deprec. Exp., Computers
Expense	6200	Insurance Expense
Expense	6300	Janitorial Expense
Expense	6325	Office Supplies Expense
Expense	6400	Rent Expense
Expense	6450	Telephone Expense
Expense	6500	Utilities Expense
Other Expense	7000	Interest Expense

The updated Chart of Accounts List appears in figure 7–M.

FIGURE 7–M

Chart of Accounts List—
Updated

NAME	TYPE	BALANCE TOTAL	ATTACH
1010 · Cash - Operating	Bank	0.00	
1200 · Accounts Receivable	Accounts Receivable	0.00	
1250 · Undeposited Funds	Other Current Asset	0.00	
1265 · Inventory of Draperies	Other Current Asset	0.00	
1270 · Inventory of Lamps	Other Current Asset	0.00	
1275 · Inventory of Mirrors	Other Current Asset	0.00	
1300 · Design Supplies	Other Current Asset	0.00	
1305 · Office Supplies	Other Current Asset	0.00	
1410 · Prepaid Advertising	Other Current Asset	0.00	
1420 · Prepaid Insurance	Other Current Asset	0.00	
1700 · Furniture	Fixed Asset	0.00	
1725 · Furniture, Cost	Fixed Asset	0.00	
1750 · Accum. Dep., Furniture	Fixed Asset	0.00	
1800 · Computers	Fixed Asset	0.00	
1825 · Computers, Cost	Fixed Asset	0.00	
1850 · Accum. Dep., Computers	Fixed Asset	0.00	
2010 · Accounts Payable	Accounts Payable	0.00	
2020 · Notes Payable	Other Current Liability	0.00	
2030 · Interest Payable	Other Current Liability	0.00	
24000 · Payroll Liabilities	Other Current Liability	0.00	
25500 · Sales Tax Payable	Other Current Liability	0.00	
30000 · Opening Balance Equity	Equity	0.00	
30800 · Owners Draw	Equity	0.00	
32000 · Owners Equity	Equity		
4010 · Design Services	Income		
4020 · Decorating Services	Income		
4060 · Sale of Carpets	Income		
4065 · Sale of Draperies	Income		
4070 · Sale of Lamps	Income		
4075 · Sale of Mirrors	Income		
4100 · Sales Discounts	Income		
5065 · Cost of Draperies Sold	Cost of Goods Sold		
5070 · Cost of Lamps Sold	Cost of Goods Sold		
5075 · Cost of Mirrors Sold	Cost of Goods Sold		
5900 · Inventory Adjustment	Cost of Goods Sold		
6020 · Accounting Expense	Expense		
6050 · Advertising Expense	Expense		
6175 · Deprec., Exp., Furniture	Expense		
6185 · Deprec. Exp., Computers	Expense		
6200 · Insurance Expense	Expense		
6300 · Janitorial Expense	Expense		
6325 · Office Supplies Expense	Expense		
6400 · Rent Expense	Expense		
6450 · Telephone Expense	Expense		
6500 · Utilities Expense	Expense		
66000 · Payroll Expenses	Expense		
7000 · Interest Expense	Other Expense		

Account ▼   Activities ▼   Reports ▼   Attach   ☐ Include inactive

HINT

If you incorrectly labeled an account as a parent or subaccount, you can edit the account or you can move the entry. To move the entry, click the diamond to the left of the account number. If you drag the diamond to the left, a subaccount will become a parent account. If you drag the diamond to the right, a parent account will become a subaccount. You can also click and drag up or down to reorganize the list.

7. Close the Add New Account and Chart of Accounts windows.

Customizing the New Company File

As previously stated, when creating a new company file using the Express Start method of New Company Setup, you first set up the preferences for the company file. As you do this, accounts are set up on the Chart of Accounts List. Then, the Chart of Accounts List is updated to add more of the accounts the company uses. The next step is to customize the new company file. This consists of customizing the system default accounts and payment terms created by QuickBooks.

Customizing System Default Accounts

As you saw in prior chapters, QuickBooks establishes default accounts and uses those accounts when recording transactions in the Activities windows. QuickBooks looks for these system default accounts in the Chart of Accounts List; if it cannot find an account, it will create one. Some system default accounts you have learned so far are Accounts Receivable, Undeposited Funds, Accounts Payable, Sales Tax Payable, Inventory Asset, and Cost of Goods Sold. Other system default accounts include the equity accounts (capital and accumulated earnings) and payroll accounts (payroll liabilities and payroll expenses).

When you created the company file and established some of the company preferences, QuickBooks created some of the system default accounts, as you saw earlier in figure 7–K.

You will now customize the system default accounts that were created by QuickBooks (sales tax payable and the equity accounts) by editing the account names and numbers to follow the company's pattern for naming and numbering accounts on the Chart of Accounts List. The payroll accounts that QuickBooks creates cannot be deleted, but since they will not be used in our sample company file, they can be marked as inactive to hide them on the Chart of Accounts List. Then you will learn how to force QuickBooks to create additional system default accounts that were not created when you created the company file and established the preferences (undeposited funds, inventory asset, and cost of goods sold). After QuickBooks creates the additional system default accounts, you will then customize these account names and numbers.

Customizing System Default Accounts Created in a New Company File and Company Preferences

When you created the company and indicated it was a sole proprietorship, QuickBooks automatically created three equity accounts: Opening Balance Equity, Owners Draw, and Owners Equity. When you activated the sales tax feature, QuickBooks created a Sales Tax Payable account. The numbers and names for each of these accounts can be edited. The Opening Balance Equity account will be renamed as Kristin Raina, Capital, and the Owners Draw account will be renamed Kristin Raina, Drawings. The Opening Balance Equity account is used by QuickBooks as an offsetting account when certain opening balances are entered in the accounts. The Owners Equity account is created for the purpose of capturing net income at the end of the fiscal year. In chapter 12, you will see how QuickBooks utilizes the Owner's Equity account in a company file. This account will be renamed as Accumulated Earnings. QuickBooks usually identifies a system default account by graying, or dimming, the account type. As you edit each of these accounts, notice that the account type is dimmed.

To edit account numbers and account names—
1. Click Lists and then click *Chart of Accounts*.
2. At the Chart of Accounts window, select *30000 Opening Balance Equity* but do not open the account.
3. Click the Account button.
4. At the Account menu, click *Edit Account*.
5. In the *Number* field, delete 30000 and then key **3010**.
6. In the *Account Name* field, delete Opening Balance Equity and then key **Kristin Raina, Capital**. (See figure 7–N.)

FIGURE 7–N

Edit Account—System
Default Account

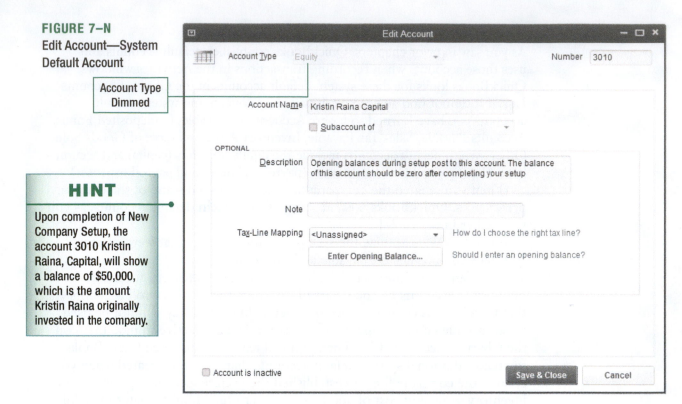

Account Type
Dimmed

7. If the information is correct, click Save & Close.
8. Edit the two other equity accounts and the Sales Tax Payable account as
   follows:

QuickBooks		Edited	
Number	Account Name	Number	Account Name
30800	Owners Draw	3020	Kristin Raina, Drawings
32000	Owners Equity	3030	Accumulated Earnings
25500	Sales Tax Payable	2200	

Hiding Inactive System Default Accounts Created in a New Company File

When you create a new company file using the Express Start method,
QuickBooks assumes by default that you will be using the payroll feature and
automatically creates a Payroll Liabilities account and a Payroll Expenses
account. Even though you subsequently turned off the payroll feature in the
Preferences window, once payroll accounts are created in QuickBooks, you
cannot delete them.

In addition, once you turned on the account numbers feature, QuickBooks
assigned the account numbers 24000 to the Payroll Liabilities account and
66000 to the Payroll Expenses account. Because payroll has not yet been
covered, you will not be using the payroll accounts at this time. You can
make them inactive, and they will not be displayed in the reports.

To mark an account as inactive—
1. At the Chart of Accounts window, select the Payroll Liabilities account.
2. Click the Account button and then click Make Account Inactive.

The Payroll Liabilities account is no longer displayed in the Chart of Accounts List.

3. Select the Payroll Expenses account.
4. Click the Account button, then click Make Account Inactive.

To see Inactive accounts listed on the Chart of Accounts List, click the Account button and then click Show Inactive Accounts. You will see the Inactive accounts with an ✖ next to the account name. To hide the accounts, click the Account button and then click Hide Inactive Accounts.

5. Close the Chart of Accounts window.

Customizing System Default Accounts Created for Use in Activities Windows

Recall that in the Create Invoices window, the system default account is a debit to Accounts Receivable, and in the Enter Bills window, the system default is a credit to Accounts Payable. When you chose an inventory item in any of the Activities windows, QuickBooks knew—from the Item List—which inventory asset account, cost of goods sold account, and sale of inventory account was the system default account to use for properly recording the transaction. You also know that you can create accounts in the Chart of Accounts List. But sometimes QuickBooks does not find the account you created; you must let QuickBooks create the account for the software to identify it as a system default account.

You have just updated the Chart of Accounts List to add accounts that will be used by Kristin Raina Interior Designs. Some of those accounts included Accounts Receivable, Undeposited Funds, Inventory, Accounts Payable, and Cost of Goods Sold. To illustrate how QuickBooks creates its own system default accounts, you will open some Activities windows and the Item List. You will then see that QuickBooks cannot locate some of the accounts you created and will create its own accounts.

<table>
<tr><td>

HINT

QuickBooks sometimes needs to create its own system default accounts. Opening and closing these windows forces QuickBooks to create system default accounts. After QuickBooks creates these accounts, you can then edit the account name and number.

</td><td>

To allow QuickBooks to create system default accounts—
1. Click Customers and then click *Create Invoices*. Close the Create Invoices window.
2. Click Customers and then click *Enter Sales Receipts*. Close the Enter Sales Receipts window.
3. Click Vendors and then click *Enter Bills*. Close the Enter Bills window.
4. Click Lists and then click *Item List*.
5. At the Item List window, click the Item button.
6. At the Item menu, click *New*.
7. At the New Item window, in the *TYPE* field, click *Inventory Part*.
8. Close the New Item window. Close the Item List.

</td></tr>
</table>

As you opened each of these windows, QuickBooks looked for certain accounts; when they could not be identified, QuickBooks created new system default accounts. Review the Chart of Accounts List and observe that QuickBooks created the following accounts:

12000	*Undeposited Funds
12100	Inventory Asset
50000	Cost of Goods Sold

(See figure 7–O.)

FIGURE 7–O

Chart of Accounts
List—Additional System
Default Accounts Created
by QuickBooks

Additional System
Default Accounts
Created by
QuickBooks

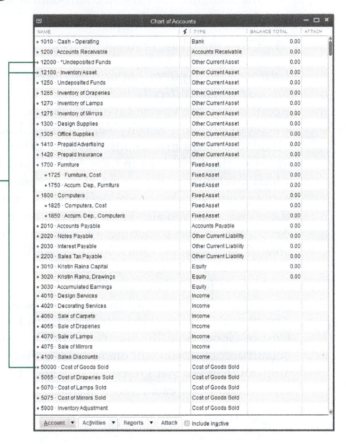

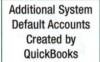

HINT

If you did not create the Accounts Receivable and Accounts Payable accounts, when you opened the Create Invoices and Enter Bills windows, these two accounts automatically would have been created and the account types dimmed. You would need to edit only the account numbers.

When you opened the Create Invoices window, QuickBooks looked for the Accounts Receivable account and was able to locate it because of the accounts receivable account type in that account. Similarly, when you opened the Enter Bills window, QuickBooks looked for the Accounts Payable account and was able to locate it because of the accounts payable account type.

But, when you opened the Enter Sales Receipts window, QuickBooks looked for an Undeposited Funds account, and even though you created this account, QuickBooks could not locate it and created a new account *Undeposited Funds. Similarly, when you chose the new inventory part type in the Item List, QuickBooks looked for an inventory asset account and cost of goods sold account. Even though you had previously created three inventory accounts and three cost of goods sold accounts, again, QuickBooks did not identify these accounts as system default accounts, and therefore, it created a new account 12100 Inventory Asset and a new account 50000 Cost of Goods Sold. Therefore, in some situations—such as these—you must allow QuickBooks to create its own accounts and then you can edit them to your liking. In all cases, accounts created by QuickBooks will have dimmed account types; you will not be able to change the account type, but you can change the account numbers and account names.

Before you can edit the accounts that QuickBooks created, delete the 1250 Undeposited Funds account you created. This account name and number can then be used when editing the accounts created by QuickBooks.

To delete an account—
1. Click Lists and then click *Chart of Accounts.*
2. At the Chart of Accounts window, select *1250 Undeposited Funds.*
3. Click the Account button and then click Delete Account.
4. At the warning, click OK.

Now edit the system default accounts created by QuickBooks, noting that for each of these accounts created by QuickBooks, the account type is dimmed:

QuickBooks		Edited	
Number	Account Name	Number	Account Name
12000	*Undeposited Funds	1250	Undeposited Funds
12100	Inventory Asset	1260	Inventory of Carpets
50000	Cost of Goods Sold	5060	Cost of Carpets Sold

See figure 7–P for the updated and customized Chart of Accounts List.

FIGURE 7–P

Chart of Accounts List— Updated and Customized System Default Accounts

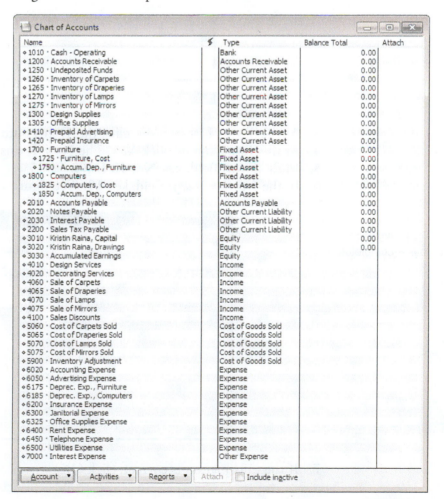

5. Close the Chart of Accounts window.

Customizing Payment Terms

In QuickBooks, a list with payment terms is accessed in customer files, vendor files, and activities windows when needed. As seen in prior chapters, payment terms such as Net 30 Days, 2/10 Net 30 Days, and so on can be identified in both the customer and vendor files if they relate to a particular customer or vendor.

When you create a new company file, QuickBooks automatically creates a list of payment terms. As with all other Lists/Centers in QuickBooks, you can add, delete, or edit the Terms List to customize it for your company.

To add a payment term—
1. Click Lists and then click *Customer & Vendor Profile Lists*.
2. At the Customer & Vendor Profile Lists submenu, click *Terms List*.

The Terms List window appears with the terms of payment that were created by QuickBooks. (See figure 7–Q.)

FIGURE 7–Q
Terms List Created by
Quickbook

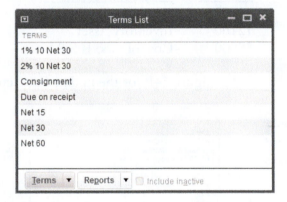

3. At the Terms List window, click the Terms button.
4. At the Terms menu, click *New*. The New Terms window appears.
5. In the *Terms* field, key **Net 10 Days**.
6. In the *Net due in days* field, key **10**. (See figure 7–R.)

FIGURE 7–R
New Terms Window—
Net 10 Days—Completed

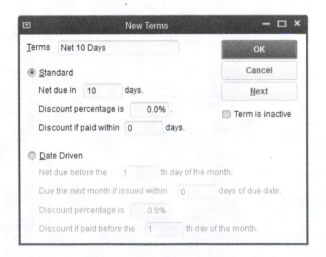

7. If the information is correct, click OK.

To delete a payment term—

1. At the Terms List, select *1% 10 Net 30*, but do not open it.
2. Click the Terms menu button. At the Terms menu, click *Delete Terms*.
3. A warning screen will appear. Click OK. The payment terms will be deleted.
4. Delete the following terms of payment:

   Consignment
   Due on Receipt
   Net 60

To edit a payment term—

1. At the Terms List, double-click *2% 10 Net 30* to open the Edit Terms window.
2. At the *Terms* field, change the name to **2/10, Net 30 Days**. (See figure 7–S.)

FIGURE 7–S
Edit Terms Window—
2/10, Net 30 Days—
Completed

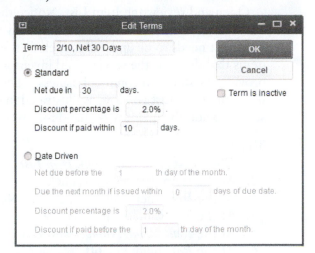

3. If the information is correct, click OK.
4. Edit the following terms of payment:

   Net 15 to **Net 15 Days**
   Net 30 to **Net 30 Days**

The updated Terms List appears in figure 7–T.

FIGURE 7–T
Terms List—Customized

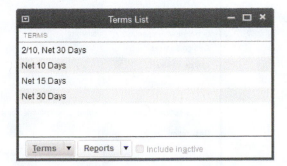

5. Close the Terms List window.

Updating the Lists and Centers

At this point, the company file has been created, preferences have been established, the Chart of Accounts List has been updated, and the system default accounts and payment terms have been customized. Since you did not use the QuickBooks Setup window to create the Customer and Vendor Centers or update the Item List, the next step is to update the Item List and the Customer and Vendor Centers using the procedures learned in prior chapters. In addition, when you update the Item List and Customer and Vendor Centers, you will be entering the beginning balances.

Updating the Item List

In QuickBooks, the Item List stores information about the service items, the inventory part items, and the sales tax. As transactions are recorded in the Activities windows, QuickBooks uses information in the Item List to record the transaction in the correct accounts.

Open and review the Item List. Notice that QuickBooks recorded the sales tax item when the sales tax feature was activated in the Preferences window. The Item List needs to be updated to include the service items and inventory part items that describe the services and inventory that Kristin Raina Interior Design provides or stocks to conduct business. These items are added to the Item List using the Item List window, as illustrated in prior chapters. The only additional step is to add the quantity on hand for inventory part items.

To add a service item—
1. Click Lists and then click *Item List*.
2. At the Item List window, click the Item button.
3. At the Item menu, click *New*. The New Item window appears.
4. At the *TYPE* field, click *Service*.
5. At the *Item Name/Number* and *Description* fields, key **Design Services**.
6. At the *Rate* field, key **60**.
7. At the *Tax Code* field, click *Non* for Non-Taxable Sales.
8. At the *Account* field, click *4010 Design Services*. Your screen should look like figure 7–U.

FIGURE 7–U

New Item Window—
Service

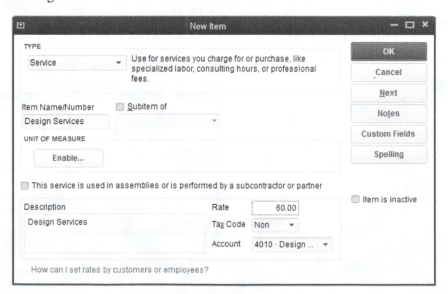

9. If the information is correct, click Next.

10. Enter the information listed below for the next service item:

TYPE:	**Service**
Item Name/Number:	**Decorating Services**
Description:	**Decorating Services**
Rate:	**50**
Tax Code:	**Non – Non-Taxable Sales**
Account:	**4020 Decorating Services**

11. Click OK.

To add inventory part items—
1. Open the Item List, if necessary, and then click *New* on the Item menu.
2. At the *TYPE* field, click *Inventory Part.*
3. Enter the information listed below for the carpets inventory:

Item Name/Number:	**Carpets**
Description on Purchase and	
Sales Transactions:	**Carpets**
Cost:	**200**
COGS Account:	**5060 Cost of Carpets Sold**
Sales Price:	**400**
Tax Code:	**Tax – Taxable Sales**
Income Account:	**4060 Sale of Carpets**
Asset Account:	**1260 Inventory of Carpets**
Reorder Point:	**5**
On Hand:	**4**
As of:	**04/01/2014**

> **HINT**
>
> In the account fields, you can key in the account number instead of using the drop-down list.

The amount of 800.00 in the *Total Value* field is computed automatically based on cost times quantity on hand. (See figure 7–V.)

FIGURE 7–V
New Item Window—Inventory Part

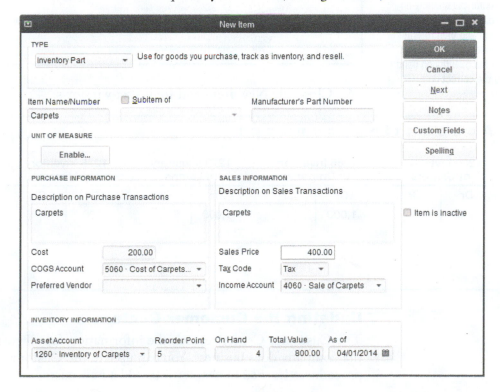

HINT

If you receive the Future Transactions message, click Yes at the message. Click Edit from the main menu bar, and then click *Preferences*. Click the Accounting icon, then click the Company Preferences tab. Remove the check marks in the *DATE WARNINGS* section and then click OK.

4. If the information is correct, click Next. The New Item window is displayed with the fields cleared for the next item.
5. Using the information in table 7–2, key in the remainder of the inventory part items. All inventory part items are taxable, and the reorder point is 5. Be sure to have the date as of 04/01/2014 on each item.

TABLE 7–2
Inventory Part Items

Item Name, Description on Purchase and Sales Transactions	Cost	COGS Account	Sales Price	Income Account	Asset Account	Reorder Point	On Hand	Total Value
Draperies	$125	5065	$250	4065	1265	5	8	$1,000
Lamps	100	5070	200	4070	1270	5	10	1,000
Mirrors	150	5075	300	4075	1275	5	6	900

The updated Item List appears in figure 7–W.

FIGURE 7–W
Item List—Updated

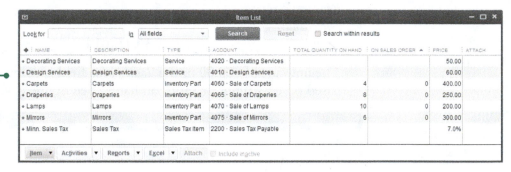

HINT

If you inadvertently do not enter the quantity on hand, delete the inventory item and then re-enter the inventory item along with the quantity on hand and the correct date.

6. Close the New Item and Item List windows.

A c c o u n t i n g   c o n c e p t

1260 Inventory of Carpets		1265 Inventory of Draperies		1270 Inventory of Lamps		1275 Inventory of Mirrors		3010 Kristin Raina, Capital	
Dr	Cr	Dr	Cr	Dr	Cr	Dr	Cr	Dr	Cr
800		1,000		1,000		900			800
									1,000
									1,000
									900

Updating the Customer Center

The Customer Center records the information for all customers with whom the company does business. You can update the Customer Center using the procedures learned in chapter 3 to add a new customer. The only additional step you need to take is to enter outstanding balances for some of these customers when recording the new customer file.

Kristin Raina has 10 customers. Two of the customers have outstanding balances.

To add a customer with an outstanding balance—
1. Click Customers and then click *Customer Center*.
2. At the Customer Center window, click the New Customer & Job button and then click New Customer. The New Customer window appears.
3. At the *CUSTOMER NAME* field, key **Berger Bakery Company**.
4. Move to the *OPENING BALANCE* field, and key **600**.
5. Move to the *AS OF* field, and choose *04/01/2014*.
6. Enter the information listed below on the Address Info tab:

HINT

On the Address Info tab, after completing the *INVOICE/BILL TO* field, click Copy to fill in the *SHIP TO* field.

Address Info		
	COMPANY NAME:	**Berger Bakery Company**
	FULL NAME:	
	First:	**Barry**
	Last:	**Berger**
	Main Phone:	**612-555-2240**
	Fax:	**612-555-2241**
	INVOICE/BILL TO:	**18 N. Grand Ave.**
		Minneapolis, MN 55403

(See figure 7–X.)

FIGURE 7–X
New Customer
Window—Address Info
Tab

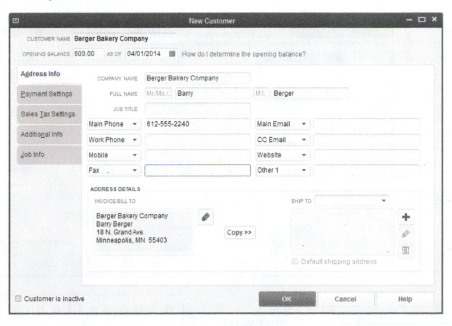

7. On the Payment Settings tab, at the *ACCOUNT NO.* field, key **R1825**.
8. At the *PAYMENT TERMS* drop-down list, click *Net 30 Days*.
9. Click OK. The new customer is added to the Customer Center.
10. Using the information in table 7–3, key in the information for all customers. Be sure to have the date as of 04/01/2014 for the customer with the opening balance.

TABLE 7–3

Customers

CUSTOMER/ COMPANY NAME	OPENING BALANCE	FULL NAME	Main Phone/ Fax	INVOICE/BILL TO	ACCOUNT NO.	PAYMENT TERMS
Alomar Company		Oliver Alomar	612-555-5757 612-555-5858	1001 Oak Lake Ave. Minneapolis, MN 55401	O1535	Net 30 Days
Barrera Bagel Barn		Belinda Barrera	612-555-1233 612-555-1234	148 46th Ave. N Plymouth, MN 53406	B0250	Net 30 Days
Cook Caterers		Stephen Cook	612-555-7896 612-555-7599	275 Oak Lake Ave. Minneapolis, MN 55401	C0360	Net 30 Days
Franco Films Co.	$940	Fred Franco	612-555-4566 612-555-4567	100 Pleasant Ave. S. Minneapolis, MN 55409	F0660	Net 30 Days
Guthrie, Jennie		Jennie Guthrie	651-555-1515	165 Terrace Ct. St. Paul, MN 55101	O1565	2/10, Net 30 Days
Hamilton Hotels		Hilda Hamilton	651-555-1050 651-555-1060	1000 York Ave. St. Paul, MN 55101	H0830	2/10, Net 30 Days
Jones, Beverly		Beverly Jones	612-555-7778	333 York Circle Bloomington, MN 54603	J1013	Net 30 Days
Omari, Maria		Maria Omari	612-555-9999 612-555-9998	210 NE Lowry Ave. Minneapolis, MN 54204	O1545	Net 30 Days
Plaza Pizza Palace		Mikey Plaza	612-555-9000 612-555-9800	360 Border Ave. N Minneapolis, MN 55401	P1650	Net 30 Days

FIGURE 7–Y

Customer Center— Updated

The updated Customer Center appears in figure 7–Y.

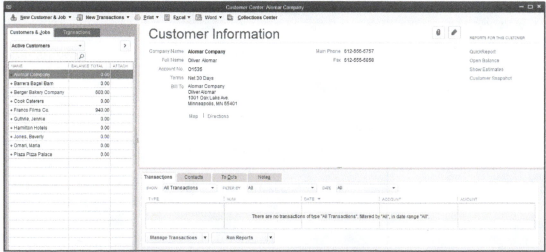

HINT

If you inadvertently do not enter the opening balance, delete the customer and re-enter with the balance and correct date.

11. Close Customer Center window.

Accounting concept

1200 Accounts Receivable		49900 Uncategorized Income	
Dr	Cr	Dr	Cr
600			600
940			940
Bal 1,540			Bal 1,540

Updating the Vendor Center

The Vendor Center records the information for all vendors with whom the company does business. Open and review the Vendor Center. There is one vendor, Minn. Dept. of Revenue, that was added to the Vendor Center when you set up the sales tax item. All other vendors need to be added to the Vendor Center.

The Vendor Center is updated using procedures learned in chapter 2 to add a new vendor. The only additional step you need to take is to enter outstanding balances for some of these vendors when recording the new vendor file.

Kristin Raina has 17 vendors. Seven of the vendors have outstanding balances.

To add a vendor with an outstanding balance—
1. Click Vendors and then click *Vendor Center*.
2. At the Vendor Center window, click the New Vendor menu button and then click New Vendor. The New Vendor window appears.
3. At the *VENDOR NAME* field, key **Ace Glass Works**.
4. At the *OPENING BALANCE* field, key **1500**.
5. At the *AS OF* field, choose *04/01/2014*.
6. Enter the information listed below:

Address Info	*COMPANY NAME:*	**Ace Glass Works**
	FULL NAME:	
	First:	**Archie**
	Last:	**Ace**
	Main Phone:	**612-555-9812**
	Fax:	**612-555-6813**
	BILLED FROM:	**25 SE Como Ave.**
		Minneapolis, MN 53602
Payment Settings	*ACCOUNT NO.:*	**1245**
	PAYMENT TERMS:	**Net 30 Days**
	PRINT NAME ON CHECK AS:	**Ace Glass Works**

(See figure 7–Z.)

FIGURE 7–Z
New Vendor Window—
Payment Settings Tab

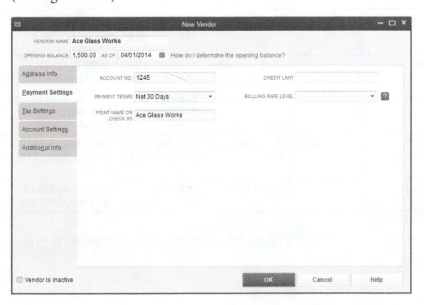

7. If the information is correct, click OK. The new vendor is added to the Vendor Center.
8. Using the information in table 7–4, key in all vendors. Be sure to have the date as of 04/01/2014 for the vendors with the opening balance.

Note: In the event that you do not have a person's name but instead have a department as a contact, you can still enter the information on the Address Info tab in the FULL NAME field. For example, if the contact is Customer Service, you can enter Customer in the first name field and Service in the last name field.

TABLE 7–4
Vendors

VENDOR/COMPANY NAME	OPENING BALANCE	FULL NAME	Main Phone/Fax	BILLED FROM	ACCOUNT NO.	PAYMENT TERMS
Bell Carpet Design	$2,000	Bill Bell	651-555-8823 651-555-8824	55 North Main Ave. St. Paul, MN 54603	66-87874	Net 30 Days
Cuza and Carl Associates	400	Carrie Cuza	651-555-8855 651-555-8856	23 W. University Ave. St. Paul, MN 54603	KR569	Net 30 Days
Darren Tapestry		Donna Darren	612-555-2221 612-555-2222	10 W. Larpenteur Ave. Minneapolis, MN 52604	2365	Net 30 Days
Galeway Computers	2,600	Roger Rivera	617-555-4747 617-555-4748	33 Route 10 Springfield, MA 24105	2455-897	Net 30 Days
Grayson Graphics		Gregg Grayson	612-555-0002 612-555-0003	56 Amity Way Bloomington, MN 53608	33-2221	Net 30 Days
Jeter Janitorial Services		Jason Jeter	612-555-4444 612-555-4445	233 Lilac Rd. Minneapolis, MN 54302	555-32	Net 30 Days
Kristin Raina		Kristin Raina				
Lumiare Lighting Company		Larry Lyght	612-555-4790 612-555-4795	123 Glenwood Ave. Minneapolis, MN 53609	36	Net 30 Days
Midwest Mutual Insurance Co.	2,400	Mike Mills	805-555-4545 805-555-4546	3566 Broadway Chicago, IL 58303	54778784	Net 30 Days
Minneapolis Electric & Gas Co.	450	Jack Watts	651-555-4949 651-555-4950	150 Douglas Ave. St. Paul, MN 55303	2001-23657	Net 30 Days
Nordic Realty		Melanie Marx	612-555-3232 612-555-3233	23 N. 12th Street Minneapolis, MN 53604	55-1212	Net 10 Days
TwinCityTelCo		Terry Ameche	651-555-6667 651-555-6668	3223 River Dr. St. Paul, MN 53908	666-6667	Net 30 Days
Weaver Fabrics		Jon Weaver	612-555-8777 612-555-8778	355 W. 70th Street Minneapolis, MN 53604	9878	Net 30 Days
Williams Office Supply Company	400	Bernard Williams	612-555-2240 612-555-2241	15 Grand Ave. S Minneapolis, MN 55404	55-8988	Net 30 Days
[Your Name] Accounting Service		Your Name	612-555-2222 612-555-2223	One Main Plaza St. Paul, MN 53602	99-2014-XX	Net 30 Days

The updated Vendor Center appears in figure 7–AA.

FIGURE 7–AA
Vendor Center—Updated

9. Close the New Vendor and Vendor Center windows.

HINT

If you inadvertently do not enter the opening balance, delete the vendor and re-enter the vendor along with the balance and the correct date.

Accounting concept

69800 Uncategorized Expenses		2010 Accts Payable	
Dr	Cr	Dr	Cr
1,500			1,500
2,000			2,000
400			400
2,600			2,600
2,400			2,400
450			450
400			400
Bal 9,750			Bal 9,750

Interim Review of New Company Setup

So far in setting up your new company file, you have created the company file, established preferences, updated and customized the Chart of Accounts, and updated the Item List and Customer and Vendor Centers.

As you added the inventory items, customers, and vendors with balances to the Lists and Centers, behind the scenes QuickBooks recorded the information in general journal format and updated the appropriate account balances. Now, display the *Journal*, *Profit & Loss Standard*, and *Balance Sheet Standard* reports to see the activity taking place behind the scenes up to this point.

Journal Report

To view and print the *Journal* report—
1. Click Reports and then click *Accountant & Taxes*.
2. At the Accountant & Taxes submenu, click *Journal*. At the Collapsing and Expanding Transactions message, read the message, and then place a check mark in the box to the left of Do not display this message in the future and click OK.

3. In the *From* and *To* fields, choose *04/01/2014* and then click the Refresh button on the top of the report.
4. To print the *Journal* report, click the Print button on the top of the report.
5. At the Print Reports dialog box, check the settings and then click Print. Your printout should look like figure 7–BB.

FIGURE 7–BB
Journal Report

CH7 [Your Name] Kristin Raina Interior Designs
Journal
April 1, 2014

Trans #	Type	Date	Num	Adj	Name	Memo	Account	Debit	Credit
1	Inventory Adjust	04/01/2014				Carpets Opening balance	3010 · Kristin Raina Capital		800.00
						Carpets Opening balance	1260 · Inventory of Carpets	800.00	
								800.00	800.00
2	Inventory Adjust	04/01/2014				Draperies Opening balance	3010 · Kristin Raina Capital		1,000.00
						Draperies Opening balance	1265 · Inventory of Draperies	1,000.00	
								1,000.00	1,000.00
3	Inventory Adjust	04/01/2014				Lamps Opening balance	3010 · Kristin Raina Capital		1,000.00
						Lamps Opening balance	1270 · Inventory of Lamps	1,000.00	
								1,000.00	1,000.00
4	Inventory Adjust	04/01/2014				Mirrors Opening balance	3010 · Kristin Raina Capital		900.00
						Mirrors Opening balance	1275 · Inventory of Mirrors	900.00	
								900.00	900.00
5	Invoice	04/01/2014			Berger Bakery Company	Opening balance	1200 · Accounts Receivable	600.00	
					Berger Bakery Company	Opening balance	49900 · Uncategorized Income		600.00
								600.00	600.00
6	Invoice	04/01/2014			Franco Films Co.	Opening balance	1200 · Accounts Receivable	940.00	
					Franco Films Co.	Opening balance	49900 · Uncategorized Income		940.00
								940.00	940.00
7	Bill	04/01/2014			Ace Glass Works	Opening balance	2010 · Accounts Payable		1,500.00
					Ace Glass Works	Opening balance	69800 · Uncategorized Expenses	1,500.00	
								1,500.00	1,500.00
8	Bill	04/01/2014			Bell Carpet Design	Opening balance	2010 · Accounts Payable		2,000.00
					Bell Carpet Design	Opening balance	69800 · Uncategorized Expenses	2,000.00	
								2,000.00	2,000.00
9	Bill	04/01/2014			Cuza and Carl Associates	Opening balance	2010 · Accounts Payable		400.00
					Cuza and Carl Associates	Opening balance	69800 · Uncategorized Expenses	400.00	
								400.00	400.00
10	Bill	04/01/2014			Galeway Computers	Opening balance	2010 · Accounts Payable		2,600.00
					Galeway Computers	Opening balance	69800 · Uncategorized Expenses	2,600.00	
								2,600.00	2,600.00
11	Bill	04/01/2014			Midwest Mutual Insurance Co.	Opening balance	2010 · Accounts Payable		2,400.00
					Midwest Mutual Insurance Co.	Opening balance	69800 · Uncategorized Expenses	2,400.00	
								2,400.00	2,400.00
12	Bill	04/01/2014			Minneapolis Electric & Gas Co.	Opening balance	2010 · Accounts Payable		450.00
					Minneapolis Electric & Gas Co.	Opening balance	69800 · Uncategorized Expenses	450.00	
								450.00	450.00
13	Bill	04/01/2014			Williams Office Supply Comp...	Opening balance	2010 · Accounts Payable		400.00
					Williams Office Supply Comp...	Opening balance	69800 · Uncategorized Expenses	400.00	
								400.00	400.00
TOTAL								**14,990.00**	**14,990.00**

Review the journal entries. They can be categorized as follows:
a. For items that are debit entries to the inventory accounts, the corresponding credit entry is to the Kristin Raina, Capital (Opening Balance Equity) account.
b. For entries that are debits to Accounts Receivable, the corresponding credit is to Uncategorized Income.
c. For entries that are credits to Accounts Payable, the corresponding debit is to Uncategorized Expenses.

6. Close the report. If you receive a message about Memorize Report, place a check mark in the box to the left of *Do not display this message in the future* and then click No.

Profit & Loss Standard (Income Statement) Report

To view the *Profit & Loss Standard* report—
1. Click Reports and then click *Company & Financial*.
2. At the Company & Financial submenu, click *Profit & Loss Standard*.
3. In the *From* and *To* fields, choose from *01/01/2014* to *04/01/2014* and then click the Refresh button on the top of the report. (See figure 7–CC.)

FIGURE 7–CC
Profit & Loss Standard Report

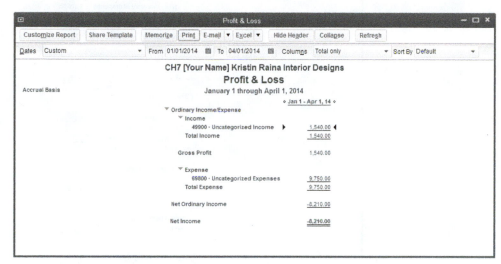

The *Profit & Loss Standard* report indicates only Uncategorized Income and Uncategorized Expenses. These amounts are offsetting amounts of the Accounts Receivable and Accounts Payable accounts. This is not a proper representation of the income and expenses of this company.

4. Close the report.

Balance Sheet Standard Report

To display the *Balance Sheet Standard* report—
1. Click Reports and then click *Company & Financial*.
2. At the Company & Financial submenu, click *Balance Sheet Standard*.
3. In the *As of* field, choose *04/01/2014* and then click the Refresh button on the top of the report. (See figure 7–DD.)

A review of the balance sheet indicates the following:
a. The only assets recorded so far are Accounts Receivable and the Inventory accounts.
b. The only liabilities recorded so far are the Accounts Payable.
c. The balance in the Kristin Raina, Capital (Opening Balance Equity) account is the same as the sum of the total inventory.
d. The net income is incorrect as seen in the Income Statement.

4. Close the report.

FIGURE 7–DD

Balance Sheet Standard
Report

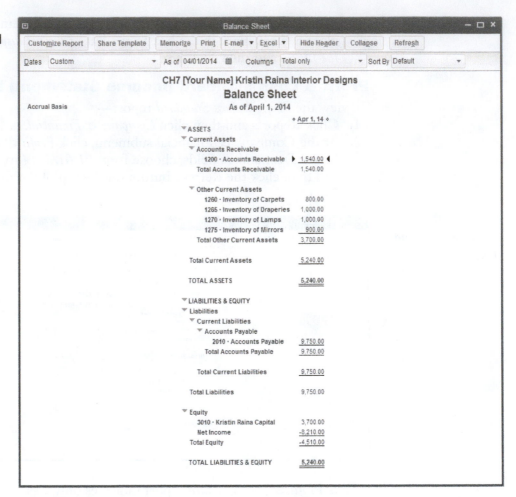

Adjusting for the Accrual Basis of Accounting

You have now created the new company file, established preferences, and updated and customized—as appropriate—the Lists and Centers. Now you must enter the remaining opening balances and prepare the company file for the **accrual basis of accounting**.

Accrual Basis of Accounting versus Cash Basis of Accounting

You may have noticed in many of the reports that there was a label *accrual basis* in the upper left-hand corner of the report. In QuickBooks, by default, the accounting reports and financial statements are prepared using the accrual basis of accounting, which records revenue when earned and expenses when incurred regardless of cash receipts and cash payments. The accrual basis of accounting follows GAAP—generally accepted accounting principles—and is the basis used in this text.

An alternative basis is called the **cash basis of accounting,** which records revenue only when the cash has been received for services provided or for a product sold, and records expenses only when cash payments have been made. QuickBooks allows you to switch individual reports from the accrual basis of accounting to the cash basis.

accrual basis of accounting
An accounting method that requires the recording of revenue when it is earned and the recording of expenses when they are incurred regardless of cash receipts or cash payments.

cash basis of accounting An accounting method that records revenue when cash is received for services provided or for a product sold, and records expenses only when payments have been made.

To view a report using the cash basis of accounting, open the report and click the Customize Report button. Then on the Display tab, choose REPORT BASIS – Cash, and click OK. The report is converted to reflect the cash basis of accounting. The accounts that are typically affected are Accounts Receivable, Accounts Payable, revenues, and expenses.

The default for all reports can be changed to the cash basis of accounting in the Preferences window. To change the default, click Edit, then click Preferences. Choose the Reports & Graphs icon and the Company Preferences tab. The SUMMARY REPORTS BASIS field is where the default can be changed to the cash basis.

Completing New Company Setup Using the Accrual Basis of Accounting

Recall that you entered the opening balances for the Inventory accounts, Accounts Receivable, and Accounts Payable accounts when you set up and updated the Lists/Centers. When you set up the Chart of Accounts List, you also could have entered the opening balances for assets (excluding Accounts Receivable), liabilities (excluding Accounts Payable), and equity accounts at that time as well. But you cannot enter opening balances for some system default accounts (such as Accounts Receivable, Accounts Payable, and Sales Tax Payable) and you cannot enter opening balances for revenue and expense accounts when creating new accounts in the Chart of Accounts List. Therefore, all opening balances (excluding inventory, accounts receivable, and accounts payable) will be entered in one journal entry.

As you saw in the *Journal* report (figure 7–BB), every time an Accounts Receivable account was recorded, a corresponding Uncategorized Income account was recorded, and every time an Accounts Payable account was recorded, a corresponding Uncategorized Expenses account was recorded. The Uncategorized Income and Uncategorized Expenses accounts are not used in the accrual basis of accounting and therefore must be reversed to eliminate them. You do this by using **reversing entries**.

reversing entries
Entries recorded in the general journal to offset a balance in an account.

To complete New Company Setup using the accrual basis of accounting, you will prepare three journal entries: entering opening balances, reversing uncategorized income account, and reversing uncategorized expenses account.

Entering Opening Balances

You will enter all opening balances for Kristin Raina Interior Designs, excluding inventory, accounts receivable, and accounts payable, as one large compound journal entry.

To enter opening balances in the Make General Journal Entries window—
1. Click Company and then click *Make General Journal Entries*. At the Assigning Numbers to Journal Entries message, place a check mark in the box to the left of *Do not display this message in the future* and then click OK. The Make General Journal Entries window appears.
2. At the *DATE* field, choose *04/01/2014*.
3. At the *ENTRY NO.* field, accept the default ENTRY NO. 1.
4. Remove the check mark from ADJUSTING ENTRY and click the Hide List icon to allow more space to record this large journal entry.

HINT

Maximize the Make General Journal Entries window and click the Hide List icon before recording this journal entry so that you can see more of the entries.

5. Enter the following accounts and amounts as debits:

Number	Account Name	Balance
1010	Cash - Operating	$50,855.38
1300	Design Supplies	200.00
1305	Office Supplies	250.00
1410	Prepaid Advertising	500.00
1420	Prepaid Insurance	2,200.00
1725	Furniture, Cost	12,000.00
1825	Computers, Cost	3,600.00
3020	Kristin Raina, Drawings	400.00
4100	Sales Discounts	84.62
5060	Cost of Carpets Sold	1,200.00
5065	Cost of Draperies Sold	500.00
5070	Cost of Lamps Sold	600.00
5075	Cost of Mirrors Sold	450.00
5900	Inventory Adjustment	150.00
6020	Accounting Expense	300.00
6050	Advertising Expense	100.00
6175	Deprec. Exp., Furniture	100.00
6185	Deprec. Exp., Computers	60.00
6200	Insurance Expense	200.00
6300	Janitorial Expense	125.00
6325	Office Supplies Expense	150.00
6400	Rent Expense	800.00
6450	Telephone Expense	275.00
6500	Utilities Expense	450.00
7000	Interest Expense	50.00

QuickCheck: $75,600

6. Enter the following accounts and amounts as credits:

Number	Account Name	Balance
1750	Accum. Dep., Furniture	$ 100.00
1850	Accum. Dep., Computers	60.00
2020	Notes Payable	7,000.00
2030	Interest Payable	50.00
4010	Design Services	4,980.00
4020	Decorating Services	3,400.00
4060	Sale of Carpets	2,400.00
4065	Sale of Draperies	1,000.00
4070	Sale of Lamps	1,200.00
4075	Sale of Mirrors	900.00

QuickCheck: $54,510

HINT

You can key in the account number for each account or use the drop-down list.

7. Record the credit balance of $54,510 as a credit to account 3010 Kristin Raina, Capital. (See figure 7–EE.)

FIGURE 7–EE
Make General Journal
Entries Window—
Opening Balances

Figure 7–EE: Make General Journal Entries Window

ACCOUNT	DEBIT	CREDIT	MEMO	NAME	BILLABLE?
1010 · Cash - Operating	50,855.38				
1300 · Design Supplies	200.00				
1305 · Office Supplies	250.00				
1410 · Prepaid Advertising	500.00				
1420 · Prepaid Insurance	2,200.00				
1700 · Furniture:1725 · Furniture, Cost	12,000.00				
1800 · Computers:1825 · Computers, Cost	3,600.00				
3020 · Kristin Raina, Drawings	400.00				
4100 · Sales Discounts	84.62				
5060 · Cost of Carpets Sold	1,200.00				
5065 · Cost of Draperies Sold	500.00				
5070 · Cost of Lamps Sold	600.00				
5075 · Cost of Mirrors Sold	450.00				
5900 · Inventory Adjustment	150.00				
6020 · Accounting Expense	300.00				
6050 · Advertising Expense	100.00				
6175 · Deprec., Exp., Furniture	100.00				
6185 · Deprec. Exp., Computers	60.00				
6200 · Insurance Expense	200.00				
6300 · Janitorial Expense	125.00				
6325 · Office Supplies Expense	150.00				
6400 · Rent Expense	800.00				
6450 · Telephone Expense	275.00				
6500 · Utilities Expense	450.00				
7000 · Interest Expense	50.00				
1700 · Furniture:1750 · Accum. Dep., Furniture		100.00			
1800 · Computers:1850 · Accum. Dep., Computers		60.00			
2020 · Notes Payable		7,000.00			
2030 · Interest Payable		50.00			
4010 · Design Services		4,980.00			
4020 · Decorating Services		3,400.00			
4060 · Sale of Carpets		2,400.00			
4065 · Sale of Draperies		1,000.00			
4070 · Sale of Lamps		1,200.00			
4075 · Sale of Mirrors		900.00			
3010 · Kristin Raina Capital		54,510.00			
Totals	75,600.00	75,600.00			

DATE 04/01/2014   ENTRY NO. 1   ADJUSTING ENTRY

HINT

If you receive the Future Transactions message, click Yes at the message. Click Edit from the main menu bar and then click *Preferences*. Click the Accounting icon, then click the Company Preferences tab. Remove the check marks in the *DATE WARNINGS* section, then click OK.

8. If the information is correct, click Save & New. If a message appears about Tracking fixed assets, place a check mark in the box to the left of *Do not display this message in the future* and then click OK.

Accounting concept

The effect of recording the opening balances is as follows:

1010-1825 Assets		
Dr		Cr
Cash - Operating	50,855.38	
Design Supplies	200.00	
Office Supplies	250.00	
Prepaid Advertising	500.00	
Prepaid Insurance	2,200.00	
Furniture	12,000.00	
Computers	3,600.00	
	69,605.38	

1750-1850 Accum Dep	
Dr	Cr
	100.00
	60.00
	160.00

2020-2030 Payables		
Dr	Cr	
	7,000.00	Notes
	50.00	Interest
	7,050.00	

3010 Kristin Raina, Capital	
Dr	Cr
	54,510.00

3020 Kristin Raina, Drawings	
Dr	Cr
400.00	

4010-4020 Service Revenue		
Dr	Cr	
	Design 4,980.00	
	Decor 3,400.00	
	8,380.00	

4060-4075 Sale of Inventory		
Dr	Cr	
	Carpets	2,400.00
	Draperies	1,000.00
	Lamps	1,200.00
	Mirrors	900.00
		5,500.00

4100 Sales Discounts	
Dr	Cr
84.62	

5060-5075,5900 Cost of Goods Sold		
Dr		Cr
Carpets	1,200.00	
Draperies	500.00	
Lamps	600.00	
Mirrors	450.00	
Invent Adj	150.00	
	2,900.00	

6020-6500 Expenses		
Dr		Cr
Accounting	300.00	
Advertising	100.00	
Dep Exp, Furniture	100.00	
Dep Exp, Computers	60.00	
Insurance	200.00	
Janitorial	125.00	
Office Supplies	150.00	
Rent	800.00	
Telephone	275.00	
Utilities	450.00	
Bal	2,560.00	

7000 Interest Exp	
Dr	Cr
50.00	

Reversing Uncategorized Income Account

Recall that in the *Journal* report of figure 7–BB, two journal entries are recorded that debit the Accounts Receivable and credit Uncategorized Income for two customers as follows:

Berger Bakery Company	$ 600
Franco Films Co.	940
	$1,540

The debit entries to the Accounts Receivable account are correct and will stay in that account. The credits to the Uncategorized Income account will be reversed by debiting Uncategorized Income for the total of $1,540 and crediting the account 3010 Kristin Raina, Capital (formerly the Opening Balance Equity account) for $1,540.

HINT

As part of customizing the Chart of Accounts, the account Opening Balance Equity, created by QuickBooks, was changed to 3010 Kristin Raina, Capital.

To reverse the Uncategorized Income account—

1. At the Make General Journal Entries window, choose the date, *04/01/2014*, and at the *ENTRY NO.* field, accept ENTRY NO. 2.
2. Remove the check mark from ADJUSTING ENTRY, if necessary.
3. Debit account 49900 Uncategorized Income for 1,540, and credit account 3010 Kristin Raina, Capital, for 1,540. (See figure 7–FF.)

FIGURE 7–FF
Make General Journal Entries Window—Reverse Uncategorized Income

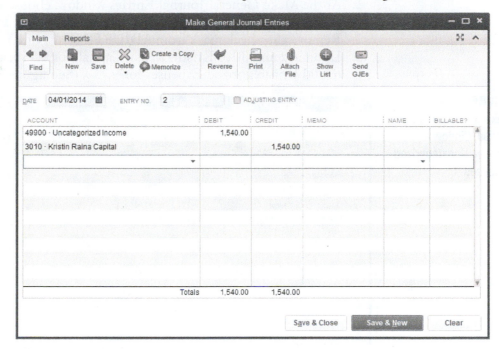

4. If the information is correct, click Save & New.

Accounting concept

49900 Uncategorized Income		3010 Kristin Raina, Capital	
Dr	Cr	Dr	Cr
Rev 1,540	1,540		1,540
	Bal 0		

Reversing the Uncategorized Expenses Account

In the *Journal* report shown in figure 7–BB, there are seven journal entries that credit Accounts Payable and debit Uncategorized Expenses for seven vendor balances as follows:

Ace Glass Works	$1,500
Bell Carpet Design	2,000
Cuza and Carl Associates	400
Galeway Computers	2,600
Midwest Mutual Insurance Co.	2,400
Minneapolis Electric & Gas Co.	450
Williams Office Supply Company	400
	$9,750

The credit entries to the Accounts Payable account are correct and will stay in that account. The debits to the Uncategorized Expenses, however, have to be reversed by crediting Uncategorized Expenses for the total of $9,750 and debiting the 3010 Kristin Raina, Capital, account for $9,750.

To reverse the Uncategorized Expenses account—
1. At the Make General Journal Entries window, choose the date *04/01/2014*, and at the *ENTRY NO.* field, accept ENTRY NO. 3.
2. Remove the check mark from ADJUSTING ENTRY, if necessary.
3. Debit account 3010 Kristin Raina, Capital, for 9,750, and credit account 69800 Uncategorized Expenses for 9,750. (See figure 7–GG.)

FIGURE 7–GG
Make General Journal Entries Window— Reverse Uncategorized Expenses

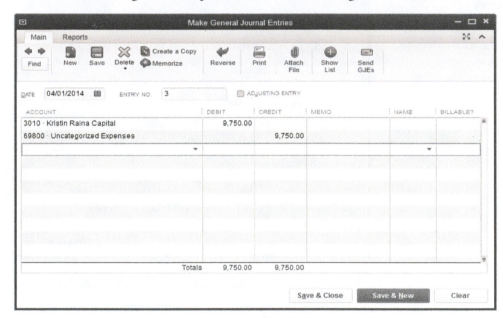

4. If the information is correct, click Save & Close.

Accounting concept

69800 Uncategorized Expenses			3010 Kristin Raina, Capital	
Dr	Cr		Dr	Cr
9,750	Rev 9,750		9,750	
0				

REPORTS:

Accounting Reports and Financial Statements

Upon completing the New Company Setup, you should display and print the accounting reports and financial statements.

Accounting Reports

The accounting reports you need to print and review consist of the *Journal* and the *Trial Balance*.

HINT

To display only the last three journal entries in the *Journal* report, click the Customize Report button. Then click the Filters tab. In the *CHOOSE FILTER* field, click *Transaction Type* field. In the *Transaction Type*, click *Journal*. Then click OK.

Journal Report

You displayed and printed the *Journal* report after the initial company setup was completed (figure 7–BB). After recording the opening balances and reversing the Uncategorized Income and Uncategorized Expenses accounts, three more journal entries have been added to the *Journal* report. You can view and print all journal entries for April 1, 2014. Figure 7–HH displays only the additional three journal entries.

FIGURE 7–HH
Additional Journal Entries

CH7 [Your Name] Kristin Raina Interior Designs
Journal
April 1, 2014

Trans #	Type	Date	Num	Adj	Name	Memo	Account	Debit	Credit
14	General Journal	04/01/2014	1				1010 · Cash - Operating	50,855.38	
							1300 · Design Supplies	200.00	
							1305 · Office Supplies	250.00	
							1410 · Prepaid Advertising	500.00	
							1420 · Prepaid Insurance	2,200.00	
							1725 · Furniture, Cost	12,000.00	
							1825 · Computers, Cost	3,600.00	
							3020 · Kristin Raina, Drawings	400.00	
							4100 · Sales Discounts	84.62	
							5060 · Cost of Carpets Sold	1,200.00	
							5065 · Cost of Draperies Sold	500.00	
							5070 · Cost of Lamps Sold	600.00	
							5075 · Cost of Mirrors Sold	450.00	
							5900 · Inventory Adjustment	150.00	
							6020 · Accounting Expense	300.00	
							6050 · Advertising Expense	100.00	
							6175 · Deprec., Exp., Furniture	100.00	
							6185 · Deprec. Exp., Computers	60.00	
							6200 · Insurance Expense	200.00	
							6300 · Janitorial Expense	125.00	
							6325 · Office Supplies Expense	150.00	
							6400 · Rent Expense	800.00	
							6450 · Telephone Expense	275.00	
							6500 · Utilities Expense	450.00	
							7000 · Interest Expense	50.00	
							1750 · Accum. Dep., Furniture		100.00
							1850 · Accum. Dep., Computers		60.00
							2020 · Notes Payable		7,000.00
							2030 · Interest Payable		50.00
							4010 · Design Services		4,980.00
							4020 · Decorating Services		3,400.00
							4060 · Sale of Carpets		2,400.00
							4065 · Sale of Draperies		1,000.00
							4070 · Sale of Lamps		1,200.00
							4075 · Sale of Mirrors		900.00
							3010 · Kristin Raina Capital		54,510.00
								75,600.00	75,600.00
15	General Journal	04/01/2014	2				49900 · Uncategorized Income	1,540.00	
							3010 · Kristin Raina Capital		1,540.00
								1,540.00	1,540.00
16	General Journal	04/01/2014	3				3010 · Kristin Raina Capital	9,750.00	
							69800 · Uncategorized Expenses		9,750.00
								9,750.00	9,750.00
TOTAL								86,890.00	86,890.00

HINT

If you display all the journal entries, the total debits and total credits is $101,880.

Trial Balance Report

Next, view and print the *Trial Balance* report for April 1, 2014. (It should look like figure 7–II.) The accounts and balances on this trial balance should match the trial balance of March 31, 2014, after transactions were recorded in chapters 2 through 5.

FIGURE 7–II
Trial Balance Report

CH7 [Your Name] Kristin Raina Interior Designs
Trial Balance

Accrual Basis

As of April 1, 2014

	Apr 1, 14	
	Debit	Credit
1010 · Cash - Operating	50,855.38	
1200 · Accounts Receivable	1,540.00	
1260 · Inventory of Carpets	800.00	
1265 · Inventory of Draperies	1,000.00	
1270 · Inventory of Lamps	1,000.00	
1275 · Inventory of Mirrors	900.00	
1300 · Design Supplies	200.00	
1305 · Office Supplies	250.00	
1410 · Prepaid Advertising	500.00	
1420 · Prepaid Insurance	2,200.00	
1700 · Furniture:1725 · Furniture, Cost	12,000.00	
1700 · Furniture:1750 · Accum. Dep., Furniture		100.00
1800 · Computers:1825 · Computers, Cost	3,600.00	
1800 · Computers:1850 · Accum. Dep., Computers		60.00
2010 · Accounts Payable		9,750.00
2020 · Notes Payable		7,000.00
2030 · Interest Payable		50.00
3010 · Kristin Raina Capital		50,000.00
3020 · Kristin Raina, Drawings	400.00	
4010 · Design Services		4,980.00
4020 · Decorating Services		3,400.00
4060 · Sale of Carpets		2,400.00
4065 · Sale of Draperies		1,000.00
4070 · Sale of Lamps		1,200.00
4075 · Sale of Mirrors		900.00
4100 · Sales Discounts	84.62	
49900 · Uncategorized Income	0.00	
5060 · Cost of Carpets Sold	1,200.00	
5065 · Cost of Draperies Sold	500.00	
5070 · Cost of Lamps Sold	600.00	
5075 · Cost of Mirrors Sold	450.00	
5900 · Inventory Adjustment	150.00	
6020 · Accounting Expense	300.00	
6050 · Advertising Expense	100.00	
6175 · Deprec., Exp., Furniture	100.00	
6185 · Deprec. Exp., Computers	60.00	
6200 · Insurance Expense	200.00	
6300 · Janitorial Expense	125.00	
6325 · Office Supplies Expense	150.00	
6400 · Rent Expense	800.00	
6450 · Telephone Expense	275.00	
6500 · Utilities Expense	450.00	
69800 · Uncategorized Expenses	0.00	
7000 · Interest Expense	50.00	
TOTAL	**80,840.00**	**80,840.00**

Recall that QuickBooks created the Uncategorized Income and Uncategorized Expenses accounts when you entered outstanding accounts receivable and accounts payable balances in the Customer Center and Vendor Center, respectively. The balances in these uncategorized accounts were subsequently reversed when the company file was prepared for the accrual basis of accounting. These accounts are no longer needed and can be marked inactive in the Chart of Accounts List.

Financial Statements

The financial statements consist of the *Profit & Loss Standard* report (see figure 7–JJ) and the *Balance Sheet Standard* report (see figure 7–KK). Upon completion of the New Company Setup, these reports should be the same as the financial reports printed at the end of chapter 5.

FIGURE 7–JJ
Profit & Loss Standard Report

CH7 [Your Name] Kristin Raina Interior Designs
Profit & Loss
Accrual Basis   January 1 through April 1, 2014

	Jan 1 – Apr 1, 14
Ordinary Income/Expense	
Income	
4010 · Design Services	4,980.00
4020 · Decorating Services	3,400.00
4060 · Sale of Carpets	2,400.00
4065 · Sale of Draperies	1,000.00
4070 · Sale of Lamps	1,200.00
4075 · Sale of Mirrors	900.00
4100 · Sales Discounts	-84.62
49900 · Uncategorized Income	0.00
Total Income	13,795.38
Cost of Goods Sold	
5060 · Cost of Carpets Sold	1,200.00
5065 · Cost of Draperies Sold	500.00
5070 · Cost of Lamps Sold	600.00
5075 · Cost of Mirrors Sold	450.00
5900 · Inventory Adjustment	150.00
Total COGS	2,900.00
Gross Profit	10,895.38
Expense	
6020 · Accounting Expense	300.00
6050 · Advertising Expense	100.00
6175 · Deprec., Exp., Furniture	100.00
6185 · Deprec. Exp., Computers	60.00
6200 · Insurance Expense	200.00
6300 · Janitorial Expense	125.00
6325 · Office Supplies Expense	150.00
6400 · Rent Expense	800.00
6450 · Telephone Expense	275.00
6500 · Utilities Expense	450.00
69800 · Uncategorized Expenses	0.00
Total Expense	2,560.00
Net Ordinary Income	8,335.38
Other Income/Expense	
Other Expense	
7000 · Interest Expense	50.00
Total Other Expense	50.00
Net Other Income	-50.00
Net Income	8,285.38

FIGURE 7–KK

Balance Sheet Standard
Report

CH7 [Your Name] Kristin Raina Interior Designs

Balance Sheet

Accrual Basis   **As of April 1, 2014**

	Apr 1, 14
ASSETS	
Current Assets	
Checking/Savings	
1010 · Cash ☐Operating	50,855.38
Total Checking/Savings	50,855.38
Accounts Receivable	
1200 · Accounts Receivable	1,540.00
Total Accounts Receivable	1,540.00
Other Current Assets	
1260 · Inventory of Carpets	800.00
1265 · Inventory of Draperies	1,000.00
1270 · Inventory of Lamps	1,000.00
1275 · Inventory of Mirrors	900.00
1300 · Design Supplies	200.00
1305 · Office Supplies	250.00
1410 · Prepaid Advertising	500.00
1420 · Prepaid Insurance	2,200.00
Total Other Current Assets	6,850.00
Total Current Assets	59,245.38
Fixed Assets	
1700 · Furniture	
1725 · Furniture, Cost	12,000.00
1750 · Accum. Dep., Furniture	-100.00
Total 1700 · Furniture	11,900.00
1800 · Computers	
1825 · Computers, Cost	3,600.00
1850 · Accum. Dep., Computers	-60.00
Total 1800 · Computers	3,540.00
Total Fixed Assets	15,440.00
TOTAL ASSETS	**74,685.38**
LIABILITIES & EQUITY	
Liabilities	
Current Liabilities	
Accounts Payable	
2010 · Accounts Payable	9,750.00
Total Accounts Payable	9,750.00
Other Current Liabilities	
2020 · Notes Payable	7,000.00
2030 · Interest Payable	50.00
Total Other Current Liabilities	7,050.00
Total Current Liabilities	16,800.00
Total Liabilities	16,800.00
Equity	
3010 · Kristin Raina Capital	50,000.00
3020 · Kristin Raina, Drawings	-400.00
Net Income	8,285.38
Total Equity	57,885.38
TOTAL LIABILITIES & EQUITY	**74,685.38**

Hybrid Method of New Company Setup and QuickBooks Setup Window

You have now learned two methods of new company setup: Detailed Start and Express Start. In addition, in chapter 6 you learned how to use the QuickBooks Setup window to enter information for customers, vendors, and items, but the QuickBooks Setup window could also have been used in chapter 7. Instead, in chapter 7, you learned to enter service items, and inventory part items, customers, and vendors by going directly to the Item List, Customer Center, and Vendor Center to enter the appropriate information bypassing the QuickBooks Setup window.

However, once you create the new company file with either the Detailed Start or the Express Start, you can then use any combination of entering company information for service items, inventory part items, customers, and vendors. That is, you can use the QuickBooks Setup window or the Lists/Center in any combination. For instance, you could use the QuickBooks Setup window to enter the customers and vendors, but you may choose to use the Item List to enter the service and inventory part items, or you could use the QuickBooks Setup window to enter the inventory part items and use the Item List to enter the service items. QuickBooks will accept any variation of using the QuickBooks Setup window or Lists/Centers for entering the information for customers, vendors, service items, and inventory part items.

Backing Up the New Company File

You should make a backup copy of the new company file in the event there is damage to the file or the computer, or you are working on a different computer. Using the procedures learned in previous chapters, make a backup copy of the new company file to your subfolder and/or a removable storage device, and name it **EX7 [*Your Name*] Kristin Raina Interior Designs**. Restore the backup copy and change the company name to **EX7 [*Your Name*] Kristin Raina Interior Designs**.

Upon completion of the New Company Setup level of operation, customizing and updating the Lists/Centers, viewing and printing Reports, and making a backup copy of the new company file, your accounting records are now ready for recording daily activities. Activities would be recorded in the new company file using the procedures illustrated in the prior chapters.

Chapter Review and Assessment

Procedure Review

To begin New Company Setup and create a new company file using Express Start—

1. Open QuickBooks.
2. At the No Company Open window, click the *Create a new company* button or click File and then click *New Company*. The QuickBooks Setup window appears with the Let's get your business set up quickly! page displayed. This is the page where you select the method of New Company Setup.
3. At the QuickBooks Setup window on the Let's get your business set up quickly! page, click the Express Start button. The Tell us about your business page appears.
4. At the Tell us about your business page, in the *Company Name* field, key the company name.
5. Move to the Industry field and click *Help me choose*. The Select Your Industry page appears.
6. At the Select Your Industry page, in the *Industry* field, scroll to the bottom and select *Other/None*.
7. Click OK. You are returned to the Tell us about your business page.
8. In the *Company Type* field, click the drop-down arrow and choose *Sole Proprietorship*.
9. At the *Tax ID#* field, key in the tax identification number.
10. Click Continue. You are moved to the Enter your business contact information page.
11. At the Enter your business contact information page, key in the appropriate information.
12. Click the Preview Your Settings button.
13. At the Preview Your Company Settings page, click the Company File Location tab.
14. On the Company File Location tab, click the Change Location button. You are moved to the Browse For Folder window.
15. At the Browse For Folder window, scroll through the list and choose the folder where you save your files, and then click OK. You are returned to the Company File Location tab with the path and folder displayed.
16. If the path and folder are correct, click OK. You are returned to the Enter your business contact information page.
17. Click the Create Company File button. The company file is saved in the path and folder you indicated above. The QuickBooks Setup window appears.
18. Click the X to close the QuickBooks Setup window. The home page and left icon bar appear. Click the X to close the home page. To remove the left icon bar, click View and then click Hide Icon Bar.

To activate the account numbers feature—
1. Click Edit and then click *Preferences*.
2. Along the left frame of the Preferences window, click the *Accounting* icon.
3. Click the Company Preferences tab.
4. At the *ACCOUNTS* field, place a check mark in the box to the left of *Use account numbers* to turn on the account numbers feature.
5. Click OK.

To activate the inventory feature—
1. Click Edit and then click *Preferences*.
2. Along the left frame of the Preferences window, click the *Items & Inventory* icon.
3. Click the Company Preferences tab.
4. At the *PURCHASE ORDERS AND INVENTORY* section, place a check mark in the box to the left of *Inventory and purchase orders are active* to turn on the inventory feature.
5. Click OK.

To activate the sales tax feature—
1. Click Edit and then click *Preferences*.
2. Along the left frame of the Preferences window, click the *Sales Tax* icon.
3. Click the Company Preferences tab.
4. At the *Do You Charge Sales Tax?* field, click *Yes*.
5. Move to the *Your most common sales tax item* field, and click the drop-down arrow.
6. Click < Add New >. The New Item window appears.
7. Key in the sales tax item information.
8. Move to the *Tax Agency* field and click the drop-down arrow.
9. At the Tax Agency drop-down list, click < Add New >. The New Vendor window appears.
10. Enter the appropriate vendor information and then click OK.
11. Click OK at the completed New Item window and then click OK at the Preferences window.
12. At the Updating Sales Tax dialog box, click OK.

To disable the payroll feature—
1. Click Edit and then click *Preferences*.
2. Along the left frame of the Preferences window, click the *Payroll & Employees* icon.
3. Click the Company Preferences tab.
4. At the *QUICKBOOKS PAYROLL FEATURES* field, click *No Payroll*.
5. Click OK.

To update the Chart of Accounts List—
1. Click Lists and then click *Chart of Accounts*.
2. Click the Account menu button.
3. At the Account menu, click *New*.
4. At the Add New Account: Choose Account Type window, choose the type and then click Continue.
5. At the Add New Account window, key the information and then click Save and New or Save and Close.

To allow QuickBooks to create system default accounts—

1. Open and close the Activities windows, such as the Create Invoices, Enter Sales Receipts, and Enter Bills windows. Open the Item List and the New Item window, and select *Inventory Part*.

   This process will create the system default accounts: Undeposited Funds, Inventory Asset, and Cost of Goods Sold. After QuickBooks creates these accounts, you can edit the account number and name. If you created an accounts receivable–type account and an accounts payable–type account, QuickBooks will accept the accounts. If you did not previously create them, when you open and close the Create Invoices and Enter Bills windows, QuickBooks will create the accounts receivable and accounts payable accounts, respectively.

2. Follow the steps to customize the system default accounts.

To customize the system default accounts—

1. Click Lists and then click *Chart of Accounts*.
2. Select the account to edit.
3. Click the Account button.
4. At the Account menu, click *Edit Account*.
5. Make any necessary changes to the account, then click Save and Close.

To make an account inactive—

1. Click Lists and then click *Chart of Accounts*.
2. Select the account to make inactive.
3. Click the Account button.
4. At the Account menu, click *Make Account Inactive*.

To customize payment terms—

1. Click Lists and then click *Customer & Vendor Profile Lists*.
2. At the Customer & Vendor Profile Lists submenu, click *Terms List*.
3. At the Terms List window, select the terms created by QuickBooks that you wish to edit.
4. Click the Terms menu button; from the Terms menu, click *Edit Terms*.
5. Change the appropriate information, then click OK.
6. At the Terms List window, select the terms created by QuickBooks that you wish to delete.
7. Click the Terms menu button; from the Terms menu, click *Delete Terms*. Click OK at the warning.
8. At the Terms List window, click the Terms menu button.
9. At the Terms menu, click *New*.
10. At the New Terms window, key the appropriate information for any terms QuickBooks did not create that you wish to create.
11. Click Next or OK.

To update the Item List—

1. Click Lists and then click *Item List*.
2. At the Item List window, click the Item menu button.
3. At the Item menu, click *New*.
4. At the New Item window, key the information and then click Next or OK.

To update the Customer Center—
1. Click Customers and then click *Customer Center.*
2. At the Customer Center window, click the New Customer & Job button and then click New Customer.
3. At the New Customer window, enter the background data for the customer including the opening balance, if any, and the correct date.
4. Click Next or OK.

To update the Vendor Center—
1. Click Vendors and then click *Vendor Center.*
2. At the Vendor Center window, click the New Vendor button and then click New Vendor.
3. At the New Vendor window, enter the background data for the vendor including the opening balance, if any, and the correct date.
4. Click Next or OK.

To enter opening balances in the Make General Journal Entries window—
1. Click Company and then click *Make General Journal Entries.*
2. Choose the date, and make or accept an entry in the *ENTRY NO.* field.
3. Remove the check mark from ADJUSTING ENTRY.
4. Enter the accounts and amounts to be debited.
5. Enter the accounts and amounts to be credited.
6. Record the balancing amount as a credit (or debit) to the capital account.
7. Click Save & Close.

To reverse the Uncategorized Income account—
1. Click Company and then click *Make General Journal Entries.*
2. Choose the date, and make or accept an entry in the *ENTRY NO.* field.
3. Remove the check mark from ADJUSTING ENTRY.
4. Debit the Uncategorized Income account for the full amount in that account, and credit the Capital account for the same amount.
5. Click Save & Close.

To reverse the Uncategorized Expenses account—
1. Click Company and then click *Make General Journal Entries.*
2. Choose the date, and make or accept an entry in the *ENTRY NO.* field.
3. Remove the check mark from ADJUSTING ENTRY.
4. Debit the Capital account for the full amount in the Uncategorized Expenses account, and credit the Uncategorized Expenses account for the same amount.
5. Click Save & Close.

To view and print accounting reports from the Reports menu—
1. Click Reports and then click *Accountant & Taxes.*
2. At the Accountant & Taxes submenu, choose a report.
3. Indicate the start and end dates for the report.
4. Click the Print button on the top of the report.
5. At the Print Reports dialog box, review the settings and then click Print.
6. Close the report.

To view and print financial statements from the Reports menu—
1. Click Reports and then click *Company & Financial.*
2. At the Company & Financial submenu, choose a financial report.
3. Indicate the start and end dates for the report.
4. Click the Print button on the top of the report.
5. At the Print Reports dialog box, review the settings and then click Print.
6. Close the report.

Key Concepts

Select the letter of the item that best matches each definition.

a. Most Common Sales Tax
b. Inactive
c. Uncategorized Income
d. Preferences - Accounting
e. Inventory Asset and Cost of Goods Sold

f. Preferences - Items & Inventory
g. Express Start
h. System Default Accounts
i. Uncategorized Expenses
j. Customer & Vendor Profile Lists

_____ 1. An alternative method of New Company Setup.
_____ 2. Accounts automatically created by QuickBooks when you choose an inventory item part in the New Item window.
_____ 3. An option you can choose so accounts not in use are not displayed in the reports.
_____ 4. Window used to activate account numbers.
_____ 5. Accounts automatically created by QuickBooks.
_____ 6. Account created by QuickBooks as an offsetting amount of Accounts Receivable.
_____ 7. Window used to activate the inventory feature.
_____ 8. Submenu used to open the Terms List window.
_____ 9. Field that must be completed to activate the sales tax feature.
_____ 10. Account created by QuickBooks as an offsetting amount of Accounts Payable.

Procedure Check

1. You are setting up a new company file, and you wish to use the Express Start method. Which preferences should be established before recording data?
2. When you first choose Inventory Part item in the New Item window of the Item List, which two accounts does QuickBooks look for on the Chart of Accounts List? Can you customize these accounts? If so, explain how.
3. What is the Opening Balance Equity account? Can you customize this account? If so, explain how.
4. If you set up a new company file using the Express Start method and you choose not to use the QuickBooks Setup window to enter information, how are the accounts receivables and accounts payables recorded?
5. If you set up a new company file using the Express Start method, which journal entries would you normally record to complete the New Company Setup process?

6. Your manager is just learning QuickBooks. He asked you if it is necessary to use the Detailed Start method with the EasyStep Interview window or the QuickBooks Setup window for New Company Setup. Provide the manager with a written explanation of how he could set up the new company file using the Express Start method and not using the EasyStep Interview and QuickBooks Setup windows.

Case Problems
Case Problem 1

On April 1, 2014, Lynn Garcia began her business, called Lynn's Music Studio. In the first month of business, Lynn set up the music studio, provided guitar and piano lessons, and recorded month-end activity. In May, the second month of business, Lynn started purchasing and selling inventory items of guitars, keyboards, music stands, and sheet music. In April and May, Lynn was recording the financial activities using a manual accounting system. On June 1, 2014, Lynn decides to switch her accounting method to QuickBooks. Lynn has organized the information about the company but has hired you to convert the accounting records to QuickBooks.

1. Use the information below to create and set up the company file using the Express Start method (skip the QuickBooks Setup window after the new company file is created):

Company Name:	**CH7 [*Your Name*] Lynn's Music Studio**
Industry:	**Other/None**
Company Type:	**Sole Proprietorship**
Tax ID #:	**45-6123789**
Legal Name:	**CH7[*Your Name*] Lynn's Music Studio**
Address:	**228 Pearl Street**
City:	**Scranton**
State:	**PA**
Zip:	**18501**
Country:	**U.S.**
Phone:	**570-555-0400**
Email:	**LYNN@emcp.net**

2. Activate the account numbers, inventory, and sales tax features. For sales tax, use the following information:

TYPE:	**Sales Tax Item**
Tax Name:	**PA Sales Tax**
Description:	**Sales Tax**
Tax Rate (%):	**7**
Tax Agency:	**PA Dept. of Revenue**

3. Disable the payroll.

4. Open and close the following windows to allow QuickBooks to create default accounts.

Create Invoices
Enter Sales Receipts
Enter Bills
Item List: New Item: Inventory Part

5. Customize the system default accounts:

QuickBooks		Edited	
Number	Account Name	Number	Account Name
11000	Accounts Receivable	1200	
12000	Undeposited Funds	1250	
12100	Inventory Asset	1260	Inventory of Guitars
20000	Accounts Payable	2010	
25500	Sales Tax Payable	2200	
30000	Opening Balance Equity	3010	Lynn Garcia, Capital
30800	Owners Draw	3020	Lynn Garcia, Drawings
32000	Owners Equity	3030	Accumulated Earnings
50000	Cost of Goods Sold	5060	Cost of Guitars Sold

6. Mark the Payroll Liabilities and Payroll Expenses accounts as inactive.

7. Customize the payment Terms List to list only the following:

2/10, Net 30 Days
Net 10 Days
Net 15 Days
Net 30 Days

8. Use the information in table LMS—Accounts to update the Chart of Accounts List.

TABLE LMS—Accounts

Account Type	Number	Account Name
Bank	1010	Cash - Operating
Other Current Asset	1265	Inventory of Keyboards
Other Current Asset	1270	Inventory of Music Stands
Other Current Asset	1275	Inventory of Sheet Music
Other Current Asset	1300	Music Supplies
Other Current Asset	1305	Office Supplies
Other Current Asset	1410	Prepaid Advertising
Other Current Asset	1420	Prepaid Insurance
Fixed Asset	1700	Music Instruments
Fixed Asset	1725	Music Instruments, Cost [Subaccount of 1700]
Fixed Asset	1750	Accum. Dep., Music Instruments [Subaccount of 1700]
Fixed Asset	1800	Furniture

continued

Account Type	Number	Account Name
Fixed Asset	1825	Furniture, Cost [Subaccount of 1800]
Fixed Asset	1850	Accum. Dep., Furniture [Subaccount of 1800]
Fixed Asset	1900	Computers
Fixed Asset	1925	Computers, Cost [Subaccount of 1900]
Fixed Asset	1950	Accum. Dep., Computers [Subaccount of 1900]
Other Current Liability	2020	Notes Payable
Other Current Liability	2030	Interest Payable
Income	4010	Piano Lessons
Income	4020	Guitar Lessons
Income	4060	Sale of Guitars
Income	4065	Sale of Keyboards
Income	4070	Sale of Music Stands
Income	4075	Sale of Sheet Music
Income	4100	Sales Discounts
Cost of Goods Sold	5065	Cost of Keyboards Sold
Cost of Goods Sold	5070	Cost of Music Stands Sold
Cost of Goods Sold	5075	Cost of Sheet Music Sold
Cost of Goods Sold	5900	Inventory Adjustment
Expense	6075	Deprec. Exp., Music Instruments
Expense	6085	Deprec. Exp., Furniture
Expense	6095	Deprec. Exp., Computers
Expense	6150	Instrument Tuning Expense
Expense	6200	Insurance Expense
Expense	6300	Music Supplies Expense
Expense	6325	Office Supplies Expense
Expense	6400	Rent Expense
Expense	6450	Telephone Expense
Expense	6500	Utilities Expense
Other Expense	7000	Interest Expense

9. Use the information in table LMS—Items to update the Item List. For the Inventory Part Items, be sure to use the date June 1, 2014.

TABLE LMS—Items

Item Name and Description on Purchase and Sales Transactions	Cost	COGS Acct	Rate/ Sales Price	Income Acct	Asset Acct	Reorder Point	On Hand	Total Value
Service Items (nontaxable):								
Guitar Lessons			$ 30	4020				
Piano Lessons			35	4010				
Inventory Part Items (taxable):								
Guitars	$50	5060	100	4060	1260	10	6	$ 300
Keyboards	75	5065	150	4065	1265	10	17	1,275
Music Stands	20	5070	40	4070	1270	10	17	340
Sheet Music	3	5075	6	4075	1275	50	165	495

10. Use the information in table LMS—Customers to update the Customer Center.

TABLE LMS—Customers

CUSTOMER/COMPANY NAME	OPENING BALANCE	FULL NAME	Main Phone/Fax	INVOICE/BILL TO	PAYMENT TERMS
Douglaston Senior Center	175.00	Herbie Richardson	570-555-7748 570-555-8800	574 S Beech Street Scranton, PA 18506	Net 30 Days
Highland School		Asst. Principal Office	570-555-6963 570-555-6970	115 Forrest Street Waymart, PA 18472	2/10, Net 30 Days
Jefferson High School		Music Department	570-555-9600 570-555-9700	500 Apple Street Dunmore, PA 18512	2/10, Net 30 Days
Mulligan Residence	1575.90	Adam Smith	570-555-3325 570-555-3500	299 Hickory Lane Scranton, PA 18504	2/10, Net 30 Days
Musical Youth Group		Dana Thompson	570-555-6642 570-555-6700	550 Marion Lane Scranton, PA 18504	Net 30 Days
Patel Family		Ari Patel	570-555-1132	574 Kenwood Drive Dickson City, PA 18519	Net 30 Days
Patterson Family		Jonathan Patterson	570-555-6321	650 Memory Lane Dickson City, PA 18519	Net 30 Days
Schroeder Family		Betty Schroeder	570-555-1897	98 Belmont Rd. Carbondale, PA 18407	Net 30 Days
Twin Lakes Elementary		Miss Brooks	570-555-4474 570-555-4485	515 Hobson Street Honesdale, PA 18431	2/10, Net 30 Days

11. Use the information in table LMS—Vendors to update the Vendor Center.

TABLE LMS—Vendors

VENDOR/COMPANY NAME	OPENING BALANCE	FULL NAME	Main Phone/Fax	BILLED FROM	PAYMENT TERMS
Computer Town	2,000.00	Customer Service	570-555-1500 570-555-1550	1000 Carbondale Highway Scranton, PA 18502	Net 30 Days
Katie's Keyboards	1,500.00	Katie Shea	570-555-7777 570-555-8888	158 Clay Road Scranton, PA 18505	Net 30 Days
Lynn Garcia					
Melody Music Equipment		Melody Arhmand	570-555-1120 570-555-1125	780 Roselyn Ave. Scranton, PA 18505	Net 30 Days
Mills Family Furniture	1,500.00	Edna Mills	570-555-7144 570-555-7200	150 Amelia Street Scranton, PA 18503	Net 30 Days
Music Instruments, Inc.		Matilda Molloy	570-555-9630 570-555-9635	25 Monroe Ave. Scranton, PA 18505	Net 30 Days
Mutual Insurance Company	1,200.00	Bob Maxwell	570-555-5600 570-555-5900	1 Main Street Honesdale, PA 18431	Net 30 Days

continued

VENDOR/ COMPANY NAME	OPENING BALANCE	FULL NAME	Main Phone/ Fax	BILLED FROM	PAYMENT TERMS
Paper, Clips, and More	350.00	Justin Daves	570-555-8558 570-555-5555	157 Waymart Lane Waymart, PA 18472	Net 30 Days
Pioneer Phone		Customer Service	570-555-6000 570-555-6500	1000 Route 6 Carbondale, PA 18407	Net 15 Days
Steamtown Electric		Customer Service	570-555-2500 570-555-3000	150 Vine Lane Scranton, PA 18501	Net 15 Days
Strings, Sheets & Such		Manuela Perez	570-555-3636 570-555-3700	250 Lincoln St. Scranton, PA 18505	Net 30 Days
Tune Tones		Tony Tune	570-555-1111 570-555-2222	500 Monroe Ave. Dunmore, PA 18512	Net 30 Days
Viewhill Realty		Matt Snyder	570-555-1000 570-555-1200	100 Commerce Blvd. Scranton, PA 18501	Net 15 Days

12. Make three journal entries on June 1, 2014 (accept the default Entry Nos.):
   a. Enter the opening balances listed below. Enter the following accounts and amounts as debits:

Number	Account Name	Balance
1010	Cash - Operating	$14,615.18
1300	Music Supplies	430.00
1305	Office Supplies	300.00
1420	Prepaid Insurance	1,100.00
1725	Music Instruments	4,000.00
1825	Furniture	2,500.00
1925	Computers	3,000.00
3020	Lynn Garcia, Drawings	1,000.00
4100	Sales Discounts	188.92
5060	Cost of Guitars Sold	1,150.00
5065	Cost of Keyboards Sold	2,475.00
5070	Cost of Music Stands Sold	460.00
5075	Cost of Sheet Music Sold	1,305.00
5900	Inventory Adjustment	50.00
6075	Deprec. Exp., Music Instruments	60.00
6085	Deprec. Exp., Furniture	40.00
6095	Deprec. Exp., Computers	35.00
6150	Instrument Tuning	100.00
6200	Insurance Expense	100.00
6300	Music Supplies Expense	70.00
6325	Office Supplies Expense	50.00
6400	Rent Expense	600.00
6450	Telephone Expense	50.00
6500	Utilities Expense	70.00
7000	Interest Expense	15.00

Enter the following accounts and amounts as credits:

Number	Account Name	Balance
1750	Accum. Dep., Music Instruments	$ 60.00
1850	Accum. Dep., Furniture	40.00
1950	Accum. Dep., Computers	35.00
2020	Notes Payable	2,000.00
2030	Interest Payable	15.00
4010	Piano Lessons	3,535.00
4020	Guitar Lessons	2,910.00
4060	Sale of Guitars	2,300.00
4065	Sale of Keyboards	4,950.00
4070	Sale of Music Stands	920.00
4075	Sale of Sheet Music	2,610.00

   b. Make a journal entry to reverse the Uncategorized Income account.
   c. Make a journal entry to reverse the Uncategorized Expenses account.

13. Display and print the following reports for June 1, 2014:

   a. *Journal*
   b. *Trial Balance*
   c. *Profit & Loss Standard* (04/01/2014–06/01/2014)
   d. *Balance Sheet Standard*
   e. *Item Listing*
   f. *Customer Contact List*
   g. *Vendor Contact List*

14. Make a backup copy of the new company file. Use the name **LMS7 [*Your Name*] Lynn's Music Studio**. Restore the backup copy, and change the company name to **LMS7 [*Your Name*] Lynn's Music Studio**.

Case Problem 2

On June 1, 2014, Olivia Chen began her business, called Olivia's Web Solutions. In the first month of business, Olivia set up the office, provided web page design and Internet consulting services, and recorded month-end activity. In July, the second month of business, Olivia began to purchase and sell inventory items of computer hardware and software. In June and July, Olivia was recording the financial activities using a manual accounting system. On August 1, 2014, Olivia decides to switch her accounting method to QuickBooks. Olivia has organized the information about the company but has hired you to convert the accounting records to QuickBooks.

1. Use the information below to create and set up the company file using the Express Start method (skip the Quickbooks Setup window after the new company file is created):

Company Name:	**CH7 [*Your Name*] Olivia's Web Solutions**
Industry:	**Other/None**
Company Type:	**Sole Proprietorship**
Tax ID #:	**55-5656566**
Legal Name:	**CH7 [*Your Name*] Olivia's Web Solutions**
Address:	**547 Miller Place**
City:	**Westport**
State:	**NY**
Zip:	**11858**
Country:	**U.S.**
Phone:	**516-555-5000**
Email:	**LIV@emcp.net**

2. Activate the account numbers, inventory, and sales tax features. For sales tax, use the following information:

TYPE:	**Sales Tax Item**
Tax Name:	**NYS Sales Tax**
Description:	**Sales Tax**
Tax Rate (%):	**8**
Tax Agency:	**NYS Tax Dept.**

3. Disable the payroll.
4. Open and close the following windows to allow QuickBooks to create default accounts.

Create Invoices
Enter Sales Receipts
Enter Bills
Item List: New Item: Inventory Part

5. Customize the system default accounts:

QuickBooks		Edited	
Number	Account Name	Number	Account Name
11000	Accounts Receivable	1200	
12000	Undeposited Funds	1250	
12100	Inventory Asset	1260	Inventory of Computers
20000	Accounts Payable	2010	
25500	Sales Tax Payable	2200	
30000	Opening Balance Equity	3010	Olivia Chen, Capital
30800	Owners Draw	3020	Olivia Chen, Drawings
32000	Owners Equity	3030	Accumulated Earnings
50000	Cost of Goods Sold	5060	Cost of Computers Sold

6. Mark the Payroll Liabilities and Payroll Expenses accounts as inactive.
7. Customize the payment Terms List to list only the following:

2/10, Net 30 Days
Net 10 Days
Net 15 Days
Net 30 Days

8. Use the information in table OWS—Accounts to update the Chart of Accounts List.

TABLE OWS—Accounts

Account Type	Number	Account Name
Bank	1010	Cash - Operating
Other Current Asset	1265	Inventory of Scanners
Other Current Asset	1270	Inventory of HTML Software
Other Current Asset	1275	Inventory of Desktop Pub. Soft.
Other Current Asset	1300	Computer Supplies
Other Current Asset	1305	Office Supplies
Other Current Asset	1410	Prepaid Advertising
Other Current Asset	1420	Prepaid Insurance
Fixed Asset	1700	Computers
Fixed Asset	1725	Computers, Cost [Subaccount of 1700]
Fixed Asset	1750	Accum. Dep., Computers [Subaccount of 1700]
Fixed Asset	1800	Furniture
Fixed Asset	1825	Furniture, Cost [Subaccount of 1800]
Fixed Asset	1850	Accum. Dep., Furniture [Subaccount of 1800]
Fixed Asset	1900	Software
Fixed Asset	1925	Software, Cost [Subaccount of 1900]
Fixed Asset	1950	Accum. Dep., Software [Subaccount of 1900]
Other Current Liability	2020	Notes Payable
Other Current Liability	2030	Interest Payable
Income	4010	Web Page Design Fees
Income	4020	Internet Consulting Fees
Income	4060	Sale of Computers
Income	4065	Sale of Scanners
Income	4070	Sale of HTML Software
Income	4075	Sale of Desktop Pub. Software
Income	4100	Sales Discounts
Cost of Goods Sold	5065	Cost of Scanners Sold
Cost of Goods Sold	5070	Cost of HTML Software Sold
Cost of Goods Sold	5075	Cost of Desktop Pub. Soft. Sold
Cost of Goods Sold	5900	Inventory Adjustment

continued

Account Type	Number	Account Name
Expense	6050	Advertising Expense
Expense	6075	Deprec. Exp., Computers
Expense	6085	Deprec. Exp., Furniture
Expense	6095	Deprec. Exp., Software
Expense	6100	Insurance Expense
Expense	6300	Computers Supplies Expense
Expense	6325	Office Supplies Expense
Expense	6350	Online Service Expense
Expense	6400	Rent Expense
Expense	6450	Telephone Expense
Expense	6500	Utilities Expense
Other Expense	7000	Interest Expense

9. Use the information in table OWS—Items to update the Item List. For the Inventory Part Items, be sure to use the date August 1, 2014.

TABLE OWS—Items

Item Name and Description on Purchase and Sales Transactions	Cost	COGS Acct	Rate/ Sales Price	Income Acct	Asset Acct	Reorder Point	On Hand	Total Value
Service Items (nontaxable):								
Internet Consulting Services			$ 100	4020				
Web Page Design Services			125	4010				
Inventory Part Items (taxable):								
Computers	$1,000	5060	2,000	4060	1260	3	10	$10,000
Scanners	300	5065	600	4065	1265	5	12	3,600
HTML Software	75	5070	150	4070	1270	5	18	1,350
Desktop Pub. Software	100	5075	200	4075	1275	5	10	1,000

10. Use the information in table OWS—Customers to update the Customer Center.

TABLE OWS—Customers

CUSTOMER/ COMPANY NAME	OPENING BALANCE	FULL NAME	Main Phone/ Fax	INVOICE/BILL TO	PAYMENT TERMS
Artie's Auto Repair	800.00	Leon Artie	516-555-1221 516-555-1231	32 W. 11th Street New Hyde Park, NY 11523	Net 30 Days
Breathe Easy A/C Contractors		Allen Scott	516-555-6868 516-555-6869	556 Atlantic Ave. Freeport, NY 11634	Net 30 Days
Long Island Water Works		Customer Service	516-555-4747 516-555-4748	87-54 Bayview Ave. Glen Cove, NY 11563	2/10, Net 30 Days
Miguel's Restaurant		Miguel Perez	516-555-3236 516-555-3237	30 Willis Ave. Roslyn, NY 11541	2/10, Net 30 Days
Schneider Family	1,000.00	Johnny Schneider	516-555-8989 516-555-8990	363 Farmers Rd. Syosset, NY 11547	Net 15 Days

continued

CUSTOMER/ COMPANY NAME	OPENING BALANCE	FULL NAME	Main Phone/ Fax	INVOICE/BILL TO	PAYMENT TERMS
Sehorn & Smith Attorneys	800.00	Jerry Sehorn	212-555-3339 212-555-3338	510 Fifth Ave. New York, NY 10022	Net 30 Days
Singh Family		David Singh	718-555-3233 718-555-3239	363 Marathon Parkway Little Neck, NY 11566	Net 15 Days
South Shore School District	12,056.00	Joseph Porter	516-555-4545 516-555-4546	3666 Ocean Ave. South Beach, NY 11365	2/10, Net 30 Days
Thrifty Stores	1,500.00	William Way	718-555-2445 718-555-2446	23 Boston Ave. Bronx, NY 11693	Net 30 Days

11. Use the information in table OWS—Vendors to update the Vendor Center.

TABLE OWS—Vendors

VENDOR/COMPANY NAME	OPENING BALANCE	FULL NAME	Main Phone/ Fax	BILLED TO	PAYMENT TERMS
ARC Management		Alvin R. Clinton	516-555-6363 516-555-6364	668 Lakeville Ave. Garden City, NY 11678	Net 30 Days
Chrbet Advertising	1,200.00	Chris Chrbet	212-555-8777 212-555-8778	201 E. 10th Street New York, NY 10012	Net 30 Days
Comet Computer Supplies		Customer Service	631-555-4444 631-555-4455	657 Motor Parkway Center Island, NY 11488	Net 15 Days
Computec Computers	10,000.00	Customer Service	702-555-6564 702-555-6563	3631 Gate Blvd. Greenboro, NC 27407	Net 30 Days
Eastel	350.00	Customer Service	212-555-6565 212-555-6566	655 Fifth Ave. New York, NY 10012	Net 30 Days
Eastern Mutual Insurance		Customer Service	212-555-6363 212-555-6364	55 Broadway Room 55 New York, NY 10001	Net 30 Days
InterSoft Development Co.		Customer Service	631-555-3634 631-555-3635	556 Route 347 Hauppauge, NY 11654	Net 30 Days
Lewis Furniture Co.	1,700.00	Manny Lewis	631-555-6161 631-555-6162	1225 Route 110 Farmingdale, NY 11898	Net 30 Days
LI Power Company		Customer Service	516-555-8888 516-555-8889	5444 Northern Ave. Plainview, NY 11544	Net 15 Days
Martin Computer Repairs		Ken Martin	516-555-7777 516-555-7778	366 N. Franklin St. Garden City, NY 11568	Net 30 Days
Netsoft Development Co.	1,600.00	Customer Service	974-555-7873 974-555-7874	684 Mountain View Rd. Portland, OR 68774	Net 30 Days
Office Plus	375.00	Customer Service	516-555-3214 516-555-3213	45 Jericho Tpke. Jericho, NY 11654	Net 30 Days
Olivia Chen					
Scanntronix		Customer Service	617-555-8778 617-555-8776	2554 Bedford Rd. Boston, MA 02164	Net 30 Days
Systems Service		Jeremy Jones	516-555-2525 516-555-2526	36 Sunrise Lane Hempstead, NY 11004	Net 30 Days
Textpro Software, Inc.		Customer Service	615-555-4545 615-555-4546	877 Route 5 Ft. Lauderdale, FL 70089	Net 30 Days

12. Make three journal entries on August 1, 2014 (accept the default Entry Nos.):

a. Enter the opening balances listed below. Enter the following accounts and amounts as debits:

Number	Account Name	Balance
1010	Cash - Operating	$24,489.16
1300	Computer Supplies	350.00
1305	Office Supplies	325.00
1410	Prepaid Advertising	1,000.00
1420	Prepaid Insurance	1,650.00
1725	Computers	5,000.00
1825	Furniture	3,200.00
1925	Software	3,600.00
3020	Olivia Chen, Drawings	500.00
4100	Sales Discounts	179.84
5060	Cost of Computers Sold	10,000.00
5065	Cost of Scanners Sold	2,400.00
5070	Cost of HTML Software Sold	75.00
5075	Cost of Desktop Pub. Soft. Sold	500.00
5900	Inventory Adjustment	75.00
6050	Advertising Expense	200.00
6075	Deprec. Exp., Computers	75.00
6085	Deprec. Exp., Furniture	50.00
6095	Deprec. Exp., Software	100.00
6100	Insurance Expense	150.00
6300	Computer Supplies Expense	250.00
6325	Office Supplies Expense	50.00
6350	Online Service Expense	150.00
6400	Rent Expense	800.00
6450	Telephone Expense	350.00
6500	Utilities Expense	125.00
7000	Interest Expense	25.00

Enter the following accounts and amounts as credits:

Number	Account Name	Balance
1750	Accum. Dep., Computers	$ 75.00
1850	Accum. Dep., Furniture	50.00
1950	Accum. Dep., Software	100.00
2020	Notes Payable	2,500.00
2030	Interest Payable	25.00
4010	Web Page Design Fees	9,750.00
4020	Internet Consulting Fees	6,600.00
4060	Sale of Computers	20,000.00
4065	Sale of Scanners	4,800.00
4070	Sale of HTML Software	150.00
4075	Sale of Desktop Pub. Software	1,000.00

b. Make a journal entry to reverse the Uncategorized Income account.

c. Make a journal entry to reverse the Uncategorized Expenses account.

13. Display and print the following reports for August 1, 2014:

    a. *Journal*
    b. *Trial Balance*
    c. *Profit & Loss Standard (06/01/2014–08/01/2014)*
    d. *Balance Sheet Standard*
    e. *Item Listing* — No way to change Date
    f. *Customer Contact List*
    g. *Vendor Contact List*

14. Make a backup copy of the new company file. Use the name **OWS7 [*Your Name*] Olivia's Web Solutions**. Restore the backup copy, and change the company name to **OWS7 [*Your Name*] Olivia's Web Solutions**.

CHAPTER 8

Payroll Setup

Custom Setup

Chapter Objectives

- Review payroll terminology

- Activate the payroll preference

- Customize payroll system default accounts

- Customize and update the Chart of Accounts List for payroll

- Set up payroll to accept manual entries

- Customize the Payroll Item List for payroll items created by QuickBooks

- Update the Payroll Item List

- Display and print the *Payroll Item Listing* report

Introduction

QuickBooks allows you to process payroll and track payroll information for your company's employees. **Payroll** involves computing each employee's gross earnings, determining each employee's withholding and deductions, and calculating each employee's net pay. It also involves preparing employee paychecks, properly recording payroll-related transactions (journal entries), submitting payroll withholdings and deductions to the appropriate tax agency or other entity, and preparing payroll compliance reports.

To process payroll in QuickBooks, the payroll must first be set up. Payroll setup involves enabling the payroll feature, customizing and adding payroll accounts to the Chart of Accounts List, choosing a QuickBooks payroll service or activating the manual entries feature, and establishing payroll items such as compensation and payroll taxes or payroll deductions. These payroll items comprise the *Payroll Item List*.

In this chapter, our sample company, Kristin Raina Interior Designs, will set up the payroll in anticipation of hiring two employees beginning April 1, 2014. After the payroll setup is complete and the employees are hired, the payroll transactions for Kristin Raina Interior Designs will then be illustrated in chapter 9.

QuickBooks versus Manual Accounting: Payroll

In a manual accounting system, the process of preparing a payroll is laborious and time-consuming. For each employee, the company has to tally the hours worked in a pay period, compute the gross pay for the pay period, and then determine all the withholdings and deductions from that employee's pay. After completing these computations, the company has to prepare paychecks, along with pay stubs showing all the earnings, withholdings, and deductions for the pay period as well as all the year-to-date earnings, withholdings, and deductions. Without the use of computers, payroll withholdings are calculated manually using preprinted withholding tables. The gross pay, withholdings, and deductions for all employees then has to be totaled to record the payroll in a payroll journal, which subsequently is posted to the general ledger accounts. In addition, year-to-date earnings and withholdings need to be accumulated and used in preparing government-required quarterly and year-end reports. In dealing with such a quantity and variety of computations, it is easy to make a mistake.

One of the first accounting tasks to be computerized was the processing of payroll. Payroll preparation firms were formed for this sole purpose. A company simply prepares a list of each employee's name and the hours that person worked during a pay period. This information is submitted to the payroll processing firm and—usually overnight—the payroll is prepared; the company receives its properly completed paychecks and a summary report the next morning. The paychecks are distributed to the employees, and the summary report is used to record the appropriate journal entries for the payroll. The payroll processing firms also accumulate the necessary information for preparing government compliance reports. As personal computers and accounting software packages became available, companies are able to process their payroll in-house as part of their routine accounting tasks without the need to use an outside payroll preparation firm.

QuickBooks includes a payroll feature that, once activated, allows for processing a payroll with employees' earnings, withholdings, deductions, and net pay quickly and easily calculated. Simultaneously, the payroll transactions are recorded in the journal. In addition, the paychecks can be immediately printed when the printer is set up to do so. QuickBooks also simultaneously prepares reports that summarize all quarterly and annual information needed for required filings, and for required payments of employee withholdings to the appropriate agencies. Part of what makes payroll processing in QuickBooks easier than that of a manual system is the use of Lists/Centers, which you will recall function as a database. Typical gross earnings, withholdings, and deductions are detailed in the Payroll Item List. In addition, exact payroll taxes are maintained within the payroll feature and QuickBooks payroll services. When employees are to be paid, QuickBooks calls upon the information in the Payroll Item List, along with information about the employee (discussed in chapter 9) and quickly does all computations and prepares all related reports. But since the employee's pay is computed by QuickBooks accessing information from the Payroll Item List, it is of paramount importance that the Payroll Item List be accurate and complete. Any errors in the Payroll Item List will result in inaccurate computations in the payroll and the subsequent recording of incorrect entries in the general journal.

Payroll Definitions and Terms

Whether payroll is processed manually or with a software package, the laws, procedures, filing requirements, definitions, and terminology remain the same. The following is a brief review of the more common payroll definitions.

Employee Payroll Information

To properly determine an employee's gross pay, tax withholdings, deductions, and net pay, and to meet federal and state record-keeping requirements, the employer needs specific information about the employee. This information includes but is not limited to the following:

- Name
- Address
- Social Security number
- Marital status
- Gross pay amount or hourly rate
- Tax withholding allowances
- Voluntary deductions (pensions, 401K, insurance, and so on)

The employer uses this information along with the applicable tax rates to compute the employee's paycheck and track the employee's pay information.

Gross Pay

gross pay Total earnings for an employee for a specific pay period before withholdings and deductions.

Gross pay is the total earnings for the employee for a specific pay period before any withholdings and deductions. Compensation can be in the form of a salary, hourly wages, tips, commissions, bonus, and overtime earned during a pay period. If the employee is paid based on an annual salary, the annual amount is divided over the number of pay periods in the year. Gross pay for hourly workers is determined based on the number of hours worked during the pay period multiplied by the employee's hourly pay rate. The gross pay will be subject to payroll taxes, for both the employer and employee.

FICA Tax (Social Security) and Medicare Tax

The Federal Insurance Contribution Act (FICA) tax, also known as Social Security, is a tax imposed on both the employer and employee at a rate of 6.2% of the first $113,700 (year 2013) of wages for each employee. (For

2011 and 2012, the rate was temporarily reduced to 4.2% for employees only.) Medicare tax is also imposed on both the employer and the employee at a rate for each of 1.45%—there is no wage maximum for the Medicare tax. Beginning in 2013, there will be an Additional Medicare Tax of .9% (.009), which has different thresholds for different taxpayers ($250,000/$125,000/$200,000). The employer periodically remits both the employer and employee portion of the tax to the federal government.

Federal Income Tax (FIT)

Employers are required to withhold from each employee's pay the appropriate amount of federal income tax (FIT). The Internal Revenue Service (IRS) publishes tables and instructions to assist employers in determining the proper withholding amount for each employee. The withholding amount is determined based on the employee's gross pay, marital status, and exemption allowances claimed. The employer periodically forwards the tax withheld to the federal government along with the Social Security and Medicare taxes.

State Income Tax (SIT)

Many states impose an income tax and require employers to withhold the tax from the employees' pay, in a manner similar to that used for FIT. The employer will remit this tax periodically to the appropriate state taxing authority. Some local governments (city, county) may also impose income taxes. Rules for withholding local taxes for local governments are similar to those used by federal and state governments.

Federal Unemployment Tax Act (FUTA)

The Federal Unemployment Tax Act (FUTA) imposes a tax on the employer only. The tax is used to fund unemployment insurance programs administered by the federal government. The effective rate of the tax has been .8% (.008) (which included a .02% (.002) surcharge) of the first $7,000 of each employee's wages. As of July 2011, the surcharge expired and the rate was reduced to .6% (.006).

State Unemployment Insurance (SUI)

In addition to paying the FUTA tax, employers are required by all states to contribute to a state unemployment insurance (SUI) fund. Rates and regulations vary from state to state. However, most states impose the tax only on the employer. The rates can vary from 1% to 10% based on the employer's location and unemployment experience, and the taxable amount will vary from state to state.

State Disability Insurance (SDI)

Most states require employers to purchase an insurance policy, sometimes called state disability insurance (SDI), that will compensate employees if they are unable to work for an extended period due to illness or injury. Some states allow employers to withhold a small amount from each employee's pay to defray the employer's insurance premium cost.

Company Deductions

Many employers will sponsor various fringe benefit programs and deduct amounts from an employee's pay to fund or offset the costs of the benefits. Programs such as 401k plans, medical and dental insurance, pension and profit-sharing plans, long-term disability, life insurance, and so on may be partially funded by a deduction made by the company from an employee's paycheck.

Net Pay

Net pay is the amount of the employee's gross pay less all employee withholdings and deductions. As anyone who has worked knows, net pay is only a fraction of the gross pay earned.

United States Treasury

The United States Treasury is the tax-collecting agency of the federal government. The United States Treasury is responsible for collecting the FICA tax, Medicare tax, FIT, and the FUTA tax. Most states have a similar department for collecting SIT, SUI, and SDI.

Chapter Problem

In this chapter, Kristin Raina Interior Designs will set up the payroll in anticipation of hiring two employees during the month of April 2014. The April 1 beginning balances for the company are contained in the company file CH8 Kristin Raina Interior Designs.

Before you begin, open the company file CH8 Kristin Raina Interior Designs. QBW. Make a backup copy of the file, name it **EX8 [*Your Name*] Kristin Raina Interior Designs**, and then restore the file. Finally, change the company name in the file to **EX8 [*Your Name*] Kristin Raina Interior Designs**.

NEW COMPANY SETUP:

Payroll Setup

If you set up a new company file using the Express Start method, QuickBooks automatically activates the payroll feature. However, if you set up a new company file using the Detail Start method (using the EasyStep Interview window), you have the choice of disabling the payroll feature. In the company file for this chapter problem, the payroll feature was disabled and needs to be activated in the Preferences window on the Edit menu.

To activate the QuickBooks payroll feature—
1. Click Edit and then click *Preferences*.
2. Along the left frame of the Preferences window, click the *Payroll & Employees* icon.
3. Click the Company Preferences tab. If the payroll processing feature is not activated, the No payroll button is selected.
4. Click the Full payroll button. (See figure 8–A.)

FIGURE 8–A
Preferences Window—
Payroll & Employees—
Company Preferences

Full Payroll Button

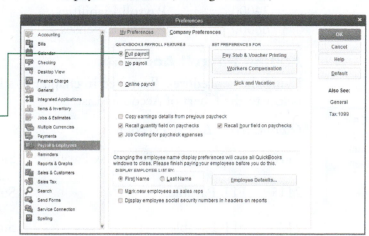

5. Accept the defaults and click OK.

Once you have activated the Payroll feature, QuickBooks automatically creates two default general ledger accounts: Payroll Liabilities and Payroll Expenses.

LISTS/CENTERS: ──○ **Updating the Chart of Accounts List for Payroll**

When the payroll feature is activated, QuickBooks establishes one default general ledger liability posting account for *all* payroll-related liabilities and one expense account for *all* payroll expenses. Open and review the Chart of Accounts List. The accounts created by QuickBooks are 24000 Payroll Liabilities and 66000 Payroll Expenses. When these accounts are created, the account type is dimmed in the Edit Account window to indicate that QuickBooks has created each account and that each account is a system default account. Recall that you must allow QuickBooks to create its own accounts in some situations, but then you can edit the account name and account number.

QuickBooks creates one payroll liability account and one payroll expense account to be used in the payroll processing transactions (chapter 9). However, most companies usually create separate payroll liability accounts for FIT, SIT, Social Security, Medicare, and so on. Similarly, most companies usually create separate payroll expense accounts for Social Security, Medicare, FUTA, SUI, and so on. For our sample company, Kristin Raina Interior Designs, you will create separate payroll liability accounts that will be subaccounts of the system default Payroll Liabilities account created by QuickBooks. Similarly, you will create separate payroll expense accounts that will be subaccounts of the system default Payroll Expenses account created by QuickBooks. Before creating the additional payroll accounts, you will customize the system default accounts to change the account numbers to follow the company pattern for numbering accounts on the Chart of Accounts List.

Customize the Payroll System Default Accounts

Using the procedures illustrated in chapter 4, customize the payroll system default accounts in the Chart of Accounts List as follows:

	QuickBooks		Edited
Number	Account Name		Number
24000	Payroll Liabilities		2100
66000	Payroll Expenses		6560

Adding Payroll Accounts

Using the procedures illustrated in chapter 4, add the payroll accounts listed below to the Chart of Accounts List.

Other Current Liability account type:

2110	Social Sec/Medicare Tax Payable	Subaccount of 2100 Payroll Liabilities
2115	FIT Payable	Subaccount of 2100 Payroll Liabilities
2120	SIT Payable	Subaccount of 2100 Payroll Liabilities

> **HINT**
>
> To add an account, click the Account button in the Chart of Accounts List window and then click New.

| 2125 | FUTA Payable | Subaccount of 2100 Payroll Liabilities |
| 2130 | SUI Payable | Subaccount of 2100 Payroll Liabilities |

Expense account type:

6565	Salaries and Wages Expense	Subaccount of 6560 Payroll Expenses
6610	Social Sec/Medicare Tax Expense	Subaccount of 6560 Payroll Expenses
6625	FUTA Expense	Subaccount of 6560 Payroll Expenses
6630	SUI Expense	Subaccount of 6560 Payroll Expenses

HINT

Use *Edit* from the Account menu in the Chart of Accounts List window to correct any errors.

QuickCheck: The updated Chart of Accounts List appears in figure 8–B.

FIGURE 8–B
Updated Charts of Accounts List

Chart of Accounts

NAME	TYPE	BALANCE TOTAL	ATTACH
1010 · Cash - Operating	Bank	43,355.38	
1020 · Cash - Payroll	Bank	7,500.00	
1200 · Accounts Receivable	Accounts Receivable	1,540.00	
1250 · Undeposited Funds	Other Current Asset	0.00	
1260 · Inventory of Carpets	Other Current Asset	800.00	
1265 · Inventory of Draperies	Other Current Asset	1,000.00	
1270 · Inventory of Lamps	Other Current Asset	1,000.00	
1275 · Inventory of Mirrors	Other Current Asset	900.00	
1300 · Design Supplies	Other Current Asset	200.00	
1305 · Office Supplies	Other Current Asset	250.00	
1410 · Prepaid Advertising	Other Current Asset	500.00	
1420 · Prepaid Insurance	Other Current Asset	2,200.00	
1700 · Furniture	Fixed Asset	11,900.00	
1725 · Furniture, Cost	Fixed Asset	12,000.00	
1750 · Accum. Dep., Furniture	Fixed Asset	-100.00	
1800 · Computers	Fixed Asset	3,540.00	
1825 · Computers, Cost	Fixed Asset	3,600.00	
1850 · Accum. Dep., Computers	Fixed Asset	-60.00	
2010 · Accounts Payable	Accounts Payable	9,750.00	
2020 · Notes Payable	Other Current Liability	7,000.00	
2030 · Interest Payable	Other Current Liability	50.00	
2100 · Payroll Liabilities	Other Current Liability	0.00	
2110 · Social Sec/Medicare Tax Payable	Other Current Liability	0.00	
2115 · FIT Payable	Other Current Liability	0.00	
2120 · SIT Payable	Other Current Liability	0.00	
2125 · FUTA Payable	Other Current Liability	0.00	
2130 · SUI Payable	Other Current Liability	0.00	
2200 · Sales Tax Payable	Other Current Liability	0.00	
3010 · Kristin Raina, Capital	Equity	50,000.00	
3020 · Kristin Raina, Drawings	Equity	-400.00	
3030 · Accumulated Earnings	Equity		
4010 · Design Services	Income		
4020 · Decorating Services	Income		
4060 · Sale of Carpets	Income		
4065 · Sale of Draperies	Income		
4070 · Sale of Lamps	Income		
4075 · Sale of Mirrors	Income		
4100 · Sales Discounts	Income		
5060 · Cost of Carpets Sold	Cost of Goods Sold		
5065 · Cost of Draperies Sold	Cost of Goods Sold		
5070 · Cost of Lamps Sold	Cost of Goods Sold		
5075 · Cost of Mirrors Sold	Cost of Goods Sold		
5900 · Inventory Adjustment	Cost of Goods Sold		
6020 · Accounting Expense	Expense		
6050 · Advertising Expense	Expense		
6175 · Deprec. Exp., Furniture	Expense		
6185 · Deprec. Exp., Computers	Expense		
6200 · Insurance Expense	Expense		
6300 · Janitorial Expenses	Expense		
6325 · Office Supplies Expense	Expense		
6400 · Rent Expense	Expense		
6450 · Telephone Expense	Expense		
6500 · Utilities Expense	Expense		
6560 · Payroll Expenses	Expense		
6565 · Salaries and Wages Expense	Expense		
6610 · Social Sec/Medicare Tax Expense	Expense		
6625 · FUTA Expense	Expense		
6630 · SUI Expense	Expense		
7000 · Interest Expense	Other Expense		

Account ▾   Activities ▾   Reports ▾   Attach   ☐ Include inactive

Payroll Liabilities—
Parent Account and
Subaccounts

Payroll Expenses—
Parent Account and
Subaccounts

QuickBooks Payroll Services versus Calculating Payroll Manually

Like most computerized accounting packages, QuickBooks offers several payroll services: QuickBooks Basic Payroll, QuickBooks Enhanced Payroll, QuickBooks Assisted Payroll, Full Service Payroll, and Online Payroll Basic or Payroll Enhanced. A company would choose the service that best fits the company's needs from the Basic service, which allows the company to prepare and issue paychecks or direct deposit, to the Enhanced service, which also prepares the federal and state tax reporting information. If a company prefers, it could use the Assisted Payroll service where the company prepares the paychecks or direct deposits and QuickBooks takes care of the tax reporting issues, or the Full Service Payroll, which does the same and also does the payroll setup. If a company chooses to use one of the QuickBooks payroll services, it either purchases the package or subscribes to the service and pays a monthly fee. Once a company purchases a QuickBooks payroll service, the taxes imposed on employers and the employee withholdings are automatically computed based on the information in the Payroll Item List, the employee's file (chapter 9), and the QuickBooks payroll service. If the company has not purchased or subscribed to a QuickBooks payroll service, then the firm's payroll withholdings and payroll taxes must be entered manually.

Part of the payroll setup is to indicate either that a specific payroll service will be used or that the payroll will be processed manually. In business, it is commonly advisable to subscribe to a payroll service. However, in the classroom environment, the payroll withholdings and payroll taxes will be entered manually. The payroll for manual processing is set up using the Help menu.

To set up payroll for manual processing using the Help menu—
1. Click Help and then click *QuickBooks Help*. The Have a Question? and Help Article windows appear.
2. In the Have a Question? window, in the Search box, key **Payroll options** and press Enter or click the search icon. The Payroll options topics are listed below in the Results in Help section. (See figure 8–C.)

FIGURE 8–C

Have a Question? Window—Payroll Options Topics Listed

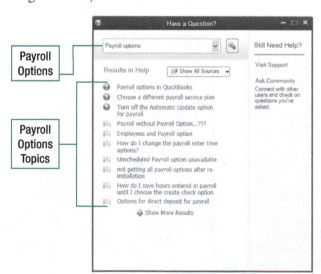

3. At the Results in Help section, click *Payroll options in QuickBooks.* The Payroll options in QuickBooks information appears in the Help Article window. (See figure 8-D.)

FIGURE 8–D

Help Article Window— Payroll Options in QuickBooks Information

Subscribe to QuickBooks Payroll link

Manually calculate and enter payroll withholdings for each paycheck link

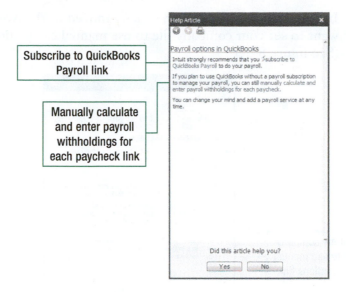

If you click the Subscribe to QuickBooks Payroll link, the Intuit Payroll Solutions window, which provides a comparative anaylsis of the QuickBooks payroll services appears. (You may have to move or close the Have a Question? or Help Article windows to view the Intuit Payroll Solutions window.)

4. At the Help Article window with the Payroll options in QuickBooks Payroll information displayed, click the *manually calculate and enter payroll witholdings for each paycheck* link. The Calculate payroll taxes manually (without a subscription to QuickBooks Payroll) information now appears in the Help Article window. (See figure 8-E.)

FIGURE 8–E

Help Article Window— Calculate Payroll Taxes Manually (without a Subscription to QuickBooks Payroll) Information

Manual payroll calculations link

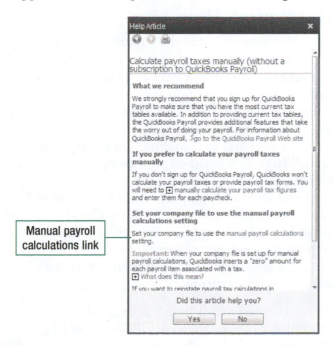

5. In the Help Article window, under the Set your company file to use the manual payroll calculations setting section, click the *manual payroll calculations* link.

In the Help Article window, you are moved to the Are you sure you want to set your company file to use manual calculations? information. (See figure 8–F.)

HINT

If you inadvertently click *manually calculate your payroll tax figures* in the If you prefer to calculate your payroll taxes manually section, you are moved to another section of the Help Article window. In the Help Article window, scroll down to the Set your company file to use the manual payroll calculations settings, and then click the *manual payroll calculations* link.

Set my company file to use manual calculations link

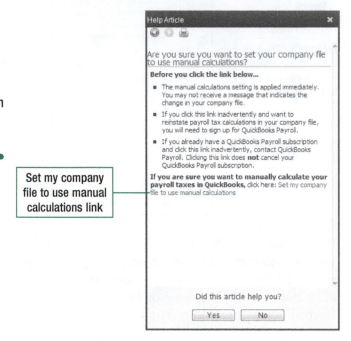

6. Click the *Set my company file to use manual calculations* link.
7. Close the Have a Question? and Help Article windows, then click OK at the QuickBooks Information message.

LISTS/CENTERS: ○ **The Payroll Item List**

Once you have activated the payroll feature and the manual calculations feature, QuickBooks automatically sets up a Payroll Item List, which you may now access. The Payroll Item List contains a file for each type of payroll item that affects the company's employees. QuickBooks automatically creates several standard payroll items, including Social Security Company (FICA tax), Social Security Employee, Medicare Company (Medicare tax), Medicare Employee, federal withholding, and so on. Typically, you must modify the Payroll Item List based on your company's geographic location, company deductions, and pay policies.

As you know, the second level of operation in QuickBooks is to update the background information in the Lists/Centers. In earlier chapters, you added, deleted, or edited vendor, customer, accounts, and inventory item files to keep each Lists/Centers current for your company. Now you will be customizing and updating the Payroll Item List to match the payroll information unique to your company.

To review the Payroll Item List created by QuickBooks—
1. Click Lists and then click *Payroll Item List*.
2. The Payroll Item List appears. (See figure 8–G.)

FIGURE 8–G
Payroll Item List

ITEM NAME	TYPE	AMOUNT	ANNUAL LIMIT	TAX TRACKING	PAYABLE TO	ACCOUNT ID
Advance Earned Income Credit	Federal Tax			Advance EIC Payment		33-4777781
Federal Unemployment	Federal Tax	0.6%	7,000.00	FUTA		33-4777781
Federal Withholding	Federal Tax			Federal		33-4777781
Medicare Company	Federal Tax	1.45%		Comp. Medicare		33-4777781
Medicare Employee	Federal Tax	1.45%		Medicare		33-4777781
Social Security Company	Federal Tax	6.2%	110,100.00	Comp. SS Tax		33-4777781
Social Security Employee	Federal Tax	4.2%	-110,100.00	SS Tax		33-4777781

Notice that the payroll items initially created by QuickBooks are the ones generally applicable to all payroll situations, such as Social Security tax, Medicare tax, Federal Withholding tax, Federal Unemployment tax, and so on.

To view a specific payroll item, such as Federal Withholding—
1. Double-click *Federal Withholding.* The Edit payroll item (Federal Withholding) window appears. (See figure 8–H.)

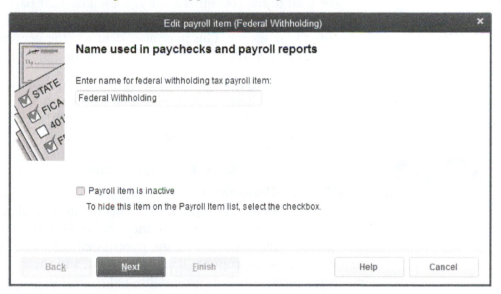

This window displays the name used in paychecks and payroll reports. The Edit payroll item window for each payroll item file displays several pages of information that are displayed each time you click Next.

2. Click Next, and the Agency for employee-paid liability page appears. (See figure 8–I.) (This information will be filled in later.)

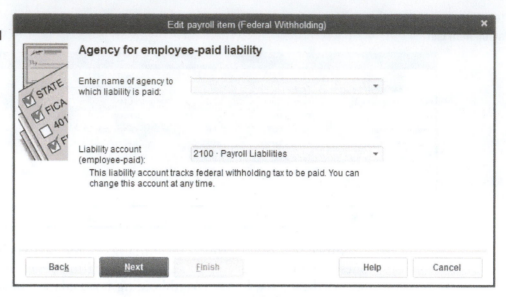

This page displays the government agency to which payment should be forwarded as well as the general ledger account for the tax liability. Remember, federal income tax withheld from the employees' paycheck is counted as a liability to the employer that must at some time be paid to the appropriate tax agency. The Edit payroll item (Federal Withholding) window—Agency for employee-paid liability page identifies that agency. This page also identifies the general ledger liability account that will be used for this payroll item.

3. Click Next to move to the next page, Taxable compensation. This page indicates all items subject to federal income tax withholdings.
4. Click Finish. You are returned to the Payroll Item List window.
5. Close the Payroll Item List.

LISTS/CENTERS: ○ # Customizing the Payroll Item List

When you activated the payroll feature and the manual calculations feature, QuickBooks created several payroll items required of all companies, as seen in figure 8–G. You will customize these items for Kristin Raina Interior Designs to include identifying the government agency to which payment will be directed, the appropriate liability account, and the appropriate expense account for each of these pre-established payroll items.

Customizing a Payroll Item

Kristin Raina wishes to enter the vendor for Social Security Company tax payments. She also wants to change the general ledger posting accounts for the expense and the liability on the Payroll Item List.

Recall that Social Security tax is withheld from the employee's paycheck and that the employer must also pay an amount, which is an expense to the company. QuickBooks creates two payroll items: Social Security Company and Social Security Employee. When you edit one of these payroll items, the changes you make in one of the payroll items is carried over to the other payroll item.

To customize the Social Security Company payroll item—
1. Click Lists and then click *Payroll Item List*.
2. Choose the *Social Security Company* payroll item by double-clicking. The payroll item is opened in Edit mode. (See figure 8–J.)

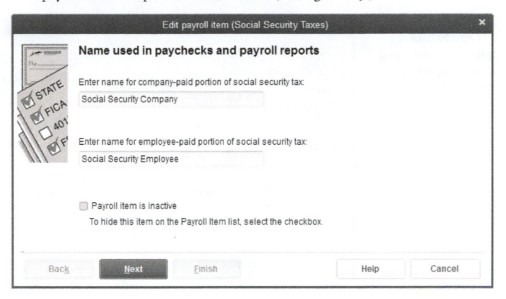

3. Accept the default names and then click Next. The Liability agency page appears.

   This payroll item, Social Security Company, represents the social security tax that the employer must pay. This tax, both the employee's withholding and the employer's portion, is subsequently paid to the United States Treasury. Since the company will be writing a check to this government agency, QuickBooks considers it a vendor of the company; thus, it must be included in the Vendor Center. Once the agency is included in the Vendor Center, it can then be selected from this drop-down list.

4. At the *Enter name of agency to which liability is paid* field, click *United States Treasury* from the drop-down list.

   For all payroll items, you will need to indicate general ledger accounts. For some payroll items you will select a liability account, for some you will select an expense account, and for some you will select both a liability account and an expense account. When selecting accounts, be careful to choose the correct liability account or expense account, and then be careful to choose the proper subaccount. The general ledger accounts in the Payroll Item List are eventually used by QuickBooks to record the payroll journal entries. If an incorrect general ledger account is recorded in the Payroll Item List, the payroll journal entries will be incorrect.

   This page also asks for the liability account that will be used for both the amount to be paid by the employer and the amount withheld from the employees' paychecks. These can be different liability accounts, but Kristin Raina uses the same liability account for both the employer and employee. Notice that you must enter two liability accounts on this page.

5. At both the *Liability account (company-paid)* field and the *Liability account (employee-paid)* field, click *2110 Social Sec/Medicare Tax Payable*. Both the parent account 2100 Payroll Liabilities and the subaccount 2110 Social Sec/Medicare Payable are displayed. (See figure 8–K.)

FIGURE 8–K
Edit Payroll Item
(Social Security Taxes)
Window—Liability
Agency Page

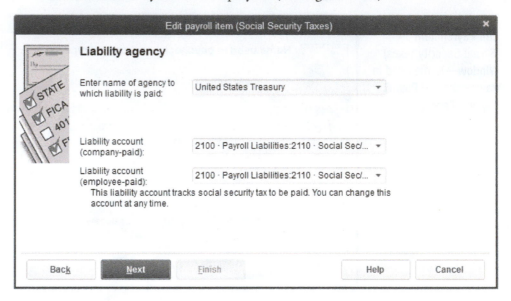

6. If the information is correct, click Next. The Expense account page appears.

   Only the employer's portion of Social Security and Medicare is considered an expense for the company. The portion withheld from the employee's paycheck is not.

7. At the *Enter the account for tracking this expense* field, click *6610 Social Sec/Medicare Tax Expense*. Both the parent account 6560 Payroll Expenses and the subaccount 6610 Social Sec/Medicare Expense are displayed. (See figure 8–L.)

FIGURE 8–L
Edit Payroll Item
(Social Security Taxes)
Window—Expense
Account Page

8. If the information is correct, click Next. The Company and employee tax rates page appears, displaying the current tax rates. Notice that these tax rates are dimmed. These rates are established for the current year by the federal government and cannot be changed.
9. Click Next to accept. The Taxable compensation page appears.
10. Click Finish. You will be returned to the Payroll Item List with all changes saved.

As stated previously, QuickBooks creates both a Social Security Company payroll item and a Social Security Employee payroll item. Changes made to one payroll item are carried over to the other payroll item. Review the Social Security Employee payroll item to observe that the changes were carried over.

To review the Social Security Employee payroll item—
1. Open the Payroll Item List if necessary.
2. Choose the Social Security Employee item by double-clicking.
3. Review each page, and compare the pages with figures 8–J to 8–L.
4. Close the Payroll Item List.

P r a c t i c e   E x e r c i s e

On the Payroll Item List, customize the Medicare Company and Medicare Employee payroll items.

Liability Agency:	**United States Treasury**
Liability Account:	**2110 Social Sec/Medicare Tax Payable**
Expense Account:	**6610 Social Sec/Medicare Tax Expense**

Kristin Raina wishes to enter the vendor for the Federal Unemployment tax payments. She also wants to change the general ledger posting accounts for the expense and liability in the Payroll Item List.

To customize the Federal Unemployment payroll item—
1. Click Lists, and then click *Payroll Item List*.
2. Choose the *Federal Unemployment* payroll item by double-clicking. The payroll item is opened in the Edit mode.
3. Accept the default name Federal Unemployment by clicking Next. The Agency for company-paid liability page appears.
4. In the *Enter name of agency to which the liability is paid* field, click United States Treasury from the drop-down list.
5. In the *Liability account* field, click *2125 FUTA Payable*. Both the parent account 2100 Payroll Liabilities and the subaccount 2125 FUTA Payable are displayed.
6. In the *Expense account* field, click *6625 FUTA Expense*. Both the parent account 6560 Payroll Expenses and the subaccount 6625 FUTA Expense are displayed. Notice on this page that you are listing one liability account and one expense account. (See figure 8–M.)

FIGURE 8–M

Edit Payroll Item
(Federal Unemployment)
Window—Agency for
Company-Paid Liability
Page

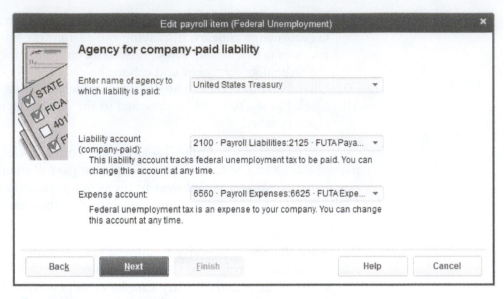

Notice for this payroll item the liability and expense accounts are recorded on the same page, whereas with the Social Security and Medicare items, two liability accounts were recorded on one page and the expense account was recorded on a second page.

7. If the information is correct, click Next.
8. At the Federal unemployment tax rate page, accept the default rate by clicking Next.
9. At the Taxable Compensation page, click Finish.
10. Close the Payroll Item List.

Practice Exercise

On the Payroll Item List, customize the Federal Withholding payroll item.

Liability Agency:	**United States Treasury**
Liability Account:	**2115 FIT Payable**

LISTS/CENTERS:

Updating the Payroll Item List

In QuickBooks, there are two methods for adding a payroll item set up—EZ Setup and Custom Setup. The EZ Setup method guides you in setting up payroll items using the QuickBooks Payroll Setup window. The Custom Setup method allows you to directly enter information in the Payroll Item List. The Custom Setup method is used in this chapter.

In Custom Setup, the steps to set up the Payroll Items of salary and wages are slightly different from the steps to set up the Payroll Items of payroll withholdings and employer payroll taxes.

HINT

See Appendix G for the steps to set up payroll, including the Payroll Item List, using the alternative method of the QuickBooks Payroll Setup window.

Adding a Salary and Wage Payroll Item

Kristin Raina wishes to add Salary to the Payroll Item List.

To add Salary to the Payroll Item List—
1. Click Lists and then click *Payroll Item List*.
2. At the Payroll Item List window, click the Payroll Item menu button.

3. At the Payroll Item menu, click New. The Add new payroll item window with the Select setup method page appears.

    Similar to editing a payroll item when you create a new payroll item, several pages of information are displayed each time you click Next.

4. At the Select setup method page, click the Custom Setup option. (See figure 8–N.)

5. Click Next.

    This second page in the Add new payroll item window—Payroll item type page—lists the types of payroll items you can create.

    There are seven payroll item types: Wage, Addition, Deduction, Company Contribution, Federal Tax, State Tax, and Other Tax. For each of these types, there are several subtypes, listed in parenthesis, next to each of the payroll item types. When adding new payroll items, you will first select the payroll item type on this page; then, on the next page, you will select the subtype.

6. At the Payroll item type page, click *Wage (Hourly Wages, Annual Salary, Commission, Bonus)*. (See figure 8–O.)

FIGURE 8–O

Add New Payroll Item
Window—Payroll Item
Type Page—Wages Type
Selected

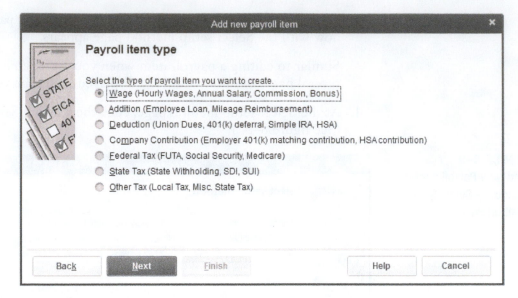

7. Click Next.

The Wages page appears with the subtypes listed. Observe that the subtypes on this page are the choices noted in parentheses on the previous Payroll item type page (compare with figure 8–O.)

8. Choose the *Annual Salary* subtype. (See figure 8–P.)

FIGURE 8–P

Add New Payroll Item
Window—Wages Page—
Annual Salary Subtype
Selected

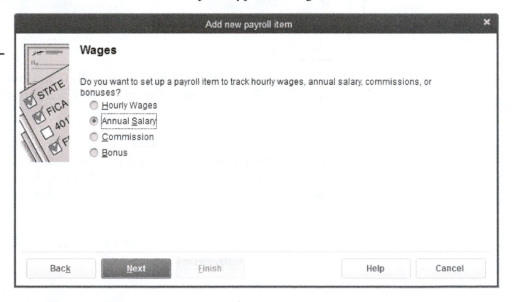

9. Click Next. The next page lets you indicate the form of pay: regular, sick, or vacation.
10. Choose *Regular Pay*. (See figure 8–Q.)

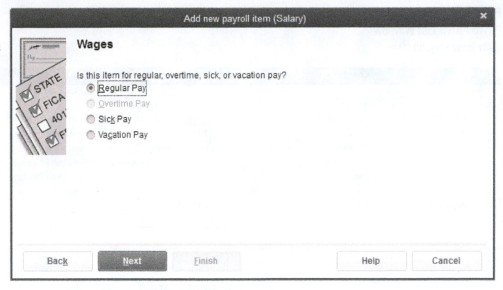

11. Click Next. The Name used in paychecks and payroll reports page appears. This step is where you assign a name for the item on paychecks and reports.

12. At the *Enter name for salary item* field, key **Salary** and then click Next. The Expense account page appears. This step is where you assign the general ledger account for Salary expense.

13. At the *Enter the account for tracking this expense* field, click *6565 Salaries and Wages* from the drop-down list. Both the parent account 6560 Payroll Expenses and the subaccount 6565 Salaries and Wages are displayed. (See figure 8–R.)

FIGURE 8–R

Add New Payroll Item
(Salary:Salary) Window—
Expense Account Page

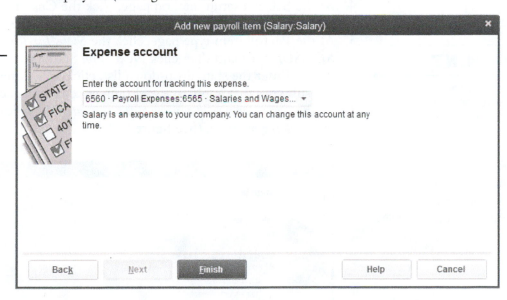

14. If the information is correct, click Finish. You are returned to the Payroll Item List window with the new payroll item included. (See figure 8–S.)

FIGURE 8–S
Payroll Item List Window
with New Payroll Item

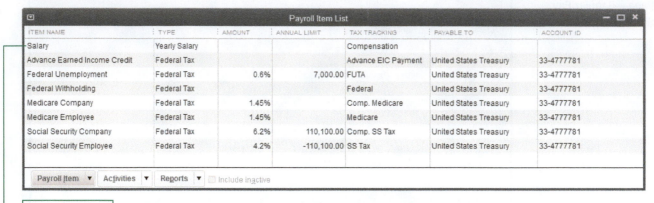

ITEM NAME	TYPE	AMOUNT	ANNUAL LIMIT	TAX TRACKING	PAYABLE TO	ACCOUNT ID
Salary	Yearly Salary			Compensation		
Advance Earned Income Credit	Federal Tax			Advance EIC Payment	United States Treasury	33-4777781
Federal Unemployment	Federal Tax	0.6%	7,000.00	FUTA	United States Treasury	33-4777781
Federal Withholding	Federal Tax			Federal	United States Treasury	33-4777781
Medicare Company	Federal Tax	1.45%		Comp. Medicare	United States Treasury	33-4777781
Medicare Employee	Federal Tax	1.45%		Medicare	United States Treasury	33-4777781
Social Security Company	Federal Tax	6.2%	110,100.00	Comp. SS Tax	United States Treasury	33-4777781
Social Security Employee	Federal Tax	4.2%	-110,100.00	SS Tax	United States Treasury	33-4777781

Payroll Item ▼   Activities ▼   Reports ▼   ☐ Include inactive

New Payroll Item

15. Close the Payroll Item List.

Adding a Payroll Withholding Payroll Item

Kristin Raina wishes to add Minnesota state income tax to the Payroll Item List.

To add Minnesota state income tax to the Payroll Item List—
1. Click Lists, and then click *Payroll Item List*.
2. At the Payroll Item List window, click the Payroll Item menu button.
3. At the Payroll Item menu, click *New*. The Add a new payroll item window with the Select setup method page appears.
4. At the Select a setup method page, click the Custom Setup option and then click Next. The Payroll item type page appears.
5. At the Payroll item type page, click the *State Tax (State Withholding, SDI, SUI)* type and then click Next. The State tax page appears.
6. At the Enter the state drop-down list, click *MN*. After you select a state, the subtypes that apply to the chosen state become active.
7. At the *Select the type of tax you want to create* field, click the *State Withholding* subtype. (See figure 8–T.)

HINT

To choose the state, use the drop-down list or key **M**. Keep keying **M** until *MN* appears.

FIGURE 8–T
Add New Payroll Item
Window—State Tax
Page—Subtype Selected

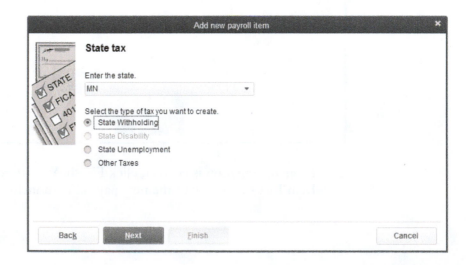

8. If the information is correct, click Next.

The Name used in paychecks and payroll reports page appears; it assigns a name for the tax for paycheck and payroll reporting purposes.

9. Accept the default name assigned and click Next. The Agency for employee-paid liability page, which records information for tax vendors and general ledger posting accounts, appears.

10. At the *Enter name of agency to which liability is paid* field, click *Minn. Dept. of Revenue* from the drop-down list.

This payroll item, Minnesota State Withholding Tax, represents the state income tax withheld from the employee's check that must subsequently be paid to the Minnesota Department of Revenue. Since the company will be writing a check to this government agency, QuickBooks identifies it as a vendor of the company; therefore, it must be included in the Vendor Center.

11. At the *Enter the number that identifies you to agency* field, key **33-4777781**.

12. At the *Liability account (employee-paid)* field, click *2120 SIT Payable*. Both the parent account, 2100 Payroll Liabilities, and the subaccount, 2120 SIT Payable, are displayed. (See figure 8–U.)

FIGURE 8–U
Add New Payroll Item (MN-State Withholding Tax) Window—Agency for Employee-paid Liability Page

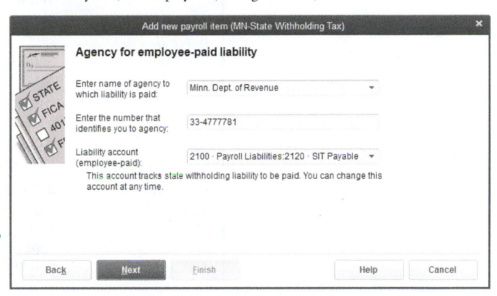

HINT

QuickBooks provides a Schedule Payments feature if you subscribe to one of the QuickBooks payroll services. The Schedule Payments feature allows you to keep track of your payroll tax and other payroll liabilities amounts, due dates, and payments.

13. If the information is correct, click Next. The Taxable compensation page appears; it shows the types of income subject to the tax. At this time, the only payroll item for Kristin Raina Interior Designs subject to state income tax is Salary. This item should be checked.

14. Click Finish. At the Schedule Payments message, click OK. You are returned to the Payroll Item List window with the new tax included.

15. Close the Payroll Item List.

Practice Exercise

On the Payroll Item List, add the following two new payroll items:

Hourly Wages

Payroll Item Type:	**Wage (Hourly Wages, Annual Salary, Commission, Bonus)**
Payroll Item Subtype—Wages:	**Hourly Wages**
Wages:	**Regular Pay**
Name:	**Hourly Wages**
Expense Account:	**6565 Salaries and Wages Expense**

Minnesota State Unemployment (SUI)

Payroll Item Type:	**State Tax (State Withholding, SDI, SUI)**
State:	**MN**
Payroll Item Subtype—State Tax:	**State Unemployment**
Name:	**MN - Unemployment Company**
Agency:	**Minn. Dept. of Revenue**
ID Number:	**ER-12343**
Liability Account:	**2130 SUI Payable**
Expense Account:	**6630 SUI Expense**
Rate:	**3.4715% each quarter (if a different rate appears, accept the default rate)**

QuickCheck: The updated Payroll Item List appears in figure 8–V.

FIGURE 8–V
Updated Payroll Item List

Payroll Item List

ITEM NAME	TYPE	AMOUNT	ANNUAL LIMIT	TAX TRACKING	PAYABLE TO	ACCOUNT ID
Salary	Yearly Salary			Compensation		
Hourly Wages	Hourly Wage			Compensation		
Advance Earned Income Credit	Federal Tax			Advance EIC Payment	United States Treasury	33-4777781
Federal Unemployment	Federal Tax	0.6%	7,000.00	FUTA	United States Treasury	33-4777781
Federal Withholding	Federal Tax			Federal	United States Treasury	33-4777781
Medicare Company	Federal Tax	1.45%		Comp. Medicare	United States Treasury	33-4777781
Medicare Employee	Federal Tax	1.45%		Medicare	United States Treasury	33-4777781
Social Security Company	Federal Tax	6.2%	110,100.00	Comp. SS Tax	United States Treasury	33-4777781
Social Security Employee	Federal Tax	4.2%	-110,100.00	SS Tax	United States Treasury	33-4777781
MN - Withholding	State Withholding Tax			SWH	Minn. Dept. of Revenue	33-4777781
MN - Unemployment Company	State Unemployment Tax	3.4715%	28,000.00	Comp. SUI	Minn. Dept. of Revenue	ER-12343

Payroll Item ▼   Activities ▼   Reports ▼   ☐ Include inactive

REPORTS: ──○ **Payroll Reports**

Reports, the fourth level of operation in QuickBooks, allows you to display and print a number of payroll reports, both for internal payroll management and for government and payroll tax compliance.

The payroll management reports provide the company with valuable information, most of which reflects payroll processing (chapter 9). One of the reports reflects payroll setup—the *Payroll Item Listing*.

Payroll Item Listing

The *Payroll Item Listing* report lists the payroll item, type, rates, and limits for some of the mandatory taxes, and the expense and liability accounts relating to the payroll item.

To view the *Payroll Item Listing* report—
1. Click Reports and then click *Employees & Payroll*.
2. At the Employees & Payroll submenu, click *Payroll Item Listing*. The *Payroll Item Listing* report is displayed. (See figure 8–W.)

FIGURE 8–W
Payroll Item Listing Report

Payroll Item Listing

Customize Report | Share Template | Memorize | Print | E-mail ▼ | Excel ▼ | Hide Header | Refresh   Sort By Default

EX8 [Your Name] Kristin Raina Interior Designs
Payroll Item Listing

Payroll Item	Type	Amount	Limit	Expense Account	Liability Account	Tax Tracking
Salary	Yearly Salary			6560 · Payroll Expenses:6565 · Salaries and Wages Expense		Compensation
Hourly Wages	Hourly Wage			6560 · Payroll Expenses:6565 · Salaries and Wages Expense		Compensation
Advance Earned Income Credit	Federal Tax				2100 · Payroll Liabilities	Advance EIC Payment
Federal Unemployment	Federal Tax	0.6%	7,000.00	6560 · Payroll Expenses:6625 · FUTA Expense	2100 · Payroll Liabilities:2125 · FUTA Payable	FUTA
Federal Withholding	Federal Tax				2100 · Payroll Liabilities:2115 · FIT Payable	Federal
Medicare Company	Federal Tax	1.45%		6560 · Payroll Expenses:6610 · Social Sec/Medicare Tax Expense	2100 · Payroll Liabilities:2110 · Social Sec/Medicare Tax Payable	Comp. Medicare
Medicare Employee	Federal Tax	1.45%			2100 · Payroll Liabilities:2110 · Social Sec/Medicare Tax Payable	Medicare
Social Security Company	Federal Tax	6.2%	110,100.00	6560 · Payroll Expenses:6610 · Social Sec/Medicare Tax Expense	2100 · Payroll Liabilities:2110 · Social Sec/Medicare Tax Payable	Comp. SS Tax
Social Security Employee	Federal Tax	4.2%	110,100.00		2100 · Payroll Liabilities:2110 · Social Sec/Medicare Tax Payable	SS Tax
MN - Withholding	State Withholding Tax				2100 · Payroll Liabilities:2120 · SIT Payable	SWH
MN - Unemployment Company	State Unemployment Tax	3.4715%	28,000.00	6560 · Payroll Expenses:6630 · SUI Expense	2100 · Payroll Liabilities:2130 · SUI Payable	Comp. SUI

3. Close the report.

Chapter Review and Assessment

Procedure Review

To activate the QuickBooks payroll feature—
1. Click Edit and then click *Preferences*.
2. Along the left frame of the Preferences window, click the *Payroll & Employees* icon.
3. Click the Company Preferences tab.
4. Click the Full payroll features option.
5. Accept the defaults.
6. Click OK.

To set up payroll for manual processing using the Help menu—
1. Click Help and then click *QuickBooks Help*.
2. In the Have a Question? window, in the Search box, key **Payroll options** and press Enter or click the search icon. The Payroll options topics are listed below in the Results in Help section.
3. At the Results in Help section, click *Payroll options in QuickBooks*. The Payroll Options in QuickBooks information appears in the Help Article window.
4. At the Help Article window with the Payroll options in QuickBooks information displayed, click *manually calculate and enter payroll withholdings for each paycheck*. The Calculate payroll taxes manually (without a subscription to QuickBooks Payroll) information now appears in the Help Article window.
5. In the Help Article window under the Set your company file to use the manual payroll calculations setting section, click *manual payroll calculations*. In the Help Article window, you are moved to the Are you sure you want to set your company file to use manual calculations? information.
6. Click *Set my company file to use manual calculations*.
7. Close the Have a Question? and Help Article windows, and click OK at the QuickBooks Information message.

To customize the Social Security Company payroll item—
1. Click Lists and then click *Payroll Item List*.
2. Choose the *Social Security Company* payroll item by double-clicking. The payroll item is opened in Edit mode.
3. Accept the default names and click Next.
4. At the Liability agency page, at the *Enter name of agency to which liability is paid* field, click *United States Treasury* from the drop-down list.
5. At both the *Liability account (company-paid)* field and the *Liability account (employee-paid)* field, choose the correct liability accounts and then click Next.
6. At the Expense account page, choose the correct expense account and then click Next.
7. At the Company and employee tax rates page, click Next.

8. At the Taxable compensation page, click Finish.
9. Close the Payroll Item List.

To add a salary and wages payroll item—
1. Click Lists and then click *Payroll Item List*.
2. At the Payroll Item List window, click the Payroll Item menu button.
3. At the Payroll Item menu, click *New*.
4. At the Select setup method page, click the Custom Setup option and then click Next.
5. At the Payroll item type page, click the *Wage (Hourly Wages, Annual Salary, Commission, Bonus)* type and then click Next.
6. At the Wages page, choose the *Annual Salary* or *Hourly Wages* subtype and click Next.
7. Choose *Regular Pay* and click Next.
8. At the Name used in paychecks and payroll reports page, in the *Enter name for salary item* field, key **Salary** or **Hourly Wages** and then click Next.
9. At the Expense account page, choose the expense account to track this item and then click Finish.
10. Close the Payroll Item List.

To add a withholding or tax payroll item—
1. Click Lists and then click *Payroll Item List*.
2. At the Payroll Item List page, click the Payroll Item menu button.
3. At the Payroll Item menu, click *New*.
4. At the Select setup method page, click the Custom Setup option and then click Next.
5. At the Payroll item type page, choose the applicable tax type and click Next.
6. At the State page, enter the state. After you select a state, the subtypes that apply to the chosen state become active.
7. At the *Select the type of tax you want to create* field, click the appropriate withholding or tax subtype, then click Next.
8. At the Name used in paychecks and payroll reports page, in the *Enter name for state withholding tax* field, accept the default and then click Next.
9. At the Agency for employee-paid liability page, in the *Enter name of agency* field, click the tax agency from the drop-down list.
10. Key the tax ID number.
11. At the Liability account field, choose the liability account for the tax. If it is a tax payroll item, choose the expense account and then click Next.
12. If it is a tax payroll item, accept the default tax rates and then click Next.
13. The Taxable compensation page shows which types of income are subject to tax. Click Finish to accept.
14. Close the Payroll Item List.

To view and print the *Payroll Item Listing* from the Reports menu—
1. At the Reports menu, click *Employees & Payroll*.
2. At the Employees & Payroll submenu, click *Payroll Item Listing*. The *Payroll Item Listing* report is displayed.

3. Click the Print button on the top of the report.
4. At the Print Reports dialog box, review the settings and then click Print.
5. Close the report.

Key Concepts

Select the letter of the item that best matches each definition.

a. Payroll
b. Social Security Tax, Medicare Tax, FUTA, and SUI
c. Manual Payroll Calculations
d. Payroll Item List
e. Social Security Tax, Medicare Tax, Federal Withholding, and State Withholding
f. Payroll Items
g. Payroll Liabilities and Payroll Expenses
h. Government Agency
i. Social Security and Medicare
j. QuickBooks Payroll Services

_____ 1. Payroll taxes imposed on the employer.

_____ 2. A variety of services offered by QuickBooks; includes automatic processing of payroll and requires a purchase price or a monthly service fee.

_____ 3. Two default general ledger accounts created by QuickBooks when the payroll feature is activated.

_____ 4. Payroll taxes imposed on the employee and collected by the employer.

_____ 5. Contains a file for each type of payroll item that affects the payroll computation.

_____ 6. Listed on the Vendor Center and included in Payroll Item List; identifies where the employee's payroll withholdings should be sent.

_____ 7. An option that must be activated to access the Payroll Item List when a company does not subscribe to QuickBooks Payroll Services.

_____ 8. Payroll items that require identifying two liabilities accounts and one expense account in the Payroll Item List.

_____ 9. Compensation, payroll taxes, or payroll withholdings created by QuickBooks that you can customize or add to; each requires identifying related liability accounts, expense accounts, and government agency.

_____ 10. Involves computing each employee's gross earnings, withholdings and deductions, and net pay; preparing paychecks; recording payroll journal entries; and submitting payroll withholdings to the appropriate agency.

Procedure Check

1. You have decided to use the payroll feature of QuickBooks. How do you activate the payroll feature in an existing company file, and what does QuickBooks automatically set up?
2. After activating the payroll feature, what must you do to access the Payroll Item List?
3. What items on the Payroll Item List are automatically created by QuickBooks, and how would you customize them for your company?
4. What types of payroll items does QuickBooks allow to be created, and which types and subtypes would a company be interested in adding to the Payroll Item List?
5. Describe the steps to set up a withholding and tax payroll item.
6. Your company has been using the services of an outside payroll processing firm. You, as a junior accountant, know that QuickBooks has a payroll feature; you wish to recommend to your manager that your company process payroll within the company. In anticipation of making a recommendation to your manager, prepare a summary of the steps involved in setting up payroll in QuickBooks.

Case Problems

Case Problem 1

In June, the third month of business for Lynn's Music Studio, Lynn Garcia has decided to hire two employees. To prepare for this, Lynn wishes to set up the payroll feature. The company file includes information for Lynn's Music Studio as of June 1, 2014.

1. Open the company file CH8 Lynn's Music Studio.QBW.
2. Make a backup copy of the company file LMS8 [*Your Name*] Lynn's Music Studio.
3. Restore the backup copy of the company file. In both the Open Backup Copy and Save Company File as windows, use the file name LMS8 [*Your Name*] Lynn's Music Studio.
4. Change the company name to **LMS8 [*Your Name*] Lynn's Music Studio**.
5. Activate the payroll feature for Lynn's Music Studio.
6. Customize the system default accounts:

	QuickBooks	Edited
Number	Account Name	Number
24000	Payroll Liabilities	2100
66000	Payroll Expenses	6560

7. Add the following accounts to the Chart of Accounts List:

2110	Social Sec/Medicare Tax Payable	Subaccount of 2100 Payroll Liabilities
2115	FIT Payable	Subaccount of 2100 Payroll Liabilities

2120	SIT Payable	Subaccount of 2100 Payroll Liabilities
2125	FUTA Payable	Subaccount of 2100 Payroll Liabilities
2130	SUI Payable	Subaccount of 2100 Payroll Liabilities
6565	Salaries and Wages Expense	Subaccount of 6560 Payroll Expenses
6611	Social Sec/Medicare Tax Expense	Subaccount of 6560 Payroll Expenses
6625	FUTA Expense	Subaccount of 6560 Payroll Expenses
6630	SUI Expense	Subaccount of 6560 Payroll Expenses

8. Select the manual payroll calculations option.
9. Customize each of the payroll items listed below. For each item, proceed as follows:

- Accept the name listed.
- Choose United States Treasury as the agency to which the liability will be paid.
- Select the liability and expense accounts indicated below.
- Accept all tax rates.
- Accept all taxable compensation defaults.

Payroll Item	Liability Account	Expense Account
Federal Unemployment	2125 FUTA Payable	6625 FUTA Expense
Federal Withholding	2115 FIT Payable	
Medicare Company	2110 Social Sec/ Medicare Tax Payable	6611 Social Sec/ Medicare Tax Expense
Medicare Employee	2110 Social Sec/ Medicare Tax Payable	6611 Social Sec/ Medicare Tax Expense
Social Security Company	2110 Social Sec/ Medicare Tax Payable	6611 Social Sec/ Medicare Tax Expense
Social Security Employee	2110 Social Sec/ Medicare Tax Payable	6611 Social Sec/ Medicare Tax Expense

10. Add the following payroll items:

Salary

Payroll Item Type:	**Wage (Hourly Wages, Annual Salary, Commission, Bonus)**
Payroll Item Subtype—Wages:	**Annual Salary**
Wages:	**Regular Pay**
Name:	**Salary**
Expense Account:	**6565 Salaries and Wages Expense**

Wages

Payroll Item Type:	**Wage (Hourly Wages, Annual Salary, Commission, Bonus)**
Payroll Item Subtype—Wages:	**Hourly Wages**
Wages:	**Regular Pay**
Name:	**Hourly Wages**
Expense Account:	**6565 Salaries and Wages Expense**

State Tax Withholding

Payroll Item Type:	**State Tax (State withholding, SDI, SUI)**
State:	**PA**
Payroll Item Subtype—State Tax:	**State Withholding**
Name Used in Paychecks:	**PA – Withholding**
Agency for Liabilities:	**PA Dept. of Revenue**
Identifying Number:	**45-6123789**
Liability Account:	**2120 SIT Payable**
Taxable Compensation:	**Accept defaults**

SUI

Payroll Item Type:	**State Tax (State withholding, SDI, SUI)**
State:	**PA**
Payroll Item Subtype—State Tax:	**State Unemployment**
Name Used in Paychecks:	**PA – Unemployment Company**
Agency for Liabilities:	**PA Dept. of Revenue**
Identifying Number:	**ER-76558**
Liability Accounts:	**2130 SUI Payable**
Expense Account:	**6630 SUI Expense**
Company Tax Rate:	**3.703% each quarter**
Employee Tax Rate:	**.08% each quarter**
Taxable Compensation:	**Accept defaults**

11. Display and print the *Payroll Item Listing* report.

Case Problem 2

In August, the third month of business for Olivia's Web Solutions, Olivia Chen has decided to hire two employees. To prepare for this, Olivia wishes to set up the payroll feature. The company file includes information for Olivia's Web Solutions as of August 1, 2014.

1. Open the company file CH8 Olivia's Web Solutions.QBW.
2. Make a backup copy of the company file OWS8 [*Your Name*] Olivia's Web Solutions.
3. Restore the backup copy of the company file. In both the Open Backup Copy and Save Company File as windows, use the file name OWS8 [*Your Name*] Olivia's Web Solutions.
4. Change the company name to **OWS8 [*Your Name*] Olivia's Web Solutions**.
5. Activate the payroll feature for Olivia's Web Solutions.

6. Customize the system default accounts:

	QuickBooks		Edited
Number	Account Name		Number
24000	Payroll Liabilities		2100
66000	Payroll Expenses		6560

7. Add the following accounts to the Chart of Accounts List:

2110	Social Sec/Medicare Tax Payable	Subaccount of 2100 Payroll Liabilities
2115	FIT Payable	Subaccount of 2100 Payroll Liabilities
2120	SIT Payable	Subaccount of 2100 Payroll Liabilities
2125	FUTA Payable	Subaccount of 2100 Payroll Liabilities
2130	SUI Payable	Subaccount of 2100 Payroll Liabilities
6565	Salaries and Wages Expense	Subaccount of 6560 Payroll Expenses
6611	Social Sec/Medicare Tax Expense	Subaccount of 6560 Payroll Expenses
6625	FUTA Expense	Subaccount of 6560 Payroll Expenses
6630	SUI Expense	Subaccount of 6560 Payroll Expenses

8. Select the manual payroll calculations option.
9. Customize each of the payroll items listed below. For each item, proceed as follows:

- Accept the name listed.
- Choose United States Treasury as the agency to which the liability will be paid.
- Select the liability and expense accounts indicated below.
- Accept all tax rates.
- Accept all taxable compensation default.

Payroll Item	Liability Account	Expense Account
Federal Unemployment	2125 FUTA Payable	6625 FUTA Expense
Federal Withholding	2115 FIT Payable	
Medicare Company	2110 Social Sec/ Medicare Tax Payable	6611 Social Sec/ Medicare Tax Expense
Medicare Employee	2110 Social Sec/ Medicare Tax Payable	6611 Social Sec/ Medicare Tax Expense
Social Security Company	2110 Social Sec/ Medicare Tax Payable	6611 Social Sec/ Medicare Tax Expense
Social Security Employee	2110 Social Sec/ Medicare Tax Payable	6611 Social Sec/ Medicare Tax Expense

10. Add the following payroll items:

Salary

Payroll Item Type:	**Wage (Hourly Wages, Annual Salary, Commission, Bonus)**
Payroll Item Subtype—Wages:	**Annual Salary**
Wages:	**Regular Pay**
Name:	**Salary**
Expense Account:	**6565 Salaries and Wages Expense**

Wages

Payroll Item Type:	**Wage (Hourly Wages, Annual Salary, Commission, Bonus)**
Payroll Item Subtype—Wages:	**Hourly Wages**
Wages:	**Regular Pay**
Name:	**Hourly Wages**
Expense Account:	**6565 Salaries and Wages Expense**

State Tax Withholding

Payroll Item Type:	**State Tax (State Withholding, SDI, SUI)**
State:	**NY**
Payroll Item Subtype—State Tax:	**State Withholding**
Name Used on Paychecks:	**NY – Withholding**
Agency for Liabilities:	**NYS Tax Department**
Identifying Number:	**55-5656566**
Liability Account:	**2120 SIT Payable**
Taxable Compensation:	**Accept defaults**

SUI

Payroll Item Type:	**State Tax (State Withholding, SDI, SUI)**
State:	**NY**
Payroll Item Subtype—State Tax:	**State Unemployment**
Name Used on Paychecks:	**NY – Unemployment Company**
Agency for Liabilities:	**NYS Tax Department**
Identifying Number:	**ER-4877**
Liability Account:	**2130 SUI Payable**
Expense Account:	**6630 SUI Expense**
Company Tax Rate:	**4.025% each quarter**
Taxable Compensation:	**Accept defaults**

11. Display and print the *Payroll Item Listing* report.

CHAPTER 9

Payroll Processing

Pay Employees, Pay Payroll Liabilities, and Process Payroll Forms

Chapter Objectives

- Review accounting for payroll transactions

- Update the Employee Center

- Record payroll in the Pay Employees windows

- Record payments of payroll taxes in the Pay Liabilities window

- Display and print payroll-related reports, accounting reports, and financial statements

Introduction

In chapter 8, you learned to activate the payroll feature, customize and update the Chart of Accounts List to include the appropriate payroll accounts required for payroll processing, set up the payroll to accept manual entries, and customize and add various payroll items to the Payroll Item List. Once payroll is activated and set up, QuickBooks allows you to process payroll and track payroll information for your company's **employees**. You can establish a file for each employee and then process payroll transactions. These employee files comprise the *Employee Center*.

Once you have established an employee file, you can enter transactions for payroll (Activities) in the *Pay Employees* and *Pay Liabilities* windows. Every time your company processes payroll for employees in the activities windows, QuickBooks simultaneously updates the information in the Employee Center. In addition, QuickBooks changes balance sheet and income statement accounts based on payroll transactions entered in the payroll activities windows.

In this chapter, our sample company, Kristin Raina Interior Designs, will hire and pay two employees beginning April 1, 2014. Kristin Raina will have to establish an employee file for each employee in the Employee List.

QuickBooks versus Manual Accounting: Payroll Transactions

In a manual accounting system, employee pay transactions are usually recorded in a **payroll journal** or **register**. The employee's gross pay, tax withholding, and other payroll deductions are calculated in the journal using the employee's background information (pay rate, marital status, state of residency, and so on) along with the applicable tax schedules. Payroll checks and tax remittance checks are usually recorded in a cash payments journal.

In QuickBooks, the Employee Center contains background information for each employee, such as name, address, Social Security number, pay rate, and applicable tax deductions. The Payroll Item List contains a file for all payroll items such as taxes and withholdings affecting the pay computation for the company (chapter 8).

When the company processes payroll, the transactions are recorded in the Pay Employees window. QuickBooks uses the information entered in the Employee Center along with the items on the Payroll Item List applicable to the employee to determine gross pay, payroll deductions, and net pay in the Pay Employees windows.

When payroll tax liabilities are paid, the Pay Liabilities window is used to record the transaction. These transactions update the Chart of Accounts List (general ledger) while at the same time updating the employee's file.

In both manual and computerized systems, payroll reports will be generated and forwarded periodically to the appropriate federal and state tax authorities. In QuickBooks, these payroll forms are prepared using the Process Payroll Forms window if you subscribe to a QuickBooks payroll service.

---

employee Someone hired by a company who will receive salary or wages on a regular basis.

payroll journal (register) A journal used to calculate payroll and record payroll entries for each employee.

Accounting for Payroll Transactions

When a company generates a paycheck, the transaction affects a number of expense and liability accounts.

The employee's gross pay is an expense the company records at the payroll date. Additional expenses for the company include the various taxes imposed on the employer including, but not limited to, Social Security tax (FICA), Medicare tax, Federal Unemployment Tax Act (FUTA) tax, and state unemployment insurance (SUI) recorded in the appropriate expense accounts at the payroll date.

The employee, at a minimum, will have amounts for FICA, Medicare, federal income tax, and state income tax (if applicable) deducted from his or her paycheck by the employer. These withheld taxes, along with the taxes imposed on the employer, are recorded as liabilities on the books of the company because the company is responsible for remitting these taxes to the appropriate governmental tax-collecting agency at a later date.

The gross pay less the employee deductions results in a net payroll check to the employee. The following example illustrates the effect one paycheck has on the general ledger:

> Company A has one employee who earns an annual salary of $48,000 per year. The company pays its employees semimonthly, on the 15th and last day of the month. Therefore, there are 24 pay periods in the year. Consequently, our employee will earn $2,000 of salary income for each pay period. The employee is subject to FICA (6.2% of $2,000 = $124), Medicare tax (1.45% of $2,000 = $29), FIT ($300), and SIT ($100)—with a resulting net pay of $1,447. The employer is also subject to the matching FICA tax and Medicare tax along with FUTA (.8% of $2,000 = $16) and SUI (3% of $2,000 = $60).

The journal entry to record the employee's earnings, deductions, and net pay is as follows:

			Debit	Credit
	Salaries Expense		2000	
	Social Sec/Medicare Tax Payable			153
	($124 + $29)			
	FIT Payable			300
	SIT Payable			100
	Cash – Payroll			1447

Many companies use a separate checking account for payroll transactions. Periodically, funds are transferred into this account from the operating account. Having a separate checking account helps track payroll transactions.

In addition, the journal entry of the employer's payroll tax expenses is recorded on the paycheck date as follows:

			Debit	Credit
	Social Sec/Medicare Tax Expense		153	
	FUTA Expense (.008 × $2,000)		16	
	SUI Expense (.03 × $2,000)		60	
	Social Sec/Medicare Tax Payable			153
	FUTA Payable			16
	SUI Payable			60

When the company remits the employer and employee taxes to the federal and local governments, it records several journal entries. Payment for the employer and employee Social Security tax and Medicare tax, the employee federal withholding, and the FUTA tax will be forwarded to the federal government. The journal entry is as follows:

	Social Sec/Medicare Tax Payable		3 0 6				
	($153 + $153)						
	FIT Payable		3 0 0				
	FUTA Payable		1 6				
	Cash – Payroll					6 2 2	

Payment for the state withholding tax and the SUI is usually made with one check payable to the state taxing authority responsible for these taxes. In some states, two checks have to be sent because two different tax agencies are responsible.

	SIT Payable		1 0 0				
	SUI Payable		6 0				
	Cash – Payroll					1 6 0	

As you can see, the journal entries for the foregoing transactions can be complex, as several general ledger accounts are affected. In addition, federal and state payroll and compliance laws are detailed and burdensome, with costly penalties for noncompliance. As a result, payroll accounting is a time-consuming process that can result in costly errors and omissions.

Before the availability of low-cost, off-the-shelf accounting software, most small companies either processed payroll manually or used outside computerized payroll services that charged per check. With the coming of QuickBooks and other general ledger software packages, small companies can now process payroll; determine gross pay, tax expenses, and tax liabilities; and prepare employee paychecks and payroll data in compliance with federal and state payroll regulations.

Chapter Problem

In this chapter, Kristin Raina Interior Designs will hire two employees and begin to process payroll during the month of April 2014. You will enter information for each employee in the Employee Center. The April 1 beginning balances for the company are contained in the company file CH9 Kristin Raina Interior Designs.

Before you begin, open the company file CH9 Kristin Raina Interior Designs.QBW. Make a backup copy of the file, name it **EX9 [*Your Name*] Kristin Raina Interior Designs**, and restore the file. Finally, change the company name in the file to **EX9 [*Your Name*] Kristin Raina Interior Designs**.

LISTS/CENTERS: ○ ## The Employee Center

The Employee Center contains a file for each employee of the company. Information such as name, address, Social Security number, hire date, pay rate, and applicable payroll taxes are indicated for each employee.

QuickBooks uses the information contained in each employee's file, along with the information in the Payroll Item List, to calculate the employee's gross pay, deductions, and net paycheck.

Like all other Lists and Centers, in QuickBooks, the Employee Center needs to be updated as new employees are hired, employees leave the company, or information about an employee changes and needs to be revised.

Employee Center

To view the Employee Center—
1. Click Employees and then click *Employee Center.*

The Employee Center appears. (See figure 9–A.)

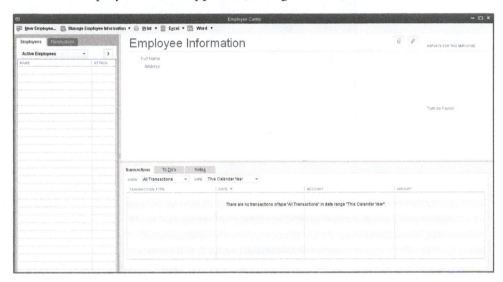

The Employee Center contains the following parts:

Employees tab	Lists all current employees. You can display active employees, all employees, or only released employees.
Transactions tab	Lists all transactions for selected employees.
New Employee button	Used to add a new employee.
Employee Information	Displays background and transaction information for the employee selected in the Employees tab.
Edit icon	Used to edit background information for the employee selected in the Employees tab.
Notes tab	Used to include narrative information specific to an employee.

Kristin Raina has hired two employees, Harry Renee and Richard Henderson, beginning April 1, 2014. Since our sample company did not previously have employees, the only updating to the Employee Center at this time is to add the new employees.

To add an employee—

1. Click Employees and then click *Employee Center*.
2. At the Employee Center window, click the New Employee button. The New Employee window appears. (See figure 9–B.)

FIGURE 9–B
New Employee Window

The New Employee window has six information tabs: Personal, Address & Contact, Additional Info, Payroll Info, Employment Info, and Workers' Comp. The Personal tab is the initial display.

3. Enter the information listed below on the Personal tab.

First Name:	**Harry**
Last Name:	**Renee**
PRINT ON CHECKS AS:	**Harry Renee**
SOCIAL SECURITY NO.:	**112-55-9999**
GENDER:	**Male**
DATE OF BIRTH:	**2/17/58**

(See figure 9–C.)

FIGURE 9–C

New Employee
Window—Personal
Tab—Completed

4. Click the Address and Contact tab. Enter the information listed below.

ADDRESS:	**323 S. Main Ave.**
	St. Paul, MN 54120
MAIN PHONE:	**651-555-3311**
Mobile:	**651-555-0001**

(See figure 9–D.)

FIGURE 9–D

New Employee
Window—Address and
Contact Tab—Completed

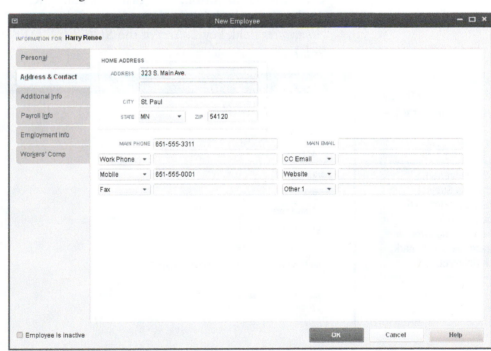

5. Click the Payroll Info tab
6. In the *PAY FREQUENCY* field, click *Semimonthly* from the drop-down list
7. In the *EARNINGS—ITEM NAME* field, click *Salary* from the drop-down list.
8. In the *HOURLY/ANNUAL RATE* field, key **24000**. (See figure 9–E.)

FIGURE 9–E

New Employee Window—Payroll Info Tab—Partially Completed

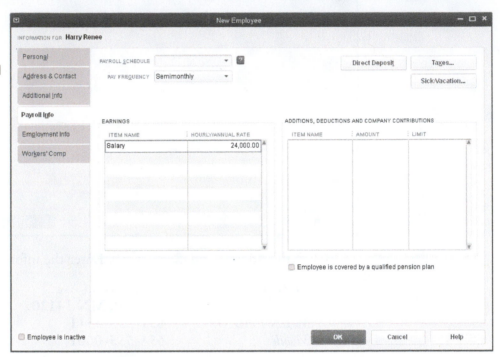

9. Click the Taxes button. The Taxes for Harry Renee window appears.
10. At the Federal tab, at the *Filing Status* field, accept *Single;* at the *Allowances* field, key **1**. Accept the *SUBJECT TO* defaults. (See figure 9–F.)

FIGURE 9–F

Taxes for Harry Renee Window—Federal Tab

HINT

If you inadvertently uncheck a Subject to tax, a window will appear warning of a possible setup error. To replace the check mark, click Reselect.

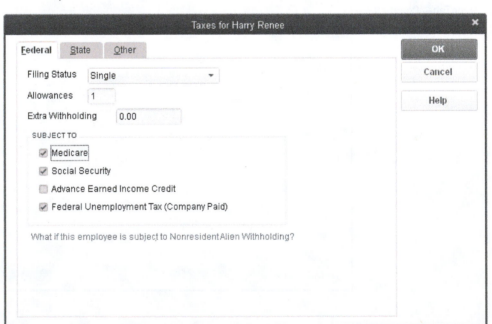

11. Click the State tab. In both the *STATE WORKED* and *STATE SUBJECT TO WITHHOLDING* sections, click *MN*. When you move to the next field, additional fields appear.
12. Accept *Single* in the *Filing Status* field; at the allowances field, key **1**. (See figure 9–G.)

FIGURE 9–G
Taxes for Harry Renee
Window—State Tab

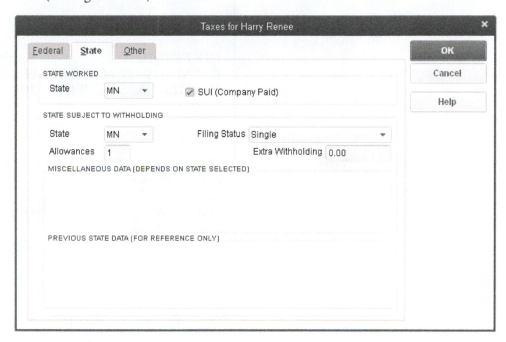

13. If the information is correct, click OK.

If the QuickBooks Information window appears, read the information and then click OK. Click the Delete button to remove the tax added by the QuickBooks program.

14. Click OK to close the window. At the QuickBooks for Windows message, click *No*. You are returned to the Payroll Info tab.
15. Click OK. The New Employee: Payroll Info (Other) window appears.
16. Click *Leave As Is*.

Practice Exercise

Add the following employee:

Personal tab	
First Name:	**Richard**
Last Name:	**Henderson**
PRINT ON CHECKS AS:	**Richard Henderson**
SOCIAL SECURITY NO.:	**333-44-5555**
GENDER:	**Male**
DATE OF BIRTH:	**8/1/75**

Address and Contact tab	*ADDRESS:*	23 Ashland Rd. St. Paul, MN 54120
	MAIN PHONE:	**651-555-6868**
	Mobile:	**651-555-2541**

Payroll Info tab

PAY FREQUENCY:	**Semimonthly**
EARNINGS-ITEM NAME:	**Hourly Wages**
HOURLY/ANNUAL RATE:	**20**

Taxes

Federal Filing Status:	**Married**
Federal Allowances:	**2**
State Worked/Subject to Withholding:	**MN**
Subject to SUI?:	✓
State Filing Status:	**Married**
State Allowances:	**2**
Not Subject to Local Taxes	

QuickCheck: The updated Employee Center appears in figure 9–H.

FIGURE 9–H
Updated Employee Center

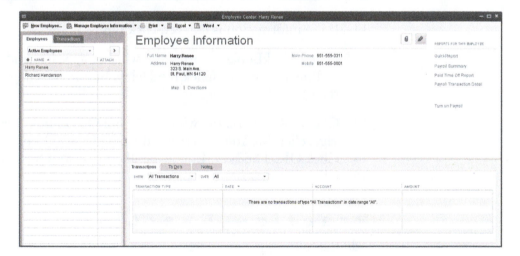

○ **The Pay Employees Windows**

You use the Pay Employees windows to calculate gross pay, taxes, and net payroll for employees, a daily business activity that is part of the third order of operations in QuickBooks. As in a manual accounting system, when you process payroll through the Pay Employees window, a number of general ledger accounts are affected by the transaction.

As illustrated earlier in the chapter, it is common in a manual accounting system to record payroll using two journal entries. One journal entry records the salaries/wages expense, the employees' withholdings as liabilities, and the net pay. The second journal entry usually records the employer's related tax expense and related liabilities.

In QuickBooks, the transaction is recorded as one compound journal entry instead of two separate journal entries. The transaction is recorded as follows:

Salaries Expense (Gross pay)	XXX		
Social Sec/Medicare Tax Expense	XXX		
FUTA Expense	XXX		
SUI Expense	XXX		
Social Sec/Medicare Tax Payable			XXX
Federal Withholding Tax Payable			XXX
State Withholding Tax Payable			XXX
FUTA Payable			XXX
SUI Payable			XXX
Cash – Payroll			XXX

At the same time you record the transaction, QuickBooks updates the Employee Center and payroll reports to reflect pay earned to date and taxes withheld.

There are three Pay Employees windows: Enter Payroll Information, Preview Paycheck, and Review and Create Paychecks. The Enter Payroll Information window is used to select the employee(s) to be paid at the current pay date. (See figure 9–I.)

FIGURE 9–I
Enter Payroll Information
Window

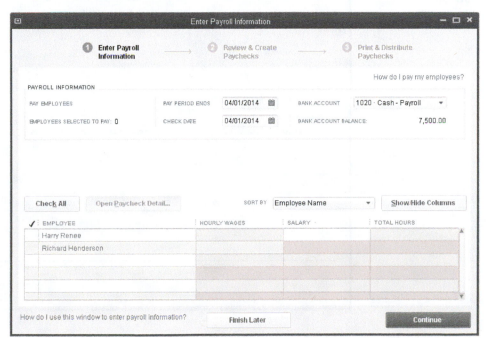

Once an employee is selected, you move to the Preview Paycheck window. (See figure 9–J.)

FIGURE 9–J
Preview Paycheck Window

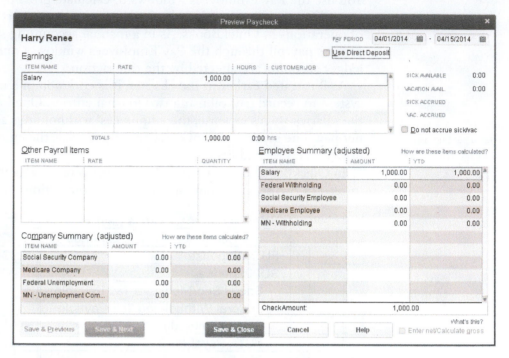

If the company has subscribed to a QuickBooks payroll service, tax figures and deductions would be calculated and displayed automatically in the taxes and deductions columns. If you do not subscribe to a payroll service, which is assumed in this text, you will need to key in the amount for the taxes in the Preview Paycheck window. Once all payroll information has been entered, you will move to the Review and Create Paychecks window. (See figure 9-K.)

FIGURE 9–K
Review and Create Paychecks Window

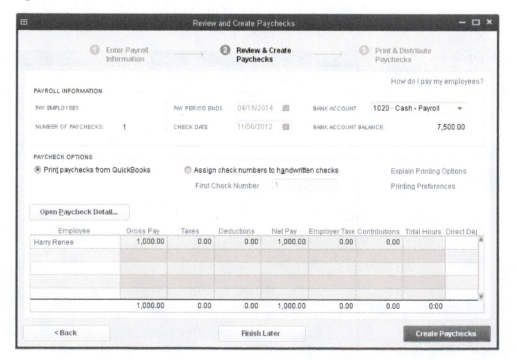

Paying an Employee

On April 15, 2014, Kristin Raina will pay the company's two employees. Harry Renee will be paid first. When Harry Renee was entered in the Employee Center, an annual salary of $24,000 was entered and the semi-monthly pay period was indicated. Semimonthly pay periods result in 24 paychecks per year. Based on this information, QuickBooks determines that Harry Renee is to be paid $1,000 ($24,000/24 pay periods) per pay period.

HINT

Remember that many companies set up a separate checking account dedicated to payroll transactions.

To pay an employee—

1. Click Employees and then click *Pay Employees*. The Enter Payroll Information window appears.
2. At the *PAY PERIOD ENDS* and *CHECK DATE* fields, choose *04/15/2014*.
3. At the *BANK ACCOUNT* field, click *1020 Cash - Payroll*.
4. Select Harry Renee by placing a check mark next to the name. (See figure 9–L.)

FIGURE 9–L
Enter Payroll Information Window—Completed

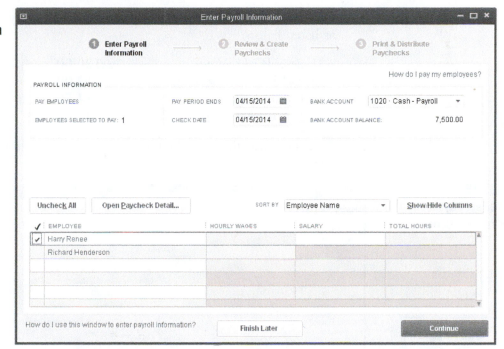

5. If the information is correct, click *Open Paycheck Detail*. The Preview Paycheck window appears.
6. Make sure the *ITEM NAME* field lists *Salary*, the *RATE* field shows *1,000*, and the *PAY PERIOD* fields display *04/01/2014* and *04/15/2014*.
7. Move to the Company Summary (adjusted) section.

   In the Company Summary (adjusted) section, you enter the employer's payroll-related tax expenses. When you key information in this section, use the mouse or Tab key to move to each field, not the Enter key. If you press the Enter key, QuickBooks assumes the pay information is complete, exits you out of this window, and will not let you re-enter it.

8. Key the employer's taxes in the Company Summary (adjusted) section as listed below:

Social Security Company:	**62.00**
Medicare Company:	**14.50**
Federal Unemployment:	**8.00**
MN - Unemployment Company:	**40.00**

9. Move to the Employee Summary (adjusted) section.

In the Employee Summary (adjusted) section, you enter the amount of taxes withheld from the employee's paycheck. As in the Company Summary (adjusted) section, use the mouse or Tab key to move to each field; do not press Enter. You do not have to precede the amount with a minus sign; QuickBooks automatically enters the minus sign before each amount.

10. Key the employee's taxes in the Employee Summary (adjusted) section as listed below:

Federal Withholding:	**120.00**
Social Security Employee:	**62.00**
Medicare Employee:	**14.50**
MN - Withholding:	**46.00**

After entering all taxes, the Check Amount total should be displayed as *757.50*. (See figure 9–M.)

FIGURE 9–M
Preview Paycheck Window—Completed

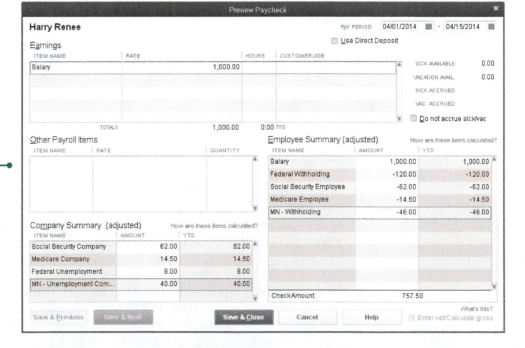

HINT

See Appendix H to review steps to track sick and vacation paid time off.

11. If the information is correct, click Save & Close. You will be returned to the Enter Payroll Information window.
12. Click Continue. You move to the Review and Create Paychecks window with the taxes columns completed.

13. In the *PAYCHECK OPTIONS* section, click *Assign check numbers to hand-written checks;* in the *First Check Number* field, key **1**. (See figure 9–N.)

FIGURE 9–N

Review and Create Paychecks Window—Completed

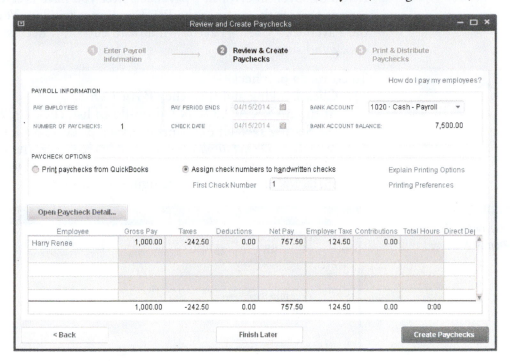

14. If the information is correct, click *Create Paychecks*.
15. At the Confirmation and Next Steps window, click Close.

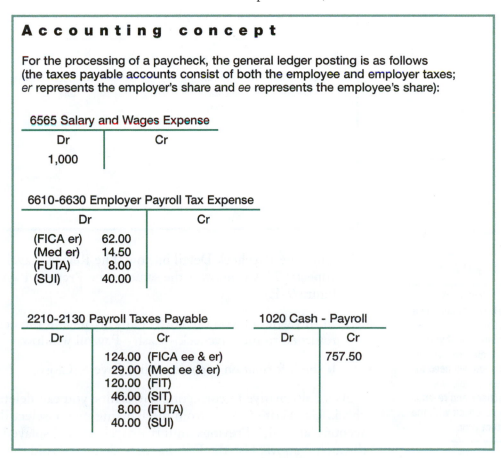

Accounting concept

For the processing of a paycheck, the general ledger posting is as follows (the taxes payable accounts consist of both the employee and employer taxes; *er* represents the employer's share and *ee* represents the employee's share):

6565 Salary and Wages Expense

Dr	Cr
1,000	

6610-6630 Employer Payroll Tax Expense

Dr		Cr
(FICA er)	62.00	
(Med er)	14.50	
(FUTA)	8.00	
(SUI)	40.00	

2210-2130 Payroll Taxes Payable

Dr	Cr	
	124.00	(FICA ee & er)
	29.00	(Med ee & er)
	120.00	(FIT)
	46.00	(SIT)
	8.00	(FUTA)
	40.00	(SUI)

1020 Cash - Payroll

Dr	Cr
	757.50

Correcting an Error in a Paycheck

If you discover an error in a paycheck after you have created the check, you cannot correct the error in the Pay Employees window. You will have to use the Paycheck - Cash - Payroll window to edit or, if necessary, delete the paycheck and start over.

To correct a paycheck—
1. Click Banking and then click *Write Checks*.
2. At the BANK ACCOUNT drop-down list, click *1020 Cash - Payroll*. At the Setting Default Accounts message, place a check mark in the box to the left of *Do not display this message in the future*, then click OK.
3. Click the Previous arrow on the Find button until you arrive at the check for Harry Renee. (See figure 9–O.)

FIGURE 9–O
Paycheck - Cash - Payroll Window

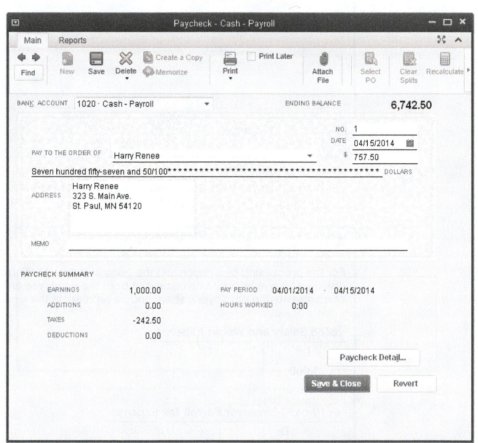

4. Click the Paycheck Detail button. The Review Paycheck window appears. This window is the same as the Preview Paycheck window. (See figure 9–P.)

In this window, you can correct any errors and then click OK. You are returned to the Paycheck - Cash - Payroll window.

5. If the information is correct, click Save & Close.

As an alternative to correcting any errors, you can delete the entire paycheck. Use Write Checks from the Banking menu, select the Cash - Payroll account, and click Previous until the paycheck is displayed as in steps 1 through 3 above. Use the Edit menu to delete or void the paycheck.

> **HINT**
>
> QuickBooks will not allow you to change a paycheck outside the current year. If you make an error with the year, you will need to delete or void the paycheck and re-enter the paycheck with the correct year.

FIGURE 9–P
Review Paycheck
Window

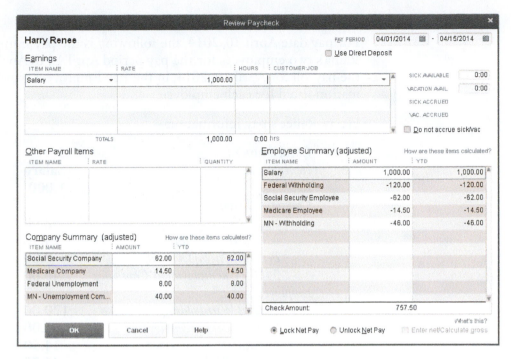

Practice Exercise

Process the pay for Richard Henderson for the pay period ending April 15, 2014, in the Pay Employees windows using the information listed below.

Richard Henderson's pay information:

Item Name:	**Hourly Wages**
Rate:	**20**
Hours:	**80**

Richard is an hourly employee. You must key the actual number of hours he has worked in the *HOURS* field. QuickBooks then computes the gross pay by multiplying his hourly pay rate (previously entered in the Employee Center and displayed in this window) by the number of hours worked for this pay period.

Company Taxes		
	Social Security Company:	**99.20**
	Medicare Company:	**23.20**
	Federal Unemployment:	**12.80**
	MN - Unemployment Company:	**64.00**
Employee Taxes		
	Federal Withholding:	**120.00**
	Social Security Employee:	**99.20**
	Medicare Employee:	**23.20**
	MN - Withholding:	**54.00**

QuickCheck: The check amount should be $1,303.60.

Additional Payroll Journal Entries

For pay date April 30, 2014, the following is the pay information for Kristin Raina's two employees for the pay period April 16 to April 30, 2014. Record the payroll for April 30, 2014, in the Pay Employees window using the information listed for each employee.

Harry Renee's pay information—

Check Number:	**3**
Item Name:	**Salary**
Rate:	**1,000**
Company Taxes:	
Social Security Company:	**62.00**
Medicare Company:	**14.50**
Federal Unemployment:	**8.00**
MN - Unemployment Company:	**40.00**
Employee Taxes:	
Federal Withholding:	**120.00**
Social Security Employee:	**62.00**
Medicare Employee:	**14.50**
MN - Withholding:	**46.00**

QuickCheck: The check amount should be $757.50.

Richard Henderson's pay information—

Check Number:	**4**
Item Name:	**Hourly Wages**
Rate:	**20**
Hours:	**88**
Company Taxes:	
Social Security Company:	**109.12**
Medicare Company:	**25.52**
Federal Unemployment:	**14.08**
MN - Unemployment Company:	**70.40**
Employee Taxes:	
Federal Withholding:	**132.00**
Social Security Employee:	**109.12**
Medicare Employee:	**25.52**
MN - Withholding:	**61.00**

QuickCheck: The check amount should be $1,432.36.

ACTIVITIES: **The Pay Liabilities Window**

Activities identified as paying employees were recorded in the Pay Employees window. Subsequently, Activities identified as paying payroll liabilities are then recorded in the *Pay Liabilities* window. As you process paychecks in the Pay Employees windows, QuickBooks tracks all payroll liabilities as they accumulate from each paycheck. The Pay Liabilities window then displays all payroll liabilities existing at a specified date and allows you to pay each to its appropriate tax-collecting agency.

The Pay Liabilities window is designed for the payment of federal and local payroll tax liabilities. The default accounts are the various payroll tax liability accounts that have been credited during the payroll processing in the Pay Employees window. Once a liability is selected for payment, the transaction is recorded as follows:

| | | Payroll Tax Payable | | XXX | | | |
| | | Cash – Payroll | | | | XXX | |

The QuickBooks Pay Liabilities window appears in figure 9–Q.

FIGURE 9–Q
Pay Liabilities Window

Once you enter the period of time, QuickBooks displays all payroll tax liabilities accrued during that period that remain unpaid. Because of this, you can pay all liabilities payable to a given taxing authority with a single check.

On April 30, 2014, Kristin Raina wishes to remit the federal employer and employee payroll taxes owed to the United States Treasury for the April payroll. The company and employee FICA, the company and employee Medicare tax, the employee's FIT, and the employer's FUTA tax are to be remitted to the federal government.

To pay federal payroll tax liabilities—
1. Click Employees and then click *Payroll Taxes and Liabilities*.
2. At the Payroll Taxes and Liabilities submenu, click *Pay Payroll Liabilities*.
3. At the Select Date Range For Liabilities dialog box, choose from *04/01/2014* through *04/30/2014* and then click OK. The Pay Liabilities window is displayed, showing all payroll tax liabilities accumulated during the selected period. The company can pay the entire liability or only a portion as needed.

4. Make sure the *To be printed* box is unchecked, the *Review liability check to enter expenses/penalties* option is selected, and the correct date range appears.
5. At the Bank Account drop-down list, click *1020 Cash - Payroll*.
6. At the Check Date box, choose *04/30/2014*.
7. Place a check mark next to the liabilities listed below, all of which are payable to the United States Treasury:

> *Federal Unemployment*
> *Federal Withholding*
> *Medicare Company*
> *Medicare Employee*
> *Social Security Company*
> *Social Security Employee*

The Amt. To Pay column should total $1,354.96. (See figure 9–R.)

FIGURE 9–R
Pay Liabilities Window—Completed

8. If all information is correct, click *Create*. The Liability Check - Cash - Payroll window will be displayed. (See figure 9–S.)
9. If the information on the check is correct, click Save & Close.

Like other Write Check windows in QuickBooks, even though a check is not printed, the liability is paid and a check is recorded in the system.

FIGURE 9–S
Liability Check - Cash -
Payroll Window

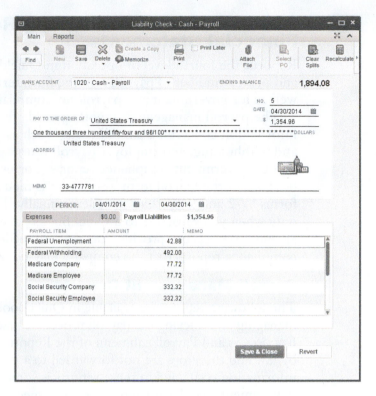

HINT

If you make an error in the Pay Liabilities window, you cannot correct it in this window once you have saved the information. You must use the Paycheck - Cash - Payroll window (Write Checks) in the Banking menu. Click the Cash - Payroll account, and click the Previous arrow until the check with the error is displayed. Then, make any corrections, or delete the entire check using the Edit menu.

Accounting concept

For a payment of payroll liability, the general ledger posting is as follows:

2110 Social Security/MedicareTaxes Payable

Dr	Cr
Pmt 820.08	820.08
	Bal 0

2115 FIT Payable

Dr	Cr
Pmt 492.00	492.00
	Bal 0

2125 FUTA Payable

Dr	Cr
Pmt 42.88	42.88
	Bal 0

1020 Cash in Bank - Payroll

Dr	Cr
	1,354.96

Practice Exercise

On April 30, 2014, pay the payroll tax liabilities for MN - Unemployment Company and MN Withholding.

QuickCheck: The amount due and to pay is $421.40.

Payroll Reports, Accounting Reports, and Financial Statements

Reports, the fourth level of operation in QuickBooks, allows you to display and print a number of payroll reports, for internal payroll management as well as for government and payroll tax compliance.

The payroll management reports provide the company with valuable information concerning payroll costs—such as gross pay; payroll liabilities and withholding; and employer payroll taxes.

The government compliance reports (Forms 941, W-2, and 940) are replications of the federal form 941, which is filed quarterly, and the federal forms W-2 and 940, which are filed annually. These reports are available only when you subscribe to a QuickBooks payroll service, but payroll management reports can provide information needed to complete state and local compliance reports that the company may be required to submit.

Payroll Management Reports

The following reports are available in QuickBooks to assist the company in managing and tracking the payroll process. These reports are accessed from the Employees and Payroll submenu of the Reports menu. They are not required by law and therefore are not forwarded to a government agency. However, information contained in these reports is sometimes used to complete government-mandated payroll reports, especially at the state or local level.

Payroll Summary Report

The *Payroll Summary* report lists the earnings, deductions, and employer payroll taxes for each employee for a specified period of time.

To view and print the *Payroll Summary* report—
1. Click Reports and then click *Employees & Payroll*.
2. At the Employees & Payroll submenu, click *Payroll Summary*.
3. At the *From* and *To* fields, choose *04/01/2014* to *04/30/2014* and then click Refresh. The report will be displayed for the period.
4. To print the report, click the Print button from the top of the report, check the settings in the Print Reports dialog box, and click Print. Your report should look like figure 9–T.
5. Close the report.

> **HINT**
>
> You can also view payroll management reports from the Reports menu of the Payroll Item List or the Employee Center window.

FIGURE 9–T
Payroll Summary Report

EX9 [Your Name] Kristin Raina Interior Designs
Payroll Summary
April 2014

	Harry Renee			Richard Henderson			TOTAL		
	Hours	Rate	Apr 14	Hours	Rate	Apr 14	Hours	Rate	Apr 14
Employee Wages, Taxes and Adjustments									
Gross Pay									
Salary			2,000.00			0.00			2,000.00
Hourly Wages			0.00	168	20.00	3,360.00	168.00		3,360.00
Total Gross Pay			2,000.00	168		3,360.00	168.00		5,360.00
Adjusted Gross Pay			2,000.00	168		3,360.00	168.00		5,360.00
Taxes Withheld									
Federal Withholding			-240.00			-252.00			-492.00
Medicare Employee			-29.00			-48.72			-77.72
Social Security Employee			-124.00			-208.32			-332.32
MN - Withholding			-92.00			-115.00			-207.00
Total Taxes Withheld			-485.00			-624.04			-1,109.04
Net Pay			1,515.00	168		2,735.96	168.00		4,250.96
Employer Taxes and Contributions									
Federal Unemployment			16.00			26.88			42.88
Medicare Company			29.00			48.72			77.72
Social Security Company			124.00			208.32			332.32
MN - Unemployment Company			80.00			134.40			214.40
Total Employer Taxes and Contributions			249.00			418.32			667.32

Payroll Liability Balances Report

The *Payroll Liabilities Balances* report lists all payroll liabilities owed and unpaid for a specified period of time. If liabilities have been accrued and paid, a zero will appear for that liability.

To view and print the *Payroll Liability Balances* report—
1. Click Reports and then click *Employees & Payroll.*
2. At the Employees & Payroll submenu, click *Payroll Liability Balances.*
3. At the *From* and *To* fields, choose *04/01/2014* to *04/30/2014* and then click Refresh. The report will be displayed for the period. (See figure 9–U.)

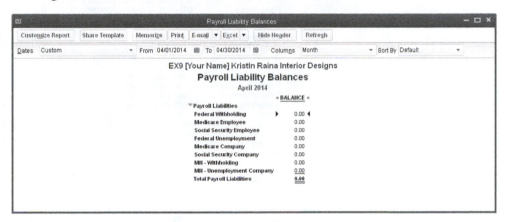

4. To print the report, click the Print button from the top of the report, check the settings in the Print Reports dialog box, and click Print.
5. Close the report.

Payroll Transaction Detail Report

The *Payroll Transaction Detail* report provides detailed information for each payroll transaction (paychecks and payroll liability payments) recorded during the period. Information such as employee salary per paycheck, tax withholding, net pay, employer-paid taxes, and taxes remitted are presented in this report.

To view and print the *Payroll Transaction Detail* report—
1. Click Reports and then click *Employees & Payroll.*
2. At the Employees & Payroll submenu, click *Payroll Transaction Detail.*
3. At the *To* and *From* fields, choose *04/01/2014* and *04/30/2014*, then click Refresh. The report will display all payroll transactions recorded during the specified period.
4. To print the report, click the Print button from the top of the report, check the settings in the Print Reports dialog box, and Print. (See figure 9–V.)
5. Close the report.

FIGURE 9-V
Payroll Transaction Detail
Report

Date	Num	Type	Source Name	Payroll Item	Wage Base	Amount
04/15/2014	1	Paycheck	Harry Renee	Salary	0.00	1,000.00
			Harry Renee	Federal Withholding	1,000.00	-120.00
			Harry Renee	Social Security Company	1,000.00	62.00
			Harry Renee	Social Security Company	1,000.00	-62.00
			Harry Renee	Social Security Employee	1,000.00	-62.00
			Harry Renee	Medicare Company	1,000.00	14.50
			Harry Renee	Medicare Company	1,000.00	-14.50
			Harry Renee	Medicare Employee	1,000.00	-14.50
			Harry Renee	Federal Unemployment	1,000.00	8.00
			Harry Renee	Federal Unemployment	1,000.00	-8.00
			Harry Renee	MN - Withholding	1,000.00	-46.00
			Harry Renee	MN - Unemployment Company	1,000.00	40.00
			Harry Renee	MN - Unemployment Company	1,000.00	-40.00
						757.50
04/15/2014	2	Paycheck	Richard Henderson	Hourly Wages	0.00	1,600.00
			Richard Henderson	Federal Withholding	1,600.00	-120.00
			Richard Henderson	Social Security Company	1,600.00	99.20
			Richard Henderson	Social Security Company	1,600.00	-99.20
			Richard Henderson	Social Security Employee	1,600.00	-99.20
			Richard Henderson	Medicare Company	1,600.00	23.20
			Richard Henderson	Medicare Company	1,600.00	-23.20
			Richard Henderson	Medicare Employee	1,600.00	-23.20
			Richard Henderson	Federal Unemployment	1,600.00	12.80
			Richard Henderson	Federal Unemployment	1,600.00	-12.80
			Richard Henderson	MN - Withholding	1,600.00	-54.00
			Richard Henderson	MN - Unemployment Company	1,600.00	64.00
			Richard Henderson	MN - Unemployment Company	1,600.00	-64.00
						1,303.60
04/30/2014	3	Paycheck	Harry Renee	Salary	0.00	1,000.00
			Harry Renee	Federal Withholding	1,000.00	-120.00
			Harry Renee	Social Security Company	1,000.00	62.00
			Harry Renee	Social Security Company	1,000.00	-62.00
			Harry Renee	Social Security Employee	1,000.00	-62.00
			Harry Renee	Medicare Company	1,000.00	14.50
			Harry Renee	Medicare Company	1,000.00	-14.50
			Harry Renee	Medicare Employee	1,000.00	-14.50
			Harry Renee	Federal Unemployment	1,000.00	8.00
			Harry Renee	Federal Unemployment	1,000.00	-8.00
			Harry Renee	MN - Withholding	1,000.00	-46.00
			Harry Renee	MN - Unemployment Company	1,000.00	40.00
			Harry Renee	MN - Unemployment Company	1,000.00	-40.00
						757.50
04/30/2014	4	Paycheck	Richard Henderson	Hourly Wages	0.00	1,760.00
			Richard Henderson	Federal Withholding	1,760.00	-132.00
			Richard Henderson	Social Security Company	1,760.00	109.12
			Richard Henderson	Social Security Company	1,760.00	-109.12
			Richard Henderson	Social Security Employee	1,760.00	-109.12
			Richard Henderson	Medicare Company	1,760.00	25.52
			Richard Henderson	Medicare Company	1,760.00	-25.52
			Richard Henderson	Medicare Employee	1,760.00	-25.52
			Richard Henderson	Federal Unemployment	1,760.00	14.08
			Richard Henderson	Federal Unemployment	1,760.00	-14.08
			Richard Henderson	MN - Withholding	1,760.00	-61.00
			Richard Henderson	MN - Unemployment Company	1,760.00	70.40
			Richard Henderson	MN - Unemployment Company	1,760.00	-70.40
						1,432.36
04/30/2014	5	Liability Check	United States Trea...	Federal Unemployment		42.88
			United States Trea...	Federal Withholding		492.00
			United States Trea...	Medicare Company		77.72
			United States Trea...	Medicare Employee		77.72
			United States Trea...	Social Security Company		332.32
			United States Trea...	Social Security Employee		332.32
						1,354.96
04/30/2014	6	Liability Check	Minn. Dept. of Rev...	MN - Unemployment Company		214.40
			Minn. Dept. of Rev...	MN - Withholding		207.00
						421.40
TOTAL						**6,027.32**

Employee State Taxes Detail Report

As mentioned previously, federal and state compliance reports are available only when you subscribe to a QuickBooks payroll service. However, the *Employee State Taxes Detail* report provides most, if not all, information most states will require a company to submit on a periodic basis.

Information such as type of state tax, amount of income subject to tax, and amount of each tax will be displayed in this report.

To view and print the *Employee State Taxes Detail* report—
1. Click Reports and then click *Employees & Payroll*.
2. At the Employees & Payroll submenu, click *Employee State Taxes Detail*.
3. Since most states require quarterly filings, at the *To* and *From* fields, choose *04/01/2014* and *06/30/2014*, then click Refresh. The report will be displayed for the period. (See figure 9–W.)

FIGURE 9–W
Employee State Taxes
Detail Report

Source Name	SSN/Tax ID	Date	Payroll Item	Income Subject To Tax	Wage Base	Amount
Harry Renee						
Harry Renee	112-55-9999	04/15/2014	MN - Withholding	1,000.00	1,000.00	-48.00
Harry Renee	112-55-9999	04/15/2014	MN - Unemployment Company	1,000.00	1,000.00	-40.00
Harry Renee	112-55-9999	04/30/2014	MN - Withholding	1,000.00	1,000.00	-48.00
Harry Renee	112-55-9999	04/30/2014	MN - Unemployment Company	1,000.00	1,000.00	-40.00
Total Harry Renee				4,000.00	4,000.00	-172.00
Richard Henderson						
Richard Henderson	333-44-5555	04/15/2014	MN - Withholding	1,600.00	1,600.00	-54.00
Richard Henderson	333-44-5555	04/15/2014	MN - Unemployment Company	1,600.00	1,600.00	-64.00
Richard Henderson	333-44-5555	04/30/2014	MN - Withholding	1,760.00	1,760.00	-61.00
Richard Henderson	333-44-5555	04/30/2014	MN - Unemployment Company	1,760.00	1,760.00	-70.40
Total Richard Henderson				6,720.00	6,720.00	-249.40
TOTAL				10,720.00	10,720.00	-421.40

4. To print the report, click the Print button from the top of the report, check the settings in the Print Reports dialog box, and click Print.
5. Close the report.

Payroll Government Compliance Reports

The Employees menu contains the basic government compliance reports all companies with payroll are required to file with the federal government (Internal Revenue Service).

To display and print government payroll compliance reports, you will need to subscribe to a QuickBooks payroll service.

Form 941
Form 941—Employer's Quarterly Federal Tax Return is forwarded to the Internal Revenue Service quarterly. This report summarizes the total wages paid to all employees for the quarter, along with the federal tax withheld and employer's and employee's Social Security and Medicare tax liabilities.

Form 940
Form 940—Employer's Annual Federal Unemployment (FUTA) Tax Return is filed annually with the Internal Revenue Service. This form computes the FUTA tax liability for the company for the year and reconciles the amount to the tax payments made by the company toward the tax during the year.

Form W-2
Form W-2—Wage and Tax Statement is prepared annually and furnished to each employee. This report totals the employee's earnings and tax withholding for the year. The employee uses this form to complete his or her personal income

tax return. A copy of this form is also forwarded to the federal government to be reconciled with the quarterly Form 941 filings.

Accounting Reports and Financial Statements

At the end of the month, the *Journal* report, *Profit & Loss Standard* report, and the *Balance Sheet Standard* report should be displayed and printed. See figures 9–X through 9–Z.

FIGURE 9–X

Journal Report—Partial
April 1, 2014 – April 30, 2014

EX9 [Your Name] Kristin Raina Interior Designs
Journal
April 2014

Trans #	Type	Date	Num	Name	Memo	Account	Debit	Credit
52	Transfer	04/01/2014			Funds Transfer	1010 · Cash - Oper...		7,500.00
					Funds Transfer	1020 · Cash - Payroll	7,500.00	
							7,500.00	7,500.00
53	Paycheck	04/15/2014	1	Harry Renee		1020 · Cash - Payroll		757.50
				Harry Renee		6565 · Salaries and ...	1,000.00	
				Harry Renee		2115 · FIT Payable		120.00
				Harry Renee		6610 · Social Sec/...	62.00	
				Harry Renee		2110 · Social Sec/...		62.00
				Harry Renee		2110 · Social Sec/...		62.00
				Harry Renee		6610 · Social Sec/...	14.50	
				Harry Renee		2110 · Social Sec/...		14.50
				Harry Renee		2110 · Social Sec/...		14.50
				Harry Renee		6625 · FUTA Expen...	8.00	
				Harry Renee		2125 · FUTA Payable		8.00
				Harry Renee		2120 · SIT Payable		46.00
				Harry Renee		6630 · SUI Expense	40.00	
				Harry Renee		2130 · SUI Payable		40.00
							1,124.50	1,124.50
54	Paycheck	04/15/2014	2	Richard Henderson		1020 · Cash - Payroll		1,303.60
				Richard Henderson		6565 · Salaries and ...	1,600.00	
				Richard Henderson		2115 · FIT Payable		120.00
				Richard Henderson		6610 · Social Sec/...	99.20	
				Richard Henderson		2110 · Social Sec/...		99.20
				Richard Henderson		2110 · Social Sec/...		99.20
				Richard Henderson		6610 · Social Sec/...	23.20	
				Richard Henderson		2110 · Social Sec/...		23.20
				Richard Henderson		2110 · Social Sec/...		23.20
				Richard Henderson		6625 · FUTA Expen...	12.80	
				Richard Henderson		2125 · FUTA Payable		12.80
				Richard Henderson		2120 · SIT Payable		54.00
				Richard Henderson		6630 · SUI Expense	64.00	
				Richard Henderson		2130 · SUI Payable		64.00
							1,799.20	1,799.20
55	Paycheck	04/30/2014	3	Harry Renee		1020 · Cash - Payroll		757.50
				Harry Renee		6565 · Salaries and ...	1,000.00	
				Harry Renee		2115 · FIT Payable		120.00
				Harry Renee		6610 · Social Sec/...	62.00	
				Harry Renee		2110 · Social Sec/...		62.00
				Harry Renee		2110 · Social Sec/...		62.00
				Harry Renee		6610 · Social Sec/...	14.50	
				Harry Renee		2110 · Social Sec/...		14.50
				Harry Renee		2110 · Social Sec/...		14.50
				Harry Renee		6625 · FUTA Expen...	8.00	
				Harry Renee		2125 · FUTA Payable		8.00
				Harry Renee		2120 · SIT Payable		46.00
				Harry Renee		6630 · SUI Expense	40.00	
				Harry Renee		2130 · SUI Payable		40.00
							1,124.50	1,124.50
56	Paycheck	04/30/2014	4	Richard Henderson		1020 · Cash - Payroll		1,432.36
				Richard Henderson		6565 · Salaries and ...	1,760.00	
				Richard Henderson		2115 · FIT Payable		132.00
				Richard Henderson		6610 · Social Sec/...	109.12	
				Richard Henderson		2110 · Social Sec/...		109.12
				Richard Henderson		2110 · Social Sec/...		109.12
				Richard Henderson		6610 · Social Sec/...	25.52	
				Richard Henderson		2110 · Social Sec/...		25.52
				Richard Henderson		2110 · Social Sec/...		25.52
				Richard Henderson		6625 · FUTA Expen...	14.08	
				Richard Henderson		2125 · FUTA Payable		14.08
				Richard Henderson		2120 · SIT Payable		61.00
				Richard Henderson		6630 · SUI Expense	70.40	
				Richard Henderson		2130 · SUI Payable		70.40
							1,979.12	1,979.12
57	Liability Check	04/30/2014	5	United States Treas...	33-4777781	1020 · Cash - Payroll		1,354.96
				United States Treas...	33-4777781	2125 · FUTA Payable	42.88	
				United States Treas...	33-4777781	2115 · FIT Payable	492.00	
				United States Treas...	33-4777781	2110 · Social Sec/...	77.72	
				United States Treas...	33-4777781	2110 · Social Sec/...	77.72	
				United States Treas...	33-4777781	2110 · Social Sec/...	332.32	
				United States Treas...	33-4777781	2110 · Social Sec/...	332.32	
							1,354.96	1,354.96
58	Liability Check	04/30/2014	6	Minn. Dept. of Reve...	ER-12343, 3...	1020 · Cash - Payroll		421.40
				Minn. Dept. of Reve...	ER-12343, 3...	2130 · SUI Payable	214.40	
				Minn. Dept. of Reve...	ER-12343, 3...	2120 · SIT Payable	207.00	
							421.40	421.40
TOTAL							15,303.68	15,303.68

EX9 [Your Name] Kristin Raina Interior Designs
Profit & Loss
January through April 2014

	Jan – Apr 14
Ordinary Income/Expense	
Income	
4010 · Design Services	4,980.00
4020 · Decorating Services	3,400.00
4060 · Sale of Carpets	2,400.00
4065 · Sale of Draperies	1,000.00
4070 · Sale of Lamps	1,200.00
4075 · Sale of Mirrors	900.00
4100 · Sales Discounts	-84.62
Total Income	13,795.38
Cost of Goods Sold	
5060 · Cost of Carpets Sold	1,200.00
5065 · Cost of Draperies Sold	500.00
5070 · Cost of Lamps Sold	600.00
5075 · Cost of Mirrors Sold	450.00
5900 · Inventory Adjustment	150.00
Total COGS	2,900.00
Gross Profit	10,895.38
Expense	
6020 · Accounting Expense	300.00
6050 · Advertising Expense	100.00
6175 · Deprec. Exp., Furniture	100.00
6185 · Deprec. Exp., Computers	60.00
6200 · Insurance Expense	200.00
6300 · Janitorial Expenses	125.00
6325 · Office Supplies Expense	150.00
6400 · Rent Expense	800.00
6450 · Telephone Expense	275.00
6500 · Utilities Expense	450.00
6560 · Payroll Expenses	
6565 · Salaries and Wages Expense	5,360.00
6610 · Social Sec/Medicare Tax Expense	410.04
6625 · FUTA Expense	42.88
6630 · SUI Expense	214.40
Total 6560 · Payroll Expenses	6,027.32
Total Expense	8,587.32
Net Ordinary Income	2,308.06
Other Income/Expense	
Other Expense	
7000 · Interest Expense	50.00
Total Other Expense	50.00
Net Other Income	-50.00
Net Income	**2,258.06**

FIGURE 9–Z
Balance Sheet Standard Report
April 30, 2014

Accrual Basis

EX9 [Your Name] Kristin Raina Interior Designs
Balance Sheet
As of April 30, 2014

	Apr 30, 14
ASSETS	
Current Assets	
Checking/Savings	
1010 · Cash □Operating	43,355.38
1020 · Cash □Payroll	1,472.68
Total Checking/Savings	44,828.06
Accounts Receivable	
1200 · Accounts Receivable	1,540.00
Total Accounts Receivable	1,540.00
Other Current Assets	
1260 · Inventory of Carpets	800.00
1265 · Inventory of Draperies	1,000.00
1270 · Inventory of Lamps	1,000.00
1275 · Inventory of Mirrors	900.00
1300 · Design Supplies	200.00
1305 · Office Supplies	250.00
1410 · Prepaid Advertising	500.00
1420 · Prepaid Insurance	2,200.00
Total Other Current Assets	6,850.00
Total Current Assets	53,218.06
Fixed Assets	
1700 · Furniture	
1725 · Furniture, Cost	12,000.00
1750 · Accum. Dep., Furniture	-100.00
Total 1700 · Furniture	11,900.00
1800 · Computers	
1825 · Computers, Cost	3,600.00
1850 · Accum. Dep., Computers	-60.00
Total 1800 · Computers	3,540.00
Total Fixed Assets	15,440.00
TOTAL ASSETS	**68,658.06**
LIABILITIES & EQUITY	
Liabilities	
Current Liabilities	
Accounts Payable	
2010 · Accounts Payable	9,750.00
Total Accounts Payable	9,750.00
Other Current Liabilities	
2020 · Notes Payable	7,000.00
2030 · Interest Payable	50.00
Total Other Current Liabilities	7,050.00
Total Current Liabilities	16,800.00
Total Liabilities	16,800.00
Equity	
3010 · Kristin Raina, Capital	50,000.00
3020 · Kristin Raina, Drawings	-400.00
Net Income	2,258.06
Total Equity	51,858.06
TOTAL LIABILITIES & EQUITY	**68,658.06**

Chapter Review and Assessment

Procedure Review

To add an employee—

1. Click Employees and then click *Employee Center.*
2. At the Employee Center window, click the New Employee button.
3. Enter the information on the Personal tab.
4. Click the Address and Contact tab. Enter the information.
5. Click the payroll Info tab.
6. At the Payroll Info tab, enter the information for the *ITEM NAME, HOURLY/ANNUAL RATE,* and *PAY FREQUENCY* fields.
7. Click Taxes. The Taxes window will be displayed.
8. At the Federal tab, enter the information for federal withholding tax.
9. Click the State tab, and enter the state withholding tax information.
10. Click OK. If the Information window appears, click OK to close it, and click the Delete button to remove the tax added by the program.
11. Click OK.
12. At the question box, click *No.*
13. Click OK.
14. Click *Leave As Is.*
15. Close the Employee Center.

To pay an employee—

1. Click Employees and then click *Pay Employees.* Click *No* at the QuickBooks Payroll Services message, if it appears. The Enter Payroll Information window appears.
2. Enter the correct dates at the *PAY PERIOD ENDS* and *CHECK DATE* fields.
3. At the *BANK ACCOUNT* field, click *1020 Cash - Payroll.*
4. Select the employee to be paid by placing a check mark next to the name.
5. If the information is correct, click Open Paycheck Detail. The Preview Paycheck window appears.
6. Enter the needed information in the Earnings section.
7. At the Company Summary (adjusted) section, enter the company tax information.
8. At the Employee Summary (adjusted) section, enter the employee taxes.
9. If the information is correct, click Save & Close. You will be returned to the Enter Payroll Information window.
10. Click Continue. The Review and Create Paychecks window appears with the taxes columns completed.
11. If the information is correct, click *Create Paychecks.*

To pay payroll liabilities—

1. Click Employees and then click *Payroll Taxes and Liabilities.*
2. At the Payroll Taxes and Liabilities submenu, click *Pay Payroll Liabilities.*
3. At the Select Date Range For Liabilities dialog box, choose the date range and then click OK.

4. Make sure the *To be printed* box is unchecked, the *Review liability check* option is selected, and the correct date range appears.
5. At the Bank Account drop-down list, click *1020 Cash - Payroll*.
6. Enter the payment date.
7. Place a check mark next to the liabilities you wish to pay.
8. If all information is correct, click *Create*. The liability check will be displayed.
9. If the information on the check is correct, click Save & Close.

To view and print reports from the Reports menu—
1. At the Reports menu, click *Employees & Payroll*.
2. At the Employees & Payroll submenu, click a report.
3. Indicate the appropriate dates.
4. Click the Print button on the top of the report.
5. At the Print Reports dialog box, review the settings and then click Print.
6. Close the report.

Key Concepts

Select the letter of the item that best matches each definition.

a. Pay Employee windows
b. Payroll Info tab
c. Employee Center
d. Preview Paycheck window
e. New Employee button
f. *Payroll Summary* report
g. Form 941
h. *Employee State Taxes Detail* report
i. *Payroll Liability Balances* report
j. Pay Liabilities window

_____ 1. Tab in the New Employee window where pay information is entered.
_____ 2. Quarterly payroll report forwarded to the Internal Revenue Service.
_____ 3. Series of three windows.
_____ 4. Button in Employee Center used to access New Employee window.
_____ 5. Window used to enter pay and tax information to calculate net pay.
_____ 6. Report that lists all payroll liabilities unpaid as of a specified date.
_____ 7. Contains a file with each employee's payroll background information.
_____ 8. Report that displays information concerning state taxes imposed on the employer and employee.
_____ 9. Window used to pay payroll liabilities accumulated when pay is processed.
_____ 10. Report that displays the earnings, deductions, and employer payroll taxes for each employee.

Procedure Check

1. Your company plans to convert from a manual payroll process to a computerized payroll processing system. What information must be assembled before you can process the first payroll check?
2. Your company has hired a new employee. Describe the steps to add this employee to the Employee Center.
3. After setting up a new employee in the Employee Center, you want to prepare a paycheck for the employee. Describe the steps to pay an employee.
4. Your company's management wishes to have a report of the amount of each local payroll tax the company is subject to. How would you use QuickBooks to gather this information?
5. Your company wishes to have a report that displays the earnings, deductions, and employer payroll taxes paid for each employee for a specific period of time. Describe how you would use QuickBooks to obtain this information.

6. Your company's newly hired college intern has just received her first paycheck. She is disappointed that her net check is only a fraction of what she thought she was earning. Prepare a brief memo, describing the taxes that must be withheld from her check.

Case Problems

Case Problem 1

In June, the third month of business for Lynn's Music Studio, Lynn Garcia has decided to hire two employees. One employee will be the studio manager, who will be paid a salary. The other employee, an assistant instructor, will be paid on an hourly basis. The company file includes information for Lynn's Music Studio as of June 1, 2014.

1. Open the company file CH9 Lynn's Music Studio.QBW.
2. Make a backup copy of the company file LMS9 [*Your Name*] Lynn's Music Studio.
3. Restore the backup copy of the company file. In both the Open Backup Copy and Save Company File as windows, use the file name LMS9 [*Your Name*] Lynn's Music Studio.
4. Change the company name to **LMS9 [*Your Name*] Lynn's Music Studio**.
5. Add the following employees:

First Name:	**Wei**
Last Name:	**Chan**
PRINT ON CHECKS AS:	**Wei Chan**
SOCIAL SECURITY NO.:	**159-89-2527**
GENDER:	**Female**
DATE OF BIRTH:	**3/23/80**
ADDRESS:	**417 Willow Street**
	Scranton, PA 18505
MAIN PHONE:	**570-555-3980**
Mobile:	**570-555-9898**

ITEM NAME:	**Salary**
HOURLY/ANNUAL RATE:	**$18,000**
PAY FREQUENCY:	**Semimonthly**
Federal Filing Status:	**Married**
Federal Allowances:	**1**
State Worked/Subject to Withholding:	**PA**
Subject to SUI?:	**Yes**
State Filing Status:	**Withhold**
State Allowances:	**1**

Not Subject to Local Taxes

First Name:	**Michelle**
Last Name:	**Auletta**
PRINT ON CHECKS AS:	**Michelle Auletta**
SOCIAL SECURITY NO.:	**291-08-7433**
GENDER:	**Female**
DATE OF BIRTH:	**8/9/55**
ADDRESS:	**23 Grand Ave.**
	Scranton, PA 18505
MAIN PHONE:	**570-555-4872**
Mobile:	**570-555-4949**
ITEM NAME:	**Hourly Wages**
HOURLY/ANNUAL RATE:	**12**
PAY FREQUENCY:	**Semimonthly**
Federal Filing Status:	**Single**
Federal Allowances:	**1**
State Worked/Subject to Withholding:	**PA**
Subject to SUI?:	**Yes**
State Filing Status:	**Withhold**
State Allowances:	**1**

Not Subject to Local Taxes

6. Process pay for June 15, 2014, using the following information:

Check No.:	**1**
Check Date:	**06/15/2014**
Pay Period Ends:	**06/15/2014**
Employee:	**Michelle Auletta**
Item Name:	**Hourly Wages**
Rate:	**12**
Hours:	**30**
Company Taxes:	
Social Security Company:	**22.32**
Medicare Company:	**5.22**
Federal Unemployment:	**2.88**
PA - Unemployment Company:	**14.40**
Employee Taxes:	
Federal Withholding:	**32.40**
Social Security Employee:	**22.32**
Medicare Employee:	**5.22**
PA - Withholding:	**10.80**
PA - Unemployment Employee:	**0**

Check No.:	**2**
Check Date:	**06/15/2014**
Pay Period Ends:	**06/15/2014**
Employee:	**Wei Chan**
Item Name:	**Salary**
Rate:	**750.00**
Company Taxes:	
Social Security Company:	**46.50**
Medicare Company:	**10.88**
Federal Unemployment:	**6.00**
PA - Unemployment Company:	**30.00**
Employee Taxes:	
Federal Withholding:	**82.50**
Social Security Employee:	**46.50**
Medicare Employee:	**10.88**
PA – Withholding:	**22.50**
PA – Unemployment Employee:	**0**

7. Process pay for June 30, 2014, using the following information:

Check No.:	**3**
Check Date:	**06/30/2014**
Pay Period Ends:	**06/30/2014**
Employee:	**Michelle Auletta**
Item Name:	**Hourly Wages**
Rate:	**12**
Hours:	**45**
Company Taxes:	
Social Security Company:	**33.48**
Medicare Company:	**7.83**
Federal Unemployment:	**4.32**
PA - Unemployment Company:	**21.60**
Employee Taxes:	
Federal Withholding:	**48.60**
Social Security Employee:	**33.48**
Medicare Employee:	**7.83**
PA - Withholding:	**16.20**
PA - Unemployment Employee:	**0**

Check No.:	**4**
Check Date:	**06/30/2014**
Pay Period Ends:	**06/30/2014**
Employee:	**Wei Chan**
Item Name:	**Salary**
Rate:	**750.00**
Company Taxes:	
Social Security Company:	**46.50**
Medicare Company:	**10.88**
Federal Unemployment:	**6.00**
PA - Unemployment Company:	**30.00**

Employee Taxes:

Federal Withholding:	**82.50**
Social Security Employee:	**46.50**
Medicare Employee:	**10.88**
PA - Withholding:	**22.50**
PA - Unemployment Employee:	**0**

8. On June 30, 2014, pay all payroll tax liabilities owed to the United States Treasury for the period June 1, 2014, to June 30, 2014, Check No. 5.
9. Display and print the following reports for June 1, 2014, to June 30, 2014:
   a. *Payroll Summary*
   b. *Payroll Transaction Detail*
   c. *Journal*
   d. *Employee State Taxes Detail*

Case Problem 2

In August, the third month of business for Olivia's Web Solutions, Olivia Chen has decided to hire two employees. One employee will be a web page designer, who will be paid hourly. The other employee, an administrative assistant, will be paid on a salary. The company file includes information for Olivia's Web Solutions as of August 1, 2014.

1. Open the company file CH9 Olivia's Web Solutions.QBW.
2. Make a backup copy of the company file OWS9 [*Your Name*] Olivia's Web Solutions.
3. Restore the backup copy of the company file. In both the Open Backup Copy and Save Company File as windows, use the file name OWS9 [*Your Name*] Olivia's Web Solutions.
4. Change the company name to **OWS9 [*Your Name*] Olivia's Web Solutions**.
5. Add the following employees:

First Name:	**Fiona**
Last Name:	**Ferguson**
PRINT ON CHECKS AS:	**Fiona Ferguson**
SOCIAL SECURITY NO.:	**449-99-3333**
GENDER:	**Female**
DATE OF BIRTH:	**8/8/81**
ADDRESS:	**23 E. 14th Street**
	Westport, NY 11858
MAIN PHONE:	**631-555-1020**
Mobile:	**631-555-3814**
ITEM NAME:	**Salary**
HOURLY/ANNUAL RATE:	**19,200**
PAY FREQUENCY	**Semimonthly**
Federal Filing Status:	**Single**
Federal Allowances:	**1**
State Worked/Subject to Withholding:	**NY**

Subject to SUI?:	**Yes**
Subject to SDI?:	**No** (Press Continue at the potential setup error window)
State Filing Status:	**Single**
State Allowances:	**1**
Not Subject to Local Taxes	(Press the Delete button five times to remove taxes.)
First Name:	**Gary**
Last Name:	**Glenn**
PRINT ON CHECKS AS:	**Gary Glenn**
SOCIAL SECURITY NO.:	**101-55-3333**
GENDER:	**Male**
DATE OF BIRTH:	**12/23/75**
ADDRESS:	**1050 York Ave.**
	Westport, NY 11858
MAIN PHONE:	**631-555-5447**
Mobile:	**631-555-7111**
ITEM NAME:	**Hourly Wages**
HOURLY ANNUAL RATE:	**25**
PAY FREQUENCY:	**Semimonthly**
Federal Filing Status:	**Married**
Federal Allowances:	**2**
State Worked/Subject to Withholding:	**NY**
Subject to SUI?:	**Yes**
Subject to SDI?:	**No**
State Filing Status:	**Married**
State Allowances:	**2**
Not Subject to Local Taxes	(Press the Delete button five times to remove taxes.)

6. Process pay for August 15, 2014, using the following information:

Check No.:	**1**
Check Date:	**08/15/2014**
Pay Period Ends:	**08/15/2014**
Employee:	**Fiona Ferguson**
Item Name:	**Salary**
Rate:	**800**
Company Taxes:	
Social Security Company:	**49.60**
Medicare Company:	**11.60**
Federal Unemployment:	**6.40**
NY - Unemployment Company:	**32.00**
Employee Taxes:	
Federal Withholding:	**110.00**
Social Security Employee:	**49.60**
Medicare Employee:	**11.60**
NY - Withholding:	**40.00**

Check No.:	**2**
Check Date:	**08/15/2014**
Pay Period Ends:	**08/15/2014**
Employee:	**Gary Glenn**
Item Name:	**Hourly Wages**
Rate:	**25**
Hours:	**80**
Company Taxes:	
Social Security Company:	**124.00**
Medicare Company:	**29.00**
Federal Unemployment:	**16.00**
NY - Unemployment Company:	**80.00**
Employee Taxes:	
Federal Withholding:	**360.00**
Social Security Employee:	**124.00**
Medicare Employee:	**29.00**
NY - Withholding:	**98.00**

7. Process pay for August 31, 2014, using the following information:

Check No.:	**3**
Check Date:	**08/31/2014**
Pay Period Ends:	**08/31/2014**
Employee:	**Fiona Ferguson**
Item Name:	**Salary**
Rate:	**800**
Company Taxes:	
Social Security Company:	**49.60**
Medicare Company:	**11.60**
Federal Unemployment:	**6.40**
NY - Unemployment Company:	**32.00**
Employee Taxes:	
Federal Withholding:	**110.00**
Social Security Employee:	**49.60**
Medicare Employee:	**11.60**
NY – Withholding:	**40.00**

Check No.:	**4**
Check Date:	**08/31/2014**
Pay Period Ends:	**08/31/2014**
Employee:	**Gary Glenn**
Item Name:	**Hourly Wages**
Rate:	**25**
Hours:	**88**

Company Taxes:

Social Security Company:	**136.40**
Medicare Company:	**31.90**
Federal Unemployment:	**17.60**
NY - Unemployment Company:	**88.00**

Employee Taxes:

Federal Withholding:	**400.00**
Social Security Employee:	**136.40**
Medicare Employee:	**31.90**
NY - Withholding:	**105.00**

8. On August 31, 2014, pay all payroll tax liabilities owed to the United States Treasury for the period August 1, 2014, to August 31, 2014, Check No. 5.

9. Display and print the following reports for August 1, 2014, to August 31, 2014:

a. *Payroll Summary*

b. *Payroll Transaction Detail*

c. *Journal*

d. *Employee State Taxes Detail*

CHAPTER 10

Banking

Transfer Funds, Reconcile Accounts, and Enter Credit Card Charges

Chapter Objectives

- Transfer funds between accounts using the Transfer Funds between Accounts window

- Reconcile cash accounts using the Reconcile window

- Enter credit card charges using the Enter Credit Card Charges window

- Pay credit card charges using the Write Checks window

- Display and print banking-related reports, accounting reports, and financial statements

Introduction

An integral part of operating any business is effectively managing cash. This usually involves maintaining cash in one or more bank accounts. In addition, it involves transferring funds among the bank accounts, reconciling account balances, using credit cards for business purchases, and making credit card payments. QuickBooks allows you to transfer funds from one bank account to another, process the month-end bank reconciliation, and enter and pay credit card charges.

Many companies have more than one checking account. The regular checking account, commonly known as the operating account, is used for paying bills and collecting and depositing receivables and other funds. Usually, a company maintains a separate checking account solely for payroll transactions. Periodically, funds from the operating checking account are transferred to the payroll checking account to pay employees and payroll taxes.

As a business grows in complexity, the need for special-purpose accounts grows correspondingly. For example, many companies have interest-bearing money market accounts that are designed to hold excess funds temporarily. These funds earn interest until they are needed for an operating activity, at which time they are transferred to a checking account.

transfer funds The movement of money from one account to another account.

Companies can **transfer funds** as needed among the different accounts, often via online banking connections. With QuickBooks, you can use the *Transfer Funds Between Accounts* window to record and monitor the transfer of funds between accounts.

Companies typically receive a statement from the bank at the end of the month detailing the activity the bank has recorded in the company's checking account, along with a month-end balance. Often, this balance does not agree with the company's records. Differences in the account balance usually occur because the bank has recorded transactions that the company does not know about. **Bank reconciliation** is a procedure used to determine the correct cash balance by accounting for these differences and ensuring that they are not a result of errors, either by the bank or the company, or from theft of funds. In addition, if the bank makes changes to the company's account, the company will have to record transactions in the general ledger accounts to reflect these changes. In QuickBooks, the *Reconcile* window is used to reconcile the balance per the bank statement to the balance per the accounting records.

bank reconciliation Procedure used to determine the correct cash balance in an account by comparing the activity recorded in the account with the activity recorded on the bank statement.

credit card charges Expenditures charged to a credit card to be paid at a later date.

Many companies use credit cards to pay bills. These **credit card charges** allow the company to track expenses of a specific nature, such as travel and entertainment expenses, and to defer payment of expenses as needed. In QuickBooks, the *Enter Credit Card Charges* window is used to record credit card expenditures.

In this chapter, our sample company, Kristin Raina Interior Designs, will transfer funds between accounts, process bank reconciliations, and use a credit card to pay for expenses.

QuickBooks versus Manual Accounting: Banking

Banking activities in both manual and computerized accounting systems require a company to record transfers of funds among bank accounts, reconcile each bank account balance to the company's balances, and track charges and payments by credit card.

Transfer Funds

In a manual accounting system, when funds are transferred to or from one cash account to another, the transaction can be handled in several ways. Transfers from the company's operating account can be recorded in the cash payments journal or the general journal. If the cash payments journal is used for transfers out of the cash accounts, the cash receipts journal will be used for transfers into the cash accounts. Similarly, if the general journal is used to record the transfer out of the cash accounts, it also will be used to record the transfers into the cash accounts. A cash payments journal procedure is used when a check is drawn from a cash account to accomplish the transfer. If the transfer is accomplished via a bank credit and debit memo or phone transfer, the general journal procedure is used.

In QuickBooks, transfers among bank accounts, if not done by check, are recorded in the Transfer Funds Between Accounts activity window. This window indicates the cash accounts involved in the transfer and the amount of the transfer.

Bank Reconciliation

The steps to completing a bank reconciliation in QuickBooks are similar to those in a manual accounting system. The company receives a statement from the bank detailing the activity in the account for the month. The statement shows the deposits (or other additions) to the account along with the checks that have cleared (were paid by) the bank. If the account has earned interest, it is added to the balance by the bank. If the bank has charged any fees, called service charges, they will be deducted from the account. Other items that may appear are non-sufficient funds (NSF) checks, credit memos (additions), or debit memos (subtractions). The bank statement is compared with the company's accounting records, and any differences are identified. Generally, these differences, called **reconciling items**, fall into three categories: timing differences, such as **deposits in transit** or **outstanding checks**; omissions, such as the interest recorded by the bank not yet recorded by the company; or errors by either party. The first two are normal differences that are expected as part of the reconciliation process. If all timing differences and omissions are accounted for, and there are no errors, the adjusted bank balances will agree with the adjusted balance for the company's books. The account is then said to be reconciled. However, if there is an error, a difference will remain until the source of the mistake is found.

In QuickBooks, the bank reconciliation procedure is carried out using the Reconcile windows. Once a cash account is identified, the windows display all activity to the account, including deposits or other additions (debits), and checks or other reductions (credits). This information is compared with the bank statement to reconcile the account.

reconciling items
Differences between the bank statement and the company's records that have to be reconciled so that the cash balance in the company's accounting records agrees with the balance in its bank statement.

deposit in transit
A deposit recorded on the company's books, usually at the end of the month, yet deposited too late to be on the current month's bank statement.

outstanding check
A check written and recorded by a company that has not yet been paid by the bank.

Credit Card Charges

In a manual accounting system, a credit card charge is usually recorded when the bill is paid by the company or tracked as part of accounts payable. This often results in expenses being recorded in periods after they are actually incurred. In QuickBooks, a credit card charge can be recorded immediately when it is incurred by using the Enter Credit Card Charges window. The program also tracks the resulting credit card liability, which will be paid at a later date and separate from accounts payable. This method ensures that assets and/or expenses are recorded in the proper time period and that the credit card liability is tracked.

Chapter Problem

In this chapter, Kristin Raina Interior Designs will transfer funds among the company's bank accounts, prepare a reconciliation of the cash accounts, and enter credit card transactions. The balances as of April 30, 2014, are contained in the company file CH10 Kristin Raina Interior Designs. Open that file, make a backup copy, name it **EX10 [*Your Name*] Kristin Raina Interior Designs**, restore the backup copy, and change the company name to **EX10 [*Your Name*] Kristin Raina Interior Designs**.

LISTS/CENTERS:

Updating the Chart of Accounts List

Kristin Raina has decided to open and fund a money market cash account because the bank offers a higher rate of interest on money market funds than it offers on a Cash - Operating account. Typically, a company will have a separate general ledger account for each bank account to facilitate the bank reconciliation process. Kristin Raina needs to add another cash account as well as accounts that reflect the adjustments resulting from the bank reconciliation. Kristin also will begin using a credit card to pay for travel-related expenses, so accounts must be added for this additional expense and liability. You will need to update Kristin Raina's Chart of Accounts List to include the new accounts necessary for the additional banking procedures.

Follow the procedures presented in chapter 4 to add these accounts:

Type	Number	Account Name
Bank	1050	Cash - Money Market
Credit Card	2015	American Travel Card
Expense	6100	Bank Service Charges
Expense	6475	Travel Expense
Other Income	6900	Interest Income

The revised Account Listing appears in figure 10–A.

FIGURE 10–A
Updated Account Listing

EX10 [Your Name] Kristin Raina Interior Designs
Account Listing
April 30, 2014

Account	Type	Balance Total	Accnt. #
1010 · Cash - Operating	Bank	43,355.38	1010
1020 · Cash - Payroll	Bank	1,472.68	1020
1050 · Cash - Money Market	Bank	0.00	1050
1200 · Accounts Receivable	Accounts Receivable	1,540.00	1200
1250 · Undeposited Funds	Other Current Asset	0.00	1250
1260 · Inventory of Carpets	Other Current Asset	800.00	1260
1265 · Inventory of Draperies	Other Current Asset	1,000.00	1265
1270 · Inventory of Lamps	Other Current Asset	1,000.00	1270
1275 · Inventory of Mirrors	Other Current Asset	900.00	1275
1300 · Design Supplies	Other Current Asset	200.00	1300
1305 · Office Supplies	Other Current Asset	250.00	1305
1410 · Prepaid Advertising	Other Current Asset	500.00	1410
1420 · Prepaid Insurance	Other Current Asset	2,200.00	1420
1700 · Furniture	Fixed Asset	11,900.00	1700
1700 · Furniture:1725 · Furniture, Cost	Fixed Asset	12,000.00	1725
1700 · Furniture:1750 · Accum. Dep., Furniture	Fixed Asset	-100.00	1750
1800 · Computers	Fixed Asset	3,540.00	1800
1800 · Computers:1825 · Computers, Cost	Fixed Asset	3,600.00	1825
1800 · Computers:1850 · Accum. Dep., Computers	Fixed Asset	-60.00	1850
2010 · Accounts Payable	Accounts Payable	9,750.00	2010
2015 · American Travel Card	Credit Card	0.00	2015
2020 · Notes Payable	Other Current Liability	7,000.00	2020
2030 · Interest Payable	Other Current Liability	50.00	2030
2100 · Payroll Liabilities	Other Current Liability	0.00	2100
2100 · Payroll Liabilities:2110 · Social Sec/Medicare Tax Payable	Other Current Liability	0.00	2110
2100 · Payroll Liabilities:2115 · FIT Payable	Other Current Liability	0.00	2115
2100 · Payroll Liabilities:2120 · SIT Payable	Other Current Liability	0.00	2120
2100 · Payroll Liabilities:2125 · FUTA Payable	Other Current Liability	0.00	2125
2100 · Payroll Liabilities:2130 · SUI Payable	Other Current Liability	0.00	2130
2200 · Sales Tax Payable	Other Current Liability	0.00	2200
3010 · Kristin Raina, Capital	Equity	50,000.00	3010
3020 · Kristin Raina, Drawings	Equity	-400.00	3020
3030 · Accumulated Earnings	Equity		3030
4010 · Design Services	Income		4010
4020 · Decorating Services	Income		4020
4060 · Sale of Carpets	Income		4060
4065 · Sale of Draperies	Income		4065
4070 · Sale of Lamps	Income		4070
4075 · Sale of Mirrors	Income		4075
4100 · Sales Discounts	Income		4100
5060 · Cost of Carpets Sold	Cost of Goods Sold		5060
5065 · Cost of Draperies Sold	Cost of Goods Sold		5065
5070 · Cost of Lamps Sold	Cost of Goods Sold		5070
5075 · Cost of Mirrors Sold	Cost of Goods Sold		5075
5900 · Inventory Adjustment	Cost of Goods Sold		5900
6020 · Accounting Expense	Expense		6020
6050 · Advertising Expense	Expense		6050
6100 · Bank Service Charges	Expense		6100
6175 · Deprec. Exp., Furniture	Expense		6175
6185 · Deprec. Exp., Computers	Expense		6185
6200 · Insurance Expense	Expense		6200
6300 · Janitorial Expenses	Expense		6300
6325 · Office Supplies Expense	Expense		6325
6400 · Rent Expense	Expense		6400
6450 · Telephone Expense	Expense		6450
6475 · Travel Expense	Expense		6475
6500 · Utilities Expense	Expense		6500
6560 · Payroll Expenses	Expense		6560
6560 · Payroll Expenses:6565 · Salaries and Wages Expense	Expense		6565
6560 · Payroll Expenses:6610 · Social Sec/Medicare Tax Expense	Expense		6610
6560 · Payroll Expenses:6625 · FUTA Expense	Expense		6625
6560 · Payroll Expenses:6630 · SUI Expense	Expense		6630
6900 · Interest Income	Other Income		6900
7000 · Interest Expense	Other Expense		7000

The Transfer Funds Window

As you know, the third level of operations in QuickBooks is to record the daily transactions of the business. In QuickBooks, you use the Transfer Funds Between Accounts window (or Transfer Funds window, for short) to record the movement of funds among the cash accounts of the business. If you transfer funds by writing a check from one cash account to be deposited into another cash account, you can use the Write Checks window. However, when you transfer funds via bank memo, telephone, or online services, you use the Transfer Funds window to record the transaction. In this window, since there are no default accounts, you identify the source (transferor) cash account, the receiving account (transferee), and the amount to be transferred. The transaction is recorded as follows:

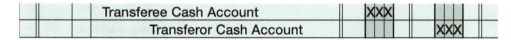

		Transferee Cash Account		XXX	
		Transferor Cash Account			XXX

The QuickBooks Transfer Funds window appears in figure 10–B.

FIGURE 10–B
Transfer Funds Between Accounts Window

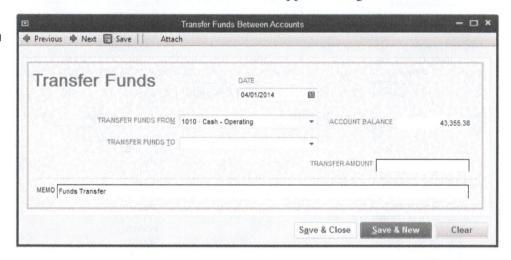

This window allows you to identify the source (transferor) cash account, the receiving (transferee) account, and the amount to be transferred. It also displays the current balance of the source account, thus preventing you from overdrawing it. The Previous and Next arrows—and the Save & Close, Save & New, and Clear buttons—all have the same function in this window as in other Activity windows.

On April 30, 2014, Kristin Raina wants you to transfer $7,000 from the company's Cash - Operating account to its Cash - Payroll account so there are sufficient funds in that account to pay May's payroll and payroll tax liabilities.

To transfer funds—

1. Click Banking and then click *Transfer Funds*.
2. At the *DATE* field, choose *04/30/2014*.
3. At the TRANSFER FUNDS FROM drop-down list, click *1010 Cash - Operating*. The balance in the account is displayed.
4. At the TRANSFER FUNDS TO drop-down list, click *1020 Cash - Payroll*.
5. At the *TRANSFER AMOUNT* field, key **7000**. (See figure 10–C.)
6. If the information is correct, click Save & New.

FIGURE 10–C

Transfer Funds Between Accounts Window—Completed

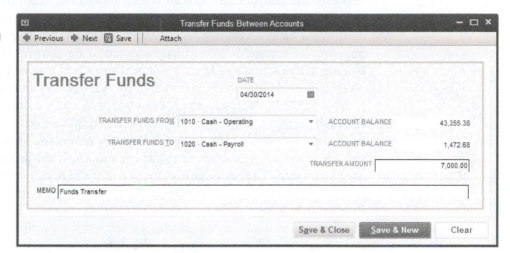

Accounting concept

For a transfer of funds between accounts, the general ledger posting is as follows:

1010 Cash - Operating				1020 Cash - Payroll		
	Dr	Cr			Dr	Cr
Bal	43,355.38	Trf	7,000	Bal	1,472.68	
				Trf	7,000.00	
Bal	36,355.38			Bal	8,472.68	

Practice Exercise

On April 30, 2014, transfer $10,000 from the Cash - Operating account to the Cash - Money Market account.

The Reconcile Windows

In QuickBooks, Activities identified as bank reconciliation are processed in the Reconcile windows. The reconciliation procedure in QuickBooks accomplishes two purposes. First, it ensures that the company's cash records are correct and agree with that of the bank. Second, transactions missing from the company's records that are discovered during the reconciling process can be recorded at this time.

The Reconcile windows display all additions to a given account, such as deposits and transfers in, and all reductions to the account, such as checks written and transfers out. Using these windows, you can compare the information for each account with the bank statement for that account. You can indicate the transactions that have cleared or have been paid by the bank by placing a check mark next to the transaction, and you can add transactions recorded on the bank statement that are not yet on the company's books.

As part of the reconciling process, you may need to make adjustments to the cash account. For example, the bank may have deducted service charges from the company's bank account during the month. This deduction is reflected on the bank statement but has not yet been recorded in the company's records. The same holds true for any interest income earned on the company's bank account. While performing the bank reconciliation in the Reconcile windows, you have the opportunity to identify and record these transactions and adjust the company's accounts accordingly.

When you add service charges, the default accounts are the Bank Service Charges account and the Cash account. QuickBooks records the transaction as follows:

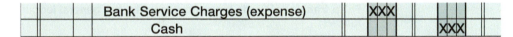

When you record interest income, the default accounts are the Cash account and the Interest Income account. QuickBooks records the transaction as follows:

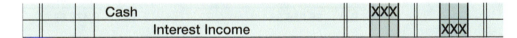

If the bank records an NSF check from a customer, QuickBooks does not automatically record the transaction. Instead, you must record the transaction in the Create Invoices window to re-establish the accounts receivable for this customer and deduct the cash that was never actually collected.

Recall that the system default account in the Create Invoices window is a debit to Accounts Receivable. When you select an item, usually a service or inventory part item, the appropriate revenue account is credited. If you are using QuickBooks to reconcile accounts, you create an item for NSFs in the Item List. When you establish an NSF item, you will identify the default account as Cash. When you record an NSF in the Create Invoices window, the Accounts Receivable is debited for the amount of the NSF still due the company; the corresponding credit, based on the NSF item, will be to Cash.

The QuickBooks Reconcile window consists of two parts. The first window, called the Begin Reconciliation window, allows you to select a bank account to reconcile, add transactions such as service charges and interest income, and enter the bank statement balance. (See figure 10–D.)

FIGURE 10–D
Begin Reconciliation Window

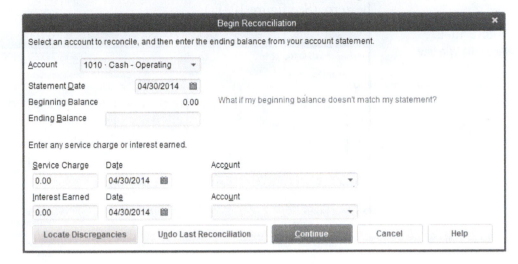

Special note should be made of the following fields:

Account	QuickBooks allows you to reconcile all cash accounts set up by the company. Once you select an account from the drop-down list, all activity for only that account is displayed.
Beginning Balance	Indicates the opening balance for the bank statement. If this is the first time you are reconciling the account, the figure will be zero. **Do not edit this number**.
Ending Balance	Used to enter the ending balance appearing on the bank statement.
Service Charge	Used to enter the amount of the service charges appearing on the bank statement. You also indicate the account the service charge will be charged to here. When you click *Reconcile Now* in the Reconcile window, QuickBooks automatically posts the expense and reduces the cash account.
Interest Earned	Used to enter the amount of interest shown on the bank statement along with the appropriate income account for interest. When you click *Reconcile Now*, QuickBooks automatically posts the increase to both Cash and Interest Income.
Locate Discrepancies button	Used to locate changes to previously cleared transactions.
Undo Last Reconciliation	Used to undo the previous reconciliation to correct errors or omissions.

Once the information is entered in the first window, the second window, called the Reconcile window, will be used to indicate which transactions recorded on the company's books have cleared the bank. Once all cleared or missing transactions have been accounted for, the difference amount should be zero. (See figure 10–E.)

FIGURE 10–E
Reconcile Window

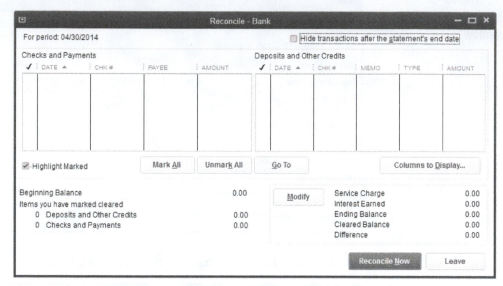

Special note should be made of the following fields:

Difference	If all reconciling items are accounted for, the difference will be zero. If after completing the reconciliation process a difference remains, it is probably due to an error by either the bank or the company. You must identify the error and correct it before completing the reconciliation.
Reconcile Now	Click this button if the Difference amount is zero. The account is now reconciled, and a *Reconciliation* report can be printed.

On April 30, 2014, Kristin Raina receives the bank statement for the Cash - Operating account from her bank. After a review of the bank statement, you determine the following:

1. The cash balance per the bank statement is $20,675.00.
2. The cash balance per the company's books is $ 26,355.38.

   You can review the Chart of Accounts List, the trial balance, or the general ledger for the Cash - Operating account to determine the balance on the company's books.

3. The bank charged the account $35 for bank service charges.
4. The bank credited the account for $10 of interest income.
5. All deposits, except the deposit of March 31, 2014, have cleared the bank.
6. All checks and payments, except Check Nos. 10 and 11, have cleared the bank.
7. A check for $600 from Berger Bakery Company, included in the deposit of February 28, 2014, was returned as NSF. The bank deducted the amount from the bank statement.

HINT

Do not edit the Beginning Balance figure.

To reconcile the Cash - Operating account with the bank statement—
1. Click Banking, and then click *Reconcile*. The Begin Reconciliation window appears.
2. At the Account drop-down list, click *1010 Cash - Operating*.
3. At the *Statement Date* field, choose *April 30, 2014*.
4. At the *Ending Balance* field, key **20,675**.
5. At the *Service Charge* field, key **35**.
6. At the *Date* field, choose *April 30, 2014*.
7. At the Account drop-down list, click *6100 Bank Service Charges*.
8. At the *Interest Earned* field, key **10**.
9. At the *Date* field, choose *April 30, 2014*.
10. At the Account drop-down list, click *6900 Interest Income*. (See figure 10–F.)

FIGURE 10–F
Begin Reconciliation Window—Completed

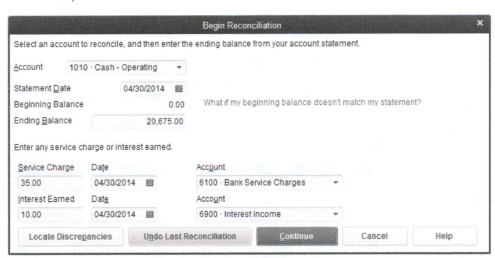

11. If the information is correct, click Continue. The Reconcile - Cash - Operating window appears. The activity for that account will be displayed.

12. Click to place a check mark next to all deposits, except the deposit of March 31, to indicate that all have cleared. (See figure 10–G.)

FIGURE 10–G
Reconcile - Cash - Operating
Window with Cleared Deposits

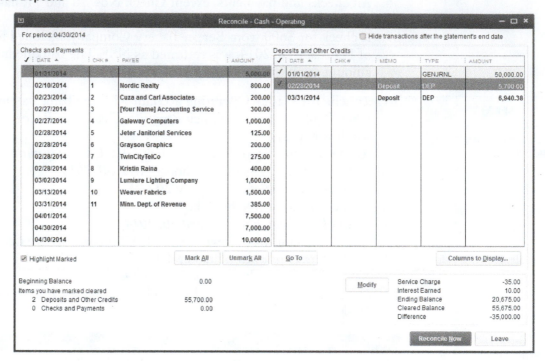

13. Click to place a check mark next to all checks and payments except Check Nos. 10 and 11, as they have not cleared the bank. The Difference is now *-600.00*, which is the amount of the NSF. (See figure 10–H.)

FIGURE 10–H
Reconcile - Cash - Operating Window with Cleared Checks and Payments

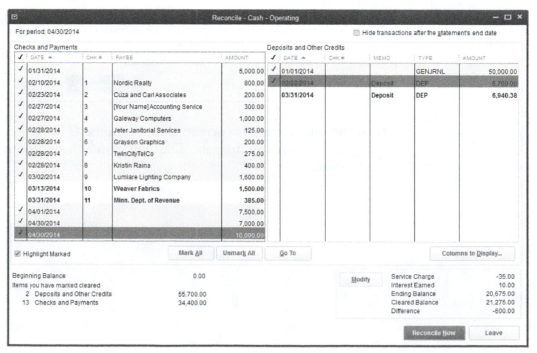

14. Click the deposit of 02/28/2014 to select it, then click *Go To*. The Make Deposits window appears, listing the checks that were included in the deposit of February 28. Notice the $600 check from Berger Bakery Company is included in the deposit. (See figure 10–I.)

FIGURE 10–I
Make Deposits Window

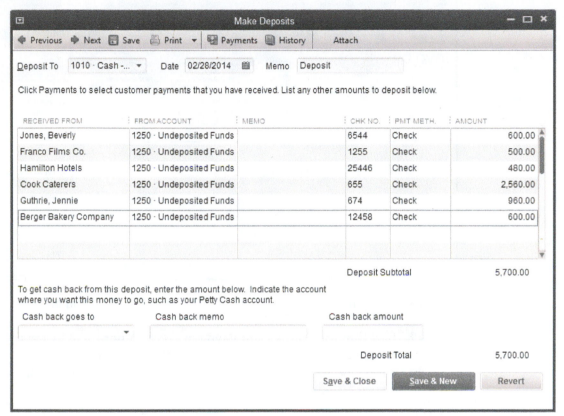

When this deposit was made on February 28, the bank recorded the total deposit and increased the bank balance by $5,700. When the Berger Bakery Company check was returned due to NSFs, the bank then deducted the $600 from the bank balance. To reconcile with the bank account, the $600 must be deducted from the Cash - Operating account.

15. Close the Make Deposits window. If the check mark was removed from the February 28 deposit, click the deposit to replace the check mark.
16. With the Reconcile window open, on the main menu click *Customers* and then click *Create Invoices*.
17. In the Create Invoices window, enter the following information:

> *CUSTOMER:JOB:*   **Berger Bakery Company**
> *Date:*   **04/30/2014**
> *Invoice #:*   **NSF1**
> *ITEM CODE:*   **NSF**
> *AMOUNT:*   **600**
> *TAX:*   **Non**

(See figure 10–J.)

HINT

If you leave the Reconcile window at this point, the items checked off will be saved; however, all other information, such as ending balance, service charge, and interest income, will be lost.

FIGURE 10–J
Create Invoices Window

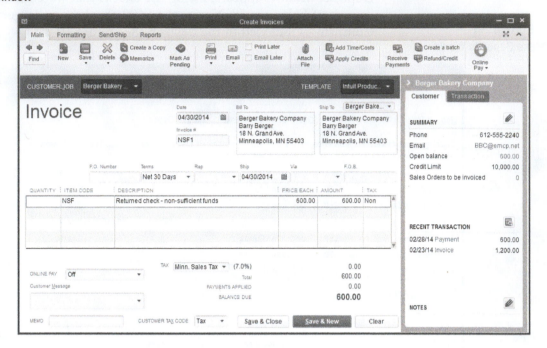

18. If the information is correct, click Save & Close. You are returned to the Reconcile window.
19. Scroll in the Checks and Payments section until you locate the $600 adjustment to the Cash account for the NSF check.
20. Place a ✓ next to the 600 NSF. The difference is now zero. (See figure 10–K.)

FIGURE 10–K
Reconcile - Cash - Operating Window—Completed

21. If the information is correct, click *Reconcile Now*. At the Information message, click OK if it appears. The account is now reconciled, and the missing transactions for service charges and interest are now posted to the appropriate accounts.
22. At the Select Reconciliation Report dialog box, click *Detail* and then click Print.
23. At the Print Lists dialog box, choose the Portrait orientation and then click Print. The report will be printed, and it should look like figure 10–L.

FIGURE 10–L

Reconciliation Detail Report—
Cash - Operating Account

Ex10 [Your Name] Kristin Raina Interior Designs
Reconciliation Detail
1010 · Cash - Operating, Period Ending 04/30/2014

Type	Date	Num	Name	Clr	Amount	Balance
Beginning Balance						0.00
Cleared Transactions						
Checks and Payments - 15 items						
General Journal	01/31/2014			X	-5,000.00	-5,000.00
Bill Pmt -Check	02/10/2014	1	Nordic Realty	X	-800.00	-5,800.00
Bill Pmt -Check	02/23/2014	2	Cuza and Carl Associates	X	-200.00	-6,000.00
Bill Pmt -Check	02/27/2014	4	Galeway Computers	X	-1,000.00	-7,000.00
Bill Pmt -Check	02/27/2014	3	[Your Name] Accounting Service	X	-300.00	-7,300.00
Check	02/28/2014	8	Kristin Raina	X	-400.00	-7,700.00
Check	02/28/2014	7	TwinCityTelCo	X	-275.00	-7,975.00
Check	02/28/2014	6	Grayson Graphics	X	-200.00	-8,175.00
Check	02/28/2014	5	Jeter Janitorial Services	X	-125.00	-8,300.00
Check	03/02/2014	9	Lumiare Lighting Company	X	-1,600.00	-9,900.00
Transfer	04/01/2014			X	-7,500.00	-17,400.00
Transfer	04/30/2014			X	-10,000.00	-27,400.00
Transfer	04/30/2014			X	-7,000.00	-34,400.00
Invoice	04/30/2014	NSF1	Berger Bakery Company	X	-600.00	-35,000.00
Check	04/30/2014			X	-35.00	-35,035.00
Total Checks and Payments					-35,035.00	-35,035.00
Deposits and Credits - 3 items						
General Journal	01/01/2014			X	50,000.00	50,000.00
Deposit	02/28/2014			X	5,700.00	55,700.00
Deposit	04/30/2014			X	10.00	55,710.00
Total Deposits and Credits					55,710.00	55,710.00
Total Cleared Transactions					20,675.00	20,675.00
Cleared Balance					20,675.00	20,675.00
Uncleared Transactions						
Checks and Payments - 2 items						
Check	03/13/2014	10	Weaver Fabrics		-1,500.00	-1,500.00
Sales Tax Payment	03/31/2014	11	Minn. Dept. of Revenue		-385.00	-1,885.00
Total Checks and Payments					-1,885.00	-1,885.00
Deposits and Credits - 1 item						
Deposit	03/31/2014				6,940.38	6,940.38
Total Deposits and Credits					6,940.38	6,940.38
Total Uncleared Transactions					5,055.38	5,055.38
Register Balance as of 04/30/2014					25,730.38	25,730.38
Ending Balance					**25,730.38**	**25,730.38**

You should print the report immediately. The *Reconciliation Detail* report is available from the Reports menu. However, this option is available only until you do the next reconciliation.

Accounting concept

For a bank reconciliation, the postings to the general ledger are as follows:

Cash - Operating			Accts Rec	
Dr	Cr		Dr	Cr
26,355.38	600 NSF		600	
Int Inc 10.00	35 SC			
Bal 25,730.38				

Bank Service Charges			Interest Income	
Dr	Cr		Dr	Cr
35.00				10.00

Adjusted Bank Statement Balance:

Ending Balance	$20,675.00	
Deposit-in-transit	6,940.38	
Outstanding Checks:		
No. 10	1,500.00	
No. 11	385.00	(1,885.00)
		$25,730.38

In addition, the customer file for Berger Bakery Company will reflect the increased asset amount:

Berger Bakery Company	
Dr	Cr
600	

Practice Exercise

On April 30, 2014, reconcile the company's Cash - Payroll account. The following information relates to this account:

1. The cash figure per the bank statement is $3,224.04 as of 4/30/14.
2. The bank charged the account $25 for bank service charges.
3. No interest was earned on this account.
4. The deposit of $7,000 on April 30, 2014, did not clear the bank statement.
5. Check Nos. 5 and 6 did not clear the bank.

QuickCheck: See the bank reconciliation report in figure 10–M.

FIGURE 10–M
Reconciliation Detail
Report—Cash - Payroll
Account

Ex10 [Your Name] Kristin Raina Interior Designs
Reconciliation Detail
1020 · Cash - Payroll, Period Ending 04/30/2014

Type	Date	Num	Name	Clr	Amount	Balance
Beginning Balance						0.00
Cleared Transactions						
Checks and Payments - 5 items						
Paycheck	04/15/2014	2	Richard Henderson	X	-1,303.60	-1,303.60
Paycheck	04/15/2014	1	Harry Renee	X	-757.50	-2,061.10
Paycheck	04/30/2014	4	Richard Henderson	X	-1,432.36	-3,493.46
Paycheck	04/30/2014	3	Harry Renee	X	-757.50	-4,250.96
Check	04/30/2014			X	-25.00	-4,275.96
Total Checks and Payments					-4,275.96	-4,275.96
Deposits and Credits - 1 item						
Transfer	04/01/2014			X	7,500.00	7,500.00
Total Deposits and Credits					7,500.00	7,500.00
Total Cleared Transactions					3,224.04	3,224.04
Cleared Balance					3,224.04	3,224.04
Uncleared Transactions						
Checks and Payments - 2 items						
Liability Check	04/30/2014	5	United States Treas...		-1,354.96	-1,354.96
Liability Check	04/30/2014	6	Minn. Dept. of Reve...		-421.40	-1,776.36
Total Checks and Payments					-1,776.36	-1,776.36
Deposits and Credits - 1 item						
Transfer	04/30/2014				7,000.00	7,000.00
Total Deposits and Credits					7,000.00	7,000.00
Total Uncleared Transactions					5,223.64	5,223.64
Register Balance as of 04/30/2014					8,447.68	8,447.68
Ending Balance					**8,447.68**	**8,447.68**

If there are errors in a previous bank reconciliation, QuickBooks allows you to undo that reconciliation and make corrections.

To undo the last reconciliation of the Cash - Operating account—

1. Click Banking and then click *Reconcile*. The Begin Reconciliation window appears.
2. At the account drop-down list, click *1010 Cash - Operating*.
3. The Statement Date should read *May 31, 2014*.
4. The Beginning Balance should read *$20,675*. (See figure 10–N.)

FIGURE 10–N
Begin Reconciliation
Window

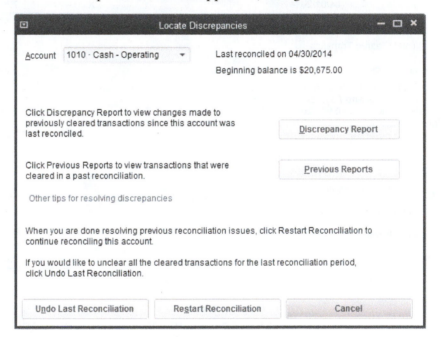

5. If the information is correct, click the Locate Discrepancies button. The Locate Discrepancies window appears. (See figure 10–O.)

FIGURE 10–O
Locate Discrepancies
Window

6. Click *Undo Last Reconciliation*. At the Undo Previous Reconciliation message, click Cancel.

If you wish to undo the April reconciliation, you would click Continue. At this time do not click Continue. If you undo the April reconciliation, the service charge, interest income, and NSF transactions entered as part of the original reconciliation would not be removed, although their cleared status would be changed to unclear. If you wish to reconcile the April bank statement again, do not re-enter these items; instead, check them off as cleared in the Reconcile window.

7. Close the Locate Discrepancies window.

⊸ The Enter Credit Card Charges Window

Activities identified as credit card purchases of goods or services are recorded in the Enter Credit Card Charges window. When a credit card is used to purchase goods from a vendor, the asset purchased or expense incurred is recorded as if the goods were purchased with cash or on account. The purchase creates a liability in the form of a credit card balance that will be paid at a later date. The default account is a Credit Card Liability account. Since the liability is not posted to the Accounts Payable account, Accounts Payable is not used to track the credit card liability. The transaction is recorded as follows:

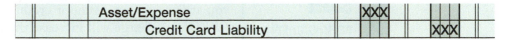

Asset/Expense	XXX	
Credit Card Liability		XXX

When the credit card bill is paid, the credit card liability is reduced by a cash payment. The default accounts are the Credit Card Liability account and the Cash account. The journal entry is as follows:

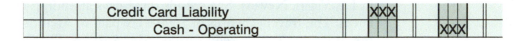

Credit Card Liability	XXX	
Cash - Operating		XXX

The QuickBooks Enter Credit Card Charges window appears in figure 10–P.

FIGURE 10–P
Enter Credit Card Charges Window

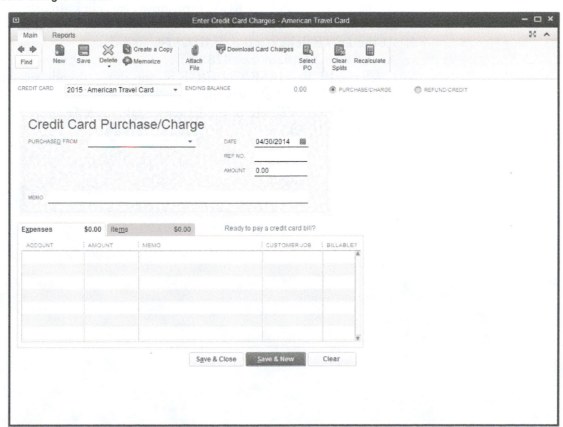

The procedures for this window are similar to those of the Enter Bills and Write Checks windows. Make special note of the following fields:

CREDIT CARD	QuickBooks allows you to track the activity of more than one credit card. Choose the credit card for the current transaction from the drop-down list.
PURCHASED FROM	Used to choose the vendor that the item or expense was purchased from with the selected credit card.
PURCHASE/ CHARGE **REFUND/CREDIT**	If this is a purchase, click *PURCHASE/CHARGE*. If you are processing a vendor credit, click *REFUND/ CREDIT*. A charge will increase the liability; a credit will reduce the liability.

Entering a Credit Card Charge

On May 1, 2014, Kristin Raina travels to a decorator's convention being held in Las Vegas, Nevada. She spends three days attending meetings and conferences. The travel expenses of $600 were paid to Atlantis Business Travel with the American Travel credit card on May 1, 2014. The Ref. No. is 47887.

To enter a credit card charge—

1. Click Banking and then click *Enter Credit Card Charges*.
2. At the CREDIT CARD drop-down list, accept *2015 American Travel Card*.
3. At the PURCHASED FROM drop-down list, click *Atlantis Business Travel*.
4. At the *DATE* field, choose *05/01/2014*.
5. At the *REF NO.* field, key **47887**.
6. Click the PURCHASE/CHARGE button if not already selected.
7. At the *AMOUNT* field, key **600**.
8. At the *ACCOUNT* field of the Expenses tab, click *6475 Travel Expense*. (See figure 10–Q.)

FIGURE 10–Q
Enter Credit Card Charges—
Completed

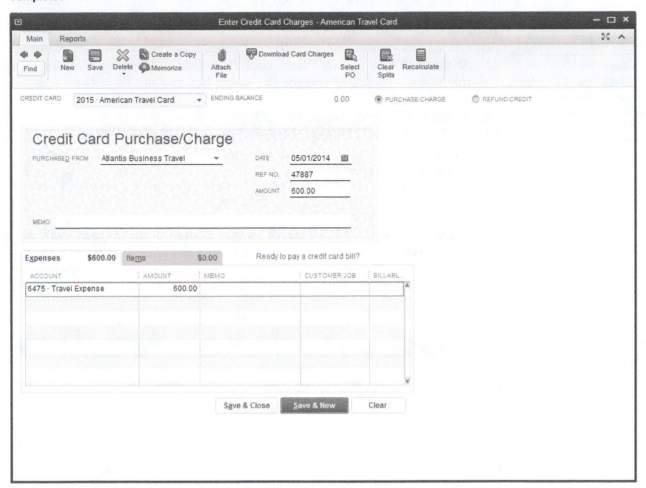

9. If the information is correct, click Save & New.

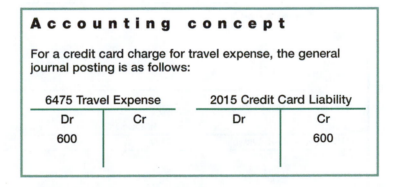

Accounting concept

For a credit card charge for travel expense, the general journal posting is as follows:

6475 Travel Expense		2015 Credit Card Liability	
Dr	Cr	Dr	Cr
600			600

Practice Exercise

On May 17, 2014, Kristin Raina traveled to St. Louis, Missouri, to meet with a new client. The travel costs of $350 were paid to Atlantis Business Travel with the American Travel Card, Ref No. 84441.

Paying a Credit Card Charge

On May 22, 2014, Kristin Raina wishes to pay the $600 credit card charge incurred on May 1, 2014, Check No. 12.

HINT

Remember that since the vendor was paid via a credit card, the liability for the charge is now with the credit card company.

To pay a credit card charge—

1. Click Banking and then click *Write Checks*.
2. At the *BANK ACCOUNT* field, click *1010 Cash - Operating*. Make sure the *NO.* field reads *12* and the *Pay Online* box and the *Print Later* box are not checked.
3. At the *DATE* field, choose *05/22/2014*.
4. At the PAY TO THE ORDER OF drop-down list, click *American Travel Card*.
5. At the *$* field, key **600**.
6. At the Expenses tab in the *ACCOUNT* field, click *2015 American Travel Card*.

   Do not choose the 6475 Travel Expense account in the Expenses tab, as that account had already been debited when the charges were recorded. When paying a credit card bill, always choose the credit card liability account. (See figure 10–R.)

7. If the information is correct, click Save & New.

FIGURE 10–R
Write Checks Window—Completed

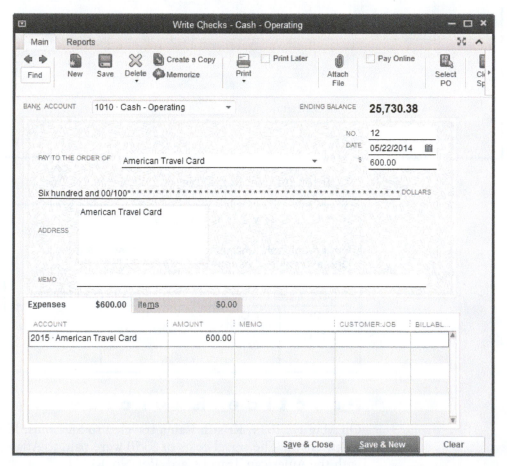

2015 Credit Card Liability		1010 Cash - Operating	
Dr	Cr	Dr	Cr
Pmt 600	600		600
	Bal 0		

Practice Exercise

On May 31, 2014, pay the remaining credit card balance to American Travel, $350, Check No. 13.

REPORTS:

Banking Reports, Accounting Reports, and Financial Statements

As you know, in QuickBooks, the fourth level of operation is to view and print reports. As we reviewed in prior chapters, reports for an activity can be accessed from both the Reports menu and the Lists menu.

Banking Reports from the Reports Menu

The *Reconciliation Detail* reports are printed as part of the reconciliation process. The company, in addition to the *Reconciliation* reports, uses the following reports:

Deposit Detail Report

The *Deposit Detail* report displays the components of all deposits to each cash account for a specified period of time. The report will show the payee's name, amount of each payment, nature of payment, and date of payment and deposit. This report is helpful in tracing a collection from a customer to the actual bank deposit.

To view and print the *Deposit Detail* report—
1. Click Reports and then click *Banking*.
2. From the Banking submenu, click *Deposit Detail*.
3. At the *From* and *To* date fields, choose *02/01/2014* and *04/30/2014*.
4. Click Refresh. The report for the period will be displayed. (See figure 10–S.)
5. Close the report.

FIGURE 10–S
Deposit Detail Report

Ex10 [Your Name] Kristin Raina Interior Designs
Deposit Detail
February through April 2014

Type	Num	Date	Name	Account	Amount
Deposit		02/28/2014		**1010 · Cash - Operating**	**5,700.00**
Payment	6544	02/13/2014	Jones, Beverly	1250 · Undeposited Funds	-600.00
Payment	1255	02/20/2014	Franco Films Co.	1250 · Undeposited Funds	-500.00
Sales Receipt	1007	02/24/2014	Hamilton Hotels	1250 · Undeposited Funds	-480.00
Payment	655	02/27/2014	Cook Caterers	1250 · Undeposited Funds	-2,560.00
Payment	674	02/28/2014	Guthrie, Jennie	1250 · Undeposited Funds	-960.00
Payment	12458	02/28/2014	Berger Bakery Company	1250 · Undeposited Funds	-600.00
TOTAL					-5,700.00
Deposit		03/31/2014		**1010 · Cash - Operating**	**6,940.38**
Sales Receipt	1009	03/22/2014	Jones, Beverly	1250 · Undeposited Funds	-1,163.00
Payment	2453	03/23/2014	Guthrie, Jennie	1250 · Undeposited Funds	-2,384.34
Sales Receipt	1011	03/29/2014	Franco Films Co.	1250 · Undeposited Funds	-1,631.00
Payment	6555	03/30/2014	Hamilton Hotels	1250 · Undeposited Funds	-1,762.04
TOTAL					-6,940.38
Deposit		04/30/2014		**1010 · Cash - Operating**	**10.00**
				6900 · Interest Income	-10.00
TOTAL					-10.00

Missing Checks Report

The title of this report is somewhat misleading. The *Missing Checks* report actually displays detailed information for all checks written from a specified cash account. The report includes the check number, date written, payee, and purpose (type) of check. Since it lists each check, the report is helpful in finding missing or duplicate checks.

To view and print the *Missing Checks* report—
1. Click Reports and then click *Banking*.
2. At the Banking submenu, click *Missing Checks*. The Missing Checks dialog box will appear. (See figure 10–T.)

FIGURE 10–T
Missing Checks Dialog
Box

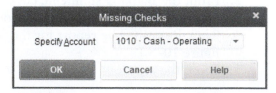

3. At the Specify Account drop-down list, click *1010 Cash - Operating* and then click OK. The report will display all checks written since the account was opened. (See figure 10–U.)
4. Close the report.

FIGURE 10–U
Missing Checks Report

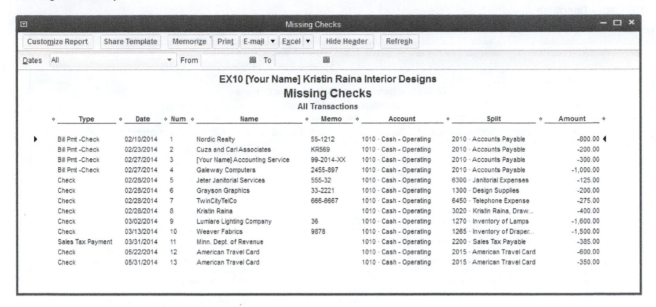

Banking Reports from the Lists Menu

QuickBooks allows you to view and print banking reports from the Lists windows. Once you access a List, you can view a list of available reports by clicking the Reports button in the List window.

HINT

The report can be displayed for any cash account and for any time period specified.

To view and print a QuickReport of the cash account—
1. Click Lists and then click *Chart of Accounts*.
2. Select (highlight) *1010 Cash - Operating*, but do not open the account.
3. Click the Reports button.
4. At the Reports menu, click *QuickReport: 1010 Cash - Operating*. The report will be displayed. (See figure 10–V.)

FIGURE 10–V
Account QuickReport—
1010 Cash - Operating

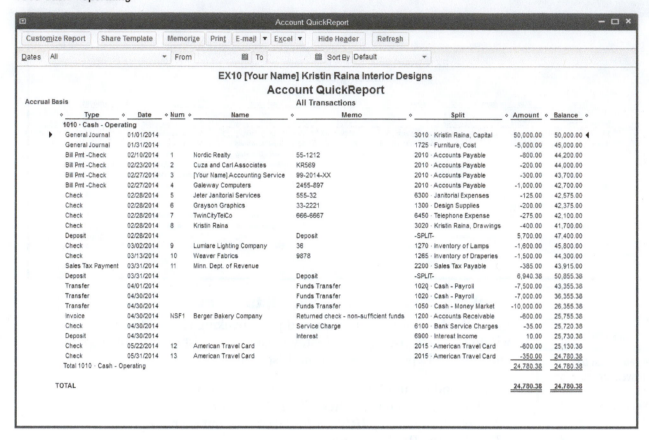

This report displays all of the activity affecting the account. The default setting is for all transactions for the fiscal year. However, you can set any period. If you scroll down the window, you will notice that the transactions for bank service charges and interest income have been included in the account activity.

5. Close the report.
6. Close the Chart of Accounts list.

Accounting Reports and Financial Statements

In addition to the banking reports, there are other reports related to the company's banking that can be viewed and printed at the end of the month.

Transaction Detail by Account Report

An additional report that can be helpful in the reconciliation process is the *Transaction Detail by Account* report. This report will display, for the cash accounts, all checks written by the company. It will also indicate if the checks have cleared the bank. This report is similar to the *General Ledger* report.

To view and print the *Transaction Detail by Account* report—

1. Click Reports and then click *Accountant & Taxes*.
2. From the Accountant & Taxes submenu, click *Transaction Detail by Account*.
3. At the *From* and *To* fields, choose *01/01/2014* and *05/31/2014* and then click Refresh. The report for the period will be displayed. (See figure 10–W.)

FIGURE 10–W
Transaction Detail by
Account Report

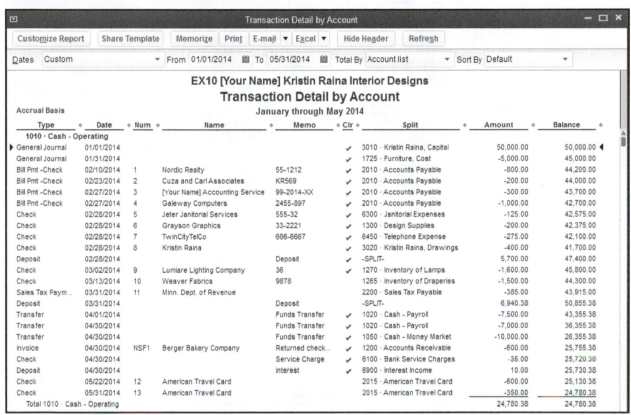

Notice that in the 1010 Cash - Operating account and the 1020 Cash - Payroll account, the cleared items have a check in the *Clr* column to indicate that they have cleared.

4. Close the report.

Journal Report and Financial Statements

At the end of each month, the *Journal* report, the *Profit & Loss Standard* report, and the *Balance Sheet Standard* report should be viewed and printed. These reports are displayed in figures 10–X, 10–Y, and 10–Z.

FIGURE 10–X
Journal Report
April 30, 2014 – May 31, 2014, page 3

Ex10 [Your Name] Kristin Raina Interior Designs
Journal
April 30 through May 31, 2014

Trans #	Type	Date	Num	Name	Memo	Account	Debit	Credit
56	Paycheck	04/30/2014	3	Harry Renee		1020 · Cash - Payroll		757.50
				Harry Renee		6565 · Salaries and Wages Expense	1,000.00	
				Harry Renee		2115 · FIT Payable		120.00
				Harry Renee		6610 · Social Sec/Medicare Tax Expense	62.00	
				Harry Renee		2110 · Social Sec/Medicare Tax Payable		62.00
				Harry Renee		2110 · Social Sec/Medicare Tax Payable		62.00
				Harry Renee		6610 · Social Sec/Medicare Tax Expense	14.50	
				Harry Renee		2110 · Social Sec/Medicare Tax Payable		14.50
				Harry Renee		2110 · Social Sec/Medicare Tax Payable		14.50
				Harry Renee		6625 · FUTA Expense	8.00	
				Harry Renee		2125 · FUTA Payable		8.00
				Harry Renee		2120 · SIT Payable		46.00
				Harry Renee		6630 · SUI Expense	40.00	
				Harry Renee		2130 · SUI Payable		40.00
							1,124.50	1,124.50
57	Paycheck	04/30/2014	4	Richard Henderson		1020 · Cash - Payroll		1,432.36
				Richard Henderson		6565 · Salaries and Wages Expense	1,760.00	
				Richard Henderson		2115 · FIT Payable		132.00
				Richard Henderson		6610 · Social Sec/Medicare Tax Expense	109.12	
				Richard Henderson		2110 · Social Sec/Medicare Tax Payable		109.12
				Richard Henderson		2110 · Social Sec/Medicare Tax Payable		109.12
				Richard Henderson		6610 · Social Sec/Medicare Tax Expense	25.52	
				Richard Henderson		2110 · Social Sec/Medicare Tax Payable		25.52
				Richard Henderson		2110 · Social Sec/Medicare Tax Payable		25.52
				Richard Henderson		6625 · FUTA Expense	14.08	
				Richard Henderson		2125 · FUTA Payable		14.08
				Richard Henderson		2120 · SIT Payable		61.00
				Richard Henderson		6630 · SUI Expense	70.40	
				Richard Henderson		2130 · SUI Payable		70.40
							1,979.12	1,979.12
58	Liability Check	04/30/2014	5	United States Treasury	33-4777781	1020 · Cash - Payroll		1,354.96
				United States Treasury	33-4777781	2125 · FUTA Payable	42.88	
				United States Treasury	33-4777781	2115 · FIT Payable	492.00	
				United States Treasury	33-4777781	2110 · Social Sec/Medicare Tax Payable	77.72	
				United States Treasury	33-4777781	2110 · Social Sec/Medicare Tax Payable	77.72	
				United States Treasury	33-4777781	2110 · Social Sec/Medicare Tax Payable	332.32	
				United States Treasury	33-4777781	2110 · Social Sec/Medicare Tax Payable	332.32	
							1,354.96	1,354.96
59	Liability Check	04/30/2014	6	Minn. Dept. of Revenue	ER-12343, 3...	1020 · Cash - Payroll		421.40
				Minn. Dept. of Revenue	ER-12343, 3...	2130 · SUI Payable	214.40	
				Minn. Dept. of Revenue	ER-12343, 3...	2120 · SIT Payable	207.00	
							421.40	421.40
60	Transfer	04/30/2014			Funds Transfer	1010 · Cash - Operating		7,000.00
					Funds Transfer	1020 · Cash - Payroll	7,000.00	
							7,000.00	7,000.00
61	Transfer	04/30/2014			Funds Transfer	1010 · Cash - Operating		10,000.00
					Funds Transfer	1050 · Cash - Money Market	10,000.00	
							10,000.00	10,000.00
62	Invoice	04/30/2014	NSF1	Berger Bakery Company		1200 · Accounts Receivable	600.00	
				Berger Bakery Company	Returned che...	1010 · Cash - Operating		600.00
				Minn. Dept. of Revenue	Sales Tax	2200 · Sales Tax Payable	0.00	
							600.00	600.00
63	Check	04/30/2014			Service Charge	1010 · Cash - Operating		35.00
					Service Charge	6100 · Bank Service Charges	35.00	
							35.00	35.00
64	Deposit	04/30/2014			Interest	1010 · Cash - Operating	10.00	
					Interest	6900 · Interest Income		10.00
							10.00	10.00
65	Check	04/30/2014			Service Charge	1020 · Cash - Payroll		25.00
					Service Charge	6100 · Bank Service Charges	25.00	
							25.00	25.00
66	Credit Card C...	05/01/2014	47887	Atlantis Business Travel		2015 · American Travel Card		600.00
				Atlantis Business Travel		6475 · Travel Expense	600.00	
							600.00	600.00
67	Credit Card C...	05/17/2014	84441	Atlantis Business Travel		2015 · American Travel Card		350.00
				Atlantis Business Travel		6475 · Travel Expense	350.00	
							350.00	350.00
68	Check	05/22/2014	12	American Travel Card		1010 · Cash - Operating		600.00
				American Travel Card		2015 · American Travel Card	600.00	
							600.00	600.00
69	Check	05/31/2014	13	American Travel Card		1010 · Cash - Operating		350.00
				American Travel Card		2015 · American Travel Card	350.00	
							350.00	350.00
TOTAL							24,449.98	24,449.98

FIGURE 10-Y
Profit & Loss Standard Report
January 1, 2014 – May 31, 2014

Ex10 [Your Name] Kristin Raina Interior Designs
Profit & Loss
January through May 2014

Accrual Basis

	Jan - May 14
Ordinary Income/Expense	
Income	
4010 · Design Services	4,980.00
4020 · Decorating Services	3,400.00
4060 · Sale of Carpets	2,400.00
4065 · Sale of Draperies	1,000.00
4070 · Sale of Lamps	1,200.00
4075 · Sale of Mirrors	900.00
4100 · Sales Discounts	-84.62
Total Income	13,795.38
Cost of Goods Sold	
5060 · Cost of Carpets Sold	1,200.00
5065 · Cost of Draperies Sold	500.00
5070 · Cost of Lamps Sold	600.00
5075 · Cost of Mirrors Sold	450.00
5900 · Inventory Adjustment	150.00
Total COGS	2,900.00
Gross Profit	10,895.38
Expense	
6020 · Accounting Expense	300.00
6050 · Advertising Expense	100.00
6100 · Bank Service Charges	60.00
6175 · Deprec. Exp., Furniture	100.00
6185 · Deprec. Exp., Computers	60.00
6200 · Insurance Expense	200.00
6300 · Janitorial Expenses	125.00
6325 · Office Supplies Expense	150.00
6400 · Rent Expense	800.00
6450 · Telephone Expense	275.00
6475 · Travel Expense	950.00
6500 · Utilities Expense	450.00
6560 · Payroll Expenses	
6565 · Salaries and Wages Expense	5,360.00
6610 · Social Sec/Medicare Tax Expense	410.04
6625 · FUTA Expense	42.88
6630 · SUI Expense	214.40
Total 6560 · Payroll Expenses	6,027.32
Total Expense	9,597.32
Net Ordinary Income	1,298.06
Other Income/Expense	
Other Income	
6900 · Interest Income	10.00
Total Other Income	10.00
Other Expense	
7000 · Interest Expense	50.00
Total Other Expense	50.00
Net Other Income	-40.00
Net Income	**1,258.06**

FIGURE 10-Z
Balance Sheet Standard Report
May 31, 2014

Ex10 [Your Name] Kristin Raina Interior Designs
Balance Sheet
As of May 31, 2014

	May 31, 14
ASSETS	
Current Assets	
Checking/Savings	
1010 · Cash ☐Operating	24,780.38
1020 · Cash ☐Payroll	8,447.68
1050 · Cash ☐Money Market	10,000.00
Total Checking/Savings	43,228.06
Accounts Receivable	
1200 · Accounts Receivable	2,140.00
Total Accounts Receivable	2,140.00
Other Current Assets	
1260 · Inventory of Carpets	800.00
1265 · Inventory of Draperies	1,000.00
1270 · Inventory of Lamps	1,000.00
1275 · Inventory of Mirrors	900.00
1300 · Design Supplies	200.00
1305 · Office Supplies	250.00
1410 · Prepaid Advertising	500.00
1420 · Prepaid Insurance	2,200.00
Total Other Current Assets	6,850.00
Total Current Assets	52,218.06
Fixed Assets	
1700 · Furniture	
1725 · Furniture, Cost	12,000.00
1750 · Accum. Dep., Furniture	-100.00
Total 1700 · Furniture	11,900.00
1800 · Computers	
1825 · Computers, Cost	3,600.00
1850 · Accum. Dep., Computers	-60.00
Total 1800 · Computers	3,540.00
Total Fixed Assets	15,440.00
TOTAL ASSETS	**67,658.06**
LIABILITIES & EQUITY	
Liabilities	
Current Liabilities	
Accounts Payable	
2010 · Accounts Payable	9,750.00
Total Accounts Payable	9,750.00
Other Current Liabilities	
2020 · Notes Payable	7,000.00
2030 · Interest Payable	50.00
Total Other Current Liabilities	7,050.00
Total Current Liabilities	16,800.00
Total Liabilities	16,800.00
Equity	
3010 · Kristin Raina, Capital	50,000.00
3020 · Kristin Raina, Drawings	-400.00
Net Income	1,258.06
Total Equity	50,858.06
TOTAL LIABILITIES & EQUITY	**67,658.06**

Chapter Review and Assessment

Procedure Review

To transfer funds between accounts—

1. Click Banking and then click *Transfer Funds.*
2. At the *DATE* field, enter the transfer date.
3. At the TRANSFER FUNDS FROM drop-down list, click the cash account from which the funds are transferring.
4. At the TRANSFER FUNDS TO drop-down list, click the cash account to which the funds are transferring.
5. Enter the transfer amount in the *TRANSFER AMOUNT* field.
6. Click Save & Close.

To reconcile a cash account—

1. Click Banking and then click *Reconcile.*
2. At the Begin Reconciliation window, in the Account drop-down list, click the account to reconcile.
3. Enter the date in the *Statement Date* field.
4. Enter the bank statement ending balance in the *Ending Balance* field.
5. Enter the bank service charges in the *Service Charge* field.
6. Enter the reconciliation date in the *Date* field.
7. Click the expense account for the service charges from the Account drop-down list.
8. Enter the interest income in the *Interest Earned* field.
9. Enter the reconciliation date in the *Date* field.
10. Click the revenue account for interest income at the Account drop-down list.
11. If the information is correct, click Continue. The Reconcile window appears. The activity for that account will be displayed.
12. Place a ✓ next to all deposits that have cleared the bank.
13. Place a ✓ next to checks and payments that have cleared the bank.
14. If there are any NSF checks, record them in the Create Invoices window while the Reconcile window is open.
15. In the Create Invoices window, click Save & Close and then return to the Reconcile window.
16. Place a ✓ next to any NSF amounts in the *Checks and Payments* field.
17. Check to see if the *Difference* field reads zero.
18. If the information is complete, click *Reconcile Now.*
19. At the Select Reconciliation Detail Report dialog box, click *Detail* and then click Print.
20. At the Print dialog box, click Print.

To enter a credit card charge—

1. Click Banking and then click *Enter Credit Card Charges.*
2. At the CREDIT CARD drop-down list, click the appropriate credit card.
3. At the PURCHASED FROM drop-down list, click the vendor name.
4. Choose the charge date at the *DATE* field.
5. Enter the vendor reference number at the *REF NO.* field.
6. Click the PURCHASE/CHARGE button.
7. Enter the charge amount at the *AMOUNT* field.

8. At the *ACCOUNT* field of the Expenses tab, click the account to be debited.
9. Click Save & New.

To pay a credit card charge—
1. Click Banking and then click *Write Checks*.
2. At the *BANK ACCOUNT* field, click the appropriate cash account.
3. Choose the check date in the *DATE* field.
4. Click the credit card vendor from the PAY TO THE ORDER OF drop-down list.
5. At the *$* field, enter the amount of the check.
6. At the Expenses tab in the *ACCOUNT* field, click the appropriate credit card liability account.
7. Click Save & New.

To view and print banking reports from the Reports menu—
1. Click Reports and then click *Banking*.
2. At the Banking submenu, click a report.
3. Indicate the appropriate dates of the report.
4. Click Refresh.
5. Click the Print button at the top of the report.
6. Close the report.

To view and print banking reports from the Lists menu—
1. Click Lists and then click *Chart of Accounts*.
2. Highlight the appropriate cash account.
3. Click the Reports menu button.
4. Click a report.
5. Indicate the appropriate dates for the report, if necessary.
6. Click the Print button at the top of the report.
7. Close the report.

Key Concepts

Select the letter of the item that best matches each definition.

a. Bank Reconciliation
b. *Missing Checks* report
c. Reconcile windows
d. Reconciling Items
e. *Deposit Detail* report
f. Transfer Funds Between Accounts window
g. Banking Menu
h. Enter Credit Card Charges window
i. Cleared Checks
j. QuickReport

_____ 1. Menu that contains the Write Checks, Reconcile, and Transfer Funds choices.
_____ 2. The procedure to account for all differences between the company's cash account record and the bank statement.
_____ 3. Report from the Chart of Accounts List window that displays all activity within an account.
_____ 4. Activity windows used to reconcile a cash account.
_____ 5. Activity window used to transfer funds among cash accounts.
_____ 6. Report that displays detailed information for each check written.

_____ 7. Activity window used to enter credit card charges.

_____ 8. Report from the Reports menu that displays details of each deposit for a specified period of time.

_____ 9. Items, such as deposits in transit, outstanding checks, bank charges, and interest income, that account for differences in cash between the company's books and the bank statement.

_____ 10. Checks written by the company that have cleared the bank.

Procedure Check

1. Your company has four cash accounts. How would you use QuickBooks to move funds from one account to another without having to write a check?

2. Your company wishes to verify the accuracy of the accounting records concerning its cash accounts. How would you use QuickBooks to accomplish this?

3. What is an NSF, and how is it treated?

4. Your company has given all sales personnel a company credit card for travel and entertainment expenses. How would you use QuickBooks to record the sales force's expenses?

5. You wish to print a list of all checks written for the year. How would you use QuickBooks to prepare this list?

6. Describe the steps to prepare a bank reconciliation that are common to both a manual accounting system and QuickBooks.

Case Problems

Case Problem 1

On June 30, 2014, Lynn's Music Studio will open a new bank account and transfer funds among the various cash accounts. At the end of June, after receiving the bank statement for the company's Cash - Operating account, Lynn Garcia will prepare a bank reconciliation. In addition, during the month of July, Lynn Garcia will begin using a credit card for travel and seminar expenses. The company file includes the information for Lynn's Music Studio as of June 30, 2014.

1. Open the company file CH10 Lynn's Music Studio.QBW.

2. Make a backup copy of the company file LMS10 [*Your Name*] Lynn's Music Studio.

3. Restore the backup copy of the company file. In both the Open Backup Copy and Save Company File as windows, use the file name LMS10 [*Your Name*] Lynn's Music Studio.

4. Change the company name to **LMS10 [*Your Name*] Lynn's Music Studio**.

5. Add the following accounts:

Type	Number and Name
Bank	1050 Cash - Money Market
Credit Card	2015 Harmony Club Card
Expense	6060 Bank Service Charges
Expense	6475 Travel and Seminars
Other Income	6900 Interest Income

6. Using the Transfer Funds Between Accounts window, record the following transactions:

Jun. 30	Transfer $3,000 from the Cash - Operating account to the Cash - Payroll account.
Jun. 30	Transfer $6,000 from the Cash - Operating account to the Cash - Money Market account.

7. Using the Reconcile window, prepare a bank reconciliation for the Cash - Operating account as of June 30, 2014, based on the information listed below. Remember, since this is the first reconciliation, the opening balance is zero.
   a. The cash figure per the bank statement is $5,464.78 as of June 30.
   b. The cash balance per the company's books is $2,615.18.
   c. The bank charged the account $20 for bank service charges.
   d. The bank credited the account $10 for interest income.
   e. All deposits cleared the bank.
   f. Check Nos. 14 and 15 did not clear the bank.
   g. A check from Mulligan Residence included in the April 30 deposit was returned NSF (nontaxable).
8. Print a bank reconciliation report using the full detail report choice. Statement closing date is June 30, 2014.
9. Using the Enter Credit Card Charges window, enter the following transaction:

Jul. 16	Travel and seminar expenses of $400 to attend an instructor's convention in Philadelphia were paid to Express Business Travel with the Harmony Club credit card. Ref. No. 2718.

10. Using the Write Checks window, enter the following transaction:

Jul. 27	Paid in full: $400, for the Harmony Club Card charge incurred on July 16; Check No. 16.

11. Display and print the following reports:
    a. *Deposit Detail* for April 1, 2014, to June 30, 2014
    b. *Missing Checks* for the Cash - Operating account
    c. *Journal* for June 30, 2014, to July 31, 2014

Case Problem 2

On August 31, 2014, Olivia's Web Solutions will open a new bank account and transfer funds among the various cash accounts. At the end of August, after receiving the bank statement for the company's Cash - Operating account, Olivia Chen will prepare a bank reconciliation. In addition, during the month of September, Olivia Chen will begin using a credit card for travel and entertainment expenses. The company file includes the information for Olivia's Web Solutions as of August 31, 2014.

1. Open the company file CH10 Olivia's Web Solutions.QBW.
2. Make a backup copy of the company file OWS10 [*Your Name*] Olivia's Web Solutions.
3. Restore the backup copy of the company file. In both the Open Backup Copy and the Save Company File as windows, use the file name OWS10 [*Your Name*] Olivia's Web Solutions.
4. Change the company name to **OWS10 [*Your Name*] Olivia's Web Solutions**.
5. Add the following accounts:

Type	Number and Name
Bank	1050 Cash - Money Market
Credit Card	2015 Travelers Express Card
Expense	6060 Bank Service Charges
Expense	6475 Travel & Entertainment
Other Income	6900 Interest Income

6. Using the Transfer Funds Between Accounts window, record the following transactions:

   Aug. 31   Transfer $6,000 from the Cash - Operating account to the Cash - Payroll account.

   Aug. 31   Transfer $4,000 from the Cash - Operating account to the Cash - Money Market account.

7. Using the Reconcile window, prepare a bank reconciliation for the Cash - Operating account as of August 31, 2014, based on the information below. Remember, since this is the first reconciliation, the opening balance is zero.
   a. The cash figure per the bank statement was $14,487.16 as of August 31.
   b. The cash balance per the company's books was $7,989.16.
   c. The bank charged the account $30 for bank service charges.
   d. The bank credited the account $20 for interest income.
   e. All deposits cleared the bank.
   f. Check Nos. 12 and 14 did not clear the bank.
   g. A check from Breathe Easy from the July 31 deposit was returned NSF (nontaxable).

8. Print a bank reconciliation report using the full detail report choice. Statement closing date is August 31, 2014.
9. Using the Enter Credit Card Charges window, enter the following transaction:

   Sep. 15   Travel and entertainment expenses of $750 to attend a sales convention in Florida were paid to Reliable Business Travel with the Travelers Express credit card. Ref. No. 6554.

10. Using the Write Checks window, enter the following transaction:

Sep. 28   Paid $400 toward the Travelers Express credit card charge incurred on September 15, Check No. 15.

11. Display and print the following reports:
   a. *Deposit Detail* for June 1, 2014, to August 31, 2014
   b. *Missing Checks* for the Cash - Operating account
   c. *Journal* for August 31, 2014, to September 30, 2014

CHAPTER 11

Jobs and Time Tracking

Record Job Income, Record Job Payroll Expenses, Track Time for Employees and Jobs, and Create Customer Statements

Chapter Objectives

- Add a job to the Customer Center

- Record and allocate payroll incurred for a specific job in the Pay Employees windows

- Record and allocate services rendered for a specific job in the Create Invoices windows

- Set up Time Tracking

- Track employee time for each job using the Weekly Timesheet window

- Pay employees using Time Tracking data

- Create Invoices using Time Tracking data

- Create Customer Statements

- Display and print job and time tracking reports, accounting reports, and financial statements

Introduction

job A project, assignment, or any identifiable segment of work for a customer.

QuickBooks allows you to allocate income and expenses for a specific job for a customer. A **job** is a project, assignment, or any identifiable segment of work for a customer. Identifying jobs allows the company to measure the profitability of individual customer projects or assignments. When you record revenue in windows such as the Create Invoices or Enter Sales Receipts windows, you can indicate the job for which the revenue was earned. When you record expenses such as payroll in the Pay Employees windows, you can also allocate employee pay and payroll tax expenses to a job.

Most service businesses track employee hours as part of the invoicing process. Customers are billed, usually at an hourly rate, for services provided by various company personnel. This is called billable time or billable hours. Time tracking mechanisms can vary from a simple manual system, using handwritten timesheets, to stand-alone time-and-billing software. The billable hours are used to allocate expenses to a job, determine the invoice to be billed for the job, and ultimately determine the profit (job revenue less job expenses) for the job.

To allocate the revenue and expenses to a specific job, you can either maintain the details manually or use QuickBooks *Time Tracking* feature. When activated, this feature allows you to record time spent by company personnel for customers and specific jobs by entering data in the *Weekly Timesheet* window. This data is then used to allocate payroll expenses to those jobs and to bill customers for work done.

QuickBooks versus Manual Accounting: Jobs and Time Tracking

In a manual accounting system, when revenue is recorded in a sales or cash receipts journal, an additional step must be taken to identify the job earning the revenue and to record that revenue in a jobs subsidiary ledger. Similarly, when job expenses are recorded in the purchases, cash payments, or payroll journals, they also must be posted to the jobs subsidiary ledger. These steps must be taken in addition to the customer and vendor subsidiary ledger posting.

In QuickBooks, the job file in the Customer Center serves as the jobs subsidiary ledger for the company. When it is desirable to track revenues and expenses for a particular job, that job is created as part of the customer's file in the Customer Center. Relevant information—such as job name, status, start date, and job description—is entered when the job file is created and is updated as necessary.

When the company earns revenue from the job, the revenue is recorded in much the same manner as previously recorded in the Create Invoices window or the Enter Sales Receipts window. However, when the revenue is identified with a particular job in each window, it is automatically allocated to the job while the transaction is recorded. These transactions simultaneously update the general ledger for the revenue earned, the customer file for the account receivable (in the Create Invoices window), and the job file for the job revenue. If employees work on a specific job, the Pay Employees windows themselves allow you to identify the time spent or salary expense related to the job.

In addition, QuickBooks has a Time Tracking feature that is integrated into the existing accounting software. Time tracking is used to track the billable time allocated to the jobs. Billable time by job is recorded in the Weekly Timesheet window for each employee. This information is then carried to the Pay Employees window when payroll is processed; there, the payroll expense is allocated to the identified jobs. This information is also used in the Create Invoices or Enter Sales Receipts windows to bill customers by job based on the billable time.

Chapter Problem

In this chapter, our sample company, Kristin Raina Interior Designs, will track revenue and expenses for several jobs for a customer. As revenue is generated, you will identify the job earning the revenue and allocate the revenue to that job. You will also charge selected payroll to a specific job. Although not an employee, Kristin Raina also will track and allocate her time to specific jobs.

The time tracking feature is an optional feature; you can track revenue and expenses with or without using it. For the first half of the month, you will allocate revenues and expenses to jobs without using the time tracking feature. In the second half of the month, you will activate the time tracking feature that will be used to allocate revenues and expenses to jobs. Additionally, at the end of the month, Kristin Raina will display and print a customer statement for the company that she is invoicing for the jobs.

Beginning balances for May 1, 2014, are contained in company file CH11 Kristin Raina Interior Designs. Open that file, make a backup copy, name it **EX11 [*Your Name*] Kristin Raina Interior Designs**, restore the backup copy, and change the company name to **EX11 [*Your Name*] Kristin Raina Interior Designs**.

LISTS/CENTERS: ─o **The Customer Center**

As you know, the Customer Center contains a file for each customer with which the company does business. If there are specific jobs for a customer, or multiple jobs for that customer, you identify those jobs in the customer file. *A job must always be associated with a customer.* Once a job is added, it will have its own file—separate but part of the customer's file. It carries over the customer information from the customer's file (name, address, telephone, and so on). In addition, the job file will contain important information such as job name, description, start and expected completion dates, and status.

On May 1, 2014, Kristin Raina Interior Designs was awarded a contract to redesign the lobbies of the three hotels owned by Hamilton Hotels. Kristin Raina wishes to track the revenue and payroll expenses for each of the three jobs by using the jobs feature of QuickBooks.

HINT

To select is to highlight something by clicking once. To choose is to activate a command, usually by double-clicking.

To add a job—
1. Click Customers and then click *Customer Center*.
2. At the Customer Center window, select (highlight) *Hamilton Hotels*, but do not open the file. (See figure 11–A.)

FIGURE 11–A
Hamilton Hotels File Selected

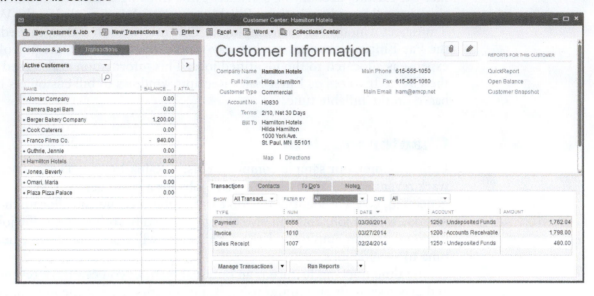

3. Click the New Customer & Job button.
4. At the New Customer & Job menu, click *Add Job*. The New Job window opens. Notice that the New Job window carries over information from the Hamilton Hotels file. (See figure 11–B.)

FIGURE 11–B
New Job Window

5. At the *JOB NAME* field, key **Lakeside Hotel**.
6. At the Job Info tab, choose or key the following data:

JOB DESCRIPTION	**Lakeside Hotel Lobby Redesign**
JOB STATUS:	**Awarded**
START DATE:	**05/01/2014**
PROJECTED END DATE:	**08/31/2014**

(See figure 11–C.)

FIGURE 11–C
New Job Window—
Completed

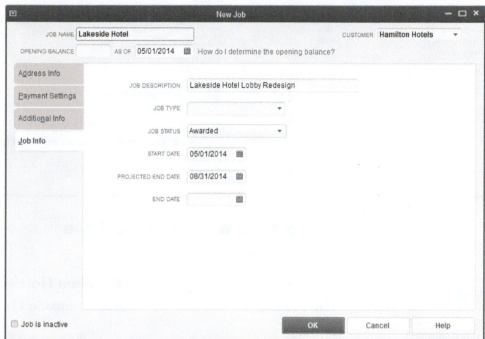

7. If the information is correct, click OK. You will be returned to the Customer Center. Notice that the Lakeside Hotel job is listed below the Hamilton Hotels file as a subfile. (See figure 11–D.)

FIGURE 11–D
Customer Center

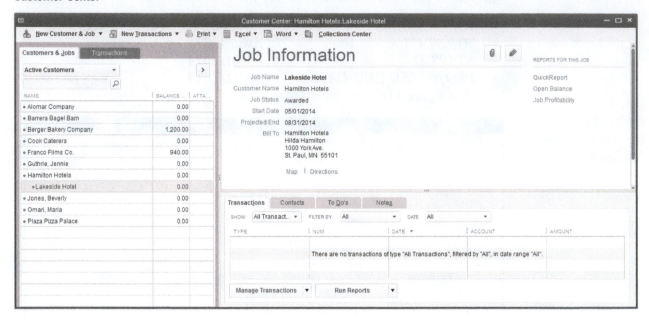

Practice Exercise

Add the following jobs:

CUSTOMER:	**Hamilton Hotels**
JOB NAME:	**Mountainside Hotel**
Job Info:	
JOB DESCRIPTION:	**Mountainside Hotel Lobby Redesign**
JOB STATUS:	**Awarded**
START DATE:	**05/01/2014**
PROJECTED END DATE:	**08/31/2014**

CUSTOMER:	**Hamilton Hotels**
JOB NAME:	**Riverside Hotel**
Job Info:	
JOB DESCRIPTION:	**Riverside Hotel Lobby Redesign**
JOB STATUS:	**Awarded**
START DATE:	**05/01/2014**
PROJECTED END DATE:	**08/31/2014**

QuickCheck: The updated Customer Center appears in figure 11–E.

FIGURE 11–E
Updated Customer
Center

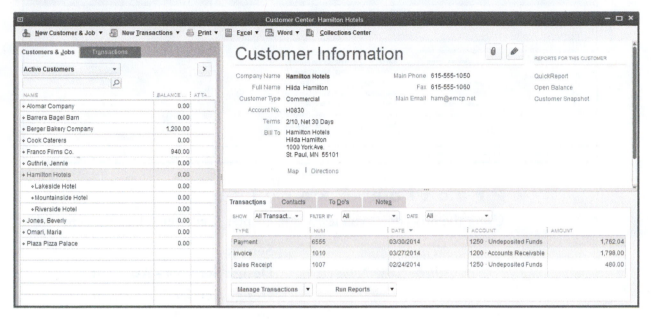

Moving Entries

Notice in figure 11-E that the three jobs are indented under the customer name, Hamilton Hotels, with which those jobs are associated. If you have incorrectly placed the job with the wrong customer, QuickBooks allows you to move the entry. To move an entry, click the diamond to the left of the job name and drag to the correct customer. Often, when entering a series of jobs for one customer, a job is inadvertently listed under another job, instead of the customer. You can easily correct the error by clicking and dragging the diamond to the left, which will correctly list all jobs under the customer name.

LISTS/CENTERS: ---o ## The Item List

Beginning this month, Kristin Raina will be billing customers for design and decorating work done by both her and one of her employees. Recall that the rate for Design Services is $60 per hour and the rate for Decorating Services is $50 per hour. These rates apply to work done by Kristin Raina, the owner. The work done by the employee, Richard Henderson, will be billed at $40 per hour for both Design and Decorating Services.

Since the company will now bill customers at different rates depending on who is doing the work, separate items have to be set up for each rate. The Item List in the company file has been modified to reflect the foregoing changes. The Design Services item has been changed to Design Services - Owner. Decorating Services has been similarly changed. A new item has been added: Decorating Services - Assistant, which reflects the services performed and billed for Richard Henderson with a rate of $40 per hour. (See figure 11–F.)

FIGURE 11–F
Item List

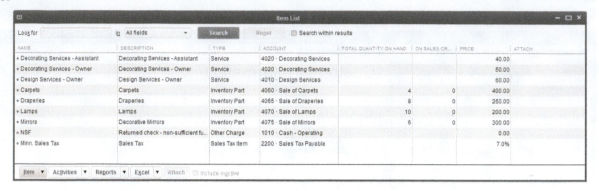

FIGURE 11–G
Item List—Updated

Practice Exercise

Using the procedures you learned in chapter 5, add the following item:

Type:	**Service**
Item Name/Number:	**Design Services - Assistant**
Description:	**Design Services - Assistant**
Rate:	**40**
Tax Code:	**Non-taxable Sales**
Account:	**4010 Design Services**

QuickCheck: The updated Item List appears in figure 11–G.

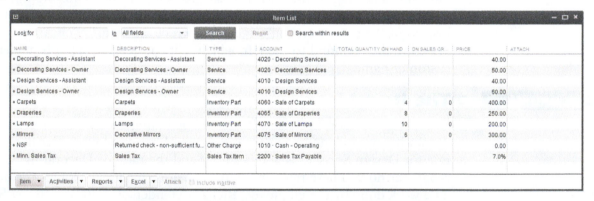

ACTIVITIES: ─○ **Allocating Payroll Expenses to a Job**

As you recall from chapter 9 on payroll, Kristin Raina has two employees, Harry Renee and Richard Henderson. Harry Renee is an administrative assistant whose time is not billable. Richard Henderson is a design assistant who, along with the owner Kristin Raina, provides design and decorating services to customers. Both Richard Henderson and Kristin Raina will be spending time working on the Hamilton Hotels projects.

Kristin Raina wishes to charge the payroll expense to each project to measure the profitability of each project. For the first payroll in May, Kristin Raina has kept track of the hours spent on each job, by both Richard Henderson and herself, on a manual system.

On May 15, 2014, Kristin Raina pays Richard Henderson, who spent all of his time during the pay period working on the Hamilton Hotels jobs. He worked 25 hours at Lakeside Hotel, 35 hours at Mountainside Hotel, and 28 hours at Riverside Hotel, for a total of 88 hours. In preparing the payroll for May 15, 2014, allocate the 88 hours he worked to the different jobs. This will allow you to keep track of the payroll costs by job.

To pay an employee and allocate to jobs—

1. Click Employees and then click *Pay Employees*. The Enter Payroll Information window appears.
2. At the *PAY PERIOD ENDS* and *CHECK DATE* fields, choose *05/15/2014*.
3. At the *BANK ACCOUNT* field, click *1020 Cash - Payroll*.
4. Select Richard Henderson by placing a ✓ next to the name.
5. If the information is correct, click *Open Paycheck Detail*. You will move to the Preview Paycheck window.
6. Make sure the item name is *Hourly Wages*, the rate is *20*, and the pay period is *05/01/2014* to *05/15/2014*.
7. At the first line of the *HOURS* column, key **25**.
8. At the CUSTOMER:JOB drop-down list, click *Lakeside Hotel*. (See figure 11–H.)

FIGURE 11–H
Preview Paycheck Window

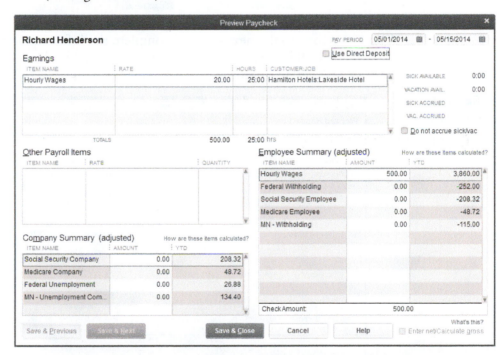

9. Move to the second line of the *ITEM NAME* field, and click *Hourly Wages* from the drop-down list.
10. At the *HOURS* field, key **35**.
11. At the CUSTOMER:JOB drop-down list, click *Mountainside Hotel*. Notice that there are now two hourly wages totals. (See figure 11–I.)

FIGURE 11–I
Preview Paycheck
Window

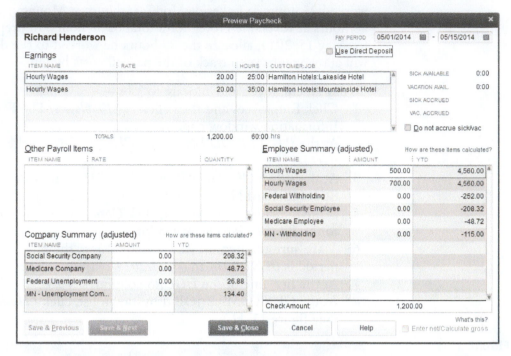

12. Move to the next line and complete the information for Riverside Hotel for 28 hours. Notice that there are three hourly wage amounts totaling $1,760 (88 hours @ $20 per hour). (See figure 11–J.)

FIGURE 11–J
Preview Paycheck
Window—Completed

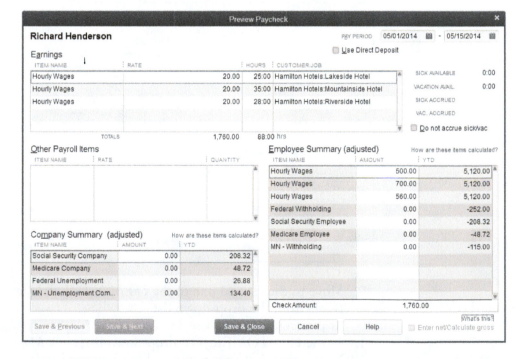

13. Complete the remainder of the window using the information listed below, following the procedure learned in chapter 9.

Company Taxes		
	Social Security Company:	109.12
	Medicare Company:	25.52
	Federal Unemployment:	14.08
	MN - Unemployment Company:	70.40
Employee Taxes		
	Federal Withholding:	132.00
	Social Security Employee:	109.12
	Medicare Employee:	25.52
	MN - Withholding:	61.00

QuickCheck: Check Amount $1,432.36.

(See figure 11–K.)

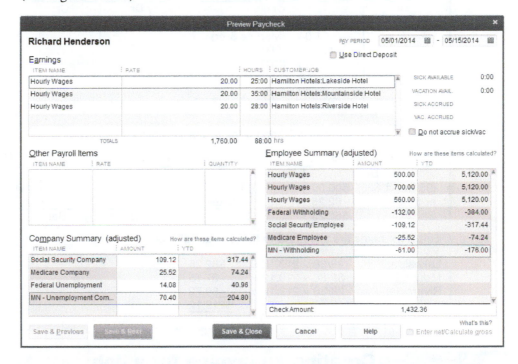

FIGURE 11–K
Preview Paycheck Window—Completed

14. If the information is correct, click Save & Close. You will be returned to the Enter Payroll Information window.
15. Click Continue. You will move to the Review and Create Paychecks window, and the taxes and net pay columns are now completed.
16. If the information is correct, click *Create Paychecks*.
17. At the Confirmation and Next Steps window, click Close.

As a result of this transaction, payroll expense (including the employer payroll tax expense) is allocated to each job in proportion to the hours worked for each.

Accounting concept

For the processing of a paycheck, the general ledger posting is as follows:
(The taxes payable accounts consist of both the employee and employer taxes; *er* represents the employer's share, and *ee* represents the employee's share.)

6565 Salaries and Wages Expense

Dr	Cr
(88 hrs @ $20) 1,760	

6610-6630 Employer Payroll Tax Expense

Dr		Cr
(FICA er)	109.12	
(Med er)	25.52	
(FUTA)	14.08	
(SUI)	70.40	
Bal	219.12	

2210-2130 Payroll Taxes Payable

Dr		
	218.24	(FICA ee & er)
	51.04	(Med ee & er)
	132.00	(FIT)
	61.00	(SIT)
	14.08	(FUTA)
	70.40	(SUI)
	Bal 546.76	

1020 Cash - Payroll

Dr	Cr
	1,432.36

In addition, the job files will keep track of the expenses as follows:

Lakeside

Dr		Cr
(25 hrs @ $20)	500.00	
er taxes	62.25	
Bal	562.25	

Mountainside

Dr		Cr
(35 hrs @ $20)	700.00	
er taxes	87.15	
Bal	787.15	

Riverside

Dr		Cr
(28 hrs @ $20)	560.00	
er taxes	69.72	
Bal	629.72	

Employer taxes are allocated to the jobs as follows:

Lakeside:	25/88 × 219.12 =	$62.25
Mountainside:	35/88 × 219.12 =	87.15
Riverside:	28/88 × 219.12 =	69.72
		$219.12

ACTIVITIES: ○ **Creating an Invoice for a Job**

In chapter 3, you learned how to create an invoice using the Create Invoices window. When invoices are prepared for specific jobs, the procedure will be similar but with one important difference. At the Customer:Job drop-down list, you will select the *Job* rather than the Customer.

On May 15, 2014, Kristin Raina is preparing an invoice for the Lakeside Hotel job. During the period from May 1, 2014, to May 15, 2014, Kristin Raina and Richard Henderson spent the following time on Design Services for each job:

Job	Kristin Raina Hours	Richard Henderson Hours
Lakeside Hotel	15	25
Mountainside Hotel	5	35
Riverside Hotel	20	28

The hours for Richard are the same hours you used to record the payroll, which allocates the payroll expenses to each job. QuickBooks now uses these hours to bill the customer for the job, which will record the revenue to each job.

Kristin Raina will invoice the client for the work done on the Lakeside Hotel project by her and her staff, Invoice No. 1011.

To create an invoice for a job—
1. Click Customers and then click *Create Invoices*.
2. At the CUSTOMER:JOB drop-down list, click *Lakeside Hotel*. Although the Lakeside Hotel job is selected, the bill will be forwarded to Hamilton Hotels.
3. At the Billable Time/Costs window, choose the second option, *Exclude outstanding billable time and costs at this time?* and then click OK.
4. At the TEMPLATE drop-down list, click *Intuit Service Invoice*.
5. At the *Date* field, choose the date *05/15/2014*, and at the *Invoice #* field, key **1011**. Accept the terms shown.
6. At the ITEM drop-down list, click *Design Services - Owner*.
7. At the *QUANTITY* field, key **15**.
8. Move to the second line of the *ITEM* field and click *Design Services - Assistant* from the drop-down list.

   Recall that when you process pay for the period, Richard Henderson, the design assistant, spent 25 hours on this project. Kristin Raina will invoice the customer for these hours at a rate of $40 per hour. *At present, this information is maintained manually.* Later in the chapter, we will use the QuickBooks Time Tracking feature to incorporate this information into the company file.

9. At the *QUANTITY* field, key **25**. (See figure 11–L.)

FIGURE 11–L
Create Invoices Window—Completed

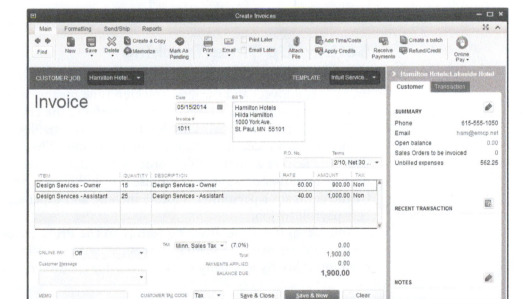

10. The *Print Later* and *Email Later* boxes should not be checked, and *ONLINE PAY* should say Off.
11. If the information is correct, click Save & New.

Practice Exercise

May 15	Create Invoice No. 1012 for Mountainside Hotel for work done from May 1, 2014, to May 15, 2014, based on hours devoted to that job by Kristin Raina and Richard Henderson. *QuickCheck:* Total Invoice $1,700.
May 15	Create Invoice No. 1013 for Riverside Hotel for work done from May 1, 2014, to May 15, 2014, based on hours devoted to that job by Kristin Raina and Richard Henderson. *QuickCheck:* Total Invoice $2,320.

Accounting concept

For design services provided on account, the general ledger postings are as follows:

1200 Accounts Receivable			4010 Design Services	
(Lakeside)	1,900			1,900
(Mountainside)	1,700			1,700
(Riverside)	2,320			2,320
Bal	5,920		Bal	5,920

The Hamilton Hotels customer file is updated for the three invoices. In addition, the job files are updated for the revenues as follows:

Lakeside	Mountainside	Riverside
1,900	1,700	2,320

Setting Up Time Tracking

The Time Tracking feature of QuickBooks allows you to track hours worked by both employees and owners. Tracking time means recording the hours worked by company personnel while identifying the customer or job for which they spend their working hours. Many companies maintain manual timesheets or timecards to record employee time. The QuickBooks Time Tracking feature automates that process and enables you to use the resulting data in a number of ways. You can use it to bill clients by job for work done by the company's personnel, allocate income and expenses to jobs, and process payroll by job.

You set up the Time Tracking feature in the Preferences window. Once you have done that, the Weekly Timesheet window is available, and you can then input hourly and daily work activity for customers and/or jobs.

To set up Time Tracking—

1. Click Edit and then click *Preferences*. The Preferences window appears.
2. Along the left frame of the Preferences window, click the *Time & Expenses* icon. You may have to scroll down the frame to find it.
3. Click the Company Preferences tab.
4. At the *Do you track time?* field, click *Yes*. Accept *Monday* at the *First Day of Work Week* field.
5. Place a check in the box *Mark all time entries as billable*. (See figure 11–M.)

FIGURE 11–M
Preferences Window—
Time & Expenses—
Company Preferences
Tab

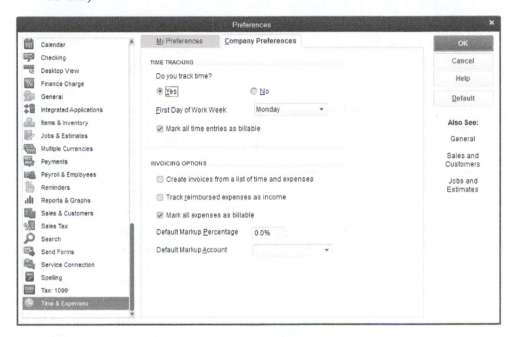

6. If the information is correct, click OK.

ACTIVITIES: ## The Weekly Timesheet Window

In QuickBooks, you can use the Weekly Timesheet window to enter the daily work activity of employees and owners on a weekly basis. Each employee or owner indicates the number of hours worked for a customer or job. You enter the daily hours along with the customer or job name and the type of service that is performed in the Weekly Timesheet window. This information does not in itself generate a transaction or journal entry. Instead, when you wish to invoice a customer for the work and to prepare the payroll for the employees, QuickBooks uses the information in the Weekly Timesheet to automatically complete fields in the Create Invoices, Enter Sales Receipts, and Pay Employee windows. The QuickBooks Weekly Timesheet window appears in figure 11–N.

FIGURE 11–N
Weekly Timesheet Window

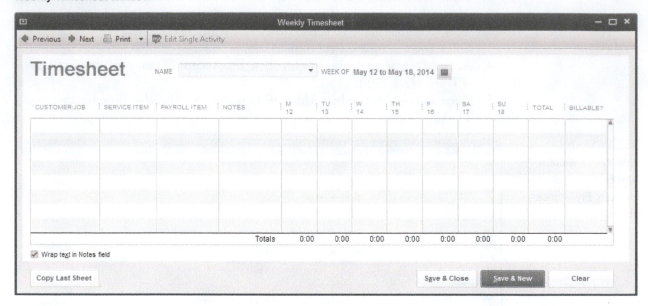

The Weekly Timesheet window allows you to select the name of the employee or owner doing the work, the type of service to be invoiced, the type of payroll item (salary or hourly pay), and the daily hours spent for each customer or job. Ideally, this information is entered daily by the employee/owner. However, in this chapter, you will enter the data for an entire pay period at one time. The box on the right side of the timesheet titled *Billable?* is check marked if the hours are billable to a customer and unchecked if they are not. The hours for employees always default as billable. The hours for the owner always default as non-billable. When recording data for the owner, click to place a check mark in the box to indicate that the hours are billable.

Kristin Raina has been tracking time manually. Beginning May 20, she wants to use the Time Tracking feature and the Weekly Timesheet.

On May 31, 2014, Richard Henderson submitted the following time data for the period May 19, 2014, to May 31, 2014, for Design Services.

Job	Hours per Job for May by Date											Totals
	19	20	21	22	23	24	27	28	29	30	31	
Lakeside Hotel	2	2	2	3			2	4	2	2	2	21
Mountainside Hotel	3	4	4	1		4	2	2	4	4		28
Riverside Hotel	3	2	2	4	8	4	4	2	2	2	6	39

To enter time tracking in the Weekly Timesheet—
1. Click Employees and then click *Enter Time*.
2. At the Enter Time submenu, click *Use Weekly Timesheet*.
3. At the NAME drop-down list, click *Richard Henderson*. Click *Yes* at the Transfer Activities to Payroll window message box.
4. Click the calendar icon. The Set Date dialog box appears.
5. Choose *05/19/2014*. (See figure 11–O.)

FIGURE 11–O
Set Date Dialog Box

6. Click May 19 on the calendar to return to the Weekly Timesheet window.
7. At the first line of the CUSTOMER:JOB drop-down list, click *Lakeside Hotel*.
8. At the SERVICE ITEM drop-down list, click *Design Services - Assistant*.
9. At the PAYROLL ITEM drop-down list, click *Hourly Wages*.
10. At the M 19 column, key **2**.
11. At the TU 20 column, key **2**.
12. At the W 21 column, key **2**.
13. At the TH 22 column, key **3**. Notice that the *Billable?* box correctly indicates billable. (See figure 11–P.)

FIGURE 11–P
Weekly Timesheet Window—Partially Complete

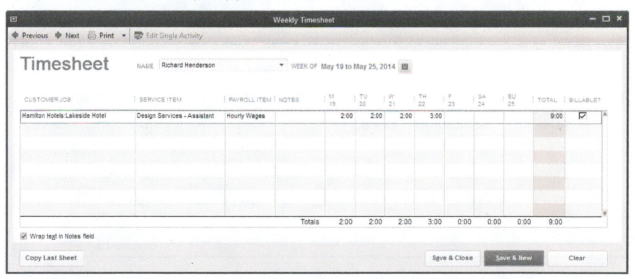

14. Move to the second line of the *CUSTOMER:JOB* field, and from the drop-down list, click *Mountainside Hotel*.
15. At the SERVICE ITEM drop-down list, click *Design Services - Assistant*.
16. Accept the *Hourly Wages* default for PAYROLL ITEM.
17. Key the hours for the appropriate dates. (See figure 11–Q.)

FIGURE 11–Q
Weekly Timesheet Window—Partially Complete

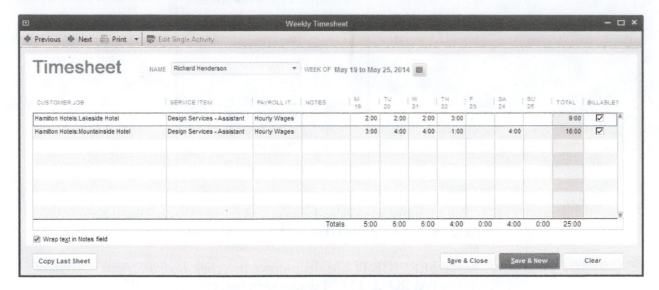

18. Move to the third line of the *CUSTOMER:JOB* field, and from the drop-down list, click *Riverside Hotel*.
19. Complete the balance of the line by repeating steps similar to steps 15 through 17. (See figure 11–R.)

FIGURE 11–R
Weekly Timesheet Window—Completed

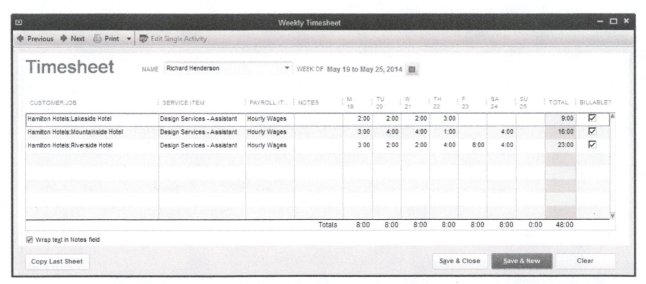

> **HINT**
>
> It is not necessary to enter zero where no work is indicated for a job.

20. If the information is correct, click the Next arrow. You will be moved to the next week.
21. Enter the information for May 27, 2014, to May 31, 2014, for all three jobs. (See figure 11–S.)
22. If the information is correct, click Save & Close.

FIGURE 11–S
Weekly Timesheet Window—Completed

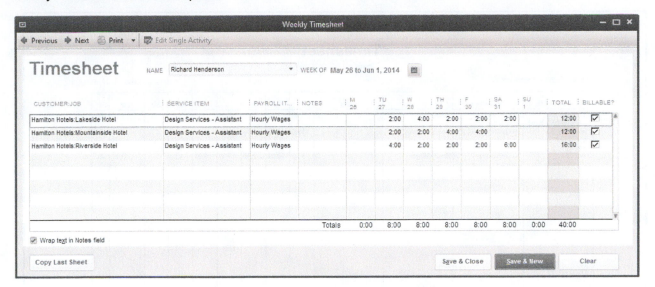

The time records for Richard Henderson are now stored in the system for later use. When you bill Hamilton Hotels for the work done, QuickBooks will retrieve this information to assist in calculating billable time as part of creating an invoice for the work. In addition, this information will be part of the payroll processing and job allocation procedures. Since the time is billable, this information will be needed to create invoices for this customer.

Practice Exercise

May 31 | Kristin Raina submitted the following data for Design Services time spent on each project. Enter the information in the Weekly Timesheet window. Since the *Mark all time entries as billable* box is checked in the Time and Expenses Preference, the BILLABLE? box will automatically fill.

Job	19	20	21	22	23	24	27	28	29	30	31	Totals
Hours per Job for May by Date												
Lakeside Hotel	2	1	2				4				2	11
Mountainside Hotel		1		1	1		3	2	2			10
Riverside Hotel	1		2	1	1	2	1	3	4	1	3	19

To review the data entered in the Weekly Timesheet, you can print the timesheets—

1. In the Weekly Timesheet, click Print. The Select Timesheets to Print dialog box appears.
2. In the *Dates* field, choose *05/19/2014* through *05/25/2014* and then move to the next field. All personnel for whom time data has been entered are listed and selected.
3. Click OK. A timesheet is printed for each person for each week. One of the timesheets is shown in figure 11–T.
4. Close the Weekly Timesheet.

FIGURE 11–T
Timesheet

Timesheet

Printed on: 5/25/2014

Name: Richard Henderson

May 19 to May 25, 2014

Customer:Job	Service Item	Payroll Item	Notes	M	Tu	W	Th	F	Sa	Su	Total	Bill*
Hamilton Hotels:Lakeside Hotel	Design Services - Assistant	Hourly Wages		2:00	2:00	2:00	3:00				9:00	B
Hamilton Hotels:Mountainside Hotel	Design Services - Assistant	Hourly Wages		3:00	4:00	4:00	1:00		4:00		16:00	B
Hamilton Hotels:Riverside Hotel	Design Services - Assistant	Hourly Wages		3:00	2:00	2:00	4:00	8:00	4:00		23:00	B
			Totals	8:00	8:00	8:00	8:00	8:00	8:00	0:00	48:00	

Signature _____

Review the timesheets to make sure the hours are correct and the correct service item is listed. The data on these timesheets will flow through to the Pay Employees and Create Invoices windows. If there is an error, the payroll and invoices generated will be incorrect. Once you have recorded payroll and invoices, any subsequent changes you make to the timesheets will *not* flow through to correct them.

ACTIVITIES:

Paying an Employee and Allocating Payroll Expense to a Job

On May 15, 2014, when Kristin Raina processed the pay for Richard Henderson, the hours spent for each job were manually entered in the Review Paycheck window. This was necessary because the QuickBooks Time Tracking feature had not yet been set up. Now the Time Tracking feature has been set up, and daily work activity has been entered into the Weekly Timesheet window. This information can now be used to assist in the payroll process and to allocate employee payroll costs to specific customer jobs.

On May 31, 2014, Kristin Raina will process the pay for Richard Henderson, who worked on all three jobs during the pay period.

To pay an employee and allocate payroll costs using Time Tracking—
1. Click Employees and then click *Pay Employees*. The Enter Payroll Information window appears.
2. At the *PAY PERIOD ENDS* and *CHECK DATE* fields, choose *05/31/2014*. At the Pay Period Change message, click Yes to update the hours for the new pay period.
3. At the *BANK ACCOUNT* field, click *1020 Cash - Payroll*.
4. Select Richard Henderson by placing a ✓ next to the name.
5. If the information is correct, click *Open Paycheck Detail*. You will move to the Preview Paycheck window. Notice that QuickBooks has automatically filled the data for the hours worked on each job and for the amount paid. (See figure 11–U.)

FIGURE 11–U
Preview Paycheck
Window—Partially
Completed

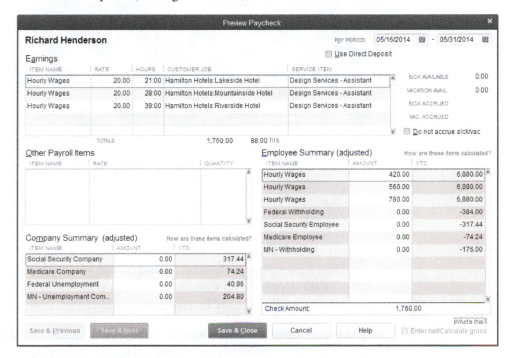

6. Complete the tax information with the information below using the procedures you learned in chapter 9.

Company Taxes	
Social Security Company:	109.12
Medicare Company:	25.52
Federal Unemployment:	14.08
MN - Unemployment Company:	70.40
Employee Taxes	
Federal Withholding:	132.00
Social Security Employee:	109.12
Medicare Employee:	25.52
MN - Withholding:	61.00

QuickCheck: Check Amount $1,432.36.

(See figure 11–V.)

FIGURE 11–V

Preview Paycheck
Window—Completed

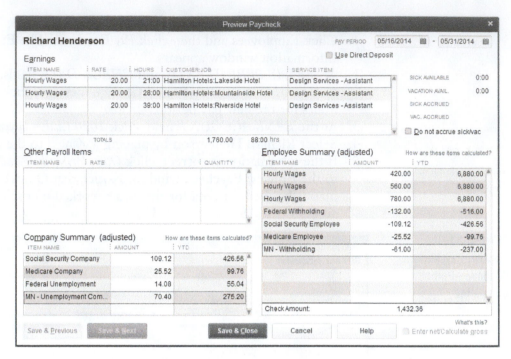

7. If there is an error in the Preview Paycheck window, close the Pay Employees window. Open the Time Worksheet, choose the employee, and set the date. Use the Previous and Next buttons to display the data for each week. Correct any errors, save the corrections, close the Time Worksheet, and return to the Pay Employees windows to continue processing the payroll.

8. If the information is correct, click Save & Close. When you return to the Enter Payroll Information window, click Continue.

9. At the Review and Create Paychecks window, if the information is correct, click *Create Paychecks* and then click Close.

As a result of this transaction, all payroll expenses for Richard Henderson (including employer payroll taxes) have been allocated to each job based on the hours entered in the Weekly Timesheet window.

ACTIVITIES: ─○ **Creating an Invoice with Time Tracking**

You have entered the daily work information for Kristin Raina and Richard Henderson in the Weekly Timesheet window. When you processed the payroll for Richard Henderson, QuickBooks used the information from the Weekly Timesheet window to total the hours spent on each job and to allocate the payroll expense accordingly. QuickBooks also uses the timesheet data to bill customers for services rendered and to allocate revenue earned to each job.

On May 31, 2014, Kristin Raina will bill Hamilton Hotels for work done by the company personnel from May 16, 2014, to May 31, 2014, for each job at the rates established in the Item List for Design Services, Invoice Nos. 1014, 1015, and 1016.

To create an invoice using Time Tracking—

1. Click Customers and then click *Create Invoices*.
2. At the *Date* field, choose *5/31/2014*.
3. Make sure the invoice number is 1014 and the Template reads *Intuit Service Invoice*.
4. At the CUSTOMER:JOB drop-down list, click *Lakeside Hotel*. The Billable Time/Costs window appears. (See figure 11–W.)

FIGURE 11–W

Billable Time/Costs Message

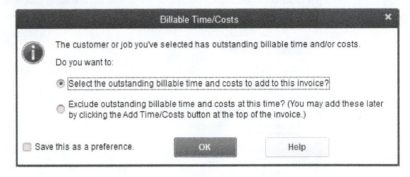

5. At the Billable Time/Costs window, accept the first option: *Select the outstanding billable time and costs to add to this invoice?*
6. Click OK. The Choose Billable Time and Costs window appears with the time information for Richard Henderson and Kristin Raina entered on the Time tab. (See figure 11–X.)

FIGURE 11–X

Choose Billable Time and Costs Window—Time Tab

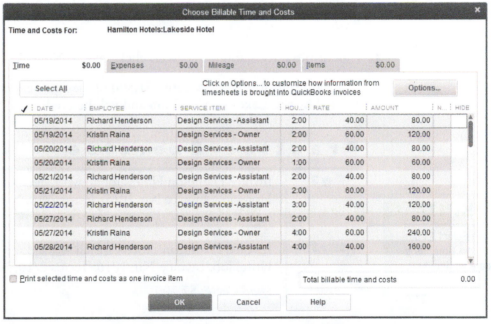

7. Click Select All. A ✓ will be placed next to all items listed.
8. Click OK and then click OK at the Invoicing for Vendor Time window. You will be returned to the Create Invoices window with all billable hours entered at the appropriate rate and time. (See figure 11–Y.)

FIGURE 11–Y
Create Invoices
Window—Completed

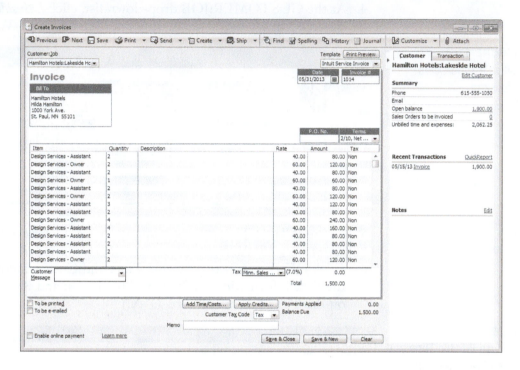

9. If the information is correct, click Save & New.

As a result of this transaction, $1,500 of Design Services revenue has been earned by the Lakeside Hotel job and will be credited to that job file.

Practice Exercise

May 31	Invoice Hamilton Hotels for all work done on the Mountainside Hotel job. Invoice No. 1015. Terms 2/10, Net 30.
	QuickCheck: $1,720
May 31	Invoice Hamilton Hotels for all work done on the Riverside Hotel job. Invoice No. 1016. Terms 2/10, Net 30.
	QuickCheck: $2,700

HINT

Use the Select All button on the Time tab to allocate all time to the job.

ACTIVITIES: —○ **Creating a Customer Statement**

As part of the management of accounts receivable it is often advisable to forward a statement of activity to a customer. The statement will list all activity of that customer's account, such as sales on account or sales for cash, collections of receivables and open balances, if any. This will act as a reminder to the customer if there is a balance due, especially if the balance is greater than 30 days old. Often, the presentation of a statement will result in the payment of open invoices.

In QuickBooks, customer statements are prepared using the Create Statements window of the Customers menu. Statements can be prepared for a specific period and for selected customers. Alternately, statements can be prepared for all customers at one time, whether they have an open balance or not.

On May 31, 2014, Kristin Raina wishes to forward a statement to Hamilton Hotels, due to the increased activity with that customer during May.

To create a customer statement-
1. Click Customers and then click *Create Statement*.
2. At the *Statement Date* field, choose *05/31/2014*.
3. At the *Statement Period From* and *To* fields, choose *02/01/2014* to *05/31/2014*.
4. At the *SELECT CUSTOMERS* field, click the *One Customer* button and from the drop-down list click *Hamilton Hotels*. (See figure 11-Z).

FIGURE 11–Z

Create Statements Window—Hamilton Hotels Selected

5. Make sure the *Intuit Standard Statement* Template is selected and the *Print due date on transactions* box is checked.
6. If the information is correct, click *Preview*. The statement will display all activity with this customer along with an aging of open receivables. (See figure 11-AA).

FIGURE 11–AA
Customer Statement—
Hamilton Hotels

Statement

EX11 [Your Name] Kristin Raina Interior Designs
25 NE Johnson Street
Minneapolis, MN 53402

Date
5/31/2014

To:
Hamilton Hotels
Hilda Hamilton
1000 York Ave.
St. Paul, MN 55101

Amount Due	Amount Enc.
$11,840.00	

Date	Transaction	Amount	Balance
01/31/2014	Balance forward		0.00
03/27/2014	INV #1010. Due 04/26/2014.	1,798.00	1,798.00
03/30/2014	PMT #6555.	-1,762.04	35.96
03/30/2014	Discount #6555.	-35.96	0.00
	Lakeside Hotel-		
05/15/2014	INV #1011. Due 06/14/2014.	1,900.00	1,900.00
05/31/2014	INV #1014. Due 06/30/2014.	1,500.00	3,400.00
	Mountainside Hotel-		
05/15/2014	INV #1012. Due 06/14/2014.	1,700.00	5,100.00
05/31/2014	INV #1015. Due 06/30/2014.	1,720.00	6,820.00
	Riverside Hotel-		
05/15/2014	INV #1013. Due 06/14/2014.	2,320.00	9,140.00
05/31/2014	INV #1016. Due 06/30/2014.	2,700.00	11,840.00

CURRENT	1-30 DAYS PAST DUE	31-60 DAYS PAST DUE	61-90 DAYS PAST DUE	OVER 90 DAYS PAST DUE	Amount Due
11,840.00	0.00	0.00	0.00	0.00	$11,840.00

7. Click Print to print the report. If the statement printed OK, click *Yes* at the *Did statement(s) print OK* window. If a window appears titled Sending forms by e-mail, place a check mark in the box to the left of *Do not display this message in the future*, and click OK.

8. Close the report and the Create Statements window.

Job and Time Tracking Reports, Accounting Reports, and Financial Statements

Both the Job and Time Tracking features produce reports that companies find helpful in measuring job profit and managing employee time. The job reports focus on profitability, while the time tracking reports analyze time spent by each person or for each job.

Job and Time Tracking Reports

Several reports can be accessed from the Reports menu that analyze information related to jobs. Two of these reports are the *Profit & Loss by Job* report and the *Time by Job Summary* report.

Profit & Loss by Job Report

The *Profit & Loss by Job* report provides information on the profitability of customer and job activity. The report shows the type of revenue earned and the expenses incurred for each job for a specified period of time.

To view and print the *Profit & Loss by Job* report—
1. Click Reports and then click *Jobs, Time & Mileage*.
2. At the Jobs, Time & Mileage submenu, click *Profit & Loss by Job*.
3. At the *To* and *From* fields, choose *05/01/2014* and *05/31/2014* and then click Refresh. The report for the three jobs is displayed.
4. Print the report. (See figure 11–BB.)

FIGURE 11–BB
Profit & Loss by Job Report

EX11 [Your Name] Kristin Raina Interior Designs
Profit & Loss by Job
May 2014

Accrual Basis

	Lakeside Hotel (Hamilton Hotels)	Mountainside Hotel (Hamilton Hotels)	Riverside Hotel (Hamilton Hotels)	Total Hamilton Hotels
Ordinary Income/Expense				
Income				
4010 · Design Services	3,400.00	3,420.00	5,020.00	11,840.00
Total Income	3,400.00	3,420.00	5,020.00	11,840.00
Gross Profit	3,400.00	3,420.00	5,020.00	11,840.00
Expense				
6560 · Payroll Expenses				
6565 · Salaries and Wages Expense	920.00	1,260.00	1,340.00	3,520.00
6610 · Social Sec/Medicare Tax Expense	70.38	96.39	102.51	269.28
6625 · FUTA Expense	7.36	10.08	10.72	28.16
6630 · SUI Expense	36.80	50.40	53.60	140.80
Total 6560 · Payroll Expenses	1,034.54	1,416.87	1,506.83	3,958.24
Total Expense	1,034.54	1,416.87	1,506.83	3,958.24
Net Ordinary Income	2,365.46	2,003.13	3,513.17	7,881.76
Net Income	2,365.46	2,003.13	3,513.17	7,881.76

5. Close the report.

Time by Job Summary Report

The *Time by Job Summary* report lists hours spent by job for a specified period of time. The report lists the job and the time each employee devoted to each job.

To view and print the *Time by Job Summary* report—
1. Click Reports and then click *Jobs, Time & Mileage*.
2. At the Jobs, Time & Mileage submenu, click *Time by Job Summary*.
3. At the *To* and *From* fields, choose *05/01/2014* and *05/31/2014* and then click Refresh. The report will be displayed for the period. (See figure 11–CC.)

FIGURE 11–CC
Time by Job Summary
Report

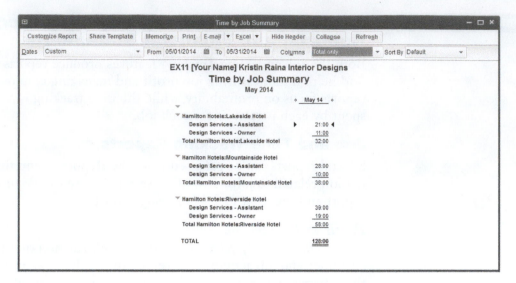

4. Print the report.
5. Close the report.

Accounting Reports and Financial Statements

At the end of the month, the *Journal* report, *Profit & Loss Standard* report, and *Balance Sheet Standard* report should be viewed and printed. The *Journal* report is displayed in figure 11–DD, the *Profit & Loss Standard* report is displayed in figure 11–EE, and the *Balance Sheet Standard* report is shown in figure 11–FF.

FIGURE 11–DD

Journal Report
May 1, 2014–May 31, 2014

EX11 [Your Name] Kristin Raina Interior Designs
Journal
May 2014

Trans #	Type	Date	Num	Name	Memo	Account	Debit	Credit
66	Credit Card C...	05/01/2014	47887	Atlantis Business Travel		2015 · American Travel Card		600.00
				Atlantis Business Travel		6475 · Travel Expense	600.00	
							600.00	600.00
67	Credit Card C...	05/17/2014	84441	Atlantis Business Travel		2015 · American Travel Card		350.00
				Atlantis Business Travel		6475 · Travel Expense	350.00	
							350.00	350.00
68	Check	05/22/2014	12	American Travel Card		1010 · Cash - Operating		600.00
				American Travel Card		2015 · American Travel Card	600.00	
							600.00	600.00
69	Check	05/31/2014	13	American Travel Card		1010 · Cash - Operating		350.00
				American Travel Card		2015 · American Travel Card	350.00	
							350.00	350.00
70	Paycheck	05/15/2014	7	Richard Henderson		1020 · Cash - Payroll		1,432.36
				Hamilton Hotels:Lakeside Hotel		6565 · Salaries and Wages Expense	500.00	
				Hamilton Hotels:Mountainside Hotel		6565 · Salaries and Wages Expense	700.00	
				Hamilton Hotels:Riverside Hotel		6565 · Salaries and Wages Expense	560.00	
				Richard Henderson		2115 · FIT Payable		132.00
				Hamilton Hotels:Lakeside Hotel		6610 · Social Sec/Medicare Tax Expense	31.00	
				Hamilton Hotels:Mountainside Hotel		6610 · Social Sec/Medicare Tax Expense	43.40	
				Hamilton Hotels:Riverside Hotel		6610 · Social Sec/Medicare Tax Expense	34.72	
				Richard Henderson		2110 · Social Sec/Medicare Tax Payable		109.12
				Richard Henderson		2110 · Social Sec/Medicare Tax Payable		109.12
				Hamilton Hotels:Lakeside Hotel		6610 · Social Sec/Medicare Tax Expense	7.25	
				Hamilton Hotels:Mountainside Hotel		6610 · Social Sec/Medicare Tax Expense	10.15	
				Hamilton Hotels:Riverside Hotel		6610 · Social Sec/Medicare Tax Expense	8.12	
				Richard Henderson		2110 · Social Sec/Medicare Tax Payable		25.52
				Richard Henderson		2110 · Social Sec/Medicare Tax Payable		25.52
				Hamilton Hotels:Lakeside Hotel		6625 · FUTA Expense	4.00	
				Hamilton Hotels:Mountainside Hotel		6625 · FUTA Expense	5.60	
				Hamilton Hotels:Riverside Hotel		6625 · FUTA Expense	4.48	
				Richard Henderson		2125 · FUTA Payable		14.08
				Richard Henderson		2120 · SIT Payable		61.00
				Hamilton Hotels:Lakeside Hotel		6630 · SUI Expense	20.00	
				Hamilton Hotels:Mountainside Hotel		6630 · SUI Expense	28.00	
				Hamilton Hotels:Riverside Hotel		6630 · SUI Expense	22.40	
				Richard Henderson		2130 · SUI Payable		70.40
							1,979.12	1,979.12
71	Invoice	05/15/2014	1011	Hamilton Hotels:Lakeside Hotel		1200 · Accounts Receivable	1,900.00	
				Hamilton Hotels:Lakeside Hotel	Design Servi...	4010 · Design Services		900.00
				Hamilton Hotels:Lakeside Hotel	Design Servi...	4010 · Design Services		1,000.00
				Minn. Dept. of Revenue	Sales Tax	2200 · Sales Tax Payable	0.00	
							1,900.00	1,900.00
72	Invoice	05/15/2014	1012	Hamilton Hotels:Mountainside Hotel		1200 · Accounts Receivable	1,700.00	
				Hamilton Hotels:Mountainside Hotel	Design Servi...	4010 · Design Services		300.00
				Hamilton Hotels:Mountainside Hotel	Design Servi...	4010 · Design Services		1,400.00
				Minn. Dept. of Revenue	Sales Tax	2200 · Sales Tax Payable	0.00	
							1,700.00	1,700.00
73	Invoice	05/15/2014	1013	Hamilton Hotels:Riverside Hotel		1200 · Accounts Receivable	2,320.00	
				Hamilton Hotels:Riverside Hotel	Design Servi...	4010 · Design Services		1,200.00
				Hamilton Hotels:Riverside Hotel	Design Servi...	4010 · Design Services		1,120.00
				Minn. Dept. of Revenue	Sales Tax	2200 · Sales Tax Payable	0.00	
							2,320.00	2,320.00
74	Paycheck	05/31/2014	8	Richard Henderson		1020 · Cash - Payroll		1,432.36
				Hamilton Hotels:Lakeside Hotel		6565 · Salaries and Wages Expense	420.00	
				Hamilton Hotels:Mountainside Hotel		6565 · Salaries and Wages Expense	560.00	
				Hamilton Hotels:Riverside Hotel		6565 · Salaries and Wages Expense	780.00	
				Richard Henderson		2115 · FIT Payable		132.00
				Hamilton Hotels:Lakeside Hotel		6610 · Social Sec/Medicare Tax Expense	26.04	
				Hamilton Hotels:Mountainside Hotel		6610 · Social Sec/Medicare Tax Expense	34.72	
				Hamilton Hotels:Riverside Hotel		6610 · Social Sec/Medicare Tax Expense	48.36	
				Richard Henderson		2110 · Social Sec/Medicare Tax Payable		109.12
				Richard Henderson		2110 · Social Sec/Medicare Tax Payable		109.12
				Hamilton Hotels:Lakeside Hotel		6610 · Social Sec/Medicare Tax Expense	6.09	
				Hamilton Hotels:Mountainside Hotel		6610 · Social Sec/Medicare Tax Expense	8.12	
				Hamilton Hotels:Riverside Hotel		6610 · Social Sec/Medicare Tax Expense	11.31	
				Richard Henderson		2110 · Social Sec/Medicare Tax Payable		25.52
				Richard Henderson		2110 · Social Sec/Medicare Tax Payable		25.52
				Hamilton Hotels:Lakeside Hotel		6625 · FUTA Expense	3.36	
				Hamilton Hotels:Mountainside Hotel		6625 · FUTA Expense	4.48	
				Hamilton Hotels:Riverside Hotel		6625 · FUTA Expense	6.24	
				Richard Henderson		2125 · FUTA Payable		14.08
				Richard Henderson		2120 · SIT Payable		61.00
				Hamilton Hotels:Lakeside Hotel		6630 · SUI Expense	16.80	
				Hamilton Hotels:Mountainside Hotel		6630 · SUI Expense	22.40	
				Hamilton Hotels:Riverside Hotel		6630 · SUI Expense	31.20	
				Richard Henderson		2130 · SUI Payable		70.40
							1,979.12	1,979.12
75	Invoice	05/31/2014	1014	Hamilton Hotels:Lakeside Hotel		1200 · Accounts Receivable	1,500.00	
				Hamilton Hotels:Lakeside Hotel		4010 · Design Services		80.00
				Hamilton Hotels:Lakeside Hotel		4010 · Design Services		120.00
				Hamilton Hotels:Lakeside Hotel		4010 · Design Services		80.00
				Hamilton Hotels:Lakeside Hotel		4010 · Design Services		60.00
				Hamilton Hotels:Lakeside Hotel		4010 · Design Services		80.00
				Hamilton Hotels:Lakeside Hotel		4010 · Design Services		120.00
				Hamilton Hotels:Lakeside Hotel		4010 · Design Services		120.00
				Hamilton Hotels:Lakeside Hotel		4010 · Design Services		80.00
				Hamilton Hotels:Lakeside Hotel		4010 · Design Services		240.00
				Hamilton Hotels:Lakeside Hotel		4010 · Design Services		160.00

Page 2

continued

FIGURE 11–DD
Continued

EX11 [Your Name] Kristin Raina Interior Designs
Journal
May 2014

Trans #	Type	Date	Num	Name	Memo	Account	Debit	Credit
				Hamilton Hotels:Lakeside Hotel		4010 · Design Services		80.00
				Hamilton Hotels:Lakeside Hotel		4010 · Design Services		80.00
				Hamilton Hotels:Lakeside Hotel		4010 · Design Services		80.00
				Hamilton Hotels:Lakeside Hotel		4010 · Design Services		120.00
				Minn. Dept. of Revenue	Sales Tax	2200 · Sales Tax Payable	0.00	
							1,500.00	1,500.00
76	Invoice	05/31/2014	1015	Hamilton Hotels:Mountainside Hotel		1200 · Accounts Receivable	1,720.00	
				Hamilton Hotels:Mountainside Hotel		4010 · Design Services		120.00
				Hamilton Hotels:Mountainside Hotel		4010 · Design Services		160.00
				Hamilton Hotels:Mountainside Hotel		4010 · Design Services		60.00
				Hamilton Hotels:Mountainside Hotel		4010 · Design Services		160.00
				Hamilton Hotels:Mountainside Hotel		4010 · Design Services		40.00
				Hamilton Hotels:Mountainside Hotel		4010 · Design Services		60.00
				Hamilton Hotels:Mountainside Hotel		4010 · Design Services		160.00
				Hamilton Hotels:Mountainside Hotel		4010 · Design Services		60.00
				Hamilton Hotels:Mountainside Hotel		4010 · Design Services		80.00
				Hamilton Hotels:Mountainside Hotel		4010 · Design Services		180.00
				Hamilton Hotels:Mountainside Hotel		4010 · Design Services		80.00
				Hamilton Hotels:Mountainside Hotel		4010 · Design Services		120.00
				Hamilton Hotels:Mountainside Hotel		4010 · Design Services		160.00
				Hamilton Hotels:Mountainside Hotel		4010 · Design Services		120.00
				Hamilton Hotels:Mountainside Hotel		4010 · Design Services		160.00
				Minn. Dept. of Revenue	Sales Tax	2200 · Sales Tax Payable	0.00	
							1,720.00	1,720.00
77	Invoice	05/31/2014	1016	Hamilton Hotels:Riverside Hotel		1200 · Accounts Receivable	2,700.00	
				Hamilton Hotels:Riverside Hotel		4010 · Design Services		120.00
				Hamilton Hotels:Riverside Hotel		4010 · Design Services		60.00
				Hamilton Hotels:Riverside Hotel		4010 · Design Services		80.00
				Hamilton Hotels:Riverside Hotel		4010 · Design Services		80.00
				Hamilton Hotels:Riverside Hotel		4010 · Design Services		120.00
				Hamilton Hotels:Riverside Hotel		4010 · Design Services		160.00
				Hamilton Hotels:Riverside Hotel		4010 · Design Services		60.00
				Hamilton Hotels:Riverside Hotel		4010 · Design Services		320.00
				Hamilton Hotels:Riverside Hotel		4010 · Design Services		60.00
				Hamilton Hotels:Riverside Hotel		4010 · Design Services		160.00
				Hamilton Hotels:Riverside Hotel		4010 · Design Services		120.00
				Hamilton Hotels:Riverside Hotel		4010 · Design Services		160.00
				Hamilton Hotels:Riverside Hotel		4010 · Design Services		60.00
				Hamilton Hotels:Riverside Hotel		4010 · Design Services		80.00
				Hamilton Hotels:Riverside Hotel		4010 · Design Services		180.00
				Hamilton Hotels:Riverside Hotel		4010 · Design Services		80.00
				Hamilton Hotels:Riverside Hotel		4010 · Design Services		240.00
				Hamilton Hotels:Riverside Hotel		4010 · Design Services		80.00
				Hamilton Hotels:Riverside Hotel		4010 · Design Services		60.00
				Hamilton Hotels:Riverside Hotel		4010 · Design Services		240.00
				Hamilton Hotels:Riverside Hotel		4010 · Design Services		180.00
				Minn. Dept. of Revenue	Sales Tax	2200 · Sales Tax Payable	0.00	
							2,700.00	2,700.00
TOTAL							**17,698.24**	**17,698.24**

EX11 [Your Name] Kristin Raina Interior Designs
Profit & Loss
January through May 2014

Accrual Basis

	Jan – May 14
Ordinary Income/Expense	
Income	
4010 · Design Services	16,820.00
4020 · Decorating Services	3,400.00
4060 · Sale of Carpets	2,400.00
4065 · Sale of Draperies	1,000.00
4070 · Sale of Lamps	1,200.00
4075 · Sale of Mirrors	900.00
4100 · Sales Discounts	-84.62
Total Income	25,635.38
Cost of Goods Sold	
5060 · Cost of Carpets Sold	1,200.00
5065 · Cost of Draperies Sold	500.00
5070 · Cost of Lamps Sold	600.00
5075 · Cost of Mirrors Sold	450.00
5900 · Inventory Adjustment	150.00
Total COGS	2,900.00
Gross Profit	22,735.38
Expense	
6020 · Accounting Expense	300.00
6050 · Advertising Expense	100.00
6100 · Bank Service Charges	60.00
6175 · Deprec. Exp., Furniture	100.00
6185 · Deprec. Exp., Computers	60.00
6200 · Insurance Expense	200.00
6300 · Janitorial Expenses	125.00
6325 · Office Supplies Expense	150.00
6400 · Rent Expense	800.00
6450 · Telephone Expense	275.00
6475 · Travel Expense	950.00
6500 · Utilities Expense	450.00
6560 · Payroll Expenses	
6565 · Salaries and Wages Expense	8,880.00
6610 · Social Sec/Medicare Tax Expense	679.32
6625 · FUTA Expense	71.04
6630 · SUI Expense	355.20
Total 6560 · Payroll Expenses	9,985.56
Total Expense	13,555.56
Net Ordinary Income	9,179.82
Other Income/Expense	
Other Income	
6900 · Interest Income	10.00
Total Other Income	10.00
Other Expense	
7000 · Interest Expense	50.00
Total Other Expense	50.00
Net Other Income	-40.00
Net Income	9,139.82

FIGURE 11–FF
Balance Sheet
Standard Report
May 31, 2014

Accrual Basis

EX11 [Your Name] Kristin Raina Interior Designs
Balance Sheet
As of May 31, 2014

	May 31, 14
ASSETS	
Current Assets	
Checking/Savings	
1010 · Cash - Operating	24,780.38
1020 · Cash - Payroll	5,582.96
1050 · Cash - Money Market	10,000.00
Total Checking/Savings	40,363.34
Accounts Receivable	
1200 · Accounts Receivable	13,980.00
Total Accounts Receivable	13,980.00
Other Current Assets	
1260 · Inventory of Carpets	800.00
1265 · Inventory of Draperies	1,000.00
1270 · Inventory of Lamps	1,000.00
1275 · Inventory of Mirrors	900.00
1300 · Design Supplies	200.00
1305 · Office Supplies	250.00
1410 · Prepaid Advertising	500.00
1420 · Prepaid Insurance	2,200.00
Total Other Current Assets	6,850.00
Total Current Assets	61,193.34
Fixed Assets	
1700 · Furniture	
1725 · Furniture, Cost	12,000.00
1750 · Accum. Dep., Furniture	-100.00
Total 1700 · Furniture	11,900.00
1800 · Computers	
1825 · Computers, Cost	3,600.00
1850 · Accum. Dep., Computers	-60.00
Total 1800 · Computers	3,540.00
Total Fixed Assets	15,440.00
TOTAL ASSETS	**76,633.34**
LIABILITIES & EQUITY	
Liabilities	
Current Liabilities	
Accounts Payable	
2010 · Accounts Payable	9,750.00
Total Accounts Payable	9,750.00
Other Current Liabilities	
2020 · Notes Payable	7,000.00
2030 · Interest Payable	50.00
2100 · Payroll Liabilities	
2110 · Social Sec/Medicare Tax Payable	538.56
2115 · FIT Payable	264.00
2120 · SIT Payable	122.00
2125 · FUTA Payable	28.16
2130 · SUI Payable	140.80
Total 2100 · Payroll Liabilities	1,093.52
Total Other Current Liabilities	8,143.52
Total Current Liabilities	17,893.52
Total Liabilities	17,893.52

Reconciliation of Data to Reports

As you have seen in this chapter, income and expenses can be allocated to jobs either by entering data directly into the Create Invoices window and Payroll window or by activating the Time Tracking feature and using the Weekly Timesheet. When data is entered manually or into the Weekly Timesheet, QuickBooks, behind the scenes, calculates the amounts per job that appear in the Create Invoice window, Payroll windows, Job files, and Job reports. To better understand some of the behind-the-scenes computations, refer to figure 11–GG. This figure displays how the amounts are calculated by QuickBooks.

FIGURE 11–GG

Reconciliation of Data to Reports

RECONCILIATION OF DATA TO REPORTS

		Lakeside Hotel		Mountainside Hotel		Riverside Hotel		Total
Design Services:								
May 15, 2014 Kristin Raina	(15 x $60) =	$900	(5 x $60) =	$300	(20 x $60) =	$1,200		$2,400
Richard Henderson	(25 x $40) =	1,000	(35 x $40) =	1,400	(28 x $40) =	1,120		3,520
		$1,900		$1,700		$2,320		$5,920
May 31, 2014 Kristin Raina	(11 x $60) =	$660	(10 x $60) =	$600	(19 x $60) =	$1,140		$2,400
Richard Henderson	(21 x $40) =	840	(28 x $40) =	1,120	(39 x $40) =	1,560		3,520
		$1,500		$1,720		$2,700		$5,920
Total Income		$3,400		$3,420		$5,020		$11,840
Payroll Expenses:								
May 15, 2014 Salaries Expense	(25 x $20) =	500.00	(35 x $20) =	700.00	(28 x $20) =	560.00		$1,760.00
PR Tax Expense		$62.25		87.15		69.72		219.12
		562.25		787.15		629.72		$1,979.12
May 31, 2014 Salaries Expense	(21 x $20) =	420.00	(28 x $20) =	560.00	(39 x $20) =	780.00		$1,760.00
PR Tax Expense		52.29		69.72		97.11		219.12
		472.29		629.72		877.11		$1,979.12
Total Expenses		1,034.54		1,416.87		1,506.83		3,958.24
Net Income		$2,365.46		$2,003.13		$3,513.17		$7,881.76

Allocation of Payroll Tax Expense:

Company Payroll Tax Expense:			Allocation of payroll tax expense based on hours to each job:				
May 15, 2014 Social Security Company	$109.12						
Medicare Company	25.52		Lakeside Hotel	(25 ÷ 88) x	$219.12 =	$62.25
Federal Unemployment	14.08		Mountainside Hotel	(35 ÷ 88) x	$219.12 =	87.15
MN - Unemployment Company	70.40		Riverside Hotel	(28 ÷ 88) x	$219.12 =	69.72
	$219.12		Total			$219.12
May 31, 2014 Social Security Company	$109.12					
Medicare Company	25.52		Lakeside Hotel	(21 ÷ 88) x	$219.12 =	$52.29
Federal Unemployment	14.08		Mountainside Hotel	(28 ÷ 88) x	$219.12 =	$69.72
MN - Unemployment Company	70.40		Riverside Hotel	(39 ÷ 88) x	$219.12 =	$97.11
	$219.12		Total			$219.12

Chapter Review and Assessment

Procedure Review

To add a job—

1. Click Customers and then click *Customer Center*.
2. At the Customer Center window, select (highlight) the customer to which the job is associated, but do not open the file.
3. Click the New Customer & Job button.
4. At the New Customer & Job menu, click *Add Job*. The New Job window opens. The New Job window carries over information from the customer's file.
5. At the *JOB NAME* field, key the job name.
6. At the Job Info tab, key the appropriate data in the following fields:

   JOB DESCRIPTION
   JOB STATUS
   START DATE
   PROJECTED END DATE

7. If the information is correct, click OK.

To allocate payroll expenses to a job (without the Time Tracking feature)—

1. Click Employees and then click *Pay Employees*. Click *No* at the QuickBooks Payroll Services message, if it appears. The Enter Payroll Information window appears.
2. Enter the appropriate dates in the *PAY PERIOD ENDS* and *CHECK DATE* fields.
3. At the *BANK ACCOUNT* field, click the appropriate bank account.
4. Select the appropriate employee by placing a ✓ next to the name.
5. Click Open Payroll Detail. You will move to the Preview Paycheck window.
6. Make sure the correct payroll item appears.
7. At the first line of the *HOURS* column, key the hours for the first job.
8. At the CUSTOMER:JOB drop-down list, click the job.
9. Move to the second line of the *ITEM NAME* field, and click the payroll item from the drop-down list.
10. At the *HOURS* field, key the hours for the second job.
11. At the CUSTOMER:JOB drop-down list, click the second job.
12. Repeat this procedure for all remaining jobs.
13. Complete the balance of the window in the manner explained in chapter 9 for company taxes and employee taxes.
14. If the information is correct, click Save & Close. You will be returned to the Enter Payroll Information window.
15. Click Continue. The Review and Create Paychecks window appears with the taxes columns completed.
16. If the information is correct, click the Create Paychecks button.
17. At the Confirmation and Next Steps window, click Close.

Creating an invoice for a job (without the Time Tracking feature)—
1. Click Customers and then click *Create Invoices*.
2. At the CUSTOMER:JOB drop-down list, click the job name.
3. At the Billable Time/Costs window, choose *Exclude outstanding billable time and costs at this time?* and then click OK.
4. At the TEMPLATE drop-down list, click *Intuit Service Invoice*.
5. Enter the date and invoice number and accept the terms.
6. Click the appropriate items from the ITEM drop-down list.
7. Enter the quantity. The *Print Later* and *Email Later* boxes should not be checked.
8. Click Save & Close.

Setting up Time Tracking—
1. Click Edit and then click *Preferences*. The Preferences window appears.
2. Along the left frame of the Preferences window, click the *Time Tracking* icon. You will have to scroll down the frame to find it.
3. Click the Company Preferences tab.
4. At the *Do You Track Time?* field, click *Yes*. Accept *Monday* as the first day of the work week
5. Place a check in the *Mark all time entries as billable* box.
6. If the information is correct, click OK.

Entering Time Tracking data—
1. Click Employees and then click *Enter Time*.
2. At the Enter Time submenu, click *Use Weekly Timesheet*.
3. At the NAME drop-down list, click the employee name and then click *Yes* at the Transfer Activities to Payroll window message box.
4. Click the calendar icon. The Set Date dialog box appears.
5. Choose the start date.
6. Click the date to return to the Weekly Timesheet window.
7. At the first line of the CUSTOMER:JOB drop-down list, click the job name.
8. At the SERVICE ITEM drop-down list, click the service item.
9. At the PAYROLL ITEM drop-down list, click the payroll item for this employee.
10. At the column for first day of work, key the hours for that job.
11. Continue entering the hours for that job for the period of time displayed.
12. Note the BILLABLE? box is checked.
13. Move to the second line of the *CUSTOMER:JOB* field, and click the second job from the drop-down list.
14. Repeat the process for all successive jobs for this time period.
15. If the information is correct, click the Next arrow.
16. Repeat the process for the employee for the next week.
17. If this is the final period of work, click Save & Close.

Paying an employee and allocating time with Time Tracking—
1. Click Employees and then click *Pay Employees*. The Enter Payroll Information window appears.

2. Enter the appropriate dates in the *PAY PERIOD ENDS* and *CHECK DATE* fields. At the Pay Period Change window, click Yes to update the hours for the new pay period.
3. At the *BANK ACCOUNT* field, click the appropriate bank account.
4. Select the appropriate employee by placing a ✓ next to the name.
5. Click Open Paycheck Detail. You will move to the Preview Paycheck window.
6. Notice that the data for the hours worked on each job and the pay amount have been filled automatically.
7. Complete the tax information in the usual manner.
8. If the information is correct, click Save & Close. You will be returned to the Enter Payroll Information window.
9. Click Continue. The Review and Create Paychecks window appears with the taxes columns completed.
10. If the information is correct, click *Create Paychecks*.
11. At the Confirmation and Next Steps window, click Close.

To create an invoice with Time Tracking—
1. Click Customers and then click *Create Invoices*.
2. Select the date, invoice number, and template.
3. At the CUSTOMER:JOB drop-down list, click the job name.
4. At the Billable Time/Costs window, choose the first option: *Select the outstanding billable time and costs to add to this invoice?*
5. Click OK. The Choose Billable Time and Costs window appears, and the hours billed by all company employees for the job are displayed.
6. Click Select All. A ✓ will be placed next to all items listed.
7. Click OK and then click OK at the message. You will be returned to the Create Invoices window with all billable hours entered at the appropriate rate and time.
8. Click Save & Close.

To create a customer statement—
1. Click Customers and then click *Create Statement*.
2. At the *Statement Date* field, choose the statement date.
3. At the *Statement Period From* and *To* fields, enter the period of time covered by the statement.
4. At the *SELECT CUSTOMERS* field, click the button for the statement you wish to create.
5. Make sure the *Intuit Standard Statement* Template is selected and the *Print due date on transactions* box is checked.
6. If the information is correct, click *Preview*. The statement will display all activity with this customer along with an aging of open receivables.
7. Click Print to print the report. If the statement printed OK, click *Yes* at the *Did statement(s) print OK* window.
8. Close the report and the Create Statements window.

To view and print the *Profit & Loss by Job* report—
1. Click Reports and then click *Jobs, Time & Mileage*.
2. At the Jobs, Time & Mileage submenu, click *Profit & Loss by Job*.
3. Enter the report dates.
4. Print the report and then close it.

To view and print the *Time by Job Summary* report—
1. Click Reports and then click *Jobs, Time & Mileage*.
2. At the Jobs, Time & Mileage submenu, click *Time by Job Summary*.
3. Enter the dates of the report.
4. Print the report and then close it.

Key Concepts

Select the letter of the item that best matches each definition.

a. Job	f. Weekly Timesheet window
b. Time Tracking	g. Job Profit
c. Customer Center	h. *Profit & Loss by Job* report
d. Job Revenue	i. *Time by Job Summary* report
e. Time tab	j. Billable Time

_____ 1. Tab on the Choose Billable Time and Costs window that lists billable hours worked for a specific job.

_____ 2. Center that contains a file for each customer job.

_____ 3. Report that displays the revenues, expenses, and net profit for each job for a specified period of time.

_____ 4. Time worked by company personnel that can be billed to customers.

_____ 5. Process by which a company maintains records of time worked by employees for various customers or jobs.

_____ 6. Job revenue less job expenses.

_____ 7. Report that displays employee time spent on each job.

_____ 8. Can be a project, assignment, or any identifiable segment of work for a customer.

_____ 9. Window where time worked by company personnel is entered.

_____ 10. Income earned for a particular job.

Procedure Check

1. Your company is a construction contractor working on several projects for one customer. How would you use QuickBooks to determine which jobs are making money?
2. Describe the steps to add a job to the Customer Center.
3. Your company wishes to keep a record of the time worked by company personnel to bill customers for service provided. How would you use QuickBooks to track time information?
4. Upper management requests a report showing the profit or loss for each project the company is currently working on. How would you use QuickBooks to develop the information?
5. You wish to see how many hours the company's personnel are spending on each job. How would you use QuickBooks to develop this information?
6. Explain why it is so important for a service business to keep accurate records of the time employees and others are spending for each job or customer.

Case Problems
Case Problem 1

In July, the fourth month of business for Lynn's Music Studio, one of Lynn Garcia's clients, Highland School, has asked her to organize, coordinate, and supervise an eight-week intensive music program. All classes will be held at the schools, but they will be offered to three levels of students: beginning, intermediate, and progressive. Highland School needs separate invoices each month for each level of students, so Lynn has decided that it is necessary to track income and expenses for each level. To aid in this process, she has decided to activate the Time Tracking feature of QuickBooks so that the time spent by herself and one of her employees, Michelle Auletta, can be tracked and allocated to each level of student and then billed to the client, Highland School. She has added two service items to the Item List for Michelle Auletta's billable time as an assistant. The company file includes information for Lynn's Music Studio as of July 1, 2014.

1. Open the company file CH11 Lynn's Music Studio.QBW.
2. Make a backup copy of the company file: LMS11 [*Your Name*] Lynn's Music Studio.
3. Restore the backup copy of the company file. In both the Open Backup Copy and Save Company File as windows, use the file name LMS11 [*Your Name*] Lynn's Music Studio.
4. Change the company name to **LMS11 [*Your Name*] Lynn's Music Studio**.
5. Set up the Time Tracking feature for Lynn's Music Studio. Monday is the first day of the work week.
6. Add the following jobs to the Customer Center:

CUSTOMER:	**Highland School**
JOB NAME:	**Beginner Level**
JOB DESCRIPTION:	**Beginner Level Summer Program Job**
STATUS:	**Awarded**
START DATE:	**07/01/2014**
PROJECTED END DATE:	**08/31/2014**
JOB NAME:	**Intermediate Level**
JOB DESCRIPTION:	**Intermediate Level Summer Program**
JOB STATUS:	**Awarded**
START DATE:	**07/01/2014**
PROJECTED END DATE:	**08/31/2014**
JOB NAME:	**Progressive Level**
JOB DESCRIPTION:	**Progressive Level Summer Program**
JOB STATUS:	**Awarded**
START DATE:	**07/01/2014**
PROJECTED END DATE:	**08/31/2014**

7. Enter the following hours worked in the Weekly Timesheet window (remember to click *Yes* at the Transfer Activities to Payroll window message box):

Michelle Auletta: Piano Lessons—Assistant

Job	\underline{Hours per Job for July by Date}									
	1	**2**	**3**	**5**	**7**	**8**	**9**	**10**	**11**	**Totals**
Beginner Level	2	2	2	2	2	2	2	2	2	18
Intermediate Level						2		2		4
Progressive Level				2					2	4

Lynn Garcia: Piano Lessons—Owner

Job	\underline{Hours per Job for July by Date}									
	1	**2**	**3**	**5**	**7**	**8**	**9**	**10**	**11**	**Totals**
Beginner Level		2	2				2			6
Intermediate Level	2	2	2	2	2	2	2	2	2	18
Progressive Level	2	2	2	2	2	2	2	2	2	18

8. Process pay and allocate time for July 11, 2014, for Michelle Auletta (click *Yes* at the Pay Period Change window):

Check No.:	**6**
Item Name:	**Hourly Wages**
Rate:	**12**
Company Taxes:	
Social Security Company:	**19.34**
Medicare Company:	**4.52**
Federal Unemployment:	**2.50**
PA - Unemployment Company:	**12.48**
Employee Taxes:	
Federal Withholding:	**28.08**
Social Security Employee:	**19.34**
Medicare Employee:	**4.52**
PA - Withholding:	**9.36**
PA - Unemployment Employee:	**0.00**

9. Create the following invoices:

Jul. 11   Create invoice for Highland School Beginner Level piano lessons provided by Lynn Garcia and Michelle Auletta for the period July 1, 2014, to July 11, 2014. Invoice No. 2020. Terms 2/10, Net 30 Days.

Jul. 11   Create invoice for Highland School Intermediate Level piano lessons provided by Lynn Garcia and Michelle Auletta for the period July 1, 2014, to July 11, 2014. Invoice No 2021. Terms 2/10, Net 30 Days.

Jul. 11   Create invoice for Highland School Progressive Level piano lessons provided by Lynn Garcia and Michelle Auletta for the period July 1, 2014, to July 11, 2014. Invoice No. 2022. Terms 2/10, Net 30 Days.

10. Enter the following hours worked in the Weekly Timesheet window:

Michelle Auletta: Piano Lessons—Assistant

Job	Hours per Job for July by Date										
	14	15	16	17	18	21	22	23	24	25	Totals
Beginner Level	3	3	2	3	2	3	2	2	2	2	24
Intermediate Level	3		3			3		3			12
Progressive Level		2		2	2		3		3	2	14

Lynn Garcia: Piano Lessons—Owner

Job	Hours per Job for July by Date										
	14	15	16	17	18	21	22	23	24	25	Totals
Beginner Level	2				2					2	6
Intermediate Level	2	2	2	2	2	2	2		2	2	18
Progressive Level	2	3	2	2	2	3	2	2	2	2	22

11. Process pay and allocate time for July 25, 2014, for Michelle Auletta:

Check No.:	**7**
Item Name:	**Hourly Wages**
Rate:	**12**
Company Taxes:	
Social Security Company:	**37.20**
Medicare Company:	**8.70**
Federal Unemployment:	**4.80**
PA - Unemployment Company:	**24.00**
Employee Taxes:	
Federal Withholding:	**54.00**
Social Security Employee:	**37.20**
Medicare Employee:	**8.70**
PA - Withholding:	**18.00**
PA - Unemployment Employee:	**0.00**

12. Create the following invoices:

Jul. 25   Create invoice for Highland School Beginner Level piano lessons provided by Lynn Garcia and Michelle Auletta for the period July 14, 2014, to July 25, 2014. Invoice No. 2023. Terms Net 30 Days.

Jul. 25   Create invoice for Highland School Intermediate Level piano lessons provided by Lynn Garcia and Michelle Auletta for the period July 14, 2014, to July 25, 2014. Invoice No. 2024. Terms Net 30 Days.

Jul. 25   Create invoice for Highland School Progressive Level piano lessons provided by Lynn Garcia and Michelle Auletta for the period July 14, 2014, to July 25, 2014. Invoice No. 2025. Terms Net 30 Days.

13. Display and print a customer statement for Highland School for April 1, 2014 to July 31, 2014.

14. Display and print the following reports for July 1, 2014, to July 31, 2014:
    a. *Profit & Loss by Job*
    b. *Time by Job Summary*

Case Problem 2

In September, the fourth month of business for Olivia's Web Solutions, one of Olivia Chen's customers, Thrifty Stores, has decided to expand to three stores. Each store will need its own web page design services, as the stores carry different products. Olivia Chen has decided that it is necessary to track income and expenses for each store. In addition, she wishes to activate the Time Tracking feature of QuickBooks so that the time spent by herself and one of her employees, Gary Glenn, can be tracked and allocated to each job and then billed to the customer. She has added two service items to the Item List for Gary Glenn's billable time as an assistant. The company file includes information for Olivia's Web Solutions as of September 1, 2014.

1. Open the company file CH11 Olivia's Web Solutions.QBW.
2. Make a backup copy of the company file OWS11 [*Your Name*] Olivia's Web Solutions.
3. Restore the backup copy of the company file. In both the Open Backup Copy and the Save Company File as windows, use the file name OWS11 [*Your Name*] Olivia's Web Solutions.
4. Change the company name to **OWS11 [*Your Name*] Olivia's Web Solutions**.
5. Set up the Time Tracking feature for Olivia's Web Solutions. Monday is the first day of the work week.
6. Add the following jobs to the Customer Center:

CUSTOMER:	**Thrifty Stores**
JOB NAME:	**Bronx Store**
JOB DESCRIPTION:	**Thrifty Bronx Store Web Page Design**
JOB STATUS:	**Awarded**
START DATE:	**09/01/2014**
PROJECTED END DATE:	**10/31/2014**
JOB NAME:	**Brooklyn Store**
JOB DESCRIPTION:	**Thrifty Brooklyn Store Web Page Design**
JOB STATUS:	**Awarded**
START DATE:	**09/01/2014**
PROJECTED END DATE:	**10/31/2014**
JOB NAME:	**Queens Store**
JOB DESCRIPTION:	**Thrifty Queens Store Web Page Design**
JOB STATUS:	**Awarded**
START DATE:	**09/01/2014**
PROJECTED END DATE:	**10/31/2014**

7. Enter the following hours worked in the Weekly Timesheet window (remember to click *Yes* at the Transfer Activities to Payroll window message box):

Gary Glenn: Web Page Design—Assistant

Job	Hours per Job for September by Date										
	2	3	4	5	6	8	9	10	11	12	Totals
Bronx Store	4	3	1		5	2	4		1	2	22
Brooklyn Store		1	4	4	3	2	1	6	4	6	31
Queens Store	4	4	3	4		4	3	2	3		27

Olivia Chen: Web Page Design—Owner

Job	Hours per Job for September by Date										
	2	3	4	5	6	8	9	10	11	12	Totals
Bronx Store		2		2	2	2	1	4	2		15
Brooklyn Store		1	2		3		1	2	2	4	15
Queens Store	2	1	1	2		1	2	2	3		14

8. Process pay and allocate time for September 12, 2014, for Gary Glenn (click *Yes* at the Pay Period Change window):

Check No.:	**6**
Item Name:	**Hourly Wages**
Rate:	**25**
Company Taxes:	
Social Security Company:	**124.00**
Medicare Company:	**29.00**
Federal Unemployment:	**16.00**
NY - Unemployment Company:	**80.00**
Employee Taxes:	
Federal Withholding:	**360.00**
Social Security Employee:	**124.00**
Medicare Employee:	**29.00**
NY - Withholding:	**98.00**

9. Create the following invoices:

Sep. 12   Create invoice for Web Page Design Services for Thrifty Bronx Store for services provided by Olivia Chen and Gary Glenn for the period September 1, 2014, to September 12, 2014. Invoice No. 1017. Terms Net 30 Days.

Sep. 12   Create invoice for Web Page Design Services for Thrifty Brooklyn Store for services provided by Olivia Chen and Gary Glenn for the period September 1, 2014, to September 12, 2014. Invoice No. 1018. Terms Net 30 Days.

Sep. 12   Create invoice for Web Page Design Services for Thrifty Queens Store for services provided by Olivia Chen and Gary Glenn for the period September 1, 2014, to September 12, 2014. Invoice No. 1019. Terms Net 30 Days.

10. Enter the following hours worked in the Weekly Timesheet window (remember to click *Yes* at the Transfer Activities to Payroll window message box):

Gary Glenn: Web Page Design—Assistant

Job	Hours per Job for September by Date										
	15	16	17	18	19	22	23	24	25	26	Totals
Bronx Store	4	3	6	4	2		1	2	3		25
Brooklyn Store	2	3	1	2	4	6	5	5	4	1	33
Queens Store	2	2	1	2	2	2	2	1	1	7	22

Olivia Chen: Web Page Design—Owner

Job	Hours per Job for September by Date										
	15	16	17	18	19	22	23	24	25	26	Totals
Bronx Store	1	2	5	2	3	4		2	2		21
Brooklyn Store	2	2	2	2	2		4		2		16
Queens Store	4	3		3	1	4	2	1	1		19

11. Process pay and allocate time for September 26, 2014, for Gary Glenn:

Check No.:	7
Item Name:	**Hourly Wages**
Rate:	25
Company Taxes:	
Social Security Company:	**124.00**
Medicare Company:	**29.00**
Federal Unemployment:	**16.00**
NY - Unemployment Company:	**80.00**
Employee Taxes:	
Federal Withholding:	**360.00**
Social Security Employee:	**124.00**
Medicare Employee:	**29.00**
NY - Withholding:	**98.00**

12. Create the following invoices:

Sep. 26   Create invoice for Web Page Design Services for Thrifty Bronx Store for services provided by Olivia Chen and Gary Glenn for the period September 15, 2014, to September 26, 2014. Invoice No. 1020. Terms Net 30 Days.

Sep. 26   Create invoice for Web Page Design Services for Thrifty Brooklyn Store for services provided by Olivia Chen and Gary Glenn for the period September 15, 2014, to September 26, 2014. Invoice No. 1021. Terms Net 30 Days.

Sep. 26   Create invoice for Web Page Design Services for Thrifty Queens Store for services provided by Olivia Chen and Gary Glenn for the period September 15, 2014, to September 26, 2014. Invoice No. 1022. Terms Net 30 Days.

13. Display and print a customer statement for Thrifty Stores for June 1, 2014 to September 30, 2014.

14. Display and print the following reports for September 1, 2014, to September 30, 2014:
    a. *Profit & Loss by Job*
    b. *Time by Job Summary*

CHAPTER 12

Customizing Your Company File

Desktop, Invoices, Letters, Memorized Transactions, Graphs, and Fiscal Year

Chapter Objectives

- Customize the desktop with the home page and icon bars

- Customize Lists/Centers including subaccounts, merge entries, and custom fields

- Customize Activities including activity window display and related invoice, QuickBooks Letter in Microsoft Word, memorize transactions

- Customize Reports including the appearance of reports, memorize settings, export a report into Microsoft Excel, process multiple reports, change report default settings, view and print a graph

- View fiscal year closing, set closing date, prepare for new fiscal year

Introduction

At this point, you should have a good understanding of operating QuickBooks and be able to create and set up a new company file, update the Lists and Centers, record transactions in the Activities windows, and view and print a variety of management reports, accounting reports, and financial statements.

In this final chapter, you will learn how to customize the desktop; customize Lists/Centers by changing subaccount default settings, merging entries, and creating custom fields; customize Activities by customizing the Create Invoices window and related printed invoices, prepare a QuickBooks Letter in Microsoft Word, and memorize transactions; and customize Reports and memorize the settings, export a report to Microsoft Excel, process multiple reports, change report default settings, and view and print graphs. Finally, you will conclude the accounting cycle in QuickBooks by viewing fiscal year closing, setting the closing date, and preparing for the new fiscal year.

Chapter Problem

Begin by opening the company file CH12 Kristin Raina Interior Designs.QBW. Make a backup copy and name it **EX12 [*Your Name*] Kristin Raina Interior Designs**. Restore the backup copy and then change the company name to **EX12 [*Your Name*] Kristin Raina Interior Designs**.

Customize the Desktop

There are many different ways to access Lists/Centers, Activities windows, and Reports in QuickBooks. Throughout the text only the main menu bar was used to illustrate accessing the Lists/Centers, Activities windows, and Reports. You can customize your desktop to use the home page and the icon bars as alternative ways of accessing these items.

Home Page

By default, when you create a new company file, and each time you open a company file, the home page is displayed. If the default was changed and the home page is not automatically displayed, it can be accessed for the current work session or the default can be changed so that the home page displays each time the company file is opened. In addition, the home page can be customized to your choices.

Using the Home Page
To display the home page if it is not displayed—
1. Click Company.
2. Click Home Page. (See figure 12–A.)

FIGURE 12–A
Home Page

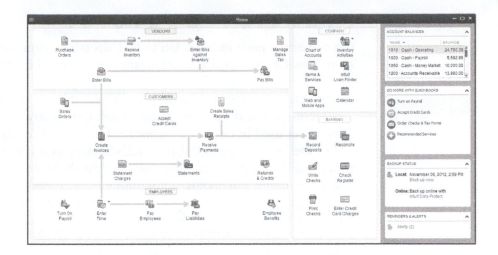

There are five sections of the home page that are labeled with tabs: VENDORS, CUSTOMERS, EMPLOYEES, COMPANY, and BANKING. Recall that VENDORS, CUSTOMERS, and EMPLOYEES are the Centers presented in prior chapters. If you click any of these tabs you are moved to the respective Center.

The home page also displays icons for certain tasks and the workflow related to each Center. You can click the icon to move to the respective window. In some cases, a drop-down menu will appear with additional choices.

To access a window using the icons on the home page—
1. On the home page in the VENDORS section, click the Enter Bills icon. The Enter Bills window – Expenses tab appears.
2. Close the Enter Bills window.
3. In the VENDORS section, click the Receive Inventory icon. A drop-down list displays two choices: Receive Inventory with Bill and Receive Inventory without Bill. (See figure 12–B.)

FIGURE 12–B
Receive Inventory
Drop-Down List

> Receive Inventory with Bill
> Receive Inventory without Bill

HINT

Recall that there is only one Enter Bills window. When you choose Enter Bills, the Enter Bills window opens with the Expenses tab displayed. When you choose Receive Inventory with Bill, the Enter Bills window opens with the Items tab displayed. If the incorrect tab is displayed, simply click the tab to display the desired tab.

---

4. On the Receive Inventory drop-down menu, click *Receive Inventory with Bill*. The Enter Bills window – Items tab is opened.

In chapter 5 – Inventory – when inventory was purchased and received, the transaction was recorded in the Enter Bills window – Items tab. The Enter Bills window – Items tab was accessed using the Vendors menu and choosing Receive Items and Enter Bill. When you use the home page and choose Receive Inventory with Bill from the drop-down menu, the Enter Bills window – Items tab opens.

5. Close the Enter Bills window.

In addition to the VENDORS, CUSTOMERS, and EMPLOYEES tab sections on the home page that represent the Centers, there is a tab section labeled COMPANY and a tab section labeled BANKING. Both of these sections offer icons related to the Company and Banking tasks.

Practice Exercise

On the home page in the CUSTOMERS tab section, click the *Create Invoices* icon. The Create Invoice window appears. Close the Create Invoices window.

On the home page in the EMPLOYEES tab section, click the *Enter Time* icon. At the drop-down menu, click *Use Weekly Timesheet*. The Weekly Timesheet used in chapter 11 appears. Close the Weekly Time Sheet.

On the home page in the BANKING tab section, click *Reconcile*. You are moved to the Begin Reconciliation window that was used in chapter 10. Close the Begin Reconciliation window.

Customize the Home Page

Icons are added or removed from the home page depending on the preferences for the company file. Recall in the New Company Setup chapters, that when creating a new company file the preferences, or features, of QuickBooks are turned on (enabled) or turned off (disabled). In chapter 6, the preferences were enabled or disabled as you answered questions in the EasyStep Interview window. In chapter 7, you went directly to the Preferences window to enable or disable preferences. As a preference is enabled, choices appear on the drop-down menus on the main menu bar and also on the home page. If a preference is enabled, you cannot remove the icon from the home page. In chapter 12, most preferences for our sample company Kristin Raina Interior Designs have been enabled. If you look at the home page for a company file in the earlier chapters, you will see fewer icons on the home page. For example, look at figure 1–H on page 1-12.

Currently, Kristin Raina is not using Estimates. Look at the company home page (figure 12–A) and observe in the Customers section that there isn't an Estimates icon. Upon enabling the Estimates preference, the Estimates icon will appear on the home page.

To enable a preference to customize the home page—
1. Click Edit, then click Preferences.
2. Along the left frame of the Preferences window, click the Desktop View icon.
3. Click the Company Preferences tab. (See figure 12–C.)

FIGURE 12–C

Preferences Window – Desktop View – Company Preferences

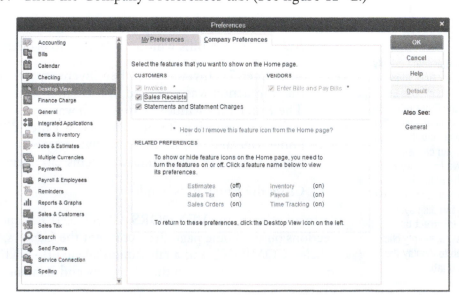

The RELATED PREFERENCES section of this page indicates if a feature is enabled (on) or disabled (off). If a preference is enabled, you cannot remove the icon from the home page. To remove the icon from the home page you would have to disable the preference (off). The Estimates preference is off. When it is enabled, the Estimates icon will appear on the home page.

4. In the RELATED PREFERENCES section, click Estimates. You are moved to the Job & Estimates page.
5. At the *DO YOU CREATE ESTIMATES?* field, click Yes, and then click OK. At the Warning message, click OK.
6. Open the home page from the Company menu, if necessary. The Estimates feature is now enabled and the Estimates icon now appears on the home page in the CUSTOMERS tab section.

Along the right side of the home page are four areas of information: ACCOUNT BALANCES, DO MORE WITH QUICKBOOKS, BACKUP STATUS, and REMINDERS & ALERTS. While you cannot remove these categories from the home page, you can minimize the detail below each heading by clicking the up arrow ⌃. When you click this arrow, only the information title is displayed. To see the information below the title, click the down arrow ⌄.

Changing the Default for the Home Page
The Preferences window is used to change the default setting for displaying the home page when opening a new company file.

To change the default setting for the home page—
1. Click Edit, then click Preferences. The Preferences window appears.
2. Along the left frame of the Preferences window, click the Desktop View icon.
3. Click the My Preferences tab.
4. Place or remove a check mark in the box to the left of Show Home page when opening a company file.
5. Click OK to save the default setting.
6. Close the home page.

Icon Bars

In addition to the home page, there are two icon bars that can be used to access Lists/Centers, Activities windows, and Reports.

Left Icon Bar
To view the left icon bar—
1. Click View. On the View drop-down menu, when a check mark appears to the left of Left Icon Bar, the left icon bar is enabled. If there is no check mark, the left icon bar is disabled.
2. Click Left Icon Bar if there is no check mark. The left icon bar is displayed. (See figure 12-D.)

FIGURE 12–D
Left Icon Bar

There are four sections on the left icon bar: Search, Content, Categories, and Do More With QuickBooks. The information in the Content section changes depending on which Category is selected. By default, the My Shortcuts category is selected. Next to each icon in the Content section is the text for the icon. Move the mouse pointer over the icons listed in the Content section and the entire text for each icon is displayed.

The left icon bar can be customized to add, delete, or edit the icons in the My Shortcuts Content list.

To add an icon to the left icon bar—

1. Click View and then click Customize Icon Bar. The Customize Icon Bar window appears. (See figure 12-E.)

You are provided the choices to Add, Edit, or Delete icons from the left icon bar. You can also change the order the icons are displayed in the Content section of the left icon bar.

2. At the Customize Icon Bar window, click the Add button. The Add Icon Bar Item window appears.
3. At the Add Icon Bar Item window, scroll through the list until you see Calculator.
4. Click Calculator. The Calc icon is added to the left icon bar at the bottom of the list in the Content section.
5. Click OK at the Add Icon Bar Item window, and then click OK at the Customize Icon Bar window to save the change.

An additional way to add icons to the Icon bar is when a QuickBooks window is open. For many windows, when a window is open, you can click the View menu, and there will be a choice to Add Window to Icon Bar.

To edit an icon on the left icon bar—

1. Click View, then click Customize Icon Bar.
2. In the Customize Icon Bar window, in the ICON BAR CONTENT field, scroll through the list and click *Accnt* once to highlight it, and then click Edit.
3. At the Edit Icon Bar Item window, in the *Label* field, delete Accnt, and key **Chart Accts**.
4. Click OK in the Edit Icon Bar window and then click OK in the Customize Icon Bar window. In the Content section of the left icon bar, the Accnt icon text changed to Chart Accts.

To remove an icon from the Icon bar—

1. Click View and then click Customize Icon Bar.
2. In the Customize Icon Bar window, in the ICON BAR CONTENT field, scroll up through the list and click Calendar once to highlight.
3. Click the Delete button. The Calendar icon is removed from the left icon bar.
4. Delete the following items from the left icon bar:
   Reg
   Rmnd
   Feedback
   User Licenses
   Services
   Add Payroll
   Docs
5. Click OK to save the changes.

In the Category section of the left icon bar, after My Shortcuts, other choices are My Apps, which allows you to find apps that work with QuickBooks; Do Today, which allows you to set up and view Reminders and Alerts; View Balances, which allows you to view the balances in cash/bank accounts, accounts receivable, and liabilities accounts; Run Favorite Reports, which allows you to list customized reports that have been saved as favorites; and Open Windows, which provides a list of windows that may be open.

The last section, Do More With QuickBooks, provides for additional features that QuickBooks offers online. This section also appears on the home page when the left icon bar is not displayed.

Top Icon Bar

To view the Icon bar—

1. Click View.
   On the View drop-down menu, when a check mark appears to the left of Top Icon Bar, the top icon bar is enabled. If there is no check mark, then the Top Icon bar is disabled.
2. Click Top Icon bar if there is no check mark.

The top icon bar is displayed under the menu bar when it is enabled. When the top icon bar is chosen, the left icon bar is no longer displayed. Under each icon is the text for the top icon bar. (See figure 12–F.)

FIGURE 12–F
Top Icon Bar

The top icon bar can be customized to add, edit, and delete icons the same way the left icon bar was customized. Changes made to the icons on the left icon bar are carried over to the top icon bar. In addition, the top icon bar can be customized to add a space and vertical line between the icons. This is done using the Add Separator button in the Customize Icon Bar window. With QuickBooks update R4, the background color of the top icon bar can be changed using the Preferences window, Desktop View, My Preferences tab.

The left icon bar or top icon bar can be removed by clicking View and then Hide Icon Bar.

LISTS/CENTERS ## Customize Subaccounts Presentation

As you know, accounts in the Chart of Accounts List can be denoted as sub-accounts. When an account is a subaccount, the account of which it is a subaccount is referred to as the parent account. Accounts are marked as subaccounts to show a subtotal or net amount of the parent account on the financial statements. This procedure was illustrated with fixed assets, where the accumulated depreciation account (subaccount) was deducted from the fixed asset cost account (subaccount) to show the net book value of the fixed asset account (parent) on the *Balance Sheet*.

When you have a parent and related subaccounts in the Chart of Accounts List, by default, QuickBooks displays the parent account first, followed by the subaccount. However, sometimes when you are reviewing the *Account Listing* or choosing an account in an Activity window, the default listing of first the parent account and then the subaccount can be cumbersome. Therefore, you can change the default settings to simplify the presentation of the parent and subaccounts.

Chart of Accounts List Window Presentation

Open the Chart of Accounts List window. Scroll down to the fixed asset section. Look at the cost and accumulated depreciation accounts. These subaccounts are indented under the parent accounts. This is referred to as the hierarchical view. (See figure 12–G.)

FIGURE 12–G
Chart of Accounts Window—Hierarchical View

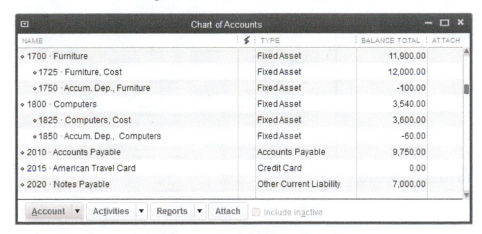

If you do not like the subaccounts indented, you can change the format to list all accounts aligned to the left of the window. This is referred to as the flat view.

To change to flat or hierarchical view—
1. In the Chart of Accounts window, click the Account menu button. Notice that *Hierarchical View* is checked.
2. Click *Flat View*.
3. Scroll down the Chart of Accounts window until the fixed assets are again displayed. The subaccounts are no longer indented; they are now left-aligned in the window. Notice each line lists both the parent account and subaccount. (See figure 12–H.)

FIGURE 12–H
Chart of Accounts
Window—Flat View

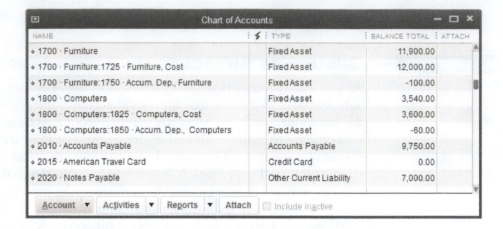

FIGURE 12–H
Chart of Accounts
Window—Flat View

4. Click the Account button and then click *Hierarchical View.* The presentation changes back to indent the subaccounts.
5. Close the window.

These changes to the view settings in the Chart of Accounts List window affect only this window.

Lists and Activities Windows Presentation

Open the Account Listing Report by clicking Reports and then List. (See Figure 12-I.)

FIGURE 12–I
Account Listing - Parent
Account Listed to Left of
Subaccount

Parent and Subaccounts
for Fixed Assets

Review the subaccounts listed in the *Account Listing* in figures 12–I. Notice that the subaccounts 1725, 1750, 1825, and 1850—the cost and accumulated depreciation accounts—are listed next to their respective parent accounts 1700 and 1800.

Open the Make General Journal Entries window; in the *ACCOUNT* field on the first line, click the account *Furniture 1725, Cost,* and then tab to the next field. In the *ACCOUNT* field, the parent account is listed first. Because the field is small, you see the parent account and only a small part of the subaccount. (See figure 12–J.)

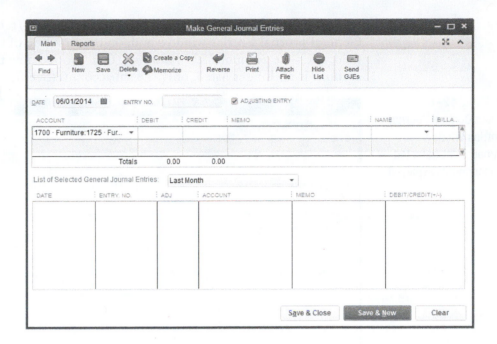

Close the Make General Journal Entries window.

In the Lists, Activities, and Reports windows, the default setting is to display the subaccounts to the right of the parent account. This default setting can be changed in the Preferences window.

To change the default setting of subaccounts—
1. Click Edit and then click *Preferences*.
2. Along the left frame of the Preferences window, click the *Accounting* icon.
3. Click the Company Preferences tab.
4. In the *ACCOUNTS* section, place a check mark in the box next to *Show lowest subaccount only*. (See figure 12–K.)

FIGURE 12–K

Preferences Window—
Accounting—Company
Preferences Tab

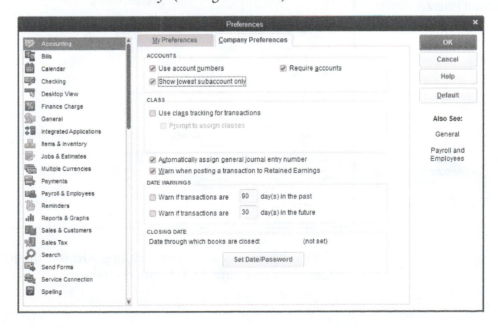

5. If the information is correct, click OK.

To see the effect of this default setting change, first, reopen the Make General Journal Entries window and, on the first line of the *ACCOUNT* field, click the account *1725 Furniture, Cost*. Notice now that the parent account is no longer listed, only the subaccount. (See figure 12–L.)

FIGURE 12–L

Make General Journal Entries Window—
Subaccount Selected—
Subaccount Displayed

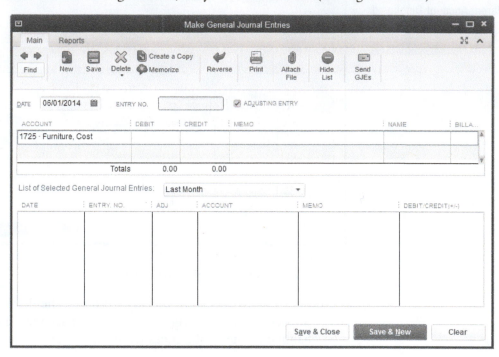

6. Close the Make General Journal Entries window.

Second, view the *Account Listing* report. (See figure 12–M.)

FIGURE 12–M

Account Listing Report—
Subaccounts Listed
Without Parent Accounts

The subaccounts are listed on a line without the parent account. Compare to figure 12-I. Close the report.

Merge Entries

You have previously learned to add, delete, or modify vendors, customers/jobs, accounts, service items, and inventory part items in the appropriate Lists/Centers. You can also combine or merge vendors, customers, accounts, service items, and inventory part items. To do so, you simply use a name already in use and QuickBooks will inquire if you wish to merge two items.

Kristin Raina currently has a 6450 Telephone Expense account and a 6500 Utilities Expense account. Kristin Raina decides to combine (that is, merge) the two accounts into the one account 6500 Utilities Expense.

Open the Journal Report from 02/28/2014 to 02/28/2014. Scroll through the journal entries until you see the TwinCityTelCo journal entry, which records $275 to the account 6450 Telephone Expense. Leave the journal report open.

To merge two accounts—
1. Open the Chart of Accounts List. Notice the accounts 6450 Telephone Expense and 6500 Utilities Expense.
2. Select 6450 Telephone Expense but do not open it.
3. Click the Account button, then click Edit Account. The Edit Account window opens.
4. In the account number field, change the number to 6500, and then click Save and Close. A Merge message appears informing you the account is already in use and inquiring if you wish to merge the accounts.
5. At the Merge message, click Yes. Look at the Chart of Accounts List. Notice there is no longer an account 6450 Telephone Expense.
6. Close the Chart of Account List.

Now look at the Journal Report for February 28, 2014. Notice the transaction for TwinCityTelCo now has the transaction recorded as 6500 Utilities Expense instead of 6450 Telephone Expense. Close the Journal report.

The same process can be used to combine vendors, customers/jobs, service items, and inventory part items. QuickBooks will update all information based on the merge.

Create Custom Fields

In prior chapters, you displayed and printed reports including filtering reports using fields of information already included in the report. QuickBooks allows you to create your own custom fields of information for later display in a report. Custom fields can be created for customers, vendors, employees, or items and are created in the appropriate List or Center.

Most of Kristin Raina's customers are located in either Minneapolis or St. Paul. She would like to sort her customers by region so when she and her assistant visit the customers, they can each go to all the customers in one city at a time. To do this, Kristin Raina will create a custom field named Region and then will edit each customer's account to identify the region for that customer. Finally, Kristin Raina will filter the Customer Center to list only the customers in a specified region.

To create a custom field—

1. Open the Customer Center and choose the first customer, Alomar Company, by double-clicking the customer name. The Edit Customer window appears. Notice the city in the ADDRESS DETAILS section for this customer is Minneapolis.
2. Click the Additional Information tab.
3. On the Additional Information tab, in the CUSTOM FIELDS section, click the Define Fields button. The Set up Custom Fields for Names window appears.
4. On the first line in the Label column, key **Region**.
5. In the Use for: field, place a check mark in the Cust (customer) column. (See figure 12–N.)

FIGURE 12–N
Set Up Custom Fields for Names Window

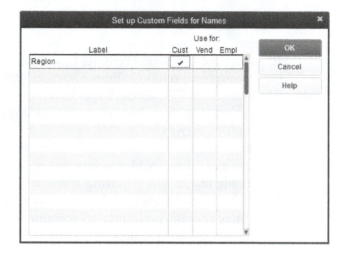

6. If the information is correct, click OK.
7. At the Information message, place a check mark in the box to the left of *Do not display this message in the future* and click OK. The Region field text box is now displayed in the CUSTOM FIELDS section on the Additional Info tab.
8. In the REGION field text box, key **Minneapolis**. (See figure 12–O.)

FIGURE 12–O
Edit Customer Window—
Additional Info Tab—
Region Field Added and
Completed

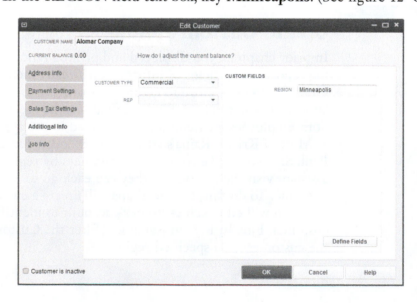

9. If the information is correct, click OK to save the information

HINT

The Region field can also be viewed in the Customer Contact List report. Open the report and click the Customize Report button. In the Modify Report dialog box, click the Filters tab. In the CHOOSE FILTER field, scroll through the list and choose Region.

In the Region text box, key Minneapolis and then click OK. The Customer Contact List is updated to display only the customers that have Minneapolis as their Region.

10. Edit each customer and key in their city in the Region text box on the Additional Info tab.
11. Close the Customer Center

The Customer Center can now be customized to display only the customers in a specified region.

To display customers in the Customer Center in the Minneapolis region—
1. Open the Customer Center.
2. On the Customer & Jobs tab, click the Search icon 🔍. The Custom Filter dialog box appears.
3. In the Customer Filter dialog box, click or key the following information:

Search:	*Active Customers*
in:	*Custom Fields*
For:	**Minneapolis**

4. Click Go. The Customer Center is updated to display only the customers that have Minneapolis as their Region on the Additional Information tab. (See figure 12–P.)

FIGURE 12–P
Customer Center Filtered for Region Field

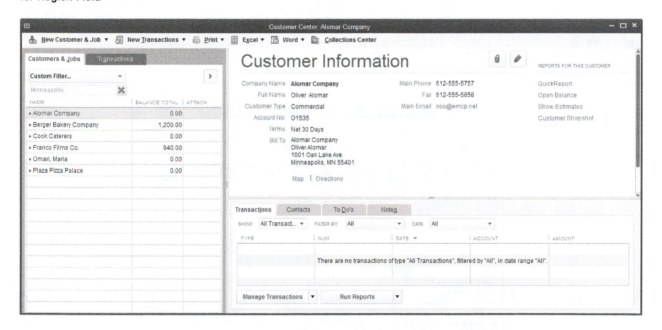

5. In the field where Minneapolis is displayed, click the X. The Customer Center returns to the list of all Active Customers.
6. Close the Customer Center.

Practice Exercise

In the Customer Center, display the customers in the St. Paul Region.
QuickCheck: Five customers and jobs should be displayed in the Customer Center.

Similar procedures can be used to create custom fields for vendors, employees, and items. If you wanted to include the Region field in the Vendor Center, open any vendor in the Edit Vendor window. On the Additional Info tab, click Define Fields. The Set up Custom Fields for Names window will appear with the Region label listed. Place a check mark in the Vend (vendor) column, which will activate the Region text box on the Additional Info tab for each vendor.

ACTIVITIES:

Customize Activities Windows and Printed Documents

In all chapters, the Activities windows displayed were based on default settings. QuickBooks allows you to change the default settings of a window as well as those of a document that can be printed because of data entered in a window.

Recall in chapter 11 that when you used time tracking, the data you entered in the Weekly Timesheet window was carried forward to the Create Invoices window. The Create Invoices window displayed by default did not display all relevant information carried over to that window. By changing the default settings in the Create Invoices window, more of the important information can be displayed.

To view the default settings and preview an invoice—
1. Click Customers and then click *Create Invoices.*
2. Click the Find Previous button to display Invoice No. 1016. Click the Formatting tab. (See figure 12–Q.)

FIGURE 12–Q
Create Invoices Window—Invoice No. 1016

Manage Templates Icon

Customize Data Layout Icon

Preview Icon

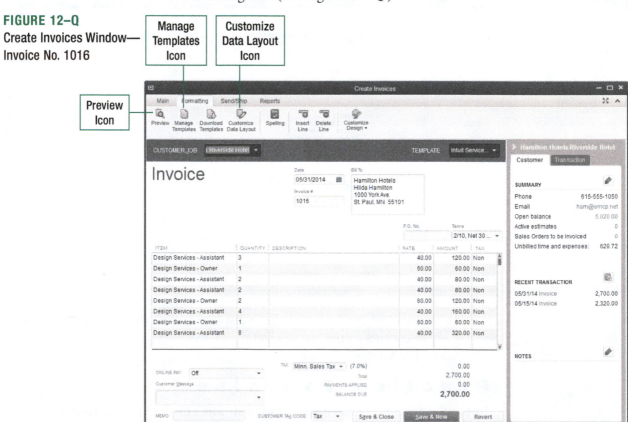

In QuickBooks you can preview and print invoices that can be sent to customers.

3. On the Formatting tab, click the Preview button. The invoice should look like figure 12–R.

FIGURE 12–R
Invoice No. 1016

EX12 [Your Name] Kristin Raina Interior Designs	**Invoice**

25 NE Johnson Street
Minneapolis, MN 53402

Date	Invoice #
5/31/2014	1016

Bill To

Hamilton Hotels
Hilda Hamilton
1000 York Ave.
St. Paul, MN 55101

P.O. No.	Terms	Project
	2/10, Net 30 Days	Riverside Hotel

Quantity	Description	Rate	Amount
3		40.00	120.00
1		60.00	60.00
2		40.00	80.00
2		40.00	80.00
2		60.00	120.00
4		40.00	160.00
1		60.00	60.00
8		40.00	320.00
1		60.00	60.00
4		40.00	160.00
2		60.00	120.00
4		40.00	160.00
1		60.00	60.00
2		40.00	80.00
3		60.00	180.00
2		40.00	80.00
4		60.00	240.00
2		40.00	80.00
1		60.00	60.00
6		40.00	240.00
3		60.00	180.00
	Sales Tax	7.00%	0.00

Total	**$2,700.00**

In both the Create Invoices window and the invoice itself, all the detail information is not displayed. In addition, the printed invoice does not indicate the items for which you are billing. This is not an invoice you would want to send to a customer. You can customize both the Create Invoices window and the invoice so that all detailed information is adequately displayed. QuickBooks provides several pre-established invoices. Two invoices previously used are the *Intuit Service Invoice* and *Intuit Product Invoice*. These invoices are based on templates. You can create your own invoice by customizing a template. To do this, you will first make a copy of the existing template and then customize the copy. This is done using the Manage Templates icon on the Formatting tab in the Create Invoices window.

4. Close the Print Preview.

To customize the Create Invoices window and a printed invoice—

1. With the Create Invoices window open and Invoice No. 1016 displayed, on the Formatting tab, click the *Manage Templates icon.* You are moved to the Manage Templates dialog box.

2. In the SELECT TEMPLATE section, select *Intuit Service Invoice* and then click the Copy button.

A copy of the Intuit Service Invoice is made. It is labeled Copy of: Intuit Service Invoice in both the SELECT TEMPLATE section and in the PREVIEW section—*Template Name* field. (See figure 12–S.)

FIGURE 12–S

Manage Templates Dialog Box—Template Name— Copy of: Intuit Service Invoice

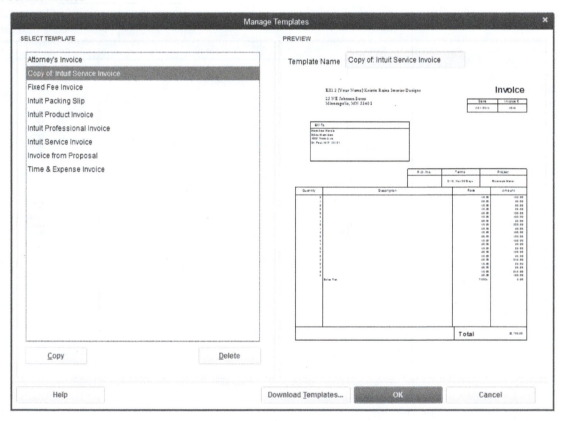

You will create your own invoice using the Copy of: Intuit Service Invoice as a guideline. But you will first assign a new name to the invoice.

3. In the PREVIEW section, at the *Template Name* field, delete the name Copy of: Intuit Service Invoice, key **Job Invoice**, and press the Tab key. Notice the invoice name is also changed in the SELECT TEMPLATE section. (See figure 12–T.)

FIGURE 12–T

Manage Templates Dialog Box—Template Name—Job Invoice

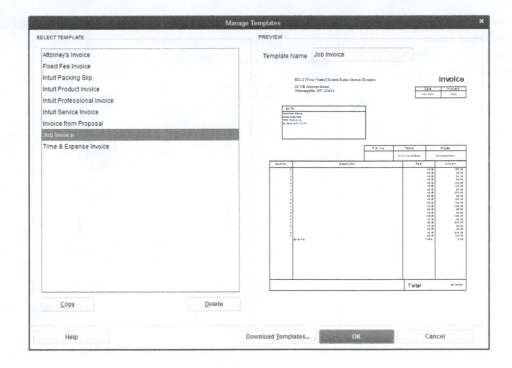

4. If the information is correct, click OK. You are moved to the Basic Customization dialog box.
5. Click the Additional Customization button. You are moved to the Additional Customization dialog box.
6. At the Additional Customization dialog box, click the Columns tab.

The Columns tab lists the pre-established settings for the service invoice. Next to each of the pre-established settings, you will see four columns of boxes. The Screen column applies to the settings that appear in the Create Invoices window. The Print column applies to the settings that appear on the printed invoice. Boxes containing check marks indicate whether the setting will appear on the screen (in the Create Invoices window), on the printed invoice, or both. The Order column applies to the order of display on both the screen and printed invoice. The Title column is the title for the column to be displayed in both the screen and printed invoice.

Since nothing was listed in the *Description* field, we will remove this column from both the window and the invoice, which will allow more room for the columns where data is displayed. In addition, we will indicate that the *Item* field should appear on the printed invoice.

7. At the *Description* field, in the Screen column, remove the check mark. At the Layout Designer message, place a check mark to the left of *Do not display this message again* and then click OK.
8. At the *Description* field, in the Print column, remove the check mark.
9. Place a check mark in the Print column box to the right of the *Item* field. At the Overlapping Fields message, click *Continue*.
10. On the Service Date line, place a check mark in both the *Screen* and *Print* boxes. At the Overlapping Fields message, click *Continue*. QuickBooks automatically assigns an order number of 4. (See figure 12–U.)

FIGURE 12–U

Additional Customization
Window Dialog Box—
Columns Tab

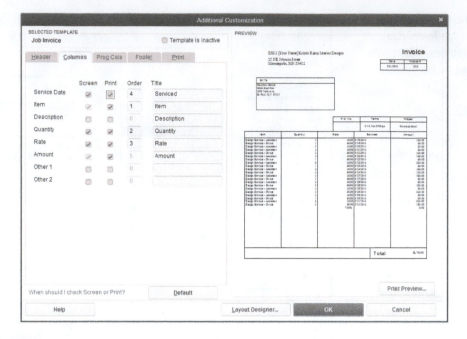

11. If the information is correct, click OK. You are returned to the Basic Customization dialog box.
12. Click OK. You are returned to the Create Invoices window. The *TEMPLATE* field displays the new format created: *Job Invoice*. The Description column has been removed, and the Serviced column has been added. (See figure 12–V and compare with figure 12–Q.)

FIGURE 12–V

Create Invoices
Window—Job Invoice—
Service Dates Added

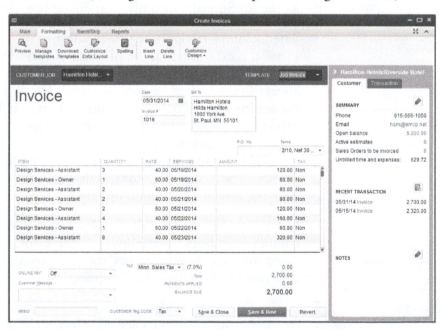

> **HINT**
>
> At the Formatting tab, you could also choose Manage Templates. At the Manage Template dialog box, select *Job Invoice* and then click OK. You move to the Basic Customization dialog box. At the Basic Customization dialog box, click *Additional Customization*.

Upon reviewing the Create Invoices window, you realize the order of data fields should be different. You will further customize the Job Invoice you just created.

13. On the Formatting tab in the Create Invoices window, click the *Customize Data Layout* icon. You are moved to the Additional Customization dialog box for the Job Invoice.

14. At the Additional Customization dialog box, click the Columns tab.
15. Change the order of the data fields as follows:

Service Date:	**2**	*Quantity:*	**3**
Item:	**1**	*Rate:*	**4**

The Amount order is automatically changed to 5. (See figure 12–W.)

FIGURE 12–W

Additional Customization Dialog Box—Columns Tab—Order

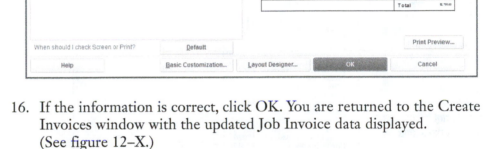

HINT

If the revised order does not appear in the PREVIEW, in the Additional Customization dialog box for the Job Invoice, click the Columns tab, recheck the Description screen and print boxes, then uncheck them, and click OK, and the order will be updated.

16. If the information is correct, click OK. You are returned to the Create Invoices window with the updated Job Invoice data displayed. (See figure 12–X.)

FIGURE 12–X

Create Invoices Window—Job Invoice—Updated Order

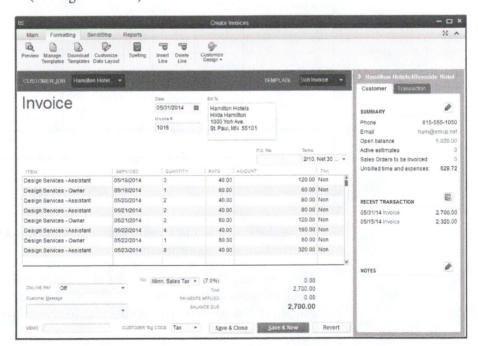

17. If the information is correct, on the Formating tab click the Preview icon. If the Recording Transaction message appears, click *Yes* to save the Job Invoice format for this invoice.

18. The invoice is displayed using the custom-designed Job Invoice format. (See figure 12–Y and compare with figure 12–R.)

FIGURE 12–Y
Invoice No. 1016—
Job Invoice Format

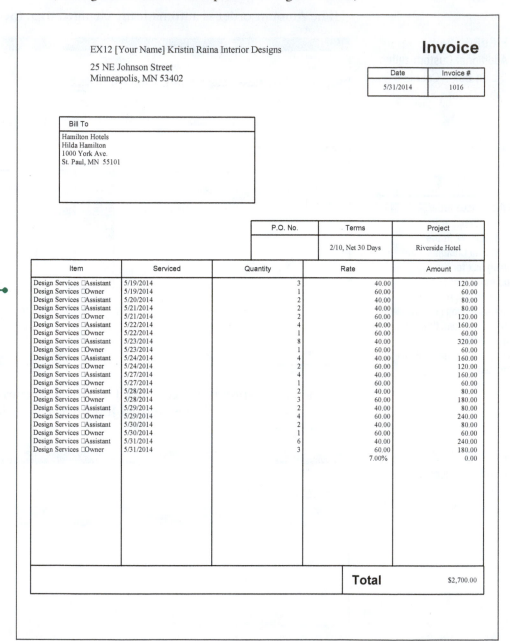

HINT

If the revised order does not appear on the printed invoice, go back to the Additional Customization for the Job Invoice, click the Columns tab, re-check the Description screen and print boxes, then uncheck them, and click OK.

EX12 [Your Name] Kristin Raina Interior Designs

Invoice

25 NE Johnson Street
Minneapolis, MN 53402

Date	Invoice #
5/31/2014	1016

Bill To
Hamilton Hotels
Hilda Hamilton
1000 York Ave.
St. Paul, MN 55101

P.O. No.	Terms	Project
	2/10, Net 30 Days	Riverside Hotel

Item	Serviced	Quantity	Rate	Amount
Design Services ☐Assistant	5/19/2014	3	40.00	120.00
Design Services ☐Owner	5/19/2014	1	60.00	60.00
Design Services ☐Assistant	5/20/2014	2	40.00	80.00
Design Services ☐Assistant	5/21/2014	2	40.00	80.00
Design Services ☐Owner	5/21/2014	2	60.00	120.00
Design Services ☐Assistant	5/22/2014	4	40.00	160.00
Design Services ☐Owner	5/22/2014	1	60.00	60.00
Design Services ☐Assistant	5/23/2014	8	40.00	320.00
Design Services ☐Owner	5/23/2014	1	60.00	60.00
Design Services ☐Assistant	5/24/2014	4	40.00	160.00
Design Services ☐Owner	5/24/2014	2	60.00	120.00
Design Services ☐Assistant	5/27/2014	4	40.00	160.00
Design Services ☐Owner	5/27/2014	1	60.00	60.00
Design Services ☐Assistant	5/28/2014	2	40.00	80.00
Design Services ☐Owner	5/28/2014	3	60.00	180.00
Design Services ☐Assistant	5/29/2014	2	40.00	80.00
Design Services ☐Owner	5/29/2014	4	60.00	240.00
Design Services ☐Assistant	5/30/2014	2	40.00	80.00
Design Services ☐Owner	5/30/2014	1	60.00	60.00
Design Services ☐Assistant	5/31/2014	6	40.00	240.00
Design Services ☐Owner	5/31/2014	3	60.00	180.00
			7.00%	0.00

Total	$2,700.00

19. Close the Preview and Create Invoices windows. If the Recording Transaction message appears, click *Yes*.

After creating this new format for an invoice, you could review the other invoices in the Create Invoices window that used Time Tracking and apply the new Job Invoice format to those invoices.

QuickBooks Letters

QuickBooks provides pre-formatted letters that may be used in certain business circumstances. You can use these letters as they are or customize them based on your personal preferences. You must have Microsoft Word installed on your computer to use this feature.

Kristin Raina wants to send a letter to Berger Bakery Company regarding the check that was returned as non-sufficient funds (NSF) with the April 30 bank statement. She will use QuickBooks Letters to do this.

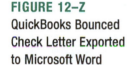

HINT

To refresh your memory, open the Create Invoices window and use the Find Previous button until you come to the transaction of 04/30/2014, Invoice # NSF1. This transaction was recorded when the bank reconciliation was prepared. Close the Create Invoices window.

To prepare a business letter using QuickBooks Letters—

1. Click Company and then click *Prepare Letters with Envelopes*.
2. At the Prepare Letters with Envelopes submenu, click *Customer Letters*.

   If you see the Find Letter Templates message box, click *Copy*.

3. At the Review and Edit Recipients page, click *Unmark All* to remove all check marks from the customer names.
4. Click *Berger Bakery Company* to select that customer, then click Next.
5. At the Choose a Letter Template page, click *Bounced check* and then click Next.
6. At the Enter a Name and Title page, enter the following data:

Name:	**[Your Name]**
Title:	**Assistant Accountant**

7. Click Next. Microsoft Word opens, and the bounced check letter is displayed with your company name and customer name included. (See figure 12–Z.)

FIGURE 12–Z
QuickBooks Bounced Check Letter Exported to Microsoft Word

8. Close Microsoft Word. Do not save the letter.
9. Close the Letters and Envelopes window.

Memorized Transactions

Many routine business activities are repeated, often at daily, weekly, and monthly intervals. QuickBooks allows you to *memorize* repetitive transactions. Once a transaction is memorized, you can recall the transaction at the appropriate time to record it, or you can have QuickBooks automatically record the transaction on certain dates.

An example of a transaction that could be memorized is the monthly rent Kristin Raina Interior Designs pays for its space.

On June 1, 2014, Kristin Raina Interior Designs is ready to pay the monthly rent of $800 to Nordic Realty. Since this is a routine bill, Kristin Raina decides to have you set it up as a memorized transaction. To memorize a transaction, you first enter the data for the transaction as a regular transaction, then, before saving it, you set it up as a memorized transaction.

To set up and memorize a transaction—
1. Click Banking and then click *Write Checks.*
2. Enter the following data for the rent expense, as you have previously learned:

Bank Account:	**1010 - Cash - Operating**
No.:	**14**
Date:	**06/01/2014**
Pay to the Order of:	**Nordic Realty**
Amount:	**800**
Account:	**6400 Rent Expense**

(See figure 12–AA.)

FIGURE 12–AA
Write Checks - Cash - Operating Window— Rent Expense

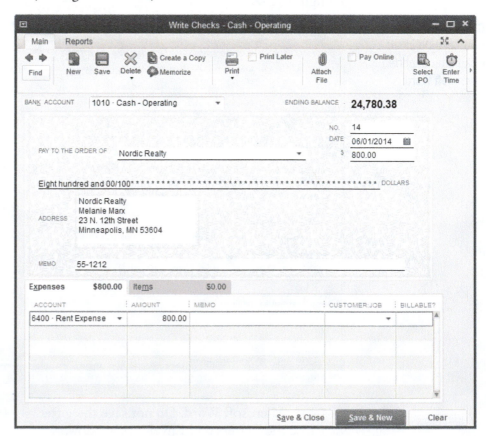

3. If the information is correct, click Edit on the main menu bar and then click *Memorize Check*. The Memorize Transaction dialog box appears.
4. In the *How Often* field, click *Monthly*.
5. In the *Next Date* field, choose *07/01/2014*. (See figure 12–BB.)

FIGURE 12–BB
Memorize Transaction
Dialog Box

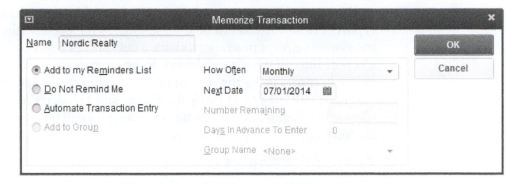

6. If the information is correct, click OK. The transaction is memorized.
7. At the Write Checks window, click Save & Close.

Assume it is now July 1, 2014, and time to pay the rent for July. You can recall the memorized transaction.

To recall a memorized transaction—
1. Click Lists and then click *Memorized Transaction List*. The Memorized Transaction List window appears. (See figure 12–CC.)

FIGURE 12–CC
Memorized Transaction
List Window

2. To recall the transaction, select *Nordic Realty* and then click *Enter Transaction*.

The Write Checks window appears with the correct date and the next check number automatically entered.

3. Do not record the transaction at this time. Close the Write Checks window. Click *No* at the warning.
4. Close the Memorized Transaction List window.

Customize the Appearance of Reports

As you have seen, QuickBooks contains a large variety of pre-established management reports, accounting reports, and financial statements, many of which you have displayed and printed throughout this text.

When you display a report, there is a row of buttons along the top of the report. These buttons can be used to change the presentation of the report, memorize settings in a report, share a customized report template, and export a report into an Excel spreadsheet. In prior chapters, you displayed and printed reports using the pre-established settings—except in chapter 4, where you modified the report using the Filters and Header/Footer tabs of the Customize Report button. In this chapter, you will use most of the remaining buttons along the top of the report.

Customize Report Button

The Customize Report button is used to adjust the appearance of the report. The Customize Report button moves you to the Modify Report dialog box, which consists of four tabs: Display, Filters, Header/Footer, and Fonts & Numbers. A report can be modified to add or delete fields of information displayed in a report (Display tab); to filter (select) which categories of information should be included in a report (Filters tab); to indicate which information should be displayed in the headers or footers (Header/Footer tab); and to indicate the fonts and formats of the numbers in the reports (Fonts & Numbers tab).

Modify Report—Display Tab

Open the *Account Listing* report by clicking Reports and then List. (See figure 12–DD.)

FIGURE 12–DD

Account Listing Report

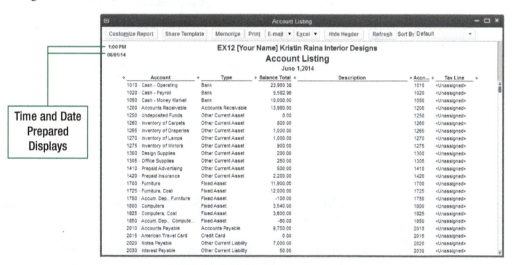

Time and Date
Prepared
Displays

To modify a report using the Display tab—

1. In the *Account Listing* report, click the Customize Report button on the top of the report. The Modify Report dialog box appears.

   In the Modify Report dialog box, the default tab is Display. The Display tab is used to indicate the fields of information that can be displayed in the columns in a report. Any column title that is checked is displayed.

When adding new accounts to the Chart of Accounts List, you did not use the *Description* field; therefore, this field of information is blank. In the *Tax Line* field, all accounts are marked unassigned. Since you do not need the information in these two fields, you can remove these fields from this report.

2. Remove the check marks from the field titles *Description* and *Tax Line*. (See figure 12–EE.)

FIGURE 12–EE
Modify Report: Account
Listing—Display Tab

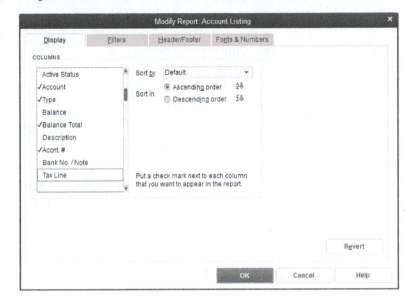

3. If the information is correct, click OK. The report is revised to exclude those two fields of information.

4. Widen the *Account* name and *Accnt. #* columns to display the entire account names and the Accnt. # title. (See figure 12–FF.)

FIGURE 12–FF
Account Listing—
Customized

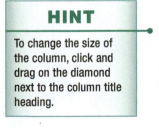

HINT

To change the size of the column, click and drag on the diamond next to the column title heading.

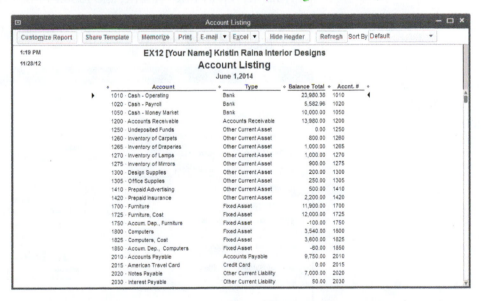

Modify Report—Header/Footer Tab

The Header/Footer tab is used to establish the presentation of the headers (including titles) and footers (including page numbers) to be displayed in a report. Two items in the heading of a report you can format are the Date Prepared and Time Prepared items. You may have noticed that when reports are displayed, by default, the date and time the report is prepared are always displayed in the upper left corner. The *Date Prepared* and *Time Prepared* fields are where you tell the software to display the current date and time on each report. By default this field is activated, which tells the software to display the current date and time as maintained by your computer.

If you print reports often, it is useful to have the date and time you print a report listed to avoid confusion among the many printouts. But there may be times you do not want the date or time displayed on the report. The printouts reproduced in this text did not include a current date or time because the *Date Prepared* and *Time Prepared* fields defaults were disabled.

To disable or change the format of the *Date Prepared* and *Time Prepared* fields and change a title in a report—

1. In the *Account Listing* report, click the Customize Report button on the top of the report. The Modify Report dialog box appears.
2. In the Modify Report dialog box, click the Header/Footer tab. The Header/Footer tab appears.
3. Click the Date Prepared drop-down list. You can use this drop-down list to change the format of the date.
4. To not display a date at all, remove the check mark from the box to the left of the *Date Prepared* field.
5. To not display the time at all, remove the check mark from the box to the left of the *Time Prepared* field.

In the Header/Footer dialog box, you can also change or remove the company name, report title, subtitle, and footer information of the report.

6. In the *Subtitle* field, delete the date provided and then key **June 30, 2014**. (See figure 12–GG.)

FIGURE 12–GG

Modify Report: Account Listing—Header/Footer Tab

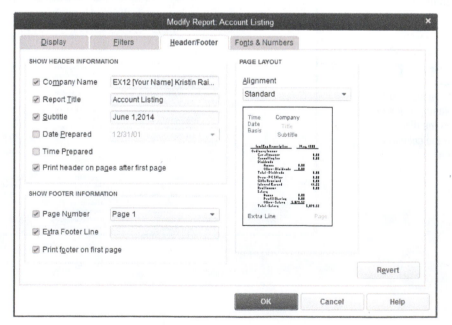

7. If the information is correct, click OK. You are returned to the *Account Listing* report. The Date Prepared and Time Prepared items have been removed, and the subtitle has been changed. (See figure 12–HH.)

FIGURE 12–HH
Account Listing Report—
Customized and Header
Modified

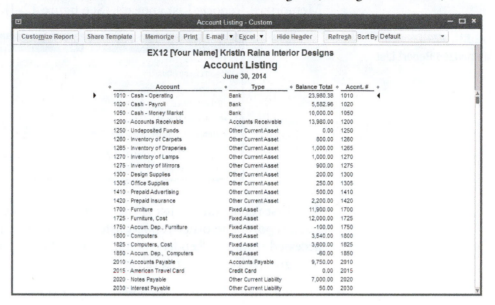

Memorize Button

The changes you just made to the report remain in place as long as the report is displayed. However, as soon as you close the report, those changes are lost. When you reopen the report, the original default settings are again displayed. Instead of having to change the settings each time you open the report, you can save the changes to a report by using the Memorize button.

To memorize the settings for a report—
1. With the *Account Listing* report open, the *Description* and *Tax Line* fields removed, and the heading format changed, click the Memorize button on the top of the report. The Memorize Report dialog box appears.
2. In the Memorize Report dialog box in the *Name* field, key **Account Listing - Custom**. (See figure 12–II.)

FIGURE 12–II
Memorize Report Dialog
Box

3. If the information is correct, click OK.
4. Close the *Account Listing* report.

Reopen the *Account Listing* report. Notice that all original default settings are used to display the report. Close the *Account Listing* report. If you wish to see the memorized report, you must open the memorized report.

To open a memorized report—

1. Click Reports and then click *Memorized Reports*.
2. At the Memorized Reports submenu, click *Memorized Report List*. The Memorized Reports List appears. (See figure 12–JJ.)

FIGURE 12–JJ
Memorized Report List

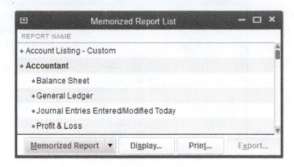

The first report on the list is the *Account Listing - Custom* memorized report. The other reports listed are the same reports that can be accessed from the Reports menu, but QuickBooks has organized them into groups for easy retrieval.

3. Double-click the report *Account Listing - Custom*.

The *Account Listing* report appears with all changes intact. If you make any changes to a memorized report, they will be stored only while the report is displayed. If you wish to memorize the new changes, you must click Memorize again. You will then be given a choice to replace the memorized report with the new changes or to create an additional memorized report.

4. Close the report and then close the Memorized Report List.

Collapse/Expand Button

Open the *Balance Sheet Standard* report for June 30, 2014. Notice that the Date Prepared and Time Prepared items appear in the report window. Remove the Date Prepared and Time Prepared items using the Customize Report button (Header/Footer tab) on the top of the report. Click the Print icon, then click Print Preview. Scroll down until the fixed assets section appears in the screen. (See figure 12-KK.)

FIGURE 12–KK
Balance Sheet Standard
Report—Expanded

Fixed Assets		
1700 · Furniture		
1725 · Furniture, Cost	12,000.00	
1750 · Accum. Dep., Furniture	-100.00	
Total 1700 · Furniture		11,900.00
1800 · Computers		
1825 · Computers, Cost	3,600.00	
1850 · Accum. Dep., Computers	-60.00	
Total 1800 · Computers		3,540.00
Total Fixed Assets		15,440.00

Recall that in the fixed assets section, the fixed asset account is the parent account and the related cost and accumulated depreciation accounts are subaccounts of the fixed asset. On the *Balance Sheet Standard* report, the amounts for each subaccount are indented to the left of the dollar value column, and the net of the two accounts is listed on the right in the dollar value column. This format is referred to as *expanded*. As an alternative, you can *collapse* the numbers, which then will display only the net amount for each fixed asset account in the dollar value column. Close the Print Preview. Click Cancel at the Print Reports dialog box.

To collapse and expand the numbers in a report—
1. In the *Balance Sheet Standard* report, click the Collapse button on the top of the report.
2. Click the Print icon, then click Print Preview. Scroll down until the fixed assets are again displayed. Only the net amount for each fixed asset is displayed. (See figure 12–LL.)

FIGURE 12–LL
Balance Sheet
Standard Report—
Collapsed

Fixed Assets	
1700 · Furniture	11,900.00
1800 · Computers	3,540.00
Total Fixed Assets	15,440.00

3. Close the Print Preview and click Cancel at the Print Reports dialog box. Notice the Collapse button on the top of the report changed into the Expand button.
4. To expand the numbers, click the Expand button on the top of the report. The report returns to the original presentation.

Share Template Button

HINT

You can also access customized report templates from the Reports menu. Click Reports and then click Contributed Reports. From the Contributed Reports menu, select any report category. You are moved to the Report Center – Contributed tab.

In addition to the Reports menu, QuickBooks includes a Report Center. The Report Center provides the same choices of reports that appear on the Reports menu. The Report Center also allows you to memorize reports, save in favorites, and view recent reports. An added feature to the Report Center is it offers a forum where customized report templates can be shared among QuickBooks users. The customized report templates are provided by both Intuit and QuickBooks users. To access the Report Center, click Reports and then click Report Center. The customized report templates are accessed on the Contributed tab in the Report Center. By default, the Intuit report templates are displayed. To access report templates prepared by other QuickBooks users, in the Report Center – on the Contributed tab – in the SORT BY field, choose *Community created* on the drop-down menu. When you customize any of your reports, the Share Template button in the report is activated, which then allows you to share your report with the community. Only the format of a report is shared, not the financial details. Close the Reports Center.

Excel Button

QuickBooks allows you to export the reports to a Microsoft Excel worksheet, where you can incorporate the report into other Excel files you may have or create a new worksheet. You can then use Excel to further customize the report. Excel must be installed on your computer to export the report.

To export a report to a new Microsoft Excel worksheet—
1. With the *Balance Sheet Standard* report (expanded) for June 30, 2014 displayed, click the Excel button on the top of the report.

   A drop-down list appears that offers two choices: Create New Worksheet and Update Existing Worksheet.

2. Choose Create New Worksheet. The Send Report to Excel dialog box appears. (See figure 12–MM.)

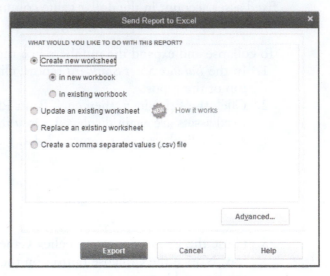

In this dialog box, you have the choice to Create a new worksheet in a new workbook or in an existing workbook, Update an existing worksheet, Replace an existing worksheet, or Create a comma separated values (.csv) file.

3. Click the Advanced button. The Advanced Excel Options dialog box appears. (See figure 12–NN.)

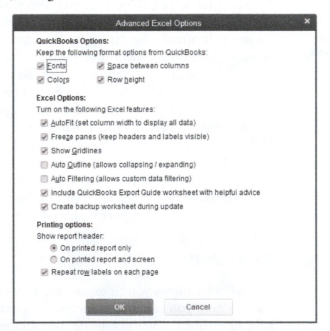

The Advanced Excel Options dialog box allows you the choice to carry over formatting from QuickBooks to Excel, or by removing the check marks, not carry over the formatting. It also provides choices to turn on Excel options and printing options. You can make these choices here in QuickBooks, or you can make them directly in the Excel worksheet after the report is exported into Excel.

4. At the Advanced Excel Options dialog box, click Cancel.
5. At the Send Report to Excel dialog box, with Create a new worksheet selected, click Export.

Excel is opened, and a worksheet is prepared with the *Balance Sheet Standard* report exported into the worksheet. (See figure 12–OO.)

FIGURE 12–OO

Balance Sheet Standard Report Exported to Microsoft Excel

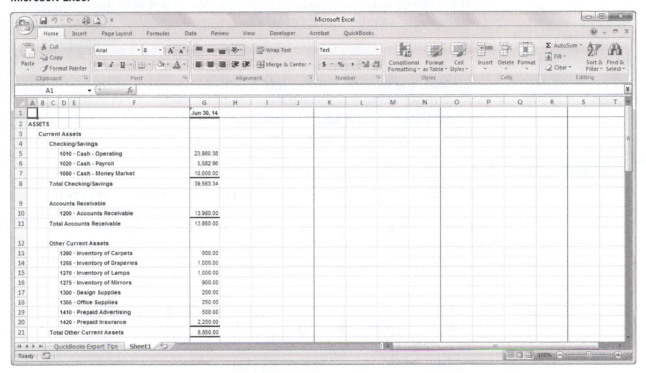

If you are familiar with Excel, you may revise the report according to your preferences.

6. Close Excel by clicking the Close (X) button.
7. At the Excel message Do you want to save the changes, click Yes. You are moved to the Save As dialog box.
8. At the Save As dialog box, choose the folder where you save your files, and in the filename field, key **EX12 [*Your Name*] QB-BS**, and then click Save. The Excel worksheet is saved and Excel is closed.

Assume at a later date, after more activities are recorded in QuickBooks, you wish to record the updated information in the Excel worksheet you just created and saved.

To export a report to an existing Microsoft Excel worksheet—
1. Open the Balance Sheet Standard report if necessary and use the date July 31, 2014.
2. Click the Excel button.
3. At the drop-down list, click *Update Existing Worksheet*.
4. At the Send Report to Excel dialog box, click the Browse button. You are moved to the Open Microsoft Excel File dialog box.

5. Select the folder where you save your files, select the file EX12 [Your Name] QB-BS, and then click Open. You are returned to the Send Report to Excel dialog box with the path filled in the first box in the *Select workbook* field.

6. In the second box in the *Select workbook* field, click the drop-down list and choose *Sheet1*, and then click Export.

An Export Report Alert message appears inquiring if you want the existing worksheet updated with new data. If you want to update the existing worksheet, click Yes. If you prefer to retain the existing worksheet intact, click No, which ends the process. Start over again using the steps above to export a report to a new worksheet.

7. At the Export Alert message, click Yes. Excel opens the existing worksheet updated with the new data. The only change in this worksheet is the date has been updated to July 31, 2014. Any previous changes in the formatting of the Excel worksheet would be retained.

8. Close Excel. Do not save the changes.

9. Close the Balance Sheet Standard report.

REPORTS: ──○ **Process Multiple Reports**

In each chapter as various reports were displayed, each report was opened one at a time. QuickBooks also allows you to open several reports at the same time. For example, Kristin Raina wishes to display the Trial Balance, Profit & Loss Standard, and Balance Sheet Standard reports for the period January 1 – June 30, 2014.

To display multiple reports—

1. Click Reports, then click Process Multiple Reports. The Process Multiple Reports window is displayed.

2. In the *Select Memorized Reports From* Field, click <All Reports>. (See figure 12–PP.)

FIGURE 12–PP
Process Multiple Reports Window

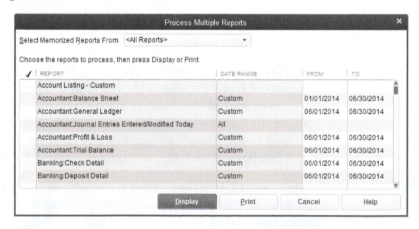

All reports are listed. In the From and To fields, the current month or the current fiscal year-to-date will be displayed. QuickBooks includes pre-established groups with which reports are classified. Custom groups can be created and reports can be memorized in a custom group. The name to the left of each report lists the pre-established group where QuickBooks locates the report. These classifications do not affect the display of the report.

3. Place a check mark to the left of Accountant: Balance Sheet, Accountant: Profit & Loss, and Accountant: Trial Balance.
4. In the From and To fields for each of these reports, choose 01/01/2014 to 06/30/2014, and then click Display. All three reports are displayed for the period of time indicated.
5. Close all the reports.

REPORTS:

Set Default Settings in Reports

You saw that each time you display a report, you can modify the display by using the Customize Report (Display, Filters, Header/Footer tabs) and Collapse/Expand buttons. You also saw that these changes are only temporary. To save the changes, you can memorize the report. Or, alternatively, you can change the default settings of *all* reports using the Preferences window. For example, you can change the Date Prepared and Time Prepared items default setting.

To turn off or change the Date Prepared and Time Prepared items default settings—

1. Click Edit and then click *Preferences*.
2. Along the left frame of the Preferences window, click the *Reports & Graphs* icon.
3. Click the Company Preferences tab. (See figure 12–QQ.)

FIGURE 12–QQ
Preferences Window—
Reports & Graphs—
Company Preferences
Tab

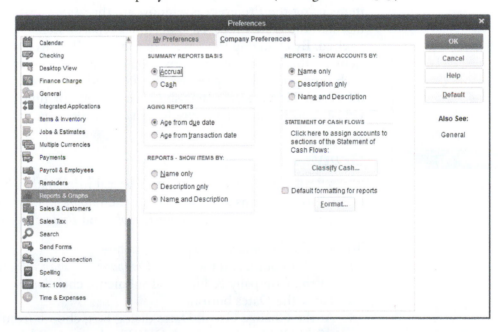

4. Click the Format button. The Report Format Preferences dialog box appears; it consists of two tabs: Header/Footer and Fonts & Numbers.
5. Click the Header/Footer tab, if necessary. You can change default formats or disable any field of information in all reports on this tab.
6. To disable the Date Prepared item, remove the check mark from the box to the left of the *Date Prepared* field.
7. To disable the Time Prepared item, remove the check mark from the box to the left of the *Time Prepared* field. (See figure 12–RR.)

FIGURE 12–RR

Report Format
Preferences Dialog
Box—Header/Footer
Tab—Date Prepared and
Time Prepared Fields
Disabled

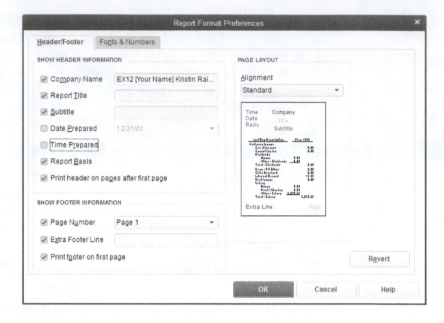

8. Click OK at the Report Format Preferences dialog box. You are returned to the Preferences window.
9. Click OK.

The steps you used to disable the Date Prepared and Time Prepared items using the Preferences window are the same steps taken when you disabled the Date Prepared and Time Prepared items while a report was opened. By changing the setting of the Date Prepared and Time Prepared items in the Preferences window, you changed the default setting. Now, each time you open any report, the date and time prepared are no longer displayed. However, if you wish to see the date or time prepared in an individual report, you can activate it for the specific report.

REPORTS: ─○ **Graphs**

QuickBooks allows you to display financial information in graph format. Graph presentations are available for the *Income and Expense, Net Worth, Accounts Receivable, Sales, Accounts Payable,* and *Budget vs. Actual* reports.

To view the Income and Expense graph—
1. Click Reports and then click *Company & Financial*.
2. At the Company & Financial submenu, click *Income & Expense Graph*.
3. Click the Dates button.
4. At the Change Graph Dates dialog box, choose from *01/01/2014* to *05/31/2014* and then click OK. The Income and Expense graphs for that period of time appear. (See figure 12–SS.)

FIGURE 12–SS
Income and Expense
Graph Window

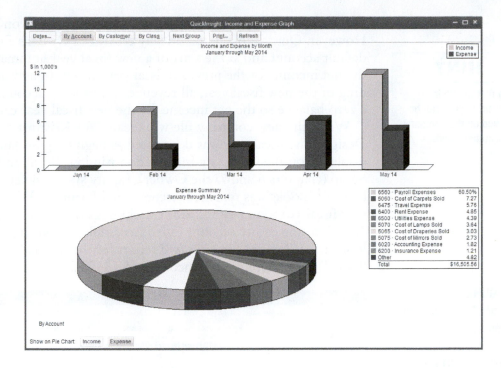

The column chart displays a comparative analysis of income and expenses. The pie chart, by default, displays the expense analysis.

5. To display the income analysis as a pie chart, click the Income button at the bottom of the window. The pie chart changes to display the income analysis.
6. Close the graph.

All graphs are displayed in the same manner. The graphs that are available can be accessed using the Reports menu on the main menu bar or the Reports button in the List windows.

Fiscal Year

Businesses must prepare their financial statements, including the Profit & Loss Report and the Balance Sheet Report, at least once per year. The year can be the calendar year or any other 12-month period. This 12-month financial reporting year for the company is called a **fiscal year**.

fiscal year The 12-month financial reporting year of the company. It can be the calendar year or any other 12-month period.

In QuickBooks, the start of the fiscal year is displayed on the Company Information page. Open the Company Information page for Kristin Raina Interior Designs and observe that the fiscal year for this company begins in January, which implies that the fiscal year for Kristin Raina is January 1 through December 31.

Fiscal Year Closing

In a manual accounting system, and most other computerized accounting software packages, the books are closed on fiscal year end. When the books are closed, the temporary accounts—usually revenues, expenses, and some equity accounts—are brought to a zero balance, and the net income for the year is transferred into a capital or retained earnings equity account for the next year. After the books are closed, pre-closing balances in the temporary accounts are no longer accessible.

QuickBooks does not require you to close the books on fiscal year end. However, QuickBooks automatically creates an Owner's Equity system default account and at the start of a new fiscal year automatically transfers the net income for the previous fiscal year into it. In addition, at the beginning of the new fiscal year, all revenue and expense accounts will begin with a zero balance so the net income for the new fiscal year can be accumulated.

When the new company file was created for Kristin Raina Interior Designs, the fiscal year was designated as beginning on January 1, which is displayed on the Company Information window. Recall in New Company Setup (chapters 6 and 7) the Owner's Equity system default account created by QuickBooks was renamed Accumulated Earnings. When you move to the new fiscal year, January 1, 2015, QuickBooks transfers the net income for 2014 into the equity account called Accumulated Earnings. For example, look at the *Profit & Loss Standard* report for the period 01/01/2014 to 06/30/2014. There is a net income of $8,339.82. (See figure 12–TT.)

HINT

The first month in your fiscal year can be viewed on the Company Information window.

FIGURE 12–TT

Profit & Loss Standard Report—
January 1, 2014–
June 30, 2014—
Net Income Section

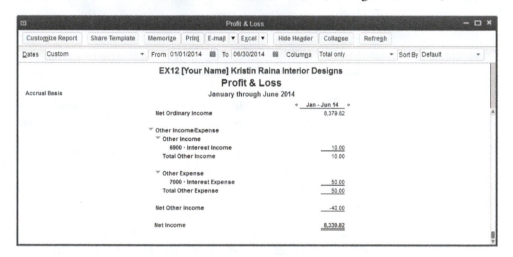

The net income is carried over to the *Balance Sheet Standard* report. (See figure 12-UU.)

FIGURE 12–UU

Balance Sheet Standard Report—
June 30, 2014—
Equity Section

2014 Net Income

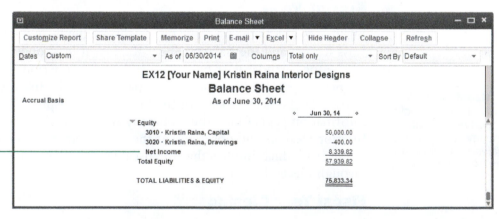

Assuming no other activity for the year 2014, look at the *Balance Sheet Standard* and *Profit & Loss Standard* reports for the first day of the new fiscal year, January 1, 2015. Notice there is no longer a line for net income, but the $8,339.82 has been transferred into the Accumulated Earnings account. (See figure 12–VV.)

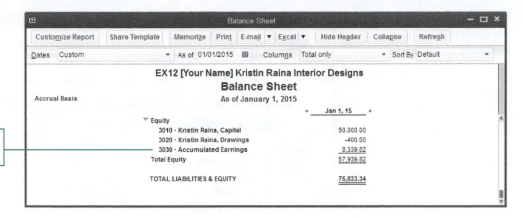

In addition, the revenue and expenses all begin with a zero balance for the start of the new fiscal year. Since there are no revenues or expenses on January 1, 2015, there is no income. (See figure 12–WW.)

FIGURE 12–WW

Profit & Loss Standard
Report—
January 1, 2015

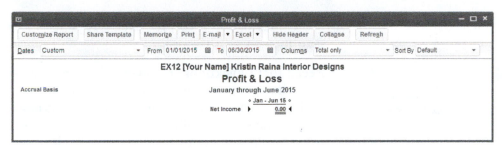

At this point, if you wanted to close the Drawings account, you would have to record an adjusting journal entry in the Make General Journal Entries window. Close all the windows.

Set Closing Date

Because QuickBooks does not actually close the books, you still have access to all records for prior years. As a precaution, however, you can protect the data for a fiscal year by restricting access to the records so no changes can be made after fiscal year end. This is accomplished when you set the closing date.

To set the closing date—
1. Click Company, then click Set Closing Date. The Preferences window appears on the Accounting page – Company Preferences.
2. Click the Set Date/Password button. The Set Closing Date and Password dialog box appears.
3. Read the page and then in the Closing Date field choose December 31, 2014.
4. In the Closing Date Password and Confirm Password, key **student** or a password of your choosing. (See figure 12–XX.)

FIGURE 12–XX
Set Closing Date and
Password Dialog Box

5. If the information is correct, click OK. The No Password Entered message appears.

HINT

See Appendix J on how
to set up passwords and
users.

Recall that QuickBooks company files can be password protected to limit the people who have access to the financial information. It is advisable to have a password in business, but passwords have not been used in the company files or exercise files in this book. This message refers to a password for the company file; it is not referring to the password just created for the Set Closing Date.

6. At the No Password Entered message, place a check mark in the box to the left of *Do not display this message in the future*, and then click No. You are returned to the Preferences window.
7. At the Preferences window, click OK.

If you need to make a change to a transaction in the company file after you set the closing date, you will receive a warning that the company file is closed and you would need to enter the password to save any changes.

To enter updated information in a company file that is closed—
1. Open the Journal Report and enter the dates from 01/01/2014 to 12/31/14.
2. Double-click the transaction for Minneapolis Electric and Gas of 02/02/2014. The transaction appears in the Enter Bills window.
3. Change the amount to $500 and then click Save & Close.
4. At the Recording Transaction message, click Yes.

   The QuickBooks message appears informing you that you are modifying a transaction in a closed accounting period. If you still wish to record the transaction, you must enter the closing date password (student).

5. Do not save the change. Click Cancel at the QuickBooks message and then close the Enter Bills window.
6. Click No at the Recording Transaction message.
7. Close the Journal Report.

New Fiscal Year

Because in QuickBooks the accounting records aren't closed, all the activities previously recorded will be retained in the company files. If you wish to continue with the company file in the new fiscal year, but do not want to carry forward the prior fiscal year activities into the new fiscal year, QuickBooks provides a utility called Condense Data. When you condense the data in a company file, the prior year activities are removed from the company file but all preferences previously established remain intact.

As part of the process, QuickBooks will make a copy of the company file before the company file is condensed. Note that this process is normally done in the year after the fiscal year end. The company file for Kristin Raina Interior Designs is 2014. If you attempt to do this process before January 1, 2015, it may not be completed.

To Condense the company file to prepare for the new fiscal year—
1. Click File, then click Utilities.
2. At the Utilities menu, click Condense Data. The Condense Data dialog box appears with the What transactions do you want to remove? page displayed.
3. Choose the Transactions before a specific date option and choose January 1, 2015 (See figure 12–YY.)

FIGURE 12–YY
Condense Data Dialog Box

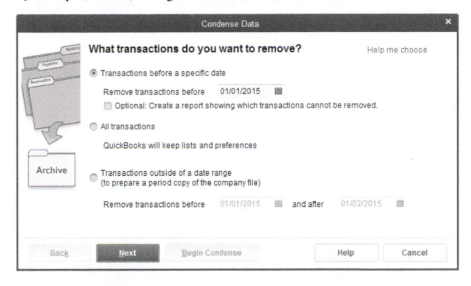

4. If the information is correct, click Next.
5. At the How Should Transactions Be Summarized page, accept the default Create one summary journal entry (recommended), and then click Next.
6. At the How Should Inventory Be Condensed? page, accept the default Summarize inventory transactions (recommended), and then click Next.
7. At the Do You Want To Remove The Following Transactions page, accept the defaults, and then click Next.
8. At the Do You Want To Remove Unused List Entries? page, accept the defaults, and then click Next.
9. At the Begin Condense page, click Begin Condense. It will take several minutes and then you will see a QuickBooks Information message. Note that QuickBooks makes a copy of the company file. (See figure 12–ZZ.)

FIGURE 12–ZZ
QuickBooks Information
Window – Condense
Complete

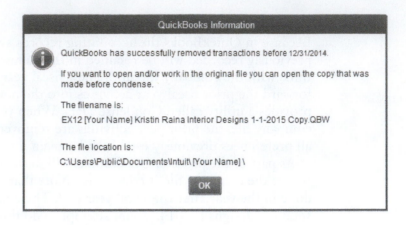

10. At the QuickBooks Information message, click OK.

The effect of condensing the file is similar to the closing entries in a manual accounting system. A closing journal entry is recorded in the general journal. Balances in asset, liability, and equity accounts are carried forward into the new fiscal year in the general ledger. Balances in revenue and expense accounts are closed and these accounts begin with a zero balance in the general ledger in the new fiscal year. The company file is now ready for the activities for the new fiscal year.

Chapter Review and Assessment

Procedure Review

To display the home page if it is not displayed—
1. Click Company.
2. Click Home Page.

To access a window using the icons on the home page—
1. On the home page, click the icon. Either a window opens or a drop-down list appears.
2. If the drop-down list appears, make a choice on the list, and then a window will open.

To enable a preference to customize the home page—
1. Click Edit, then click Preferences.
2. Along the left frame of the Preferences window, click the *Desktop View* icon.
3. Click the Company Preferences tab.
4. In the RELATED PREFERENCES section, click the item marked *off* and you are moved to the window to enable the preference. When you enable a preference the icon(s) will appear on the home page.

To view the left icon bar—
1. Click View. On the View drop-down menu, when a check mark is to the left of Left Icon Bar, the left icon bar is enabled. If there is no check mark, the left icon bar is disabled.
2. Click Left Icon Bar if there is no check mark.

To view the top icon bar—
1. Click View. On the View drop-down menu, when a check mark is to the left of Top Icon Bar, the top icon bar is enabled. If there is no check mark, the top icon bar is disabled.
2. Click Top Icon Bar if there is no check mark. If the left icon bar had been displayed, it is removed when the top icon bar is displayed.

(Only one icon bar can be displayed.)

To add an icon to an icon bar—
1. Click View, then click Customize Icon Bar. The Customize Icon Bar window appears.
2. In the Customize Icon Bar window, click the Add button. The Add Icon Bar Item window appears.
3. At the Add Icon Bar Item window, scroll through the list until you see the icon you wish to add.
4. Click the icon you wish to add.
5. Click OK at the Add Icon Bar Item window, and then click OK at the Customize Icon Bar window to save the changes.

To edit an icon on an icon bar—
1. Click View, then click Customize Icon Bar. The Customize Icon Bar window appears.
2. In the Customize Icon Bar window, in the ICON BAR CONTENT field, scroll through the list and click once on the icon you wish to edit to highlight it.
3. Click Edit.
4. At the Edit Icon Bar Item window, in the *Label* field, delete the name, and key the edited name.
5. Click OK in the Edit Icon Bar window and then click OK in the Customize Icon Bar window. In the Content section of the left icon bar, the icon text is updated to the edited name.

To remove an icon from an icon bar—
1. Click View, then click Customize Icon Bar. The Customize Icon Bar window appears.
2. In the Customize Icon Bar window, in the ICON BAR CONTENT field, scroll through the list and click once on the icon you wish to delete to highlight it.
3. Click Delete. The icon is removed from the Icon bar.
4. Click OK to save the changes.

To change to flat or hierarchical view in the Chart of Accounts List window—
1. In the Chart of Accounts List window, click the Account button. By default, *Hierarchical View* is checked.
2. Click *Flat View*. The subaccounts are no longer indented but are left-aligned in the window.
3. Click the Account button and then click *Hierarchical View*. The presentation changes to indent the subaccounts.
4. Close the window.

To change the default setting of subaccounts—
1. Click Edit and then click *Preferences*.
2. Along the left frame of the Preferences window, click the *Accounting* icon.
3. Click Company Preferences.
4. In the *ACCOUNTS* section, place a check mark in the box next to *Show lowest subaccount only*.
5. Click OK.

To merge two accounts—
1. Open the Chart of Accounts List.
2. Select the account you wish to merge but do not open it.
3. Click the Account button, then click Edit Account. The Edit Account window opens.
4. In the account number field, change the number to the desired account to merge, and then click Save and Close. A Merge message appears informing you the account is already in use and inquiring if you wish to merge the accounts.

5. At the Merge message, click Yes. The two accounts are merged. All information in QuickBooks is updated accordingly.
6. Close the Chart of Account List.

To create a custom field—
1. Open a Center and choose a customer or vendor by double-clicking on the name. The Edit window appears.
2. Click the Additional Information tab.
3. On the Additional Information tab, in the CUSTOM FIELDS section, click the Define Fields button. The Set up Custom Fields for Names window appears.
4. On the first line in the Label column, key the name of the new field you wish to create.
5. In the Use for: field, place a check mark in the appropriate column.
6. If the information is correct, click OK.
7. At the Information message, place a check mark in the box to the left of *Do not display this message in the future* and click OK. The new field text box is now displayed in the CUSTOM FIELDS section on the Additional Info tab.
8. In the new field text box, key the appropriate information.
9. If the information is correct, click OK to save the information.
10. Edit each customer or vendor and key in the information in the new field text box on the Additional Info tab.
11. Close the Center.

To display customers or vendors in the Customer or Vendor Center for the custom field—
1. Open the Center.
2. Click the Search icon. The Custom Filter dialog box appears.
3. In the Filter dialog box, click or key the appropriate information.
4. Click Go. The Center is updated to display only the customers or vendors that have been identified for the custom field on the Additional Information tab.

To customize the Create Invoices window and a printed invoice—
1. With the Create Invoices window open, on the Formatting tab, click *Manage Templates.*
2. In the SELECT TEMPLATE section, make sure the Service Invoice is selected and then click the Copy button.
3. In the PREVIEW section, at the *Template Name* field, key **Job Invoice**.
4. Click OK.
5. At the Basic Customization dialog box, click *Additional Customization.*
6. At the Additional Customization dialog box, click the Columns tab.
7. Add or delete check marks for the different fields of information.
8. Change the order of the fields, if necessary.
9. Click OK at the Additional Customization and Basic Customization dialog boxes.
10. In the Create Invoices window, click Save & Close.

To prepare a business letter using QuickBooks Letters—
1. Click Company and then click *Prepare Letters with Envelopes.*
2. At the Prepare Letters with Envelopes submenu, click *Customer Letters.* If you see the Find Letter Templates message box, click *Copy.*
3. At the Review and Edit Recipients page, click *Unmark All* to remove all check marks from the customer names.
4. Select the desired name and then click Next.
5. At the Choose a Letter Template page, select a letter and then click Next.
6. At the Enter a Name and Title page, enter the appropriate data.
7. If the information is correct, click Next. Microsoft Word opens, and the chosen letter is displayed with your company name and customer name included.
8. Save and print the letter and then close Microsoft Word.

To set up and memorize a transaction—
1. Record a transaction as usual in an Activity window, but do not click Save.
2. Click Edit and then click *Memorize Check.*
3. In the *How Often* field, click *Monthly.*
4. In the *Next Date* field, choose the date to start the memorized transaction.
5. Click OK. The transaction is memorized.
6. At the Activity window, click Save & Close.

To recall a memorized transaction—
1. Click Lists and then click *Memorized Transaction List.*
2. At the Memorized Transaction List window, select the transaction you wish to record and then click *Enter Transaction.*
3. The Activity window appears with the correct date and other information automatically entered. You may make changes if necessary.
4. If you wish to record the transaction, click Save & Close.
5. Close the Memorized Transaction List window.

To modify a report using the Display tab—
1. Open the report and then click the Customize Report button on the top of the report.
2. In the Modify Report dialog box, the default tab is Display.
3. Place or remove the check marks from the field titles you wish to add or hide.
4. Click OK at the Modify Report dialog box.

To disable or change the format of the *Date Prepared* and *Time Prepared* fields and change a subtitle in a report—
1. Open the report and then click the Customize Report button on the top of the report.
2. In the Modify Report dialog box, click the Header/Footer tab.
3. Remove the check mark from the box to the left of the *Date Prepared* and *Time Prepared* fields.

4. In the *Subtitle* field, delete the date provided and then key the new subtitle.
5. Click OK at the Modify Report dialog box.

To memorize the settings for a report—
1. Open the report and make the desired changes.
2. Click the Memorize button on the top of the report.
3. At the Memorize Report dialog box, key the new report name.
4. Click OK.

To open a memorized report—
1. Click Reports and then click *Memorized Reports.*
2. At the Memorized Reports submenu, click *Memorized Report List.* The Memorized Reports List appears.
3. In the Memorized Reports List, double-click the desired report. The memorized report appears.

To collapse and expand the numbers in a report—
1. Open the report and then click the Collapse button on the top of the report. Any account that has subaccounts is collapsed into one amount. The changes appear on the printed report.
2. To expand the numbers, click the Expand button on the top of the report. The report returns to the original presentation.

To export a report to a new Microsoft Excel worksheet—
1. Open the report and then click the Excel button on the top of the report. A drop-down list appears.
2. Choose *Create new worksheet.* The Send Report to Excel dialog box appears.
3. At the Send Report to Excel dialog box, click the Advanced button if you wish to review any Excel options.
4. At the Send Report to Excel dialog box, with Create a new worksheet selected, click Export. Excel is opened, and a worksheet is prepared using the report.
5. If you are familiar with Excel, you may revise the report according to your preferences.
6. Close Excel by clicking the Close (X) button.
7. At the Excel message Do you want to save the changes, click Yes. You are moved to the Save As dialog box.
8. At the Save As dialog box, choose the folder where you save your files, and in the filename field, key in the file name, and then click Save. The Excel worksheet is saved and Excel is closed.

To export a report to an existing Microsoft Excel worksheet—
1. Open the report and enter the correct dates.
2. Click the Excel button. A drop-down list appears.
3. Choose *Update Existing Worksheet.* The Send Report to Excel dialog box appears.
4. At the Send Report to Excel dialog box, with Update Existing Worksheet selected, click the Browse button. You are moved to the Open Microsoft Excel File dialog box.

5. Select the folder where you save your files, select the file, and then click Open. You are returned to the Send Report to Excel dialog box with the path filled in the first box in the *Select workbook* field.

6. In the second box in the *Select workbook* field, choose *Sheet1* from the drop-down list, and then click Export.

7. At the Export Alert message, click Yes. Excel opens the existing worksheet updated with the new data. Any previous changes in the formatting of the Excel worksheet would be retained.

8. Close Excel and then close the report.

To display multiple reports—

1. Click Reports, then click Process Multiple Reports. The Process Multiple Reports window is displayed.

2. In the *Select Memorized Reports From* field, click <All Reports>.

3. Place a check mark to the left of the reports you wish to view.

4. In the From and To fields for each of these reports, choose the appropriate dates and then click Display. All reports are displayed for the period of time indicated.

5. Close all the reports.

To disable or change the Date Prepared and Time Prepared items default settings—

1. Click Edit and then click *Preferences*.

2. Along the left frame of the Preferences window, click the *Reports & Graphs* icon.

3. Click the Company Preferences tab.

4. Click the Format button.

5. Click the Header/Footer tab. You can change the default formats or disable any field of information for all reports in this dialog box.

6. To disable the Date Prepared item, remove the check mark from the box to the left of the *Date Prepared* field.

7. To disable the Time Prepared item, remove the check mark from the box to the left of the *Time Prepared* field.

8. Click OK at the Report Format Preferences dialog box. You are returned to the Preferences window.

9. Click OK.

To view a graph—

1. Use the Reports menu from the main menu bar, or the Reports button in a List window, to choose a graph.

2. Click the Dates button.

3. Choose the dates and then click OK. The graph for that period of time is displayed.

4. At the Income and Expense graph, to display the income as a pie chart, click the Income button. The pie chart changes to display the income analysis.

5. Close the graph.

To set the closing date—

1. Click Company, then click Set Closing Date. The Preferences window appears on the Accounting page – Company Preferences.
2. Click the Set Date/Password button. The Set Closing Date and Password dialog box appears.
3. Read the page, and then in the Closing Date field, choose the closing date.
4. In the Closing Date Password and Confirm Password, key a password of your choosing.
5. If the information is correct, click OK. The No Password Entered message appears.
6. At the No Password Entered message, place a check mark in the box to the left of *Do not display this message in the future*, and then click No. You are returned to the Preferences window.
7. At the Preferences window, click OK.

To enter updated information in a company file that is closed—

1. Open the Journal Report and enter the appropriate dates.
2. Double-click the transaction. The transaction appears in the appropriate window.
3. Change the information and then click Save & Close.
4. At the Recording Transaction message, click Yes.
5. The QuickBooks message appears informing you that you are modifying a transaction in a closed accounting period. If you still wish to record the transaction, you must enter the closing date password.
6. Click OK or Cancel.
7. Close the Activity window and click *No* at the Recording Transaction message.
8. Close the report.

To Condense the company file to prepare for the new fiscal year—

1. Click File, then click Utilities.
2. At the Utilities menu, click Condense Data. The Condense Data dialog box appears with the What transactions do you want to remove? page displayed.
3. Choose the Transactions before a specific date option and click the date of the new fiscal year, and then click Next.
4. At the How Should Transactions Be Summarized page, accept the default Create one summary journal entry (recommended), and then click Next.
5. At the How Should Inventory Be Condensed? page, accept the default Summarize inventory transactions (recommended), and then click Next.
6. At the Do You Want To Remove The Following Transactions page, accept the defaults, and then click Next.
7. At the Do You Want To Remove Unused List Entries? page, accept the defaults, and then click Next.
8. At the Begin Condense page, click Begin Condense. It will take several minutes and then you will see a QuickBooks Information message. Note that QuickBooks made a copy of the company file.
9. At the QuickBooks Information message, click OK.

Key Concepts

Select the letter of the item that best matches each definition.

a. Excel button
b. Additional Customization dialog box—Columns tab
c. Header/Footer tab
d. Edit menu - Memorize Check
e. Accumulated Earnings
f. Display tab
g. Memorize button on the top of the report
h. Prepare Letters with Envelopes
i. Manage Templates icon
j. Collapse/Expand button

_____ 1. Used to choose fields of information and order of appearance in the Create Invoices window and on a printed invoice.

_____ 2. Command choice to use pre-formatted business letters available in QuickBooks.

_____ 3. Button used to save the changes made to the settings in a report.

_____ 4. Used to customize a pre-established invoice in QuickBooks.

_____ 5. Buttons used to list all numbers in a report in one column or to separate the subaccounts into the left column of a report.

_____ 6. Command used to save a routine transaction so you can recall it for later use.

_____ 7. Tab used to add or delete the fields of information displayed in each column in a report.

_____ 8. Account created and used by QuickBooks at the start of the new fiscal year to automatically transfer the net income of the previous year into it.

_____ 9. Button used to export a report into a spreadsheet.

_____ 10. Tab used to establish the headers and footers to be displayed in a report.

Procedure Check

1. You change the columns of information displayed in the Customer Contact List every time you display it. What steps could you take to eliminate this repetitive formatting each time you view the List?

2. The *Date Prepared* field has been disabled on all reports. How can you activate this feature on all reports?

3. You wish to display a graph representing the sales for the first quarter of the year. How can you use QuickBooks to accomplish this?

4. In the Activities windows, when you choose an account with a subaccount, only the parent account is displayed in the account field. How can you modify this display of account names?

5. On the first of each month, you write a check for $100 for the liability insurance premium. How can you use QuickBooks to simplify this monthly process?

6. Your manager is new to QuickBooks and has just used the Time Tracking feature. However, when the data was transferred into the Create Invoices window, he found it difficult to read the information in the window. Explain to the manager how QuickBooks can be used to display the information in a more meaningful presentation.

Case Problems

Case Problem 1

Lynn's Music Studio recorded the income earned on the Highland Schools jobs for the month of July 2014 in the Create Invoices window, but Lynn Garcia has not yet sent the invoices to the school. It is now August 1, 2014, and she is ready to send the invoices for the first half of July but wishes to present the detail in a more desirable format. You have been requested to prepare a job invoice format and print Invoices Nos. 2020, 2021, and 2022.

1. Open the company file CH12 Lynn's Music Studio.QBW.
2. Make a backup copy of the company file LMS12 [*Your Name*] Lynn's Music Studio.
3. Restore the backup copy of the company file. In both the Open Backup Copy and Save Company File as windows, use the file name LMS12 [*Your Name*] Lynn's Music Studio.
4. Change the company name to **LMS12 [*Your Name*] Lynn's Music Studio**.
5. Open the Create Invoices window and display Invoice No. 2020.
6. Create a Job Invoice, based on the Intuit Service Invoice, using the following information:
   a. Save the new invoice as Job Invoice.
   b. Delete the *Description* column.
   c. Add the *Item* column (Print).
   d. Add the *Service Date* column.
   e. Put the invoice columns in the following order:

Item:	1
Service Date:	2
Quantity:	3
Rate:	4
Amount:	5

7. Print Invoice No. 2020 and then save the invoice.
8. Open Invoice No. 2021, change it to the Job Invoice format, print the invoice, and save the change.
9. Open Invoice No. 2022, change it to the Job Invoice format, print the invoice, and save the change.

Case Problem 2

Olivia's Web Solutions recorded the income earned on the Thrifty Stores jobs for the month of September 2014 in the Create Invoices window, but Olivia Chen has not yet sent the invoices to the store. It is now October 1, 2014, and she is ready to send the invoices for the first half of September but wishes to present the detail in a more desirable format. You have been requested to prepare a job invoice format and print Invoice Nos. 1017, 1018, and 1019.

1. Open the company file CH12 Olivia's Web Solutions.QBW.
2. Make a backup copy of the company file OWS12 [*Your Name*] Olivia's Web Solutions.
3. Restore the backup copy of the company file. In both the Open Backup Copy and Save Company File as windows, use the file name OWS12 [*Your Name*] Olivia's Web Solutions.
4. Change the company name to **OWS12 [*Your Name*] Olivia's Web Solutions**.
5. Open the Create Invoices window and display Invoice No. 1017.
6. Create a Job Invoice, based on the Intuit Service Invoice, using the following information:
   a. Save the new invoice as Job Invoice.
   b. Delete the *Description* column.
   c. Add the *Item* column (Print).
   d. Add the *Service Date* column.
   e. Put the invoice columns in the following order:

Item:	1
Service Date:	2
Quantity:	3
Rate:	4
Amount:	5

7. Print Invoice No. 1017 and then save the invoice.
8. Open Invoice No. 1018, change it to the Job Invoice format, print the invoice, and save the change.
9. Open Invoice No. 1019, change it to the Job Invoice format, print the invoice, and save the change.

APPENDICES

APPENDIX A

Open or Restore a Company File

There is a significant difference between the option to Open a company file and the option to Restore a backup copy of a company file. The following summarizes and compares opening a company file to restoring (opening a backup copy) of a company file. Compare figure 1–F with figure 1–N, and compare figure 1–G with figure 1–O below, which are the figures and figure numbers illustrated in chapter 1. When you *open* a company file, on the Open or Restore Company window, you choose the option *Open a company file* (see figure 1–F). This window is followed by the *Open a Company* dialog box. All the files in this dialog box have the extension .QBW. (See figure 1–G.)

Choosing the *Open a company file* option:

FIGURE 1–F

Open or Restore
Company Window—
Open a company file
Selected

Open a
company file

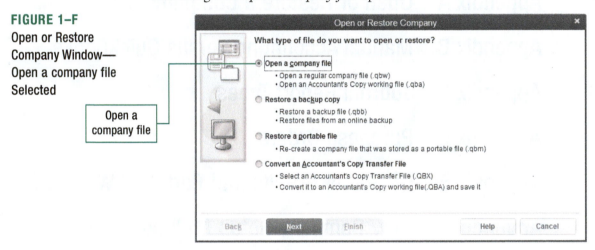

is followed by the *Open a Company* dialog box:

FIGURE 1–G

Open a Company Dialog Box

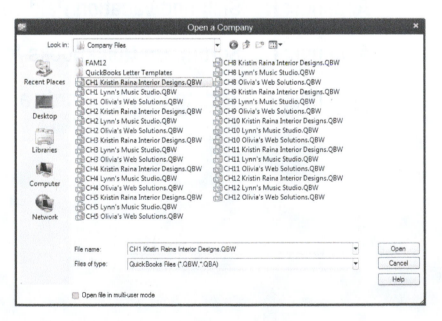

Notice all company files have the extension .QBW.

Conversely, when you want to open a backup copy of a file, you must *restore* the file. On the Open or Restore Company window, you choose the option *Restore a backup copy* (see figure 1–N). This window is followed by the *Open Backup Copy* dialog box. All the files in this dialog box have the extension .QBB. (See figure 1–O.)

You must use the *restore* command to open a *backup* copy of a file. If you do not see your backup copy file listed, you may be in the wrong dialog box. Go back to the Open or Restore Company window and be sure you selected the Restore a backup copy choice.

Choosing the *Restore a backup copy* option:

FIGURE 1–N
Open or Restore
Company Window—
Restore a backup copy
Selected

Restore a
backup copy

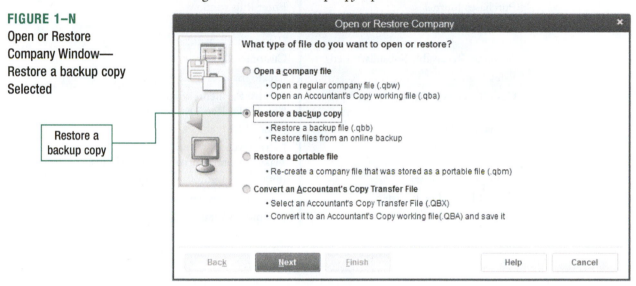

is followed by the *Open Backup Copy* dialog box:

FIGURE 1–O
Open Backup Copy
Dialog Box

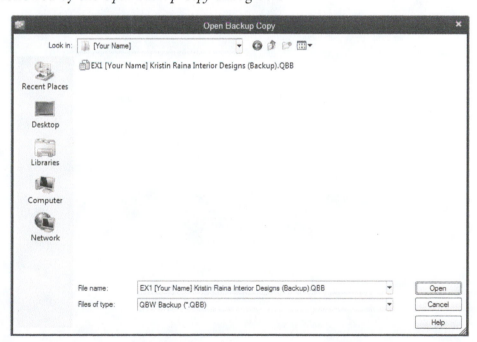

Notice all company files have the extension .QBB.

Manual Accounting versus QuickBooks

A manual accounting system uses journals and ledgers. QuickBooks uses Lists/Centers windows and reports. The following table summarizes and compares the journals and ledgers used in a manual accounting system to the Lists/Centers windows and reports used in QuickBooks as explained in the chapters.

Manual Accounting System	QuickBooks
Accounts Payable Subsidiary Ledger	Vendor Center
Purchases Journal	Enter Bills window
Cash Payments Journal	Pay Bills window Write Checks window
Accounts Receivable Subsidiary Ledger	Customer Center
Sales Journal	Create Invoices window
Cash Receipts Journal	Receive Payments window Enter Sales Receipts window
General Ledger	General Ledger Report
General Journal	Journal Report Make General Journal Entries window
Inventory Subsidiary Ledger	Item List (inventory part items)
Payroll Journal or Register	Pay Employees windows
Jobs Subsidiary Ledger	Customer Center

Journal Report Types

In a Journal report, the Type column indicates the window in which the activity was recorded. The System Default Account indicates the account that QuickBooks automatically uses to record activity. The following table summarizes the Activity window and system default accounts for each journal entry type.

Type	Activity Window	System Default Account	
		Debit	Credit
Bill	Enter Bills		Accounts Payable
Credit	Enter Bills	Accounts Payable	
Bill Pmt — Check	Pay Bills	Accounts Payable	Cash
Check	Write Checks		Cash
Invoice	Create Invoices	Accounts Receivable	
Payment	Receive Payments	Undeposited Funds	Accounts Receivable
Sales Receipt	Enter Sales Receipts	Undeposited Funds	
Deposit	Make Deposits	Cash	Undeposited Funds
General Journal	Make General Journal Entries		
Inventory Adjust	Adjust Quantity/Value on Hand		
Sales Tax Payment	Pay Sales Tax	Sales Tax Payable	Cash
Paycheck	Pay Employees	Salaries and Wages Expense Payroll Tax Expenses	Payroll Liabilities Cash — Payroll
Liability Check	Pay Payroll Liabilities	Payroll Liabilities	Cash —Payroll
Transfer	Transfer Funds Between Accounts		
Credit Card Charge	Enter Credit Card Charges		Credit Card Liability
Discount	Receive Payments	Sales Discount or Bad Debt	Accounts Receivable

Purchase Orders

Businesses commonly use a purchase order document as part of the inventory process. The Purchase Order (PO) initiates an order from a supplier of goods and services and, at the same time, gives the purchasing company a record of goods on order but not yet received. In QuickBooks, the information contained in the PO documents (items ordered, quantity, cost, vendor name, and so on) serves as the basis for completing the Receive Items and Enter Bill or Write Checks windows when goods are received.

HINT

Company name is changed to KR Interior Designs to fit the name in the PO ship to box.

Appendix Problem

Before you begin, open the company file APP D Kristin Raina Interior Designs.QBW. Make a backup copy of the file, name it **EXD [*Your Name*] Kristin Raina Interior Designs** and then restore the file. Finally, change the company name to **EXD [*Your Name*] KR Interior Designs**.

ACTIVITIES:

Creating a Purchase Order for Inventory items

On April 1, 2014, Kristin Raina orders 10 carpets from Bell Carpet Design as the Stock Status by Item report indicates that the supply of carpets is below the reorder point. The Purchase Order No. is 1.

To create a purchase order—
1. Click Vendors and then click *Create Purchase Orders*.
2. At the VENDOR drop-down list, click *Bell Carpet Design*.
3. At the *Date* field, choose *04/01/2014*.
4. At the P.O. No. field, key **1**.
5. Complete the balance of the window in the same manner as you would in the Receive Items and Enter Bill window. Note that the Ship to field contains the shipping address for Kristin Raina. (See figure D–1.)

FIGURE D–1
Create Purchase Orders Window-Completed

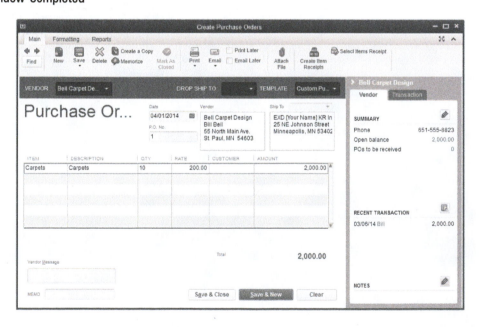

6. If the information is correct, click Save & Close.

The creation of a purchase order is not a transaction that changes general ledger posting accounts. No balances are affected. Kristin Raina can track open purchase orders through the Open Purchase Orders report contained in the Purchases submenu of the Reports menu. (See figure D–2.)

FIGURE D–2
Open Purchase Orders Report

Recording Receipt of Inventory on Purchase Order

On April 5, 2014, Kristin Raina receives the carpets ordered on April 1, from Bell Carpet Design, their invoice 12-5791. The bill is due May 5, 2014.

To record a purchase and receipt of inventory on order—

1. Click Vendors and then click *Receive Items and Enter Bill.*
2. At the VENDOR drop-down list, click *Bell Carpet Design.*

A window appears alerting you that open purchase orders exist for this vendor and asking Do you want to receive against one or more of these orders?

3. At the message, click Yes. The Open Purchase Orders window appears.
4. Choose the open purchase order by clicking in the ✓ column. (See Figure D–3.)

> **HINT**
>
> You can also access the Open Purchase Orders window by clicking the Select PO button in the Receive Items and Enter Bill window.

FIGURE D–3
Open Purchase Orders Window—Open Purchase Order Selected

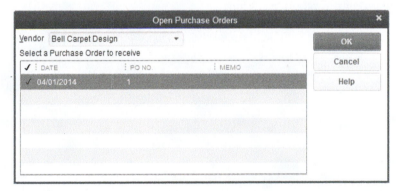

5. Click OK. The information from the Purchase Order window will fill the appropriate fields in the Enter Bills window. (See figure D–4.)

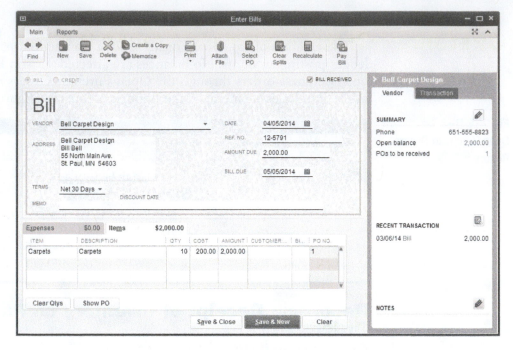

6. Complete the *DATE*, *REF. NO.*, *BILL DUE*, and *TERMS* fields in the same way as illustrated in Chapter 5.
7. If the information is correct, click Save & Close.

The same procedure can be employed if the purchase is recorded in the Write Checks window.

Customer Credits and Bad Debt Write-offs

In Chapters 3 and 5, you learned to record sales of services and inventory on account in the Create Invoices window. This transaction created an accounts receivable from the customer, which you tracked through the Customer Center and Customer & Receivable reports. Collection of receivables was recorded in the Receive Payments window.

In Appendix E you will record a credit memo for a customer return of inventory in the Create Credit Memos/Refunds window. The credit memo will reduce the balance owed by the customer and reduce sales revenue, while restoring the returned item to inventory.

In addition, in this appendix you will record the write-off of an accounts receivable that is determined to be uncollectible using the Receive Payments window. The write-off will result in the elimination of an accounts receivable and the recognition of a bad debts expense.

Appendix Problem

Before you begin, open the company file APP E Kristin Raina Interior Designs.QBW. Make a backup copy of the file, name it **EXE [*Your Name*] Kristin Raina Interior Designs** and then restore the file. Finally, change the company name to **EXE [*Your Name*] Kristin Raina Interior Designs.**

ACTIVITIES: ──o **Record a Sale of Inventory on Account**

1. **Record a Sale of Inventory on Account** (pages 5-16 to 5-18). Follow the steps under *Recording a Sale of an Inventory Item on Account* to record the following transaction in the Create Invoices window:

Mar. 31	Sold the following on account to Maria Omari. Invoice No. 1020, Terms 2/10, Net 30 Days	
	4 lamps	$ 800.00
	2 carpets	800.00
	total sale of merchandise	$ 1,600.00
	sales tax (.07 × $1,600)	112.00
	decorating services (6 hrs)	300.00
	total sale on account	$ 2,012.00

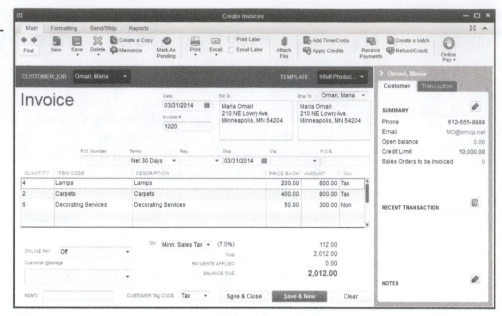

ACTIVITIES:

Record a Customer Credit in the Create Credit Memos/Refund Window

The Create Credit Memos/Refund window is used to record a credit to a customer's account as a result of transactions such as returned inventory items from prior sales, allowances against prior invoicing, and so on. The credit can be in the form of a cash refund, credit available for use against future sales, or can be applied to a specific open invoice. If a cash refund is made, a check can be created as part of the credit memo process. If the credit is applied to an open invoice, accounts receivable for that customer will be reduced.

The journal entry is as follows:

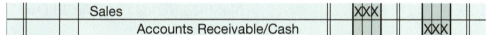

		Sales		XXX			
		Accounts Receivable/Cash					XXX

If the credit is a result of a returned inventory item, there will be an additional journal to return the item into the inventory account:

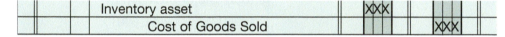

		Inventory asset		XXX			
		Cost of Goods Sold					XXX

Recording a Credit Memo and Applying It to an Open Invoice

On April 15, 2014, Maria Omari returns a lamp purchased on March 31, 2014, and a credit memo will be issued, No. 001. Because Invoice No. 1020 is still open, the credit memo will be applied against the unpaid balance.

To record a credit memo—
1. Click Customers and then click *Create Credit Memos/Refunds.*

2. At the CUSTOMER:JOB drop-down list, click *Omari, Marie*. The invoice of March 31 will be listed in the RECENT TRANSACTIONS list on the right and the open balance of $2,012.00 will appear in the SUMMARY. (See figure E–2.)

FIGURE E–2

Create Credit Memos/
Refunds Window—Maria
Omari

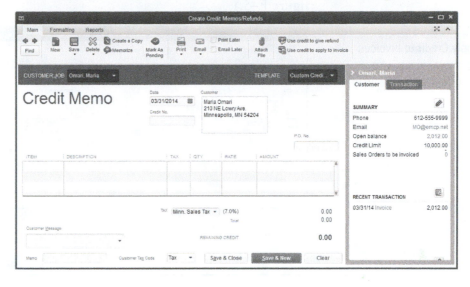

3. Enter the information listed above for the *Date* and *Credit No.* fields.
4. Click the *ITEM* field. At the ITEM drop-down list, click *Lamps*.
5. At the *QTY* field, key **1.** The word *Tax* should appear in the CustomerTax Code field, and the *Print Later* and the *Email Later* boxes should not be checked. (See figure E–3.)

FIGURE E–3

Create Credit Memos/
Refunds Window

6. If the information is correct, click Save & Close. The Available Credit window will appear asking you how this credit should be used. (See figure E–4.)

FIGURE E–4

Available Credit Window

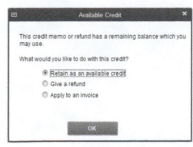

7. Click the *Apply to an invoice* option and then click OK. The Apply Credit to Invoices window appears, listing the open invoices for this customer.
8. Place a ✓ on the line of invoice No. 1020 if it not already there. (See figure E–5.)

FIGURE E–5

Apply Credit to Invoices Window—Invoice No. 1020 Selected

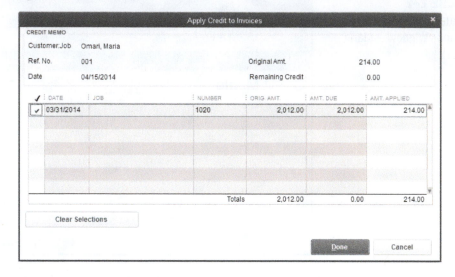

9. If the information is correct, click Done.
10. Open the Customer Center.
11. Select (highlight) *Maria Omari.*
12. At the DATE drop-down list, click *All.* A review of Maria Omari's customer file in the Customer Center shows the $214 credit, reducing her balance to $1,798. (See figure E–6.)

FIGURE E–6

Customer Center—Maria Omari File

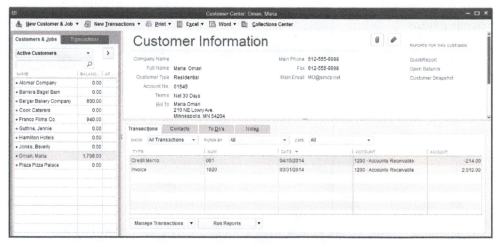

Inventory Valuation Detail Report

1. In addition, the cost of one lamp has been added back into inventory. Follow the steps under *Inventory Valuation Detail Report* (page 5-28) to view the report for the period *March 1, 2014 to April 30, 2014*. (See figure E–7.)

FIGURE E–7
Inventory Valuation Detail Report

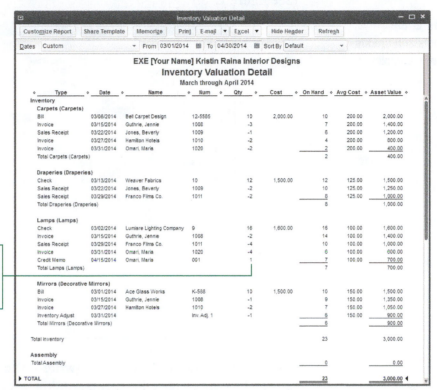

Lamps inventory adjustment due to return

Recording the Write-off of an Accounts Receivable (Bad Debt)

Often, companies that make sales on account must write off a receivable that will not be collected. Companies make every attempt to limit their losses by doing credit checks on customers, reviewing collection policies, and tracking the age of receivables. However, despite best efforts, a receivable may prove uncollectible. In QuickBooks, the write-off of an uncollectible account, called a bad debt, is accomplishing using the Receive Payments window.

On April 30, 2014, Kristin Raina determines that the remaining balance owed by Franco Films Co. has become uncollectible and she writes off the receivable and records a bad debt expense.

> **HINT**
>
> If the PMT. METHOD field indicates Check, the Reference field will be called Check #. Clearing the Pmt. Method field will change the title back to Reference #.

To record a bad debt—
1. Click Customers and then click *Receive Payments*.
2. At the RECEIVED FROM drop-down list, click *Franco Films Co.* The open invoice for the customer is displayed
3. At the *DATE* field, choose *04/30/2014*.
4. Leave the AMOUNT field at **0**.
5. In the *REFERENCE #* field, key **Bad Debt 1**.

6. Select the invoice by clicking in the ✓ column next to the open invoice.
7. Click the Discount and Credits button. This will display the Discount and Credits window.
8. In the *Amount of Discount* field, key **940**.
9. At the Discount Account drop-down list, click *6075 Bad Debt Expense*. (See figure E–8.)

10. Click Done to accept the discount (write-off) calculation. You will be returned to the Receive Payments window with the write-off amount in the Discount field. (See figure E–9.)

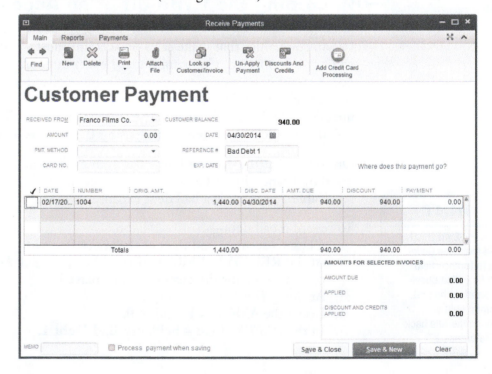

11. If the information is correct, click Save & Close.

Customer Balance Detail Report and Profit & Loss Standard Report

1. Follow the steps under *Customer Balance Detail Report* (page 3-28) to view the report. (See figure E–10.) You will note that the balance for Franco Films Co. is now 0.

FIGURE E–10

Customer Balance Detail Report

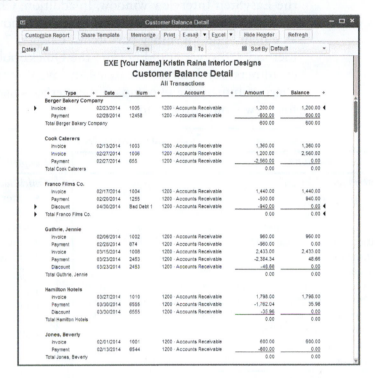

2. Follow the steps outlined in the chapters to view a *Profit & Loss Standard Report* for the period *January 1, 2014* to *April 30, 2014*. You will note Bad Debt Expense for $940. (See figure E–11.)

FIGURE E–11

Profit & Loss standard Report
January 1, 2014 – April 30, 2014

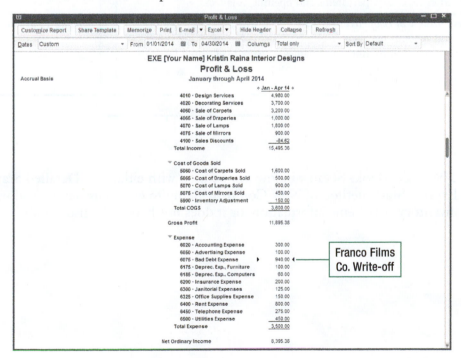

New Company Setup Methods

There are two methods of New Company Setup: Detailed Start and Express Start. Chapter 6 illustrates the Detailed Start method, which uses the EasyStep Interview window. In addition, Chapter 6 illustrates using the QuickBooks Setup window to enter information for customers, vendors, service items, and inventory part items. Chapter 7 illustrates the Express Start method. However, it did not use the QuickBooks Setup window to record customers, vendors, service items, or inventory part items. The following charts summarize and compare the methods used in chapter 6 and chapter 7 for New Company Setup.

New Company Setup	
Chapter 6 – Detailed Start	**Chapter 7 – Express Start**

EasyStep Interview Window
 • enter company information
 • select industry
 • select company organization
 • select first month of fiscal year
 • create company file
 • answer questions to establish preferences
    ➤ What do you sell? (choosing products enables inventory)
    ➤ Do you charge sales tax? (choosing yes enables sales tax)
    ➤ Do you have employees? (choosing no disables payroll)
 • start date for using QuickBooks
 • review income and expense accounts
    ➤ creates accounts in the Chart of Accounts List
	QuickBooks Setup Window
	 • enter company name
	 • select industry
	 • select company organization
	 • enter company information
	 • create company file

	Establish Preferences • add account numbers • enable inventory • enable sales tax • disable payroll
*QuickBooks Setup Window • enter customer information and opening balances • enter vendor information and opening balances • enter service items • enter inventory part items and opening balances	
Customize Chart of Accounts List • add account numbers • edit account numbers and names of accounts created by QuickBooks as part of the EasyStep Interview and QuickBooks Setup window	**Update Chart of Accounts List**

*   The QuickBooks Setup window can be used with either the Detailed Start method or the Express Start method of New Company Setup to enter customer, vendor, service items, or inventory part items information, or it does not have to be used at all.

continues

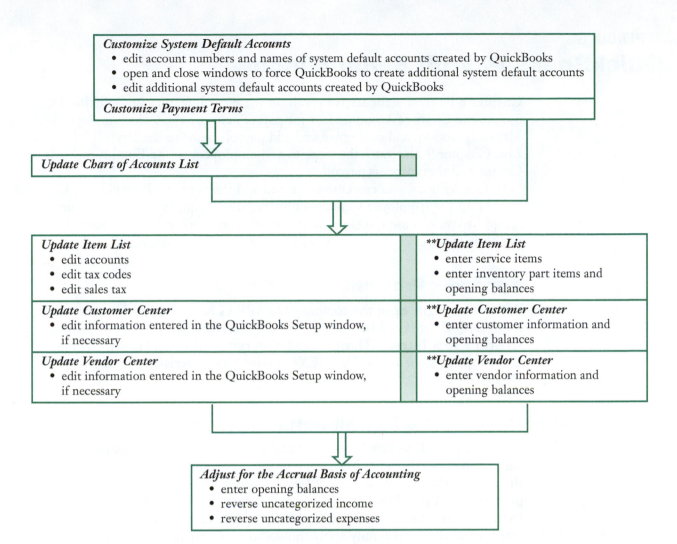

Customize System Default Accounts
- edit account numbers and names of system default accounts created by QuickBooks
- open and close windows to force QuickBooks to create additional system default accounts
- edit additional system default accounts created by QuickBooks

Customize Payment Terms

Update Chart of Accounts List

Update Item List
- edit accounts
- edit tax codes
- edit sales tax

Update Customer Center
- edit information entered in the QuickBooks Setup window, if necessary

Update Vendor Center
- edit information entered in the QuickBooks Setup window, if necessary

**Update Item List
- enter service items
- enter inventory part items and opening balances

**Update Customer Center
- enter customer information and opening balances

**Update Vendor Center
- enter vendor information and opening balances

Adjust for the Accrual Basis of Accounting
- enter opening balances
- reverse uncategorized income
- reverse uncategorized expenses

**   All information and balances can be entered directly into the Item List, Customer Center, and Vendor Center if you choose not to use the QuickBooks Setup window to enter this information.

QuickBooks Payroll Setup Window

Chapter 8 illustrates the steps to activate the payroll feature in QuickBooks, update the Chart of Accounts List for payroll, choose the Calculate Payroll Manually option, and customize and add payroll items to the Payroll Item List. Chapter 9 illustrates the steps to add employees to the Employee Center and then process payroll.

In QuickBooks, you can customize and add items to the Payroll Item List and set up the Employee Center as illustrated in chapters 8 and 9 (custom setup) or you can use the *QuickBooks Payroll Setup window*. In this appendix, the basic features of the QuickBooks Payroll Setup window are described.

Appendix Problem

Before you begin, open the company file APP G Kristin Raina Interior Designs.QBW. Make a backup copy of the file, name it **EXG [*Your Name*] Kristin Raina Interior Designs**, and then restore the file. Finally, change the company name in the file to **EXG [*Your Name*] Kristin Raina Interior Designs**.

LISTS/CENTERS ──o ## QuickBooks Payroll Setup Window

Once the payroll feature is activated and you have chosen to calculate payroll manually—which has been done in this Appendix Problem—you can then access the *QuickBooks Payroll Setup Window*. As part of this activation process, the *Payroll Item List* was created, as seen in chapter 8, The Payroll Item List (pages 8-10 to 8-12). The Payroll Item List includes typical federal tax items that generally apply to most payroll situations, such as Social Security, Medicare, Federal Withholding, and Federal Unemployment. As you enter information in the QuickBooks Payroll Setup window, additional items will be added to the Payroll Item List.

To update the Payroll Item List and the Employee Center using the QuickBooks Payroll Setup Window—

1. Click Employees, then click *Payroll Setup*. The QuickBooks Payroll Setup window appears. (See figure G–1.)

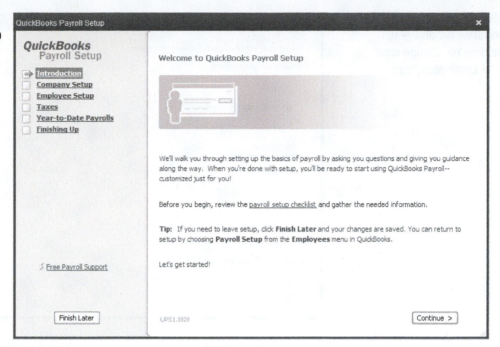

2. Read the page.

You will move through the QuickBooks Payroll Setup window by moving through pages, entering information when appropriate, and clicking Continue, Next, or Finish. As you move through the QuickBooks Payroll Setup window, you will complete steps 1 to 6 listed on the left side of the QuickBooks Payroll Setup window. Notice the link for the payroll setup checklist. You can click the *payroll setup checklist* for a checklist provided by QuickBooks (an Internet connection is needed).

3. Click Continue. You are moved to the Setup your company compensation page.

4. Read the page and then click Continue. You are moved to the Add New window – Tell us how you compensate your employees page.

At this window you will add employee compensation items. Each item you add is added to the Payroll Item List.

5. At the Tell us how you compensate your employees page, choose *Salary* and *Hourly wage and overtime*, if necessary. Remove any other check marks. (See figure G–2.)

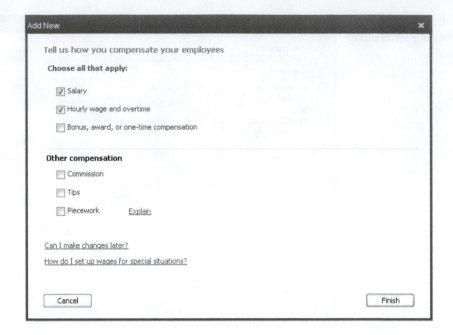

6. If the information is correct, click Finish. You are moved to the Review your Compensation list page.
7. Choose the Hourly compensation item by double-clicking Hourly. You are moved to the Edit: Hourly window.
8. At the Edit: Hourly window, in the *Show on paychecks as* field, key **Hourly Wages**.
9. In the Expense account field, on the *Account name* line, choose *Payroll Expenses: Salaries and Wages Expense* from the Account name drop-down list. (See figure G–3.)

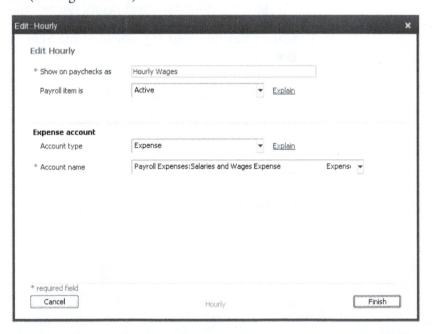

10. If the information is correct, click Finish. You are returned to the Review your Compensation list page.

11. Edit the Salary item on the Review Compensation List and choose the Account Name as *Payroll Expenses: Salaries and Wages Expense*, and then click Finish. You are returned to the Review your Compensation List page.

   Our sample company, Kristin Raina Interior Designs, only uses the Salary and Hourly Wages compensation items. QuickBooks created the Double-time hourly and Overtime (×1.5) hourly items, which Kristin Raina will not use. You will delete these two items.

12. Click Double-time hourly once to select the item and then click the Delete button. At the Delete Payroll Item message, click Yes. The Double-time hourly item is deleted.
13. Delete the *Overtime (×1.5) hourly* item.
14. After you edited or deleted each compensation item, click Continue. You are moved to the Set up employee benefits page.
15. Read the page and then click Continue. You are moved to the Add New window – Set up your insurance benefits page.
16. Accept the default *My company does not provide insurance benefits* and click Finish. You are moved to the Review your Insurance Benefits list page.
17. Click Continue. You are moved to the Add New window – Tell us about your company retirement benefits page.
18. Accept the default *My company does not provide retirement benefits* and click Finish. You are moved to the Review your Retirement Benefits list page.
19. Click Continue. You are moved to the Add New window – Set up paid time off page.
20. At the Set up paid time off page, choose *Paid sick time off* and *Paid vacation time off*. (See figure G–4.)

FIGURE G–4

Add New Window—Set Up Paid Time Off Page

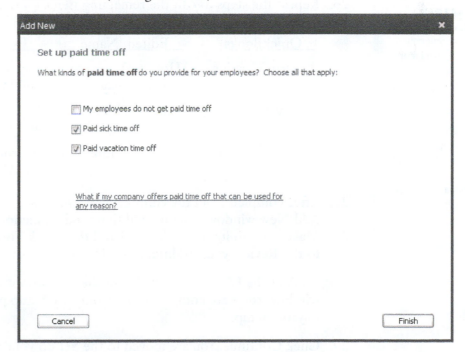

21. If the information is correct, click Finish. You are moved to the Review your Paid Time Off list page.

22. Choose the Hourly Sick paid time off item by double-clicking Hourly Sick. You are moved to the Edit: Sick Taken window.

23. In the Show on paychecks as field, key **Hourly Wages Sick Pay**.

24. In the Expense account field, choose *Payroll Expenses: Salaries and Wages Expense* from the Account name drop-down list. (See figure G–5.)

FIGURE G–5
Edit: Sick Taken Window

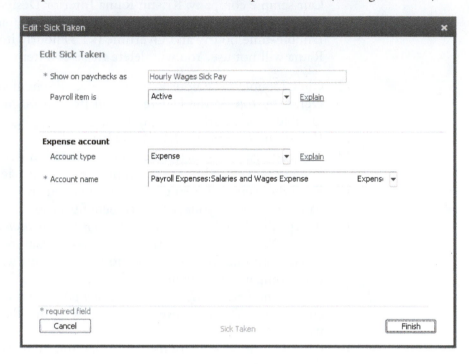

25. If the information is correct, click Finish. You are returned to the Review your Paid Time Off list page.

26. Repeat the steps to edit the remaining items on the Review your Paid Time Off list as follows:

QuickBooks	Edited Name	Expense Account
Hourly Vacation	Hourly Wages Vacation Pay	Payroll Expenses: Salaries and Wages Expense
Salary Sick	Salary Sick Pay	Payroll Expenses: Salaries and Wages Expense
Salary Vacation	Salary Vacation Pay	Payroll Expenses: Salaries and Wages Expense

27. After completing all the editing, click Continue. You are moved to the Add New window – Set up additions and deductions page.

28. Make sure no items are checked and then click Finish. You are moved to the Review your Additions and Deductions list page.

Look at the List on the left side of the QuickBooks Payroll Setup window. You have completed the Company Setup part of QuickBooks Payroll Setup.

29. Click Continue. You are moved to the Set up your employees page.

30. Read the page and then click Continue. You are moved to the New Employee window. The information you enter here will be entered in the Employee Center.

HINT

At anytime you can click the Finish Later button, which will close the QuickBooks Payroll Setup window. To return to the QuickBooks Payroll setup window, click Employees and then click Payroll Setup. You will be returned to the page where you left off.

31. Key in the following information:

First name:	Harry
Last name:	Renee
Print on check as:	Harry Renee
Employee status:	Active
Home Address:	323 S. Main Ave.
City:	St. Paul
State:	MN
Zip Code:	54120

(See figure G–6.)

FIGURE G–6

Employee Harry Renee—
Enter Employee's Name
and Address Page

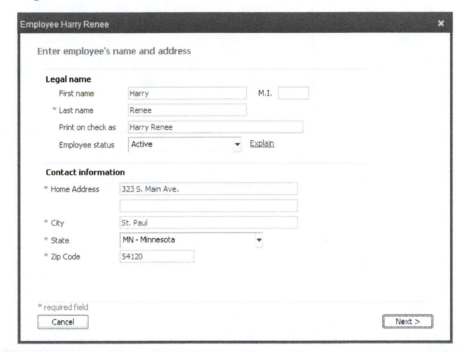

32. If the information is correct, click Next. You are moved to the
Employee Harry Renee window – Enter Harry Renee's hiring information page.
33. Enter the following information:

Employee type:	Regular
Social Security #:	112-55-9999
Hire date:	4/1/2014
Birth date:	2/17/48
Gender:	Male

(See figure G–7.)

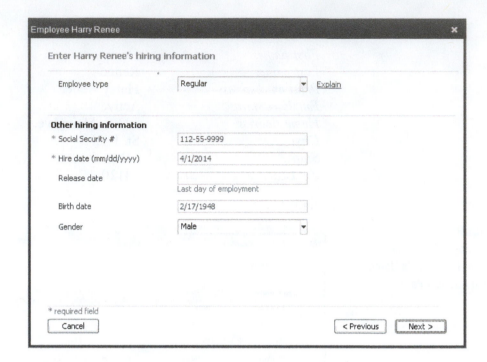

34. If the information is correct, click Next. You are moved to the Tell us
how you plan to pay Harry Renee page.
35. Enter the following information:

How often?:	Twice a month (Semimonthly)
	Salary
Salary amount:	24,000
Per:	Year

(See figure G–8.)

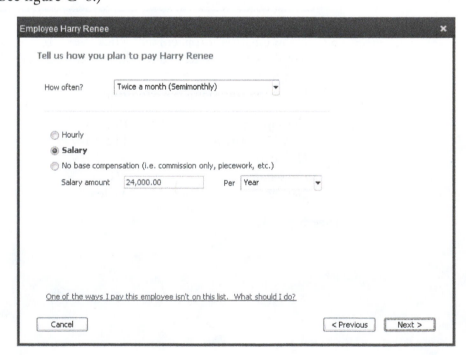

36. If the information is correct, click Next. You are moved to the How is sick time off calculated for Harry Renee? page.

37. Enter the following information using the drop-down lists when necessary:

Calculation

Harry Renee earns:	48 hours at beginning of year
Unused sick hours:	must be used or lost by end of year
Sick time accrual year starts:	January 1
Harry Renee earns:	No time off until
Earn sick time hours starting:	4/1/2014

Current Balances

Hours available as of (current date):	48
Hours used as of (current date):	0

(See Figure G–9.)

FIGURE G–9

Employee Harry Renee Window—How Is Sick Time Off Calculated For Harry Renee? Page

HINT

The date for the Current balances will be the date on your computer.

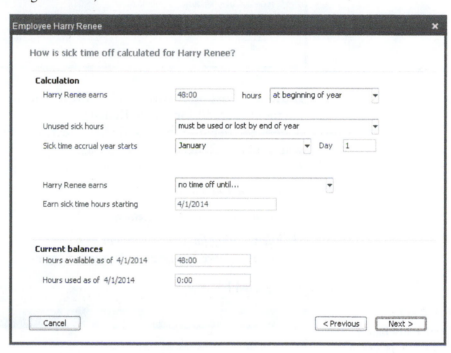

38. If the information is correct, click Next. You are moved to the How is vacation time off calculated for Harry Renee? page.

39. Enter the following information using the drop-down lists when necessary:

Calculation

Harry Renee earns:	96 hours at beginning of year
Unused vacation hours:	must be used or lost by end of year
Vacation accrual year starts:	January 1
Harry Renee earns:	No time off until
Earn vacation hours starting:	4/1/2014

Current Balances

Hours available as (current date):	96
Hours used as (current date):	0

(See Figure G–10.)

FIGURE G–10

Employee Harry Renee
Window—How is
Vacation Time Off
Calculated for Harry
Renee? Page

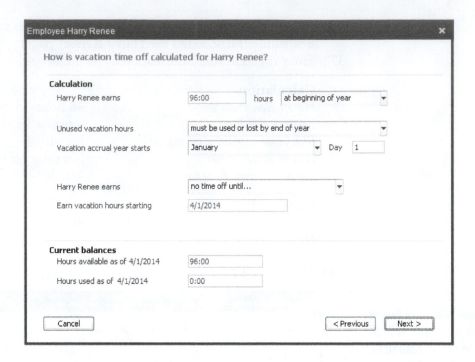

HINT

The date on the Current
Balances will be the
date on your computer.

40. If the information is correct, click Next. You are moved to the Set up payment method for Harry Renee.

41. Accept the default Check and click Next. You are moved to the Tell us where Harry Renee is subject to taxes page.

42. Enter the following information if it doesn't appear:

State subject to withholding:	MN – Minnesota
State subject to unemployment tax:	MN – Minnesota
While working for you in (current year), did Harry Renee live or work in another state?	No

(See figure G–11.)

FIGURE G–11

Employee Harry Renee
Window—Tell Us Where
Harry Renee Is Subject
To Taxes Page

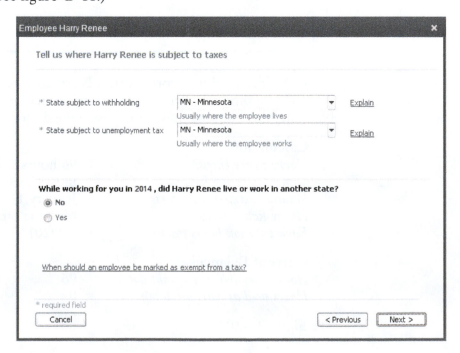

HINT

The year displayed will
be the year on your
computer.

43. If the information is correct, click Next. You are moved to the Enter federal tax information for Harry Renee page.

44. Enter the following information:

Filing Status:	Single
Allowances:	1
Subject to Medicare:	yes
Subject to Social Security:	yes
Subject to Federal Unemployment:	yes

(See figure G–12.)

(See figure G–12.)

FIGURE G–12

Employee Harry Renee Window—Enter Federal Tax Information For Harry Renee Page

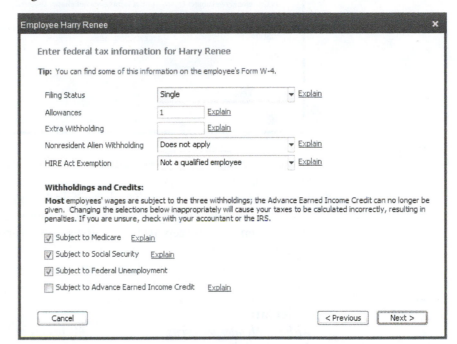

45. If the information is correct, click Next. You are moved to the Enter state tax information for Harry Renee page.

46. Enter the following information:

Filing Status:	Single
Allowances:	1
Subject to MN – Unemployment:	yes
Subject to MN – Workforce Enhancement Fee:	yes
Is this employee subject to any special local taxes not shown above?	no

(See figure G–13.)

(See figure G–13.)

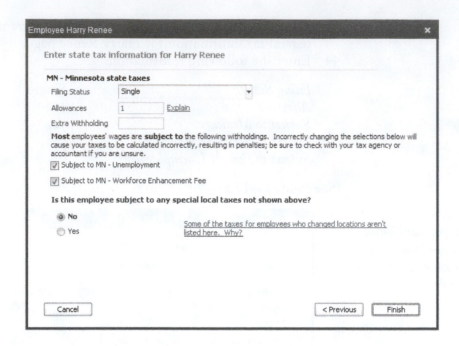

47. If the information is correct, click Finish. You are moved to the Review your Employee list page.

48. Click Add New. The New Employee window appears. Using the Practice Exercise on pages 9-9 to 9-10, along with the information in step 49 and step 50 below, enter the information for Richard Henderson, who was hired April 1, 2014.

49. At the Employee Richard Henderson window – How is sick time off calculated for Richard Henderson? page, enter the following information:

Calculation

Richard Henderson earns:	48 hours at beginning of year
Unused sick hours:	must be used or lost by end of year
Sick time accrual year starts:	January 1
Richard Henderson earns:	No time off until
Earn sick time hours starting:	4/1/2014

Current Balances

Hours available as of (current date):	48
Hours used as of (current date):	0

50. At the Employee Richard Henderson window – the How is vacation time off calculated for Richard Henderson? page, enter the following information:

Calculation

Richard Henderson earns:	96 hours at beginning of year
Unused vacation hours:	must be used or lost by end of year
Vacation accrual year starts:	January 1
Richard Henderson earns:	No time off until
Earn vacation hours starting:	4/1/2014

Current Balances

Hours available as (current date):	96
Hours used as (current date):	0

51. After entering the information for Richard Henderson, you are moved to the Review your Employee list page that lists both Harry Renee and Richard Henderson.

    Look at the List on the left side of the QuickBooks Payroll Setup window. You have completed the Employee Setup part of QuickBooks Payroll Setup.

52. Click Continue. You are moved to the Set up your payroll taxes page.
53. Read the page and then click Continue. You are moved to the Here are the federal taxes we set up for you page.

    These are the federal taxes common to most companies that QuickBooks set up on the Payroll Item List. While there is a choice here to edit these payroll items, you are not able to do so at this time.

54. Click Continue. You are moved to the Review your state taxes page.
55. Double-click MN – Unemployment. You are moved to the Edit: MN – Unemployment page.
56. Click Next. In the Company Rate field, key **3.4715**.
57. Click Finish. You are returned to the Review your state taxes page.
58. Click Continue. You are moved to the Schedule Payments – Set up payment schedule for Federal 940 page.

    QuickBooks provides a Schedule Payments feature if you subscribe to one of the QuickBooks payroll services. The Schedule Payments feature allows you to keep track of your payroll tax and other payroll liabilities amounts, due dates, and payments.

59. At the Schedule Payments window – Set up payment schedule for Federal 940 page, enter the following information:

    Payee: United States Treasury
    Payment (deposit) frequency: Quarterly

(See figure G–14.)

FIGURE G–14

Schedule Payments—Set Up Payment Schedule For Federal 940 Page

60. If the information is correct, click Next. You are moved to the Schedule Payments window – Set up payment schedule for Federal 941/944/943 page.

61. Enter the following information:

Payee:	United States Treasury
Payment (deposit) frequency:	After Each Payroll (Semiweekly)

62. Click Next. You are moved to the Set up payment schedule for MN UI and Workforce Enhancement Fee page.

63. Enter the following information:

Payee:	Minnesota UI Fund
MN Dept of Revenue Tax ID No.:	04777781-0123
Payment (deposit) frequency:	Quarterly

64. Click Next. You are moved to the Schedule Payments – Set up payment schedule for MN Withholding page.

65. Enter the following information:

Payee:	Minn. Dept. of Revenue
MN Dept of Revenue Tax ID No.:	4777781
Payment (deposit) frequency:	After Each Payroll (Semiweekly)

(See figure G–15.)

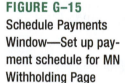
FIGURE G–15
Schedule Payments Window—Set up payment schedule for MN Withholding Page

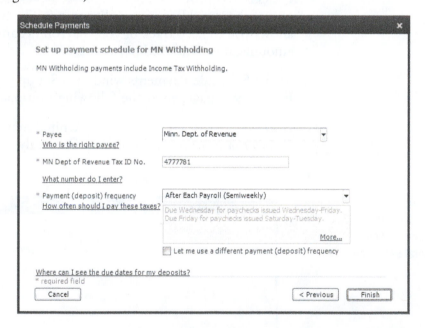

66. If the information is correct, click Finish. You are moved to the Review your Scheduled Tax Payments list page.

Look at the List on the left side of the QuickBooks Payroll Setup window. You have completed the Taxes part of QuickBooks Payroll Setup.

67. Click Continue. You are moved to the Year-to-date payrolls page. If you are setting up payroll in QuickBooks and have paid employees for the current year, you would have to enter the year-to-date payroll information for each employee.

68. Read the page and click Continue. You are moved to the Determine if you need to set up year-to-date payroll page.

69. At the Has your company issued paychecks this year? question, click No, then click Continue. You are moved to the You can now pay your employees! page.

Look at the List on the left side of the QuickBooks Payroll Setup window. You have completed the Year-to-Date Payrolls part of QuickBooks Payroll Setup.

70. Click Go to Payroll Center.

If you subscribe to a QuickBooks Payroll Service, you would move to a Payroll Center window. If you compute payroll manually, you are moved to the Employee Center window. The Employee Center should be the same as was updated in chapter 9. (See figure 9–H.)

71. Close the Employee Center.

REPORTS: ─○ **Payroll Item List**

As previously noted, when you activated the payroll feature, QuickBooks creates the Payroll Item List, which includes typical federal tax items that generally apply to most payroll situations, such as Social Security, Medicare, Federal Withholding and Federal Unemployment. As you entered information in the QuickBooks Payroll Setup window, additional items were added to the Payroll Item List, such as Salary, Hourly Wage, and State Taxes.

To open the Payroll Item List—
1. Click Lists, then click Payroll Item List. (See figure G–16.)

FIGURE G–16
Payroll Item List

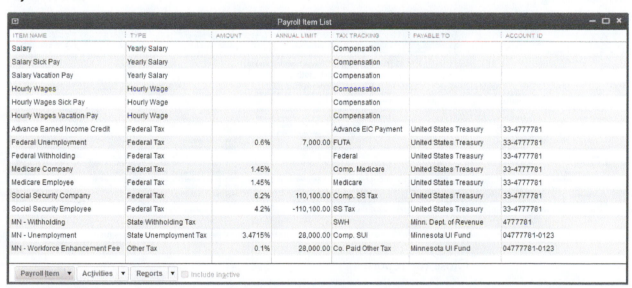

ITEM NAME	TYPE	AMOUNT	ANNUAL LIMIT	TAX TRACKING	PAYABLE TO	ACCOUNT ID
Salary	Yearly Salary			Compensation		
Salary Sick Pay	Yearly Salary			Compensation		
Salary Vacation Pay	Yearly Salary			Compensation		
Hourly Wages	Hourly Wage			Compensation		
Hourly Wages Sick Pay	Hourly Wage			Compensation		
Hourly Wages Vacation Pay	Hourly Wage			Compensation		
Advance Earned Income Credit	Federal Tax			Advance EIC Payment	United States Treasury	33-4777781
Federal Unemployment	Federal Tax	0.6%	7,000.00	FUTA	United States Treasury	33-4777781
Federal Withholding	Federal Tax			Federal	United States Treasury	33-4777781
Medicare Company	Federal Tax	1.45%		Comp. Medicare	United States Treasury	33-4777781
Medicare Employee	Federal Tax	1.45%		Medicare	United States Treasury	33-4777781
Social Security Company	Federal Tax	6.2%	110,100.00	Comp. SS Tax	United States Treasury	33-4777781
Social Security Employee	Federal Tax	4.2%	-110,100.00	SS Tax	United States Treasury	33-4777781
MN - Withholding	State Withholding Tax			SWH	Minn. Dept. of Revenue	4777781
MN - Unemployment	State Unemployment Tax	3.4715%	28,000.00	Comp. SUI	Minnesota UI Fund	04777781-0123
MN - Workforce Enhancement Fee	Other Tax	0.1%	28,000.00	Co. Paid Other Tax	Minnesota UI Fund	04777781-0123

Payroll Item ▼   Activities ▼   Reports ▼   ☐ Include inactive

In the QuickBooks Payroll Setup window you were generally, but not always, able to edit item names or account names. If there are item names or account names that you were not able to edit in the QuickBooks Payroll Setup window, you can do it in the Payroll Item List.

Follow the steps under Customizing a Payroll Item on pages 8-12 to 8-16, including the two Practice Exercises, to customize the federal tax items of Social Security (Company and Employee), Medicare (Company and Employee), Federal Unemployment, and Federal Withholding.

After the federal tax items are customized, use the same procedures to customize the state tax items that were created in the QuickBooks Payroll Setup window:

State Tax Item	Liability Account	Expense Account
MN – Withholding	2120 SIT Payable	
MN- Unemployment	2130 SUI Payable	6630 SUI Expense

2. Close the Payroll Item List.

Payroll Item Listing Report

The Payroll Item Listing Report lists the payroll item, type, rates, and limits for some of the mandatory taxes, and the expense and liability accounts relating to the payroll item.

To view the *Payroll Item Listing* report—
1. Click Reports and then click *Employees & Payroll*.
2. At the Employees & Payroll submenu, click *Payroll Item Listing*. (See figure G–17.)

FIGURE G–17
Payroll Item Listing
Report

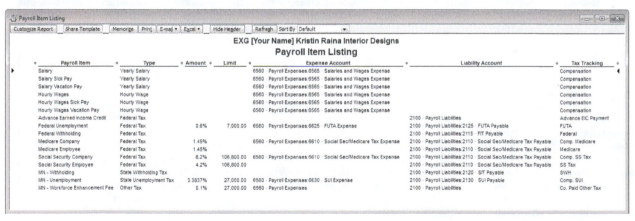

3. Close the report.

APPENDIX H
Sick and Vacation Paid Time

In Appendix G you learned to set up paid time off for Kristin Raina's employees. In this appendix you will process payroll when one employee uses sick or vacation time. You will also process payroll reports that track paid time used and paid time available.

Appendix Problem

Before you begin, open the company file APP H Kristin Raina Interior Designs.QBW. Make a backup copy of the file, name it **EXH [*Your Name*] Kristin Raina Interior Designs** and then restore the file. Finally, change the company name to **EXH [*Your Name*] Kristin Raina Interior Designs.**

ACTIVITIES: ──○ **Process Payroll**

In Chapter 9 you learned to process payroll for Kristin Raina's two employees. Employee sick and vacation hours were not available at that time. In this appendix, paid time off has been established for each employee. The amount of available paid time appears in the Preview Paycheck window every time you process pay. (See Figure H–1.)

FIGURE H–1
Preview Paycheck
Window—Paid Time Off
Hours Displayed

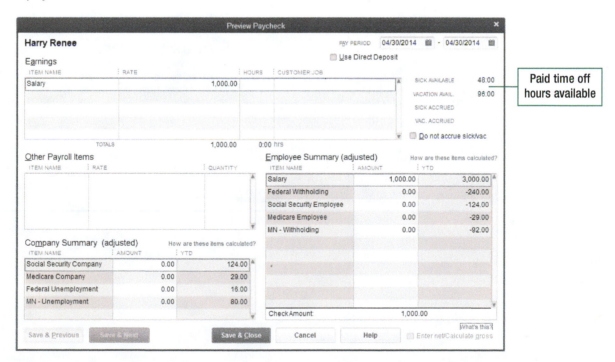

Using Banked Vacation Time Off Hours

Harry Renee plans to take a one-week vacation during the pay period ending May 15, 2014. Because he has 96 hours of paid vacation time available to him, he will use 40 of those hours and be paid during his time off.

To record the use of paid vacation time off—

1. Click Employees and then click *Pay Employees*. The Enter Payroll Information window appears.
2. At the *PAY PERIOD ENDS* and *CHECK DATE* fields, choose *05/15/2014*.
3. At the *BANK ACCOUNT* field, click *1020 Cash - Payroll*.
4. Select Harry Renee by placing a check mark next to the name.
5. If the information is correct, click *Open Paycheck Detail*. The Preview Paycheck window appears.
6. In the *ITEM NAME* field you will note that *Salary* item automatically fills for Harry Renee and the Vacation Avail. hours are 96.
7. Move to the next line and choose *Salary Vacation Pay* from the Item Name drop-down list. Notice that the $1,000 salary is now split between regular salary and vacation pay. (See Figure H–2.)

FIGURE H–2

Preview Paycheck Window—Salary Vacation Pay Entered

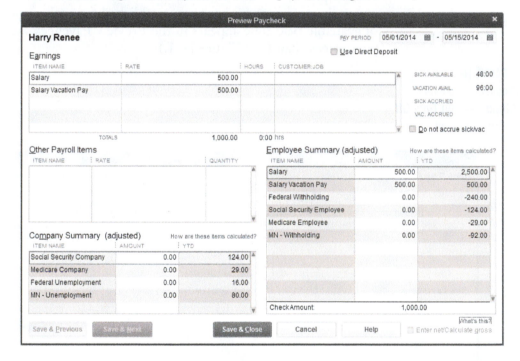

8. On both the *Salary* and *Salary Vacation Pay* lines in the hours field, key **40**.

When you move to the next field, the Vacation Avail. hours will be reduced from 96 to 56 as 40 hours of paid vacation time has now been used. In addition, the $1,000 salary for the period is now divided between the Salary item and the Salary Vacation Pay item in the Employee Summary field. (See figure H–3.)

FIGURE H–3
Preview Paycheck Window—Vacation Hours Used

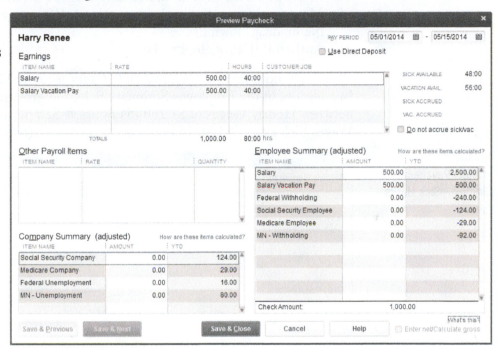

9. Complete Harry Renee's pay information—

Check Number:	**5**
Company Taxes:	
Social Security Company:	**62.00**
Medicare Company:	**14.50**
Federal Unemployment:	**8.00**
MN - Unemployment Company:	**40.00**
Employee Taxes:	
Federal Withholding:	**120.00**
Social Security Employee:	**62.00**
Medicare Employee:	**14.50**
MN - Withholding:	**46.00**

QuickCheck: The check amount should be $757.50.

ACTIVITIES: ○ **Using Banked Sick Time Off Hours**

During the pay period ending May 15, 2014, Richard Henderson used two days (16 hours) of paid sick time. His pay will be processed for that pay period with 16 of the 80 hours allocated to Hourly Wages Sick Pay and only 64 hours allocated to Hourly Wages.

To record the use of paid sick time off—

1. Click Employees and then click *Pay Employees*. The Enter Payroll Information window appears.
2. At the *PAY PERIOD ENDS* and *CHECK DATE* fields, choose *05/15/2014*, and the Bank Account *1020 Cash - Payroll*.
3. Select Richard Henderson and click *Open Paycheck Detail*. Note that Sick Available hours are 48.
4. In the HOURS field on the Hourly Wages line, key **64.**
5. Move to the next line and choose *Hourly Wages Sick Pay* from the Item Name drop-down list.
6. At the HOURS field, key **16**.

You will note that the Sick Available hours are now 32, reduced from 48. In addition, in the Employee Summary field, the gross pay is now split between Hourly Wages of $1,280 (64 hours @ $20 per hour) and Hourly Wages Sick Pay of $320 (16 hours @ 20 per hour). (See figure H–4.)

FIGURE H–4

Preview Paycheck Window—Sick Hours Used

7. Complete Richard Henderson's pay information—

Check Number:	**6**
Company Taxes:	
Social Security Company:	**99.20**
Medicare Company:	**23.20**
Federal Unemployment:	**12.80**
MN - Unemployment Company:	**64.00**
Employee Taxes:	
Federal Withholding:	**120.00**
Social Security Employee:	**99.20**
Medicare Employee:	**23.20**
MN - Withholding:	**54.00**

QuickCheck: The check amount should be $1,303.60.

Tracking Paid Time Off

The Paid Time Off List is a report that allows you to track the sick and vacation time used and the time available for each employee.

To view and print the Paid Time Off List—
1. Click Reports and then click *Employees & Payroll*.
2. At the Employees & Payroll submenu, click *Paid Time Off List*. The report will be displayed with the updated information. (See figure H–5.)

FIGURE H–5

Paid Time Off List

3. To print the report, click the Print button from the top of the report, check the settings in the Print Reports dialog box, and click Print.
4. Close the report.

Setting Up QuickBooks for Multiple Users

There are many examples of businesses in which multiple employees need access to company files to record information. QuickBooks allows the company files to be accessed by up to five people, each from their own computer. This is referred to as multi-user mode. Computers for all of the users must be networked within the company. One computer is designated as the host computer. To prepare for using the company file by multi-users, QuickBooks must be installed on each computer, multi-user access must be set up, and the company files must be prepared for multi-user access.

Install QuickBooks

HINT

To view the number of user licenses, press F2.

To use QuickBooks in multi-user mode, QuickBooks must be installed separately on each computer. Additional license fees are required for each computer. A company usually purchases the multi-user QuickBooks software, which includes the license fees for the additional users. If a company purchased single-user QuickBooks software, additional licenses can be purchased from QuickBooks.

Install QuickBooks on each computer, as described in chapter 1. For the computer designated as the host computer, select Multi-User Host Installation when prompted. For all other computers, select a standard installation.

Set Up Multi-User Access

There are several ways to set up multi-user access for a company file. One way, as stated above, is to choose Multi-user Host Installation when installing QuickBooks. If QuickBooks was previously installed, you can then set up the host computer for multi-user access.

Complete the steps below with QuickBooks open, but with no company file open.

HINT

If the choice is Stop Hosting Multi-User Access, then you are already in multi-user mode. Move to Scan Company Files for Multi-User Access.

To set up the host computer for multi-user access—
1. Click File, then click Utilities.
2. At the Utilities drop-down menu, click Host Multi-User Access. The Host multi-user access window appears.
3. Read the Start hosting multi-user access message and click Yes.
4. If the Administrator Permissions Needed message appears, click Continue.
5. If a User Account message appears, click Yes.
6. You are moved to the Multi-user setup information window. Read the message and click OK.

The host computer is now set up in multi-user mode. The company files then need to be scanned for multi-user access.

Scan Company Files for Multi-User Access

QuickBooks provides a database server manager to scan the computer files and prepare them for multi-users.

To scan the company files—
1. On your desktop, click the Start button and then click All Programs.
2. At the Programs menu, click QuickBooks and then click QuickBooks Database Server Manager.
3. If the User Account Control message appears, click Yes.
4. At the QuickBooks Database Server Manager window, on the Scan Folders tab, click the Add Folder button and select the folder where your company files are stored. The folder appears in the Folders that contain QuickBooks company files box.
5. Click the Scan button. The company files should then appear in the QuickBooks company files found box.
6. Click the Close button. The company files are now ready to be used in multi-user mode.

You then set up the users that are allowed access to the company files. It is advisable to set up the users with passwords to access company information. See Appendix J for setting up passwords and users.

Accessing the Company File in Multi-User Mode

After the host computer has been set up to allow multi-users and the company files have been set up to be accessed in multi-user mode, when opening a company file, you must indicate that you will use the company file in multi-user mode. You do this in the Open a Company window. In the lower left corner of the Open a Company window, place a check mark in the box to the left of Open file in multi-user mode.

You may be prompted to enter a user name and password or to Create New Users (click No). When the file opens, you have access as a multi-user to the company file.

If you did not open the company file in multi-user mode, you can switch to multi-user mode when the company file is open. Click File and then click Switch to Multi-user Mode. If the choice is Switch to Single-user Mode, then you are already in multi-user mode.

Setting Up Passwords and Users

To protect a company file with a password or to allow multiple users to access the company file, you must set up the users in each file. The original person that creates the company file is the Administrator (Admin) of the file. The Administrator can create a password for the company file and is also the person who determines and sets up users so they may access the company file. When the Administrator creates a user, the Administrator can then restrict access to parts of the company file or restrict access to former company information.

To set up a password for the Administrator (Admin) of the company file—

1. For any company file that you wish to protect with a password or set up for users, click Company, then click Set Up Users and Passwords.
2. At the Set Up Users and Passwords menu, click Set Up Users.
3. At the User List dialog box, in the *User Name* field, double-click Admin (logged on), or click Edit User. The Change user password and access dialog box appears.
4. At the Change user password and access dialog box, accept the default Admin, or key another name of your choosing.
5. In the *Password* and *Confirm Password* fields, key **adminpw**. (See figure J–1.)

FIGURE J–1

Change User Password and Access Dialog Box

6. Select a Challenge Question and Challenge Answer, and then click Next.
7. At the next window, click Finish, then close the User List dialog box.
8. Close the company file.

To open a company file that is password protected—

1. Open QuickBooks and open the company file that is password protected. The QuickBooks Login window appears.

2. In the *Password* field, key **adminpw**. (See figure J–2.)

FIGURE J–2
QuickBooks Login
Dialog Box

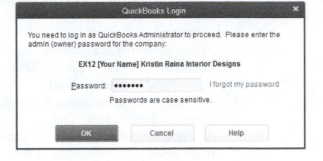

HINT

If the Administrator is the only user, only the Password field appears in the QuickBooks Login window. After additional users are set up, both the User Name and Password fields appear. If the User Name field appears, key **Admin**.

3. If the information is correct, click OK. If the Create New Users window appears, click No. The company file is opened.

To set up users in a company file—
1. Click Company, then click Set Up Users and Passwords.
2. At the Set Up Users and Passwords menu, click Set Up Users.
3. At the QuickBooks Login, key in the password **adminpw** and click OK.
4. At the User List dialog box, click Add User. The Set Up user password and access dialog box appears.
5. At the Set Up user password and access dialog box, in the *User Name* field, key **user1**.
6. Entering a password is optional but will be used in this example. In the *Password* and *Confirm Password* fields, key **user1pw**. (See figure J–3.)

FIGURE J–3
Set Up User Password and Access Dialog Box—User Name and Password Page Completed

HINT

Depending on which features are enabled in a company file, some of these pages may not appear.

7. If the information is correct, click Next.
8. At the Access for User: user1 page, choose the option *Selected areas of QuickBooks* and click Next.
9. At the Sales and Accounts Receivable page, choose the option *Full Access* and click Next.

10. At the next several pages: Purchases and Accounts Payable, Checking and Credit Cards, Inventory, Time Tracking (if displayed), and Payroll and Employees (if displayed), choose the option *No Access* and click Next.

11. At the Sensitive Accounting Activities page, choose the option *Selective Access*, then choose the option *Create transactions and create reports*, and then click Next.

12. At the Sensitive Financial Reporting page, choose the option *No Access*, and then click Next.

13. At the Changing or Deleting Transactions page, choose *Yes* at the first option and choose *No* at the second option, and then click Next. You are moved to the Access for user:user1 page, which summarizes the user's access rights. (See figure J–4.)

FIGURE J–4

Set Up User Password and Access Dialog Box— Access for User Page

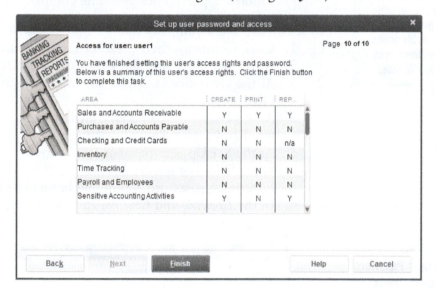

14. If the information is correct, click Finish. If you receive a warning, click OK.

15. Close the User List dialog box.

16. Close the company file.

Open the same company file as user1—

1. Open the company file. The QuickBooks Login dialog box will appear.

2. At the QuickBooks Login dialog box, in the User Name field, key **user1**, and in the Password field, key **user1pw**, and then click OK.

   Recall for user1 permission was only granted for Sales and Accounts Receivable. Open the Create Invoices window and the Sales Receipts window. These windows can be opened by user1. Now try opening other windows such as Enter Bills, Pay Employees, Journal Report, Profit & Loss Standard Report, and so on. A message will appear that you need permission to open these parts of the company file.

3. Click OK at the warning, then close the company file.

4. Close QuickBooks.

Index

NOTES

NOTES

NOTES

NOTES

NOTES

NOTES

NOTES